TRAFFIC AND TRANSPORT PSYCHOLOGY

Related books

R. ELVIK & T. VAA (eds.)	The Handbook of Road Safety Measures
FULLER & SANTOS (eds.)	Human Factors for Highway Engineers
HENSHER & BUTTON (eds.)	Handbooks in Transport Series
HAUER	Observational Before-After Studies in Road Safety
C-H. PARK et al (eds.),	World Transport Research: Selected proceedings of the 9th World Conference on Transport Research
ROTHENGATTER & VAYA (eds.)	Traffic and Transport Psychology: Theory and Application
J. SCHADE & B. SCHLAG (eds.)	Acceptability of Transport Pricing Strategies
T. ROTHENGATTER & R. D. HUGUENIN (eds)	Traffic and Transport Psychology: Theory and Application

Related Journals

Accident Analysis and Prevention
Editor: F.A. Haight

International Journal of Transport Management
Editor: A. Bristow

Transportation Research F: Traffic Psychology and Behaviour
Editors: J.A. Rothengatter and J.A. Groeger

Applied and Preventative Psychology:
Editor: D. Smith

For full details of all transportation titles published under the Elsevier imprint please go to:
www.ElsevierSocialSciences.com/transport

TRAFFIC AND TRANSPORT PSYCHOLOGY
Theory and Application

Proceedings of the ICTTP 2004

EDITED BY

GEOFFREY UNDERWOOD
School of Psychology, University of Nottingham

2005

ELSEVIER

Amsterdam – Boston – Heidelberg – London – New York – Oxford
Paris – San Diego – San Francisco – Singapore – Sydney – Tokyo

ELSEVIER B.V.
Radarweg 29
P.O. Box 211, 1000 AE
Amsterdam, The Netherlands

ELSEVIER Inc.
525 B Street, Suite 1900
San Diego, CA 92101-4495
USA

ELSEVIER Ltd
The Boulevard, Langford Lane
Kidlington, Oxford OX5 1GB
UK

ELSEVIER Ltd
84 Theobalds Road
London WC1X 8RR
UK

First edition 2005

Library of Congress Cataloging in Publication Data
A catalog record is available from the Library of Congress.

British Library Cataloguing in Publication Data
A catalogue record is available from the British Library.

ISBN: 0-08-044379-6

⊗ The paper used in this publication meets the requirements of ANSI/NISO Z39.48-1992 (Permanence of Paper).
Printed in The Netherlands.

Working together to grow
libraries in developing countries

www.elsevier.com | www.bookaid.org | www.sabre.org

ELSEVIER   BOOK AID International   Sabre Foundation

CONTENTS

Vulnerable Road Users III:

Novice Drivers

Emotion and Personality

Automation and Information Systems

DRIVING PERFORMANCE I:

Control and Workload

DRIVING PERFORMANCE II:

Perception and Awareness

VIOLATION AND REHABILITATION

TRAVEL DEMAND MANAGEMENT AND TRAVEL MODE CHOICE

EPILOGUE

PREFACE

This volume contains a selection of papers that originally formed part of the programme of the International Conference of Traffic and Transport Psychology, held in Nottingham, England, in September 2004. ICTTP2004 was the 3rd meeting in the series, following meetings in Valencia (1996) and Bern (2000). The contributions here include keynote lectures, regular platform presentation and poster presentations written for a volume that provides an overview of current developments in traffic and transport psychology.

Just as our transport systems become more and more important to our economic and social well-being, so they become more and more crowded and more at risk from congestion, disruption, and collapse. Technology and engineering can provide part of the solution, but the complete solution will need to take account of the behaviour of the users of the transport networks. Our role as psychologists is to understand how people make decisions about the alternative modes of transport and about the alternative routes to their destinations, to understand how novice and other vulnerable users can develop safe and effective behaviours, and how competent users can operate within the transport system optimally and within their perceptual and cognitive limitations. The contributions to this volume address these issues of how the use of our transport systems can be improved by taking into account knowledge of the behaviour of the people who use the systems. We start and finish, as we did at ICTTP2004 with thoughtful overviews from two senior members of our community. The opening remarks are from Denis Huguenin, the current President of the Traffic and Transportation Psychology Division of the International Association of Applied Psychology (IAAP), and appeals for interdisciplinary and integrative approaches to the understanding of traffic psychology. The concluding remarks are from Talib Rothengatter, the founding President of our IAAP Division, and the founding Editor of the journal *Transportation Research (F): Traffic Psychology and Behaviour*, and he also appeals for an integration of our approaches to traffic safety and to road safety. The opening and concluding chapters are based upon Keynote Lectures presented at ICTTP2004, as are the chapters by Oliver Carsten on automated vehicle control, by John Groeger on the cues used for speed control, by Dana Yagil on traffic law violations and by Tommy Gärling on changes in our choice of travel mode. The volume is greatly enhanced by these thoughtful and highly contemporary contributions.

Members of the ICTTP2004 Scientific Committee and session chairs actively assisted with the selection of manuscripts, and thanks are especially due to Oliver Carsten, Viola Cavallo, Peter Chapman, Luis Nunes, and Talib Rothengatter for their recommendations. The selection of papers for inclusion was not easy, with so many excellent manuscripts submitted to the IAAP/ICTTP website (http://www.psychology.nottingham.ac.uk/IAAP-div13/), and papers were selected for inclusion on the basis of forming a collection that was representative of ICTTP2004 and that would be stimulating to psychologists with interests in traffic and transport research. Peter Chapman, as Secretary of the Traffic and Transportation Psychology Division of IAAP, has developed this website, and the selection of papers for this volume was greatly facilitated by having the papers available for review in their full format. In addition to colleagues who assisted with the selection of papers for the conference and for this volume, I would like to take this opportunity of thanking Tracy Collier (Elsevier) and Jessica de Andrade Lima (University of Nottingham) for their organisational help in the running of the conference. Jessica also provided invaluable help in collating the manuscripts for the website and for this volume. The UK Government's Department for Transport provided generous financial support to ICTTP2004, and the continued dedication of their Road Safety Division merits special thanks.

Geoffrey Underwood
Nottingham, December 2004

PROLOGUE

Traffic and Transport Psychology
G. Underwood (Editor)

1

TRAFFIC PSYCHOLOGY IN A (NEW) SOCIAL SETTING

Raphael D. Huguenin[1]

INTRODUCTION

The role of traffic psychology is examined and critically reviewed from a sociological standpoint, in other words, beyond an individually centred approach. Influencing road users and diagnostics are undoubtedly justified but are, however, unequal to the tasks to be tackled at the interface between people and road traffic. Safety, environmental protection and convenience as associated factors of mobility must also be addressed in the light of social processes. This poses the question of whether traffic psychology has the right approaches to meet these factors. This question must not be seen in a void, but against a background of economic recession, persistent globalisation trends, increasing deregulation, socio-demographic changes and an accelerating gradient between rich and poor cultures. Faced with these challenges, can traffic psychology assert itself as an independent branch within the field of traffic and transport science? To what extent must it adopt a more interdisciplinary approach to create practical solutions or at least to contribute to them? Can its methods offer independent answers to new questions? Which theoretical tools are available to generate the appropriate bases essential for a mastery of new situations?

Alongside cultural changes within our society, new safety cultures are also in the course of creation, representing an additional challenge to traffic psychology. The latter must prove that it can produce application-related results and does not hamper but promotes paradigm shifts such as "Vision Zero" or "Sustainable Safety".

It has been proposed that the role of traffic psychology must be seen—to a greater degree than before—from an interdisciplinary, integrative and international viewpoint based on application in order to address changing situations and objectives and to maintain the importance of its field.

---

[1] Swiss Council for Accident Prevention bfu, Switzerland. *E-mail:* r.d.huguenin@bfu.ch (R.D. Huguenin).

Traffic Psychology

I have a very high regard for John Groeger and share his opinion on all matters in our field—except for his definition of traffic psychology. He wrote: "My own view is that there is no 'psychology' which is specific to, or peculiar to, traffic and transportation" (Groeger 2002, p. 246). For my part, I am assuming that, similar to sports psychology perhaps, traffic psychology is a branch of applied psychology and must therefore be sensibly specified by terminology and focus placed on its application. I thus define this discipline of ours as the psychological intervention or the psychological support for intervention in the field of traffic. This also includes the research that serves this purpose. The core of this chapter is thus the connection with application that works in synergy with basic work. However, I am in agreement with Groeger in that the basic principles of general psychology also apply to traffic psychology.

A few years ago, Rainer Kluwe, President of the German Psychological Society, said in a talk about the state of psychology:

(1) "Psychology is an unusually successful scientific discipline" and

(2) "In future, the further development of psychology will be marked, in particular, by three features: they will be interdisciplinary, international and application-related" (Kluwe, 2001). In my opinion, this also applies to traffic psychology. Traffic psychology has developed quickly and positively in recent years:

- Demand for knowledge in this field has increased tremendously, not just in everyday work but also in specialist bodies. Traffic psychologists are represented in the most important national and international traffic and transport committees.

- Hardly any road traffic projects in western countries are implemented without first consulting psychologists who specialise in traffic.

- Research into people's behaviour on the road as well as in cockpits or in shipping is established and a knowledge of the importance of psychology in these fields is not only recognised by those responsible for educating, training or influencing road users but is also acknowledged among laypersons.

This was not the case 50 years ago, at least not in Europe. A lot has also changed in a qualitative sense: traffic and transport psychology does not just refer to individual theoretical concepts such as perception or learning, but is based on broader approaches than before that explain behaviour on an integral basis. In addition, topics that are more relevant in practical use are being dealt with.

This summary could fool us into applauding each other and resting on our laurels. However, in his second statement, Kluwe uses the term "further development". He thus assumes that we have not yet reached the pinnacle of what we can achieve as psychologists. I would like to concentrate on this aspect in view of the current background, some of which is new—in the knowledge that I am referring to a background that does not follow the same trends everywhere. In connection with the previous expectations of being more interdisciplinary, international and application-oriented, I shall therefore focus on three topics that I consider to be important for the future of traffic and transport psychology.

MOBILITY BEHAVIOUR TODAY AND TOMORROW

In view of our level of affluence, which is increasing on the whole despite periods of recession, a change in mobility and mobility behaviour can also be anticipated at international level. According to a study conducted by Shell (2001), parallels can be drawn between the economic output of a country and the passenger kilometres travelled, which can be depicted as in relation to world regions (Figure 1). This finding is not surprising but begs the question of whether there are any consequences for traffic psychology. Figure 2 shows, with a few typical countries, how transport quality standards can be classified within these dimensions. If we follow this pattern even if it cannot be thoroughly corroborated empirically, it results in a challenge to traffic psychology. In future, it will hardly be a matter of promoting individual skills or training at the level of ability and knowledge any more, but of investigating the role of the vehicle in connection with the relevant lifestyle. Many colleagues in western countries recognised this quite some time ago and developed educational models that take this into account (e.g. Keskinen, Hattaka, Laapotti, Katila & Peräaho, 2004).

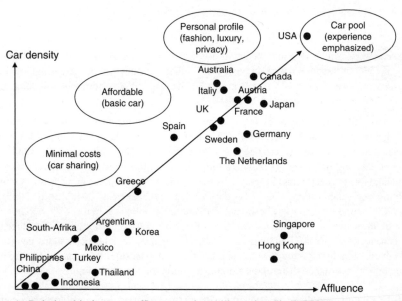

Figure 1. Relationship between affluence and mobility (after Shell, 2001).

The relationship with vehicles will also shift with the trend. Although mobility as the main purpose will not necessarily diminish, it will be increasingly linked with additional elements. These include:

- Firstly, self-portrayal and emotionalisation of the act of driving; this is already the case in some European countries as well as in Japan and North America. The new socio-culture puts the emphasis on driving fun, lifestyle and risk-seeking with technical safety (IFMO, 2002).

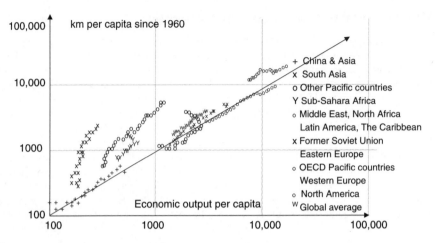

Figure 2. Transport quality standards (after Shell, 2001).

- Secondly, it can be seen that the act of driving itself—to exaggerate—is almost becoming an activity of less importance, in other words other activities will be increasingly included. This can be seen not only with phoning while driving but also from other, to some extent very dangerous, activities (AAA, 2004).

This trend will be accompanied by a second European trend that is, to some extent, in contradiction: a reluctance to drive. Since driving no longer has the cultural importance it used to have, attitudes towards cars are becoming more objective. The "cultural magic of individual transport is losing its power" (Minkmar, 2004, p. 122). Statements such as these—these are speculations—are nevertheless supported by findings in Sweden where young people are in less of a hurry to get their driving licences as they used to be (Gregersen, 2004; Murray, 2003), and Steg (2004) supports the hypotheses put forward in sociological terms with psychological findings. She shows—and this in no way makes fieldwork any easier for traffic psychologists!— that, dependent on situation, individuals combine several of the tendencies listed here within themselves. As before, young people see areas that make car driving appear to be fun, many others, however, distance themselves emotionally from the act of driving.

The latter finding leads to the question of the extent to which road use is currently more rational than it used to be. In this connection, the results of efforts connected with environmental protection and crash prevention can be incorporated as indicators. Assuming that the control of our behaviour towards environmental protection occurs rationally with the given positive motivation, willingness to act at behavioural level should be correspondingly expressed given a positive attitude. However, this is not the case, neither in the assumption that something will change on the side of action (Stradling, Meadows & Beatty, 2004a), nor effectively—primarily because the infrastructure parameters are not in place (Johansson, 2004). For example, in Switzerland, we have one of the best infrastructures in the world for mastering mobility using public transport. Nevertheless, "only" around 18% of the daily distances are covered using public transport, whereas motorised individual traffic makes up almost 70% (Microcensus,

2000; Table 1). Is this behaviour truly rational? Might psychological interventions lead to improvements?

Table 1. Choice of transport mode in
Switzerland (Microcensus, 2000).

Pedestrian	5%
Bicycle	3%
Motorbike	2%
Car	69%
Train	14%
Bus	4%
Other	3%

With regard to the question of mobility, it must be said in conclusion that traffic psychology, dependent on the country, must provide approaches to meet the needs associated with the relevant developments in road-use mobility. By means of an international exchange of experience, highly developed countries can support those that are going through an earlier stage. In this connection, more consideration should be given to the emotional aspect, which in scientific terms unfortunately receives little attention in favour of the cognitive aspect—a situation that Parker (2004) also pointed out recently. The problem is that we are noting simultaneous trends towards objectification and emotionalisation.

However, behaviour is not just determined by psychological factors in the narrower sense but also by a series of minor conditions where both ecology and safety are concerned. This knowledge must therefore be made additionally—or even particularly—available by psychologists to decision-makers and politicians. We must explain to them that low-cost or time-saving measures (Priesendörfer et al., 1999) have a chance in the field of environmental protection and add proposals for added value for safety measures, since it is mainly psychologists who know that even a positive attitude achieves little if it is not linked with other cognitions in order to be of any consequence (Gatersleben & Uzzell, 2004).

FROM AN INDIVIDUALLY FOCUSSED TO A SOCIAL APPROACH

Traffic psychologists must deal with another development step now. It can be seen that in the area of general prevention and intervention, the individually focussed approach must rightly and increasingly be abandoned and preference given to a social one. After 50 years of individually focussed traffic psychology,[2] the idea of a social approach was taken up from epidemiology only fairly recently. The criticism of the individually focussed approach, whereby the individual tends towards specific modes of behaviour based on his attitudes and/or his personality and whose behaviour can be modified individually or at least reliably diagnosed, can be discussed at a minimum of two levels in traffic psychology terms:

(1) Firstly, in connection with the idea that personal attitudes are reliable predictors of individual behaviour and that modifying them will lead to the corresponding behaviour.

---

[2] This statement must be put into perspective. In some countries, the individually focussed approach is only pursued in part-areas, in others not at all, however, in many European ones for preference.

Fishbein and Ajzen offered the theoretical basis, but when the euphoria[3] died down, criticism became rife and other socio-psychological concepts were put forward to make usable correlations between attitudes and behaviour or to achieve prognostic relevance.[4] For example, Prochaska, DiClemente and Norcross (1992) developed a transtheoretical model, as it is called, that describes the gradual process of behavioural change and aims to come closer to reality. This model takes into account the fact that, in most cases, individual behavioural modification is a time-consuming business. Frey (1996) interprets this with the words "Without patience, no substantial personality change can succeed". To this it is only necessary to add that this also applies to behaviour. In most of the measurements, time between establishing attitude and behaviour is not recorded.

Ajzen and Fishbein (with partial reference to older sources, e.g. 1980) are undergoing something of a revival in traffic psychology. Progress has undoubtedly been made and the inclusion of the social dimension as well as emotional aspects increases the validity of the predictors. In view of the specific results, the question is justified as to whether the outlay is worth it. Thanks to a complex Lisrel analysis, Aberg (2001; Figure 3) nevertheless succeeded in achieving a determination coefficient of 64% as the best figure for predicting behaviour based on attitudes and similar constructs. However, this involves items in connection with a special and methodological relative unproblematic topic (30/50 speed limits, sanctions and enforcement also play a role here) and self-reported behaviour. A large number of other authors obtained worse results—in other words, fewer associations between the two variables in question (Parker, Lajunen and Stradling, 1998).

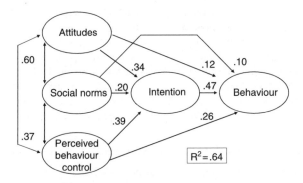

Figure 3. Prediction of behaviour (Aberg, 2001).

Let me be more specific to avoid any misunderstandings—it is not the influencing of attitudes, neither the intention nor the various techniques that is incorrect, but the expectation mostly assumed by practitioners that attitudes are consistent with behaviour. Thus, I urge a rethink of the value of attitude research and its practical application. A knowledge of attitude provides a basis for assessing an issue with a target group and is therefore not unimportant. However, the change in attitude must, in practice, merely be a basis for the introduction of measures, since these must meet with sufficient resonance and acceptance. It must be explained to politicians

---

[3] At that time, the author (Huguenin, 1978) was also a Fishbein (1966) follower.
[4] The author was also among those seeking at that time (Huguenin 1988a,b).

and decision-makers that it is wrong to expect that sufficient behavioural modification will result solely from a change in attitude. The consequence of this is: attitudes must be changed in order to incorporate other (hard) solutions.

(2) Secondly, within the framework of traffic psychological selection activities, the individually focussed approach is still used even with the worst selection. The idea of separating the wheat from the chaff is an old one and the limits of the undertaking are known, yet the theory of accident proneness is still subscribed to. Even in the times of the Old Testament, Gideon selected his warriors using a simple "drinking test" (Book of Judges 7, 5–7). In this regard traffic psychology, has unfortunately only made progress in methodology. Apart from a few special groups, for example road users who are offenders because of alcohol or excessive speed, the prognostic value of the selection is insignificant. In Switzerland, one investigation (Blaser & Schnidrig, 1993) led to loud controversy because the authors discovered that random results (by throwing dice) achieved predictions that were just as good as the traffic psychological assessment by specialists and, using clear relapse prognosis criteria, the administrator of the Traffic Office was at least on an even footing with the psychologists or even superior to them in terms of cost.

The basic question must therefore be asked as to whether traffic psychologists can appropriately solve the tasks that are to be mastered at the interface between people and road traffic. Too much is asked of them in terms of individual assessments—the expectations of the authorities and judges are excessively high. Nevertheless, judgement is passed on "traffic offenders", elderly people supposedly unfit to drive or "those in need of retraining" in a number of countries. Whether there is any legal equality or not is rarely questioned and it is argued from a commercial standpoint that psychological reports are demanded by the authorities themselves and other disciplines are unable to make any better predictions. Wherever work is carried out in this field, an attempt is usually made to seriously determine validity and reliability. Unfortunately, these studies reveal how limited the processes are. The problems can be summarised in two sentences:

(1) Even with good diagnostic methods and adequate selection, very little overall effect is achieved, since only a small (risk) group is affected.

(2) In terms of quality, the diagnostic tools are weak—with the result that the ability to make statements is restricted.

Unfortunately, too little account is taken of the findings from the discussion about the theory of accident proneness that is implicitly still used as a basis. Haight (2004) presented this in an excellent (and now accessible) essay. This does not dispute the fact that there is a rare species of accident prones; however, what is questionable is the ability to adequately detect them and that accident prevention measures would be efficient.

Let us put these problems into concrete terms with the help of two examples:

(1) In the search for better methods of detecting drivers who are offenders by nature, a test procedure was developed in Switzerland (initiated by the author himself) (Spicher & Hänsgen, 2003) that was properly organised with a great deal of methodological investment and corresponded to the principles of test design like no other tool. Yet the result from a specialist viewpoint is limited to say the least. Out of the actually unsuitable persons in terms of character (criterion "multiple offender traits"), only 60% were

correctly diagnosed, and out of the suitable persons (non-offenders), 76% were correctly allocated. Nevertheless, this still means that 24% were incorrectly diagnosed as unsuitable and possibly faced measures, while 40% could continue as road users even though the risk was high! (Table 2).

Table 2. Sensitivity and specificity of the TVP (2003), calculated according to Ewert (2004).

Character	Unsuitable (%)	Suitable (%)
Unsuitable (diagnosis)	60	24
Suitable (diagnosis)	40	76

(2)   Where older drivers as well as their selection are concerned, Hakamies-Blomqvist pointed out the problems involved (q.v. e.g. Siren & Hakamies-Blomqvist, 2004). According to their theoretical calculations (Hakamies-Blomqvist, 2004), with the assumed high risk (defined as twice as high a risk as average) of 1/10,000, avoiding an accident by selection cost 9999 safe senior citizens their mobility. The risk of accident would therefore have to rise steeply if a screening of elderly drivers were to be relevant for safety at system level. In order to achieve this, the first selection would have to be narrowed down by means of further procedure, the aim being to remove an individual group from the population as a whole. It is well known that the usual tests that exist for this purpose are so weak that they cannot be recommended because they are so unreliable.

What is more, I am against an individually focussed approach—whether it be in environmental protection or in safety work. Apart from the problem of being able to analyse the individual appropriately at all in terms of his road usage behaviour or even to predict it, it is wrong to consider the system as a given and to question whether the road user fits into the system. Exceptions to this are perhaps alcohol/drug consumption as well as extreme physical or character-based offender behaviour. In many places, the emphasis must shift [compare, for example, the EFPPA-Task Force Traffic Psychology report, in which, apart from research, only assessment and DI/counselling are listed as tasks for traffic psychology]. Our task should focus more on getting acquainted with traffic behaviour in order to change the system appropriately.

THE NEW SAFETY CULTURE

Finally, I will now get to the role of traffic psychology in terms of the demand that is starting to appear in Europe, in particular, for a new culture of safety in road traffic. The usual focus on the individual has its actual roots in the ideal of the person having sole responsibility. The attempt is now being rightly made to reduce the ballast with which the individual is burdened. The elements of vehicle, road and legislation are no longer considered as "givens"—or independent variables as it were—in the road traffic system, while the overall degree of flexibility and adaptation to these part systems is the responsibility of people. Instead, a start is being made to adapt the system to people. This is a familiar concept from the field of ergonomics, but it is nowadays being applied to the entire system. In addition, goals are being specifically set to ideally fix the number of fatalities and serious injuries at the zero limit.

The goal of road safety work thus takes on a new direction—from correcting part-elements to a determined proactive approach. In addition, the principle of the responsibility of the individual road user is at least put into perspective. No matter how attractive the ideal of individual responsibility may sound, the limit of people's ability to adapt in view of the complexity of events in traffic must also be taken into account. We are frequently overwhelmed by an information overload in traffic and the legalistic ideal of individual responsibility is just as unworkable in practice as the idea of practising Christianity, good as it may be.

Acceptance of the fact that the majority of road users are not "evil", but unreliable, led to the principle of relieving the individual in the sense of prevention being circumstantially oriented rather than behaviourally oriented. The latter must be subordinated to the former. Technology, infrastructure and legislation must be subservient to adequate behaviour. Training and further training must also be taken into account with regard to their limits, however, much their improvement in quality is to be welcomed.

The wheel thus turns full circle in line with the thesis expressed by Kluwe (2001), according to which psychology—and to this I must add: traffic psychology, too—will be practised on an increasingly interdisciplinary basis. The role of psychology must be redefined in prevention. Applied psychology means bringing in the knowledge of behaviour from research and development, combining influence with technology and legislation and ensuring that new technologies are focussed on the relevant issues, i.e. on those that serve human beings. Traffic psychologists must make sure that developments—for example, telematic developments—do not result in gags that do more harm than good in road traffic. In future, the contribution made by traffic psychology will move in the direction of system safety; the time of educational intervention is not over but it has shifted towards a more interdisciplinary and integrative approach. Good examples of these are the work done by Stradling (for instance, Stradling, Meadows & Beatty, 2004b) or Siegrist (for instance, Siegrist & Roskova, 2001) on the connections between attitudes, behaviour and enforcement.

The demand cannot be ignored; no aspect of mobility can be investigated or addressed without psychologists! While this statement is technical in orientation, it also has professional consequences and is in line with comments made by colleagues of note (Groeger & Rothengatter, 1998). Traffic psychology is not obstructed but given wings by safety concepts such as Vision Zero or Sustainable Safety, which are localised at this level, even if decision-makers will note with astonishment that traffic psychologists and not engineers demand funds for the improvement of infrastructures and technology on behalf of road users...

CONCLUDING REMARKS

ICTTP are congresses that are meaningfully organised internationally in view of their common topic, even if not all the countries individually represented here share the same bases and, to some degree, have different problems to solve. Traffic psychology cannot and must not shirk the issue of globalisation. To quote Bertrand Piccard, the first person to circumnavigate the globe in a balloon, "Globalisation should not take place solely at commercial and political levels. It must take place, in particular, in respect of an investigation into human roots, throughout all cultures..." (Jahresspiegel aus der Schweizer Prominenz, 2005, p. 8). Traffic psychology will pursue this route to an even greater degree than before and it will be operating on a different basis in 10 years from the one on which it operates today. In view of the increase in mobility and traffic volumes as well as fewer funds, I hope that we will be required and that we will be active as system consultants with even greater frequency than before—in some countries with more, in others with less regulation. Safety, environmental protection and convenience when travelling will be in even greater demand and taken even more for granted than they are today. Traffic psychology must maintain its position as an independent branch within the range of interdisciplinary traffic sciences. It can only do this if it is able to produce usable results based on applications. This must be the focus of research and practice.

REFERENCES

AAA (2004). *Distractions at the Wheel*. Washington: American Automotive Association/ Foundation for Traffic Safety.

Aberg, L. (2001). Attitudes. In Barjonet, P.-E. (Ed.), *Traffic Psychology Today*. Dordrecht: Kluwer Academic Publishers.

Ajzen, I., & Fishbein, M. (1980). *Understanding Attitudes and Predicting Social Behaviour*. Englewood Cliffs, NJ: Prentice Hall.

Blaser, A., & Schnidrig, A. (1993). *Die Experten und der Zufall—Die zufällige (Un)-Tauglichkeit von Motorfahrern und ihren Begutachtern* (vol. 76, pp. 9–12). Bern: Uni Press.

EFPPA. (2000). Some features of traffic psychology around the millennium shift—an overview with focus on Europe. EFPPA Task Force Traffic Psychology 1999–2001.

Ewert, U. (2004). *Warum werden wissenschaftliche Resultate (oft) nicht akzeptiert? Unpublished Paper of a IWIF-lecture Juni 2004*. Bern: Schweizerische Beratungsstelle für Unfallverhütung bfu.

Fishbein, M. (1966). The relationships between beliefs, attitudes and behavior. In Feldman, S. (Ed.), *Cognitive Consistency*. New York: Academic Press.

Frey, D. (1996). Der Zusammenhang von Einstellungen und Verhalten. *Die Kluft zwischen Wissen und Handeln—Eine Serie der Süddeutschen Zeitung*, 23–24.

Gatersleben, B., & Uzzell, D. (2004). Perceptions of car users and policy makers on the effectiveness and acceptability of car travel reduction measures: an attribution theory approach. In Rothengatter, T., & Huguenin, R.D. (Eds.), *Traffic and Transport Psychology, Theory and Application*. Amsterdam: Pergamon.

Gregersen (2004). Unpublished figure. VTI, Linköping.

Groeger, J.A. (2002). Trafficking in cognition: applying cognitive psychology to driving. *Transportation Research Part F, 5*, 235–248.

Groeger, J.A., & Rothengatter, J.A. (1998). Traffic psychology and behaviour. *Transportation Research Part F, 1*, 1–9.

Haight, F.A. (2004). Accident proneness: the history of an idea. In Rothengatter, T., & Huguenin, R.D. (Eds.), *Traffic and Transport Psychology, Theory and Application*. Amsterdam: Pergamon.

Hakamies-Blomqvist, L., (2004). Ageing and transportation: the challenges and opportunities for transport safety. PRI/Liikeneturva-Seminar, Helsinki www.lapri.org.

Huguenin, R.D. (1978). *Einstellungen (Attitüden) und Trinkverhalten von Automobilisten. bfu-Report 1*. Bern: Schweizerische Beratungsstelle für Unfallverhütung bfu.

Huguenin, R.D. (1988a). Fahrerverhalten im Strassenverkehr—Ein Beitrag zur Theorienbildung in der Verkehrspsychologie. Braunschweig: Faktor Mensch im Verkehr, 37, Rot-Gelb-Grün.

Huguenin, R.D. (1988b). The concept of risk and behaviour models in traffic psychology. *Ergonomics, 31*, 557–569.

IFMO (2002). In Institut für Mobilitätsforschung (Ed.), *Motives and Actions in Leisure Traffic*. Berlin: Springer.

Jahresspiegel aus der Schweizer Prominenz (2005). Bertrand Piccard. Schönbühl: Hallwag Kümmerly + Frey AG.

Johansson, M. (2004). Psychological motivation of pro-environmental travel behaviour in an urban area. In Rothengatter, T., & Huguenin, R.D. (Eds.), *Traffic and Transport Psychology, Theory and Application*. Amsterdam: Pergamon.

Keskinen, E., Hatakka, M., Laapotti, S., Katila, A., & Peräaho, M. (2004). Driver behaviour as a hierarchical system. In Rothengatter, T., & Huguenin, R.D. (Eds.), *Traffic and Transport Psychology, Theory and Application*. Amsterdam: Pergamon.

Kluwe, R.H. (2001). Zur Lage der Psychologie: Perspektiven der Fortentwicklung einer erfolgreichen Wissenschaft. *Psychologische Rundschau, 52* (1), 1–10.

Microcensus (2000). *Mobilität in der Schweiz—Ergebnisse des Mirkozensus 2000 zum Verkehrsverhalten*. Bern: ARE BFS, Bundesamt für Raumentwicklung, Bundesamt für Statistik.

Minkmar, N. (2004). Der Last-Kraftwagen. *Cicero, Magazin für Politische Kultur, 4*, 122.

Murray, A. (2003). Decreasing number of young licence holders and reduced number of accidents—a description of trends in Sweden. *Accident Analysis and Prevention, 35*, 841–850.

Parker, D. (2004). Road safety: what has social psychology to offer? In Rothengatter, T., & Huguenin, R.D. (Eds.), *Traffic and Transport Psychology, Theory and Application*. Amsterdam: Pergamon.

Parker, D., Lajunen, T., & Stradling, S. (1998). Attitudinal predictors of interpersonally aggressive violations on the road. *Transportation Research Part F, 1*, 11–24.

Priesendörfer, P., Wächter, F., Franzen, A., Diekmann, A., Schad, H., & Rommerskirchen, S. (1999). *Umweltbewusstsein und Verkehrsmittelwahl, Berichte der Bundesanstalt für Strassenwesen, Mensch und Sicherheit, Heft M 113*. Bergisch Gladbach: Bundesanstalt für Strassenwesen bast.

Prochaska, J.O., DiClemente, C.C., & Norcross, J.C. (1992). In search of how people change—applications to addictive behaviors. *American Psychologist, 47* (9), 1102–1114.

Shell (2001). *Energy needs, choices and possibilities—scenarios to 2050*. London: Exploring the Future, Global Business Environment Shell International.

Siegrist, S., & Roskova, E. (2001). The effects of safety regulations and law enforcement. In Barjonet, P.-E. (Ed.), *Traffic Psychology Today*. Dordrecht: Kluwer Academic Publishers.

Siren, A., & Hakamies-Blomqvist, L. (2004). Private car as the grand equaliser? Demographic factors and mobility in Finnish men and women aged 65 + . *Transportation Research, Part F*, 107–118.

Spicher, B., & Hänsgen, K.-D. (2003). *Test zur Erfassung verkehrsrelevanter Persönlichkeitsmerkmale TVP*. Bern: Hans Huber.

Steg, L. (2004). Car use: lust and must. In Rothengatter, T., & Huguenin, R.D. (Eds.), *Traffic and Transport Psychology, Theory and Application*. Amsterdam: Pergamon.

Stradling, S., Meadows, S., & Beatty, S. (2004a). Who will reduce their car use—and who will not? In Rothengatter, T., & Huguenin, R.D. (Eds.), *Traffic and Transport Psychology, Theory and Application*. Amsterdam: Pergamon.

Stradling, S., Meadows, S., & Beatty, S. (2004b). Characteristics and crash-involvement of speeding, violating and thrill-seeking drivers. In Rothengatter, T., & Huguenin, R.D. (Eds.), *Traffic and Transport Psychology, Theory and Application*. Amsterdam: Pergamon.

VULNERABLE ROAD USERS I:

PEDESTRIANS AND CYCLISTS

Traffic and Transport Psychology
G. Underwood (Editor)

2

USING EPIDEMIOLOGICAL DATA TO ADDRESS PSYCHOLOGICAL QUESTIONS ABOUT PEDESTRIAN BEHAVIOUR

George Dunbar[1]

INTRODUCTION

Older people are vulnerable as pedestrians, and this chapter seeks to advance our understanding of the factors influencing their risk by analysing epidemiological data about the situations that are dangerous for them. By doing this, it is possible to develop understanding about the causes of accidents. For example, some researchers have used evidence suggesting that the second half of the road crossing becomes relatively more dangerous for older people to argue that slower walking speed is a cause of accidents. The central aim of this chapter is to review the evidence for the conclusion that the second half of crossing is more dangerous, to assess this relative risk, and to evaluate possible explanations for it.

It has been realised for some time that older people are more likely to be killed or seriously injured in pedestrian accidents than younger adults (e.g. OECD 1970, 1986; WHO, 1976; see Dunbar, Holland & Maylor, 2004, for a review). For example, Hagenzieker (1996) reported that while the risk of a pedestrian fatality was 0.8 per 100 million km walked for 30–39 year olds, the corresponding rates for older people were 2.5 for 60–64 year olds, and 10.5 for those 65 and older (Netherlands data for 1992–1994).

In large measure, this is because older people are more vulnerable to physical injury. For example, Leaf and Preusser (1999) analysed data from pedestrian accidents in Florida between 1993 and 1996, and found that older people were more easily injured at all speeds. Even below 20 mph, the risk of fatality was three times greater for those over 65 than for younger adults.

[1] Department of Psychology, University of Warwick, Coventry CV4 7AL, United Kingdom. *E-mail:* G.L.Dunbar@warwick.ac.uk (G. Dunbar).

However, frailty cannot entirely explain the increase in pedestrian fatality rates. Older people are not just more likely to be killed in an accident, they are also more likely to be involved in one. Keall (1995) studied accident data from New Zealand for 1988–1991, using estimates based on Evans (1991) to take account of the additional vulnerability of older people to physical injury. Keall concluded that, after allowing for frailty, there was a substantially increased risk of involvement in accidents crossing the road from the age of 80 years.

It remains unclear what causes this increased risk of accident involvement. Previous reviews have noted that older people are over-represented in accidents involving reversing vehicles and in accidents at junctions (e.g. Hauer, 1988). It has been suggested that this may reflect difficulty coping with unexpected vehicle movements and more complex situations where attention needs to be directed in more than one direction (e.g. Staplin, Lococo, Byington & Harkey, 2001). Older people in general do show a disproportionate decline in certain attention skills (McDowd & Shaw, 2000), and the Useful Field of View test, a composite measure of visual attention, has been linked to accident rates in older drivers (e.g. Ball, Owsley, Sloane, Roenker & Bruni, 1993), making the attention decline hypothesis a plausible one.

In this study, I examine a particular facet of accident risk, the relative risk of nearside and farside accidents. This relative risk has been studied by a number of researchers who have found that older pedestrians have a relatively higher risk of being in an accident in the farside of the road than in the first part of a road crossing (see Table 1). It has been argued that older people may be more vulnerable in the latter part of road crossing for two reasons (e.g. Fontaine & Gourlet, 1997; Oxley, Fildes, Ihsen, Charlton & Day, 1997). First, older people walk more slowly and so are more likely to fail to reach the far kerb in time. Older women, in particular, walk more slowly than older men (Dunbar et al., 2004). Second, it has been suggested that, perhaps because of cognitive limitations such as those implicated in the attention decline hypothesis, older people are more likely to consider only the first lane when beginning to cross, and so may enter the road when only the first lane is safe.

Data from studies that have contrasted the two halves of road crossing is summarised in Table 1. Some of these studies do suggest that the relative risk of farside accidents increases for older people (Fontaine & Gourlet, 1997; Grayson, 1980; Oxley et al., 1997; TRRL, 1972), and one study indicates that this effect may be greater for women than men (Carthy, Packham, Salter & Silcock, 1995). However, some other studies, the largest, have shown little difference (Fildes et al., 1994; RAGB, 1981), and one suggests that any effect is in the opposite direction (Ward et al., 1994). Unfortunately, it is not straightforward to meta-analyse these data sets because of differences in methodology across studies. Only one of the studies disaggregated figures for men and women, most have not separated degrees of accident severity, and different studies have divided cases into age groups in different ways. Separation into age groups is particularly important, given Keall's finding that it is the older old, over about 80 years, who have a substantially increased accident risk. If the change in relative risk in the two halves of the road contributes to the overall increase in older people's pedestrian accident rates, then we would expect it to change at about that age.

This study analyses 10 years of British data, a much larger data set than those previously analysed, to allow us to attempt a definitive assessment of three sets of questions. First, what is the relative risk of nearside and farside pedestrian accidents for adults of different ages and

Table 1. Studies contrasting pedestrian accidents in the two halves of the road.

Study	Age group (years)	Sample size	Nearside:farside ratio
Grayson (1980)[a]	Under 60	Unknown	2.1
	60 and over	Unknown	1.7
RAGB (1981)	16–69	Unknown	1.57
	70 and over	Unknown	1.51
Fildes et al. (1994)	All ages	Unknown	1.40
	Older people	Unknown	1.40
Ward et al. (1994)	5–34	453	1.71
	35–49	63	1.86
	50–59	40	1.86
	60–64	16	1.17
	65 and over	99	3.12
Carthy et al. (1995)	Men 65–74	37	1.17
	Women 65–74	31	1.81
	Men 75 and over	25	1.50
	Women 75 and over	59	1.03
Fontaine and Gourlet (1997)	65 and over	356	0.79
Oxley et al. (1997)[b]	65 and under	33	0.85
	Over 65	19	0.29
PCA (1999)	60 and over	Unknown	1.17

Figures for all studies are for casualties, except for Fontaine and Gourlet (1997) which examined fatalities only.
[a]Grayson indicated that his data came from the same study as the widely cited TRRL (1972), which had available only part of the data. TRRL (1972) reported nearside:farside ratios of 3.6 for 15–59 years, 2.1 for 60–69 years, and 1.5 for 70 years and over; [b]Oxley et al. (1997) separated accidents stepping off the kerb, which formed a similar proportion of accidents for older and younger people. If these are counted as nearside accidents, the ratios were 1.84 and 2.66 for older and younger people, respectively.

sexes? Second, can the hypotheses that older people walk more slowly or check only the nearside lane before crossing, explain the relative risk of nearside and farside pedestrian accidents for older adults? Third, is an age-related change in this relative risk associated with the increased overall risk of a pedestrian accident?

METHOD

In Great Britain (Scotland, England and Wales), the police record details of each reported road accident that leads to a casualty using a standard form, STATS19. For this study, we considered all the pedestrian accidents from 1991 to 2000 involving a single casualty and a single vehicle in which the pedestrian had been crossing the road at the time of the accident. Cases in which there were special circumstances, such as roadworks at the accident site, or an animal in the roadway, were excluded. The STATS19 form records whether the pedestrian was struck moving from the driver's "nearside" or came from the driver's "offside", but we will label these from the perspective of the pedestrian as "nearside" and "farside" accidents for clarity of expression.

Statistical significance of contrasts between age groups was evaluated using a meta-analytic method, treating each year as a separate trial, to avoid Simpson's paradox (Altman & Deeks, 2002; Cates, 2002). However, similar results are obtained if the data is analysed as a single trial.

The fundamental statistic used, the relative risk of nearside and farside incidents, it is important to emphasise, has the particular virtue that it is unaffected by differences in exposure as these are usually treated, because it is a ratio of two risks for the same group. The usual method of allowing for exposure differences is to estimate the exposure of cases in different groups, measured as distance travelled, number of journeys, number of road crossings, or whatever, by surveying separate samples of the corresponding populations, and calculating the average exposure of those samples. However, relative risk so calculated for any given group has the same estimate of exposure in its numerator and denominator, and exposure is therefore taken out of the equation algebraically.

RESULTS

The relative risk of nearside and farside accidents for each age group was calculated for each calendar year, and the mean values are shown separately for men and women in Table 2. To compare age groups, confidence intervals on the odds ratios were determined using RevMan

Table 2. Relative risk (ratio) of nearside approach compared to farside pedestrian accidents that led to death or serious injury within 30 days, by age group and sex: averages for Great Britain 1991–2000.

Age group (years)	Men (N)	Women (N)
Under 35	1.65 (26,947)	1.62 (14,216)
35–44	1.31 (2677)	1.44 (1150)
45–54	1.35 (2196)	1.47 (1206)
55–64	1.33 (2069)	1.30 (1468)
65–74	1.33 (2369)	1.23 (2654)
75–84	1.25 (2380)	1.23 (3734)
85 years and over	1.55 (853)	1.51 (1269)

and MetaView software and combined using the Mantel-Haenszel method (The Cochrane Collaboration, 2000). In all cases, the homogeneity assumption was evaluated and was found to be satisfied (minimum $p = 0.12$).

Compared to those aged 75–84, the relative risk of being killed or seriously injured in the nearside was greater for those aged 85 and over (odds ratio = 1.24, 95% CI = 1.12–1.37, $z = 4.12$, $p < 0.01$), and for those aged under 35 years (odds ratio = 1.32, 95% CI = 1.24–1.39, $z = 9.73$, $p < 0.01$).

A very rough estimate of exposure was made by using figures for number of journeys per year for each age group given in Mitchell (2000). These figures were not broken down by sex and the age groups were not aligned perfectly with the ones used here. Based on these rough estimates, the number of deaths and serious injuries per 1000 journeys was calculated for each age group, by sex and year of study, and this was correlated with the nearside relative risk. (One outlying data point, women aged 45–54 in 1999, with a relative risk of over 2.5, was excluded.) There was a small correlation, $r = 0.17$, $p = 0.046$, $N = 139$, indicating that, across time, age and sex, a higher nearside relative risk is associated with a higher risk of death or serious injury per journey made as a pedestrian, despite the fact that nearside accidents are less severe.

DISCUSSION

The relative risk of nearside accidents is high for young people under 35 years, but declines during middle age. For the very oldest pedestrians, however, this trend is reversed and the relative risk of fatal or serious nearside accidents increases again. There is no difference in the relative risk between those aged 85 and over and those aged under 35 years.

Population rates for pedestrian accidents begin to rise from late middle age and this rise may be partly explained by differences in exposure (people in the early years of retirement may walk more) and changes in people's capacity to cope with physical harm. There is a, particularly, large rise in the fatality rate, which is several times higher for older people. However, Keall's (1995) analysis, which allowed for the effect of frailty, suggested that there was a substantial increase in accident involvement when crossing the road for the oldest old people, those aged 80 and over. On the basis of this finding, we had hypothesised that there might be a difference between the older and younger old. Consistent with that prediction, we found a pattern of greater over-representation in nearside crossing accidents for precisely the very oldest people. This finding cannot be explained by differences in exposure because the relative risk measure neutralises exposure differences as usually calculated. Indeed, one could plausibly argue that the ratio allows for exposure at the level of the individual case, because, of course, everyone who crosses a road must cross both halves.[2] That is, to a close approximation, each case will have been exposed equally often in the past to a nearside or farside crossing episode. At the case level, reliable exposure data are not normally obtainable in studies of road safety.

Existing accounts of the relative risk of the two halves of road crossing have been predicated on the assumption that the farside becomes relatively more dangerous with increasing age. The present findings force us to re-evaluate those accounts. Some of those accounts suggested that older people are more likely to consider only the nearside lane before crossing, perhaps because they have reduced attentional capacity (Carthy et al., 1995; Oxley et al., 1997). However, this could not in itself explain why the oldest pedestrians actually have a higher relative risk in the nearside lane. Indeed, the evidence for the original suggestion was not clear-cut. Carthy et al.'s observation was based on a pilot study at a limited number of locations, and some other studies have found that an older person is, if anything, more likely than an younger adult to turn their

---

[2] Strictly speaking, this is only approximately correct, for a couple of reasons. For example, in some cases a pedestrian may cross part of the way, and then retreat, creating a relatively greater exposure to the near side. Another example is crossing a one-way street.

head both ways to look for traffic before crossing (Wilson & Grayson, 1980). Similarly, although slow walking speed clearly is a problem for older pedestrians, especially on wide roads, or if signal controlled intersections and crossings do not allow sufficient time (e.g. Hoxie & Rubenstein, 1994; Zegeer, Stutts, Huang & Zhou, 1993), it cannot explain the increased relative risk of nearside accidents over 85 years.

There is an alternative cognitive hypothesis that could explain these findings, another attentional hypothesis. On this account, higher relative risk for nearside accidents arises from attentional failures which affect the beginning of crossing most, because pedestrians who fail to attend to the road environment, not just the far lane, carefully before beginning to cross are likely to fail to notice active hazards (Dunbar et al., 2004). One possible contributory factor is the increasing prevalence of dementia in the oldest age groups. The prevalence of moderate and severe dementia rises from 5% at 65 years or older to 20% over 80 (Gelder, Gath, Mayou & Cowen, 1996). Furthermore, it is now well established that older people on average have lower visual attention capacity and that this is correlated with the risk of driving accidents (Ball et al., 1993).

In conclusion, this study indicates that pedestrians aged 85 and over have an increased relative risk of nearside accidents. Some previous studies had argued that older people have a reduced relative risk of nearside accidents compared to younger adults. The data analysed here indicate that younger old women (65–84 years) do have a reduced nearside relative risk compared to women aged 35–54 years. Giving regard to differences in methodology, this aspect of the results is only broadly consistent with the earlier studies reviewed above, which tended not to differentiate the older old from the younger old, and so did not detect the rising relative risk for the very old, and which typically did not distinguish figures for men and women.

We have found a moderate association between nearside relative risk and overall accident rate. We also found that the increase in nearside relative risk occurred at around the same age that previous research had found the overall accident rate increased substantially. Taken together, these findings connect the change in nearside relative risk to the increase in overall accident rate, and indicate that by studying the reasons for the nearside increase, we have a good prospect of understanding reasons for the overall increase in accident risk with age. Methodologically, reduced nearside relative risk may provide one index of safer road crossing behaviour. The ratio is, in principle, independent of differences in population and differences in exposure to the road environment, such as the number of roads crossed by different age groups, and there is an empirical association between increasing values of this ratio and age groups believed to be at greater accident risk. However, it is clear that a reasonably large sample is needed to obtain reliable estimates of relative risk, and it remains to be seen whether the empirical link with age generalises to other countries.

This finding is important for public interventions to reduce pedestrian accidents among older people. A number of widely adopted measures, such as the provision of pedestrian refuges in the centre of the road, and increasing crossing time at signal-controlled crossings, target the reduced ability of older people to traverse the full width of the road safely. The present findings do not suggest that provision of those measures should abate. Rather, they indicate that different measures will be needed to target the extra accidents that the older old have in the first half of road crossing. Appropriate measures would include, e.g. physically separating pedestrians from the roadway using barriers, but that would be feasible in only a minority of locations.

In practice, a large part of the increase in fatality rates for older pedestrians can be attributed to the increasing frailty that the ageing process tends to bring. There is little the older person can do to compensate for this. The only way to protect them is to make the road environment safer, and the most obvious step to take is to reduce vehicle speed, a goal that could be achieved through a range of measures including educating drivers, altering the road environment and changing the regulatory framework. Other important measures, such as improving visibility, are discussed in Dunbar et al. (2004). However, a small percentage of the older population, the oldest, also have a much higher risk of accident involvement, and have an increased relative risk of nearside accidents comparable to the under 35s.

ACKNOWLEDGEMENTS

The road accident data sets (Department of the Environment Transport and the Regions Road Accidents Branch, 2001a–e; Department of Transport Road Accident Statistics Branch, 2001a–d; Department of Transport Road Accidents Branch, 2001) were gathered by the UK Government and are subject to Crown Copyright. The data sets were made available through the UK data archive (http://www.data-archive.ac.uk/). The interpretation and further analysis of the data reported here is, of course, not the responsibility of the originators of the data set. The population statistics used were revised estimates of mid-year values for Great Britain for 1991–2000, published by the Office of National Statistics in February 2003, and available from their website http://www.statistics.gov.uk/.

This paper has benefited from comments made by participants in the symposium "Interdisciplinary approaches to pedestrian safety and pedestrian behaviour" held at the third International Conference on Traffic and Transport Psychology, Nottingham, UK, September 2004.

REFERENCES

Altman, D.G., & Deeks, J.J. (2002). Meta-analysis, Simpson's paradox, and the number needed to treat. *BMC Medical Research Methodology*, 2 (3), Available online at http://www.biomedcentral.com/1471-2288/1472/1473.

Ball, K., Owsley, C., Sloane, M.E., Roenker, D.L., & Bruni, J.R. (1993). Visual attention problems as a predictor of vehicle crashes in older drivers. *Investigative Ophthalmology and Visual Science*, 34 (11), 3110–3123.

Carthy, T., Packham, D., Salter, D., & Silcock, D. (1995). *Risk and Safety on the Roads: The Older Pedestrian*. Basingstoke, Hampshire: AA Foundation for Road Safety Research.

Cates, C.J. (2002). Simpson's paradox and calculation of the number needed to treat from meta-analysis. *BMC Medical Research Methodology*, 2 (1), Available online at http://www.biomedcentral.com/1471-2288/1472/1471.

Department of the Environment Transport and the Regions Road Accidents Branch (2001a). *Road Accident Data, 1991 [computer file]*. Colchester, Essex: UK Data Archive, 10 May 2001, Retrieved, from the World Wide Web.

Department of the Environment Transport and the Regions Road Accidents Branch (2001b). *Road Accident Data, 1997 [computer file]*. Colchester, Essex: UK Data Archive, 11 May 2001, Retrieved, from the World Wide Web.

Department of the Environment Transport and the Regions Road Accidents Branch (2001c). *Road Accident Data, 1998 [computer file]*. Colchester, Essex: UK Data Archive, 11 May 2001, Retrieved, from the World Wide Web.

Department of the Environment Transport and the Regions Road Accidents Branch (2001d). *Road Accident Data, 1999 [computer file]*. Colchester, Essex: UK Data Archive, 1 May 2001, Retrieved, from the World Wide Web.

Department of the Environment Transport and the Regions Road Accidents Branch (2001e). *Road Accident Data, 2000 [computer file]*. Colchester, Essex: UK Data Archive, 17 April 2002, Retrieved, from the World Wide Web.

Department of Transport Road Accidents Branch (2001). *Road Accident Data, 1992 [computer file]*. Colchester, Essex: UK Data Archive, 11 May 2001, Retrieved, from the World Wide Web.

Department of Transport Road Accident Statistics Branch (2001a). *Road Accident Data, 1993 [computer file]*. Colchester, Essex: UK Data Archive, 11 May 2001, Retrieved, from the World Wide Web.

Department of Transport Road Accident Statistics Branch (2001b). *Road Accident Data, 1994 [computer file]*. Colchester, Essex: UK Data Archive, 11 May 2001, Retrieved, from the World Wide Web.

Department of Transport Road Accident Statistics Branch (2001c). *Road Accident Data, 1995 [computer file]*. Colchester, Essex: UK Data Archive, 11 May 2001, Retrieved, from the World Wide Web.

Department of Transport Road Accident Statistics Branch (2001d). *Road Accident Data, 1996 [computer file]*. Colchester, Essex: UK Data Archive, 10 May 2001, Retrieved, from the World Wide Web.

Dunbar, G., Holland, C.A., & Maylor, E.A. (2004). *Older pedestrians: A review*. London: Department for Transport.

Evans, L. (1991). *Traffic Safety and the Driver*. New York: Van Nostrand Reinhold.

Fildes, B., Corben, B., Kent, S., Oxley, J., Le, T.M., & Ryan, P. (1994). *Older Road User Crashes (Report No. 61)*. Melbourne, Australia: Monash University Accident Research Centre.

Fontaine, H., & Gourlet, Y. (1997). Fatal pedestrian accidents in France: a typological analysis. *Accident Analysis and Prevention, 29*, 303–312.

Gelder, M., Gath, D., Mayou, R., & Cowen, P. (1996). *Oxford Textbook of Psychiatry* (3rd ed.). Oxford: OUP.

Grayson, G.B. (1980). The elderly pedestrian. In Oborne, D.J., & Levis, J.A. (Eds.), *Human Factors in Transport Research: Volume 2 User Factors* (pp. 405–413). London: Academic Press.

Hagenzieker, M.P. (1996). *Some aspects of the safety of elderly pedestrians and cyclists, Proceedings of the Conference Road Safety in Europe, Birmingham, September 1996*. Linköping, Sweden: Swedish National Road and Transport Research Institute, pp. 51–65.

Hauer, E. (1988). *The Safety of Older Persons at Intersections* (Vol. 2,). Washington, DC: Transportation Research Board, pp. 194–252.

Hoxie, R.E., & Rubenstein, L.Z. (1994). Are older pedestrians allowed enough time to cross intersections safely. *Journal of the American Geriatric Society, 42*, 1219–1220.

Keall, M.D. (1995). Pedestrian exposure to risk of road accident in New Zealand. *Accident Analysis and Prevention, 27* (5), 729–740.

Leaf, W.A., & Preusser, D.F. (1999). *Literature Review on Vehicle Travel Speeds and Pedestrian Injuries (DOT HS 809 021)*. Washington, DC: US Department of Transportation, NHTSA.

McDowd, J.M., & Shaw, R.J. (2000). Attention and aging: a functional perspective. In Craik, F.I.M., & Salthouse, T.A. (Eds.), *The Handbook of Aging and Cognition*. Mahwah, NJ: Erlbaum.

Mitchell, C.G.B. (2000). *Some Implications of Road Safety for an Ageing Population, Transport Trends 2000*. London: DETR, pp. 26–34.

OECD (1970). *Pedestrian Safety*. Paris: OECD.

OECD (1986). *Effectiveness of Road Safety Education Programmes*. Paris: OECD.

Oxley, J.A., Fildes, B.N., Ihsen, E., Charlton, J.L., & Day, R.H. (1997). Differences in traffic judgements between young and old adult pedestrians. *Accident Analysis and Prevention*, 29 (6), 839–847.

PCA (1999). *Safety and the Older Pedestrian*. Neutral Bay, NSW: Pedestrian Council of Australia.

RAGB. (1981). Road accidents Great Britain 1980: The casualty report. London: HMSO.

Staplin, L., Lococo, K., Byington, S. & Harkey, D. (2001). *Guidelines and recommendations to accommodate older drivers and pedestrians* (FHWA-RD-01-051): Federal Highway Administration.

The Cochrane Collaboration (2000). RevMan 4.1.1 and Metaview 4.1 (Version 4.1.1): The Cochrane Collaboration.

TRRL (1972). *Accidents to Elderly Pedestrians (Leaflet LF323)*. Crowthorne, Berkshire: Transport and Road Research Laboratory.

Ward, H., Cave, J., Morrison, A., Allsop, R., Evans, A., Kuiper, C., & Willumsen, L. (1994). *Pedestrian Activity and Accident Risk*. London: AA Foundation for Road Safety Research.

WHO (1976). *The Epidemiology of Road Traffic Accidents, WHO Regional Publications European Series No. 2*. Copenhagen: WHO Regional Office for Europe.

Wilson, D.G., & Grayson, G.B. (1980). *Age-Related Differences in the Road Crossing Behaviour of Adult Pedestrians, Transport and Road Research Digest. LR 933*. Crowthorne: Transport and Road Research Laboratory.

Zegeer, C.V., Stutts, J.C., Huang, H., & Zhou, M. (1993). Analysis of elderly pedestrian accidents and recommended countermeasures. *Transportation Research Record, 1405*, 56–63.

Traffic and Transport Psychology
G. Underwood (Editor)
© 2005 Elsevier Ltd. All rights reserved.

3

RURAL AND URBAN CHILDREN'S UNDERSTANDING OF SAFETY AND DANGER ON THE ROAD

Karen Pfeffer[1]

INTRODUCTION

Pedestrian–car collisions are one of the leading causes of death and injury to children in motorised countries (Mayr et al., 2003). In the UK, the Department for Transport (2002) reports that child pedestrian casualties continue to be a significant problem, accounting for 63% of the total of children killed or seriously injured. The vast majority of casualties occur on built-up roads with children in urban areas having a high rate of pedestrian accidents due to their high exposure rate (Department for Transport, 2002). Within urban areas, approximately 80% of accidents to children less than 9 years of age occur on minor roads (Thomson, 1996) where crossing facilities are least likely to be found. Crossing facilities are also relatively scarce on rural roads.

Whether or not pedestrian crossing facilities are available, the ability to find a safe place to cross the road is an important pedestrian skill. It is a necessary precursor to other crossing skills such as judgement of traffic speed and movement, judgement of traffic gaps and estimates of time needed to cross. In an experimental investigation using table-top models and taking children to streets near their school, Ampofo-Boateng and Thompson (1991) found that 5- and 7-year-old children had very poor ability to separate safe from dangerous places to cross the road, nor could they choose a safe place for themselves when asked to do so. However, by the age of 11 years children appeared to have developed reasonable skill. Ampofo-Boateng and Thompson also noted that 5- and 7-year olds relied on the absence of cars as a major factor in their judgements of safe crossing points. If a car was visible somewhere in the vicinity, even if not directly approaching the road-crossing point, young children judged it unsafe to cross. It is

[1] University of Lincoln, Lincoln, UK. *E-mail:* kpfeffer@lincoln.ac.uk (K. Pfeffer).

not until about 9 years that children judge road-crossing sites with a restricted view of the road (such as the brow of a hill, a sharp bend, obscuring trees and bushes) as being unsafe places to cross. Demetre and Gaffin (1994) found that young children failed to take into account occluding vehicles in their choice of road-crossing sites. They found the road-crossing choices of 6-year olds to be random. However, by 10 years of age almost all children (92%) chose the site with a clear view of the road. Demetre and Gaffin also found that 8-year-old children who claimed to have experience of crossing roads alone tended to make appropriate road-crossing choices.

The majority of studies of child pedestrian capabilities and behaviour involve urban sites and/or children from urban schools. There is very little research literature relevant to road-safety measures for children living in rural areas (Department for Transport, 2003) as most road accidents involving children occur in urban environments. Results of the limited research pertaining to rural children have found that child pedestrians are more vulnerable at junctions and are likely to walk with their backs to the oncoming traffic (Department for Transport, 2003). The aim of this study was to add to the scant research literature on rural children's pedestrian capabilities by comparing rural and urban children's understanding of safe and dangerous road-crossing sites. As urban children have a higher exposure to road traffic than rural children, it was predicted that urban children would have a more accurate understanding of safe and dangerous road-crossing sites than rural children. For this investigation, two age groups of rural and urban children were compared, 5- to 6-year olds and 10- to 11-year olds. We were also interested in exploring potential relationships between children's regular road experiences (such as when walking to school, visiting the city centre, etc.) and their understanding of safe and dangerous road-crossing sites.

METHOD

Participants

A total of 78 children from two primary schools took part in the investigation. An urban school situated within 1 mile of the city centre and a rural school situated within 15 miles from the nearest city were selected. The rural school was situated in a village with a population of slightly less than 2000 to ensure a sufficiently large sample size. The village selected did not have a heavy traffic flow at any time of the day. The sample from both schools comprised all children present in the class of the required age with parental consent to participate. The age, sex and location (rural/urban) distribution of the sample is shown in Table 1.

Table 1. Demographic characteristics of the participants.

	5- to 6-year olds	*10- to 11-year olds*	*Total*
Rural	13 (5 boys, 8 girls)	18 (10 boys, 8 girls)	31
Urban	31 (19 boys, 12 girls)	16 (11 boys, 5 girls)	47
Total	44	34	78

Materials

Twelve photographs of safe and dangerous road-crossing sites were used. The photographs were selected from a pool of photographs taken in urban and rural areas. Photographs were selected in consultation with Lincolnshire County Council Road Safety Officers. The photographs were selected to represent a range of conditions which a pedestrian might be expected to encounter, relatively "safe" crossing sites such as road crossings designed for pedestrians (zebra crossing, pelican crossing, pedestrian refuge) and a quiet straight road affording a clear view (although it was recognised that no road-crossing site is entirely safe). Also dangerous sites were included to represent frequently encountered pedestrian environments such as sites with restricted or obstructed views (streets with parked cars, blind bends, etc.) as well as busy streets.

The use of photographs and drawings has been successfully used by several researchers (e.g. Joshi, MacLean & Carter, 1999; Pfeffer, 1989). One advantage of such methods is the ability to include a wide variety of road-crossing contexts and variables. In total there were four relatively safe crossing sites (with three identified pedestrian crossings) and eight dangerous sites. The dangerous sites comprised five urban scenes and three rural scenes (see Table 2). Examples of photographs are shown in Figures 1 and 2.

Table 2. Road-crossing sites depicted in the photographs.

Relatively "safe" sites	Dangerous urban sites	Dangerous rural sites
"Zebra" crossing	Blind bend	Blind bend
"Pelican" crossing	Brow of hill	Obscured view of "T" junction and blind bend
Pedestrian refuge	Busy street	Unmarked road with oncoming vehicles
Straight road with clear view and no vehicles	Complex junction	
	Street with parked vehicles obstructing view	

Parental questionnaires requested information about children's mode of transport to school, their experiences with traffic (whether they cross the road alone, with friends, with an adult, etc.), how frequently they visit the city centre and how frequently parents talk to their children about road safety.

Procedure

A practice photograph was presented to individual children; this was followed by the 12 test photographs presented in random order. Children were asked to look at the photograph and to state whether they thought the scene depicted was a safe place to cross the road. They were also asked to give the reasons for their answer. After completing the task, children were informed of any of the dangers they had not recognised in the photos.

Figure 1. Example of dangerous rural site (obscured view of junction and blind bend).

Figure 2. Straight road with clear view and no vehicles.

The photographs were scored according to the scoring procedure used by Ampofo-Boateng and Thomson (1991). A score of one point was given for correctly identifying the road-crossing site as safe or dangerous. A further one point was given for an appropriate explanation for their choice. Scoring was done independently by four assessors, a final rating being given by majority consensus.

Parents were also asked to complete a questionnaire giving information on their child's usual mode of transport to school (walking, cycling, by car, by bus) and their child's experiences with traffic. Parental questionnaires were scored as follows. A nominal scale was used for coding information about the child's usual mode of transport to school. A five-point ordinal scale was used to score the frequency with which children visit the city centre (0 = never, 1 = once a month, 2 = once a fortnight, 3 = once a week, 4 = more than once a week). A three-point ordinal scale was used to score the frequency with which parents talk to their children about road safety (0 = never, 1 = sometimes, 2 = mostly).

RESULTS

Tables 3 and 4 show the mean scores and standard deviations for the 5- to 6-year olds and the 10- to 11-year olds separately. Scores were calculated for all road-crossing sites combined (total of all 12 road-crossing sites), for the subset of "safe" photographs (four sites), for the subset of dangerous photographs (all eight dangerous sites), for the subset of dangerous urban sites (five sites) and the subset of dangerous rural photographs (three sites).

Table 3. Responses of 5- to 6-year-old children to the safe and dangerous road-crossing sites by photograph subset.

	Urban		Rural	
	Mean	Standard deviation	Mean	Standard deviation
All road-crossing sites[a]	11.27	4.24	8.93	3.51
Safe subset	4.13	1.73	4.57	2.02
Dangerous subset[b] (all dangerous sites)	7.17	3.71	4.36	3.05
Urban/danger subset[c]	5.43	2.69	3.86	2.83
Rural/danger subset[d]	1.70	1.44	0.64	0.84

[a]$t_{42} = 1.792, p = 0.04$; [b]$t_{42} = 2.468, p < 0.01$; [c]$t_{42} = 1.756, p = 0.04$; [d]$t_{42} = 2.539, p < 0.01$.

Table 4. Responses of 10- to 11-year-old children to the safe and dangerous road-crossing sites by photograph subset.

	Urban		Rural	
	Mean	Standard deviation	Mean	Standard deviation
All road-crossing sites	16.25	3.29	17.50	3.24
Safe subset	5.87	1.70	6.67	1.49
Dangerous subset (all dangerous sites)	10.37	3.59	10.83	2.72
Urban/danger subset	7.87	2.77	8.06	1.79
Rural/danger subset	2.50	1.71	2.78	1.39

A 2 (age groups) × 2 (school location) ANOVA was carried out for the total scores (all road-crossing sites) and for each subset (safe, dangerous, dangerous urban, dangerous rural). As expected, significant age effects were observed for all road-crossing sites and each subset, with the 10- to 11-year olds scoring higher than the 5- to 6-year olds. For all road-crossing sites

$F_{1,74} = 59.57, p < 0.001$; for safe sites $F_{1,74} = 21.96, p < 0.001$; for dangerous sites $F_{1,74} = 37.09, p < 0.001$; for dangerous urban sites $F_{1,74} = 29.65, p < 0.001$; and for dangerous rural sites $F_{1,74} = 19.51, p < 0.01$. There was no main effect of school location. However, there were significant interactions for all road-crossing sites ($F_{1,74} = 4.17, p < 0.05$), for dangerous crossing sites ($F_{1,74} = 4.22, p < 0.05$) and for dangerous rural crossing sites ($F_{1,74} = 4.04, p < 0.05$).

Comparisons between urban and rural children were carried out for each age group separately. Significant differences were observed for the 5- to 6-year olds (see Table 3). The urban 5- to 6-year-old children scored significantly higher than the rural 5- to 6-year-old children for all road-crossing sites, for the dangerous crossing sites and for the dangerous urban and dangerous rural sites. No significant differences were observed between the urban and rural 10- to 11-year olds (see Table 4).

Some of the most frequently occurring dangers identified by children are presented in Table 5. The older children more frequently mentioned a restricted view of the road (e.g. "can't see round the corner") than younger children. This was infrequently mentioned by the rural 5- to 6-year olds, although it featured prominently in the responses given by the rural 10- to 11-year olds. The presence of cars and potential appearance of cars were most frequently mentioned by the younger children, especially the urban children. Whether the road was considered "busy" or not featured more often in urban children's responses than rural children's responses for both age groups. A reliance on pedestrian crossing facilities in deciding whether a crossing site is dangerous was also more noticeable in the responses given by urban 5- to 6-year olds than any of the other groups. The younger children also noticed the road markings (mainly being absent in the rural photographs).

Table 5. Most frequently identified dangers by age and location expressed as a percentage of total number of "danger" responses.

	Urban 5- to 6-year-olds (%)	Rural 5- to 6-year-olds (%)	Urban 10- to 11-year-olds (%)	Rural 10- to 11-year-olds (%)
Total number of "danger" responses (n)	100 (n = 156)	100 (n = 65)	100 (n = 121)	100 (n = 124)
Restricted view	14.10	6.15	33.88	52.42
Cars present	25.64	20.00	11.57	12.90
Cars could come (fast)	10.89	16.92	4.13	4.03
Road markings (present/absent)	0.64	6.15	0.00	0.00
Busy road/main road	13.46	3.08	16.53	5.65
No crossings/lights/ nothing to tell you when to cross	17.31	9.23	2.48	2.42

The reasons children gave for deciding that a crossing site was safe to cross are presented in Table 6. The younger children, urban and rural, were most likely to comment on the presence and movement of cars. The older children considered this infrequently. However, the older urban children more frequently mentioned their impression of how quiet or busy the road appeared to be in their responses. Having a clear view of the road was more frequently mentioned by the rural 10- to 11-year olds than the other groups. Given that the majority of photographs of "safe" crossing sites were of designated pedestrian crossing sites, it is not surprising that the majority of responses concerned this as a reason for a crossing site being considered safe.

Table 6. Most frequent reasons given for "safe" explanations expressed as a percentage of total number of "safe" responses.

	Urban 5- to 6-year-olds (%)	Rural 5- to 6-year-olds (%)	Urban 10- to 11-year-olds (%)	Rural 10- to 11-year-olds (%)
Total number of "safe" responses (n)	100 ($n = 171$)	100 ($n = 88$)	100 ($n = 84$)	100 ($n = 84$)
Clear view	1.17	2.27	5.95	13.09
Cars absent	17.54	25.00	2.38	1.19
Cars could come (fast)	9.94	12.50	5.95	5.95
Cars stopped	2.92	2.27	0.00	0.00
Quiet road/ not busy	5.85	6.82	23.81	8.33
Designated crossing place	28.65	25.00	44.05	50.00

A total of 63 parents returned the questionnaires (a response rate of 79.75%). Comparing the responses from the parental questionnaires, no differences were found between the rural and urban children's mode of transport to school. Parents of the majority of children in both groups reported that their children usually walk to school. Mann–Whitney U-test comparisons found that the 5- to 6-year-old urban children had a higher frequency of visits to the city centre than rural children, as would be expected ($p < 0.027$). No significant differences were found between the frequency with which rural parents and urban parents reported talking to their children about road safety.

Spearman correlations were used to examine relationships between parental reports of children's experiences and children's test scores. Significant correlations were observed only for the younger children. No significant correlations were observed for the 10- to 11-year-olds. For the 5- to 6-year olds, a significant correlation was observed between parental reports of visits to the city centre and the scores for all road-crossing sites ($r_{s\,39} = 0.331, p < 0.02$) and for the subset of dangerous urban sites ($r_{s\,39} = 0.275$, $p < 0.04$) indicating that the more frequently children visited the city centre the better their understanding of safe and dangerous road-crossing sites, particularly the dangerous urban crossing sites.

A separate analysis was conducted for urban and rural 5- to 6-year olds. For the rural children, parental reports of the frequency of visits to the city centre were positively related to children's scores for all road-crossing sites ($r_{s\ 13} = 0.49$, $p < 0.05$). The more often children went to the city centre the better their understanding of safe and dangerous road-crossing sites. Parental reports of the frequency of visits to the city centre were also positively correlated with the frequency with which parents reported talking to their children about road safety ($r_{s\ 13} = 0.617$, $p = 0.019$). The more often children went to the city centre the more often parents talked to them about road safety. For the urban children the more frequently parents talked to their children about road safety the lower the children's scores on the "safe" subset ($r_{s\ 25} = -0.417$, $p = 0.038$). Further analysis is needed to determine whether this was due to parents warning children of the dangers of incorrect use of pedestrian crossing facilities.

DISCUSSION

The results of this study found that at 5–6 years of age, urban children were more able to identify safe and dangerous road-crossing sites than rural children. For the 10- to 11-year olds no rural–urban differences were apparent. Analysis of the reasons children gave for their choice of safe and dangerous sites showed that younger children focused on single features of the environment such as presence of cars, whether there were road markings on the road, etc. This supports well-established findings from previous studies (e.g. Ampofo-Boateng & Thomson, 1991). Younger children, especially the younger urban children, also mentioned the possible appearance of cars not actually present in the photograph (e.g. "cars might come", "cars can come fast"). The urban children of both age groups also frequently mentioned whether the road was "busy", "a main road" or "a quiet country road". Similar to Ampofo-Boateng and Thomson's findings was the less frequent mention of a restricted view of the road by bends, hedges and so on by the younger children, particularly the rural 5- to 6-year olds. Although the results for urban children were similar to the results of previous research, differences were evident between urban and rural 5- to 6-year olds in their understanding of safety and danger on the road.

Experience with traffic may be an important factor for 5- to 6-year-old children. Hill, Lewis and Dunbar (2000) found that 7- to 8-year-old children with more exposure to traffic (from walking to school or playing in the street) were more aware of danger. Demetre and Gaffin (1994) also noted that 8-year olds who walked to school alone were more aware of danger. Experience may also be important for younger children. In our sample, urban and rural children's experiences differed in some respects. No differences were observed between the urban and rural children in the mode of transport to school (the majority walked to school) or in the frequency with which parents reported talking to their children about road safety. However, there were differences in the frequency with which they visited the city centre and thus exposed to a greater volume of traffic, more complex road environments, more designated "safe" pedestrian crossing sites and so on. Significant correlations between the frequency of visits to the city centre and the road-safety test scores were found for the 5- to 6-year olds, particularly the rural 5- to 6-year olds. The more frequently children went to the city centre the better their understanding of safe and dangerous road-crossing sites. Urban children's parents reported more frequent visits to the city centre than rural children's parents. This may, in part, explain the urban children's better performance on the road-safety task. The results also indicated that, for rural children, the more often they visited the city centre the more often parents talked to their children about road safety. Although significant, the correlations were quite low, so the results should be interpreted with caution.

It might be expected that children living in rural environments would be more aware of the dangers of rural road environments than urban children. Interestingly, urban children performed better than rural children on the dangerous rural subset of road-crossing sites. Fyhri, Bjørnskau and Ulleberg (2004) also found urban children performed better than semi-urban children on a road-safety task involving identifying and understanding safe and dangerous crossing sites. In their study, this difference was evident both before and after training was carried out. One of the explanations for these results suggested by Fyhri et al. was that exposure to complex traffic situations may provide children with a wider frame of reference to associate new knowledge. Further research is needed on the role of such experiences on children's road-safety abilities, particularly research using a wider range of rural sites.

The results of this small-scale study into rural and urban children's understanding of safe and dangerous road-crossing sites have identified differences between rural and urban children that merit further investigation. Further research should involve a wider range of rural sites and more dynamic stimuli. Among the advantages of the use of photographs is the ability to include a wide range of road-crossing sites economically. Although it would be preferable to test participants in real road environments, this presents logistical problems. One of the limitations of the use of photographs is the limited view of the road afforded by a stationary camera. Hill et al. (2000) found short video segments to be preferable to photographs and line drawings for 5- to 6-year olds. Further research could use video segments of a range of sites.

Rural areas differ in the amount and type of traffic in the environment, as well as the type of speed limits imposed and whether these are adhered to. This study involved a small sample of children from one of many different rural environments. A wider range of comparisons is needed. Also, research should involve a wider range of age groups. Studies of urban children's road-safety knowledge and behaviour have involved comparisons among children between 3 and 15 years as well as adults. Relatively little is known about the development of rural children's road-safety understandings. Although the majority of child pedestrian injuries and fatalities occur in urban areas (Department for Transport, 2003), it should not be assumed that children living in rural areas are not at risk. Rural areas may be subjected to heavy traffic flow, sometimes with seasonal variations (such as tourist traffic or heavy goods vehicles) that make the road environment more difficult to predict. Rural children may also be likely to encounter urban roads and urban traffic at some time in their lives, particularly children who live close to major urban areas.

Although advances have been made in the road-safety education of urban children, the results of this study indicate that urban and rural children's road-safety understanding may differ. The road-safety education of these two groups of children may therefore require different approaches. More research is needed on the pedestrian capabilities and behaviour of rural children in order to determine the road-safety education needs of these children.

REFERENCES

Ampofo-Boateng, K., & Thomson, J.A. (1991). Children's perceptions of safety and danger on the road. *British Journal of Psychology, 82,* 487–505.

Demetre, J., & Gaffin, S. (1994). The salience of occluding vehicles to child pedestrians. *British Journal of Educational Psychology, 64,* 243–251.

Department for Transport (2002). *Child Road Safety: Achieving the 2010 Target.* London: Department for Transport.

Department for Transport (2003). *Child Road Safety in Rural Areas: Literature Review and Commentary (No. 32).* London: Department of Transport.

Fyhri, A., Bjørnskau, T., & Ulleberg, P. (2004). Traffic education for children with a tabletop model. *Transportation Research Part F: Traffic Psychology and Behaviour, 7,* 197–207.

Hill, R., Lewis, V., & Dunbar, G. (2000). Young children's concepts of danger. *British Journal of Developmental Psychology, 18,* 103–120.

Joshi, M.S., MacLean, M., & Carter, W. (1999). Children's journey to school: spatial skills, knowledge and perceptions of the environment. *British Journal of Developmental Psychology, 17,* 125–140.

Mayr, J.M., Eder, C., Berghold, A., Wernig, J., Khayati, S., & Ruppert-Kuhlmayr, A. (2003). Causes and consequences of pedestrian injuries in children. *European Journal of Pediatrics, 162* (3), 184–190.

Pfeffer, K. (1989). Children's awareness and understanding of dangers at home. *Current Psychology: Research and Reviews, 8,* 307–315.

Thomson, J.A. (1996). Child pedestrian accidents: what makes children vulnerable? In Gillham, B., & Thomson, J.A. (Eds.), *Child Safety: Problem and Prevention from Preschool to Adolescence.* London: Routledge.

Traffic and Transport Psychology
G. Underwood (Editor)

4

A THEMATIC ANALYSIS OF CHILDREN AND YOUNG ADULTS' PERCEPTIONS OF ROADWAY RISK

Jean Underwood[1], Alison Ault[1], Gayle Dillon[1] and Bill Farnsworth[1]

INTRODUCTION

One way to understand pedestrian behaviour is to investigate users' perceptions of the traffic scenes and specifically their perception of danger in the judgement of such a scene (Chapman & Underwood, 1998). The perception of road risk utilises cognitive schemata to represent features, functions and operations of the traffic system (Riemersma, 1988). The current study explored developmental trends in road risk perception, and also asked whether there were discernable sex differences in the perception of road risk.

The United Kingdom (UK) government's white paper *A New Deal for Transport: Better for Everyone* (Department of Environment, Transport and the Regions, 1998) highlighted the importance of improved road safety for all road users. Although the number of road deaths and reported serious injuries occurring on UK roads has declined in recent years (British Medical Association, 1997) the risk of being killed on the road network in any given year is one in 10,000 and over a life time all road users can expect to either cause or be involved in a road traffic accident (Petch & Henson, 2000). However, while driving a car is becoming increasingly less dangerous in terms of the risk of death or serious injury, pedestrians remain highly vulnerable, particularly children and the elderly (Yagil, 2000).

Mortality figures for children in the UK show that accidental injuries are the most common form of death in children over one year of age (Office of Population Censuses and Surveys,

---
[1] Division of Psychology, Nottingham Trent University, Burton Street, Nottingham, UK.
E-mail: jean.underwood@ntu.ac.uk (J. Underwood).

1990). In 2002, 179 children were killed in road accidents in the UK and 4417 sustained serious injuries. Boys were shown to be twice as likely to be killed or to sustain serious injury in pedestrian and cycle accidents as girls, with children in the lowest socio-economic group (SEG) five times more likely to be killed as pedestrians, rather than as vehicle passengers, than their higher SEG counterparts (Department of Transport, 2003). Overall, nearly a fifth of child pedestrian casualties happen on the school journey, but this proportion increases for secondary school aged children (Department of Transport, 2000).

Children's concept of risk

Although young children have a rudimentary concept of danger (Hill, Lewis & Dunbar, 2000), they are poor at identifying dangerous situations, that is they have not developed an adequate perception of risk. For example, young children may recognise that cars (Ampofo-Boateng & Thompson, 1991) and fire and water (Grieve & Williams, 1985) are dangerous, but cannot recognise when such aspects pose a threat. Danger is seen as an intrinsic feature of an object, so matches are dangerous, but furry animals are not. Only later comes the understanding that objects are dangerous in settings (Hill et al., 2000).

Although Hill et al. (2000) found that the salience of danger increased with age, it was still found to be low in children of 9–10 years when compared with adults, and children were also found to be poor at recognising potential danger unless cued to do so. They argue that the high accident rate for child pedestrians is not simply an outcome of a limited concept of danger, rather it is due to a failure to recognise the potential danger when unprompted, suggesting there is a failure to apply conceptual knowledge and their understanding of danger is not robust. Not surprisingly many countries have introduced educational measures, such as the UK Green Cross Code campaign (Singh, 1982), in an attempt to alleviate child pedestrian accidents but, as Hill et al. point out, their finding that children do not or cannot apply such knowledge without cuing has repercussions for road safety training of young pedestrians.

Categorising road risk

Steyvers (1993) has argued for an engineering solution to traffic accidents, stating that all roads should be self-explaining, and to achieve this we need to know what characteristics road users find salient. Once these are known and understood, the road infrastructure and environment can be manipulated to provoke the expectations one wants in drivers. However, Riemersma (1988) using a constrained categorisation task found that drivers' categorisations of the "designed to be self-explaining" Dutch road environment did not directly correspond with the in-built official categories. This suggests that features salient to drivers were at variance to the traffic engineers. Consequently, driver behaviours were likely to deviate from those deemed appropriate by the authorities, even when road categories are as unambiguous as those in the Netherlands. Riemersma found that categorisation was based on four factors: safety, urban versus rural environments, the nature of road boundaries and the presence of slip roads, and finally road markings; that is roads were classified on their objective physical characteristics rather than on official road categories.

Yagil (2000) has shown that pedestrians and drivers tend to view traffic scenes differently. For pedestrians in their study, road crossing behaviour was predicted by normative rather than instrumental motives. This suggests that the motives related to pedestrian compliance with safety rules are different from drivers' motives, in that the latter were found to be instrumental and normative to a similar degree (Yagil, 1998a,b). For example, pedestrians felt a stronger sense of control over the results of their behaviour than drivers, both regarding accidents and apprehension.

Underwood, Dillon and Farnsworth (2005) in a partial replication and an extension of Riemersma's (1988) study, explored how young adult drivers and non-drivers assess road traffic scenes using an unconstrained simple picture sort. The participants conducted two sorts, a free sort and sorting with the instruction to focus on safety, the latter providing global cueing as in Hill et al. (2000).

The results suggest important differences in emphasis in this participant pool to those emerging from the more constrained Dutch studies. The open categorisation derived two similar factors (safety and road markings) to that of Riemersma (1988). However, the urban/rural dimension was not apparent, rather there was a focus on the activity within the scene. Task two, by its nature, resulted in three factors which might be viewed as related to safety and which focused directly on the road. In this study, we used active traffic scenes and found that criteria such as road width and quality that were important in the Steyvers' (1993) study were little used when traffic was present. Non-drivers also tended to focus on vehicle size, while drivers tended to refer to vehicle size, density and direction. Unsurprisingly non-drivers were more aware of pedestrian safety than drivers. Less predictable was the very limited reference to driver safety by our driver participants.

The current study, focusing on pedestrians' perception of risk, is a further extension of Riemersma (1988) and Underwood et al. (2005). The key questions here were whether there were identifiable developmental trends in the perception of road risk assessment, and whether there were discernable sex differences in the reading of road risk.

METHOD

Design

The between subjects experimental design incorporated three independent variables: age (Year 3: Year 5: undergraduates); sex (male: female) and task (non-cued sort task 1: cued sort task 2).

Participants

The sample consisted of 120 participants, of which 80 were children attending main-stream schools in urban Nottingham, and 40 were young University undergraduates (see Table 1). There were 40 children in Year 3 (ages 7–8 years) and 40 in Year 5 (ages 9–10 years)

Table 1. Distribution of participants across the three groups.

Year 3 (n = 40)	Year 5 (n = 40)	Adults (n = 40)
Male = 18	Male = 20	Male = 8
Female = 22	Female = 20	Female = 32
Mean age = 7.90 years	Mean age = 10.01 years	Mean age = 19.58 years
(SD = 0.34)	(SD = 0.28)	(SD = 2.88)

and there were approximately equal numbers of male and female participants in each age group.

Stimuli

The stimuli were 20 colour photographs of road traffic scenes taken from a pedestrian perspective. There were four controlled stimuli sets consisting of five pictures of the same four roads defined on two dimensions: urban or rural environments and straight or curving roads. This provided five photographs each of: a rural road with bend, an urban road with bend, a rural straight road, and an urban straight road. Traffic patterns were manipulated in each set of five photographs to be: traffic free, have a single car approaching or departing, or have a single large vehicle (such as a lorry) approaching or moving away (see Table 2).

Table 2. Distribution of stimuli across the four baseline stimuli sets.

	Rural straight road	Rural bend	Urban straight road	Urban bend
No traffic	No traffic	No traffic	No traffic	No traffic
Traffic approaching	Single car	Single car	Single car	Single car
	Single large vehicle	Single large vehicle	Single large vehicle	Single large vehicle
Traffic departing	Single car	Single car	Single car	Single car
	Single large vehicle	Single large vehicle	Single large vehicle	Single large vehicle

Procedure

All participants were tested individually in a quiet working area of the school or university. Each session began with a practice trial before the two sorting tasks.

Task 1 required participants to sort the photographs into groups on self-selected criteria and there were no minimum or maximum number of categories to be generated. Participants were asked to explain, but not justify, their category selection on completion of the task. No time constraints were imposed.

Task 2 required the participants to re-categorise the photographs according to the overall safety of the scene, again using as many groupings as they felt necessary. They were asked to order their groups of photographs starting from the safest to the most dangerous environments. As with Task 1 they were asked to explain the reasons for their decisions.

RESULTS

The number of categories that participants sorted the photographs into for each of the tasks formed the first analysis (see Table 3).

Table 3. Means and standard deviations of the number of categories used in Tasks 1 and 2.

Group	Task 1		Task 2	
	Mean	*SD*	*Mean*	*SD*
Year 3 ($n = 40$)	5.15	2.70	2.35	0.70
Year 5 ($n = 40$)	6.20	2.63	2.30	0.85
Adults ($n = 40$)	6.08	2.53	5.60	2.50

A between-subjects ANOVA revealed that there were no significant differences in the number of categories that participants sorted cards into on Task 1. However, for Task 2 a significant difference was present between the three age groups: $F_{(2,117)} = 55.58$, $p < 0.01$ (Table 3) and when children (Years 3 and 5 combined) were analysed against adults: $F_{(1,118)} = 112.07$, $p < 0.01$ (children mean = 2.33, adult mean = 5.60).

The number of categories developed for the two tasks did not differ for the adults. However, significant differences were found for Year 3: $F_{(1,78)} = 40.21$, $p < 0.01$ (Task 1 mean = 5.15, Task 2 mean = 2.35); and Year 5: $F_{(1,78)} = 79.41$, $p < 0.01$ (Task 1 mean = 6.20, Task 2 mean = 2.30). Thus, the adults sorted cards into a similar number of categories for both tasks but the children used substantially fewer categories in cued sort Task 2, possibly due to a literal interpretation of instructions, to sort cards into safe or dangerous.

Coding schemes were developed for each task following the "Grounded Theory data driven" approach (Glaser & Strauss, 1967; Miles & Huberman, 1994). This method was favoured since the study was essentially exploratory in nature and enabled the data to be kept in the original context.

The coding scheme for the non-cued sort Task 1 informed the codes developed for Task 2. Thus, coding of cued sort Task 2 unsurprisingly contained many of the same codes as in Task 1, with the addition of new master codes to accommodate participants' safety emphasis. Coding for Task 1 produced 17 master codes for Years 3 and 5, and 16 for the adults. Task 2 produced 25 master codes for Years 3 and 5, and 22 for the adults. When analysing the children and adults' Task 2 codes, only those 14 master codes shared by all age groups were entered into the analyses.

The first analysis concerned the use of master codes for the two tasks. Pearson's correlation for Tasks 1 and 2 was conducted on the frequency count of the number of participants that referred to each master code (maximum score 40). For the adults significant positive correlations were found between Tasks 1 and 2 indicating that there were overlaps in the pattern of code used across the two tasks: $r = +0.54, p < 0.05$ ($n = 14$). However, for the children as a whole there was no significant correlation between Tasks 1 and 2, which demonstrates, that unlike the adults, the children developed a significantly different approach in their categorisation of the two tasks (see Table 3).

Factor analysis, with the master code frequency counts as variables, investigated whether the factors emerging from this UK study were similar to those from studies carried out in the Netherlands. Exploratory and confirmatory factor analysis allowed us to identify the factors evident in our own data whilst also allowing us to make direct comparisons with Riemersma's data.

The number of factors extracted from the factor analysis were constrained to four factors, in order to make direct comparisons with Riemersma's findings. The analysis explained 58.60% of the variance for Year 3; 62.70% for Year 5 and 58.00% for the adults. The four factors obtained for each age group by task are shown in Table 4.

The focus on vehicles and safety was confirmed for all groups. However, differences emerged in the degree to which each group focused on the pedestrian. A 2×2 ANOVA (year group: levels "3" and "5" by sub-code: levels "pedestrian" and "driver perspective") for the child participants identified no significant difference in the use of these two sub-codes between these groups. However, both children's groups used the pedestrian sub-code significantly more than the driver sub-code: $F_{(1,156)} = 35.59, p < 0.01$ ("pedestrian" mean = 2.34, "driver" mean = 0.41).

Imaginative coding, the telling of stories about what might happen in various contexts, showed a clear developmental trend. Stories were not developed by the adults but were used extensively by Year 3 and to some extent by Year 5. Age correlated negatively with the two main imaginative codes (potential damage: $r = -0.24$, $p < 0.05$ ($n = 80$) and story: $r = -0.27$, $p < 0.05$ ($n = 80$)) for the child-generated data. A 2×3 ANOVA (year group: levels "3" and "5" by sub-code: levels "injury", "fatality" and "crash") supported this correlation. Year 3 pupils were greater users of this master code than Year 5 pupils: $F_{(1,234)} = 6.04, p < 0.05$ (Year 3 mean = 0.512, Year 5 mean = 0.383). When the adults were added to the analysis this developmental trend remained. ANOVAs highlighted the children (both Years 3 and 5) as greater users of the code than the adults: $F_{(1,118)} = 9.77, p < 0.01$ (child mean = 1.138, adult mean = 0.30) and Year 3 pupils as greater users than Year 5 pupils, followed by adults: $F_{(2,117)} = 8.91, p < 0.01$ (Year 3 mean = 1.55, Year 5 mean = 0.73, adult mean = 0.30).

Two of the shared master codes for Task 2 were identified as "feature codes": road painting and road signs. Feature coding produced both developmental and sex effects. ANOVAs showed significant developmental trends in the use of the road painting master code: $F_{(1,390)} = 5.44$, $p < 0.05$ (Year 3 mean = 0.03, Year 5 mean = 0.10); and road signs master code: $F_{(2,234)} = 4.31$, $p < 0.05$ (Year 3 "road signs specified" mean = 0.05, Year 5 "road signs specified" mean = 0.40). When considering only the children's responses, the ANOVAs revealed significant sex differences for the use of road painting: $F_{(1,390)} = 4.93$, $p < 0.05$ (male

Table 4. Factor solution for (a) Task 1 and (b) Task 2 data by age group.

	Year 3	Year 5	Adults
(a) Task 1			
Factor 1	*Road features* Roadside features 0.86 Scene location specific 0.84 Road signs 0.76	*Road features with recognition of safety* Scene location specific 0.92 Roadside features 0.86 Road signs 0.79 Road painting 0.78 Safety 0.62	*Safety* Visibility 0.79 Pedestrian safety 0.76 Non-motorist facilities 0.72 Traffic/Road speed 0.54
Factor 2	*Vehicles* Vehicle type 0.89 Direction of vehicle 0.85 Presence of vehicles 0.77	*Vehicles* Vehicle type 0.94 Presence of vehicles 0.88 Direction of vehicles 0.87	*Vehicles* Vehicle direction 0.80 Vehicle type and size 0.70 Road rules 0.61 Presence of vehicles 0.52
Factor 3	*Scene characteristics* Activity within scene 0.90 Road layout 0.79	*Scene characteristics* Scene location general 0.82 Activity within scene 0.63	*Road features* Road instruction 0.85 Road layout 0.77
Factor 4	*Apparent and implied actors in the scene* Other road users 0.75	*Spatial features and positioning* Road layout 0.76 Directional focus 0.60	*Scene characteristics* Activity/amount of traffic 0.77 Pedestrian presence 0.62 Road type − 0.53 Scene layout 0.42

(continued)

Table 4. Continued.

	Year 3	Year 5	Adults
(b) Task 2			
Factor 1	*Driver aspects, behaviours and significance to safety*	*Driver aspects, behaviours, and evidence of other users of the scene*	*Road features*
	Driver behaviour 0.85	Other road users 0.90	Road instruction 0.84
	Vehicle speed 0.84	Driver behaviour 0.84	Road rules 0.76
	Vehicle type 0.82	Vehicle speed 0.75	Vehicle type and size 0.66
	Road painting 0.78	Pedestrian behaviour 0.69	Pedestrian safety features present/absent 0.60
	Safety 0.55		Speed restriction 0.48
Factor 2	*Imaginative, pedestrian view of what "might happen", incorporating overall scene layout*	*Isolated aspects and holistic, pedestrian view of overall scene layout*	*Activity*
	Story 0.90	Scene location specific 0.81	Pedestrian presence -0.90
	Perspective 0.89	Roadside features 0.73	Vehicle direction -0.87
	Potential damage 0.81	Road signs 0.70	Activity and amount of traffic -0.73
	Visibility 0.70	Visibility 0.69	Road layout -0.75
		Perspective 0.59	
		Road layout 0.53	
Factor 3	*Aspects of vehicle appearance, and its significance to pedestrian safety*	*Vehicles*	*Safe features*
	Vehicle stability 0.95	Vehicle type 0.81	Motorist safety 0.80
	Vehicle size 0.95	Vehicle direction 0.74	Scene location 0.76
	Safe to cross 0.83	Presence of vehicles 0.71	Visibility 0.70
Factor 4	*Non-driver aspects and behaviours*	*Imaginative, justified view of what "might happen"*	*Non-safe features*
	Pedestrian behaviour 0.89	Story 0.87	Potential for accident -0.69
	Other road users 0.83	Potential damage 0.86	Traffic speed 0.58
		Safety 0.64	Road width 0.54
		Vehicle stability 0.61	

mean $= 0.10$, female mean $= 0.03$) and road signs: $F_{(1,234)} = 4.51$, $p < 0.05$ (male mean $= 0.23$, female mean $= 0.08$). The developmental pattern altered when the adult data were added to the analyses. Children as a whole still emerged as greater users of the road painting code: $F_{(1,118)} = 4.02$, $p < 0.05$ (child mean $= 0.33$, adult mean $= 0.03$). However, when all three age groups were entered separately, the use of these codes peaked for the Year 5 sample, with usage being lower in Year 3 and adult participants: $F_{(2,117)} = 4.168$, $p < 0.05$ (Year 3 mean $= 0.15$, Year 5 mean $= 0.50$, adult mean $= 0.03$).

Holistic codes included visibility, scene location (either general or urban/rural) and activity within the scene. No differences were found in the use of these codes in Task 2 between Years 3 and 5, although a sex difference was found for use of the safety master code: $F_{(1,234)} = 6.01$, $p < 0.05$ ("male" mean $= 0.68$, "female" mean $= 0.83$). This was supported by a positive correlation between use of the safety master code and sex: $r = 0.28$, $p < 0.05$ ($n = 80$). This contrasts with the higher use of the feature codes road painting and road signs by the males in Years 3 and 5. When adults were included in the analyses they were the greatest users of the visibility master code compared to the children as a collective group: $F_{(1,118)} = 5.25$, $p < 0.05$ (child mean $= 0.65$, adult mean $= 1.25$). This was supported by the correlation between use of the visibility code and "group" (children and adults): $r = 0.21$, $p < 0.05$ ($n = 120$) and "year" (Years 3, 5 and adults): $r = 0.19$, $p < 0.05$ ($n = 120$).

Adults also used the scene location general master code more when compared to the children as a collective group $F_{(1,118)} = 14.63$, $p < 0.01$ (child mean $= 0.26$, adult mean $= 1.05$); and when all three age groups were entered separately: $F_{(2,117)} = 7.31$, $p < 0.01$ (Year 3 mean $= 0.23$, Year 5 mean $= 0.300$, adult mean $= 1.05$). The latter two ANOVAs were supported by a positive correlation between use of the scene location general code and "group" (children and adults together): $r = 0.33$, $p < 0.01$ ($n = 120$) and "year" (Year 3, 5 and adults): $r = 0.32$, $p < 0.01$ ($n = 120$), indicating that increasing age is matched by the use of scene location general code.

CONCLUSIONS

Subsumed under the main research questions, whether there were identifiable developmental trends in the perception of road risk assessment, and discernable sex differences in perception of road risk, is the issue of whether task instruction influences task outcome. Underwood et al. (2005) found minimal impact of task instructions for their young adult drivers and non-drivers. However, here a difference was found in the number of categories created by the three groups on Task 2, but not Task 1. The adults showed little or no variation across task, whereas Years 3 and 5 formed fewer categories in Task 2—in response to the differences in task instruction to focus on safety. The children interpreted the Task 2 instructions as a cue to construct a safe and dangerous set of photographs thus producing different solutions in Task 2 compared to Task 1. This differential decision making was not apparent for the adults. Hill et al. (2000) support this finding with their data showing that cueing in young children also had a significant effect on their judgements.

The results from the factor analyses suggest important differences in emphasis in this participant pool to those emerging from the more constrained Dutch studies. Riemersma (1988) found that categorisation was based on objective physical characteristics rather than on official road categories. For our adult sample, the open categorisation Task 1 had two similar factors (safety and road markings) to that of Riemersma (1988). However, the urban/rural dimension was not apparent, rather there was a focus on the activity within the scene and on the characteristics of the vehicles and this was substantially the case for our Year 5 children, although safety was subsumed within the factors. For the Year 3 children direct reference to safety on Task 1 was limited, rather they discussed the potential actions of actors (real or imaginary) within the scene.

Task 2, by its nature, resulted in three factors which might be viewed as related to safety and which focused directly on the road for the adult sample. Here we found that criteria such as road width and quality that were important in the Steyvers (1993) study were little used when traffic is present. For the youngest children the analysis of activity involved a strong pedestrian perspective and a tendency to project events into the scene, that is to tell "might be" stories.

The safety focus was evident at all ages. It was most apparent in Task 2 when encouraged by explicit cueing, but was also apparent at all ages in Task 1. An unanticipated finding, which is possibly a result of road training, was that for those children who do discuss key safety variables, visibility is cited more than level of activity within the scene, although the focus on the presence or absence and type of vehicles is apparent for all age groups.

The findings presented here confirm the developmental trend reported in Hill et al. (2000). Year 3 children viewed the road from a personal perspective, focusing on the pedestrian road user; a tendency to tell imaginative stories about what might happen (that declines but does not disappear with age), and also to focus on individual personally relevant details rather than holistic scenes (which declines with age and largely disappears in early adulthood). Year 5 moved away from idiosyncratic personal detail and began to focus on important features in the scene, but this was also found to decline into adulthood when noting individual factors gave way to reading the whole scene.

In addition, we found two clear differences in male and female responses to the roads. Across Years 3 and 5 males were more focused on road details than females. A corollary of this was that females were more likely to identify and use the super-ordinate category labels that were implicit in the grouping of the stimuli than males, and to see the scene as a whole. These differences might appear to be at odds with those presented by Hill et al. (2000), who found no difference between boys and girls in the salience of danger. However, this group did find some evidence that girls were better than boys at identifying dangers on the road and this suggests that girls in that study were also reading the scene and not focusing on feature identification. We speculate that the comparatively high accident rate among boys compared to girls maybe in part due to this focus on detail and subsequent failure to read the scene.

The data presented here confirm not only developmental trends in how road risk is perceived, but also some strong sex differences in how participants read the road scenes. Further it confirms that for younger age groups, task instructions can significantly change children's responses to the task in hand.

Conceptual flexibility underlies our ability to choose sets of defining features of a category dependent on context and purpose. Whilst it is important that we are able to limit our flexibility of definition in order to facilitate communication between individuals, this ability to be contextually flexible remains important. Although many potential groupings of conceptual features are seemingly arbitrary, as with our younger participants, even what appears to be an arbitrary classification can facilitate learning (Tulving, 1962). For each of the three groups investigated here there was an act of sense making of the scenes presented.

ACKNOWLEDGEMENTS

We would like to acknowledge the help of Westdale Lane Junior School and Walter Halls Primary School in Nottingham, who kindly allowed us to work with their Year 3 and 5 pupils.

REFERENCES

Ampofo-Boateng, K., & Thompson, J.A. (1991). Children's perception of danger and safety on the road. *British Journal of Psychology, 82*, 487–505.

British Medical Association (1997). *Road Transport and Health*. London: British Medical Journal Publishing Group.

Chapman, P.R., & Underwood, G. (1998). Visual search of dynamic scenes: event types and the role of experience in viewing driving situations. In Underwood, G. (Ed.), *Eye Guidance in Reading and Scene Perception* (pp. 369–393). Oxford: Elsevier.

Department of Environment, Transport and the Regions (1998). *A New Deal for Transport: Better for Everyone*. London: HMSO.

Department of Transport (2000). *Tomorrow's Roads: Safer for Everyone* http://www.dft.gov. uk/stellent/groups/dft_rdsafety/documents/source/dft_rdsafety_source_504644.doc. Accessed 2nd July 2004.

Department of Transport (2003). http://www.thinkroadsafety.gov.uk/statistics.htm, Accessed 2nd July 2004.

Glaser, B.G., & Strauss, A.L. (1967). *The Discovery of Grounded Theory: Strategies for Qualitative Research*. Chicago: Aldine.

Grieve, R., & Williams, W. (1985). Young children's perception of danger. *British Journal of Developmental Psychology, 3*, 385–392.

Hill, R., Lewis, V., & Dunbar, G. (2000). Young children's concepts of danger. *British Journal of Developmental Psychology, 18*, 103–120.

Miles, M.B., & Huberman, A.M. (1994). *An Expanded Sourcebook. Qualitative Data Analysis* (2nd ed.). London: Sage Publications.

Office of Population Censuses and Surveys (1990). *Mortality Statistics Series DH4 Injury and Poisoning (No. 16)*. London: HMSO.

Petch, R.O., & Henson, H. (2000). Child road safety in the urban environment. *Journal of Transportation Geography, 8*, 197–211.

Riemersma, J.B.J. (1988). An empirical study of subjective road categorisation. *Ergonomics, 31*, 621–630.

Singh, A. (1982). Pedestrian education. In Chapman, A.J., Wade, F.M., & Foot, H.C. (Eds.), *Pedestrian Accidents*. Chichester: Wiley.

Steyvers, J.J.M. (1993). Categorisation and appraisal of rural two-lane undivided 80-KM/H roads. In Gale, G.A., Brown, I.D., Haslegrave, C.M., & Taylor, S.P. (Eds.), *Vision in Vehicles VI* (pp. 271–287). Amsterdam: Elsevier.

Tulving, E. (1962). Subjective organisation of free recall of unrelated words. *Psychological Review, 69,* 344–354.

Underwood, J., Dillon, G., & Farnsworth, B. (2005). The categorisation of roads by drivers and non-drivers. In Gale, A.G. (Ed.), *Proceedings of Vision in Vehicles X.* Derby: Vision in Vehicles Press.

Yagil, D. (1998a). Gender and age differences in attitudes toward traffic laws and traffic violations. *Transportation Research Part F, 1,* 123–135.

Yagil, D. (1998b). Instrumental and normative motives for compliance with traffic laws among young and older drivers. *Accident Analysis and Prevention, 30,* 417–424.

Yagil, D. (2000). Beliefs, motives and situational factors related to pedestrians' self-reported behaviour at signal-controlled crossings. *Transportation Research Part F, 3,* 1–13.

Traffic and Transport Psychology
G. Underwood (Editor)
© 2005 Elsevier Ltd. All rights reserved.

5

ARE DIFFERENCES IN CHILDREN'S TRAVEL REFLECTED IN THEIR COGNITIVE MAPS?

James Paskins[1]

INTRODUCTION

Children's local environments provide the potential for a wide range of experiences, presenting opportunities for play, for learning and for exercise. While there are a great many activities that a child can take part indoors, there are some, such as energetic games, that can only take place outdoors. As well as providing an important venue for physical activity, outdoor activity provides the opportunity to observe and participate in a variety of social and environmental interactions. Travel, whether it is a journey with a definite purpose or a less-structured journey, such as those associated with children's play, extends the range of these opportunities and experiences.

Children's day-to-day travel is an important factor in their relationship with the local environment (Hillman, Adams, & Whitelegg, 1990). Different modes of travel allow for different types of interaction. When travelling by car, for instance, a child is not only deprived of an opportunity for physical activity, but is also prevented from direct interaction with the environment. There is a possibility that the differences in the style of interaction whilst travelling will be reflected in cognitive representations, leaving children who are chronic car users under-prepared for independent travel. Car use has been growing at the expense of walking for many years (Department for Transport, 2004); this can be seen in Table 1 which shows the shift from walking to car use for journeys made by 5–10 year olds in Great Britain between 1985/1986 and 2002.

It is not only children's travel patterns that are changing, there has also been a shift in the way that children play. The balance between the amount of time spent in unstructured play and the

[1] Centre for Transport Studies, University College London, London, UK. *E-mail:* james@transport.ucl.ac.uk
(J. Paskins).

Table 1. Percentage of 5–10 year olds using various modes
of travel.

	1985/1986	*2002*
Walk	67	51
Car	22	41
Bicycle	1	1
Bus	9	6
Other	2	2
All	100	100

Source: Department for Transport (2004).

amount of time spent in structured activities is changing for many children. These changes in children's play can have an effect on the amount of car travel that the family undertakes. In many cases unstructured play is being replaced by structured, supervised activities, and these types of activities often require a car trip (Mackett, Lucas, Paskins, & Turbin, 2004).

Both these changes, in part at least, have common causation. One factor that may be behind both changes is the perception that the world is a very dangerous place for children. When asked, as part of the National Travel Survey, why children were accompanied on the journey to school 57% of parents cited traffic danger and 47% cited fear of assault or molestation (Department for Transport, 2004). The work presented here was carried out as part of a larger project, "Reducing Children's Car Use: The Health and Potential Car Dependency Impacts". As part of that project parents were asked to rate a number of factors relating to the journey to school and indicate how important each factor was when deciding how their children travelled to school. The results from this part of the project are shown in Table 2, and it can be seen that they reflect the results found by the National Travel Survey: the child's "personal security" and "road traffic danger" were the two most highly rated factors.

Table 2. Factors relating to travel mode choice for the journey
to school.

	Average rating (1–5)
Personal security of your child	4.7
Road traffic danger	4.7
Health and fitness of your child	4.3
Distance to school	3.9
Possibility of bullying	3.9
Amount child has to carry	3.9
Environmental concerns	3.7
The cost of travel	2.8
Whether a car is available	2.7

Source: Reducing Children's Car Use: The Health and Potential Car
Dependency Impacts.

If parent's reactions to their concerns about personal security and road traffic danger has the ultimate effect of increasing the volume of road traffic and decreasing the number of people in public places, then the risk to children and, perhaps more importantly, the perceptions of that risk are likely to be increased.

One consequence of these changes for an individual child is that he or she is probably spending less time in the local environment, with less opportunity to take part in the social and environmental interactions that can be important learning experiences. One aspect of this learning experience is building up an understanding of how the local environment is put together, and how to navigate independently within it. The mental representation of knowledge about the environment, and the spatial relationships within it, is often referred to as a cognitive map (Tolman, 1948). This term can be used to cover any aspect of environmental knowledge, including routes, landmarks, directions, and even impressions and beliefs about places (Kitchin & Blades, 2002). In the context of this study the term is being used to cover the knowledge that children learn, store and recall about the configuration of spatial elements in their environment, the representations that are utilised when planning or recalling a route to travel from one place to another.

A number of techniques exist for assessing children's knowledge about large-scale environments, and these can be broadly separated into those that test recall memory and those that test recognition memory (Matthews, 1992). Each technique has its own strengths and weaknesses, and may involve the use of skills that mask a child's true competence. The study employed a recall task and a recognition task to assess the children's environmental knowledge; these are described in more detail below. The recall task involved drawing a map and labelling its elements, and so relies, in part, on skills that are unrelated to the child's knowledge about the environment. The recognition task did not rely on a child's ability to write or draw, it did, however, rely on the child's ability to read a map.

There are numerous factors that will have an impact on a child's performance on a spatial awareness task. The performance of different groups will vary, for instance, many studies have shown that boys perform better on these types of task than girls (Kitchin & Blades, 2002), and age would also be expected to influence performance.

Another factor that might be thought to be important for children's knowledge about the local environment is the way that they travel around within it. The different ways that children travel and play will effect the way that they interact with, and encode information about, their local environment. As passengers, children do not need to make any decisions to navigate, nor do they need to assess the road safety situation; there is a possibility that this will be reflected in their cognitive maps. Good spatial knowledge is required for successful way-finding and children who are regular car users may not be developing the skills required to become confident independent travellers.

The aim of this study was to see how the cognitive maps of children who regularly used the car differed from children who used other modes. The journey to school provides an opportunity to study a group of children who make a regular journey to a common location.

It was hypothesised that usual mode of travel to school, age and sex of the child would all influence children's representations of spatial knowledge. Children's spatial knowledge was assessed by their performance on the recognition task and the detail and accuracy of their sketch-maps. It was expected that children who usually travelled to school by car, younger children and girls would have lower recognition scores as well as less accurate and less detailed representations of the area around the school.

The participants in this study were 69 children at a primary school in Rossington, South Yorkshire. The children came from two year groups, Year 4 and Year 6 (the final year of primary school); the number of boys and girls in both year groups is shown in Table 3. The mean age of the children in Year 4 was 8.3 years, with a range of 8–9 years. The mean age of children in Year 6 was 10.1, with a range of 10–11 years.

Table 3. Sample.

	Year 4	Year 6	Overall
Male	17	19	36
Female	16	17	33
Overall	33	36	69

Each child was given a brief travel questionnaire, which included a question about the child's usual journey to school. Children in the study travelled to school by walking, cycling, as car passengers and on buses; Table 4 shows how the children in the sample travelled. It can be seen that cycling makes up a very small number of the journeys, while car was the mode used by the majority of children.

Table 4. Mode of travel to school for children in the sample.

	Walk	Car	Bus	Cycle	Total
Year 4—male	4	9	3	1	17
Year 4—female	2	12	1	1	16
Year 4—all	6	21	4	2	33
Year 6—male	9	6	4	0	19
Year 6—female	4	10	3	0	17
Year 6—all	13	16	7	0	36
Overall	19	37	11	2	69

All children were asked to complete a landmark recognition task, which involved correctly identifying which local landmark was being indicated on a map of the local area. Children were also asked to draw a map of the area around their school.

LANDMARK RECOGNITION TASK

For the landmark recognition test children were given a worksheet which asked them to identify eight landmarks taken from the area around their school. The position of each landmark that had to be identified was indicated on a map by a numbered arrow, the number on the arrow corresponded to the question number on the worksheet.

Children were required to read a map to find the location of the landmark and then identify its picture from those given on the worksheet. Each question on the worksheet presented four small black and white pictures, the correct landmark mixed with three distracters; two of the distracters were taken from the area around the school with the third being taken from a different town. The distracter from the other town was chosen to be similar to the actual landmark. Because of the small size of the pictures on the worksheet, groups of children were also given sheets with larger colour pictures of all the landmarks that were featured on the worksheet. Each picture on the worksheet was identified with a letter, which could be used to look up the larger colour version. Children worked individually but were seated together in groups at tables, so a single set of pictures could be shared by a table of children.

One point was given for each correctly identified landmark, up to a maximum score of eight, no points were deducted for wrong answers. All the children completed the task and were included in the analysis.

AREA MAPPING TASK

For the area mapping task a plan view of the school was included in the centre of an otherwise blank page. Children were told which classroom wall corresponded to North or upwards on the sheet and were asked to draw a map of the area around the school. They were encouraged to include as many objects and places from the vicinity of the school as they could remember, including buildings, roads, junctions, areas such as parks, playgrounds or car parks and any other landmarks they could think of. The children were encouraged to place the elements of the map as accurately as they could, both in relation to the school and any other elements they included. Children were also asked to name as many of the elements that they added as possible. The mean number of elements (including the school) in a completed map was 7.6 (SD = 2.9).

ANALYSING THE SKETCH-MAPS

The analysis of the area mapping task was not as straightforward as the analysis of the recognition task, which only involved counting up the right answers. The sketch-maps produced in this exercise provided a far richer set of data, one which has the potential to be analysed on a number of dimensions. There are, for instance, interesting differences in the style of maps, some children produced sketch-maps using a top-down view to represent buildings, while other children employed a view from the side, as if the building was being viewed from the street. While interesting, these stylistic aspects probably have little impact on how "good" a map is, that is, how well it represents the local environment. It was decided to focus on aspects that are more obviously linked to a child's awareness of the local environment, the detail and accuracy of their sketch-maps.

The first stage in the analysis was to convert the maps from paper into a digital format. The children's sketch-maps were digitised using a flatbed scanner. Then a Windows PC-based image editing package (Picture Window 2.5, Digital Light & Color) was used to find the centre of each identifiable element. The size of the school on the scanned maps was used to convert measurements from pixels into metres. Some of the sketch-maps had only a few unambiguously identifiable elements, positions shown in a sketch-map that could be reliably matched with positions shown on an Ordnance Survey map of the area (supplied by Ordnance Survey/Edina Digimap). A decision was taken that for a sketch-map to be included, a child should add at least four elements that could be identified on a map of the area. Details for the included sample, the 59 maps that included at least five unambiguously identifiable elements (including the school) are shown in Table 5.

Table 5. Maps with five or more elements.

	Year 4	Year 6	Overall
Male	16	16	32
Female	12	15	27
Overall	28	31	59

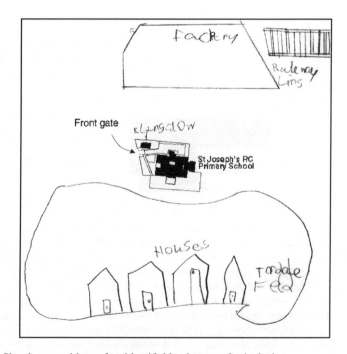

Figure 1. Sketch-map with too few identifiable elements for inclusion.

Figure 1 is an example of a map that was excluded, as only the factory, level crossing and playing field can be identified. The elements marked "houses" have not been counted, as it is not clear which houses are being represented. In contrast Figure 2 shows the most detailed sketch-map in the sample, the identifiable elements in this map include the road junctions.

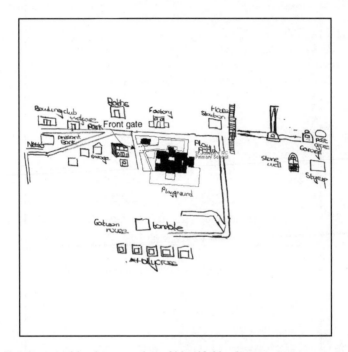

Figure 2. Sketch-map with a large number of identifiable elements.

Maps were analysed for detail and accuracy: detail was assessed by counting the number of unambiguously identifiable elements while accuracy was calculated using bidimensional regression. Bidimensional regression extends standard regression techniques to allow a best fit to be calculated for two-dimensional configurations (Tobler, 1994). In this analysis the dependent variable was the configuration of the elements in the sketch-maps, the independent variable was the real world configuration taken from Ordnance Survey data.

Friedman and Kohler (2003) describe how to calculate a measure of distortion, DI (distortion index), using bidimensional regression and this statistic has been calculated for each child's map. A high value of DI indicates a poor match between the two configurations, as DI increases the further locations in the sketch-map deviate from their locations in the real world.

Figure 3 shows an example where the elements in the sketch-map have been placed in close proximity to their real world counterparts. Figure 4 shows the same example with the addition of a series of points that represent the best fit between the real world and sketch-map positions. In this case the fit is good ($r = 0.98$) and hence the distortion is low (DI = 20.2).

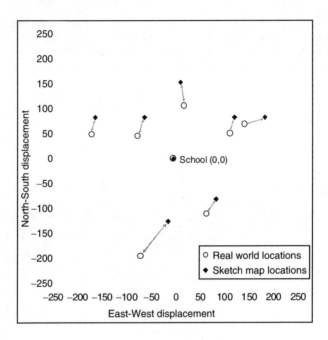

Figure 3. Comparison of sketch-map and real world element positions.

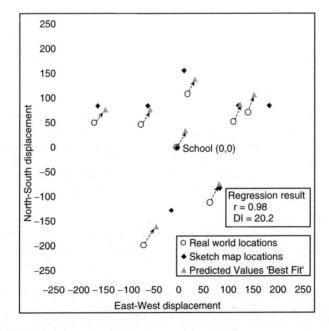

Figure 4. Best fit between sketch-map and real world positions.

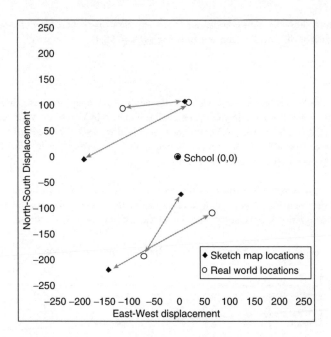

Figure 5. Comparison of sketch-map and real world element positions.

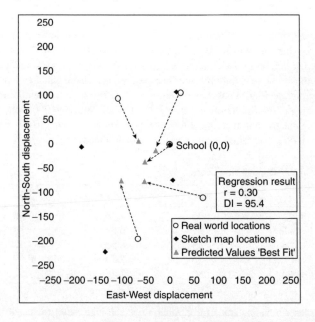

Figure 6. Best fit between sketch-map and real world positions.

Figures 5 and 6 show the same comparison for an inaccurate map: here the fit is poor ($r = 0.30$) so the measure of distortion is consequently high (DI $= 95.4$).

RESULTS

Both year groups performed very well in the landmark recognition task. Many children, especially those in the oldest age group, achieved full marks. In Year 4, the younger group, 46% of children achieved full marks, in Year 6, the older children, 79% achieved full marks. Despite evidence of ceiling effects, differences between the age groups were apparent, as were differences between users of different modes.

Table 6 shows descriptive statistics for the scores from the landmark recognition task for the different modes used to get to school. It can be seen that those who walk in each year group have the highest recognition scores, however, none of the differences between modes are significant.

Table 6. Mean recognition score by usual mode to school.

	Year 4	*Year 6*	*Overall*
Bus	6.3	7.6	7.0
Car	6.5	7.7	7.5
Walk	6.8	7.8	7.1
Overall	6.6	7.7	7.2

It can also be seen that there is a difference between the average score in Year 4 and the average score in Year 6, with the average score in Year 6 being higher. Table 7 shows descriptive statistics for recognition scores for children in Years 4 and 6, boys and girls. Independent t-tests were used to compare the recognition scores between groups, where equal variances could not be assumed appropriate adjustments have been made. The t-tests show the difference between Year 4 and Year 6 children is significant ($t = 3.46$, df $= 37.38$, $p = 0.0005$, one-tailed, equal variances not assumed), but that the difference between boys and girls is not ($t = 1.59$, df $= 44.15$, $p = 0.064$, one-tailed, equal variances not assumed).

Table 7. Recognition score.

	N	*Mean*	*SD*
Male	36	7.43	0.95
Female	33	6.84	1.94
Year 4	33	6.55	1.92
Year 6	36	7.74	0.57
Overall	69	7.15	1.52

Table 8 shows descriptive statistics for comparing sketch-map detail for usual mode for the school journey, sex of child and school year. Sketch-map detail refers to the number of identifiable elements included in a child's sketch-map.

Table 8. Level of detail—number of elements included in sketch-maps.

	N	*Mean*	*SD*
Car usually used for school journey	31	8.4	2.9
Other mode usually used	28	8.1	2.4
Male	32	8.8	3.0
Female	27	7.6	2.0
Year 4	28	8.4	3.0
Year 6	31	8.1	2.3
Overall	59	8.3	2.7

Other modes includes walk, bus and cycle.

The detail levels of the maps were compared using independent t-tests, where the dependent variable was number of identifiable elements. There were no significant differences between children in the two school years, or between those who usually travelled to school by car and those who do not. There was, however, a significant difference between boys and girls in the number of elements recalled ($t = 1.786$, df $= 57$, $p = 0.040$, one-tailed) with boys, on average, including just over one extra element in their maps. It is interesting to note, that while not significant, the differences between year groups and usual mode used are in the opposite direction to that initially predicted.

Table 9 shows descriptive statistics comparing accuracy, DI scores, for usual mode for the school journey, sex of child and school year. Sketch-map accuracy has been calculated using bidimensional regression.

Table 9. Accuracy—DI scores for sketch-maps.

	N	*Mean*	*SD*
Car usually used for school journey	31	51.7	22.6
Other mode usually used	28	41.0	18.9
Male	32	44.7	19.6
Female	27	48.9	23.5
Year 4	28	47.4	20.1
Year 6	31	45.9	22.8
Overall	59	46.6	21.4

Other modes includes walk, bus and cycle.

Independent t-tests were used to compare the groups on sketch-map accuracy, with DI as the dependent variable. Usual mode of travel to school is the only comparison that reveals a significant result ($t = 1.946$, df $= 57$, $p = 0.0285$, one-tailed), with those who usually used the car having more distorted maps. There is no significant difference between the two school years or between boys and girls.

A $2 \times 2 \times 2$ between subjects ANOVA analysed DI scores with two-level factors for mode, school year and sex. Usual mode for the school journey had a much larger influence on accuracy than school year or sex. While the main effect from car use is not significant ($F_{(1,51)} = 3.085$, $p = 0.085$) the F-ratio is far larger than for school year ($F_{(1,51)} = 0.054$, $p = 0.818$) or sex of child ($F_{(1,51)} = 0.032$, $p = 0.859$).

When the modes of transport used for the school journey are considered separately (see Table 10) it can be seen that, after the sole cyclist, it was the group who used the bus who produced the least distorted sketch-maps.

Table 10. DI scores for sketch-maps by mode.

	N	Mean	SD
Car	31	51.7	22.6
Walk	16	45.1	22.2
Bus	11	35.8	12.7
Cycle	1	33.4	–
Overall	59	46.6	21.4

This is interesting result as it is reasonable to suppose that children who used the car were at a disadvantage on this task because, on average, they lived further from the area to be mapped than those who walked. The average car user did live further away than the average walker: 2.2 km (SD = 2.9) compared to 0.65 km (SD = 0.19), but the children who used the bus lived even further away: 6.1 km (SD = 1.7).

CONCLUSIONS

The results show that mode of children's travel, in this case for the journey to school, can influence spatial knowledge. The mode of travel that was usually used for the journey to school did not have a significant impact on the detail of the maps or the performance on the recognition task. It was, however, associated with higher accuracy in the placement of the elements that were included in the sketch-maps. It is also interesting to note that when included in an analysis of variance, mode used to travel to school had a greater influence on accuracy than either the school year or the sex of child.

The expected difference in performance between boys and girls was only evident in terms of sketch-map detail, there was no significant difference in the accuracy of element placement. So while boys may be noticing, or at least recalling, more elements in their surroundings there is no evidence that their representations are more accurate. This difference was also suggested by the recognition task results, the average score for boys was higher than the average score for girls, however, this difference was not significant.

The school year of the children had a significant effect on the recognition, but did not influence sketch-map accuracy or detail. The recognition task results suggest that there is an age-related difference in spatial representations. It is possible that school year may not be sensitive enough to show age-related differences in the sketch-map task. Further work is planned employing a larger sample and an additional year group (Year 5 children), which will be able to investigate the influence of age better.

Although this paper is based on results from a small sample, there does seem to be evidence that the travel mode used for a regular journey, such as the journey to school, can have a significant effect on the accuracy of a child's spatial knowledge. It is interesting to note that the children who used the bus appear to have the most accurate cognitive representations. This raises the possibility that it may not be the mode in itself that is responsible for the effect. Instead it might be supposed that the independence of the traveller is the important factor. Children using the bus have to make a large part of the journey, and arrive at their destination, unaccompanied.

If children are going to take full advantage of open spaces, and avoid becoming car-dependent adults, it is vital that they develop the skills necessary to become confident as walkers and as users of public transport. It seems likely that those skills will rely on accurate cognitive maps.

Children often need to seek parental permission before they can travel on their own, visit a particular place or go out with friends. Parents will base their decisions, in part, on an assessment of their child's competence, and spatial knowledge will play a part in this. If children do not have experience of independent travel or unstructured play, then it is possible that their cognitive maps will be less accurate. Parents may then be less willing to let them go out alone or with friends, reinforcing the effect.

The journey to school appears to offer a useful opportunity to practice encoding and recalling spatial information, and this in turn may carry over into greater spatial awareness in other situations.

ACKNOWLEDGEMENTS

The work for this paper was conducted as part of a project entitled "Reducing Children's Car Use: The Health and Potential Car Dependency Impacts" funded by the UK Engineering and Physical Sciences Research Council under grant GR/N33638 at the Centre for Transport Studies at University College London. The co-operation of the children who took part in this exercise, as well as their parents and teachers, is greatly appreciated.

REFERENCES

Department for Transport (2004). National Travel Survey: 2002, 1999–2001 Update. *Transport Statistics Bulletin.*

Friedman, A., & Kohler, B. (2003). Bidimensional regression: assessing the configural similarity and accuracy of cognitive maps and other two-dimensional data sets. *Psychological Methods, 8,* 468–491.

Hillman, M., Adams, J., & Whitelegg, J. (1990). *One False Move: A Study of Children's Independent Mobility.* London: Policy Studies Institute.

Kitchin, M., & Blades, M. (2002). *The Cognition of Geographic Space.* London: I.B. Tauris.

Mackett, R.L., Lucas, L., Paskins, J., & Turbin, J. (2004). The health benefits of walking to school. *Proceedings of the SUSTRANS National Conference on 'Championing Safe Routes to School: Citizenship in Action'.*

Matthews, M.H. (1992). *Making Sense of Place: Children's Understanding of Large-Scale Environments.* New York: Barnes & Noble Books.

Tobler, W. (1994). Bidimensional regression. *Geographical Analysis, 26,* 187–212.

Tolman, E.C. (1948). Cognitive maps in rats and men. *The Psychological Review, 55,* 189–208.

Traffic and Transport Psychology
G. Underwood (Editor)
© 2005 Elsevier Ltd. All rights reserved.

6

CRITERIA FOR CYCLISTS' EVERYDAY ROUTE CHOICE

Carmen Hagemeister[1], Anne Schmidt[2], Tina Seidel[2] and Bernhard Schlag[2]

OBJECTIVES AND THEORETICAL BACKGROUND

When cycling routes are designed, the requirements of the cyclists should be taken into account in order to ensure that the routes are accepted. In order to make traffic planning user oriented one has to know which criteria are important for cyclists' route choice. Until now in Germany, cyclists' wishes for cycle routes have mainly been explored in west German cities and towns—even in the last 10 years (Alrutz, Bohle & Willhaus, 1998). The present study was conducted in Dresden, an east German city without a cycling tradition, little support for cycling, where cycles are used for 10% of the journeys. It is important to know which criteria have priority for the cyclists if one is to meet all criteria at the same time.

In the Netherlands, there are five main requirements for cycle routes which cover several aspects (C.R.O.W., 1993) and which were the basis for the present study. In the following sections, these main requirements and the derived criteria are listed and explained and the questions we asked are derived when they did not cover these requirements.

(1) *The first main requirement is coherence.* The cycling infrastructure forms a coherent unit and links with all departure points and destinations of cyclists.

    1.1 *Findability.* Cycle routes should have uniform planning features in order to be clearly recognisable.

    1.2 *Consistency of quality.* A cycle route is of a consistent (high) quality throughout its length.

---

[1] Department of Psychology, Dresden University of Technology, Dresden, Germany. *E-mail:* carmen.hagemeister@mailbox.tu-dresden.de (C. Hagemeister)
[2] Faculty Transport and Traffic Sciences, Dresden University of Technology, Dresden, Germany.

These criteria show a high level of planning which could not be found where the study was conducted. Neither a cycling network nor a signposting existed there, and answers to such questions could only be speculations. Possible questions concerned cycling infrastructure without gaps and clear layout at intersections, which is an aspect of findability of cycling infrastructure.

(2) *The second main requirement is directness.* The cycling infrastructure continually offers the cyclists as direct a route as possible, so detours are kept to a minimum.

    2.1 *Actual speed of flow.* The actual speed of flow is sufficient for the cycle route concerned; this means, for example, that the cycle route is wide enough.

    2.2 *Delays.* Cyclists are not delayed on a road section.

The desired and possible speed varies broadly between cyclists, but they all experience waiting times, which might be a criterion, which is more comparable for all. They were also asked about directness of the route and number and length of detours.

(3) *The third main requirement is attractiveness.* The cycling infrastructure is designed and fitted to the surroundings in such a way that cycling is attractive.

    3.1 *Visibility.* Road surface, side pavement and road making are always well visible.

    3.2 *View ahead.* Partitions on verges (wall, railing or planting) have no detrimental effect on the view ahead.

    3.3 *Chance of blinding.* The distance from and height of a cycle route in relation to the carriageway for motorised traffic is chosen so that cyclists are not blinded by car headlights.

    3.4 *Sense of social safety.* Cycling facilities are easily visible from road sections and are not obstructed by works of art.

Other aspects we asked about were a low level of traffic noise and the impression of breathing good air. Emotions can also influence the attractiveness of a route. Examples are annoyance (about other road users or inadequate construction) and fun (enjoying cycling or the surroundings). Laws and regulations can have very different consequences for cyclists, they can be experienced as senseless or as a nuisance, or they can show that cycle traffic is given priority over motor traffic. For this reason, we asked how important it is that the traffic is lead in such a way that the cyclists are not tempted to break road traffic regulations.

(4) *The fourth main requirement is safety.* The cycling infrastructure guarantees the road safety of cyclists and other road users.

    4.1 *Complexity of riding.* The chance that problems arise on encounters between cycle traffic and other traffic and on movement of a cyclist on the cycle track is minimised.

Cyclists mainly experience safety not in terms of accidents but by the conflicts they have with other road users. Depending on the perceived danger and the number of conflicts, cyclists either have to focus their attention exclusively on traffic or might attend to other things as well. How far this is possible is a measure for the safety of the route. A central problem of many conflicts is the mutual visibility of road users and the view of the route, both of which can be experienced by cyclists and were thus contained in our questionnaire. We added four aspects, which might make riding more complex: turning and crossing at intersections, overtaking distance, speed of motor vehicles and volume of motor traffic.

(5) *The fifth main requirement is comfort.* The cycling infrastructure enables a quick and comfortable flow of bicycle traffic.

    5.1 *Hilliness.* According to the design manual (C.R.O.W., 1993) the number of inclines per unit of length has no negative effect on the usage of a cycle route. Topography might have an effect in a city where some parts are rather steep.

    5.2 *Traffic impediment.* The width and location of a cycle route are chosen so as to limit traffic impediment to a minimum.

    5.3 *Weather impediment.* Impediment from adverse weather is limited as much as possible, e.g. by using vegetation or buildings as a shield against wind; areas sheltered from rain; prompt clearance of snow; prompt salting or gritting to prevent slipperiness, frost layer, black ice.

Cyclists can influence the physical demand by route and speed choice. Several questions covered the topic of impediments for cyclists, clearness of stationary objects (light posts, parked cars), clearness of the path of turning vehicles and clearness of waiting areas. The width of cycle paths and lanes influences the number of conflicts as well: the narrower a cycle track, the higher the probability of impediments by parked cars or pedestrians.

Close to the point of departure and the destination, cyclists often have no route choice. In these cases they have the option to use a stretch of the road, which is made for other road users. They might cycle on the footpath instead of the carriageway or they might avoid a cycle track, which does not meet legal standards and cycle on the carriageway for motor traffic instead. On their way to work cyclists usually make few detours (Krause, 1984); they are in general vulnerable to detours (Alrutz, Fechtel & Krause, 1991). Detours are made if they are much more attractive than the shortest way or if the detours are only small. Answers about how important various criteria are for cyclists' route choice have to be interpreted in front of this background. Routes which are experienced as pleasant can reinforce cycle use while unpleasant routes can reduce cycle use.

This study deals with the question of what the cyclists themselves see as important for route choice. If one cannot rely on a cycling infrastructure as good as that which was developed in the Netherlands over a period of decades, one has to set priorities. Fulfilling the needs of those who already go by bike might make cycling more attractive for them. On the other hand, the needs of those cyclists who are exposed to traffic and infrastructure on a daily basis might point towards something, which does not deter experienced utility cyclists but may well deter those who start to use the bike for utility cycling, for example, after a cycle tour at the weekend.

METHODS

Participants

The participants were recruited by advertisements in a city magazine, by notices put up at the university and other places and by an article in the paper of the local bicycle club. Twenty-four women and 50 men from Dresden between 17 and 71 years of age (mean 30, standard deviation 10 years) answered the questionnaire. Forty-one rated themselves as "hard-boiled everyday cyclists", 28 as "everyday cyclists" and 5 as "good-weather cyclists". Sixty-eight persons gave information concerning their education. Thirty-five per cent had a university degree, 38% were students and 12% had completed 10 years of school. Forty-five per cent were working, 38% studying, 8% unemployed, 5% attended school or an apprenticeship and 4% were pensioners. In most cases only one cyclist was present, but sometimes the time to fill in the questionnaires overlapped. If more than one cyclist was present and they started talking, the experimenter asked them to postpone discussions until after filling in the questionnaire because the intention was to get individual opinions.

Ninety-one per cent of the participants held a driving licence. Thirty-six per cent of those holding a driving licence said, they had driven less than 10,000 km, 31% 10,000–50,000 km, 16% between 50,000 and 100,000 km and 11% more than 100,000 km. Thirty-one per cent estimated their knowledge of the road traffic regulations as very good, 59% as good and 8% as sufficient.

Fifty-five persons estimated their yearly cycle distance (mostly the help of the experimenter was necessary). On average, the participants cycled 4717 km per year, 6% below 1000 km, 18% 1000–3000 km, 33% 3000–5000 km, 24% 5000–7000 km, 15% 7000–10,000 km and 6% 10,000 km and more. Sixty-eight per cent stated that they cycled daily or nearly daily all year long, 3% on workdays, 22% in the summer half of the year daily or nearly daily, 5% never use their bike in winter.

Questionnaire

In the first part of the questionnaire, biographical data and cycling habits were assessed. At the end of the first part the persons were asked which aspects signify an attractive cycle route and were required to give an open answer. Only after completing the first part did the participants receive the second part of the questionnaire, which contained the criteria. In the second part of the questionnaire, the importance of 33 criteria was rated, as well as how often they were found in the surroundings. The questions can be read in the results section together with the answers. Open questions were asked for some criteria.

RESULTS

Answers to the open questions

In the first part of the questionnaire the cyclists wrote down which aspects signify an attractive utility cycling route without having knowledge of the criteria in the following list. More than 70 criteria were mentioned and grouped for further analyses.

A good surface of the road or cycle track was mentioned most often (44 times, 12% of the answers). The next most frequent aspect was that the kerbs of cycle tracks at intersections should be reduced completely or to a minimum (mentioned 22 times). Two aspects were named 17 times each: existence of a cycle track and roads with little motor traffic. Sixteen participants mentioned the width of cycle tracks (suitable for overtaking and bicycle trailers). Three aspects were named 15 times: direct connection, no detours and coherent cycling facilities. Thirteen persons said that separation of cyclists and pedestrians by colour marking is attractive and 10 prefer cycle lanes on the level of the carriageway. Other categories were mentioned eight times or less.

Results of answers to the list of criteria

No differences were found between the "hard-boiled" and the other everyday cyclists, and the group of "good-weather cyclists" was too small to allow separate analyses. For this reason the results are given for the whole sample.

Coherence. Figure 1 shows the ratings of the criteria for coherence. Both criteria are ranked as rather important (2.19 and 2.31), and a continuous infrastructure is found seldom.

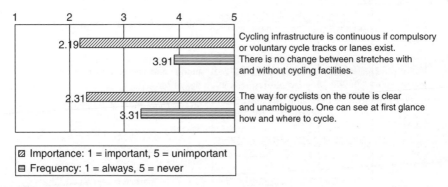

Figure 1. Importance and frequency of the criteria for coherence.

Directness. Figure 2 summarises the answers to the criteria of directness. The most important criterion was speedy progress, which is found with a medium frequency. The fact that the route contains no detours is seen as less important. For the detours the frequency question was "How often do you make a detour?" The cyclists were asked to decide between two alternative statements. Eighty-five per cent chose "If a route is more pleasant to cycle but is longer than the shortest way I prefer the longer route", 15% chose "The shortest route is always the best". Sixty-six persons said how long detours they would make if longer routes are better: the mean

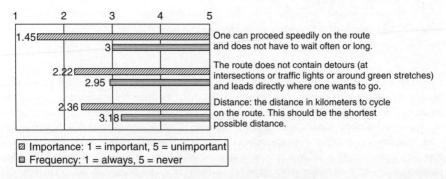

Figure 2. Importance and frequency of the criteria for directness.

value was 0.5 km for a total distance of 2 km, 1 km for a total distance of 5 km and 1.8 km for a total distance of about 10 km.

Attractiveness.   Figure 3 shows the results of the criteria for attractiveness. The second rank in this field was the impression of breathing good air. Further questions were asked about several aspects.

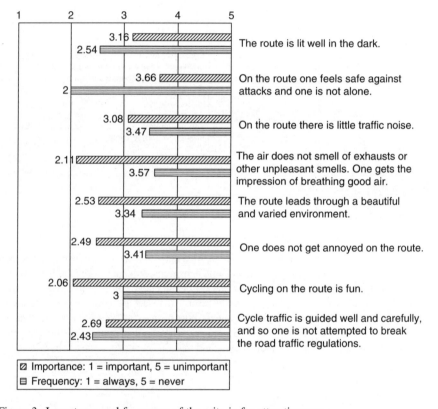

Figure 3. Importance and frequency of the criteria for attractiveness.

Fun. The most important criterion of attractiveness is fun. The cyclists were asked what makes cycling on a route fun. Twenty-five persons stated that they have fun when they cycle or roll speedily, are impeded little and have short waiting times. Twenty-four persons named infrastructure: 9 asphalt or smooth surface, 5 no kerbs. Twelve persons said that they have fun when they can cycle safely without conflict or danger. Eight persons named the related aspect that they can cycle in a relaxed way and are not forced to permanently worry about other persons' mistakes. Nineteen persons have fun when cycling on a route with little (13) or no (4) motor traffic or no fast motor traffic. Different features of the surroundings were named by

16 persons. Other aspects were mentioned by 18 persons. The answers show that fun on the route is caused by very different criteria.

Annoyance. Being not annoyed received the third rank in the field of attractiveness. The open question "What especially annoys you when you are cycling?" was answered by 48 persons in a way related to motor traffic. Fourteen persons are annoyed by close overtaking, nine by parking on the cycle track, seven by reckless drivers, six by turning car drivers, five by car doors opening into the path of the cyclist, five by thoughtless drivers. Six persons said that cyclists annoy them in different situations. Thirteen persons were especially annoyed by pedestrians, eight of them mentioned pedestrians on the cycle track. Forty-three persons are especially annoyed by the infrastructure: 24 times the surface, nine times kerbs, nine times unsafe ends of cycle tracks, seven are annoyed by bad guidance of cyclists. Eight persons are annoyed by lack of clearance of cycling facilities. Eleven persons are especially annoyed by traffic light regulations, four by road works. Other or general aspects were mentioned by 12 persons. As with fun, annoyance is related to different criteria.

Safety. Figure 4 shows how the criteria for safety were rated. Two characteristics of intersections were viewed as most important in the field of safety: a good view (1.62) and no danger when turning or crossing (1.9). The fact that the route is not dangerous as a whole was judged as rather important (2.04). The cyclists gave much information to the additional

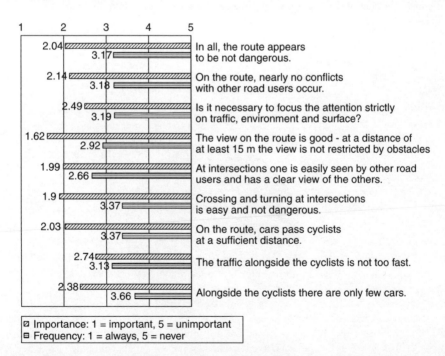

Figure 4. Importance and frequency of the criteria for safety.

questions about what they see as difficult and what as dangerous when turning and crossing at intersections.

Difficult situations at intersections. Seventeen cyclists saw encounters with motor traffic as difficult (six of them to be overlooked by drivers, four turning cars). Twenty-four answers named infrastructure (six cycle tracks which deviate away from motor traffic at intersections or lack of visibility for truck drivers, five traffic light regulation). Nineteen cyclists called left turns difficult (six direct left turns, four indirect left turns), seven lane change. Eight mentioned aspects of their own tasks as difficult.

Dangerous situations at intersections. Forty-one persons experienced cars as dangerous, most of them turning cars in general or cars turning right, six mentioned cars overtaking closely. Only one person mentioned cyclists. Seventeen persons named dangers from infrastructure: five tramlines, five bad visibility of cyclists. Ten persons regarded left turns as dangerous, two lane change.

Speed of cars.   For the question, which speed of cars the cyclists regarded as not too fast we gave three answer categories, 30 km/h is the speed limit in many residential areas, 50 km/h is the speed limit in towns, 60 km/h is the speed limit which most drivers try to keep in town in order not to be punished (Figure 5). There was also the possibility of a free answer. Eighteen per cent of the cyclists would like cars to go at speeds up to 30 km/h, 55% below 50 km/h.

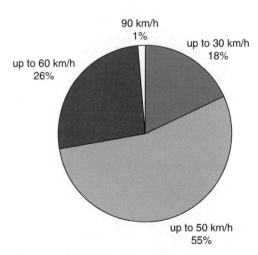

The traffic alongside the cyclists is not too fast.
What do you consider as "not too fast"?

90 km/h
1%

up to 30 km/h
18%

up to 60 km/h
26%

up to 50 km/h
55%

Figure 5. Speed of cars considered as not too fast alongside cyclists.

Comfort. Figure 6 gives an overview of the ratings for the criteria of comfort. The most important criterion was a good surface, rated as very important (1.39). The next important criterion was clearness from obstacles caused by cars and infrastructure.

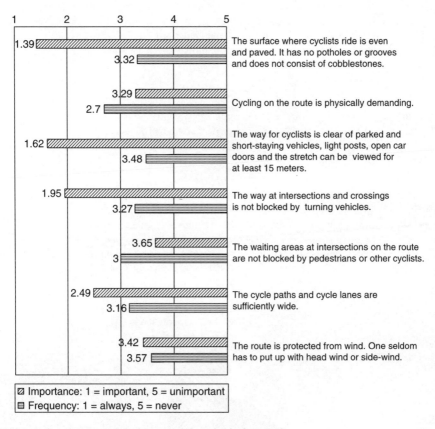

Figure 6. Importance and frequency of the criteria for comfort.

Separation of road users

Separation of cyclists and cars. Figure 7 shows the attitude towards separation of cyclists and cars. Half of the cyclists preferred a separation, a third preferred no separation, and 18% had no preference.

Turning left. Figure 8 shows the preference for direct or indirect left turns. Direct left turns were preferred to indirect left turns. Those persons who preferred direct turns named their speed and visibility as advantages. Those cyclists preferring indirect left turns considered them as safer.

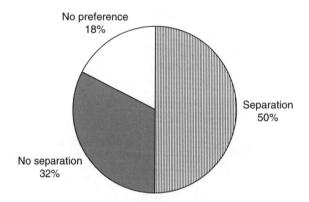

Figure 7. Attitudes towards cycle tracks separated from cars by a kerb.

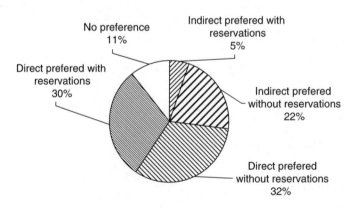

Figure 8. Preference for direct or indirect left turns.

Correlation between importance and frequency. Most correlations between importance and frequency were zero. Only four correlations were significant with $p < 0.05$. Two criteria were considered as more important the more seldom they were found: coherent infrastructure (rank correlation $\rho = -0.31$) and social safety ($\rho = -0.29$). Two criteria were seen as more important when they were experienced more often: fun ($\rho = 0.33$) and routes protected from wind ($\rho = 0.30$).

DISCUSSION

We partly found agreement between free answers and answers to the criteria list and partly large differences, which means that the method of asking might have influenced the answers. The existence of cycling facilities only had a medium range, the most important criteria were a good surface and speedy progress.

Differences between free answers and answers to the list of criteria

There were differences between the free answers and the ratings of the criteria. That means that the relative rating of importance can make a large difference to the results. The most important criterion for attractiveness and route choice was the surface. In the list, the next important criteria were speedy progress, and the fact that intersections allow a good view and are clear of obstacles. Speedy progress was on the upper ranks in the free answers whereas a good view at intersections was only seldom mentioned in the free answers. From the fact that a criterion is not mentioned in a free answer one cannot conclude that it is not important for route choice.

Alrutz et al. (1998) stated that "in a general rating of the importance, cyclists tend to rate all criteria as important" and for this reason they asked open questions. The results of this study show that cyclists neither see all criteria as equally important nor all as important for route choice. Giving cyclists a written list of criteria is a rather economic possibility of assessing the opinion of a large number of persons. Such a list of criteria allows the cyclists to give their opinion on criteria, which do not come to their mind immediately but might be important when experienced in a situation. In free answers, the cyclists depend on what comes to their mind from memory of cycling daily. In a list of criteria, they can give their opinion on things they take for granted. One has to take into account that the results might differ much depending on the chosen method.

The most important criteria and difference to prior results

In the list of criteria, the most important criterion was the surface (1.39) followed by speedy progress (1.45). Rank three was shared by sight at intersections and clearness of obstacles (1.62). On the following ranks there were turning (1.9) and crossing without danger at intersections and clear crossings (1.99). The most important criterion, surface, belongs to the criteria of comfort in the list by C.R.O.W. (1993). Bad surfaces cause a lot of falls of cyclists (Doherty, Aultman-Hall & Swaynos, 2000). This shows that they are a question not only of comfort but also of safety as well. Their study does also show that falls caused by bad surface are a problem occurring in all seasons.

Alrutz et al. (1998) found as the most important criterion the existence of cycling facilities. In our study, they belonged to the category of continuous cycling infrastructure, which only received a medium rank. The answer to another question showed that more than a quarter of the cyclists would rather ride together with the cars on the carriageway than on a separate cycle track or a mixed way for pedestrians and cyclists. This means that this proportion objects to cycle tracks. Other studies (e.g. Ellinghaus & Steinbrecher, 1993) showed that cycle paths aside footpaths cause many conflicts and dangers.

Alrutz et al. (1998) found the surface on rank two. In our study, speedy progress was on rank two, while in the study of Alrutz et al. the related criterion "few delays when cycling" was on rank seven. Krause (1984) found that the fact that a way is the fastest was the criterion mentioned most for taking a particular way, independent of the purpose of cycling. In her study, the second most important criterion was the fact that the way was the shortest, the next important criterion was the fact that the way had cycling facilities, and on rank four there was a small number of traffic lights, another aspect of progress without delays.

Differences between the rank orders of Alrutz et al. (1998) and this study can partly be explained by the circumstances in Dresden. Dresden differs largely from cities in northwest Germany, which have a better infrastructure for cyclists and a tradition where more people use their bike. Another reason for the differences between cyclists in different towns may be that only those who are willing to face the circumstances and put up with them use the bike daily.

Another difference between the studies is the focus. Alrutz et al. (1998) had stretches without intersections rated and not intersections. On stretches without intersections, cycle tracks protect from cars, which overtake too closely and for this reason such stretches are viewed as less dangerous than stretches without cycle tracks. At intersections, however, the disadvantages of cycle tracks for safety and speedy progress become visible: the cyclists in the present study named danger from turning cars, while longer delays when the traffic lights for cyclists turn red before those for cars can be observed easily. The fact that Alrutz et al. (1998) disregarded intersections might have made the rating for cycle tracks so positive. The present study included the whole route, and there the disadvantages show up as well as the advantages.

BASIC NEEDS: SPEEDY AND SAFE AT THE SAME TIME

The reasons given for preferring direct or indirect left turns show that some cyclists stress—subjectively experienced—faster cycling, and others stress—subjectively experienced—higher safety. The reasoning behind both arguments shows that basically both aspects are important for all cyclists. Cycling infrastructure for (adult) cyclists will only be a success if speed and safety are achieved at the same time. If the need for speedy progress is disregarded, cyclists will take direct left turns when indirect turns are intended, they might cycle in the wrong direction along one-way roads, they will use the carriageway instead of cycle tracks where there are obstacles like parked cars or pedestrians (Ketterer, 1990). If the need for safety is disregarded the cyclists will cycle on the footpath when it is not allowed and be a nuisance or even danger for pedestrians. Utility cyclists share the needs for speed and safety with all other road users who are on their daily journeys. However, there is no group, which is affected by such different regulations in the same city as cyclists are. If necessary, the cyclists should have the opportunity to choose between alternatives. Studies like those by Carré (2001) and Kuller, Gersemann and Ruwenstroth (1986) show how cyclists disregard traffic rules in order to proceed without delays. Carré also gives examples of how cyclists disregard traffic rules in order to achieve safety: in times with heavy traffic, 44% of the cyclists started a short time before the traffic light went green in order to get a safe distance from the following cars.

How General are the Results

If one compares utility cycling with cycling in spare time, the perspective is different: utility cyclists are exposed to conditions, which those cycling for recreation can avoid. In addition, the perspective changes if persons are exposed to a situation every day. The estimation of danger may change in general and at special places. If persons get used to situations they feel safer (Bundesanstalt für Straßenwesen, 1987). On the other hand, cyclists have learned to expect certain behaviours of other road users, where badly planned or built infrastructure makes them more likely. This is shown, for example, by the fact that the first rank in the list of accident risks mentioned in this study was an accident with a turning motor vehicle, which in fact is the most frequent severe accident for cyclists. Dangers due to the way cycle tracks are built were mentioned as well. It is very likely that persons cycling more seldom will have similar experiences when exposed to the same situations with the same frequency. The cyclists who participated in the study have, in a way, become experts, as shown by their perception of dangers.

Use of Such Studies for Practical Purposes

If a large number of cyclists are to be asked about their opinion, the number of questions in the questionnaire should be reduced. The answers show that the participants can differentiate well between a number of aspects: the answers to the questions on anger, difficulty and danger lead to different results. The answer categories turned out to be not optimal. The answers "always" and "never" were avoided which restricted the range of answers. The categories "nearly always or always" and "nearly never or never", which are less extreme, should lead to a larger range of answers. After such changes in the questionnaire, the largest differences between importance and frequencies can be discovered.

For most criteria, the ratings of importance and frequency were independent. This makes it possible to use such an instrument in a city or town in order to assess which experiences the cyclists have and what they consider as most important. Short questionnaires could also be used to assess the needs of certain subgroups of cyclists. Our results show that the needs in a group which seems to be homogeneous are very heterogeneous.

Open Questions

This study presents the view of persons who cycle often, most of them daily. Two important questions are left open concerning route choice. One is the question of strategy on the procedural level: if cyclists move to another place, how do they find the route which fits their needs, what makes them cycle on a new or a known route? The view of those who start utility cycling might be quite different than the view of the participants of our study. It would be interesting to observe how experience changes what cyclists consider as safe or attractive.

References

Alrutz, D., Fechtel, H.W., & Krause, J. (1991). *Dokumentation zur Sicherung des Fahrradverkehrs [Documentation for the Safety of Cycle-Traffic]*, *Berichte der Bundesanstalt für Straßenwesen*, Heft 74.

Alrutz, D., Bohle, W., & Willhaus, E. (1998). *Bewertung der Attraktivität von Radverkehrsanlagen [Rating the attractiveness of cycling facilities], Berichte der Bundesanstalt für Straßenwesen*, Bremerhaven: Wirtschaftsverlag NW, *Verkehrstechnik* Heft V 56.

Bundesanstalt für Straßenwesen (1987). *Situationsbezogene Sicherheitskriterien im Straßenverkehr [Criteria for Safety in Traffic in Situations], Projektgruppenberichte der BASt, Bereich Unfallforschung.*

Carré, J.-R. (2001). *RESBI. Recherche et expérimentation sur les stratégies des cyclistes dans leurs déplacements urbains [Research and experimentation on the strategies of cyclists on their ways in towns]*. Institut National de Recherche sur les Transports et leur Securité. Rapport No. 235.

C.R.O.W.—Centre for Research and Contract Standardization in Civil and Traffic Engineering—The Netherlands (Ed.) (1993). *Sign Up for the Bike. Design Manual for a Cycle-Friendly Infrastructure.* Ede, Netherlands: C.R.O.W.

Doherty, S.T., Aultman-Hall, L., & Swaynos, J. (2000). Commuter cyclist accident patterns in Toronto and Ottawa. *Journal of Transportation Engineering—ASCE, 126*, 21–26.

Ellinghaus, D., & Steinbrecher, J. (1993). *Radfahrer—Jäger und Gejagte. Untersuchung über die Unfallgefährdung von Radfahrern und der durch sie heraufbeschworenen Gefahren [Cyclists—Hunters and Hunted. Study on the Accident Risk of Cyclists and the Dangers Caused by Them], Uniroyal-Verkehrsuntersuchung 18, Köln.*

Ketterer, W. (1990). *Sicherheitsprobleme des Radverkehrs psychologisch betrachtet [Safety Problems of Cyclists Seen from a Psychological Point of View], Forschungsberichte des Psychologischen Instituts der Albert-Ludwigs-Universität Freiburg.*

Krause, J. (1984). *Radfahren in der Stadt [Cycling in the City].* Institut für Städtebau, Wohnungswesen und Landesplanung der TU Braunschweig: Braunschweig.

Kuller, E.C., Gersemann, D., & Ruwenstroth, G. (1986). *Regelabweichendes Verhalten von Fahrradfahrern [Cyclist Behaviour Deviating from Road Traffic Regulations], Forschungsberichte Bundesanstalt für Straßenwesen, Bereich Unfallforschung, 142.*

VULNERABLE ROAD USERS II:

OLDER ROAD USERS

Traffic and Transport Psychology
G. Underwood (Editor)
© 2005 Elsevier Ltd. All rights reserved.

7

THE ELDERLY PEDESTRIAN AND SOCIAL REPRESENTATIONS

Rogéria M. Sant' Anna[1] and Marilita G. C. Braga[1]

INTRODUCTION

The United Nations considers the period between 1975 and 2025 as the "Ageing Era". Developing countries are not managing to incorporate the social and economic measures necessary to facilitate and improve the quality of life of the increasing number of elderly people (Veras, 1999, 2002; WHO, 2001).

In Brazil, it was only in the 1980s that issues relating to the ageing of the population entered the public policy agenda (Veras, 1999, 2002). Presently, the elderly population (60 + years) accounts for 9% of the total, or over 14 million elderly people. Data from the World Health Organisation (WHO, 2002) suggest that between 1950 and 2025, the elderly population in Brazil will grow by 16 times.

The WHO suggests that countries, regions and international organisations will need to develop policies and programmes aiming for a more active ageing process, so that these populations remain physically and mentally healthy, independent and productive (WHO, 2002). The concept of "active ageing" emphasises quality of life and the social inclusion of this group as citizens and active members of our societies.

The main objective of this study is to identify social representations of the road environment by elderly pedestrians and to analyse the implications of such representations with regard to their security and mobility. It is an exploratory study, carried out in Rio de Janeiro, Brazil, using as a framework the Social Representations Theory (SR).

[1] Transport Engineering Group, COPPE—Federal University of Rio de Janeiro, Brazil. *E-mail:* rogeria@pet. coppe.ufrj.br (R.M. Sant' Anna); marilita@pet.coppe.ufrj.br (M.G.C. Braga).

TRANSPORT AND AGEING

Despite the main objective of transport not being to promote public health, issues such as accessibility, environmental protection and equity may provide opportunities for promoting public health. The quality of life while ageing will be strongly related to the degree of mobility enjoyed. Several aspects related to the transport system bear responsibility for their safety and mobility.

According to Metz (2000), mobility, in the traditional transport analysis, is associated with travel behaviour expressed in terms of supply and demand. Within this context, the concept of mobility and its implications for understanding the mobility of the elderly is considered to be limited. Alsnih and Hensher (2003), Banister and Bowling (2004), Metz (2000) emphasise the need to understand the concept of mobility associated with the demands of older populations. According to Alsnih and Hensher (2003), the ease with which journey destinations can be reached (accessibility) has increased, while the ease of movement (mobility) has decreased. It is crucial that the transport system and the road environment are developed to meet the needs and requirements of the elderly, allowing them a feeling of independence, security and dignity.

At present, particularly in Brazil, transport systems and traffic tend to reinforce the social exclusion of a wide range of people, including the elderly, according to the definition of social exclusion by Alsnih and Hensher (2003), Banister and Bowling (2004). There is a discrepancy between what individuals manage to do and what they would like to do; there is a spectrum of social exclusion. These authors conclude that in measuring social exclusion, one should contemplate the need to understand behaviours, so that individuals' experiences and the limitations imposed upon them can be taken into account. They recommend that in order to establish what information needs to be gathered, the end-users to be studied should be consulted. Personal contact with the researcher is essential, particularly for those who are socially excluded.

Some studies dealing with aspects of safety, traffic and ageing populations are based on the viewpoints of the elderly themselves (Banister & Bowling, 2004; Hakamies-Blomqvist, 2000; Kent & Fildes, 1997; Langlois et al., 1997). In this respect, this research ratifies these premises, of trying to obtain some indication of the point of view of the elderly.

THEORETICAL FRAMEWORK

This study adopts a qualitative and exploratory approach, taking traffic safety into account as an interdisciplinary subject, backed up by the SR.

The theoretical reference—The Social Representations Theory

The SR is a social psychology theory that refers to the way individuals think and interpret their day-to-day lives. The aim is to understand how the knowledge of certain objects is constructed by different social groups and is based on a group of images or reference systems that allows individuals to interpret their own lives and make them meaningful (Moscovici, 1978). These images should not be understood as simple copies or pictures of the exterior that individuals internalise, but as a process of symbolic construction based on the reality of certain groups. The representations are a form of construction and reconstruction of the different meanings that particular social objects may have for certain groups.

In this respect, the theoretical methodology framework adopted allows elderly pedestrians the opportunity to express their own "theories" regarding the road environment. This means understanding how this group, based on their representations, perceives the road environment and how this group relates to it.

We have adopted as a basis the theoretical framework presented in the approach of Jodelet (2001), which emphasises the genesis of Social Representation, its contents and processes of construction: anchorage (symbolic components) and objectification (figurative components). Anchorage provides an intelligible context to the object, allowing the insertion of the object of representation into existing categories. Anchorage allows knowledge to be constructed and its meaning provided simultaneously. Objectification allows a concept to become reality, giving it materiality through image. We have also utilised the theoretical framework of Abric (Sá, 1996), who considers that social representations are structured around a central core and key peripheral elements, in attributing meanings to representation.

The population and the sample

Given that this is a qualitative research, we have opted to use saturation sampling criteria to determine our sample and the number of participants taking part in the study cannot be established in advance. As long as original information is available that may lead to further investigation, the interviews should proceed. The point of saturation is established when the information obtained allows symbolic patterns, practices, classificatory systems, reality analysis categories and visions of the universe under consideration to be satisfactorily identified (Bauer & Gaskell, 2000; Sá, 1998).

Census data shows that Rio de Janeiro has the highest proportion of elderly among the country's state capitals—13.2% (IBGE, 2004). The surveys were carried out among elderly who are participants in the Open University for Studies on Ageing and Care of the Elderly (UnATI) at the Rio de Janeiro State University (UERJ). This group presents an active life-style, common among the majority of the elderly population in large Brazilian urban areas.

Fifty elderly people took part in the surveys, with ages ranging from 60 to 78, 45 of them females and only 5 of them males. The significantly higher proportion of females is relative to the profile of the elderly population in Brazil. Women account for 62.4% of these.

Data collection methodology

The first step was to apply focus group techniques (Millward, 1995) combining three stages of data collection: free association test, semi-structured interviews and image evocation test. Five focus groups were set up. The first stage comprised the application of a free word association test. This test involved presenting the groups with a phrase ("Write down whatever comes to mind when I say—the elderly pedestrian") aimed at inducing a response and then asking the participants to write down whatever came to mind.

The second stage comprised semi-structured interviews, involving three themes: (a) road safety relating to: the perception of relative risk; the diminished physical and mental performance of the elderly; the behaviour of the other road users; the road infrastructure; (b) principal difficulties of elderly pedestrians; (c) level of perceived hostility and its effect on mobility.

The third stage comprised the application of an image evocation test, complementary to the interview. This test involved presenting the groups with 14 photographs of different neighbourhoods in the city, showing elderly people in the road environment; seven of these showed hazardous traffic situations and the other seven showed safe situations. The participants were asked to select two photographs and explain the reasons for their choices. The aim was to stimulate the projective production of the elements that made up the images.

Data analysis methodology

For analysis of the Test of the Free Association of Words, the words were grouped according to their semantic similarities and the set was then analysed using the EVOC—*Ensemble de Programmes Permettant L'Analyse des Évocations (Group of Programs for the Analysis of Evoked Responses)* software, developed in France by Pierre Vergés, in 1992. This software subjects the words evoked to two criteria: frequency and average order of evocation.

The data obtained were subjected to the technique of thematic content analysis proposed by Bardin (1977). This led to the identification of the main content of social representation and its moulding processes: objectification and anchorage. For the image evocation test, the chosen photographs were analysed according to frequency of choice and the theme (safe or hazardous situation).

ANALYSIS OF THE RESULTS

In order to understand the SR of these elderly pedestrians, it was necessary to relate the focus groups' results to social, economic and cultural aspects of the context, following the guidance of Spink (1999).

Analysis of the free association test

The 202 words or expressions evoked were grouped according to semantic proximity. Hence, the data entered into the EVOC represent keywords. The EVOC software uses the criteria of average frequency (fm) and average order of evocation (ome). Thus, one can find the core and peripheral elements of the social representation: for the number of elements analysed in this case, the average values were 6 for the fm and 2.1 for the ome. The core elements are those of greater frequency and are the first to be evoked (lower average order); the peripheral system comprises elements of low frequency and higher average order of evocation. Table 1 was developed from the reports produced by the software, showing the four sections that form the structure of the social representation.

Table 1. Attributes comprising the core and peripheral elements of the Social Representation of the elderly.

OME < 2.1			OME ≥ 2.1		
Core elements	*f*	*ome*	*Peripheral elements*	*f*	*ome*
fm ≥ 6					
Walking slowly	6	1.667	Fear	6	2.333
			Buses	7	2.286
			Difficulties	8	2.125
			Pavements	9	2.667
			Fall	9	3.111
			Cross the street	10	2.400
			Traffic *signal*	16	2.500
fm < 6					
Unaware	3	1.667	Buses do not stop	3	2.667
Traffic	3	2.000	Alert	4	2.250
Difficulty walking	4	1.750	Traffic laws	4	2.750
Street	4	1.000	Kerb	4	3.500
			Sad	4	4.250
			Drivers	5	3.200
			Unsafe buses	5	3.200

One can see that *walking slowly* is the element of greatest frequency and lowest average order of evocation. Hence, it is the most representative and comprises the core of the SR for elderly pedestrians with respect to their insertion within the traffic environment, expressing perceptions of their performance as pedestrians. This question of the elderly walking more slowly is directly related to the principal biological factors involved in the human ageing process.

However, these factors involve psychological aspects as the elderly tend to become more indecisive and insecure as they tend to find that making a routine decision while walking is more difficult and entail taking greater precautions, which diminishes the walking speed still further. Analysis of the core element suggests a close link between their own perceptions of the limitations imposed by ageing and performance within the traffic environment. Walking slowly can be interpreted as a homogeneous characteristic of this social group and presents itself as potentially being shared by all the elderly.

The other boxes contain elements that comprise the peripheral system of social representation. Although these include elements related to perception of their own performance and feelings aroused by close contact with the traffic environment it can be noted that as the distance from the core augments, elements related to environmental aspects start to be included. One can say that the content of the social representation embraces physical and psychological barriers that the traffic environment imposes on elderly pedestrians.

As the free association test was carried out before the interviews, the results are related more to individual than to group representation. Consequently, at a more individual level, the elements that emerge basically involve traffic safety, with the emphasis on negative aspects of the traffic environment and a feeling of insecurity.

Analysis of the interviews

The analysis of the interviews identified the principal themes that emerged from the focus groups. Five basic categories were identified: a redefining of the social representation of old age; the forging of an "elderly" identity; the desire for mobility; the perception of the road environment as unsafe and even hostile; and the risk response of the elderly and their posture regarding "otherness".

Redefining the social representation of ageing.   The first result is linked to the transformation that has occurred in the social role of the elderly in Brazil. Ageing is endowed with negative connotations that emphasise the stereotypes of physical and emotional dependence, insecurity and isolation, although this is gradually changing for the better (Costa & Almeida, 1999; Costa & Campos, 2003; Elmôr & Madeira, 2003; Magalhães, 2003).

During the last two decades, the rapid growth of the population of the elderly has led to a rethinking of their situation and has repercussions on the government sector's definition of public policy and civil society's actions to give more prominence to specific issues involving the elderly. There are examples of successful ageing that are being experienced collectively. What was observed in the study is that, alongside this representation of problematic old age, loneliness, retirement and inactivity, there is a new generation of the elderly who go outdoors, do exercises, attend cultural events, get together at their clubs, watch their diet and work. They are active citizens, who get around in the city and take over public spaces, despite being subjected to risks.

The media, with its power to mould opinion, has played a decisive role in bringing this issue to public attention, denouncing the intergenerational conflict and prejudice that the elderly suffer, esteeming their independence and autonomy and helping to define the new identity. In addition to this group who play an active part in society, there is an enormous number of elderly people who are financially and socially excluded, tucked away and forgotten in their homes, many of them victims of violence and other forms of abuse (Minayo & Souza, 2003). But it is important to emphasise that it is primarily this group of active elderly people who are helping to redefine the concept of the elderly. They are the models for the positive connotations of ageing that other elderly people tend to identify with.

The forging of an identity.   A link was perceived between the redefinition of the social representation of old age and a process of changing identity among these people. For Soares (1997), the identity crisis among the elderly is generally experienced as an acute distress brought on by physical changes that lead to a perception that one's own body fails to correspond to the ideal imposed by the consumer society.

This redefining of the social representation of old age is a strong social benchmark. Kimmel and Weiner (1998) state that, the more developed the person's sense of identity, the more the individual appreciates the ways they are similar or different to others and the more clearly they recognise their strengths and limitations. It is mobility that enables the elderly to identify with the positive representation of old age and to feel socially included. This representation is the borderline between staying at home and going outside, between an idle, lazy, reclusive old aged and one that is vital and active.

The desire for mobility. It was seen that the need to identify with the representation of ageing that emerges leads to a growing necessity for social inclusion and, consequently, to an increase in the mobility. No significant differences were observed in travel pattern even in cases of the elderly who retire. This group goes outside their homes every weekday and the amount of trip chaining, characteristic of enhanced mobility, increased. Following retirement, they began to travel more on foot and by public transport.

Although walking is their preferred form of locomotion, it can be noted that the pleasure and autonomy derived from walking is mingled with a greater vulnerability experienced by elderly pedestrians, due to inadequate infrastructure or public/traffic violence. With regard to public transport, the bus system was the one that generated the strongest response. The interviewees emphasised the vital importance of being able to get around by bus and the impediments experienced by users of this system. It should be pointed out that, since 1999, the right to free public transport for people over 65 years of age has been enshrined in the Brazilian Constitution. However, on the whole, this service is not meeting the specific demands of this group. Buses do not meet the ergonomic requirements of the elderly population: for example, the height of the steps. With regard to the treatment of the customer, the prevailing attitude is a lack of respect on the part of drivers, who tend to reinforce the prejudice against the elderly.

For the elderly participating in the focus groups, "going by bus" is a form of "getting around in the city". This expresses that the elderly anchor this new representation of ageing in their potential for mobility and the bus emerges as an object identified with this representation. Among the population studied, their interpretation of the road environment is anchored in their potential for mobility.

With regard to objectification, the bus was the predominant symbolic image guiding the perceptions and judgment of the elderly. The bus is, therefore, a key element in understanding the representation of mobility and it is necessary to contextualise it in relation to the system of urban transport in the city where they live.

The formal public transport system that operates in the city of Rio de Janeiro is a diversified one. The rail systems were allowed to seriously deteriorate during the 1990s. The present demand for the urban railway system is around 370,000 passengers per day (4.5% of total public transport users). The subway system's operations are limited to the municipality of Rio and serve an average daily demand of around 400,000 users (Balassiano & Braga, 2000). The city has a ferry system, which carries an average of less than 30,000 passengers per day and low capacity alternatives that, according to recent studies (Vasconcellos & Balassiano, 2004), carry an average daily number of passengers similar to that of the railways and subway.

Hence, the urban bus system is identified as the principal supplier to the city's public transport demands, carrying an average of 7 million passengers per day (approximately 85% of the journeys by public transport). One can conclude, therefore, that to these elderly, the bus does not just represent a means of transport. It imposes on their very perception of mobility.

The perception of the road environment as unsafe and even hostile. The road environment was described as unsafe and hostile. Analysis of the free association test corroborates this conclusion by identifying that at the individual level, aspects linked to road infrastructure emerge as being those closest to the daily perceptions that comprise the universe of most conscious meanings. The image evocation test showed that the elderly tend to perceive conflicts in the road environment in a generalised manner. When asked to select two photographs, 36% of the elderly chose two photographs portraying hazardous traffic situations; 26% chose, in first place, photographs depicting hazardous situations and in second place, photographs showing safe situations. Thus, 62% of the participants evoked, in first place, images portraying the road environment as unsafe. When they justified their choices, it was noticed that there was a tendency to interpret the content of photos as unsafe, even when they showed a safe environment. This detail highlights their difficulty in perceiving risk.

Various aspects of the road infrastructure were criticised. Numerous examples were cited of roads and sites that were perceived as being inadequate to their necessities. Another factor identified as determinant to the perceptions of these elderly is the association between the road environment and violence. The street has associations of being the haunt of the idle, of immoral behaviour, of violence, a dangerous place.

The public authorities are seen as neglectful and incompetent. The utility of traffic laws that are not obeyed is called into question and their non-observance vindicates the insecurity felt by the elderly. Observing these wrongs being committed within the society provokes considerable indignation. It is a clash between their personal paradoxes and those of the society in which they live. To this conception is added the ambiguity of the street as a meeting place, where they can exercise their autonomy and independence.

The risk response of the elderly and their posture regarding "otherness". If the street is such a hostile, unsafe place, staying at home could be a more appropriate response. But the consequence could be diminishing self-esteem, depression and loss of positive identity. In the face of this impasse, the elderly, through a process of "otherness", anchor their insecurity in traffic in the "other". The process of objectification is directed at drivers, motorcyclists, cyclists, other pedestrians and the public authorities.

It was concluded that, for this group, "otherness" is a psychological defence mechanism adopted in response to the fear associated with a perception of insecurity within the road environment. For Joffe (1999), "otherness" is a primal form that people use to protect themselves from their fears, by projecting the responsibility for their origin onto others and thus distancing themselves from the threatening situation.

This in turn leads to the conclusion that "otherness" helps to augment the risk to this population since, upon projecting their fear of this hazardous and hostile road environment onto others, the elderly are creating a dissociation that can heighten their exposure to risk. Consequently, these elements of anchorage and objectification related to "otherness" should be taken into consideration in educational programs aimed at this segment.

CONCLUSIONS

The analysis of the results indicates a heightened potential for exposure to risk among elderly pedestrians who, although they perceive the traffic environment as hostile and unsafe, give priority to their mobility, to the detriment of their safety. In alignment with this process, the social representation of ageing is being redefined, incorporating new symbols, values and beliefs. The need to identify with a positive representation of old age is emerging and appropriating these attributes by means of greater social inclusion. Hence, this redefinition of social representation leads to an increase in the mobility of the elderly. However, in augmenting the number of journeys made, the elderly also augment constant menace from an environment that they see as hostile. But despite that, they feel impelled to go into this environment or lose their self-respect. The elderly, feeling powerless in regard to the situation, tend to comprehend and justify this risk through "otherness" and assign to the other users of the transport system and the public authorities the responsibility for their safety. This dissociation is complemented by a tendency to accentuate this population's potential exposure to risk.

Although there is a dialectic relationship between mobility and safety, in this study the terms express different representations. The more individual the level of analysis, the greater the focus is on safety; the more collective it is, the more the focus is on mobility. This verification is worrying, as the representation of mobility transcends the representation of safety. By anchoring their social inclusion on their potential for mobility, the elderly are exposing themselves more intensely to a road environment that does not meet their safety requirements. This does not mean that they are unaware of the risk.

It is possible to affirm that elderly pedestrians are exposed to greater risk, taking into consideration two factors: the failure to meet their minimum requirements (both in terms of road infrastructure and the public transport system) and the social inclusion of these elderly pedestrians (who prioritise their mobility, to the detriment of their safety in the road environment).

One of the most significant results is attention drawn to the vital importance of public transport in enabling this population to move around. The ambivalence and ambiguities that typify the conflicts pervading the relationship between the public authorities and the transport operators in Brazil need to be allayed. It necessarily involves considerations that should give emphasis to values, norms and criteria aimed at guaranteeing the rights of the elderly. Bus transport has become synonymous with public transport. Hence, any improvement in public transport, and particularly the buses, will have a significant impact on the quality of life of elderly pedestrians.

The picture of the elderly person that emerged is someone looking for a new status that confers social relevance. However, this elderly person is in a moment of transition and is battling against the restrictive representations that still predominate in our society. In this context, the priority should be to emphasise quality of life when thinking about the question of mobility and traffic safety for this population.

The results of the study confirm the importance of interdisciplinary research into traffic safety, with emphasis on the transport sector's potential to contribute with strategic approaches to promote health and social inclusion, particularly in the case of the elderly population.

ACKNOWLEDGEMENTS

We would like to thank CAPES (Foundation for the Coordination of Post-Graduate Development), a Brazilian government development agency, and UnATI (Open University for Studies on Ageing and Care of the Elderly), for their support of the research that led to this chapter.

REFERENCES

Alsnih, A., & Hensher, D.A. (2003). The mobility and accessibility expectations of seniors in an aging population. *Transportation Research Part A, 37*, 903–916.

Balassiano, R., & Braga, M.G.C. (2000). Competição no transporte rodoviário de passageiros: o caso do Rio de Janeiro. In Santos, E., & Aragão, J. (Eds.), *Transporte em Tempos de Reforma* (Vol. 1, pp. 12–20). Brasilia: L.G.E. Editora.

Banister, D., & Bowling, A. (2004). Quality of life for the elderly? The transport dimension. *Transport Policy, 11*, 105–115.

Bardin, L. (1977). *Análise de Conteúdo*, Lisboa: Edições, 70.

Bauer, M.W., & Gaskell, G. (2000). *Qualitative Researching with Text, Image and Sound*. London: Sage Publications.

Costa, W.A., & Almeida, A.M.O. (1999). Teoria das Representações Sociais: uma abordagem alternativa para se compreender o comportamento cotidiano dos indivíduos e dos grupos sociais. *Revista de Educação Pública, 8* (13), 250–280.

Costa, F.G., & Campos, P.H.F. (2003). *Representação social da velhice, exclusão e práticas institucionais, III Jornada Internacional e I Conferência Brasileira sobre Representações Sociais.* Rio de Janeiro: UERJ.

Elmôr, T.M.R., & Madeira, M.C.O. (2003). *Idoso e o aprender, III Jornada Internacional e I Conferência Brasileira sobre Representações Sociais.* Rio de Janeiro: UERJ.

Hakamies-Blomqvist, L. (2000). Recent European research on older drivers. *Accident Analysis and Prevention, 32*, 601–607.

IBGE (2004). Foundation of the Brazilian Institute for Geography and Statistics. Available from http://www.ibge.gov.br, June.

Jodelet, D. (2001). As representações sociais: um domínio em expansão. In Jodelet, D. (Ed.), *As representações sociais.* Rio de Janeiro: Editora EdUERJ.

Joffe, H. (1999). Eu não, o meu grupo não: representações sociais transculturais da AIDS. In Guareschi, P., & Jovchelovitch, S. (Eds.), *Textos em representações sociais* (Vol. 5,). Petrópolis: Vozes.

Kent, S., & Fildes, B. (1997). *A Review of Walk-with-care: An education and Advocacy Program for Older Pedestrians.* Victoria, Australia: Accident Research Centre, Monash University, Available from http://www.general.monash.edu.au/MUARC/rptsum/muarc109.pdf, June 2003.

Kimmel, D.C., & Weiner, I. (1998). *La adolescencia: una transición del desarrollo.* Barcelona: Ariel.

Langlois, J.A., Keyl, P.M., Guralnik, J.M., Foley, D.J., Marottoli, R.A., & Wallace, R.B. (1997). Characteristics of older pedestrians who have difficulty crossing the street. *American Journal of Public Health, 87*, 393–397.

Magalhães, N.C. (2003). *Máscaras e conflitos da representação social do idoso na cidade de Juiz de Fora, III Jornada Internacional e I Conferência Brasileira sobre Representações Sociais.* Rio de Janeiro: UERJ.

Metz, D.H. (2000). Mobility of older people and their quality of life. *Transport Policy, 7,* 149–152.

Millward, L. (1995). Focus groups. In Breakwell, G.M., Hammond, S., & Fife-Schaw, C. (Orgs.), *Research Methods in Psychology.* London.

Minayo, M.C., & Souza, E.R. (2003). *As múltiplas mensagens da violência contra os idosos, Violência sob o olhar da saúde: infrapolítica da contemporaneidade brasileira.* Rio de Janeiro: Editora FIOCRUZ.

Moscovici, S. (1978). *A representação social da psicanálise.* Rio de Janeiro: Zahar.

Sá, C.P. (1996). *Sobre o núcleo central das representações sociais.* Rio de Janeiro: Editora Vozes.

Sá, C.P. (1998). *A construção do objeto de pesquisa em representações sociais.* Rio de Janeiro: EdUERJ.

Soares, N.E. (1997). A velhice e suas representações sociais em duas instituições de Medicina Social, Tese de doutorado apresentada ao Instituto de Medicina da UERJ.

Spink, M.J. (1999). Desvendando as teorias implícitas: uma metodologia de análise das representações sociais. In Guareschi, P., & Jovchelovitch, S. (Eds.), *Textos em representações sociais.* Petrópolis: Vozes.

Vasconcellos, S.C., & Balassiano, R. (2004). *An Integration Proposal for the Transport System of the City of Rio de Janeiro.* CODATU XI, Bucharest, Romania, April 22–24.

Veras, R.P. (1999). *Terceira idade: alternativas para uma sociedade em transição.* Rio de Janeiro: Unati/UERJ, Relume Dumará.

Veras, R.P. (2002). A era dos idosos: os novos desafios. Iª Oficina de Trabalhos sobre desigualdades sociais e de gênero em saúde de idosos no Brasil. Available from http://www.cpqrr.fiocruz.br/nespe/Content/Ouro%20Preto/ouro-preto-anais-final.pdf, May 2004.

WHO (2001). *Spotlight on Mounting Traffic Deaths.* NMH News, WHA 54, Geneva, May.

WHO (2002). *Move for Health: Promoting a Physically Active Life Through Everyday Transport—Examples and Approaches from Europe.* World Health Organisation, Regional Office for Europe.

Traffic and Transport Psychology
G. Underwood (Editor)
© 2005 Elsevier Ltd. All rights reserved.

8

ELDERLY DRIVERS' HAZARD PERCEPTION AND DRIVING PERFORMANCE

Kazumi Renge[1], Tomikazu Ishibashi[2], Masaaki Oiri[3], Hiro Ota[4], Shigeyuki Tsunenari[5] and Marehiro Mukai[6]

INTRODUCTION

Elderly drivers' accidents become an increasingly important problem of traffic safety in Japan. The population of the elderly was 22 million in 2000 and is expected to reach 32 million in 2015, which is ca. 25% of total population. At the same time, elderly drivers could increase very rapidly from 7.2 millions in 2000 to 16.5 millions in 2015. The rate of increase of elderly drivers is much higher than that of elderly population, because the rate of elderly driving license holders increases rapidly hereafter. The number of fatal accidents involving elderly people has already increased since 1980s (Figure 1). Fatalities in particular, involving elderly motor vehicle occupants, increased from 330 in 1990 to 708 in 2003, while those involving young occupants decreased from 1562 in 1990 to 525 in 2003 (Figure 2). These changes of fatalities are much greater than population changes of each age group.

PURPOSE

The present study focuses on elderly drivers' driving performance such as drivers' searching head movements and driving speed. The performance was also evaluated by driving instructors. In particular, driving performance at several intersections was measured, because elderly drivers' accidents often occur there. The behavioral and evaluative measures were compared between

[1] Department of Psychology, Tezukayama University, Nara, Japan. *E-mail:* renge@tezukayama-u.ac.jp (K. Renge).
[2] Institute of ErgoSciences, Osaka, Japan.
[3] Kyoto Prefectural University, Kyoto, Japan.
[4] Tohoku Institute of Technology, Sendai, Japan.
[5] Department of Forensic Medicine, Kumamoto University, Kumamoto, Japan.
[6] Faculty of Psychology, Chukyo University, Nagoya, Japan.

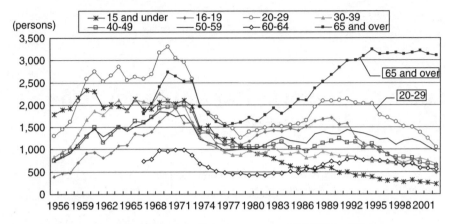

Figure 1. Changes in traffic accident fatalities by age group (ITARDA, 2004).

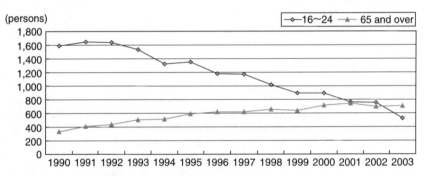

Figure 2. Changes in fatalities involving motor vehicle occupants by age group (ITARDA, 2004).

age groups such as middle-aged and elderly drivers. A hazard perception test was conducted. The scores of hazard perception were then related with the scores of driving performance.

It would be expected that elderly drivers' performance should decrease with age. They could perform lower level of searching and stopping behavior and also the driving instructors would evaluate their performance lower than middle-aged drivers. Furthermore, we will compare within the groups between semi-junior and senior-elderly drivers, so that we can estimate when such possible deterioration could start with aging.

Ota (1997) investigated the ability of hazard perception between junior-elderly and senior-elderly drivers. The senior-elderly drivers showed a lower performance of hazard perception than junior-elderly drivers. Based on the results, we expected that ability of hazard perception could also decrease with aging. The hazards were divided into three types of the hazards such as "obvious hazards", "potential hazards", and "hazards relating to prediction of other road users' behavior", of which performance were compared within groups.

METHOD

The investigation was conducted in four driving schools in Japan. Each driving school possesses a driving course and classrooms. Participants totaled 198 drivers, of which 36 were middle-aged (from 30 to 54 years old), 32 semi-elderly (from 55 to 64 years old), 88 junior-elderly (from 65 to 74 years old), and 42 senior-elderly (over 75 years old) drivers.

Drivers drove a motor vehicle of the driving school, three times on the certain course in training area of the school (Figure 3). The driving course of each driving school was slightly different, because of the design of each driving school's training area. The course, however, consisted of at least several intersections and straight course suitable for analyzing the driving performance. The intersections were those with STOP sign (left and right turn) and without STOP sign (left turn), and with restricted visibility (left turn).

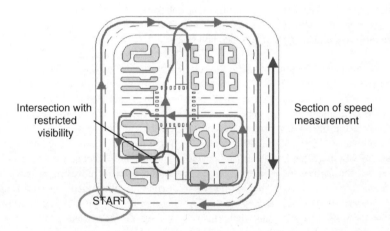

Figure 3. Driving route of a driving school in Kyoto.

Drivers' head movements and speeding in driving were chosen as behavioral measures.

Four video cameras were set in each experimental car, three of which took scenes in front of the car, speed meter, and the driver's face individually. Lastly, three scenes were gathered into one frame through a special video device (Sony YS-Q400) and recorded by a different fourth video camera (Figure 4). A car battery of each experimental car supplied with the necessary electric power through a DC–AC inverter.

At first, frequencies of drivers' head movements were counted per each trial on the basis of the video film of drivers' face. Both left and right head movements of each driver were counted as one time.

Figure 4. In-car equipment and the data recording.

Driving instructors also evaluated drivers' behavior on the basis of a checking sheet consisting of 25 items, which were at last classified into six behavioral categories such as (1) searching behavior, (2) speeding behavior, (3) signaling behavior, (4) positioning behavior, (5) lane-keeping behavior, and (6) steering behavior. Total scores, named "Driving Score by Instructors", were then calculated in percentages.

The traffic scenes in the present study were chosen from those used in the research by IATSS (2001) and Renge (1998). Every scene was videotaped from a running car. Only the daytime scenes were included and the scenes in night driving were excluded as stimuli. In total, nine scenes for experiment and one scene for training were presented to the participants. The scenes were projected using a video projector (Sony VPL-S900) and a video recorder (Sony DVCAM DSR-30) on an 80-inch wide screen in a classroom or a meeting room of each driving school. Each scene was projected first about 15 s and then continued a still picture for 5 s. After looking each scene, the participants answered on the sheets in the way of checking possible hazards (dangerous objects/road users/places). Each traffic scene was illustrated on sheets (Figure 5). They could check as many as they wanted. As the time for the answers was unlimited, the participants were able to think their answer as long as they wanted. In addition, the experimenter did not hasten their answers.

According to the contents of the hazards, the hazards were divided into three types such as "obvious hazards (OH)", "potential hazards (PH)", and "hazards relating to prediction of other road users' behavior (BH)" (see Ogawa, Renge, & Nagayama, 1993; Ota, 1997). The "obvious hazards" usually mean any moving objects in front of the car ("a pedestrian walking across the street"). If the driver would not take any evasive action, an accident and/or a traffic conflict could be expected to happen. The "potential hazards" mean any hidden objects by obstacles like a parked car or an intersection. The hazards could be anticipated to appear from blind corner to the front of the car. The third category of the hazards, "hazards relating to prediction of other road users' behavior", mean the standing or slowly moving road users on the side of streets could be really dangerous according to their possible behavior onward. Drivers should anticipate their following behavior in order to avoid potential collision with them.

Figure 5. An example of an illustrated traffic scene on the answering sheets.

Totally 31 hazards were included in the whole of the scenes, of which 18 OH, 6 PH, and 7 BH were divided. The total scores and the categorical scores were then calculated in percentages.

RESULTS AND DISCUSSION

Elderly drivers demonstrated fewer searching head movements than younger drivers (middle-aged and semi-elderly drivers) (Figure 6). As for speeding behavior, elderly drivers did not drive at higher speed on the straight course, but drove at higher speed than younger drivers at uncontrolled intersections both with restricted visibility (Figure 7) and with STOP sign. Similar results were also obtained on the evaluation scores of driving instructors. Such tendency of higher speed by elderly drivers was not found on the straight course of the range (Figure 8).

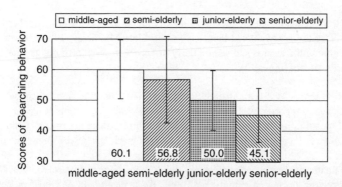

Figure 6. Scores of searching behavior by age groups.

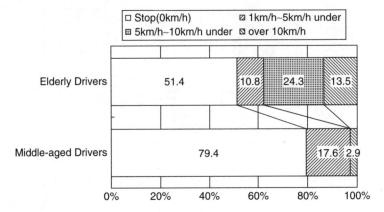

Figure 7. Passing speed at an intersection with restricted visibility between middle-aged and elderly drivers.

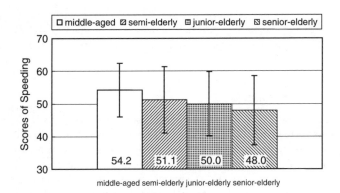

Figure 8. Speed of straight course.

Driving instructors evaluated the driving skills of elderly drivers lower than other age groups, although elderly drivers evaluated themselves very high. Middle-aged drivers were evaluated the highest among the groups and semi-elderly drivers were evaluated higher than junior- and senior-elderly drivers (Figure 9).

The evaluation scores by driving instructors to each category of driving are showed in Figures 10 and 11. The categories such as "searching behavior", "speeding behavior", "signaling behavior", "positioning behavior", and "lane keeping behavior", were found significant differences between age groups. More elderly drivers got lower scores than other age groups.

The self evaluations of elderly drivers were higher than younger drivers, while evaluations by driving instructors decreased rapidly with age. As a result, the discrepancy between self evaluations and evaluations by driving instructors increased with age (Figure 12).

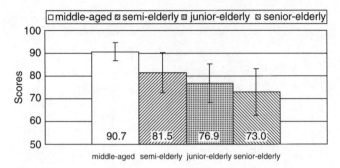

Figure 9. Evaluation scores by driving instructors to driving performance.

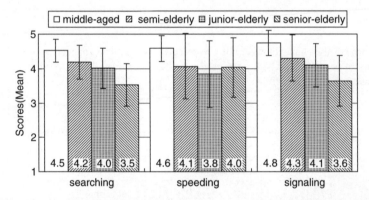

Figure 10. Evaluation scores by driving instructors in categories of driving performance by age groups (1).

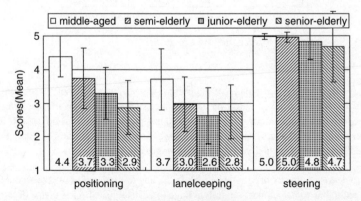

Figure 11. Evaluation scores by driving instructors in categories of driving performance by age groups (2).

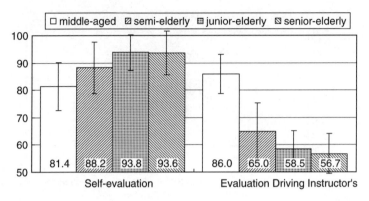

Figure 12. Evaluations of driving skills of the elderly drivers by themselves and by driving instructors.

Elderly drivers also showed lower ability to perceive hazards than younger drivers (Figure 13), especially in perception of both potential hazards and hazards relating to prediction of other road users' behavior (Figure 14).

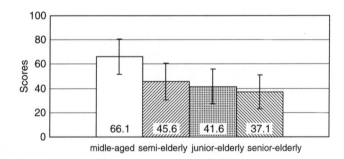

Figure 13. Scores of hazard perception by age groups.

It was concluded that the participants of the present study showed clear effect of aging. Elderly drivers drove with lower level of driving performance such as searching and speeding behavior at intersections than younger ones. They perceived less potential hazards and hazards relating to prediction of other road users' behavior than younger ones, although they evaluated their own driving skills very high (actually higher than younger drivers).

In order to decrease elderly drivers' accidental risk, any kind of driver improvement programs for them and other social supporting system have to be established. First phase of the program was developed and also the first evaluation study of the program had been finished with some positive results.

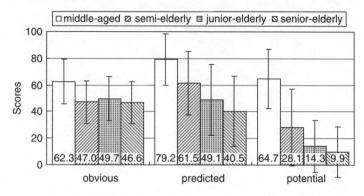

Figure 14. Scores of hazard perception in each category of hazards by age groups.

ACKNOWLEDGEMENTS

This research was executed in H381 Research Project of IATSS and also supported by a scientific research grant for the Japanese Ministry of Education in 2002–2004. We also obtained the Special Research Fund of Tezukayama University in 2002.

REFERENCES

IATSS (International Association of Traffic and Safety Sciences) (2001). Risk-taking behavior of elderly drivers. H381 Research Report. (in Japanese).

ITARDA (Institute for Traffic Accident Research and Data Analysis) (2004). Traffic Statistics 2003. ITARDA, Tokyo, Japan (in Japanese).

Ogawa, K., Renge, K., & Nagayama, Y. (1993). A positive study on the structure and the function of hazard perception. *Japanese Journal of Applied Psychology*, *18*, 37–54 (in Japanese).

Ota, H. (1997). CAI-system utilization in the re-education of older drivers' hazard perception. *Interdisciplinary Information Sciences*, *3*, 111–116.

Renge, K. (1998). Drivers' hazard and risk perception, confidence in safe driving, and choice of speed. *IATSS Research*, *22* (2), 103–110.

Traffic and Transport Psychology
G. Underwood (Editor)
© 2005 Elsevier Ltd. All rights reserved.

9

ASSESSMENT AND DECISION CRITERIA FOR DRIVING COMPETENCE IN THE ELDERLY

Helen Middleton[1], Diane Westwood[1], Jeremy Robson[2] and Dirk Kok[1]

INTRODUCTION

The opportunity to continue driving in later life provides a means to maintain mobility, independence, and quality of life, and the loss of mobility and independence in the elderly has been associated with depression (Marottoli et al., 1998). Given the importance of driving for the well being of older drivers it is not surprising that the issue of assessing fitness to drive in the elderly is both controversial and emotive. In Western society, the number of older drivers is increasing (OECD, 1985; TRBNRC, 1988). It is estimated that approximately 12% of current European drivers are elderly, and this figure is expected to increase to 20% by 2010 (EDDIT V2031). The development of a reliable and fair assessment, therefore, is becoming increasingly important.

A review of the relevant literature (Breker et al., 2003) identified age-related changes in sensory, perceptual, cognitive, and psychomotor functioning, relevant to safe driving. However, research suggests that the majority of older drivers compensate for such age-related decline in functional ability in a variety of ways, and only a minority of older drivers are involved in accidents (Hakamies-Blomqvist, Siren & Davidse, 2004; Maycock, 1997). Assessment of older drivers' fitness to drive should, therefore, aim for an appropriate balance between the opposing forces of specificity and sensitivity if assessment is to access problematic cases without inconveniencing the vast majority of older people who remain safe drivers. Developing a reliable assessment system directly tailored to cognitively impaired, at-risk older drivers would also represent a significant contribution to road safety.

---

[1] University of Sunderland, The Institute for Automotive and Manufacturing Advanced Practice, UK.
E-mail: helen.middleton@sunderland.ac.uk (H. Middleton).
[2] Northumbria University, School of Design, UK.

There is, currently, considerable variation across Europe with respect to how assessments of fitness to drive are invoked, the methodologies and tools used, and the existing criteria and thresholds applied (Middleton et al., 2003). The AGILE project is developing a pan-European assessment of functional ability in elderly drivers. AGILE proposes a multi-tiered assessment process including a standardized set of tests for assessing fitness to drive, in which the same problems and functional criteria are measured at different levels of the assessment process. The aim is to specify an assessment of functional ability most relevant to age-related problems in driving, using a selection of tests that are quick and convenient to administer and analyse, and which include indicative threshold values defining margins of unacceptable driving performance.

Pilot tests were conducted at six different sites across Europe to verify the integrated methodology, tools, criteria, and performance thresholds proposed for the AGILE assessment system. This chapter reports the outcome of tests conducted at the UK test site.

This study used specific critical road traffic scenarios identified within the project as being most appropriate for highlighting age-related problems in driving (Breker et al., 2003). The aim was to establish whether there are relative differences in the performance of younger and older drivers against scenario specific assessment criteria and thresholds (Middleton et al., 2003), and to consider aberrant driver behaviours reported by older drivers (Parker, McDonald, Rabbitt & Sutcliffe, 1999), and age differences in glance behaviour as a potential compensatory mechanism. The results of the study will be combined with results from the other AGILE test sites, and used to form the basis of further specifications in areas such as the design of in-vehicle assistive technologies, and an elderly driver re-training course (Arno, Eeckhout, Middleton, Fimm & Panou, 2003).

ELDERLY DRIVER PROBLEMS

Breker, et al. (2003) found that the age-related functional deficits with the greatest implications for safe driving in the elderly are associated with visual attention, dual task performance, selective attention, reaction time, and motor performance or sequencing. As the number of information sources and complexity of information increase; reaction time and movement time decrease (Rabbitt, 1985). In addition, younger experienced drivers are able to process multiple channels of information in parallel, whereas older drivers' processing and responses tend to be more serial in nature (Hakamies-Blomqvist, Mynttinen, Backman & Mikkonen, 1999). Parker et al. (1999) found that older drivers report more lapses than any other kind of bad driving and that this is consistent with what is known about age-related decline in cognitive capacities of older people. Cognitive changes in the efficiency of working memory, the retrieval of episodic memories, and the ability to sustain and switch attention are also highlighted by Groeger (2000); however, deterioration in cognitive functions such as semantic memory and procedural memory are less obvious.

There are a number of age-related medical conditions such as arthritis, heart diseases, arterial hypertension, diabetes, and dementia, which impact upon functional ability. The effects of functional problems upon driving may be compounded by the use of individual and multiple medications in the treatment of age-related disease (Middleton et al., 2003). Dementia is of particular relevance to driving because it is typically associated with cognitive deficits, impaired judgement, and anosagnosia (lack of insight into impairments) (Lloyd et al., 2001). The most problematic of these symptoms for driving is anosagnosia which is typically manifested in a failure to deploy ageing typical compensatory driving behaviours associated with reduced accident risk (Brouwer, Rothengatter & Wolffelaar, 1988).

COMPENSATION

Age-related deficits such as those described above impact most in complex road traffic situations. Elderly individuals drive more slowly and more cautiously than younger drivers (Alexander, Barham & Black, 2002). They also drive fewer miles (Rosenbloom, 1995), and avoid road and traffic situations with high workload, such as driving in bad weather conditions, in darkness, during rush hours, and at complex junctions (Chipman, MacGregor, Smiley & Lee-Gosselin, 1993; Hakamies-Blomqvist, 1994). These driving characteristics are interpreted as compensatory behaviours resulting from age-related functional decline (Brouwer et al., 1988).

ACCIDENTS

Evidence suggests that the vast majority of older people are safe drivers (Hakamies-Blomqvist et al., 2004; Maycock, 1997). They are, however, involved in specific types of accidents. The typical accident involving an older driver occurs at a junction where information must be processed rapidly and in parallel and where quick responses are necessary, i.e. in a forced-paced rather than a self-paced situation. In particular, older drivers experience problems turning right (left in countries where driving is on the right), at junctions and these age-related accident characteristics are more marked in drivers over the age of 65 (Hakamies-Blomqvist, 1993).

AIM

The aim of the present study was to quantify and verify elderly driver performance in simulated critical road traffic scenarios, according to specific criteria and thresholds identified as being most relevant for the AGILE assessment system (Middleton et al., 2003). An additional aim of the study was to gather preliminary data towards an investigation of aberrant driving behaviours reported by older drivers and age differences in glance behaviour as a compensatory mechanism.

In this study, healthy young and elderly participants were required to turn right through the traffic flow at an urban T-junction during simulated driving using traffic scenarios of varying complexity. Many studies have investigated drivers' choice of gap in the traffic flow when turning right at a junction using a variety of research techniques. For example, observation of traffic behaviour (Blunden, Clissold & Fisher, 1962), gap choice estimation using video footage (Lerner, Huey, McGee & Sullivan, 1995), and experimental on-road studies (Ashworth & Bottom, 1977; Darzentas, McDowell & Cooper, 1980). Studies investigating age-related differences in gap choice during simulated driving are less common, however, Alexander et al. (2002) and Skaar, Rizzo & Steirman (2003) found that older participants required a larger gap than their younger counterparts. There are no existing norms or quantitative standards for safe/unsafe performance during right turn manoeuvres in simulated driving for older drivers. The EU-funded project TRAINER was concerned with producing an educational curriculum for simulator-based driver training, proposing the following thresholds for unsatisfactory performance during turning at a junction; time-to-contact (TTC) <4 s, continuous acceleration >0.1 gravitational constant (G), collisions with street furniture or other vehicles. These thresholds were included in the present study to establish their suitability for the assessment of elderly drivers.

METHOD

Participants

There were 20 participants in two age groups: 10 in the age range 20–30 years (mean age 26.13, std. = 2.86) and 10 in the age range over 65 years (mean age 69.43, std. = 3.10). There were five male and five female participants in both groups. All had held a full UK driving licence for at least 3 years and none had taken part in advanced driver training. All were free from any medical condition or prescribed medication that might impair driving performance.

Procedure

Participants were first required to provide details about their age, licence category and status, training, health, vision, and medication. All participants were tested individually. A standardized simulated practice drive (duration 5 min) was followed immediately by the experimental trials which involved turning right during simulated driving in seven urban T-junction scenarios; once in the baseline condition (no other vehicles in simulation), and twice in each gap acceptance condition. Participants were recorded on video by a camera placed approximately 2 m behind the rig. When all seven scenarios had been completed, the participant was given a 5-min break then asked to complete two questionnaires. The first was a questionnaire about general driving habits, exposure, and experience, and the second was The Driver Behaviour Questionnaire (Parker, Manstead, Stradling & Reason, 1992). The entire procedure lasted approximately 1 hour.

Equipment

Driving simulator.   The driving simulator comprises a fixed-base driver assessment rig linked to a simulated road environment and data acquisition system.

Driver assessment rig.   The driver assessment rig consists of a car seat, steering wheel, dashboard, and pedals. It has no surrounding body shell.

Simulation system.   The simulation system is based on three Evans and Sutherlands® simFUSION image generators (Model: simFUSION PC-IG 3000Q^{TM}). Display—Three LCD projectors (model PLC-SU20E^{TM}, SANYO) are used to display the driving simulation onto three 2.29 m $\times$ 2.50 m screens creating a total viewing angle of 120°. The manipulation of eye-point offset within the software enables simulation of the drivers viewing angle of 180° without distortion.

Software. The simulated road environment was developed using CREATOR™ (real-time 3D modelling tool) and VEGA™ (advanced software environment for 3D applications) by Multigen-Paradigm®.

Data acquisition. The Master simFUSION collects signals from the primary controls on the rig via a data acquisition card (DAC) and an interface card. The DAC is the PCI 1710 from Advantech (the rig is connected to this card via a terminal wire board, PCLD-8710 also from Advantech).

Video recorder. A Sony Mini DV Cam was used to record participants' behaviour during simulated driving.

MATERIALS

- Participant details sheet
- Driving habits questionnaire
- Driver Behaviour Questionnaire (Parker et al., 1992)
- Experimental stimuli—four simulated road traffic scenarios were used in the study. One scenario was a baseline measure (Ba) requiring a right turn manoeuvre with no other traffic present. The other three scenarios required the driver to turn right at a junction through the traffic flow (traffic approaching from the right (R) (cross manoeuvre), left (L) (merge manoeuvre), or both directions (B) (cross/merge manoeuvre)). In all the cases, approaching cars passed straight through the junction (i.e. none turned into the side road).

DESIGN

The experiment employed a $2 \times 2 \times 3$ mixed design for the three gap acceptance scenarios. The between subjects variables were "age" and "sex". Each had two levels, young and old, male and female, respectively. The within subjects variable was "level of scenario" with three levels; traffic approaching from the left, traffic approaching from the right, and traffic approaching from both directions. The dependent variables were decision time in seconds (s) (measured as interval between the beginning of the scenario to first indication of gap acceptance), gap size (s), TTC (s), constant acceleration, Gravitational constant (G), and collisions with cars or road furniture (driving errors).

RESULTS

Decision time (seconds)

Results were analysed using a $2 \times 2 \times 3$ mixed ANOVA and are represented in Figure 1.

There were significant main effects of "age" ($F(1, 16) = 11.16$, $p = 0.004$) with the older group producing significantly longer decision times overall than the younger group, and "scenario" ($F(1.2, 19.4) = 24.29$, $p < 0.0005$) with decision times decreasing overall in the order Right > Left > Both. Pairwise comparisons show significant differences between all

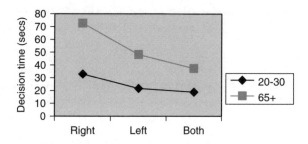

Figure 1. Decision times (seconds).

combinations for level of scenario: R > L ($p = 0.005$), Left > Both ($p = 0.007$), and R > B ($p < 0.0005$). The effect of "sex" was not significant. There was a significant age ∗ scenario interaction ($F(1.2, 19.4) = 4.23$, $p = 0.047$) with the effect of scenario being greater in the 65+ group compared to the 20–30 age group and where the difference between age groups reduces gradually across scenarios in the order Right > Left > Both. There were no other significant interaction effects.

Gap size (seconds)

Results were analysed using a $2 \times 2 \times 3$ mixed ANOVA and are represented in Figure 2.

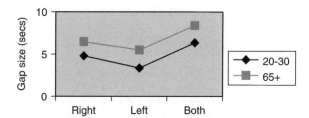

Figure 2. Gap size (seconds).

There was a significant main effect of "age" ($F(1, 16) = 12.06$, $p = 0.003$) with the younger group accepting significantly smaller gaps than the older group. There was also a significant main effect of "scenario" ($F(2, 32) = 72.89$, $p < 0.0005$) and pairwise comparison showed that R > L < B (in all cases $p < 0.0005$). There was no significant effect of "sex" and no significant interaction effects.

Time-to-contact (seconds)

It should be noted that TTC data could not be calculated in the scenario when traffic was oncoming from both directions. Results were analysed using a $2 \times 2 \times 2$ mixed ANOVA and are summarized in Figure 3.

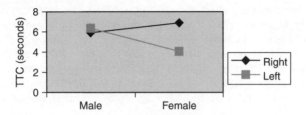

Figure 3. Time-to-contact (seconds).

There were no significant main effects. The only significant interaction effect was sex $*$ scenario ($F(1, 16) = 6.13, p = 0.025$). The interaction effect is illustrated in Figure 3 which shows that there is little effect of scenario for the male participants, whilst for females there is a significant effect of scenario with particularly low TTC values in the "left" scenario. There were no other significant interaction effects, although it should be noted that the interaction between age $*$ scenario approached significance at $p = 0.064$. This has been illustrated in Figure 4, which shows that there was no effect of scenario in the 20–30 group but the 65 + group show relatively short TTC in the "left" scenario and relatively long TTC in the "right" scenario.

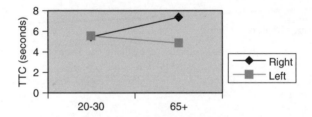

Figure 4. TTC (seconds): age $\times$ scenario.

Continuous acceleration (gravitational constant)

In this case, it was possible to use the baseline scenario (Ba) to calculate continuous acceleration around the curve when no traffic is present and to compare this with continuous acceleration in scenarios where traffic is present. The results were analysed using a $2 \times 2 \times 4$ mixed ANOVA and summarized in Figure 5.

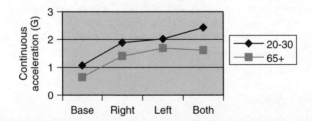

Figure 5. Continuous acceleration.

There was a significant main effect of "age" ($F(1, 16) = 5.73$, $p = 0.029$) with the 20–30 group producing higher G values overall than the over 65 age group. There was also a significant main effect of "scenario" ($F(3, 48) = 46.05$, $p < 0.0005$) with G values roughly increasing on average in the order Baseline < Right < Left < Both. Pairwise comparisons reveal that Baseline < Right ($p < 0.0005$); Baseline < Left ($p < 0.0005$) Baseline < Both ($p < 0.0005$), and Right < Both ($p = 0.047$). Baseline was significantly lower than all other conditions ($p < 0.0005$). There were no other significant differences among scenarios and no significant interaction effects.

Assessment criteria and thresholds

The performance threshold to be applied in the context of the TTC assessment criterion was <4 s The threshold for continuous acceleration was >0.1G, and collisions were also considered. Of those participants who collided with another car or infrastructure within the simulation, 80% failed on the TTC criterion and, of those who did not collide, 60% failed on the TTC criterion. There was no relationship between crashes during simulated driving and the pass/fail threshold for TTC (Fisher's exact test, $p = 0.628$, *two-tailed*). All participants failed according to the threshold for continuous acceleration.

Collisions during simulated driving

A multiple regression analysis was conducted to evaluate the extent to which AGILE criteria (TTC and continuous acceleration), decision time, and gap size, could predict number of collisions during simulated driving. A non-significant model emerged ($F(4, 15) = 1.159$, $p = 0.368$) Adjusted $R^2 = 0.236$.

Multiple regression analysis was also used to investigate whether age in years, annual mileage, and driving experience (years) might predict number of collisions during simulated driving. A non-significant model emerged ($F(3, 16) = 0.348$, $p = 0.791$) Adjusted $R^2 = 0.061$.

Collisions during on-road driving

Further, multiple regression analyses were conducted to investigate the extent to which AGILE criteria (TTC and continuous acceleration variance), decision time and gap size, could predict collisions or scrapes during on-road driving, and also whether age in years, annual mileage, and driving experience (years) predicted number of collisions or scrapes during on-road driving. Non-significant models emerged for both TTC, continuous acceleration variance, decision time and gap size ($F(4, 15) = 0.316$, $p = 0.863$) Adjusted $R^2 = 0.078$, and for age in years, annual mileage and driving experience (years) ($F(3, 16) = 0.104$, $p = 0.957$) Adjusted $R^2 = 0.019$.

Aberrant driver behaviour

A preliminary investigation to establish whether mistakes, lapse, and violations could predict drivers' age found a significant result for reported violations ($F(3, 16) = 8.834$, $p = 0.001$)

Adjusted $R^2 = 0.624$. Younger drivers average 18.56 for violations compared to 8.33 for the older group.

Glance behaviour

The video files were used to score drivers' glance behaviour, as measured by frequency of head turns to the left and right, from the start of each gap acceptance scenario until response initiation. The results show that there was no significant main effect of age for participants matched on gap size and TTC.

DISCUSSION AND CONCLUSION

In the present study, young (20–30 years) and older (over 65 years) drivers with no known pathology were required to turn right in simulated urban T-junction scenarios. The results of the study show that older drivers waited longer than younger drivers before initiating the manoeuvre. They also waited for larger gaps in the traffic. Such differences may be characteristic of ageing typical compensation. Longer decision times and choice of larger gaps may represent a compensatory mechanism for deficits in judging speed and distance, making quick decisions, and processing multiple sources of information under time constraint by increasing the time available to complete the necessary manoeuvre.

Decision times were longest for drivers in both age groups when traffic approached from the right, they were shorter for traffic approaching from the left, and even shorter still for traffic coming from both directions, and this effect was greatest for those in the over 65 age group. This finding is consistent with the relevant literature.

When selecting a safe gap in the traffic flow, both age groups selected the largest gaps when traffic approached from both directions. The smallest gaps were associated with traffic approaching from the left. This finding may be due to the fact that it is possible to build up speed whilst crossing the intersection in this scenario, making it easier to match the speed of on-coming cars before joining the traffic flow. In simulated studies where participants are required to cross the traffic flow through pre-determined gaps in the traffic, TTC is an extremely useful measure for differentiating between participants on the basis of the safety margins in their crossing behaviour. TTC can be understood as the time before two vehicles collide. In this study, there was no significant main effect of age for TTC. There was however a significant effect of sex. Females showed significantly lower TTC for the scenario where traffic approached from the left (merging manoeuvre). Gap acceptance studies show that females are more careful than males but have poorer judgement of speed (Cooper, 1976). Sex differences in spatial awareness and in judgement of speed and distance are also reported in the psychological literature (for example, Maccoby & Jacklin, 1975), suggesting that sex differences in TTC, regardless of age, may be an area worthy of further research.

Continuous acceleration was monitored to measure the gravitational constant (G) resulting from combined acceleration and steering during all scenarios (including the baseline scenario with no traffic). The results show that the older participants had a lower constant acceleration than the younger group, through all manoeuvres. Continuous acceleration was lowest in both groups for the low traffic density scenario (when no traffic was present), and increased according to the level of task difficulty (traffic approaching from the right, then the left, and then both directions).

The driving scenarios selected for the study were identified as being those scenarios most appropriate for highlighting ageing-related compensatory driving behaviours and driving-related problems. The results show that older drivers waited significantly longer than younger drivers before pulling out to turn right at the junction; waited for bigger gaps in the traffic and accelerated through the chosen gap more slowly. Such differences are widely considered to be characteristic of ageing-typical compensation and it can be concluded, therefore, that the scenarios selected are indeed useful in highlighting ageing-related compensatory driving behaviours and driving-related problems. The participants in this study had no known pathology, and none displayed driving behaviour of an erratic, dangerous or pathological nature. The results support the view that healthy older drivers are safe because they successfully compensate for normal ageing-related functional decline. It should be noted, however, that whilst this may represent an acceptable strategy for the older driver it nevertheless may create difficulties in the wider traffic context, for example, in terms of the behavioural responses of other drivers, and with respect to traffic flow, and this requires further research.

Criteria and thresholds for safe performance in simulated driving were highlighted in the AGILE project for further investigation within this study. No relationship was found between crashes during simulated driving and the proposed pass/fail thresholds for TTC or for continuous acceleration. Multiple regression analyses were also conducted to investigate the usefulness of proposed objective measures in predicting propensity to crashes in the simulator, or on-the road. In all cases, a non-significant model emerged. This raises the question of the appropriateness of the objective measures and their associated thresholds; an issue that warrants further investigation.

Although the number of participants was small, a preliminary analysis of aberrant driver behaviours was conducted and found that only reported violations predicted age, with the younger participants reporting more driving violation than the older drivers. This is consistent with the relevant literature on younger drivers (Underwood, Chapman, Wright & Crundall, 1997).

Groeger (2000) reports age-related cognitive changes in the efficiency of working memory, the retrieval of episodic memories, and in ability to sustain and switch attention. If such deficits are present in older drivers then it is possible that they are compensated for, by more frequent sampling of information from the environment. An analysis of glance behaviour, as measured by head movements to the left and right during gap acceptance scenarios, was conducted to investigate the possibility of glance behaviour as an age-related compensatory strategy. The results show that there were no significant main effects of age with regard to glances by participants matched on gap size and TTC. There are two possible explanations for this finding. The sample in this study had no known pathology and therefore may not be subject to significant levels of age-related cognitive change in the efficiency of working memory, retrieval of episodic memories, or in ability to sustain and switch attention. Alternatively, head movements are a gross measure of glance behaviour and this measure may not be sufficiently sensitive to identify subtle compensatory changes in visual sampling. It is suggested that further studies should be conducted to investigate this research question, and that eye tracking equipment be used to investigate fixations and visual scanning behaviour as a more sensitive measure of glance behaviour.

The increasing number of elderly drivers presents a new and substantial challenge to the area of driving assessment, and in automotive design. This study provides an insight into both behavioural difficulties and strengths associated with natural ageing, with implications in a wider traffic context. It compared younger and older healthy participants' performance on right turn junction manoeuvres during simulated driving, evaluated specific thresholds for safe driving performance, and gathered preliminary data towards an investigation of aberrant driving behaviours reported by older drivers, and age differences in glance behaviour as a compensatory mechanism. The results of this study will optimize preliminary AGILE results with the aim of developing a fair and reliable assessment system to meet the requirements of an increasing older driver population. This in turn should improve road safety and ensure sustained mobility for the majority of older drivers.

ACKNOWLEDGEMENTS

The AGILE project was funded by EU (number QLRT-2001-00118). We would like to thank James Middleton for transferring the video footage to hard disk and editing the trials. We would also like to thank Avanti Chandrasekera and Sevanthi Chandrasekera for their role in the analysis of the video files and Driver Behaviour Questionnaire data.

REFERENCES

Alexander, J., Barham, P., & Black, I. (2002). Factors influencing the probability of an incident at a junction: results from an interactive driving simulator. *Accident Analysis and Prevention, 34* (6), 779–792.

Arno, P., Eeckhout, G., Middleton, H., Fimm, B., & Panou, M. (2003). *Pilot Plans.* (Deliverable report D6.1), AGILE—Aged people integration, mobility, safety and quality of life enhancement through driving. EU project-part of the quality of life and management of living resources, Contract N. QLRT-2001-00118.

Ashworth, R., & Bottom, C.G. (1977). Some observations of driver gap acceptance at a priority intersection. *Traffic Engineering and Control, 18* (12), 569–571.

Blunden, W.R., Clissold, C.M., & Fisher, R.B. (1962). *Distribution of Acceptance Gaps for Crossing and Turning Manoeuvres, Australia Road Research Proceedings.*

Breker, S., Henriksson, P., Falkmer, T., Bekiaris, E., Panou, M., Eeckhout, G., Siren, A., Hakamies-Blomqvist, L., Middleton, H., & Leue, E. (2003). *Problems of the Elderly in Relation to the Driving Task and Relevant Critical Scenarios.* (Deliverable report D1.1), AGILE—Aged people integration, mobility, safety and quality of life enhancement through driving. EU project-part of the quality of life and management of living resources, Contract N. QLRT-2001-00118.

Brouwer, W., Rothengatter, T., & Wolffelaar, P.V. (1988). Compensatory potential in elderly drivers. In Rothengatter, T., & Bruin, R.D. (Eds.), *Road User Behaviour: Theory and Research.* Maastricht: van Gorcum.

Chipman, M., MacGregor, C., Smiley, A., & Lee-Gosselin, M. (1993). The role of exposure in comparisons of crash risk among different drivers and driving environments. *Accident Analysis and Prevention, 25*, 207–211.

Cooper, D.F. (1976). Traffic studies at T-junctions: three observations on gap acceptance using television. Paper presented at the Euro II Conference, Stockholm, 1976.

Darzentas, J., McDowell, M.R.C., & Cooper, D. (1980). Minimum acceptable gaps and conflict involvement in a simple crossing manoeuvre. *Traffic Engineering and Control, 21* (2), 58–61.

EDDIT. (V2031). Elderly and Disabled Drivers Information Telematics. Technical Annex.

Groeger, J.A. (2000). *Understand Driving: Applying Cognitive Psychology to a Complex Everyday Task*. London: Psychology Press.

Hakamies-Blomqvist, L. (1993). Fatal accident of older drivers. *Accident Analysis and Prevention, 25*, 19–27.

Hakamies-Blomqvist, L. (1994). Aging and fatal accidents in male and female drivers. *Journal of Gerontology, 49*, S286–S290, Social Sciences.

Hakamies-Blomqvist, L., Mynttinen, S., Backman, M., & Mikkonen, V. (1999). Age-related differences in driving: are older drivers more serial? *International Journal of Behavioral Development, 23*, 575–589.

Hakamies-Blomqvist, L., Siren, A., & Davidse, R. (2004). Older drivers: A review, VTI rapport. 497A.

Lerner, N.D., Huey, R.W., McGee, H.W., & Sullivan, A. (1995). *Older driver perception-reaction time for intersection sight distance and object detection, Report No. FHWA-RD-93-168*. Washington, DC: Federal Highway Administration.

Lloyd, S., Cormack, C.N., Blais, K., Messeri, G., McCallum, M.A., Spicer, K., & Morgan, S. (2001). Driving and dementia: a review of the literature. *Canadian Journal of Occupational Therapy, 68* (3), 149–156.

Maccoby, E.E., & Jacklin, C.N. (1975). *The Psychology of Sex Differences*. London: Oxford University Press.

Marottoli, R.A., Richardson, E.D., Stowe, M.H., Miller, E.G., Brass, L.M., Cooney, L.M., & Tinetti, M.E. (1998). Development of a test battery to identify older drivers at risk of self-reported adverse driving events. *The American Geriatrics Society, 46*, 562–568.

Maycock, G. (1997). *The Safety of Older Car-Drivers in the European Union*. Basingstoke: AA Foundation for Road Safety Research.

Middleton, H., Westwood, D., Robson, J., Henriksson, P., Falkmer, T., Siren, A., Hakamies-Blomqvist, L., Breker, S., Fimm, B., Eeckhout, G., Bekiaris, E., Panou, M., & Martin, B. (2003). *Inventory of assessment and decision criteria for elderly drivers, including particular age-related disabilities*. (Deliverable report D2.1), AGILE—Aged people integration, mobility, safety and quality of life enhancement through driving. EU project-part of the quality of life and management of living resources, Contract N. QLRT-2001-00118.

OECD (1985). *Traffic Safety of Elderly Road Users, Final report*. Paris: OECD.

Parker, D., Manstead, S.R., Stradling, S.G., & Reason, J.T. (1992). Determinants of intention to commit driving violations. *Accident Analysis and Prevention, 24*, 117–131.

Parker, D., McDonald, L., Rabbitt, P., & Sutcliffe, P. (1999). Elderly drivers and their accidents: the aging driver questionnaire. *Accident Analysis and Prevention, 32* (6), 751–759.

Rabbit, P. (1985). Sequential reactions. In Holding, D. (Ed.), *Human Skills*. Chichester: Wiley.

Rosenbloom, S. (1995). *Travel by the Elderly, Demographic Special Reports, 1990 NPTS report series*. Washington, DC: US Department of Transportation.

Skaar, N., Rizzo, M., & Steirman, L. (2003). Traffic entry judgements by ageing drivers, *Proceedings of the Second International Driving Symposium on Human Factors in Driver Assessment, Training and Vehicle Design*.

TRAINER *Development of training and assessment criteria*, Internal report T5.2, TRAINER System for Driver Training and Assessment using Interactive Evaluation Tools and Reliable Methodologies, Growth project No: GRD 1 1999 10024.

Transportation Research Board of the National Research Council (TRBNRC,1988). *Transportation in an ageing society* (Vol. 1 and 2). Washington, DC.

Underwood, G., Chapman, P., Wright, S., & Crundall, D. (1997). Estimating accident liability. In Rothengatter, J.A., & Carbonell, E. (Eds.), *Traffic and Transportation Psychology*. Oxford: Elsevier.

Traffic and Transport Psychology
G. Underwood (Editor)

10

THE ROOKWOOD DRIVING BATTERY AND THE OLDER ADULT

Pat McKenna[1], Janice Rees[2], Emily Skucek[1], Elene Nichols[3], Paul Fisher[2], Tony Bayer[3] and Vaughan Bell[4]

INTRODUCTION

It is generally accepted that brain damage, if gross or if specific to cognitive functions critical to driving, will impair driving skill. It is also accepted that some faculties decline with age and inevitably so with dementia. However, finding a simple measure of cognitive function that predicts fitness to drive has proved difficult, largely due to the complexity of pre-morbid strengths and weaknesses, both in cognitive function and in driving history. This has also been unnecessarily confounded because of methodological weakness in previous research (BPS Multi-disciplinary Working Party, 2001; Christie, 1996).

An exception is the Stroke Driver's Screening Assessment (Nouri & Lincoln, 1992, 1993) which has not only been validated but is now being adapted for use in other European countries (Lundberg, Caneman, Samuelsson, Hakamies-Blomqvist & Almkvist, 2003). This test is tailored for stroke sufferers, and its effectiveness does not extend to clients with other cerebral conditions. At the South Wales Driving Assessment Centre at Rookwood Hospital, the neuropsychological battery tests function of direct relevance to driving, i.e. visual perception (including shape, spatial and attentional perception), praxis skills (carrying out a movement on demand) and executive function including divided attention. They are also simple enough for the vast majority of normal adults to pass easily (see McKenna, 1998). The on-road test is conducted by an Advanced Driving Instructor together with a health professional experienced

[1] Rookwood Hospital, Fairwater Road, Llandaff, Cardiff, South Wales CF5 2YN, UK. *E-mail:* McKennaPK@cardiff.ac.uk (P. McKenna).
[2] Ystrad Mynach Hospital, Caerphilly Road, Ystrad Mynach, South Wales CF82 7XU, UK. *E-mail:* janice.rees@gwent.wales.nhs.uk (J. Rees).
[3] Memory Clinic, Llandough Hospital, Llandough, Cardiff, South Wales CF62 2XX, UK.
[4] School of Psychology, Cardiff University, Park Place, Cardiff, South Wales CF10 3YG, UK. *E-mail:* bellv1@cardiff.ac.uk (V. Bell).

in neurorehabilitation so the behavioural sequelae of brain damage, such as visual neglect, are not interpreted on-road as rustiness or an easily correctable habit.

Ensuring a valid on-road test is itself problematic: even when using a quantitative standardised formula, traffic conditions will vary for each client. Furthermore, the jump from observation to interpretation is significant, and varies with the experience of the assessor. At Rookwood, we have found that assessors observing the same drive most often (but not always) achieve similar score totals within 2 or 3 points, but the pattern of subtest marking on the score sheet has great variability. The final score is variable within a small range—with significant consequences for the "grey" area between pass and fail. A pass or fail judgement can be unconsciously biased towards the orientation of the assessor, whether as champion of the individual to maximise a driver's right to drive or as a representative of society to highlight disquiet about a driver's ability.

Thus the on-road test, though considered the gold-standard, is not *cast iron*. Neither has it been validated. Akinwuntan et al. (2004) attempted to examine the reliability of the on-road test using real-life observation and video recordings of the on-road driving test. They found concordance between assessors to be moderately high but with the intra-class correlation coefficient (ICC) of items varying from -0.08 to 1.0. The ICC of the overall performance was 0.62 when real-life scores were compared with video evaluations and 0.80 when two video scores were compared. Beyond these operational aspects of the on-road test, Hakamies-Blomqvist (2004) highlights the simple fact that there is no absolute threshold for driving safety, only driving risk (e.g. a very unsafe driver may never have or cause an accident). A cognitive battery to predict fitness to drive may be further hampered by the need to rely on the on-road test to establish validity.

In clinical practice at Rookwood, we have learned to be more confident in advising cessation of driving when in the "grey" area. Often Clinical Psychologists have administered the battery locally and referred on to the centre for on-road test when the driver has performed in the "grey" area on the battery. We occasionally receive feedback from such people who pass on-road but are later found to cause accidents.

McKenna, Jeffries, Dobson and Frude (2004) provide details of a validation study based on the first cohort of 142 clients attending Rookwood for assessment within a 2-year period, where the "positive predictive value" (ability to predict failure on-road) was 92% using a cut-off error score above 10 (of a possible error score of 22). However, this cut-off score was 100% accurate for predicting who would fail under age 70 but only 85% accurate for those over 70. Furthermore, 43 people were over 70, 19 of whom failed on-road even though they passed the battery. The "negative predictive value" (the ability to predict who would pass on-road) was only 36.7% for the older adult. Even without significant cognitive impairment, older adults were still failing on-road.

It was difficult for us to know to what extent failure was due to normal ageing, cerebral pathology or an interaction of age and pathology. It is generally accepted that older adults are slower to process information, slower to respond, and often restrict their driving behaviour to compensate for waning abilities in multi-tasking. Older adults coming to our centre avoid complex roads or heavy traffic, restrict their driving to their close locality, and often describe difficulties in adapting to a different car. In Sweden, Lundberg and Hakamies-Blomqvist (2003) have shown that giving older clients the opportunity to take the test in their own car meant that a significant number passed who would otherwise have failed. Following this evidence, the Swedish government now allows older adults to take the test in their own car at the discretion of the instructor when this is deemed sufficiently safe.

We were aware of a further confounding variable for older adults taking the battery. Though many of the tests on the battery were chosen because they were age free, this was only up to age around 70. Longevity is a comparatively recent phenomenon and virtually none of these tests have age norms for people in their late seventies, eighties and nineties.

This study reports on progress to date of an ongoing study to collect norms from a representative sample of healthy older adults on the cognitive battery in order to address lack of age-appropriate norms, and age–pathology interaction issues. The study originates from three clinical psychology departments in Cardiff and Newport, and the psychology department of Cardiff University. The data were collected by three psychology assistants and one senior clinical neuropsychologist. A research associate of the psychology department, Cardiff University, helped with the analysis of the data. The first stage (McKenna et al., 2004) had included normative data on the general adult population ($N = 200$). This current report presents further normative data collected to date on 116 volunteers aged over 70.

METHOD

Samples

The outline of samples from volunteers and clients attending the driving centre collected to date are as follows:

Sample 1: 200 volunteers aged 20–79 (reported in McKenna et al., 2004).

Sample 2: 142 clients (of all ages) attending for full driving assessment at the South Wales Driving Assessment Centre at Rookwood (reported in McKenna et al., 2004). These clients had mixed cerebral pathology.

Sample 3: putative 300 volunteers over 70, ongoing collection but interim report presented in this chapter.

Sample 4: the second cohort of clients attending the centre numbering 200—yet to be analysed.

Sample 5: the third cohort now attending the centre—ongoing collection.

Procedure

All people aged over 70 were eligible. Exclusion criteria were any history of acquired brain injury or brain pathology, or history of significant visual or hearing loss which clearly prevented performance on tests. Most volunteers were attendees of locality social clubs and were recruited according to procedures approved by the local Research Ethics Committees. Some were assessed in the social club centre when a quiet room was available, but most preferred to be seen at home; occasionally some preferred to come to a clinical setting.

Test battery

This comprised all the tests in the Rookwood Driving Battery plus three further tests particularly relevant to the older adult. These were the Mini Mental State Examination (MMSE; Folstein, Folstein & McHugh, 1975) and Clock-drawing (Schulman, Gold, Cohen & Zucchero, 1993) which are used to screen for dementia and general cognitive impairment. The Trail-making test (Lezak, 1983) was included as a possible additional battery test. The Rookwood Driving Battery is described and referenced in full in McKenna et al. (2004) and comprises tests of visual perception from the VOSP to test the ability to interpret shapes (Incomplete Letters) and be spatially aware (Position Discrimination and Cube Analysis) and to continually monitor the visual environment symmetrically in the horizontal plane (a visual attention task based on letter cancellation). In terms of praxis skills, tests include copying hand movements, producing common named gestures and miming the use of objects, as well as rule-dependent movement in the tapping task and learning a short sequence of hand movements (Luria, 1973). Executive function tests include non-verbal and verbal reasoning (Action Programme and Key Search from the BADS), self-monitoring and response switching (Card Rule Shift from the BADS, and the rule-dependent movement tasks described above) and divided attention (a task involving simultaneous letter cancellation while listening to a taped story and noting each time a specific word is uttered).

Participants

The age distribution of the 116 subjects, in 5-year age bands, is given in Table 1. The mean age was 80.7 with roughly half the sample under 80 and half over 80, and there were far more women (86) than men (29) with gender data missing for one person.

Table 1. Age distribution of older adult participants by percentage ($N = 116$).

Age group	71–74	75–80	81–85	86–90	91–94
Percentage	9.2	36.7	35.8	14.6	3.7

Socio-economic status, using the National Statistics Socio-economic Classifications (NS-SEC), and IQ, using the National Adult Reading Test (NART) are given in Table 2. For IQ, the mean of this group falls within the average range but is shifted a little towards the top half of the average range (106) with insufficient numbers within and below the low average range. The socio-economic distribution describes a representative spread across the range.

RESULTS

First, results on the three tests additional to the battery were analysed. Ninety-one participants completed these tests. Table 3 shows results for the MMSE and Trail-making tests.

On the MMSE, scores of 25 and above were taken to reflect intact cognition. Only eight people scored below 25/30 (three scored 22 and five scored 24). Although scores of 22 and 24 may often be accepted as indicative of mild cognitive impairment, they are not clinically diagnostic of dementia in the absence of a fuller clinical history. On the Clock-drawing test, 49 participants' performances were categorised as unimpaired (perfect or near perfect execution),

Table 2. Distribution of IQ scores and socio-economic classification of (NS-SEC) of older adult participants.

Socio-economic status	IQ band					Total N	Percentage
	Borderline/ very low	Low average	Average	High average	Superior		
Higher managerial and professional	–	–	4	9	4	17	16.5
Lower managerial and professional	–	1	4	7	2	14	13.59
Intermediate occupations	–	–	9	10	5	24	23.3
Small employers and own account workers	–	–	6	–	–	6	5.83
Lower supervisory, craft and related occupations	–	1	8	2	–	11	10.68
Semi-routine occupations	1	1	12	3	–	17	16.5
Routine occupations	–	3	5	2	–	10	9.71
Never worked and long term unemployed	–	1	1	2	–	4	3.88
Total N	1	7	49	35	11	103	100
Percentage	0.97	6.8	47.57	33.98	10.68	100	100
Theoretical normal distribution of IQ (%)	8.9	16.1	50	16.1	8.9		

Table 3. Older adult participant times for Trail-making A and B tests and Mini Mental State Examination (MMSE) score.

	Trail-making A time	Trail-making B time	MMSE score
Mean	57.82	165.86	27.53
Median	50.5	150	28
SD	26.37	80.24	2.00
Range	23–180	57–420	22–30

SD, standard deviation.

27 were borderline (errors on setting the hands and/or moderate visuospatial disorganisation), and 15 were impaired (more severe disorganisation). Therefore, up to 15 of the sample may have compromised cognitive skills. At this stage, there was evidence of only a small decline beyond normal ageing in this group.

For the Trail-making test, Table 3 presents the raw scores for times taken. Additionally some participants made numerous errors on Part B which were so gross as to indicate an overall failure on the task—sometimes despite adequate time scores. Thirty people were considered to have failed due to significant errors (26 participants), or failed to complete within a reasonable time (four participants). Eighty people were considered to have passed using this categorical scoring.

Age and demographic effects

A one-way ANOVA was used to examine the effect of group across the five age bands shown in Table 1 on performance on each of the tests. No significant effect was found for age group on performance on any of the tests, except for Trail-making A time ($F(4, 100) = 5.507, p < 0.0005$) and Trail-making B time ($F(4, 95) = 2.631, p < 0.039$).

Tukey-HSD post-hoc tests were used to look for significant difference between the youngest (ages 71–74) and oldest (ages 91–94) age group. No additional significant differences were found on any of the tests, although this is likely to be because of the small number of participants in the older group ($N = 4$).

One-way ANOVAs were used to test for the effect of socio-economic status on test performance. Socio-economic status significantly affected only NART IQ ($F(7, 95) = 7.291, p < 0.0005$), divided attention ($F(7, 95) = 2.474, p < 0.05$), Trail-making A time ($F(7, 99) = 2.733, p < 0.05$) and Trail-making B time ($F(7, 93) = 4.191, p < 0.0005$).

As can be seen from Table 4, results show significant correlations for some tests with age and IQ but these are generally weak, none reaching greater than 0.4 in either a positive or negative direction. However, the overall performance on tests as measured by the total error score correlates more strongly with age and IQ than most individual tests.

Table 4. Correlations of test performance against age and NART IQ in older adult sample.

Test	Age	NART IQ
Weigl	− 0.06	0.22*
Key Search	− 0.25*	0.27*
Action Programme	− 0.12	0.24*
Rule Shift Cards	− 0.26*	0.34*
Tapping and Sequencing	− 0.11	0.25*
Cube Analysis	− 0.14	0.06
Position Discrimination	− 0.07	0.26*
Incomplete Letters	− 0.29*	0.28*
Praxis	− 0.17	0.10*
Comprehension	− 0.32*	0.37*
Trail-making time section A	0.39*	− 0.25*
Trail-making time section B	0.32*	− 0.34*
Visual attention	− 0.21*	0.25*
Divided attention	− 0.29*	0.26*
Total errors	0.42*	− 0.41*

*Significant correlation at $p < 0.05$ or greater.

When correlated with individual test scores, the total error score on the battery showed the strongest relationship with Trail-making B time ($r = 0.66$, $p < 0.0005$) and the weakest relationship with Position Discrimination score ($r = -0.26$, $p < 0.001$). All the other tests also correlated significantly with total error score with five tests showing a relationship with a value of 0.5 or greater in either the positive or negative direction. These were Key Search ($r = -0.55$, $p < 0.0005$); Rule Shift Cards ($r = -0.53$, $p < 0.0005$); Tapping and Sequencing ($r = 0.57$, $p < 0.0005$), Comprehension ($r = -0.54$, $p < 0.0005$) and Trail-making A time ($r = 0.52$, $p < 0.0005$). This suggests that all tests are making a significant contribution to the final error score and are worthy of inclusion into the test battery.

Comparison with younger adults

The older adults were compared to the control group of adults used in the McKenna et al. (2004) study (Sample 1) on those tests common to both. These originally consisted of 200 people with an age range of 20–79 and of whom 6 were over 69. As outlined in Table 5, these six have been incorporated into the older adult group in this study and the younger adult controls now number 194, aged 20–69 inclusive. There were no significant differences in IQ between the younger group and the older group when compared using an independent samples t-test ($t(302) = 0.316$, $p = 0.239$).

The younger controls had not been given the same test of visual attention nor had they done the divided attention task and the results on the 10 tests common to both groups are also shown in Table 5. There were highly significant differences (at the $p < 0.0005$ level) between the two age groups with poorer performance by the older adult group on all tests when compared using an independent samples t-test.

Table 5. Performance on test battery of younger controls, older adult controls and clients with mixed cerebral pathology who attended a driver assessment centre.

Age/test score	Younger controls			Older adult controls			Clients		
	N	Mean	SD	N	Mean	SD	N	Mean	SD
Age	194	42.4	13.8	115	80.69	4.94	109	76.88	4.43
Weigl	194	4.00	0.00	116	3.70	0.74	109	3.39	0.96
Key Search	194	12.43	3.67	116	10.50	4.09	107	10.61	4.34
Action Programme	194	4.70	0.85	116	4.24	0.98	105	4.13	1.10
Rule Shift Cards	194	19.61	1.26	116	17.35	3.32	106	16.47	4.31
Tapping and Sequencing	194	14.48	1.06	116	13.42	2.56	109	12.12	3.27
Cube Analysis	194	9.60	0.83	116	9.12	1.45	109	8.49	2.38
Position Discrimination	194	19.71	0.85	116	19.26	1.24	109	18.77	2.21
Incomplete Letters	194	19.66	0.61	116	19.00	1.47	109	18.08	2.50
Praxis	194	15.92	0.74	116	15.26	0.95	109	15.02	1.54
Comprehension	193	7.72	0.66	116	6.60	1.55	107	5.88	2.21
NART IQ	194	104.2	10.5	112	105.76	11.60	84	106.32	13.49

SD, standard deviation. Differences between younger and older adults were significant on all tests at the $p < 0.0005$ level or greater.

Comparison with older adult clients attending the driving centre for assessment

The scores on the 12 test battery subtests obtained by healthy older adults were compared to those obtained by older adults aged 70 and above attending the driving assessment centre from March 2000 to date (Samples 2, 4 and 5). These older adults had a diagnosis of cerebral pathology, including dementia. Both groups were tested on all subtests of the battery, but clients attending the centre had not been given the MMSE, Trail-making test or Clock-drawing. Mean scores for the two groups are shown in Table 5.

There were significant differences between healthy older adults and our client group on six of the 12 tests, including the Weigl Sorting test ($t(223) = 2.668$, $p < 0.001$); Tapping and Sequencing ($t(223) = 3.342$, $p < 0.001$); Incomplete Letters ($t(223) = 3.385$, $p < 0.001$); Comprehension ($t(221) = 2.848$, $p < 0.005$); Cube Analysis ($t(223) = 2.431$, $p < 0.05$) and Position Discrimination ($t(223) = 2.057$, $p < 0.05$).

Driving status

Data on driving status was available for 88 participants. Of these, 32 people had never driven, only one of whom was a man. Of the 34 women eligible to drive, 17 had voluntarily given up (50%). In contrast, of the 22 men eligible to drive, only five had voluntarily given up (23%).

Of those eligible to drive, a comparison was made between those who had given up driving and those who were continuing to drive. Mean scores are given in Table 6. Using independent samples t-tests, no significant differences emerged between the two groups on any of the tests.

Table 6. Performance of drivers and ex-drivers in older adult sample on test battery.

	Used to drive			Drives		
	N	Mean	SD	N	Mean	SD
Age	22	81.68	4.96	34	80.56	5.12
MMSE	21	27.95	1.63	22	27.09	2.09
Clock-drawing	21	0.24	0.54	22	0.68	0.78
Weigl	22	3.73	0.7	34	3.62	0.89
Key Search	22	10.86	4.5	34	12.09	3.52
Action Programme	22	4.41	0.91	34	4.26	1.02
Rule Shift Cards	22	17.95	3.27	34	17.35	3.06
Tapping and Sequencing	22	13.95	1.73	34	13.35	2.73
Cube Analysis	22	9.32	0.89	34	9.09	1.44
Position Discrimination	22	19.14	1.39	34	19.65	0.69
Incomplete Letters	22	19.0	1.75	34	19.26	1.19
Comprehension	22	7.09	1.27	34	6.56	1.54
NART predicted IQ	20	107.75	10.94	34	109.12	9.23
Trail-making A	22	61.0	26.02	34	58.68	31.89
Trail-making B	19	158.26	66.78	34	172.06	93.12
Trail B errors	19	1.32	1.86	34	1.38	1.72
Visual attention	22	2.832	3.67	34	4.59	10.54
Divided attention	22	7.59	1.44	31	8.32	1.3
Sum of scores	22	5.91	4.6	34	6.5	4.45

SD, standard deviation.

DISCUSSION

This interim study is based on a sample of older adults who are living independently in the community, adequately representative of the normal distribution of intellectual ability and socio-economic status and largely cognitively healthy as measured by the MMSE.

In keeping with the general population in this age group, there were far more women than men. People in the low average range of ability and below were a little under-represented: such individuals might be reluctant to volunteer to undertake tasks, which they perceive to be intellectually demanding. Further group contacts are to be targeted in an attempt to address the balance.

The main aim of this interim study was to examine the effects of older age beyond 70 on performance on the cognitive tests used in the driving battery. Compared to younger adults there were significantly lower scores on every cognitive test on the battery, strongly suggesting a generalised cognitive decline across all three areas of visual perception, praxis and executive functioning. Future analysis will examine the contribution of low MMSE and Clock-drawing scores to performance on the battery.

The final data set can thus be used as more appropriate age-related norms for older adults. In particular, there were no differences across the age group within our sample of older adults, even between the youngest and oldest, which was unexpected. As the study progresses, this can be examined in larger cohorts and there will be a better representation of those adults over 90 for whom only four exist in the sample to date.

At the level of individual subtests of the battery, there were two ways in which the sensitivity of individual tests could be examined to indicate degree of cognitive impairment: correlations with overall error score, and with age. All the tests correlated with overall error score but particularly strongly for Key Search, Rule Shift Cards, Tapping and Sequencing, Comprehension and Trail-making time, and all restrict one of the tests of executive function. In terms of age correlations, these were less strong and again Comprehension and Trail-making Time were the strongest. These results suggest that the ability to process novel information and problem-solve at speed that is difficult for older adults—subjects had no difficulty in hearing and conversing, or following instructions in other tests.

This study has incorporated two tests which are useful in screening older adults in clinical settings: the MMSE and Clock-drawing. The MMSE proved to be a very effective screen to establish the health of our group in terms of cognitive functioning, confirming that our group did not contain any individuals with cognitive difficulties of a severity normally associated with established dementia. Though MMSE scores did not correlate with age, they produced one of the strongest correlations with overall error score on the battery. The MMSE may well have a screening contribution to this battery for older adults.

The Trail-making test is a useful component of a more extensive cognitive assessment with older people presenting clinically with possible dementia, but has often been rejected in research projects because scoring is problematic. The measure used in the present study for pass or fail on the Trail-making test showed that our formula for a crude pass/fail score on Trail-making B did not correlate with age or overall error score. However, time analysis showed that time taken on these tests did correlate with age. A better formula for scoring pass/fail on this test (perhaps utilising time scores) is needed in further work on this project. As with MMSE, performance on Clock-drawing did not correlate with age but did correlate strongly with overall score.

All three additional tests appear to measure general cognitive impairment but, unlike the other tests on the battery, do not target specific cognitive skills or functions. Nor is it clear how they translate to the driving situation. These aspects will need to be weighed against their statistical contribution for predicting driving safety in competing for a role in time-limited assessment.

In terms of the present battery in use at the Rookwood Driving Centre and by psychologists in South Wales, results of this study suggest that pass/fail threshold for total error score should be stricter and not more lenient for older adults. Older adult clients attending the centre often fail the on-road after having passed the cognitive battery. The results of the present study show that people over 70 do significantly worse on all tests compared to younger people even though they may not actually fail the tests. For those older adults attending for assessment, the imposition of cerebral pathology on already compromised cognitive resources appears to reduce the threshold for them to drive safely. Reducing the error score threshold may be a necessary step to obtain a better formula for predicting on-road performance. However, performance on each individual test will need to be examined in the context of the norms being collected in this study.

As well as completing the collection of normative data on healthy older adults, further work would ideally include on-road assessments for driving. Using informal methods to pilot such a venture in the course of clinical work, it has been possible to recruit older adult relatives of in-patients to do the cognitive tests, but only on-road if it were in the volunteer's own car and on their usual route. To maximise the number of recruits for an on-road test would require a multi-centre approach with plentiful resource in terms of finance and time to build up the confidence of volunteers.

Work completed on this project to date confirms that cognitive decline is real, measurable and may well have implications for driving ability in the healthy older adult population, many of whom voluntarily stop driving. Most of the people who gave up were women whose driving faded because their husbands drove, but quite a few voluntarily gave up, sometimes encouraged by family—especially when public transport was convenient. Only five men had voluntarily stopped and the remaining 17 still drove. There was no difference in cognitive ability in terms of any of the tests between those who gave up and those who continue to drive.

At present, the law in Britain makes no differentiation in the standard of driving permitted on the basis of age. Given the emerging evidence of reduction of cognitive resource, reduction of driving skill and the often compensatory driving style in the older adult, testing safety to drive is hampered without a clear political and legal appraisal of the complexities of this issue. In particular, the older adult driver who attends the driving assessment centre is disadvantaged by needing to conform to the same conditions and standards of younger adults. There is strong evidence that older people voluntarily restrict their driving, confirmed in this current study. It may be that within the self-imposed driving limitations, further restrictions may be imposed following an assessment which limits the *driving risk* for that individual (Hakamies-Blomqvist, 2004). Belgium has in some rural areas introduced "limited licences" to accommodate the mobility needs of elderly drivers in declining health, with a special identification disc so that the restrictions are publicly evident to other road users (Atkinwuntan, Leuven University Belgium, personal communication). Such a system invites exploration.

REFERENCES

Akinwuntan, A.E., De Weerdt, W., Feys, H., Arno, P., Baten, G., & Kiekens, C. (2004). Reliability of a road test after stroke. Presentation at the *International Conference of Traffic and Transport Psychology*, Nottingham, UK.

British Psychological Society (2001). Fitness to drive and cognition. *A Document of the Multi-disciplinary Working Party on Acquired Neuropsychological Deficits and Fitness to Drive*.

Christie, N. (1996). Assessing driving fitness following brain injury or illness: a research review. *Transport Research Laboratory Report 208*, obtainable from TRL, Old Wokingham.

Folstein, M.F., Folstein, S.E., & McHugh, P.R. (1975). "Mini-mental state": a practical method for grading the cognitive state of patients for the clinician. *Journal of Psychiatric Research, 12*, 189–198.

Hakamies-Blomqvist, L. (2004). Are there safe and unsafe drivers? *Third International Conference on Traffic and Transport Psychology*, Nottingham, UK.

Lezak, M.D. (1983). *Neuropsychological Assessment* (2nd ed.). Oxford: Oxford University Press.

Lundberg, C., & Hakamies-Blomqvist, L. (2003). Driving tests with older patients: effects of unfamiliar versus familiar vehicle. *Transportation Research*, Part F, Stockholm.

Lundberg, C., Caneman, G., Samuelsson, S.M., Hakamies-Blomqvist, L., & Almkvist, O. (2003). The assessment of fitness to drive after a stroke: The Nordic Stroke Driver Screening Assessment. *Scandanavian Journal of Psychology*, *44*, 23–30.

Luria, A.R. (1973). *The Working Brain*. London: Penguin.

McKenna, P. (1998). Fitness to drive: a neuropsychological perspective. *Journal of Mental Health*, *7*, 9–11.

McKenna, P., Jeffries, L., Dobson, A., & Frude, N. (2004). The use of a cognitive battery to predict who will fail an on-road driving test. *British Journal of Clinical Psychology*, *43*, 325–336.

Nouri, F.M., & Lincoln, N.B. (1992). Validation of a cognitive assessment: predicting driving performance after stroke. *Clinical Rehabilitation*, *6*, 275–281.

Nouri, F.M., & Lincoln, N.B. (1993). Predicting driving performance after stroke. *British Medical Journal*, *307*, 482–483.

Schulman, K.I., Gold, D.P., Cohen, C.A., & Zucchero, C.A. (1993). Clock-drawing and dementia in the community: a longitudinal study. *International Journal of Geriatric Psychiatry*, *8*, 487–496.

VULNERABLE ROAD USERS III:

NOVICE DRIVERS

Traffic and Transport Psychology
G. Underwood (Editor)

11

WHAT DO NOVICE DRIVERS LEARN DURING THE FIRST MONTHS OF DRIVING? IMPROVED HANDLING SKILLS OR IMPROVED ROAD USER INTERACTION?

Torkel Bjørnskau[1] and Fridulv Sagberg[1]

INTRODUCTION

One of the best documented facts in road safety research is that novice drivers are at particular high risk, and that the risk is substantially reduced with increased experience. Less known is the fact that the risk reduction of novice drivers takes place very fast. A recent report by Mayhew, Simpson and Pak (2003) shows that novice drivers' accident risk is drastically reduced during the first months of driving. Similar results are found for novice drivers in Norway. Sagberg (2000) found that the risk of an accident is reduced by 50% during the first 9 months of driving, which is in the same magnitude as the risk reduction reported by Mayhew et al. (2003).

The high risk of young drivers is often attributed to two main factors: (i) lack of driving skills and (ii) lack of safety motives (sensation seeking, speeding etc.). Given the substantial risk reduction over just a few months, it is unlikely that it can solely be ascribed to motivational factors. Hence, novice drivers must gain some specific skills enabling them to avoid accidents during the first months of driving. What exactly they learn is, however, not sufficiently known. Three hypotheses about what novice drivers learn during the first months of driving were formulated (Sagberg & Bjørnskau, 2003):

Hypothesis A: Hazard perception. Driving experience increases the ability to identify early warnings of possible dangers in traffic, making drivers able to take precautionary actions sooner.

---

[1] Institute of Transport Economics, Oslo, Norway. *E-mail:* tbj@toi.no (T. Bjørnskau).

Hypothesis B: Better car-handling skills. Driving experience increases gradual automation of handling skills in operating the car, and thus reduces the risk of potentially dangerous errors.

Hypothesis C: Improved interaction with other road users. Better understanding of the social interaction among road users and the informal rules of this interaction, results in better adjustments to other road users' behaviour, and makes one's own behaviour more predictable to others.

The present paper is limited to reporting the results concerning hypotheses B and C. The results of the hazard perception tests will be published elsewhere.

THEORETICAL BACKGROUND

There is a long tradition in safety research related to hypothesis B with focus on driver errors (Åberg & Rimmö, 1998; Karttunen & Häkkinen, 1986; Lajunen & Summala, 1995; Parker, Reason, Manstead & Stradling, 1995; Reason, Manstead, Stradling, Baxter & Campbell, 1990). Reason et al. (1990) classify errors as "mistakes" and "slips/lapses", and our hypothesis B, which focuses on the technical handling of the car, will be typically be concerned with the latter ones. Åberg and Rimmö (1998) identify some of these errors as especially typical for inexperienced drivers, and these errors will be particularly focused in our investigation of hypothesis B.

The concept of "error" has often been contrasted with "violations", which are intended actions deviating from the formal rules (Reason et al., 1990; Parker et al., 1995). Based on a survey by use of a driver behaviour questionnaire (DBQ), Parker et al. (1995) conclude that "violations", but not "errors", contribute significantly to explaining car drivers' accidents. This is, however, somewhat in contrast with the findings of Lund and Williams (1985) who found that the "defensive driving course" reduces violations, but not accidents. Groeger and Brown (1989; p. 164) conclude similarly that young drivers' problems do not seem to be risk-taking but lack of experience.

Hypothesis C, that novice drivers' risk reduction may be due to better understanding and adjustments to the social interaction in road traffic, has not been much focused upon in road safety research. The importance of road user interaction has been focused by Wilde (1976) and Rothengatter (1991), but apart from Bjørnskau (1994, 1996) this has rarely been seen as important for the high risk of novice drivers.

Bjørnskau (1994) identifies two different aspects of the ability to interact with other road users. First, one may be good at predicting how other road users will behave in specific situations and thus be able to choose an adequate action in response to these predictions. Such abilities to predict the behaviour of others might be termed "active interaction". Second, one may be easy to predict by other road users, which in general implies that one's action are in accordance with "normal" road user behaviour. This might be termed "passive interaction".

Both the ability to actively and passively interact with other road users may be of great importance to avoid accidents, and there is reason to believe that as novice drivers become more experienced they improve both active and passive interaction skills.

METHOD

Sample

The sample was composed of novice drivers with 1, 5 or 9 months of driving experience respectively and a smaller group of experienced drivers. The novice drivers were partly recruited when they conducted their driving test, and partly by letter. A questionnaire was distributed to drivers after 1, 5 or 9 months from the month they passed their driving test. The recruitment scheme adopted ensured that all three groups of novice drivers were recruited at different times throughout the year in order to avoid winter/summer bias.

Originally, we did not intend to include a sub-sample of experienced drivers, but by mistake some drivers in the sample were experienced drivers renewing their driving licence. It was then decided to add more experienced drivers to the sample. These were recruited among colleagues and by posters in the office building of the Institute of Transport Economics. Table 1 gives the number of drivers distributed by time of recruitment and driving experience.

Table 1. Total sample distributed by time of recruitment and driving experience.

Recruited	*Driving experience*				*Total*
	1 month	*5 months*	*9 months*	*Experienced*	
August 2000			63		63
December 2000			135	5	140
April 2001		137	157	10	304
August 2001	134	160	143	14	451
December 2001	134	140		12	286
April 2002	129	12		5	146
August 2002	19				19
Colleagues etc.				24	24
N	416	449	498	70	1433

Questionnaire

The questionnaire was comprised of the 32 questions of the DBQ that contributed to the four-factor solution of Åberg and Rimmö (1998). In addition the questionnaire included some questions concerning road user interaction used by Bjørnskau (1994, 1996).

As in the original DBQ, respondents should indicate how often they committed different errors on an ordinal six point scale from "Never" (1) to "Very often" (6). In addition, for some of the questions an interval scale was used. Here respondents were asked *how many times during the last month* they had committed the different errors. The alternatives were "0", "1–3", "4–6", "7–9" and "10 or more".

The following questions were used in order to measure handling skills (numbers correspond to the items in the DBQ version used by Åberg and Rimmö (1998)):

14 Forget to loosen the parking brake when driving off

29 Forget to dip the lights when driving during dark hours and is reminded by others

44 Find yourself driving in next to the highest gear although you drive fast enough to drive in the highest gear

47 Intend to reverse and find that the car is moving forward because it's in the wrong gear

63 Shift into the wrong gear while driving

70 Intend to switch on the windscreen wipers, but switch on the lights instead, or vice versa

72 Forget which gear you are currently in and have to check with your hand

86 Try to shift into a higher gear although you're already in the highest gear

Items 14, 63 and 70 were also covered by similar questions, but in another part of the questionnaire and with answer alternatives on the interval scale mentioned above. In addition, the following question was also given with interval scale answer alternatives:

"How often have you hit the wrong pedal, for instance the brake instead of the clutch?"

In order to test whether the passive ability to interact with other road users was improved during the first 9 months of driving, we used some of the violations questions from the original DBQ. The idea was that violations questions could be used to investigate whether novice drivers become more normal with increased experience. The questions selected were those that contributed most significantly to the violations factor of the four factor solution identified by Åberg and Rimmö (1998) (the numbers correspond to the items in the Swedish DBQ):

2 Deliberately disregard speed limit to follow traffic flow

3 Overtake when the car in front is lowering its speed approaching a speed-limited area

26 Drive especially close to the car in front as a signal to its driver to go faster or get out of the way

30 Speed up at traffic lights at a green/yellow phase

43 Deliberately exceed speed limit on main roads during low traffic

49 Deliberately exceed speed limit when overtaking

91 Park against parking rules because you can't find a parking lot

In order to test for active interaction skills, some of the questions used by Bjørnskau (1994) were adopted. These questions are all based on traffic situations in intersections where there might be doubts about who shall drive and who shall stop. In Norway, many intersections are governed by use of the rule of yielding to traffic from the right-hand side, but sometimes this practice is in conflict with a so-called "gentleman rule" where drivers from a smaller road give way to traffic on the larger road (Johannesen, 1984). Figure 1 shows the situation and the question that appears in the questionnaire.

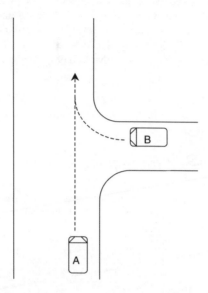

Figure 1. Situation 1: Imagine that you drive at approximately 50 km/h on a rather wide road. You are A in the figure and you approach an intersection where another car (B in the figure) approaches from the right. B is about to turn onto the road you are driving (see figure). There is no sign governing who shall give way, so the general rule of giving way for traffic from the right-hand side applies. B approaches from your right-hand side, but you drive on the larger road. Are you sometimes in doubt about who shall drive and who shall yield in such situations?

In order to investigate whether drivers differ in their effort to predict how other road users will behave, Bjørnskau (1994, 1996) used the situation in Figure 1 and asked drivers whether they looked to see if driver B signalled with his hands or otherwise, whether driver B hesitated and how fast B was approaching the junction. According to Bjørnskau (1994, 1996) those who tried to collect such information were significantly less at risk of collisions.

Analyses

On most questions, respondents were asked to indicate how often they made different errors on an ordinal six-point scale or an interval five-point scale. The ordinal scales have been given the values: "Never" = 1, "Very seldom" = 2, "Rather seldom" = 3, "Sometimes" = 4, "Often" = 5 and "Very often" = 6.

The interval scale answers had the original values "0", "1–3", "4–6", "7–9" and "10 or more". In order to compute mean values, the original values were recoded as follows: 0 = 0, 1–3 = 2,

4–6 = 5, 7–9 = 8 and 10 or more = 10. The alternative "10 or more" has not been used by more than a handful of respondents so we do not make a large mistake when recoding it into 10.

Data were analysed by use of ordinary table analysis with T-tests for comparing mean values between groups. In the literature on driver errors, this has been the standard procedure with the inclusion of factor analyses in order to establish different error types (Åberg & Rimmö, 1998; Parker et al., 1995; Reason et al., 1990). Our concern here is not whether specific errors belong to specific types, thus we have restricted the analysis to comparing means and in some instances proportions between driver groups.

RESULTS

Handling skills

Table 2 gives the main results on questions concerning handling skills.

Table 2. The frequency in which drivers make "inexperience errors" by type of error and driving experience. Means (1 = never, 6 = very often). Item numbers correspond to those of the Swedish DBQ (Åberg & Rimmö, 1998).

Error	Driving experience (time since driving test)			
	1 month	5 months	9 months	Experienced
14 Forget to loosen the parking brake	2.31^{9E}	2.24^{E}	2.14^{1}	1.96^{15}
29 Forget to dip the lights	2.25	2.34	2.35	2.30
44 Driving in too low gear	2.45^{9}	2.30	2.27^{1}	2.30
47 Intend to reverse but move forward	1.77	1.77	1.82	1.63
63 Shift into wrong gear	2.01	2.04	1.95	1.96
70 Put on wipers instead of lights etc.	1.71	1.74	1.71	1.79
72 Have to check which gear you are in	2.70^{5}	2.52^{1}	2.62	2.42
86 Try to shift into a higher gear when driving in the highest gear	1.35^{59E}	1.48^{1}	1.54^{1}	1.58^{1}

[159E] Mean values marked with elevated number/letters indicate significant differences from other groups. 1 = 1 month, 5 = 5 months, 9 = 9 months, E = Experienced. T-test, $P < 0.05$.

Table 2 gives significant differences in the expected direction only on a few items. On item 14 the most inexperienced drivers do report that this error happens more often than drivers with more experience, and the differences are significant. On items 44 and 72 there is also a similar tendency, but then on item 86 the results are opposite indicating that the most inexperienced drivers make this error more seldom than more experienced drivers. In general there seems to be quite small differences between the four driver groups, and indeed on some items the tendencies are partly opposite of what one would expect (items 70, 86).

Table 3 gives the results on the question of *how many times* during the last month drivers have made various errors.

Table 3. The frequency in which drivers make "inexperience errors" by type of error and driving experience. Means (interval scale). Item numbers correspond to those of the Swedish DBQ (Åberg & Rimmö, 1998).

Error	Driving experience (time since driving test)			
	1 month	*5 months*	*9 months*	*Experienced*
14 Forget to loosen the parking brake	0.94^{59E}	0.70^1	0.66^1	0.63^1
63 Shift into wrong gear	1.18^{59E}	0.92^1	0.82^1	0.81^1
70 Put on wipers instead of lights etc.	0.72^9	0.58	0.50^1	0.42
Hit the wrong pedal while driving	0.34^{59E}	0.17^1	0.14^1	0.11^1

^{159E} Mean values marked with elevated number/letters indicate significant differences from other groups. $1 = 1$ month, $5 = 5$ months, $9 = 9$ months, E = Experienced. T-test, $P < 0.05$.

When asked to state how many times during the last month different errors have occurred, there are significant and consistent differences between driver groups in the expected direction. There is also an expected dose–response pattern here; drivers with 1-month experience make more errors than drivers with 5-months experience, and drivers with 5 months of experience make more errors than those with 9 months of experience, etc.

The difference between answers on the ordinal and interval scale are quite dramatic, and furthermore when the ordinal scale is used the differences partly tend to go the wrong way. On all questions where the interval scale has been used, there are significant differences between driver groups according to experience in the expected direction indicating that improved handling skills indeed may be one important factor behind the risk reduction during the first months of driving.

Road user interaction

The ability to actively interact with other road users was tested by use of the situation depicted in Figure 1. Among all three groups of novice drivers approximately 55% are in doubt in the situation. Experienced drivers are, however, somewhat more in doubt (64%), and somewhat more offensive in such situations than novice drivers. Only 28% of experienced drivers report that they yield, whereas among novice drivers approximately 40% yield.

Respondents sometimes in doubt were asked whether they collected information about the other driver/car. Among experienced drivers approximately 40% did collect such information, among inexperienced drivers the proportion was around 30%. There were no differences between the three groups of inexperienced drivers.

The differences between experienced and inexperienced drivers are not significant. Nevertheless, the proportion of experienced drivers that collect information here is in the same magnitude as found by Bjørnskau (1994). Thus one might expect that with a larger sample of experienced drivers, the differences found between novice drivers and experienced drivers would be significant.

In order to test passive interaction ability, we used the seven questions with the highest loading on the violations factor according to Åberg and Rimmö (1998). Table 4 gives the main results.

Table 4. The frequency in which drivers make "violation errors" by type of violation and driving experience. Means. Item numbers correspond to those of the Swedish DBQ (Åberg & Rimmö, 1998).

Violation (1 = never, 6 = very often)	*Driving experience (time since driving test)*			
	1 month	*5 months*	*9 months*	*Experienced*
2 Disregard speed limit to follow traffic	3.55[59E]	3.88[1]	3.91[1]	3.94[1]
3 Overtaking vehicle slowing down	1.59[59E]	1.84[1E]	1.89[1]	2.14[15]
26 Drive close to car in front to signal it to go faster	1.59[59E]	1.83[1]	1.88[1]	2.01[1]
30 Speed up at traffic lights at a green/yellow phase	2.67[59E]	2.92[1E]	3.08[1]	3.37[15]
43 Deliberately exceed speed limit on main roads during low traffic	3.16[59E]	3.59[1]	3.74[1]	3.77[1]
49 Deliberately exceed speed limit when overtaking	4.13[59]	4.45[1]	4.49[1]	4.43[1]
91 Park against parking rules because you can't find a parking lot	1.67[59E]	1.80[1]	1.78	2.19[1]

[159E]Mean values marked with elevated number/letters indicate significant differences from other groups. 1 = 1 month, 5 = 5 months, 9 = 9 months, E = Experienced. T-test, $P < 0.05$.

All but one of the violations questions show that experienced drivers commit more violations than inexperienced ones. The differences are highly significant, and in most of the questions there is a consistent tendency towards more violations the more experienced drivers are.

One of the items given in Table 4, the question of how often one speeds up at traffic lights to pass on green/yellow (30) was also tested by use of an interval scale question. Respondents were asked how many out of ten occasions they drive through an intersection during the yellow period. The mean results were as follows: 1 month, 4.99 times; 5 months, 5.37 times; 9 months, 5.64 times and experienced drivers, 5.87 times. The results correspond to that of item 30 in Table 4.

The general tendency is thus that novice drivers indeed become more like ordinary drivers with increased experience. But, they make significantly *more* violations with increased experience, not less as one perhaps should expect based on previous research (Parker et al., 1995).

DISCUSSION

When we use the traditional ordinal scale from the DBQ, we do not in general find significant differences between groups on unconscious errors (slips and lapses). When using an interval scale, there are, however, clear differences in the expected direction: the more experienced drivers are, the more seldom are trivial errors like shifting into wrong gear, putting on wrong instrument, etc.

The similar results do not apply to violations. On questions of violations both ordinal scale answers and interval scale answers give similar results; novice drivers commit more violations with increased experience.

There are probably two different mechanisms operating and producing these differences between errors and violations. The first is concerned with what types of experience novice drivers have. If you ask a novice driver how often she puts in the wrong gear, she will have to answer relatively to her own experience, because she cannot know whether it happens more often to her than to other drivers. So if this happens more seldom by the time she fills in the questionnaire than before, she will perhaps answer "seldom". For novice drivers it is therefore quite likely that many of them will answer "seldom" even though they make more errors than other drivers. In fact, this mechanism could actually produce opposite results of what was in fact correct when comparing groups with different experience.

In contrast, the violations that drivers commit are normally visible to other road users, making it possible for a driver to compare himself with other drivers. Most drivers will thus be able to assess whether they, for instance, speed more often or seldom than other drivers.

The second mechanism that might be operating is that unconscious errors may be hard to remember precisely because they are unconscious; they are not something we want or plan to do. Furthermore, for most people such errors probably happen quite seldom and thus answers will lie in the never-seldom span of the answer interval. If asked about how often you break a glass it is difficult to distinguish between "seldom" and "very seldom". Many of the DBQ questions on handling skills will be subject to such problems whereas the violations questions are more evenly distributed over the scale.

Both mechanisms tend to make answers of unconscious errors more dubious when ordinal scales are used than when interval scales are used, and they might both be operating, giving the quite dramatic differences in results between ordinal scale answers and interval scale answers.

One possible implication of the results concerning technical errors is that this risk factor may also have relevance to accidents of more experienced drivers. The mechanism operating here is probably general; when people have to use tools and equipment they are not familiar with, they make more errors than when they have experience with the equipment. One of many surprises in road safety research is that new cars and better-equipped cars are more at risk of accidents than older, simpler cars (Fosser & Christensen, 1998; OECD, 1990). The explanation might be behavioural adaptation (OECD, 1990), but also the mechanism proposed here might be relevant. For any driver a new car will always be slightly different from what he is used to, hence there is reason to believe that drivers make more technical slips and lapses in new cars than in older cars. This may at least partly be the reason why new cars seem to be more at risk of accidents than older cars (Fosser & Christensen, 1998; OECD, 1990; Stamatiadis, Jones & Aultman-Hall, 1999).

An interesting result from this study is that novice drivers tend to commit more violations with increased experience, i.e. during the period that they experience a substantial risk reduction. Similar results have been reported by Lajunen and Summala (1995), but they seem to contrast the results of Parker et al. (1995). It is, however, important to remember that Parker et al. (1995) omitted drivers with less than 4 months of driving experience. It is thus possible that with more inexperienced drivers in the sample one would get another picture. Still, the results in the present study are quite clear, and on face value they seem to indicate that it is in fact favourable for novice drivers to commit violations.

The mechanism operating here is probably that as novice drivers gain experience, they also gain handling skills and confidence as drivers and adjust their driving to what they perceive as normal behaviour and perhaps abandon some of the lessons learnt during their driving education. To adjust to normal practice may be advantageous in road traffic as it is in most social systems. The main advantage of behaving "normally" in road traffic is probably that it makes it easy for other road users to predict how you will behave in different situations and to avoid misunderstandings. Thus, one might perhaps conclude that violations may be favourable to safety if they are a part of normal driver behaviour.

On the questions of active interaction skills, we did not find any substantial improvement during the first month of driving, but there were differences between experienced drivers and novice drivers as a block. One may argue that this is not surprising, given the fact that such skills include rather sophisticated and advanced types of information collection. Almost by definition such skills require experience. To be good at predicting other road user's behaviour implies to have information about local and informal rules, which can only be learned through experience in road traffic. Such informal rules will often be "violations", and we have indeed documented that there is a strong correlation between violations and driving experience.

CONCLUSION

Hypothesis B, that handling skills are improved with experience and thus errors from poor handling skills are reduced, is largely supported by the results. The more inexperienced drivers are, the more frequently they report to have used the wrong pedal, put the car in wrong gear, used wrong instruments (e.g. put on the wiper instead of the turn signal), or driven without releasing the hand brake. Poor handling skills may consequently be one important reason why inexperienced drivers have higher accident risk during the first months of driving.

As for hypothesis C, on road user interaction, the results show quite clearly that inexperienced drivers change significantly during the first 9 months of driving: the more experience they get, the more violations they commit. Thus one might conclude that their ability to passively interact with other road users is improved during the first months of driving. Their ability to actively interact with others seems, however, not to be improved during the first 9 months of driving; they are not as good as more experienced drivers when it comes to recognising traffic situations of doubt. The difference between inexperienced drivers and drivers with long driving experience indicate that this skill takes longer time to develop.

The decline in accident risk during the first months of driving is probably a consequence of a combination of changes in the behaviours and skills shown here. The relative importance of these factors in explaining the risk reduction may be investigated in detailed studies of factors contributing to accidents during the first months of driving. If the changes in behaviour that have been documented here in fact contribute to reduced accident risk during the first months of driving, it follows that increased driver training before licensing may reduce young drivers' accident risk.

Perhaps one problem within the road safety research of novice drivers is that this group is rather mixed, and their driving skills change very rapidly over a short time. A typical 18-year-old female driver with only a few months of driving experience is probably quite insecure in road traffic, and puts herself at risk by making slips and errors but rarely any violations. On the other hand, a young male driver in his early twenties may be very good at handling the car, but also at great risk because of speeding and other violations. The safety problem is thus quite different for different sub-groups of young drivers and this ought to be addressed more prominently in future research.

ACKNOWLEDGEMENTS

The Norwegian Public Roads Administration has financed the study.

REFERENCES

Åberg, L., & Rimmö, P.-A. (1998). Dimensions of aberrant driver behaviour. *Ergonomics*, *41*, 39–56.

Bjørnskau, T. (1994). *Game theory, road traffic and accidents: a theory of road user interaction*. Doctoral dissertation, University of Oslo, TØI report 287/1994, Institute of Transport Economics (in Norwegian with summary in English).

Bjørnskau, T. (1996). Why are the 'safest' norms, attitudes and types of behaviour not typical for the safest drivers? *Transport Reviews*, *16*, 169–181.

Fosser, S., & Christensen, P. (1998). *Automobile Age and Risk*, TØI report 386/1998. Oslo: Institute of Transport Economics (in Norwegian with summary in English).

Groeger, J.A., & Brown, I.D. (1989). Assessing one's own and other's driving ability: Influences of sex, age, and experience. *Accident Analysis and Prevention*, *21*, 155–168.

Johannesen, S. (1984). *Driving behaviour in unregulated T-junctions. Right hand priority rule or yield sign?* Report STF63 A84009. Trondheim: Sintef (in Norwegian).

Karttunen, R., & Häkkinen, S. (1986). *Road accident investigation teams in Finland: research on accidents involving personal injuries in 1979–1983*. Helsinki: Helsinki University of Technology.

Lajunen, T., & Summala, H. (1995). Driving experience, personality, and skill and safety-motive dimensions in drivers' self-assessments. *Personality and Individual Differences, 19*, 307–318.

Lund, A.K., & Williams, A.F. (1985). A review of the literature evaluating the defensive driving course. *Accident Analysis and Prevention, 17*, 449–460.

Mayhew, D.R., Simpson, H.M., & Pak, A. (2003). Changes in collision rates among novice drivers during the first months of driving. *Accident Analysis and Prevention, 35*, 683–691.

OECD, (1990). Behavioural adaptations to changes in the road transport system. Paris.

Parker, D., Reason, J.T., Manstead, A.S.R., & Stradling, S.G. (1995). Driving errors, driving violations and accident involvement. *Ergonomics, 38*, 1036–1048.

Reason, J.T., Manstead, A.S.R., Stradling, S., Baxter, J., & Campbell, K. (1990). Errors and violations on the roads: a real distinction? *Ergonomics, 33*, 1315–1332.

Rothengatter, J.A. (1991). Normative behaviour is unattractive if it is abnormal: relationships between norms, attitudes and traffic law. *Proceedings of the International Road Safety Symposium* (pp. 91-93). Leidschendam: SWOV.

Sagberg, F. (2000). *Novice drivers' crash risk before and after the age limit for driver training in Norway was lowered from 17 to 16 years*. TØI report 498/2000. Oslo: The Institute of Transport Economics (in Norwegian with summary in English).

Sagberg, F., & Bjørnskau, T. (2003). *Inexperienced behind the wheel. Errors driving behaviour and hazard perception among novice drivers*. TØI report 656/2003. Oslo: The Institute of Transport Economics (in Norwegian with summary in English).

Stamatiadis, N., Jones, S., & Aultman-Hall, L. (1999). Causal factors for accidents on southeastern low-volume rural roads. *Transportation Research Record, 1652*, 111–117.

Wilde, G.J.S. (1976). Social interaction patterns in driver behavior: an introductory review. *Human Factors, 18*, 477–492.

Traffic and Transport Psychology
G. Underwood (Editor)

12

"TRAINER" PROJECT: PILOT APPLICATIONS FOR THE EVALUATION OF NEW DRIVER TRAINING TECHNOLOGIES

Dimitrios Nalmpantis[1], Aristotelis Naniopoulos[2], Evangelos Bekiaris[3], Maria Panou[3], Nils Petter Gregersen[4], Torbjörn Falkmer[5], Guido Baten[6] and Juan F. Dols[7]

INTRODUCTION

In 2000, road accidents killed over 40,000 people in the European Union (EU) and injured more than 1.7 million. The age group most affected is the 14–25 year olds, for whom road accidents are the prime cause of death (European Commission (EC), 2001, p. 66).

Research suggests that at the system of road safety the human factor is a sole or a contributory factor in up to 95% of road accidents (Rumar, 1985; Sabey & Taylor, 1980; Treat, 1980). Moreover, analyses of traffic accident databases have revealed that 92% of the accidents were preceded by the violation of at least one traffic law (Rothengatter, 1991). Obviously, in order to promote road safety and to reach "the ambitious goal of reducing the number of deaths on the road by half" (EC, 2001, p. 66) in the EU during this decade, more emphasis should be placed on the human factor: "from modifying roads and vehicles to modifying people!" (Jolly, 1986, p. 69).

Among the several ways of influencing the human factor (e.g. police enforcement, traffic campaigns, etc.), education and training are still the main ways to influence young and novice

[1] Transport Engineering Laboratory, Civil Engineering Department, Aristotle University of Thessaloniki (AUTh), Thessaloniki, Greece. *E-mail:* naniopou@spark.net.gr (D. Nalmpantis).
[2] Aristotle University of Thessaloniki (AUTh), Thessaloniki, Greece.
[3] Hellenic Institute of Transport (HIT) of the Centre for Research and Technology Hellas (CERTH), Thessaloniki, Greece.
[4] Swedish National Road and Transport Research Institute (VTI), Linköping, Sweden.
[5] Linköping University (LiU), Linköping, Sweden.
[6] Belgian Road Safety Institute (BIVV), Brussels, Belgium.
[7] Polytechnic University of Valencia (UPV), Valencia, Spain.

drivers. A modified training curriculum which would place more emphasis on the higher hierarchical levels of the driving task, according to "Michon Model" and "GADGET Matrix", incorporating new technologies such as multimedia tools and simulators, might have a positive effect on road safety.

"TRAINER" is a research project that aims to address the traffic accidents of novice drivers through a series of initiatives leading to a new, improved and yet cost-effective pan-European driver training methodology. TRAINER developed innovative and yet cost-effective tools in order not to substitute but to support the driver training procedure. Both a multimedia tool and a modular driver training simulator, which is available in a low-cost and a mean-cost edition, have been developed and appropriate curricula for their integration into the training systems of four countries (viz. Belgium, Greece, Spain, and Sweden) have been issued.

Four pilot applications have been conducted for the evaluation of TRAINER tools, one in each country mentioned above. In these pilot applications, trainees trained according to the new TRAINER curricula with TRAINER tools have been compared with trainees trained according to the official curriculum of each country.

METHOD

Apparatus

"TRAINER MultiMedia Tool" (MMT): this tool is a multimedia software, which includes 31 scenarios for theoretical driver training translated into eight languages (viz. Dutch, English, French, German, Greek, Italian, Spanish, and Swedish) (TRAINER, 2003a). Although it is to be integrated into theoretical driver training, its interactivity and contents provide useful experience for practical driver training too. Two modes of operation are possible: a "Training Mode" and a "Test Mode".

Table 1. MMT Training Mode sessions.

Block 1: basic knowledge	Block 2: manoeuvring and safety	Block 3: particular situations: special states	Block 4: particular situations: new technologies
Vehicle safety check	Braking	Alcohol issues	ABS issues
Traffic signs and rules	Gap acceptance	Effects of drugs	Ecological driving
Visibility issues	Road obstacles	Drowsiness effects	ADA systems
Safety belt	Safety distance		
	Hazard perception		
	Unexpected behaviour of road users		
	Lane change		
	Speed choice and adjustment		

During Training Mode its 31 scenarios are presented in 18 different sessions clustered in four blocks. Each session is composed of theoretical training content and one or more relevant tests. In each test, feedback on the trainee's performance is provided (Table 1).

During Test Mode there is a sequence of 26 tests that cover sessions on which the trainee has already been trained. No performance feedback is provided but log files are produced and stored automatically (TRAINER, 2003b).

"TRAINER Simulator Software" (SIS): this software has been designed for the two types of TRAINER simulator. It includes 31 scenarios for practical driver training translated in eight languages (viz. Dutch, English, French, German, Greek, Italian, Spanish, and Swedish). The system offers a "Training Mode" and a "Test Mode".

During Training Mode the trainee can perform each of the 31 scenarios separately, although they are clustered in five blocks. Explanation texts are given (Table 2).

During Test Mode the trainee has to drive, following a sequence of 24 scenarios on which the trainee has already been trained and a score is given afterwards. Log files are produced and stored automatically.

"TRAINER Mean Cost Simulator" (MCS): This is a semi-dynamic driving simulator with three screens (i.e. 120° horizontal view angle) which is able to simulate lateral motions as well as vibrations.

"TRAINER Low Cost Simulator" (LCS): This is a static driving simulator with one screen (i.e. 40° horizontal view angle).

"TRAINER connecting Database and Measurement Tool" (DBT): This is a database management tool which collects the log files from the MMT and the SIS and processes the data.

"Statistical tool for Results Analysis and Presentation" (SRAP): This tool performs the analysis of the data gathered and stored on the DBT, providing the results in graphical and numerical format.

Participants

In each country, the participants in TRAINER pilot applications were trainees recruited from driving schools. The total number of trainees from the Experimental Group (EG) and the Control Group (CG) that successfully participated in TRAINER pilot applications was 215 for the MMT but only 211 for the SIS since some quit due to simulator sickness or other reasons (Table 3).

Design

Four full sets of TRAINER tools were developed and installed in Belgium, Greece, Spain, and Sweden. Tests were conducted at each site with an EG and a CG matched by age, gender, and education level. The choice of countries accounts for social and cultural differences between different EU regions and also for different types of driver training system (Figure 1).

Table 2. SIS Training Mode scenarios.

Block 1: basic control	Block 2: manoeuvring and safety (divided attention)	Block 3: manoeuvring and safety (hazard perception)	Block 4: particular situations with higher risk	Block 5: particular situations: new technology—personality aspect
Traffic rules	Following situation on a country road	Search strategy	Stopping distance at low friction	ABS and steering ability in critical situations
Start and gear shift (straight on)	Following situation on a country road (following distance and tailgating)	Gap acceptance (when turning left)	Skid control at low friction	ABS and braking distance
Negotiating a curve	Platoon situation with oncoming car, which overtakes in a risky manner on a country road	Left junction at light regulated junction	Split friction	Economical/ecological driving
Reaction time and stopping distance during normal driving	Speed adaptation when turning	Left junction at light regulated junction with oncoming car	Aquaplaning	Mental workload and use of stereo and mobile phone
Reaction time and stopping distance applying brake alertness	Overtaking manoeuvres—learning sequence	Parked car with cue for hazard perception	Shifting beams	Influence of dangerous motives on driving
	Overtaking manoeuvres—higher risk	Parked car without cue for hazard perception	Car stopping on the road in darkness	
	Overtaking manoeuvres—varying the risk	Pedestrians crossing in a junction when dark and rainy	Overtaking manoeuvres—darkness	

Table 3. Participants per tool, group and country.

	MMT		MCS		LCS	
	EG	CG	EG	CG	EG	CG
Belgium	34	25	10	10	10	12
Greece	30	30	15	15	15	15
Spain	28	20	20	10	20	10
Sweden	33	15	18	8	15	8
Total	125	90	63	43	60	45
	215		106		105	
			211			

For the test procedure both groups initially underwent the standard theoretical driver training in a local driving school. The EG was then trained for an additional 2–3 h using the MMT. After that, all trainees were tested using the MMT for about 15 min and also underwent the official national theoretical driving license test.

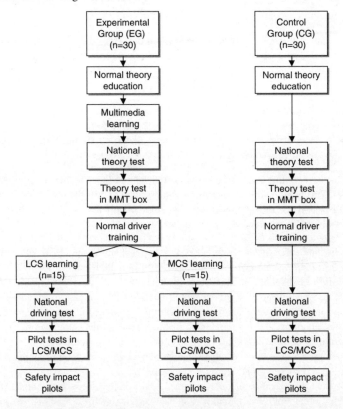

Figure 1. General design of TRAINER pilot applications.

At the second stage, all trainees were trained on the road by the local driving school using a driving school vehicle. The training lasted until the driving instructor was satisfied that the candidate was fit for the driving license test. During this training, the EG was randomly divided into two groups. Both groups underwent 2–3 h of training, one with the MCS and the other with the LCS. Both the groups as well as the CG, which was also randomly divided into two groups, were then tested in the MCS and LCS, respectively. In some pilot sites, trainees also underwent the official national practical driving license test as well as safety impact tests (TRAINER, 2003b).

Initially, the pilot application plans anticipated a total of 60 trainees per country, 30 of whom would form the EG and the other 30 the CG. Furthermore, 15 trainees from each group would use the MCS and the other 15 the LCS. The actual numbers of trainees that participated in TRAINER pilot applications reached the anticipated goal.

RESULTS

MMT results

Given that the highest possible score is 85.03, the 90% threshold to pass the MMT test is 76.53 points, rounded down to 76 points (i.e. 89.38%) (Table 4).

In Belgium, none of the trainees from the EG passed the test and the maximum score obtained was 73 (i.e. 86%). This is three points below the minimum score needed to pass the test. None of the trainees from the CG passed the test and the maximum score obtained was 59 (i.e. 69%). This is far below the minimum score needed to pass the test.

In Greece, four trainees from the EG passed the test (i.e. 13.3%) and the maximum score obtained was 80 (i.e. 94%). This is four points over the minimum score needed to pass the test. None of the trainees from the CG passed the test and the maximum score obtained was 66 (i.e. 78%). This is far below the minimum score needed to pass the test.

In Spain, none of the trainees from the EG passed the test and the maximum score obtained was 64 (i.e. 75%). This is far below the minimum score needed to pass the test. None of the trainees from the CG passed the test and the maximum score obtained was 44 (i.e. 52%). This is far below the minimum score needed to pass the test.

In Sweden, none of the trainees from the EG passed the test and the maximum score obtained was 70 (i.e. 82%). This is six points below the minimum score needed to pass the test. None of the trainees from the CG passed the test and the maximum score obtained was 58 (i.e. 68%). This is far below the minimum score needed to pass the test.

There are clear differences between the performances of the EG and the CG in every country (Figure 2):

- Belgium: EG − CG = 62.68 − 56.14% = 6.54%

- Greece: EG − CG = 74.77 − 56.04% = 18.73%

- Spain: EG − CG = 74.06 − 50.57% = 23.49%

- Sweden: EG − CG = 70.94 − 55.98% = 14.96%

Table 4. MMT Test Mode results per group and country.

	Number of participants[a]		Average test score[a]		Standard deviation[a]		Differences[b]	Student's t-test[c]			
	EG	CG	EG	CG	EG	CG	EG − CG	Value	dl	p	Sign
Belgium	34	25	53.30 (62.68%)	47.74 (56.14%)	8.58 (10.09%)	5.49 (6.46%)	5.56 (6.54%)	−2.920	57	0.00250	**
Greece	30	30	63.58 (74.77%)	47.65 (56.04%)	12.85 (15.11%)	9.52 (11.20%)	15.93 (18.73%)	−5.349	58	0.00000	***
Spain	28	20	62.97 (74.06%)	43.00 (50.57%)	7.85 (9.23%)	5.18 (6.09%)	19.97 (23.49%)	−10.438	46	0.00000	***
Sweden	33	15	60.32 (70.94%)	47.60 (55.98%)	4.77 (5.61%)	9.03 (10.62%)	12.72 (14.96%)	−5.139	46	0.00000	***

[a]The numbers of participants, the average test scores and the standard deviation have been extracted from the DBT and SRAP tools and have been rounded to the second decimal point; [b]The differences are based on the previous results; [c]The student's t-test is based on the results from each session separately extracted from the DBT. The signs used represent the following levels of statistical significance: NS: $p > 0.05$, *: $0.05 > p > 0.01$, **: $0.01 > p > 0.001$, ***: $0.001 > p$.

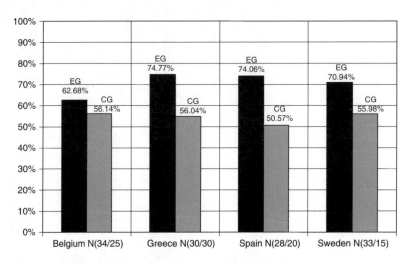

Figure 2. Average MMT Test Mode scores per country and group.

SIS results

The SIS Test Mode has a different approach from the MMT Test Mode. In case of a crash or another fatal error, the trainee fails the test immediately. Due to the fact that very few trainees passed, it was decided that the best way to thoroughly compare the differences between the two groups was to check the percentages of the trainees that started each one of the four blocks of the SIS Test Mode (Table 5).

Table 5. SIS Test Mode results per type of simulator, group and country.

	Number of participants				Passed				Differences	
	MCS		LCS		MCS		LCS		MCS	LCS
	EG	CS	EG	CG	EG	CS	EG	CG	EG − CG	EG − CG
Belgium	10	10	10	12	0 (0%)	0 (0%)	0 (0%)	0 (0%)	0 (0%)	0 (0%)
Greece	15	15	15	15	0 (0%)	0 (0%)	0 (0%)	0 (0%)	0 (0%)	0 (0%)
Spain	20	10	20	10	2 (10%)	0 (0%)	1 (5%)	0 (0%)	2 (10%)	1 (5%)
Sweden	18	8	15	8	5 (28%)	0 (0%)	1 (7%)	0 (0%)	5 (28%)	1 (7%)
Total	63	43	60	45	7 (11%)	0 (0%)	2 (3%)	0 (0%)	7 (11%)	2 (3%)

In Belgium, 42 trainees participated in total. From those that were tested with the MCS none passed the test from either group. From those that were tested with the LCS none passed the test from either group.

In Greece, 60 trainees participated in total. From those that were tested with the MCS none passed the test from either group. From those that were tested with the LCS none passed the test from either group.

In Spain, 60 trainees participated in total. From those that were tested with the MCS two (i.e. 10%) passed the test from the EG and none from the CG. From those that were tested with the LCS one (i.e. 5%) passed the test from the EG and none from the CG.

In Sweden, 49 trainees participated in total. From those that were tested with the MCS five (i.e. 28%) passed the test from the EG and none from the CG. From those that were tested with the LCS one (i.e. 7%) passed the test from the EG and none from the CG.

In total, 211 trainees participated. From those that were tested with the MCS seven (i.e. 11%) passed the test from the EG and none from the CG. From those that were tested with the LCS two (i.e. 3%) passed the test from the EG and none from the CG.

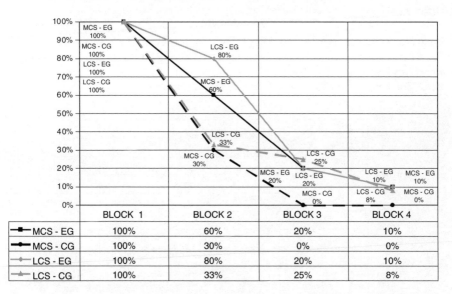

	BLOCK 1	BLOCK 2	BLOCK 3	BLOCK 4
MCS - EG	100%	60%	20%	10%
MCS - CG	100%	30%	0%	0%
LCS - EG	100%	80%	20%	10%
LCS - CG	100%	33%	25%	8%

Figure 3. SIS Test Mode results per block, type of simulator and group in Belgium.

In Belgium, the EG of the MCS performed better than the CG of the MCS on every test block. The EG of the LCS also performed better than the CG of the LCS on every test block, apart from Block 3. The trainees that were tested with the LCS performed better than those that were tested with the MCS in both groups, a result that was unexpected. This result occurred only in Belgium and perhaps was due to the lower number of participants compared to the other pilot sites (Figure 3).

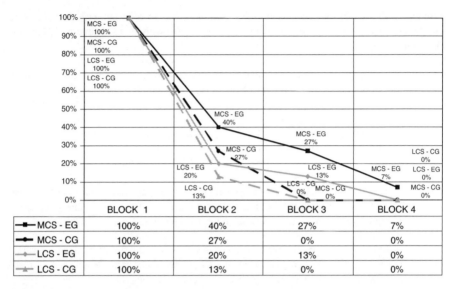

Figure 4. SIS Test Mode results per block, type of simulator and group in Greece.

In Greece, the EG of the MCS performed better than the CG of the MCS on every test block. The EG of the LCS also performed better than the CG of the LCS on every test block. The trainees that were tested with the MCS performed better than those that were tested with the LCS in both groups. These results were expected (Figure 4).

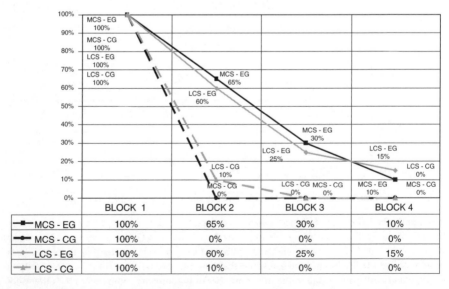

Figure 5. SIS Test Mode results per block, type of simulator and group in Spain.

In Spain, the EG of the MCS performed better than the CG of the MCS on every test block. The EG of the LCS also performed better than the CG of the LCS on every test block. There were no significant differences in the performances of the trainees that were tested with the MCS compared to those that were tested with the LCS in both groups (Figure 5).

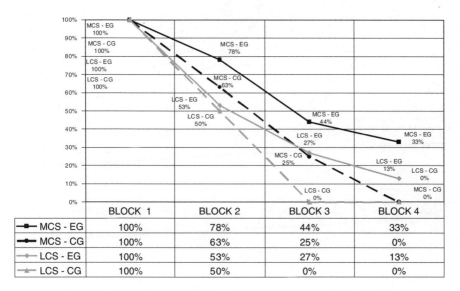

	BLOCK 1	BLOCK 2	BLOCK 3	BLOCK 4
MCS - EG	100%	78%	44%	33%
MCS - CG	100%	63%	25%	0%
LCS - EG	100%	53%	27%	13%
LCS - CG	100%	50%	0%	0%

Figure 6. SIS Test Mode results per block, type of simulator and group in Sweden.

In Sweden, the EG of the MCS performed better than the CG of the MCS on every test block. The EG of the LCS also performed better than the CG of the LCS on every test block. The trainees that were tested with the MCS performed better than those that were tested with the LCS in both groups. These results were expected (Figure 6).

The following figure presents the total results from all TRAINER pilot sites in detail (Figure 7). This is the most important figure of the SIS results since the total results are presented with a higher level of statistical significance.

In total, the EG of the MCS performed better than the CG of the MCS on every test block. The EG of the LCS also performed better than the CG of the LCS on every test block. These results were expected. It is interesting that although the EG of the MCS performed better than the EG of the LCS, this is not the case for the CGs where the respective results showed no significant differences.

From the previous figures it is obvious that the training with both types of simulator had a positive effect on the performances of the trainees. The differences in the performances per block and type of simulator are presented below. All the differences are positive as expected, apart from Block 3 of the LCS from Belgium (Table 6).

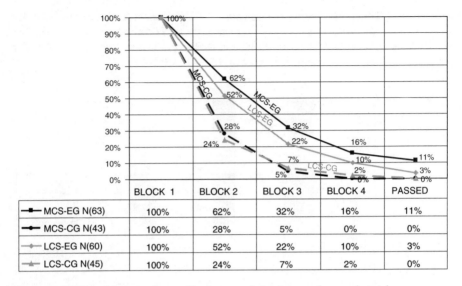

	BLOCK 1	BLOCK 2	BLOCK 3	BLOCK 4	PASSED
MCS-EG N(63)	100%	62%	32%	16%	11%
MCS-CG N(43)	100%	28%	5%	0%	0%
LCS-EG N(60)	100%	52%	22%	10%	3%
LCS-CG N(45)	100%	24%	7%	2%	0%

Figure 7. SIS Test Mode results per block, type of simulator and group in total.

Table 6. SIS Test Mode differences (EG − CG) per block, country and type of simulator.

	Block 1	Block 2	Block 3	Block 4	Passed
Belgium					
MCS (%)	0	30	20	10	0
LCS (%)	0	47	− 5	2	0
Greece					
MCS (%)	0	13	27	7	0
LCS (%)	0	7	13	0	0
Spain					
MCS (%)	0	65	30	10	10
LCS (%)	0	50	25	15	5
Sweden					
MCS (%)	0	15	19	33	28
LCS (%)	0	3	27	13	7
Total					
MCS (%)	0	34	27	16	11
LCS (%)	0	28	15	8	3

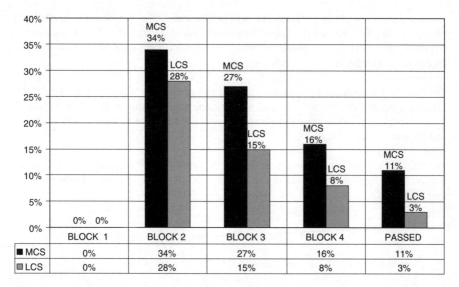

	BLOCK 1	BLOCK 2	BLOCK 3	BLOCK 4	PASSED
■ MCS	0%	34%	27%	16%	11%
▣ LCS	0%	28%	15%	8%	3%

Figure 8. Differences (EG − CG) per block and type of simulator.

The above figure presents the differences between the two groups per type of simulator (Figure 8). This is a useful figure for comparing the MCS with the LCS.

DISCUSSION

MMT discussion

In total, only four (i.e. 3.2%) trainees passed the MMT test from the EG and none from the CG. As the MMT is to be integrated into the theoretical driver training, the percentage of successful participants of the EG would be better to be near to the average of the official national theoretical tests in the EU. Therefore, it is clear that the passing threshold of 76 points (i.e. 89.38%) has to be lowered. A further optimisation step could be to simplify the Test Mode (e.g. fewer choices on multiple choice tests, no ambiguous questions, etc.).

Of the four countries compared, Spain (23.49%) and Greece (18.73%) had the biggest differences between the EG and the CG. This may reflect some social and cultural differences between the southern and northern parts of Europe. Also, it may reflect differences in training approaches since in Greece driver training at driving schools is compulsory and in Spain most trainees prefer training at driving schools. This may suggest that trainees from Greece and Spain faced the procedure of the TRAINER pilot applications more seriously than the rest.

The previous conclusion seems to be true since the EGs from Greece and Spain had the highest average scores, 74.77 and 74.06%, respectively, although there is more awareness about road safety in northern European countries.

The average score of the EG from Belgium (62.68%) was significantly lower compared to the other countries. This was not the case in Sweden, the EG of which also had a low average score (70.94%) but was closer to Greece and Spain. Perhaps the high standards of road safety and awareness in Sweden are the reasons for this.

The CGs of all countries had similar results, apart from Spain. Belgium (56.14%), Greece (56.04%), and Sweden (55.98%) had very close average scores and Spain followed (50.57%). This was expected since all these trainees had been trained with the national official curriculum and content of each country.

Finally, the EGs performed better than the CGs in every country with statistically significant results. This reflects the positive effects of training with the MMT, proving that it is an efficient training tool.

SIS discussion

In total, only seven (i.e. 11%) trainees passed the MCS test and two (i.e. 3%) the LCS test, all of them from the EG. None from the CG passed the test for either type of simulator. As the SIS is to be integrated into the practical driver training, the percentage of successful participants of the EG would be better to be near to the average of the official national practical driving tests in the EU. This way the SIS will not only be an efficient training tool but also an efficient evaluation tool. Another suggestion about the optimisation of the SIS Test Mode is that it would be better if it did not stop once there was a fatal error. It could grade the specific scenario in which the fatal error occurred with zero points and continue with the next one. This way the trainer could evaluate the trainee in all scenarios and thus spot and cure weaknesses in specific scenarios in relation to hierarchical driver models. It is difficult to do this on the road since training on the road must meet certain safety standards. Thus, evaluation is more difficult and usually remains at lower hierarchical levels.

At the MCS Test Mode, Sweden's EG had by far the best performance (28% passed) in comparison to the other countries. This may reflect the high standards of road safety and awareness in Sweden. Drivers in northern European countries generally drive safer than those in southern European countries but Sweden goes even further with its excellent road safety indicators and "Vision Zero" policy. Normally Belgium would be next according to social and cultural differences between northern and southern countries, but none from Belgium passed the MCS test. This may be due to the fact that Belgium had a small sample, just 10 trainees in its EG of MCS. The EG of Spain performed well (10% passed). None passed the test from the EG of Greece. This was expected since in Greece it is forbidden to drive before the age of 18 and any driving before obtaining a driving licence is permitted only with a professional driving trainer. Thus, the trainees of the EG of Greece did not have much driving experience when tested with the MCS. None from the CGs of any country passed the MCS Test Mode. None even started Block 3 from any country, apart from Sweden.

Once again, at the LCS Test Mode, Sweden's EG had the best performance (7% passed), perhaps for the same reasons described above. Spain came next (5% passed). As for Belgium and Greece, none passed the LCS test. None from the CGs of any country passed the LCS Test Mode. None even started Block 3 from any country, apart from Belgium.

Looking at the performances per test block, Belgium had rather unexpected results. Both the EG and the CG trainees that used the LCS performed better than those that used the MCS. Moreover, on Block 3 the CG of the LCS had even better results than the EG of the LCS. Perhaps, once again, the reason for this was the small sample from Belgium compared to the other countries. The results from the other countries were generally as expected.

In total, the results were as expected. The EG of the MCS performed better on all blocks compared to the CG of the MCS and the same went for the LCS. Moreover, the EG of the MCS performed better on all blocks compared to the EG of the LCS. The CGs of both types of simulator performed similarly, a result that was expected since the SIS Test Mode is very difficult without previous training for both simulators and the differences between the simulators are actually the hardware components, not the scenarios.

Another objective of the TRAINER pilot applications was to compare the MCS to the LCS. As mentioned, the performance of the EG of the MCS was better than the performance of the EG of the LCS on every test block. Moreover, 11% of the EG passed the MCS Test Mode in comparison to 3% that passed the LCS Test Mode. Comparing the differences (i.e. EG − CG) per test block and type of simulator, they are much higher for the MCS on every test block. As expected, the MCS is a more effective training tool than the LCS because it has a wider field of view (i.e. 120°) than the LCS (i.e. 40°) and it simulates accelerations and decelerations, making driving more realistic.

Finally, in every country, the EG performed better than the CG with both types of simulator. This reflects the positive effects that training with the SIS has with both types of simulator and that the MCS and the LCS are efficient training tools.

General discussion

After the MMT and SIS tests, a comparison was made between the performances of the two groups of Greece and Belgium and the results of the official national on-road practical driving tests. In Belgium, there was not enough time for the official on-road test to take place, so a simulation was performed. On these tests only the EG of the LCS performed better in comparison to the CG of the LCS but the results were not statistically significant. In other words, the EG did not perform better on these tests. This was expected, as the main criticism of the TRAINER project concerning official driving examinations is that they focus too much on the operational aspects of driving, whereas the aim of TRAINER tools is to be a complement to traditional driver training by focusing on higher order skills (e.g. hazard perception).

It is for this reason that traffic safety impact analyses have been conducted in Greece and Sweden. The results from these analyses indicate that the trainees from the EG indeed drive safer, but the effect on road safety impact will be apparent after 3 years, when accident analyses are scheduled for both groups. The TRAINER Consortium expects that, in the long term, trainees from the EG will be safer drivers than trainees from the CG.

CONCLUSIONS

The TRAINER project has been the first attempt to integrate new technologies into driver training at a pan-European level emphasising road safety and higher order skills.

From the results of the TRAINER pilot applications presented here it is obvious that there are high expectations concerning the application of TRAINER tools and the integration of new technologies into driver training.

In case there are positive results from the scheduled accident analyses, the TRAINER project will have been a successful start, which hopefully will be followed-up at the Sixth Framework Programme, contributing to the promotion of road safety and to "the ambitious goal of reducing the number of deaths on the road by half" (EC, 2001, p. 66) during this decade in EU.

More information about TRAINER project is available at the TRAINER project website (http://www.trainer.iao.fraunhofer.de).

ACKNOWLEDGEMENTS

TRAINER project has been co-funded by the European Commission (Directorate General for Energy and Transport, Fifth Framework Programme, Competitive, and Sustainable Growth Programme).

REFERENCES

European Commission (2001C). *White Paper—European Transport Policy for 2010: Time to Decide*. Luxembourg: Office for Official Publications of the European Communities.

Jolly, K. (1986). *Educating the teenage driver*. Proceedings of the Second World Congress of the International Road Safety Organisation, Luxembourg, 16–19 September 1986, (pp. 65–71). Luxembourg: International Road Safety Organisation.

Rothengatter, J.A. (1991). Automatic policing and information systems for increasing traffic law compliance. *Journal of Applied Behavior Analysis, 24* (1), 85–87.

Rumar, K. (1985). The role of perceptual and cognitive filters in observed behaviour. In Evans, L., & Schwing, R.C. (Eds.), *Human Behaviour and Traffic Safety* (pp. 151–165). New York: Plenum Press.

Sabey, B.E., & Taylor, H. (1980). *The Known Risks We Run: The Highway, Supplementary Report SR 567*. Crowthorne: Transport and Road Research Laboratory.

TRAINER (2003a). *Deliverable 6.2: Pilot Evaluation*. Brussels: P. Arno & E. Strypstein.

TRAINER (2003b). *Final Technical Report*. Brussels: G. Baten & E. Bekiaris.

Treat, J.R. (1980). A study of precrash factors involved in traffic accidents. *Highway Safety Research Institute Research Review, 10* (6), see also *11* (1), 1–35.

Traffic and Transport Psychology
G. Underwood (Editor)
© 2005 Elsevier Ltd. All rights reserved.

13

PROFILE OF THE BRITISH LEARNER DRIVER

Lynne F. Crinson[1] and Graham B. Grayson[1]

INTRODUCTION

It has long been known that young drivers are over-represented in accidents, and as a result have been a major focus of research and policy in traffic safety in the developed countries of the world for many years. More recently, research has shown that much of this problem is associated with inexperience, in that both younger and older new drivers have an elevated risk of accident involvement in the early stages of their driving careers (Forsyth, Maycock, & Sexton, 1995; Grayson & Sexton, 2002; Maycock, 2002; Maycock, Lockwood, & Lester, 1991; Mayhew, Simpson, & Pak, 2000; Sagberg, 1998). This raises the question of just what happens in the first 2 or 3 years of driving to turn a high-risk novice into a lower risk experienced driver and invites us to search for ways of:

- enhancing the learning process,

- preventing people from driving unsupervised until it has taken effect, and

- influencing behaviour or reducing exposure to risk during the early months of solo driving to counter the effects of inexperience and immaturity.

In Britain, the driving test is the main policy tool for inducing learner drivers to build up training and experience before driving solo, and to screen out drivers who have not reached a standard acceptable for solo driving. The provisional licence is available to people aged 17. It is the choice of the learner driver how they learn to drive, but they must be accompanied by someone who has held their licence for at least 3 years, and is at least aged 21. This person may be a professional driving instructor. Before a driver can take their Practical Test, they must pass a Theory Test.

The first investigation into the new driver problem on a large scale in this country was started in 1988 in the Cohort I study (Forsyth, 1992a,b; Forsyth et al., 1995; Maycock & Forsyth, 1997). Every person who took a driving test on 1 of 4 days (two in November 1988 and two in

---

[1] TRL Limited, UK. *E-mail:* lcrinson@trl.co.uk (L.F. Crinson) and ggrayson@trl.co.uk (G.B. Grayson).

July 1989) was sent a questionnaire 2 weeks after taking the test. Information on accidents and offences was collected at annual intervals for the first 3 years of driving. In addition, surveys of attitudes and opinions were carried out at intervals over 2 years, though respondents only participated once. A small sub-sample of respondents were given test drives to assess the development of driving skills.

The results of the Cohort I study provided valuable input to policy on driver training and testing. However, with the passage of time there have been changes to the training and testing regime, and a Cohort II project has therefore been carried out in order to provide up to date information about learner and novice drivers that can inform Department for Transport (DfT) policy.

The objectives of the Cohort II project as defined by DfT are:

- to carry out a detailed analysis of performance in both the theory and the practical driving tests in relation to candidate characteristics;

- to investigate the methods used and experience gained while learning to drive, and in preparation for each part of the test, and following test failure;

- to investigate the relationship between learning methods and driving test performance;

- to investigate the attitudes and reported behaviour of drivers in the early post-test period;

- to gather information about exposure to traffic situations, accidents, near accidents and traffic offences committed during the first 3 years after passing the driving test;

- to carry out an evaluation, based on data collected, of the effectiveness of measures introduced during the period of the contract, e.g. the introduction of hazard perception testing in the Theory Test in Autumn 2002; and

- to provide recommendations for the improvement of novice drivers' safety records.

This chapter presents some interim results on learning to drive and taking the driving test from the Cohort II project. It is important to recognise the interim nature of the results. This is a long term, longitudinal study and data accumulates throughout the project period. In most of the analyses presented in this report, data from several groups has been combined to provide more substantial samples. However, for some stages of the study there is only data from a limited number of groups. This limits the level of analysis that is possible. There are a number of analyses for which only small amounts of data have been collected. For example, there may be seasonal changes in learner and novice drivers' experience and exposure which have not yet been picked up because there is insufficient data.

The next section "Project Design" of this chapter describes the project design; and the section "Sample" discusses the samples, including response rates. The section "Selected Results from LTDQ" contains some interim results, and the last section "Future Work" discusses future work.

PROJECT DESIGN

The cohort study is a questionnaire survey of learner and newly qualified drivers. The main part of the study contacts new drivers at the time they take their test and follows up those who pass their test for up to 3 years. Information about driving test performance (both for those who pass and who fail their test) is obtained from DSA and linked to the questionnaire data. A smaller supporting study looks at learner drivers at the time they take their Theory Test. The project is designed to run for 4 years, with a new cohort every 3 months, allowing 14 cohort of novice drivers to be incorporated.

The study uses six different questionnaires:

- Learning To Drive Questionnaire (LTDQ)

- Driving Experience Questionnaire 1 (6 months)

- Driving Experience Questionnaire 2 (12 months)

- Driving Experience Questionnaire 3 (24 months)

- Driving Experience Questionnaire 4 (36 months)

- Theory Test Questionnaire (TTQ)

The first element of the project is to investigate methods used in learning to drive. The LTDQ is the first contact with respondents, and is a key part of the study. It includes questions about preparation for both the theory and practical elements of the driving test, including time spent in different types of driving environment and whether this is with an instructor or with a friend/relation. It also includes some basic attitude questions. This chapter focuses on information from this questionnaire.

The second element follows the experiences of new drivers in the early part of their driving careers. The Driver Behaviour Questionnaires (DEQs) cover accidents, exposure and offences as well as attitudes and reported behaviour, and these are sent out at 6, 12, 24 and 36 months after drivers pass the Practical Test. The repeated questionnaires allow an accident history to be built up which will track the changes in risk as drivers become more experienced. We are also able to track behavioural and attitudinal development. The results from the Driving experience questionnaires are not included in this chapter. Results from these questionnaires will be presented elsewhere.

A third element of the project involves the TTQ, which collects information about preparation for the Theory Test, previous performance (if the subject has failed a previous test), and intentions for the future (if they have just failed the test). There are also questions about preparation for the Theory Test in the LTDQ. These questionnaires were updated to reflect the introduction of the Hazard Perception element of the Theory Test in November 2002.

As well as the questionnaire data we have access to the DL25 records (the form used by driving examiners to record candidate performance during their practical driving test) which are linked for analysis purposes to the LTDQ data. The DL25 record includes data on all the driving faults committed by candidates. Subjects who passed their Practical Test are still likely to have a number of faults but these will not have been sufficient (in number or severity) to result in test failure.

SAMPLE

The main cohort study sample consists of 14 cohort, each of 8000 candidates, taken at 3-monthly intervals over the period of the project. Each cohort sample is selected from practical driving test booking data for a single week. Since, about 24,000 candidates take a practical driving test each week, this represents approximately one-third of candidates in our test weeks. The cohort are labelled from A to N (see Table 1). The sample method makes use of the DSA booking system, which holds the names and addresses of people that have booked their L-driver practical driving test. The cohort samples are selected using a randomised sample of the DSA booking system spread across each day of the week to ensure representativeness.

Those who return their LTDQ and pass their practical driving test will be sent a DEQ at 6, 12, 24, and 36 months after passing their test. The DEQ covers attitudes, driver behaviour, accidents, offences, violations and exposure to driving. Recent research suggests that much of the novice driver accident excess, and much of the post-test learning, happens in the very early months. This means that the 6-month questionnaires are an important element which was not present in the Cohort I project, where the first follow-up was at 12 months after the test. The TTQ is sent out to a different sample of 800 people every 6 months.

The project is currently planned to run for 4 years, which means that it will be possible to have 14 cohort at 3-monthly intervals. The number of follow-ups completed within the contract period will vary depending upon when the cohort entered the study. Table 1 shows the data available in September, and at the end of the project. The first questionnaire (LTDQ-A) was sent out in November 2001, and the final questionnaires are due to be sent out in February 2005. An estimate for the total number of questionnaires returned at the end of the project is shown, which is based on the response rate of the questionnaires returned to date.

The first DEQ4 questionnaires will be sent out in November 2004, and by the end of the project, only cohort A and B will have received DEQ4. Six cohort will have received DEQ3.

Table 1. Availability of data.

Question-naire	A	B	C	D	E	F	G	H	I	J	K	L	M	N	Respondents September 2004	End of project estimate
LTDQ	■	■	■	■	■	■	■	■	■	■	■	▨	▨	▨	29,100	~40,700
DEQ1	■	■	■	■	■	■	■	■	▨	▨	▨	▨	□	□	5500	~8300
DEQ2	■	■	■	■	■	■	▨	▨	▨	▨	□	□	□	□	3100	~5200
DEQ3	■	■	▨	▨	▨	▨	□	□	□	□	□	□	□	□	800	~2400
DEQ4	▨	▨	□	□	□	□	□	□	□	□	□	□	□	□	0	?
TTQ	■	■	■	■	■	■	■	□	□	□	□	□	□	□	1800	~2500

■ Data available September 2004; ▨ data available at end of project.

This is a major project in which logistics are an important factor. A total of 112,000 LTDQs will be sent out over the period of the project, and an estimated 45,000 DEQs. In order to ensure that the huge volumes of data are controlled, TRL has developed systems using Access databases and statistical analysis tools. These offer rapid and flexible procedures for extracting information. Questions can be selected for analysis from more than one cohort and more than one questionnaire, which are linked through an ID number. The system is designed for people who have no knowledge of databases.

Figure 1 shows the age and gender distribution for the DSA sample. Forty-four per cent of the DSA sample was less than 20 years of age, and 53% were female. The pass rate for the sample was 43%.

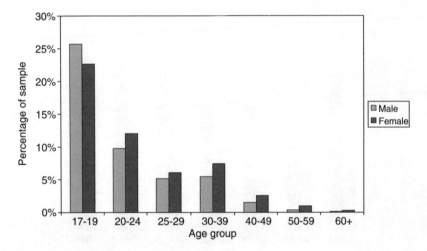

Figure 1. Age distribution of the DSA sample.

A total of 29,073 responses to the LTDQ were received from the first 10 cohort, a response rate of 38%. The response rate for each cohort is shown in Table 2.

The response rate was greater for females; 43% of females responded, compared with only 29% of males. The response rate by age and gender is shown in Figure 2. For both males and females, the response rate of the 20–24 age group was lower than that of the 17–19 group, then increased for each age group. The group with the highest response rate was females aged 60 and over, where 121 people responded, giving a response rate of 55%. The group with the lowest response was males aged 20–24, with a response rate of 22%. It was also the case that people who passed their driving test were more likely to respond to the questionnaire; for cohort A–H, 41% of people who passed responded compared with only 31% of people who failed.

Table 2. LTDQ response rates by cohort.

Cohort	LTDQ issued	LTDQ returned	Response rate (%)
A	8000	3001	37.5
B	8000	3118	39.0
C	8000	3082	38.5
D	8000	3086	38.6
E	8000	2805	35.1
F	8000	2956	37.0
G	8000	2792	34.9
H	8000	2883	36.0
I	8000	2574	32.2
J	8000	2776	34.7
Total	80,000	29,073	37.6

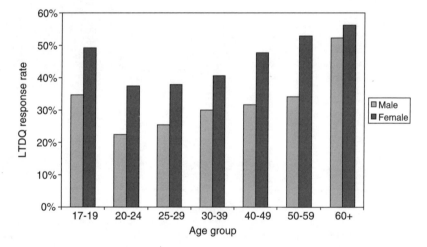

Figure 2. LTDQ response rates by age group and gender.

SELECTED RESULTS FROM LTDQ

Time to learn

Respondents were asked to say when they first started to learn to drive a car and if they had taken any breaks of longer than 6 months when they did no driving. If they had taken a break from driving they were asked to state how long this was for in total for all such breaks. The "active" learning time was then calculated as the number of months between starting to learn and taking their test, minus the total of any breaks.

The average active learning time was 15 months. Figure 3 shows that the number of months spent learning increases steadily by age, and is very similar for males and females for age groups up to 50. After 50 years of age the number of months still increases, but much more steeply for males than for females. Males over 50 took on average an extra 25 months compared with females in the same age group, however, the number of candidates over 50 was small, so these results can only be indicative of the behaviour of these older learners.

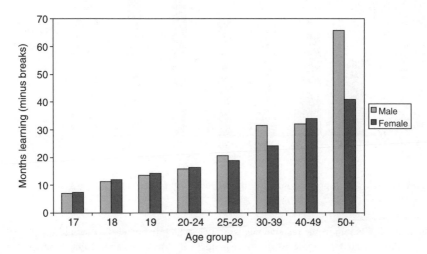

Figure 3. Months learning (minus breaks) for males and females by age group.

Hours of tuition and practice

The questionnaire asked subjects how many hours of driving with a professional driving instructor and with friends and relations they had before taking their test. Overall, 99.5% of respondents received some professional driving instruction, and 63% of respondents had some practice with friends or relations. Figure 4 shows the average number of hours of professional instruction by age group. It can be seen that the average number of hours with a professional instructor increases with the age of the candidate, and that females tend to take more professional instruction than do males, regardless of age. Professional tuition was most commonly taken for between 31 and 40 h by both males and females.

The key finding is that the older the learner driver, the longer time period they spend in preparing for their driving test (or driving tests if they fail), and that older men take longer than older women. It is important to note that this refers to *all* candidates; whether they passed or failed the test for which they were responding.

Passing the Practical Test

There are many factors that can influence the pass rate of candidates taking their practical driving test. This discussion looks at influences on the pass rate for candidates. The overall pass rate for the sample was 43%.

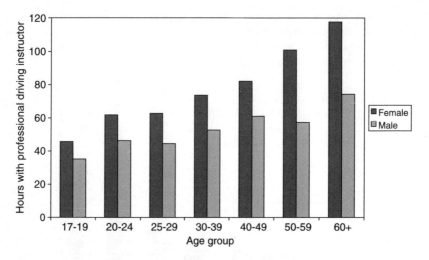

Figure 4. Hours with professional driving instructor by gender and age group.

The overall pass rate of the respondents was 50%, which is higher than for the sample, since those who passed were more likely to respond to the questionnaire. Table 3 below shows the mean values of a number of key variables for those respondents who passed their Practical Test.

Table 3. Mean values of selected variables for test pass respondents.

Variable	Female	Male	Total
Age (in years)	23.0	21.2	22.3
Time to learn (months) minus breaks	14.6	12.0	13.5
Which number practical driving test was this	2.12	1.87	2.0
Hours of professional driving tuition	51.9	36.2	45.3
Friend and relations hours driving (total sample)	22.7	21.2	22.1
Friend and relations hours driving (for those candidates who had some)	32.3	32.9	32.5

Age and gender. There are many candidates who start learning to drive as soon as they can obtain a provisional licence at 17 years of age and take their test as soon as they consider they are to the required standard. Nearly 54% of respondents to the LTDQ were in the 17–19 year age group, and 28% were aged 17 years when the test was taken.

For respondents aged 17 the pass rate is the highest of all at 56% for females and 60% for males. Overall, males have a higher pass rate than females up to 50 years of age; for candidates over 50 years of age the pass rates are about the same. This is illustrated in Figure 5.

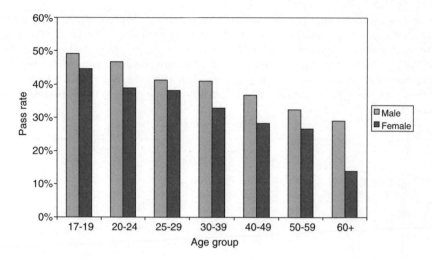

Figure 5. Pass rate by age group and gender.

Previous Practical Tests and experience. Forty-six per cent of respondents had just taken their first driving test. Respondents who had taken but failed previous tests generally had a slightly higher pass rate than those taking their test for the first time. First time test takers had a pass rate of nearly 49%, those taking their second test had a 52% pass rate, third test takers a 51% pass rate, and fourth test takers a 54% pass rate. Those taking their test for more than a fourth time had a 48% pass rate, which is slightly worse than for those taking it for the first time. This suggests that there is either a learning effect in taking the test, or that the extra training taken after failing confers some benefit when taking the next test. The exception to this applies to those candidates who perhaps find driving difficult and may struggle to pass the test, even though they take four tests or more.

Those respondents with some previous experience on the roads because they regularly rode a motorcycle before learning to drive a car found passing the car test easier. These respondents had nearly a 54% pass rate compared to a 50% pass rate for those who had not ridden a motorcycle.

Tuition. Respondents prepare for their practical driving test in various ways that may depend upon the availability of a vehicle, the cost of driving lessons from an approved driving instructor and the time they have available. The great majority (99.5%) of respondents received some professional instruction from an ADI. Just over 65% of respondents received professional instruction as well as practice with friends or relations, and nearly 35% of respondents only received professional instruction.

The number of hours of tuition or driving with friends or relations is related to success in taking the driving test. On average, the respondents had 45 h driving with a professional driving instructor, and 22 h with friends or relations Figure 6 shows the hours of tuition or practice that male and female respondents received from ADIs and from friends or relations. It shows that as the number of hours of professional tuition increases, so the pass rate increases, up to about 15 h, after which there is then a gradual reduction. Similarly, the pass rate by hours driven with friends or relations increases up to about 25 h and then flattens for higher practice levels. After those levels, if more tuition/practice is being taken then it is probably by those respondents who have failed the test at least once.

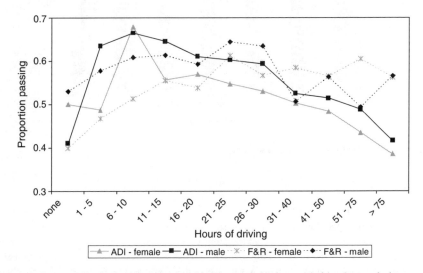

Figure 6. Pass rate by hours of professional tuition and driving with friends or relations.

The total number of hours spent driving was calculated as the sum of the number of hours of professional instruction plus the number of hours of practice with friends and relations. The average number of hours driving was analysed by the age of the candidate and gender. Overall, female respondents who failed had an average of just over 76 h of driving, 86% of which was professional instruction. Male respondents who failed had on average 13 h less driving than females, and 82% was with an ADI. The total number of hours driven increased with age, from an average of 60 h for 17–19 year olds to 180 h for those aged over 60 years. The average proportion of time driving in professional instructor's car varied from 79 (for 17–19 year olds and 60+ year old males) to 90% for 50–59 year old males.

Figure 7 shows the pass rate by total hours of driving with an ADI or friends or relations. Up to about 80 h, the pass rate for females increases with the total hours of tuition or driving, but the pass rate for males decreases. There were only 4% of females who had less than 20 h in total, and they had a pass rate of just 44%, whereas there were nearly 11% of males with less than 20 h in total and they had a 59% pass rate.

An examination of the ways in which respondents prepared for their driving test showed that if respondents could afford to take the tuition that they wanted, and have practice when they

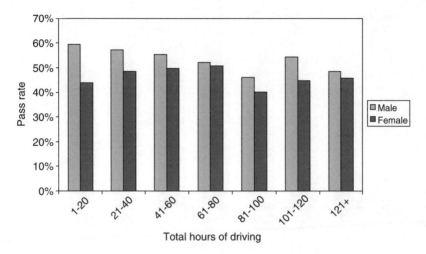

Figure 7. Practical Test pass rate by total hours of tuition or driving.

wanted, then they had a better chance of passing than those who were constrained in some way. Further, those respondents who were keen to take their test as soon as possible and those who said they found learning to drive easy had a higher pass rate than those who did not. Interestingly, those respondents who felt that they had a good chance of passing when they applied for their test (88% of the sample) had a lower pass rate (48%) than those who did not feel they had a good chance (68% passing). This also applied to a lesser extent to those who felt they had a good chance (84% of the sample) when they came to take the test, with a pass rate of 50% as compared to those who did not think they had a good chance, but achieved a pass rate of 53%.

Mileage before taking driving test. Figure 8 shows that initially pass rate increases with mileage driven up to the 300–499 mileage group. Thereafter, the pass rate is fairly stable for males and increases slightly for females until the highest mileage group—respondents who have driven more than 2000 miles prior to taking this test. It is likely that many of the respondents in this group have previously failed one or more driving tests and may well be those respondents who find driving difficult.

Piloting of the questionnaires suggested that respondents might well have had difficulties in reporting the mileage driven when learning, and that this could affect the reliability of the estimates given. When dealing with grouped data this may not pose a serious problem, but it could affect the data at an individual level.

Time spent learning prior to taking this test. Respondents were asked when they started to learn to drive a car. From this, the number of months they had been learning prior to taking their latest test was calculated. Respondents were also asked if they had taken a break of more than 6 months during which they did no driving, and if so what length of break was taken. This information was used to calculate their "active" learning to drive period in months. Just under

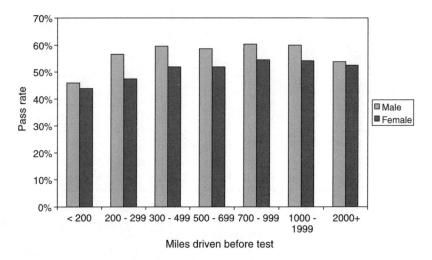

Figure 8. Pass rate by mileage before taking Practical Test.

7% of all respondents (where there were data) had taken 3 months or less to prepare, nearly 28% of all respondents took up to 6 months, and two-thirds of all respondents had taken up to 1 year before taking this test.

Figure 9 shows that the pass rate decreased with time taken after 6 months. This result applied for males and females, although the highest pass rates were after 4–6 months of learning time

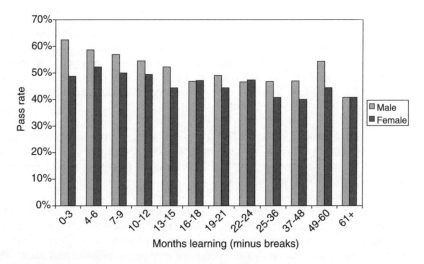

Figure 9. Pass rate by months spent learning (minus breaks).

for females and 0–3 months for male respondents. Candidates who take their test after a short time are likely to be the most able, so have a high pass rate.

Driving faults

Data from the DL25 (the form used by driving examiners to record candidate performance during their driving test) is also available, and linked to the LTDQs. There are 50 items that are assessed during the practical driving test. These items are grouped into different categories, such as control, moving away, use of mirrors, etc. Where the driver has a fault, it is marked as either a driving fault, a serious fault or a dangerous fault. The examiner notes how many of each type of fault occur for each item; if the candidate makes more than 15 driving faults in total or any serious or dangerous faults then the test is failed.

An analysis of the faults made by those respondents who failed their test shows that the most frequent category of error made is reversing or turning in the road (reverse left or right, turn in the road or reverse parking) with 45% of female respondents and 32% of male candidate making a serious or dangerous error. The next most frequent category of error is at junctions (either on approach speed, observation, turning right, turning left or cutting corners) with a third of both males and females who failed making an error.

Respondents who take the practical driving test and make fewer than 16 driving faults will pass (provided that they make no serious or dangerous faults). To analyse the average number of driving faults made in each category, the average number has been used to standardise the comparison, since some categories have more items than others (for example, there are seven items in the control category, but only three items in the judgement category). For each candidate the average per category was calculated by summing the driving faults for all items within the category and dividing by the number of items. Hence, in the control category (with seven items) if a candidate made a total of 14 faults he would be given an average of two for the category.

The categories with the highest average number of driving faults were "maintaining progress" (i.e. driving at an appropriate speed or avoiding undue hesitation) and "use of mirror".

FUTURE WORK

The final questionnaires are due to be sent out in February 2005. This will enable us to do more multivariate analysis with large data sets.

The relationship between learning methods and test performance will be studied further, and analysis will be carried out that links the questionnaires together, so that the method of learning to drive can be linked with driver performance in the first few years of driving.

The hazard perception test was introduced as part of the Theory Test in November 2002. The effect of this will be studied, in terms of preparation for the Theory Test, the performance in the Practical Test and subsequent accident rates.

REFERENCES

Forsyth, E. (1992a). *Cohort Study of Learner and Novice Drivers Part 1: Learning to Drive and Performance in the Driving Test, TRL Report RR338*. Crowthorne: Transport Research Laboratory.

Forsyth, E. (1992b). *Cohort Study of Learner and Novice Drivers Part 2: Attitudes, Opinions and the Development of Driving Skills in the First 2 Years, TRL Report RR372*. Crowthorne: Transport Research Laboratory.

Forsyth, E., Maycock, G., & Sexton, B. (1995). *Cohort Study of Learner and Novice Drivers Part 3: Accidents, Offences and Driving Experience in the First Three Years of Driving, TRL Report PR111*. Crowthorne: Transport Research Laboratory.

Grayson, G.B., & Sexton, B.F. (2002). *The Development of Hazard Perception Testing, TRL Report 558*. Crowthorne: TRL Limited.

Maycock, G.M. (2002). *Novice Driver Accidents and the Driving Test, TRL Report 527*. Crowthorne: TRL Limited.

Maycock, G., & Forsyth, E. (1997). *Cohort Study of Learner and Novice Drivers Part 4: Novice Driver Accidents in Relation to Methods of Learning to Drive, Performance in the Driving Test and Self Assessed Driving Ability and Behaviour, TRL Report 275*. Crowthorne: Transport Research Laboratory.

Maycock, G., Lockwood, C.R., & Lester, J. (1991). *The Accident Liability of Car Drivers, TRRL Report RR315*. Crowthorne: Transport and Road Research Laboratory.

Mayhew, D.R., Simpson, H.M., & Pak, A. (2000). *Changes in Collision Rates Among Novice Drivers During the First Months of Driving*. Arlington, VA: Insurance Institute for Highway Safety.

Sagberg, F. (1998). *Young Drivers: A Dramatic Decrease in Accident Risk During the First Few Months of Driving*. Nordic Road and Transport Research, 1.

Traffic and Transport Psychology
G. Underwood (Editor)
© 2005 Elsevier Ltd. All rights reserved.

14

EFFECTS OF LOWERING THE AGE LIMIT FOR DRIVER TRAINING

Fridulv Sagberg[1] and Nils P. Gregersen[2]

INTRODUCTION

The crash risk of novice drivers decreases sharply during the first few months of autonomous driving. This has been shown clearly in several studies in different countries, in the UK (Maycock, Lockwood & Lester, 1991), Sweden (Gregersen et al., 2000), Norway (Sagberg, 1998), and Canada (Mayhew, Simpson & Pak, 2003).

The time course of post-licence crash risk can be adequately fitted by a decreasing power function, as shown schematically in Figure 1, or by a decreasing logarithmic function. The decreasing risk has both an age-related component and an experience-related component, as demonstrated by Maycock et al. (1991). In the present study, focus is on the experience component. The time perspective will be the first 2 years after licensing, and we assume that the decrease during this short period is mainly a function of driving experience and increased traffic skills, whereas the age-related changes in life-style and social, motivational and emotional factors influencing crash risk are noticeable only on a time scale of several years.

Since the risk curve illustrated in Figure 1 reflects the development of skills in traffic, it may be appropriate to use the term *traffic skills curve* about the inverse function of the risk curve, which is an increasing power function.

Since the risk decreases so sharply during a short period after licensing, a pertinent question is whether the high initial crash risk of novice drivers can be attenuated by increasing the amount of pre-licence driver training (i.e. providing the necessary skills at an earlier stage), and whether the risk effect of added training can be predicted from the shape of the traffic skills curve.

[1] Institute of Transport Economics, Oslo, Norway. *E-mail:* fs@toi.no (F. Sagberg).
[2] Swedish Road and Transport Research Institute, Linköping, Sweden.

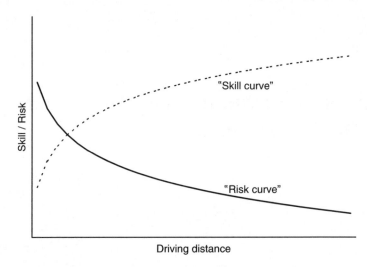

Figure 1. Schematic illustration of the risk decrease and traffic skill increase with increasing driving experience.

A hypothesis that can be tested is that by increasing the amount of *pre-licence* training by a certain amount, the initial risk is reduced to the level corresponding to the same amount of post-licence driving. This hypothesis can be illustrated by performing a backward parallel displacement of the risk curve by an amount corresponding to the increase in training. This is shown in Figure 2.

The solid line in Figure 2 shows the actual risk as a function of post-licence driving experience. The right part of the displaced curve shows the hypothetical risk curve after adding an amount of pre-licence driving corresponding to the length of the arrow. The left part of the displaced curve (in the pre-licence phase) indicates the risk in case the driving students were allowed to drive alone. (However, the pre-licence training is supposed to be accompanied driving, which has been shown to entail a very much lower risk than driving alone.)

The shaded area between the two curves indicates the expected total gain in post-licence safety, in terms of reduced number of crashes.

Providing better opportunity for more accompanied driving before getting a licence to drive alone, in order to reduce the notoriously high crash risk among novice drivers, was one of the main motivations when the Swedish and the Norwegian road authorities decided to lower the age limits for driver training. In 1993, the age limit in Sweden was lowered from 17.5 to 16 years, and in 1994, the age limit in Norway was lowered from 17 to 16 years. The licensing age was maintained at 18 years in both countries. In Norway, previous geographical restrictions on training with a lay instructor were removed, whereas Sweden did not have any such restrictions. This means that after the reform, both training when accompanied by a layperson and training with a professional driving instructor were allowed everywhere. A requirement for training with a lay instructor was that the instructor had held a licence for 5 consecutive years and was at least 25 (Norway) or 24 (Sweden) years old.

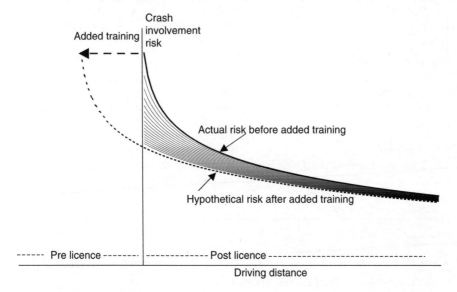

Figure 2. Schematic illustration of hypothesised effect of added pre-licence driver training onpost-licence crash risk.

Before vs. after assessments of changes in the amount of training and in post-licensing crash risk were carried out in both Sweden (Gregersen et al., 2000) and Norway (Sagberg, 2000).

The present chapter has two main purposes. First, the findings reported from the two countries will be compared regarding the changes in the amount of driver training and in the post-licence crash risk from before to after the lowering of the age limit. Second, the relationship between the amount of training and the change in crash risk will be analysed on the background of the risk curve presented in Figure 2, in order to see if the change in risk is compatible with the hypothesis that added pre-licence accompanied driving is equivalent to autonomous driving regarding the effects on subsequent crash risk.

METHOD

The methodological details of each study have been described in the respective assessment reports from the two countries. As shown in Table 1, the comparison was based on crash data from the national registers of police reported crashes, whereas data on the amount of training and on post-licensing exposure were collected by means of postal questionnaires administered to random samples of the relevant driver populations, drawn from the national registers of licence holders.

Table 1. Sources of data on crashes, exposure and amount of training.

	Sweden	*Norway*
Driver population	All drivers getting a licence at the age of 18	All drivers getting a licence in the calendar year of their 18th birthday
Year of licensing		
"Before" group	1992–1993	1994–1995
"After" group	1994–1997	1998
Crash involvement data	All police reported crash involvements during the first 2 years after licensing for the defined driver populations	
Data on amount of training and on post-licensing exposure	Postal questionnaires to driver samples drawn from the national registers of licence holders	
Sample size before change	$n = 1011$	$n = 16,985$
Sample size after change	$n = 1446$	$n = 7221$

RESULTS

Crash risk before the age limit was lowered

Figure 3 shows the month-by-month crash risk for the first 2 years after licensing. The risk decreases rather sharply, amounting to about a 50% reduction during the first 8–10 months. This development can be appropriately fitted by a power function or a logarithmic function. It turned out that a logarithmic trend line provided a better fit than a power function for both the Norwegian and the Swedish data. Therefore, the logarithmic function is used here. The sharp decrease during the first few months indicates a dramatic effect of driving experience on safety. Although the risk is somewhat higher in the Norwegian data, the decrements over time correspond closely.

Changes in the amount of training

The average number of driving lessons before and after the age limit was lowered is shown in Table 2. The amount of private driver training was considerably larger in Sweden than in Norway even before the reduction of the age limit, although the limit in Sweden was higher than in Norway (17.5 vs. 17 years). After the reduction of the age limit to 16 years, the amount of private training was doubled in Sweden, whereas there was only a modest increase in Norway.

On the other hand, the amount of training in traffic schools was larger in Norway than in Sweden both before and after the reduction of the age limit. This is obviously related to the fact that there was a mandatory minimum amount of driver training in a traffic school in Norway, whereas there was no such requirement in Sweden at the time of the assessment.

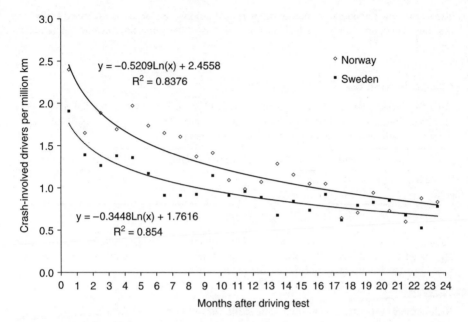

Figure 3. Month-by-month crash involvement risk of novice drivers in Norway and Sweden during the first 2 years of post-licence driving.

Table 2. Average amount (km) of pre-licence driver training with a private instructor and in traffic schools, respectively.

	Sweden	*Norway*
Private driving		
Before	1890	974
After	3795	1153
Change	1905	179
Traffic school		
Before	426	673
After	450	600
Change	24	− 73
Total		
Before	2316	1647
After	4245	1753
Change	1929	106

The slight reduction in the amount of traffic school training in Norway is explained by the fact that the mandatory number of lessons was reduced at the same time as the age limit was lowered.

Changes in crash risk

Table 3. Crash involvement risk among drivers licensed at 18 years, for the first 2 years after licensing, before and after lowering of the age limits for driver training in Sweden and Norway. Crash involvements per million vehicle kilometres.

	Before	*After*	*Percent change*	*Statistical significance*
Sweden	0.98	0.81	− 17	$p < 0.05$
Norway	1.31	1.28	− 2	ns

Table 3 shows the crash risk before and after the reduction of the age limit, for the first 2 years after licensing for drivers who got their licences at the age of 18. It appears clearly that there was a notable risk decrease in Sweden and practically no change in Norway.

Risk changes estimated from the traffic skills curve

On the background of the larger increase in training in Sweden, it was expected that the decrease in post-licensing crash risk was larger in Sweden than in Norway. To compare the actual changes in risk with theoretically expected changes, the expected effect on crash risk in the two countries was estimated from the risk curve as was illustrated schematically in Figure 2. The risk curves for Norway and Sweden as shown in Figure 3 were displaced to the left by an amount corresponding to the increase in driving distance during training, which was shown in Table 2, 1929 km in Sweden and 106 km in Norway.

The gain in safety was estimated by computing the percentage reduction of the area below the risk curve by displacing the curve to the left. For the Norwegian data this procedure yielded an estimate of a 1% reduction, which accords well with the non-significant actual reduction of 2%.

For Sweden the predicted reduction was 13%, compared to a 17% observed change. Figure 4 shows the month-by-month predicted crash risk for Sweden, based on displacing the risk curve for the before period, by an amount corresponding to the increase in training. The average increase of 1929 km corresponds to 2.4 months of post-licence driving, and the arrow in Figure 4 shows this displacement. The area between the two curves indicates the predicted reduction in accidents. The figure also shows the actual month-by-month risk in the after period, and it appears that the actual risk is lower than the predicted risk for the whole 2-year period.

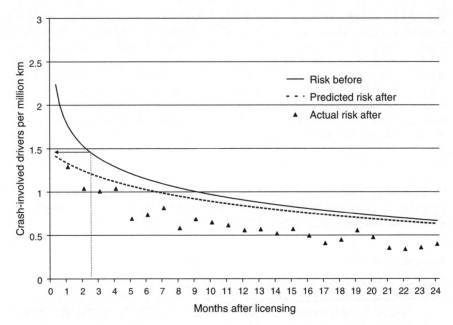

Figure 4. Actual month-by-month post-licence crash involvement risk after the reduction of the age limit for driver training, compared to predicted risk based on the increased amount of training and on the risk before the change (Swedish data).

DISCUSSION AND CONCLUSIONS

The comparison between the Norwegian and Swedish results gave some support to the assumption that accompanied pre-licence driver training is comparable to post-licence autonomous driving in terms of its effects on subsequent crash involvement risk. The observed decreases in crash risk after the reduction of the age limit tended to be somewhat larger than the changes predicted on the basis of the risk curve after licensing. If this is a reliable and replicable effect, it may imply that the accompanied training is more effective in reducing the subsequent crash risk than driving alone. In the least, there are no indications that accompanied driving is less effective. Therefore, the reduction of the age limit for training seems to be an efficient measure for reducing novice drivers' crash risk, provided that the reduced age limit is utilised to increase the amount of accompanied driving before getting a licence. The experiences from Norway indicate that decreasing the age limit is not a sufficient precondition for getting more training. Therefore, the road authorities should stimulate future drivers to increase their amount of training, e.g. by providing incentives and/or setting minimum requirements regarding the amount of training, to be documented by carrying a logbook.

An argument sometimes voiced against increasing the amount of private driver training (with a lay instructor), is that it results in an increase in the number of accidents during the training itself. To assess the total effect of this kind of training on accidents, one needs to take into account both the expected risk decrease after licensing, and the risk increase during training. However, the available evidence indicates that during training is not a large problem, for two reasons. First, as shown by Gregersen and Nyberg (2002), the risk during accompanied driving is only about one-tenth the risk during the first 2 years of post-licence driving. Second, a large amount of the accompanied driving is driving where the primary purpose is not training, but the son or daughter is allowed to drive for shopping, vacation, visits, etc. This way of combining driver training with other travel purposes does not add to the exposure, and probably not to the number of accidents either, since the risk during accompanied driving possibly is not higher than it would be if the accompanying person should drive him-/herself. A recent Norwegian study (Ulleberg, 2003) showed that as much as 60% of the accompanied driver training lessons were combined with other purposes for driving.

By way of conclusion, the results from the Swedish and Norwegian studies in combination show that lay driver training holds a high promise as an efficient measure to reduce the risk among novice drivers during the first critical period of autonomous driving.

REFERENCES

Gregersen, N.P., & Nyberg, A. (2002). *Lay instruction during driver training—a study on how it is carried out and its impact on road safety (Swedish language, with summary in English), VTI Report 481.* Linköping: Swedish National Road and Transport Research Institute.

Gregersen, N.P., Berg, H.Y., Engström, I., Nolén, S., Nyberg, A., & Rimmö, P.A. (2000). Sixteen years age limit for learner drivers in Sweden—an evaluation of safety effects. *Accident Analysis and Prevention, 32,* 25–35.

Maycock, G., Lockwood, C.R., & Lester, J.F. (1991). *The accident liability of car drivers, Research Report 315.* Crowthorne: Transport and Road Research Laboratory.

Mayhew, D.R., Simpson, H.M., & Pak, A. (2003). Changes in collision rates among novice drivers during the first months of driving. *Accident Analysis and Prevention, 35,* 683–691.

Sagberg, F. (1998). *Month-by-month changes in accident risk among novice drivers, 24th International Conference of Applied Psychology, San Francisco.*

Sagberg, F. (2000). *Novice drivers' crash risk before and after the age limit for driver training in Norway was lowered from 17 to 16 years (Norwegian language, with summary in English), TØI Report 498.* Oslo: Institute of Transport Economics.

Ulleberg, P. (2003). *Amount of driver training with a lay instructor among adolescents aged 16 and 17 (Norwegian language, with summary in English), TØI Report 675.* Oslo: Institute of Transport Economics.

EMOTION AND PERSONALITY

Traffic and Transport Psychology
G. Underwood (Editor)
© 2005 Elsevier Ltd. All rights reserved.

181

15

THE ROLE OF ATTRIBUTIONS AND ANGER IN AGGRESSIVE DRIVING BEHAVIOURS

Évelyne F. Vallières[1], Jacques Bergeron[2] and Robert J. Vallerand[3]

INTRODUCTION

Over the past decade, aggressive driving has moved into the spotlight in the media in many industrial countries (American Automobile Association, 1997; Mitchell, 1997; Sample Surveys Ltd, 1996; Taylor, 1997). Not only is aggressive driving worrisome for the general population, it is also a concern for governments because of its significant association with an increase in motor vehicle accidents (Furnham & Saipe, 1993; Hansen, 1988; Matthews, Dorn & Glendon, 1991; Mayer & Treat, 1977; Roy & Choudhary, 1985; Wells-Parker et al., 2002).

In order to understand this phenomenon, researchers have examined aggressive driving in terms of several levels of variables such as the sociocultural, situational or personal level. Recently, a general psychological model on aggressive driving has been proposed (Bergeron, 2000) that integrates variables at different levels and of various types, and takes into account their possible dynamic relations (see Figure 1). As can be seen, the model posits a "cognitions-emotions-aggressive driving" sequence and its underlying process as the central focus. While parts of this model have been the subject of much research, such as those concerned with the situational, the sociocultural and the personal variables, very few studies have focused specifically on the cognitive-emotional-aggressive driving behaviour sequence. Yet if we really want to plan effective prevention campaigns and interventions, it is of prime importance to have a better understanding of the psychological processes implied by this sequence.

Among the theoretical frameworks that emphasize cognitive and affective processes, Weiner's theory of social conduct (1995, 1996, 2001) seems particularly well suited to the study of

[1] Télé-université, Canada. *E-mail:* evallier@teluq.uquebec.ca
[2] Université de Montréal, Canada.
[3] Université du Québec à Montréal, Canada.

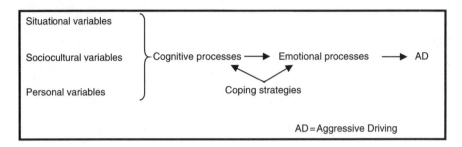

Figure 1. A general model on aggressive driving (Bergeron, 2000).

aggressive driving. More precisely, following Weiner (1995, 1996), given the context of a negative interaction between two people, it can be hypothesized that the more one of the protagonists perceives the action of the other as intentional, the more responsibility will be attributed to the other, the more angered he might feel and, eventually, the more likely he might react negatively. Weiner also adds that the more unexpected an event, the stronger the motivation to find a cause to explain it. Weiner's model appears specifically suited for the study of retaliatory or reactive rather than proactive aggression.

Let us take as an example someone who is driving a car (car *a*) on a highway when another car (car *b*), which has been tailgating for some time, finally overtakes it, moves just in front of car *a* and then slows down, forcing car *a* to slow down also. In Weiner's model (1995, 1996), such a negative incident will motivate the driver of car *a* to start a causal search.

Let us say that driver *a* attributes the situation to the driver of car *b*. The more the driver of car *a* perceives the behaviour of the other driver as intentional, the more the driver of car *a* will judge the driver of car *b* as responsible, and the more he will be angered and likely to react aggressively. In contrast, if the driver of car *a* perceives the behaviour of the driver of car *b* as unintentional, he will attribute less responsibility and will be less likely to be angry and to experience an aggressive reaction. Thus, an action perceived as intentional is associated with more responsibility attributed to a wrongdoer which, in turn, provokes anger and possibly aggressive behaviours.

In spite of the interest of Weiner's theory of social conduct (Weiner, 1996), the present authors propose that a simplified version of Weiner's model might better apply to aggressive driving reactions. In this simplified model, intentionality relates directly to anger which in turn relates to aggressive driving. It might be easier and less cognitively demanding to make intentional or unintentional attributions on the spur of the moment than to reach a responsibility judgment, in part because aggressive driving occurs in contexts where events happen rapidly and spontaneously. On this subject, Weiner speculates that in such situations "...it is probable that responsibility is immediately imposed..." (Weiner, 1995, p. 11). However, since Weiner (1996) himself describes responsibility as an encompassing inference (e.g. Was it controllable? Was it intentional? Are there mitigating factors?) and intentionality as a simple motive or goal (e.g. Is it intended? If it is, I will retaliate), it is thus likely that in spontaneous situations where others are involved, such as in aggressive driving, perceived intentionality, rather than responsibility, is the important factor leading to anger. Furthermore, previous research supports the hypothesis of a link between perceived intentionality and anger in interpersonal contexts (Averill, 1983; Ferguson & Rule, 1983; Weiner, Graham & Chandler, 1982). Therefore, the purpose of the present study was to investigate how perceived intentionality[4] relates to feelings of anger and reported aggressive driving behaviours.

METHOD

Participants and design

Participants were 55 men, 10 women and 3 individuals (sex unknown) for a total of 68 French-speaking undergraduate students with a mean age of 31.9 years (SD = 9.3 years). The study preceded another study on aggressive driving and used a methodology with hypothetical scenarios in a self-report questionnaire. Six scenarios were selected from among 18 others on the basis of the results from a pilot study. Two scenarios were selected for their higher intentionality score (intentional scenarios), two for their lower intentionality score (unintentional scenarios), and two for their in-between intentionality score (ambiguous scenarios).

Procedures and questionnaire

Participants were tested during class and were given the questionnaire containing the six hypothetical scenarios describing various situations that one might experience while driving. They were asked to read each of the six scenarios and to indicate on the appropriate scales their perceptions of each of the six other drivers' behaviour: the level of intentionality attributed to the other driver (one item: Do you think the other driver's action is intentional?) and the extent of their own reactions in such a situation (five items: yelling insults, screaming names, screaming at the other driver, behaving in a hostile way, sending a message one way or the other: alphas = 0.68–0.84). Answers were rated on a 5-point scale ranging from 1 (not at all) to 5 (entirely). Participants also rated their own level of anger in such a situation (four items: To what extent does this situation make you feel furious? angry? stressed? frustrated? Alphas = 0.79–0.88). These answers were also rated on a 5-point scale ranging from 1 (not at all) to 5 (extremely). In order to avoid order effects, four versions of the questionnaire with random orders of the scenarios were administered.

DESCRIPTION OF EACH SCENARIO TYPE

Intentional scenarios

(1) "You are driving in town. You stop at a red light. The driver behind you in an SUV starts to honk at you in a hostile way. However, the light is still quite obviously red."

---

[4] In addition, results from a previous study (Vallières, Bergeron & Vallerand, 2004) indicated that contrary to Weiner (1995), responsibility attributions did not play a significant role when applied to aggressive driving. Therefore, responsibility attributions were not included in the present study.

(2) "You are driving on the highway and the traffic is moving freely. The driver in the car behind you is tailgating you. After a while, the car overtakes you. As soon as he has passed, he deliberately slows down abruptly in front of you and you almost ram into his car."

Unintentional scenarios

(1) "You are driving on a one-way street at night when another car suddenly comes at you from the wrong direction. You have to slam on the brakes to avoid an accident."

(2) "You are driving behind another vehicle that tries to pass a truck on the right side at the same time as it starts to climb a hill. The driver seems to have a problem maintaining speed, and the motor makes funny sounds. You therefore have to slow down and forget about trying to overtake the truck."

Ambiguous scenarios

(1) "You are driving downhill on a one-way street at night when the driver in the car behind you starts to speed up, turns on his high-intensity beams, forcing you to accelerate."

(2) "You have been in a traffic jam on the highway for 30 min and nothing is moving. The driver in the car behind you starts to honk aggressively and gesticulates, urging you to move on."

RESULTS

The scores on the different scales were summed by the type of scenario. The means by type of scenario (intentional/non-intentional/ambiguous) are presented in Table 1. As can be seen, the experimental manipulation worked as expected for the intentional and unintentional scenarios. However, ambiguous scenarios were perceived as more intentional than expected. These results differ from results obtained in a previous pilot study. These differences could be due to the fact that the present study contained a higher percentage of male subjects and subjects from an older

Table 1. Mean intentionality causal dimension score, anger score, and behavioural reaction score as a function of type of scenario.

Types of scenario	Variables					
	Intentionality perceived		Anger feelings		Reported behavioural reactions	
	M	SD	M	SD	M	SD
Intentional	4.16$_a$	0.76	2.26$_a$	1.01	2.26$_a$	0.99
Unintentional	1.61$_b$	0.60	1.81$_b$	0.79	1.77$_b$	0.62
Ambiguous	4.13$_a$	0.80	2.63$_a$	0.90	2.29$_a$	0.92

Note: The higher the number, the greater the perceived intentionality, the greater the experienced anger, and the stronger the reactions. All variables were assessed on 5-point scales. Means in the same column that do not share the same subscripts differ at the $p < 0.001$.

population. However, since the purpose of the present study was to focus on the sequence "Intentional attributions → anger feelings → reported behavioural reactions" in the context of aggressive driving, and since only the intentionality attribution measures were used in the analyses, results from the three types of scenarios are presented.

Secondly, path analyses were performed through multiple regression analyses in order to investigate the mediating role of anger between attributions and reported aggressive driving behavioural reactions. Each time and for each type of scenario, analyses were first conducted by entering the intentionality measures while anger was used as the criterion variable. In the second step, the intentionality and anger measures were regressed on the criterion variable of behavioural reactions. Results of the paths for each type of scenario are presented in Figures 2–4.

Figure 2 presents the results obtained with the intentional scenarios. Non-significant relations are not presented in the figure. As can be seen, the intentionality attribution ($\beta = 0.34$) is significantly related to anger. In turn, anger ($\beta = 0.73$) is related to behavioural reactions. The results show an F change of 40.26, $p < 0.0001$ when anger is added to the model, increasing the adjusted R^2 to 0.54 for behavioural reactions. (See Figure 2 for the ΔR^2 of anger and behavioural reactions.)

In Figure 3, we present the results obtained with the unintentional scenarios. As can be seen, the intentionality attribution ($\beta = 0.20$, $p = 0.10$) is not significantly related to anger. However,

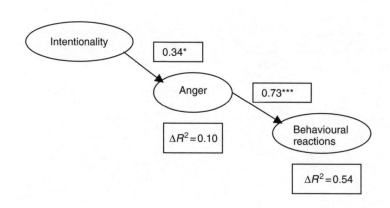

*$p<0.01$ **$p<0.001$ ***$p<0.0001$

Figure 2. Intentional scenarios: path model relating perception of intentionality to anger feelings and reported behavioural driving reactions.

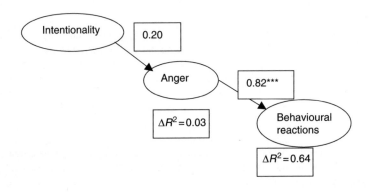

*p<0.01   **p<0.001   ***p<0.0001

Figure 3. Unintentional scenarios: path model relating perception of intentionality to anger feelings and reported behavioural driving reactions.

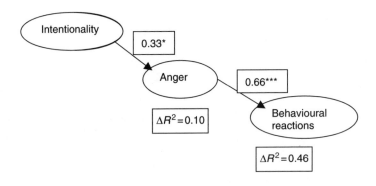

*p<0.01   **p<0.001   ***p<0.0001

Figure 4. Ambiguous scenarios: path model relating perception of intentionality to anger feelings and reported behavioural driving reactions.

anger ($\beta = 0.82$) strongly relates to behavioural reactions. Accordingly, we find an F change of 60.72, $p < 0.0001$ when anger is added to the model, increasing the adjusted R^2 to 0.64 for behavioural reactions. (See Figure 3 for the ΔR^2 of anger and behavioural reactions.)

Figure 4 shows the results obtained with the ambiguous scenarios. Similar to the intentional scenarios, the intentionality attribution ($\beta = 0.33$) is significantly related to anger which, in turn, relates ($\beta = 0.66$) to reported behavioural reactions. The F change is 28.46, $p < 0.0001$ when anger is added to the model, increasing the adjusted R^2 to 0.46 for behavioural reactions. (See Figure 4 for the ΔR^2 of anger and behavioural reactions.)

Finally, a path analysis was performed through multiple regression analyses for repeated measures (see Pedhazur, 1982), in order to investigate the sequence again. In order to control for within effects of the repeated measures, the procedure suggested by Pedhazur (1982) was followed. See Figure 5 for the results of this last path analysis. Once the within effects are controlled, the results confirm the ones obtained previously with the non-repeated measures analyses. Indeed, the intentionality attributions ($\beta = 0.25$) are significantly related to anger ($F = 97.37$, $p < 0.0001$) which, in turn, relates to behavioural reactions ($\beta = 0.38$), with an F change of 124.38, $p < 0.0001$ when anger was added to the model, increasing the adjusted

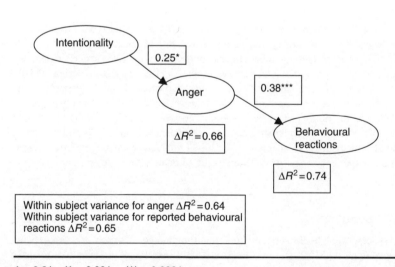

*p<0.01   **p<0.001   ***p<0.0001

Figure 5. Repeated measures: path model relating perception of intentionality to anger feelings and reported behavioural driving reactions.

R^2 to 0.74 for behavioural reactions. (See Figure 5 for the ΔR^2 of anger and behavioural reactions.)

DISCUSSION

These results provide support for the sequence "Intentionality attributions $\rightarrow$ anger feelings $\rightarrow$ reported aggressive behaviours", as only in the unintentional scenarios did the beta between intentionality and anger not reach significance. They also corroborate results obtained in a previous similar study where it was found that only perceived intentionality (and not the responsibility judgments) related significantly to anger feelings (Vallières, Bergeron & Vallerand, 2004). Therefore, the results of both of these studies seem to indicate that a simplified attributional model might better apply to aggressive reactions in the driving context.

The mediating role of anger feelings between perceived intentionality and reported aggressive reactions is also evidenced in the repeated measures analyses as well as in the conventional regression analyses conducted with each of the three types of scenarios. In cases where the relation between intentionality and reported aggressive behavioural reactions was significant, when anger was included in the equation, this relation became non-significant, which provides support for the mediating role of anger.

One finding pertaining to the variance explained by the within subject effects seems to suggest that some other variables may play a determining role in producing anger. For this reason, future studies should really explore the role of different personality variables in producing aggressive driving.

The present study is limited by the small number of participants and by the type of methodology used. Indeed, correlational studies do not permit a true test of the predictive value of the sequence. It would be important that other studies conducted on the same sequence include a greater number of participants, use other methodologies and a prospective design. Finally, further studies should explore the impact of personality characteristics on the variables of the model. Some studies have looked at personality variables such as Type A personality (e.g. Perry & Baldwin, 2000) or trait driving anger (e.g. Deffenbacher, Lynch, Oetting, & Yingling, 2001). However, the role of other characteristics such as narcissism (Emmons, 1987) or obsessive passion could also be explored (Vallerand et al., 2003), thus increasing our understanding of how one is led to experience anger while driving and, ultimately, to drive aggressively.

ACKNOWLEDGEMENTS

We gratefully acknowledge the support from the Programme d'Action concertée Fonds Nature et Technologies—MTQ—SAAQ: Project 2002-SR-86395. We would like to thank Pierre McDuff (Université de Montréal) for his participation in conducting the statistical analyses. Requests for reprints should be addressed to Evelyne Vallières, Télé-université, Université du Québec, 4750 avenue Henri-Julien, bureau 100, Montréal, Québec, Canada, H2T 3E4. Electronic mail may be sent to evallier@teluq.uquebec.ca.

REFERENCES

American Automobile Association (1997). *Aggressive Driving: Three Studies*. Washington, DC: American Automobile Association Foundation for Traffic Safety.

Averill, J.R. (1983). Studies on anger and aggression. *American Psychologist, 38*, 1145–1160.

Bergeron, J. (2000). La rage au volant et les caractéristiques psychologiques des conducteurs agressifs sur la route. *Psychologie Québec, 18* (3), 33–36.

Deffenbacher, J.L., Lynch, R.S., Oetting, E.R., & Yingling, D.A. (2001). Driving anger correlates and a test of state-trait theory. *Personality and Individual Differences, 31*, 1321–1331.

Emmons, R.A. (1987). Narcissism: theory and measurement. *Journal of Personality and Social Psychology, 52*, 11–17.

Ferguson, T., & Rule, B. (1983). An attributional perspective on anger and aggression. In Geen, R., & Donnerstein, E. (Eds.), *Aggression: Theoretical and Empirical Reviews: Vol. 1 Theoretical and Methodological Issues* (pp. 41–74). San Diego, CA: Academic.

Furnham, A., & Saipe, J. (1993). Personality correlates of convicted drivers. *Personality and Individual Differences, 14*, 329–336.

Hansen, C.P. (1988). Personality characteristics of the accident involved employee. *Journal of Business Psychology, 2*, 346–365.

Matthews, G., Dorn, I., & Glendon, A.I. (1991). Personality correlates of driver stress. *Personality and Individual Differences, 12*, 535–549.

Mayer, R.E., & Treat, J.R. (1977). Psychological, social and cognitive characteristics of high-risk drivers: a pilot study. *Accident Analysis and Prevention, 9* (1), 1–8.

Mitchell, B. (1997). Road rage in GTA [Greater Toronto Area]. *Toronto Star, November 22*, A2.

Pedhazur, E.J., (1982). *Multiple Regression in Behavioral Research*. New York: Holt, Rinehart and Winston.

Perry, A.R., & Baldwin, D.A. (2000). Further evidence of associations of Type A personality scores and driving-related attitudes and behaviours. *Perceptual and Motor Skills, 91*, 147–154.

Roy, G.S., & Choudhary, R.K. (1985). Driver control as a factor in road safety. *Asian Journal of Psychology and Education, 16* (3), 33–37.

Sample Surveys Ltd (1996). *Road Rage: A Study of Attitudes and Behaviour*. West Malling, Kent: Sample Survey Ltd.

Taylor, B. (1997). Life in the slow lane. *Toronto Star, August 25*, D1.

Vallerand, R.J., Blanchard, C.M., Mageau, G.A., Koestner, R., Ratelle, C., Leonard, M., Gagné, M., & Marsolais, J. (2003). Les passions de l'âme: on obsessive and harmonious passion. *Journal of Personality and Social Psychology, 685*, 756–767.

Vallières, E.F., Bergeron, J., & Vallerand, R.J. (2004). A preliminary test of an attributional motivational sequence leading to aggressive driving. *7th World Conference on Injury Prevention and Safety Promotion*, Vienna, June 2004, *Abstract Book* (p. 816).

Weiner, B. (1995). Inferences of responsibility and social motivation. In Zanna, M. (Ed.), *Advances in Experimental Social Psychology* (Vol. 27, pp. 1–47). New York: Academic Press.

Weiner, B. (1996). Searching for order in social motivation. *Psychological Inquiry, 7*, 197–214.

Weiner, B. (2001). Responsibility for social transgression: an attributional analysis. In Malle, B.F., Moses, L.J., & Baldwin, D.A. (Eds.), *Intentions and Intentionality: Foundations of Social Cognition*. Cambridge, MA: MIT Press.

Weiner, B., Graham, S., & Chandler, C. (1982). Causal antecedents of pity, anger, and guilt. *Personality and Social Psychology Bulletin, 8*, 226–232.

Wells-Parker, E., Ceminsky, J., Hallberg, V., Snow, R-W., Dunaway, G., Guiling, S., Williams, M., & Anderson, B. (2002). An exploratory study of the relationship between road rage and crash experience in a representative sample of US drivers. *Accident Analysis and Prevention, 34* (3), 271–278.

Traffic and Transport Psychology
G. Underwood (Editor)
© 2005 Elsevier Ltd. All rights reserved.

16

DEVELOPING THE DRIVING ANGER SCALE

Mark J. M. Sullman[1] and Peter H. Baas[2]

INTRODUCTION

Recent research and media reports appear to indicate that incidents of road rage and angry drivers are relatively common (Vest, Cohen & Tharp, 1997; Parker, Lajunen & Stradling, 1998; Underwood, Chapman, Wright & Crundall, 1999; Oliver, 2003; Pepper, 2003). Therefore, one important question is what sorts of situations provoke anger amongst drivers. The Driving Anger Scale (DAS) is one approach for measuring driver anger, and the situations that cause anger amongst drivers. The DAS was developed in the United States by Deffenbacher, Oetting and Lynch (1994), and contains 33 potentially anger provoking situations. Factor analysis of the 33-item scale produced six subscales; hostile gestures, illegal driving, police presence, slow driving, discourtesy, and traffic obstructions.

The DAS was subsequently used to measure driver anger amongst UK drivers (Lajunen, Parker, & Stradling, 1998). Lajunen et al. found a number of the original items did not evoke anger amongst UK drivers, with the main difference being that the situations without other motorists involved (e.g. encountering road works) evoked very little anger. With the removal of non-anger evoking situations, a 21-item UK version of the DAS was produced, which consisted of; "progress impeded", "direct hostility", and "reckless driving". The "direct hostility" subscale contained the same items as the factor labelled "hostile gestures" by Deffenbacher et al. (1994), while the "reckless driving" subscale consisted of a combination of items originally classified as illegal driving and discourteous driving. The "progress impeded" subscale consisted of a combination of items originally categorised as "slow driving" and "discourteous driving". These dissimilar findings raise some doubts as to whether all 33 situations would provoke anger amongst New Zealand drivers, and also the factor structure of the DAS.

---

[1] Massey University, Palmerston North, New Zealand. *E-mail:* M.Sullman@massey.ac.nz (M.J.M. Sullman).
[2] Transport Engineering Research, New Zealand, Manukau City, New Zealand.

Although road rage does not appear to be a problem in New Zealand, very little is known about the factors that cause drivers to become angry. Therefore, this research investigated how much of a problem driver anger is in New Zealand and the situations which cause New Zealand drivers to experience anger. The factor structure of the DAS was also investigated, in order to develop an appropriate set of items for a New Zealand version of the scale. Furthermore, the data were tested for relationships between driver anger, demographics, and descriptive variables.

METHOD

Materials and participants

The data reported in this article were collected as a part of a larger survey of driving behaviour. The questionnaire measured a number of variables, including; age, gender, preferred driving speed, annual mileage, and driver anger. Driver anger was measured using the original 33-item version of the DAS (Deffenbacher et al., 1994).

Procedure

The questionnaires and reply paid envelopes were distributed at petrol stations in four urban areas (two large and two smaller centres) in the North Island of New Zealand. The researcher(s) approached almost all drivers who pulled into the petrol station. The researchers introduced themselves to the customers and informed them of the research. The customers were asked to take away the questionnaire, fill it out, and return it in a reply paid envelope. To help ensure an acceptable response rate, participants were offered the chance of going into a draw to win one of the five vouchers for a NZ$50 first aid kit. In order to be entered into the draw, they were asked to write their name and address on a separate piece of paper, which was sent in with the questionnaire, but was immediately separated upon receipt. In total, just over 1700 questionnaires were distributed and 861 responses were received, giving a response rate of just over 50%.

RESULTS

Demographic and descriptive variables

The vast majority of the participants (61.4%) were in the largest age category (26–59 years old), with just over a quarter being in the 15–25 year age group and 13.2% in the 60+ age group. Over half of the participants (56.4%) were male and 43.6% female. Participants had between 0.3 and 69 years experience driving cars, with the average being almost 22 years, and had an average annual mileage of 19,944 km/year.

Driver anger

Table 1 presents the means and standard deviations of the 33 DAS items. Unlike the British data (Lajunen et al., 1998), there were no items with means less than 1.5, meaning that all items were kept for further analysis. The single item with the highest anger rating was having someone driving very close to their bumper (3.95 ± 1.09). This was followed closely by someone behind with bright lights on (3.85 ± 1.05) and someone cutting in and taking the park they had been

Table 1. Driving Anger Scale item scoring, means and standard deviation.

Item	Mean	SD
Discourtesy		
Someone is driving very close to your rear bumper	3.95	1.09
At night someone is driving right behind you with bright lights on	3.85	1.05
Someone cuts in and takes the parking spot you have been waiting for	3.77	1.18
Someone coming towards you does not dim their headlights at night	3.62	1.05
Someone speeds up when you try to pass them	3.59	1.09
Someone backs out right in front of you without looking	3.52	1.10
Someone cuts in right in front of you on the motorway	3.34	1.12
Someone pulls our right in front of you when there is no one behind you	3.12	1.13
A cyclist is riding in the middle of the lane and slowing traffic	2.86	1.16
Traffic obstructions		
Driving behind a vehicle that is smoking badly or giving off diesel fumes	3.17	1.21
A truck kicks up sand or gravel on the car you are driving	3.02	1.20
You hit a deep pothole that was not marked	2.94	1.26
Driving behind a truck which has material flapping around in the back	2.85	1.20
Driving behind a large truck and you cannot see around it	2.49	1.14
You are stuck in a traffic jam	2.44	1.12
You encounter road works and detours	1.95	0.96
Hostile gestures		
Someone makes an obscene gesture towards you about your driving	3.02	1.25
Someone shouts at you about your driving	2.70	1.21
Someone beeps at you about your driving	2.48	1.11
Slow driving		
A slow vehicle on a winding road will not pull over and let people pass	3.54	1.09
Someone is driving more slowly than is reasonable for the traffic flow	3.27	1.04
Someone is driving too slowly in the outside lane, and holding up traffic	3.21	1.09
A pedestrian walks slowly across the middle of the street	2.24	1.00
Someone is slow in parking and holds up traffic	2.21	0.99
Someone does not move off straight away when the light turns green	2.18	0.85
Police presence		
A police officer pulls you over	2.04	1.19
You see a police car watching traffic from a hidden position	1.95	1.20
You pass a speed camera	1.78	1.04
A police car is driving in traffic close to you	1.64	0.95
Illegal driving		
Someone runs a red light or stop sign	3.44	1.25
Someone is weaving in and out of traffic	3.37	1.23
Someone is driving well above the speed limit	3.16	1.27
Someone is driving too fast for the road conditions	3.14	1.17

waiting for (3.77 ± 1.18). This ordering is fairly similar to the UK research which found that someone cutting in and taking your parking spot produced the highest mean, followed by someone driving very close to your rear bumper (Lajunen et al., 1998). Table 1 also shows the least anger provoking situation was having a police car driving in traffic nearby (1.64 ± 0.95), followed by passing a speed camera (1.78 ± 1.04). This also was similar to Lajunen et al.'s findings, as the two items with the lowest means were having a police car watching from a hidden position and a police car driving in traffic nearby.

Using the six factors identified in the original DAS research (Deffenbacher et al., 1994), the subscale means found here were compared with the US and UK findings (Table 2). This appears to show that New Zealand drivers report more anger than UK drivers on all six factors, but report lower levels of anger than US drivers on all but the illegal driving factor. As with the US and UK samples, the discourtesy factor produced the highest mean amongst New Zealand drivers (3.51 ± 0.77), followed closely by the illegal driving scale (3.28 ± 0.97). The police presence scale had the lowest mean, as it did in Lajunen et al.'s (1998) research. For New Zealand drivers the category of illegal driving was substantially higher than that found in the UK and also the USA. In other words it would seem that NZ drivers appear to be angered more by illegal driving than both UK and US drivers.

Table 2. Means for USA (Deffenbacher et al., 1994), UK (Lajunen et al., 1998) and NZ.

	Number of items	USA	UK	NZ (SD)
Discourtesy	9	3.9	2.7	3.51 (± 0.77)
Traffic obstructions	7	3.3	2.0	2.69 (± 0.82)
Hostile gestures	3	3.2	2.3	2.73 (± 1.07)
Slow driving	6	3.2	2.0	2.77 (± 0.72)
Police presence	4	3.0	1.4	1.86 (± 0.86)
Illegal driving	4	2.7	2.3	3.28 (± 0.97)

Factor analysis. Factor analysis of the 33 DAS items produced a five-factor solution. As the factors were correlated the oblimin method of rotation was used. The five factor solution accounted for 57.8% of the variance and is shown in Table 3. All factors had good internal reliability with alpha coefficients ranging from 0.78 to 0.89.

Apart from the absence of the "Slow driving" factor, the New Zealand data produced a similar factor structure to that found using the US data (Deffenbacher et al., 1994). The "police presence" and "hostile gestures" factors consisted of exactly the same items found in the US sample (Deffenbacher et al., 1994). "Traffic obstructions" consisted of all seven items included in the US factor, plus one item previously placed in the "slow driving" factor. However, this item "someone is slow in parking and holds up traffic" fits very well in this factor. The "discourtesy" factor contained seven of the original nine variables that loaded on this factor, plus a further three items that were placed in the "slow driving" factor in the original research. The three additional items ("a slow vehicle on a winding road will not pull over and let people pass", "someone is driving more slowly than is reasonable for the traffic flow", and "someone is

Table 3. Factor structure of the DAS.

Item number	Item	Factor loading
Factor 1—traffic obstruction 34.5% of variance, alpha = 0.85		
31	A truck kicks up sand or gravel on the car you are driving	0.754
32	You are driving behind a large truck and you cannot see around it	0.705
30	You are driving behind a vehicle that is smoking badly or giving off diesel fumes	0.655
33	You encounter road works and detours	0.562
26	You are driving behind a truck which has material flapping around in the back	0.484
22	You hit a deep pothole that was not marked	0.453
19	You are stuck in a traffic jam	0.432
18	Someone is slow in parking and holds up traffic	0.407
Factor 2—police presence 8.7% of variance, alpha = 0.78		
16	You pass a speed camera	0.834
11	You see a police car watching traffic from a hidden position	0.814
29	A police officer pulls you over	0.676
23	A police car is driving in traffic close to you	0.648
Factor 3—discourtesy 6.6% of variance, alpha = 0.89		
10	A slow vehicle on a winding road will not pull over and let people pass	−0.820
9	Someone is driving more slowly than is reasonable for the traffic flow	−0.810
4	Someone is driving too slowly in the outside lane, and holding up traffic	−0.742
17	Someone speeds up when you try to pass them	−0.592
20	Someone pulls our right in front of you when there is no one behind you	−0.542
8	Someone cuts in and takes the parking spot you have been waiting for	−0.540
12	Someone backs out right in front of you without looking	−0.426
14	Someone coming towards you does not dim their headlights at night	−0.401
28	A cyclist is riding in the middle of the lane and slowing traffic	−0.400
15	At night someone is driving right behind you with bright lights on	−0.394

(*continued*)

Table 3. Continued

Item number	Item	Factor loading
Factor 4—hostile gestures 4.4% of variance, alpha = 0.88		
27	Someone shouts at you about your driving	−0.937
21	Someone makes an obscene gesture towards you about your driving	−0.872
24	Someone beeps at you about your driving	−0.831
Factor 5—illegal driving 3.6% of variance, alpha = 0.82		
6	Someone is weaving in and out of traffic	0.790
2	Someone is driving too fast for the road conditions	0.780
25	Someone is driving well above the speed limit	0.677
13	Someone runs a red light or stop sign	0.665
5	Someone is driving very close to your rear bumper	0.567
7	Someone cuts in right in front of you on the motorway	0.401

driving too slowly in the outside lane, and holding up traffic") also fit well in the "discourtesy" factor. The two items that were not included in the "discourtesy" factor were "someone is driving very close to your rear bumper" and "someone cuts in right in front of you on the motorway". These were placed in the "illegal driving" factor. Although both these items could be classified as discourteous driving (as they were in the US sample), they are also both illegal driving behaviours and, therefore, also appeared to be correctly classified in the New Zealand sample. The "illegal driving" factor consisted of all four illegal driving items, plus the two additional items (as mentioned above).

Anger by gender. Table 4 shows the mean reported anger for the five different factors by gender. The relative order of five anger-inducing factors was the same for both males and females, however, there were significant differences in the means. Female participants reported significantly more anger provoked by; illegal driving ($p < 0.01$), being the recipient of a hostile

Table 4. Anger by gender.

	M (SD)		t	Significance
	Males	Females		
Discourtesy	3.44 (± 0.77)	3.43 (± 0.79)	0.219	0.827
Illegal driving	3.32 (± 0.85)	3.51 (± 0.87)	−3.281	0.001***
Hostile gesture	2.61 (± 1.08)	2.89 (± 1.05)	−3.715	0.000***
Obstruction	2.56 (± 0.78)	2.73 (± 0.81)	−3.121	0.002**
Police presence	1.87 (± 0.87)	1.84 (± 0.85)	0.565	0.572
Overall	2.87 (± 0.63)	2.96 (± 0.66)	−2.037	0.042*

*$p < 0.05$, **$p < 0.01$, ***$p < 0.001$.

gesture ($p < 0.001$) and coming across a traffic obstruction ($p < 0.01$). Overall, females reported a higher mean level of anger than males ($p < 0.05$). These findings are in line with previous research, which has also found that females report higher overall levels of anger than males (Lajunen & Parker, 2001; Lajunen et al., 1998). Males reported a slightly higher level of anger induced by police presence (possibly due to the fact that they are more likely to be breaching the law), which was not statistically significant.

Anger by age group.   Previous research has found that reported anger varies with age (Lajunen & Parker, 2001; Lajunen et al., 1998). As shown in Table 5, the average reported anger clearly declines with age in four of the five factors. Illegal driving was the only factor where this pattern was not repeated. Table 5 shows that the 15–25 year age group reported more anger overall and on the traffic obstruction, police presence, dangerous driving, and hostile gestures factors than the two age groups. Also, the 26–59-year-old age group report more anger overall than the 60+ age group on all of the five factors.

An ANOVA revealed significant age differences in overall levels of reported anger ($F(2, 850) = 20.80$, $p < 0.001$). Post hoc tests found that overall, drivers in the 15–25-year age group reported significantly higher levels of anger than 26–59 year olds ($p < 0.01$) and the 60+ age group ($p < 0.001$). The 26–59 age group also reported a significantly higher level of anger than the 60 + age group ($p < 0.001$).

A comparison of the five different anger factors also revealed significant age differences for traffic obstruction ($F(2, 850) = 10.18$, $p < 0.001$), police presence ($F(2, 850) = 11.69$, $p < 0.001$), discourteous driving ($F(2, 851) = 33.19$, $p < 0.001$), and hostile gestures ($F(2, 850) = 18.96$, $p < 0.001$). The illegal driving factor was the only factor that did not significantly reduce with age. This would tend to indicate that illegal driving causes drivers to experience similar levels of anger, regardless of their age. Post hoc tests of the four significantly different factors revealed that all comparisons were significant at $p < 0.05$, with the majority being significant at $p < 0.01$. Thus, in line with previous research there was a significant decline in anger with age (Lajunen et al., 1998; Lajunen & Parker, 2001).

Table 5. Average reported anger by age group.

	Traffic obstruction	*Police presence*	*Discourteous driving*	*Hostile gestures*	*Illegal driving*	*Overall anger*
15–25	2.78 (0.78)	2.05 (0.93)	3.64 (0.64)	3.06 (1.09)	3.33 (0.79)	3.05 (0.57)
26–59	2.63 (0.78)	1.83 (0.83)	3.45 (0.77)	2.68 (1.02)	3.45 (0.86)	2.91 (0.63)
60+	2.37 (0.79)	1.59 (0.74)	2.94 (0.86)	2.33 (1.14)	3.29 (1.00)	2.58 (0.72)
Total	2.63 (0.79)	1.85 (0.86)	3.43 (0.78)	2.73 (1.07)	3.40 (0.87)	2.90 (0.65)

Standard deviation in brackets.

Level of anger by urban centre size.   The data were analysed for differences in the level and situations provoking anger in the two types of urban centres. Table 6 shows that participants from the main urban areas reported higher levels of anger overall and across the five different factors.

Table 6. Anger by urban classification.

	Obstruction	Police presence	Discourtesy	Hostile gestures	Illegal driving	Overall Anger
Main urban	2.73 (0.79)	1.98 (0.87)	3.52 (0.74)	2.81 (1.05)	3.48 (0.84)	3.00 (0.63)
Secondary urban	2.57 (0.79)	1.77 (0.84)	3.37 (0.80)	2.67 (1.09)	3.35 (0.88)	2.84 (0.65)
Total	2.64 (0.79)	1.86 (0.86)	3.43 (0.78)	2.73 (1.07)	3.40 (0.87)	2.91 (0.65)

Standard deviation in brackets.

An ANOVA found that participants from secondary urban areas reported significantly lower levels of anger for traffic obstructions ($p < 0.01$), police presence ($p < 0.001$), discourteous driving ($p < 0.01$) and illegal driving ($p < 0.05$). Although hostile gestures evoked a lower level of anger in the secondary urban areas, this was not significant ($p = 0.062$). The overall level of anger was also significantly lower in the secondary urban area ($F(1, 858) = 12.54$, $p < 0.001$).

Anger by descriptive variables.   The correlations between the five anger factors, overall anger and the remaining descriptive variables were examined through the calculation of Pearson's correlation coefficients (Table 7). The overall level of anger was positively correlated with annual mileage (0.095, $p < 0.01$), and preferred speed (0.099, $p < 0.01$), while the length of time a driver had been driving (experience) was negatively correlated with overall anger (-0.189, $p < 0.001$). Therefore, overall driver anger was significantly higher for those participants driving more kilometres a year and lower for those drivers who had held their drivers license longer (this may be due to a very strong correlation with age, $0.968, p < 0.001$). Annual mileage was also correlated with police presence (0.112, $p < 0.001$) and discourteous driving (0.125, $p < 0.001$), meaning that drivers who reported travelling more kilometres per year also report more anger from the presence of the police and discourteous drivers.

Table 7. Correlation coefficients for driver anger and descriptive variables.

	Obstruction	Police	Discourtesy	Hostile	Illegal	Overall
Mileage	0.022	0.112**	0.125***	0.049	0.036	0.095**
Experience	−0.131***	−0.131***	−0.244***	−0.227***	0.015	−0.189***
Speed	0.021	0.110**	0.256***	0.040	−0.157***	0.099**

**$p < 0.01$, ***$p < 0.001$.

The length of time a participant had been driving (experience) was also negatively correlated with traffic obstruction (-0.131, $p < 0.001$), police presence (-0.131, $p < 0.001$), discourteous driving ($-0.244, p < 0.001$), and hostile gestures ($-0.227, p < 0.001$). This means that drivers with more driving experience reported less anger caused by traffic obstructions, police presence, discourteous driving, and hostile gestures. However, this again may be due to the fact that experience was very strongly correlated with age (0.968, $p < 0.001$).

Preferred driving speed had significant positive correlations with police presence (0.110, $p < 0.01$) and discourtesy (0.256, $p < 0.001$), while there was also a significant negative correlation with illegal driving (-0.157, $p < 0.001$). This means that drivers who report higher preferred driving speeds also report more anger from discourteous driving and police presence, but report lower levels of anger provoked by illegal driving. This is not particularly surprising, as those drivers who report higher preferred driving speeds are also likely to be the drivers actually engaging in the illegal driving behaviour.

DISCUSSION

This study found five different kinds of anger; police presence, traffic obstructions, illegal driving, hostile gestures, and discourteous driving which was very similar to that found in the original American research (Deffenbacher et al., 1994). However, the factor structure found here was very different from that found amongst the UK drivers (Lajunen et al., 1998). This is due mainly to the fact that, unlike the UK drivers, New Zealand drivers reported anger evoked by impersonal situations (e.g. you encounter road works) in addition to the situations involving another person (e.g. someone speeds up when you go to overtake them). There were, however, differences in the factor structure and item placement found here and that found by Deffenbacher et al., with the main difference being that the New Zealand data did not produce a "slow driving" factor. However, overall the differences were outweighed by the similarities in the factor structure.

The findings of this research also have implications for the later research carried out by Parker, Lajunen and Summala (2002), as they used a 22-item scale to measure driver anger in three different countries, including the UK. Their conclusion that similar situations angered drivers in Britain, Finland, and The Netherlands may be limited by the fact that the drivers in Finland and The Netherlands did not have the opportunity to rate the anger evoked by situations, which did not involve another person. Although Parker et al. (2002) found more similarities than differences, there were some differences between the three countries. Therefore, it would be interesting to test whether the items omitted from the original scale would have evoked anger amongst the Finnish and Dutch drivers, as they did with the New Zealand drivers. Future research should attempt a cross-cultural comparison using the 33-item version of the DAS.

The overall levels of driver anger reported here appeared to be higher than that found in the UK, but were mostly lower than that found in America. Female drivers reported significantly more anger overall and in three of the five different categories of driver anger (illegal driving, hostile gestures, and traffic obstruction). These findings are in line with previous research, which has also found that females report higher overall levels of anger (Lajunen et al., 1998; Lajunen & Parker, 2001). However, although Lajunen et al. found that females reported higher levels of anger on two of the three factors, and overall, these differences were not statistically significant. Parker et al. (2002) also found that females reported more anger on four of the five factors they measured using a 22-item measure of driver anger. Furthermore, in the US sample females reported significantly more anger induced by illegal driving, discourtesy, and traffic obstructions, two of the three which were significantly different in the New Zealand sample (Deffenbacher et al., 1994). Therefore, New Zealand females were similar to the US sample, in that illegal driving and traffic obstructions were significantly higher for females. However, unlike in the US sample (Deffenbacher et al., 1994) New Zealand females were not more angered by discourteous driving than males. The US research also found that males reported significantly more anger induced by police presence, which was not found here.

Participants from the main urban areas reported more anger than those from the secondary urban areas both overall and across the five different factors. Researchers have found that drivers are more likely to report anger when traffic congestion was present (Underwood et al., 1999). Furthermore, Parker et al. (2002) reported that anger induced by their "impatient driving" factor was highest in the two countries with the highest traffic density. As the main urban areas of New Zealand are more congested than the secondary urban areas this research provides further limited support of a relationship between traffic density and driver anger.

There may be a number of other possible explanations for the different levels of anger by centre size. For example, it may be that the type of individuals living in the main urban areas differ significantly from those living in the secondary areas. Those living in the main urban centres may lead more rushed, busy and stressful lives and are thus more prone to anger. In support of this potential explanation is the fact that research has found some individuals have a greater propensity to become angry whilst driving (Deffenbacher et al., 2001; DePasquale, Geller, Clarke & Littleton, 2001). In addition, research has also found that those residing in urban areas report greater life stress than those residing in more rural areas (Paykel, Abbott, Jenkins, Brugha & Meltzer, 2003). It may also be that individuals attracted to main urban areas are more anger prone than individuals living in the less populated areas of New Zealand.

There was a similar pattern with the ordering of the five categories of anger across the three age groups. Furthermore, the level of reported anger declined with age for all categories of anger provoking situations, except "illegal driving". Therefore, it would seem that drivers find illegal driving to be equally anger provoking, regardless of their age. These findings support previous research which has also found that anger declines with age (Lajunen et al., 1998; Lajunen & Parker, 2001).

As with all research that relies on self-report, this study potentially suffers the normal limitations associated with self-report. It is possible that some participants exaggerated or were modest with the truth regarding the situations that provoked anger whilst driving. However, as all participants were assured of anonymity and their responses were completely confidential, there were no external pressures preventing them from answering truthfully.

REFERENCES

Deffenbacher, J.L., Oetting, E.R., & Lynch, R.S. (1994). Development of a driver anger scale. *Psychological Reports, 74*, 83–91.

Deffenbacher, J.L., Lynch, R.S., Oetting, E.R., & Yingling, D.A. (2001). Driving anger: correlates of a test of state–trait theory. *Personality and Individual Differences, 31*, 1321–1331.

DePasquale, J.P., Geller, E.S., Clarke, S.W., & Littleton, L.C. (2001). Measuring road rage: development of the propensity for angry driving scale. *Journal of Safety Research, 32,* 1–16.

Lajunen, T., & Parker, D. (2001). Are aggressive people aggressive drivers? A study of the relationship between self-reported general aggressiveness, driver anger and aggressive driving. *Accident Analysis and Prevention, 33,* 243–255.

Lajunen, T., Parker, D., & Stradling, S.G. (1998). Dimensions of driver anger, aggressive and highway code violations and their mediation by safety orientation in UK drivers. *Transportation Research Part F, 1,* 107–121.

Oliver, M. (2003). Poll reveals prevalence of road rage. Retrieved August 26, 2003 from the http://www.guardian.co.uk/uk_news/story/0,3604,1017254,00.html

Parker, D., Lajunen, T., & Stradling, S.G. (1998). Attitudinal predictors of aggressive driving violations. *Transportation Research Part F, 1,* 11–24.

Parker, D., Lajunen, T., & Summala, H. (2002). Anger and aggression among drivers in three European countries. *Accident Analysis & Prevention, 34,* 229–235.

Paykel, E., Abbott, R., Jenkins, R., Brugha, T., & Meltzer, H. (2003). Urban–rural mental health differences in Great Britain: findings from the National Morbidity Survey. *International Review of Psychiatry, 15,* 97–107.

Pepper, M. (2003). Road rage. Retrieved August 28, 2003 from http://www.drivers.com/cgi-bin/go.cgi?type=ART&id=000000167&static=1

Underwood, G., Chapman, P., Wright, S., & Crundall, D. (1999). Anger while driving. *Transportation Research Part F, 2,* 55–68.

Vest, K., Cohen, W., & Tharp, M. (1997). Road rage. Retrieved 28 August, 2003 from http://www.drivers.com/article/169/

Traffic and Transport Psychology
G. Underwood (Editor)
© 2005 Elsevier Ltd. All rights reserved.

17

EFFECTS OF EMOTIONS ON OPTIMISM BIAS AND ILLUSION OF CONTROL IN TRAFFIC

Jolieke Mesken[1,2], Marjan P. Hagenzieker[1] and Talib Rothengatter[2]

INTRODUCTION

Anger is related to aggression in traffic, which in turn may lead to risky driving (e.g. Lajunen, Parker & Stradling, 1998; Deffenbacher, Huff, Lynch, Oetting & Salvatore, 2000; Parker, Lajunen & Summala, 2002; Deffenbacher, Lynch, Filetti, Dahlen & Oetting, 2003). Anger may also lead directly to risk taking behaviour. Although evidence for the link between anger and risk exists in areas outside traffic (Lerner & Keltner, 2001; Lerner, Gonalez, Small & Fischoff, 2003), the research that has been carried out in the area of traffic is mostly correlational and therefore leaves space for alternative explanations. For example, Arnett, Offer and Fine (1996) showed that people who are in an angry state exceed the speed limit to a greater degree than people who are not angry. This might imply that an angry state leads to speeding behaviour. An alternative explanation is that certain types of people are more inclined to both experience anger and to exceed the speed limit. For example, Sensation Seeking (defined by Zuckerman (1994) as "the need to seek novel, varied, complex and intense sensations and experiences") has been associated with both anger (Zuckerman, 1994; Iversen & Rundmo, 2002) and risk (Jonah, 1997; Jonah, Thiessen & Au-Yeung, 2001; Iversen & Rundmo, 2002; Roberti, 2004). In the present study, the effects of anger on cognitive processes related to risk will be investigated.

Two types of emotion effects on performance can be distinguished. Emotion may consciously trigger actions or action tendencies (Frijda, 1986), as is the case in aggression, or emotions may cause a bias in cognition (Clore & Gasper, 2000). A number of cognitive processes may be affected by emotions, for instance memory (Parrot & Spackman, 2000) and social judgement

---
[1] SWOV Institute for Road Safety Research, Leidschendam, Netherlands. *E-mail:* Jolieke.Mesken@swov.nl (J. Mesken).
[2] University of Groningen, Groningen, The Netherlands.

(Forgas, 1995, 1998). However, not all of these processes are related to risk taking behaviour and as such relevant for traffic safety. Two cognitive processes that are related to risk can be distinguished: optimism bias and illusion of control. Optimism (or optimistic) bias refers to the extent to which people are biased about their chances of getting involved in good or bad events. The term is also referred to as unrealistic optimism and was first described by (Weinstein, 1980). In two studies, Weinstein showed that people rate their chances to experience positive events as higher than average and their chances to experience negative events as lower than average. It is important to keep in mind that optimism bias can only be determined at group level. An individual person may rate his or her risk as lower than average and may actually be correct. However, on a group level, it is unlikely that the risk of the majority is below average.

Also in the area of traffic, research shows that people tend to overestimate their driving skills and underestimate their risk of getting involved in a car crash. Several studies (Svensson, 1981; Svensson, Fischhoff & MacGregor, 1985; Dejoy, 1989;) showed that drivers are optimistically biased: they rate themselves as more skillful and safer than the average driver, and they rate their accident likelihood as less than the average driver. Perceived controllability of the accident is a strong predictor of optimism in these studies. Also McKenna (1993) found that the optimism bias disappears when taking perceived control into account. So, people think they are better drivers only when they think they have control over the situation.

In general, people tend to overestimate the degree of control they can exert on a situation. Langer (1975) called this phenomenon the illusion of control. In her studies, the concept of illusion of control refers to situations in which the control is really absent. However, in traffic related studies, the concept is mostly used to refer to situations where the control is genuine, but the benefits of the control are illusory. Horswill and McKenna (1999a,b) found differences in preferred speed when people were asked to imagine they were driving themselves, and when people were asked to imagine they were a passenger. As drivers, people accepted higher speeds than as passengers, presumably because as passengers they thought their hypothetical driver was less able to cope with higher speed than themselves. The control as a driver is genuine, but this control does not necessarily lead to a decreased risk level.

Several studies have shown relations between emotions and these cognitive processes. Dewberry and Richardson (1990) and Dewberry, Ing, James, Nixon and Richardson (1990) showed an inverse relationship between anxiety and optimism bias: people who were more anxious about negative life events were less inclined to be unrealistically optimistic. The authors conclude that anxiety reduces optimism, and as anxiety is an example of negative affect, the authors furthermore generalise that not only anxiety, but also negative affect in general, reduces optimism.

Several studies have examined the effect of specific emotions, as opposed to general positive or negative affect, on cognitive processes. Some older studies investigated the relationship between emotions and illusion of control. Alloy and Abramson (1979) and Alloy, Abramson and Viscusi (1982) found that depressed persons are less vulnerable to the illusion of control than non-depressed persons. Lerner and Keltner (2001) found opposing effects of fear and anger on risk perception: angry respondents rated situations as less risky than fearful respondents. Hemenover and Zhang (2004) showed that anger is related to optimistic evaluations, which is contrary to the conclusion of Dewberry that general negative affect reduces optimism. The last two studies used the appraisal tendency framework (Lerner & Keltner, 2000) to explain emotion-specific effects on cognitive processes. According to this framework, people who are in a specific emotional state are likely to interpret other (not necessarily related) events in line with the emotions. For example, as anger is associated with a high level of perceived control, angry people will rate situations as more controllable and therefore less risky than non-angry individuals. Sad and fearful respondents will rate situations as less controllable and therefore as more risky, whereas happy persons will display the same pattern as angry respondents.

The general aim of the study reported here was to investigate the effect of anger on cognitive bias in traffic. An experimental design was used in which subjects either did or did not receive an emotion induction procedure. All subjects made judgements of traffic situations and the performance of the two groups was compared. The emotions that people experience and express in certain situations are different from person to person. As mentioned before, sensation seeking has been shown to be related to the experience of anger (Zuckerman, 1994). Therefore, in the current study the sensation seeking scale is included. It is a personality scale that aims to measure the tendency of people to engage in exciting or thrilling activities. Within the sensation seeking scale, four subscales can be distinguished: Thrill and adventure seeking, experience seeking, boredom susceptibility and disinhibition. It is expected that the emotion manipulation procedure works best with people who score high on sensation seeking. Another reason to include sensation seeking in the experiment, is that relations have been shown between sensation seeking and risk taking behaviour (Horvath & Zuckerman, 1993; Heino, 1996; Jonah et al., 2001).

METHOD

The general design of the study was a pretest–posttest design with an experimental group and a control group. The order of the tasks was the same for both groups and included a computer task in which videofragments were judged and questions were answered (pretest), an emotion induction procedure, and a second computer task with videofragments and questionnaires (posttest). In Table 1 the design of the study is portrayed.

Table 1. Design of the study.

	Time = 1	*Time = 2*	*Time = 3*	*Time = 4*
Experimental group (*n* = 75)	Pretest	Emotion induction	Posttest	Post-task questionnaire
Control group (*n* = 82)	Pretest	Short break	Posttest	Post-task questionnaire

Respondents

One hundred fifty-seven respondents were recruited by media advertisements in a local newspaper. They were told that during the experiment they would be asked to evaluate traffic scenarios showed on video and to participate in a traffic quiz. The sample included 70 males (44.6%) and 87 females. The mean age was 44.3 years. All respondents were holders of a driving license. The average time that respondents held their driver license was 22.5 years. The percentage respondents that drove less than 5000 km in 2002 was 35.7%, 21.0% drove 5000–10,000 km; 18.5% drove 10,000–15,000 km; 10.8% drove 15,000–20,000 and 14.0% drove more than 20,000 km in 2001.

Pretest and posttest

The pretest and the posttest were identical with regard to all variables. This was necessary because of the emotion manipulation, which will be discussed in the next paragraph. Questions were asked regarding general background information (age, gender, driving experience, etc.). Sensation seeking was measured using a 20-items version of Zuckerman's sensation seeking scale in a Dutch translation. A series of 12 videofragments was recorded using an instrumented car equipped with a video camera mounted behind the front window. The fragments showed a 2 × 2 lane highway from the camera car driver's perspective. In the fragments the following distance to the lead car that was visible on the videofragments was varied. Each videofragment was shown on the computer screen for about 15 s. After each videofragment, questions were asked regarding risk perception ("How safe or unsafe do you evaluate the situation?"), optimism bias ("Compare yourself to the average driver. Do you have more, less or the same chance of getting involved in a (near)accident in this situation?"), illusion of control ("Say, the driver in front of you hits the brakes suddenly. How likely is it that you are able to react in time in this situation?"), and behaviour intention ("How likely is it that you would drive like the driver in the video?"). Respondents answered these questions by using a 7-point rating scale, in which the lowest score meant unsafe (risk perception), more chance (optimism bias), and not likely (illusion of control and behaviour intention). After the videofragments emotional state was measured by using a Dutch translation of Izard's (1977) Discrete Emotions Scale without the subscale of disgust. Finally, general questions regarding optimism bias and illusion of control were asked.

Emotion induction and procedure

Respondents were tested in groups of eight. Each group was randomly assigned to either the experimental or the control group. The respondents in the experimental group were told that they would first watch a series of videofragments at the computer and that they were supposed to answer several questions about the fragments. They were also told that after watching the fragments, they were supposed to answer questions in a traffic quiz, testing their knowledge and understanding of traffic situations. This study, the respondents were told, was developed to see if performance on a quiz is influenced by reward. Therefore, it was told, all respondents were divided in two groups. One group would not receive any reward, the other group would receive 5 euro extra on top of the 10 euro they would receive anyway by participating in the experiment, but only if they would answer 20 out of 30 questions correctly. After explaining this procedure to the respondents, they were asked to proceed with the first part of the experiment: watching the videofragments and answering the accompanying questions. When all participants had watched all videofragments and had answered the questions, the experiment leader informed respondents that data were not saved to the network, and asked if anyone of the respondents had pressed the escape key during the experiment. None of the respondents agreed to have done so. The experiment leader then said that since the first part of the experiment (the videofragments) was very important, the respondents would have to do the task for a second time. The second part (the traffic quiz, with which extra money could have been earned) was cancelled. The respondents then did the video task for the second time. In reality, the data from both sessions were recorded without any problems. The first time served as the pretest and the second time as a posttest. It was expected that the combination of having to do a rather boring task twice, the missed chance of earning 5 euro extra and the implicit blame that the experimenter put on the respondents (by asking if anyone had hit the escape key) would induce sufficiently high levels of negative emotions.

Respondents in the control group were told that the study was partly meant to study the reliability of the scales. Therefore, they were told that they had to do the video fragment task twice. They were warned that it could be a bit boring task in the end, but they were free to have a short break between the first and second time, to get some coffee or tea. It was expected that the respondents would not experience any anger or annoyance, because they knew exactly how long the task would last and what would happen during the experiment.

Post-task questionnaire

Both the experimental and the control group filled out a post-task questionnaire. Respondents were asked whether they thought the experiment was fun to do or boring, rated on 5-point scales. Also, they were asked whether they had tried to replicate their answers during the second time they watched the videofragments (yes or no). Respondents in the experimental group answered some additional questions. They were asked whether they felt bad about having to do the boring task twice, about missing the additional award, and about being blamed by the experiment leader (all these questions were rated on a 5-point rating scale). Also, they were asked how they felt immediately after they heard that they had to do the task for a second time. Items were "annoyed", "angry" and "frustrated", rated on a 5-point scale.

RESULTS

Manipulation check

Figure 1 shows the means of the 15 emotion items for experimental (a) and control (b) group. For the experimental group, for the emotions "annoyed", "angry" and "frustrated" the means in the post-task questionnaire are displayed as well. These are the mean results of the question "how did you feel immediately after you found out you had to do the video test again?"

From the figure it is clear that the differences between pretest and posttest are small; both in the experimental and in the control group. Only for "annoyed" results showed a group × measure × sensation seeking interaction ($F(1, 88) = 4.08$; $p < 0.05$). Respondents in the experimental group who scored high on sensation seeking were more annoyed in the posttest than in the pretest. There was no difference in annoyance between pretest and posttest for respondents in the experimental group who scored low on sensation seeking. Neither was there a difference in annoyance between pretest and posttest for respondents in the control group regardless of level of sensation seeking (see Figure 2).

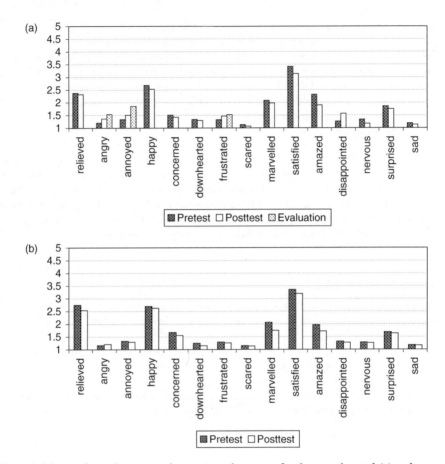

Figure 1. Means of emotions scores in pretest and posttest, for the experimental (a) and control (b) group.

From these data it can be concluded that the manipulation was somewhat effective, but the differences between pretest and posttest are small and only significant for one emotion item (annoyance). Even for annoyance the difference is only significant for the group of high sensation seekers. Also, the mean level of annoyance is in this group only 1.8 on a scale from 1 to 5. Therefore, again no differences on the dependent measures can be expected. Just to be sure, repeated measures analyses were carried out with group (experimental, control) as between respondents factor, measure (pretest, posttest) as within respondents factor and the four sum scores of the video ratings (risk perception, optimism bias, illusion of control and behaviour intention) as dependent variables. For all four dependent variables there were main effects of measure: these were all in the direction that the videofragments were considered less safe in the posttest than in the pretest. However, no interaction effects were found between group and measure, indicating that the difference between pretest and posttest was the same for respondents from both the experimental and the control group.

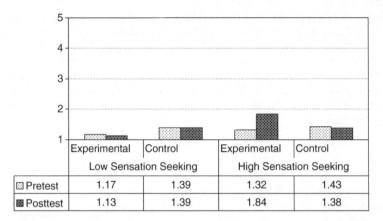

	Experimental	Control	Experimental	Control
	Low Sensation Seeking		High Sensation Seeking	
⊠ Pretest	1.17	1.39	1.32	1.43
▨ Posttest	1.13	1.39	1.84	1.38

Figure 2. Pre- en posttest scores for annoyance, distinguished by experimental group and level of sensation seeking.

Exploratory analyses

Since comparisons of the experimental groups were not possible, because the emotion manipulation was not sufficiently successful, several exploratory analyses were conducted. First, a factor analysis was carried out on the 15 emotion items, which resulted in five factors with eigenvalues over 1. Factor 1 was labelled anger/disappointment. Items measuring anger and sadness loaded on this factor. Factor 2 was labelled surprise, factor 3 was labelled worry, factor 4 was labelled happiness and factor 5 was called fear/anxiety. Together, the five factors explained 74.5% of the variance. Respondents' scores on each of the factors were saved as new variables. For each factor, a group of low scorers and high scorers was selected; respondents scoring below the 25th percentile were considered scoring low on the factor, respondents scoring over the 75th percentile were considered high on the factor. Then, analyses of variance were carried out using the new variables of high versus low factor scores as independent variables and the sum scores of risk perception, optimism bias, illusion of control and behaviour intention as dependent variables. No significant effects were revealed. This is presumably due to the fact that the negative emotion scores were low for all respondents: for example even the 25% of the respondents with the highest scores on the factor anger/disappointment had mean scores of only 2.1 (on a scale from 1 to 5) for reported anger and 2.3 for reported disappointment.

Second, respondents were divided in two groups, regardless of initial experimental group. Respondents who had turned *more* angry in the posttest than in the pretest were compared with respondents who had not turned more angry in the posttest than in the pretest. For this reason, sum scores of the items "angry", "annoyed", "frustrated" were calculated for pretest and posttest. Next, respondents whose score in the posttest was at least two points higher than in the pretest were considered "angry", all others were considered "not angry". With regard to risk perception, angry respondents showed no difference on pretest ($M = 39.2$) and posttest ($M = 39.1$) whereas not angry respondents considered the video fragments as less safe in the posttest ($M = 38.5$) than in the pretest ($M = 42.2$); this difference approached significance

($F(1, 153) = 3.7$; $p = 0.056$). Angry respondents felt they had more control in the posttest ($M = 47.5$) than in the pretest ($M = 45.8$), whereas respondents who were not angry felt they had less control in the posttest ($M = 44.1$) than in the pretest ($M = 46.6$; $F(1, 153) = 4.3$; $p < 0.05$). Finally, angry respondents did not differ much in behaviour intention in the pretest ($M = 35.8$) and posttest ($M = 36.2$) whereas respondents who were not angry had a lower score on behaviour intention in the posttest ($M = 36.6$) than in the pretest ($M = 39.9$; $F(1, 153) = 4.1$; $p < 0.05$). No results of anger on optimism bias were shown. These results are portrayed in Figure 3.

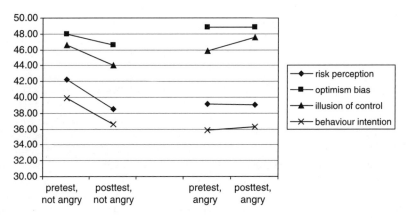

Figure 3. Scores of risk perception, optimism bias. Illusion of control and behaviour intention for pretest and posttest in relation to anger change.

A problem with this analysis is that there were clear differences between the angry and not angry respondents on the dependent measures already in the pretest, suggesting that some other variable or random variations may have influenced the results. To investigate this, the "angry" and "not angry" groups were compared on several variables. Angry respondents had less driving experience ($M = 16.1$ years) than non-angry respondents ($M = 23.4$ years; $F(1, 155) = 4.2$; $p < 0.05$). Angry respondents also had a higher score on sensation seeking ($M = 60.8$) than non-angry respondents ($M = 54.4$; $F(1, 155) = 5.0$; $p < 0.05$). Angry and non-angry respondents did not differ significantly on age, gender and kilometrage.

Post-task questionnaire

The analyses of the post-task questionnaires showed that most people thought the experiment was fun to do (79%). Only 21% thought the experiment was boring. About one third (31.2%) of the respondents felt bad about having to do the same task twice. Almost half of the respondent (45.9%) had tried to replicate their answers the second time. However, this did not result in actual different scores: the videofragments were evaluated more risky in the posttest than in the pretest and this was the same for respondents who had and had not tried to replicate their answers.

DISCUSSION

The research question of this study was whether emotion leads to cognitive bias when evaluating traffic situations. The results show that the emotion manipulation was not sufficiently successful. Although some effects of the manipulation were shown for respondents scoring high on sensation seeking, still the mean differences were rather small. As expected, no effects of emotion manipulation on cognitive biases were found.

Three aspects were central in the emotion manipulation procedure. First, respondents had to do a task twice; a task that was thought to be rather boring. Results from the post-task analyses showed, however, that most of the respondents did not find the task very boring, instead, most people considered the experiment fun to do. The second aspect was that respondents were implicitly blamed by the experimenter. Only a few respondents indicated that they felt bad about this. The third aspect was that respondents were led to believe they could win extra money in a traffic knowledge test: a possibility that was denied to them later on by the experimenter. About 40% felt bad about not being able to earn the extra money, and almost 75% felt bad about not being able to participate in the traffic knowledge test. The situation seems to be that participants liked to participate in the experiment and most were only disappointed about the cancelled quiz. They were not so much affected by the financial reward. They just followed the instructions of the experimenter, and when it turned out the experiment developed a bit different than planned, they easily accepted this change.

The post-task analyses also showed that although the effect of the emotion manipulation procedure was limited, it was stronger immediately after the emotion induction than later, when they performed the manipulation check. This suggests that if emotions would have been present, they had probably faded away when emotion was actually measured. If this has been the case and emotions have lasted only a few minutes, then they could not have affected the dependent measures because it took about 20 min to evaluate the videofragments.

Results from the exploratory analyses showed, first, that the evaluation of the traffic situations was different in the posttest than in the pretest. This measurement effect was present for all four dependent variables (risk perception, optimism bias, illusion of control and behaviour intention) for both experimental and control group. The videofragments were consistently rated in a more conservative way in the posttest than in the pretest: respondents evaluated the fragments as less safe and less controllable in the posttest than in the pretest. They were less optimistically biased about their chances to be involved in a (near)accident in the posttest than in the pretest. And finally, they rated the probability to perform unsafe behaviour as less likely in the posttest than in the pretest. An explanation for this general measurement effect could be that respondents, after evaluating the fragments for the second time, knew the range of following distances appearing in the videofragments. The first series of fragments may have served as an anchor on which the second series of fragments were evaluated. Therefore, respondents might have been better capable of making accurate judgements. Inspection of the standard deviations of the video evaluations supports this hypothesis: they were consistently larger in the posttest than in the pretest.

A second result from the exploratory analyses was that this general measurement effect did not occur for those respondents who had become angry during the experiment. These respondents gave similar ratings of the videofragments in the posttest and pretest. This could mean that the angry state prevented these respondents from adjusting their evaluation in a more risk-averse direction. It could also mean that respondents who become angry during an experiment are a different type of persons than respondents who do not become angry. The fact that there were differences between angry and non-angry respondents already in the pretest supports this. Also, the scores on sensation seeking of the two groups differed.

In summary, this study showed that although causal links between anger and cognitive bias could not be made, there does seem to be a relation between affective state and judgement. The question remains to which extent this is due to actual state anger or an underlying personality characteristic.

REFERENCES

Alloy, B., & Abramson, L.Y. (1979). Judgment of contingency in depressed and nondepressed students: sadder but wiser? *Journal of Experimental Psychology, 108*, 441–485.
Alloy, B., Abramson, L.Y., & Viscusi, D. (1981). Induced mood and the illusion of control. *Journal of Personality and Social Psychology, 41*, 1129–1140.
Arnett, J.J., Offer, D., & Fine, M.A. (1996). Reckless driving in adolescence: 'State' and 'Trait' factors. *Accident Analysis and Prevention, 29*, 57–63.
Clore, G.L., & Gasper, K. (2000). Feeling is believing: some affective influences on belief. In Frijda, N.H., Manstead, A.S.R., & Bem, S. (Eds.), *Emotions and Beliefs: How Feelings Influence Thoughts* (pp. 10–44). Cambridge, UK: Cambridge University Press.
Deffenbacher, J.L., Huff, M.E., Lynch, R.S., Oetting, E.R., & Salvatore, N.F. (2000). Characteristics and treatment of high-anger drivers. *Journal of Counseling Psychology, 47*, 5–17.
Deffenbacher, J.L., Lynch, R.S., Filetti, L.B., Dahlen, E.R., & Oetting, E.R. (2003). Anger, aggression, risky behaviour, and crash-related outcomes in three groups of drivers. *Behaviour Research and Therapy, 41*, 333–349.
Dejoy, D.M. (1989). The optimism bias and traffic accident risk perception. *Accident Analysis and Prevention, 21*, 333–340.
Dewberry, C., & Richardson, S. (1990). Effect of anxiety on optimism. *The Journal of Social Psychology, 130*, 731–738.
Dewberry, C., Ing, M., James, S., Nixon, M., & Richardson, S. (1990). Anxiety and unrealistic optimism. *The Journal of Social Psychology, 130*, 151–156.
Forgas, J.P. (1995). Strange couples: mood effects on judgements and memory about prototypical and atypical targets. *Personality and Social Psychology Bulletin, 21*, 747–765.
Forgas, J.P. (1998). The effects of mood on responding to more of less polite requests. *Personality and Social Psychology Bulletin, 24*, 173–185.
Frijda, N. (1986). *The Emotions*. Cambridge, UK: Cambridge University Press.
Heino, A. (1996). Risk taking in car driving: perceptions, individual differences and effects of safety incentives. PhD Thesis. Groningen: University of Groningen.
Hemenover, S.H., & Zhang, S. (2004). Anger, personality, and optimistic stress appraisals. *Cognition and Emotion, 18*, 363–382.

Horswill, M.S., & McKenna, F.P. (1999a). The development, validation, and application of a video-based technique for measuring an everyday risk-taking behavior: drivers' speed choice. *Journal of Applied Psychology, 84,* 977–985.

Horswill, M.S., & McKenna, F.P. (1999b). The effect of perceived control on risk taking. *Journal of Applied Social Psychology, 29,* 377–391.

Horvath, P., & Zuckerman, M. (1993). Sensation seeking, risk appraisal, and risky behavior. *Personality and Individual Differences, 14,* 41–52.

Iversen, H., & Rundmo, T. (2002). Personality, risky driving and accident involvement among Norwegian drivers. *Personality and Individual Differences, 33,* 1251–1263.

Izard, C.E. (1977). *Human Emotions.* New York: Plenum Press.

Jonah, B.A. (1997). Sensation seeking and risky driving. In Rothengatter, T., & Carbonell Vaya, E. (Eds.), *Traffic and Transport Psychology: Theory and Application* (pp. 259–267). Oxford: Pergamon.

Jonah, B.A., Thiessen, R., & Au-Yeung, E. (2001). Sensation seeking, risky driving and behavioral adaptation. *Accident Analysis and Prevention, 33,* 679–684.

Lajunen, T., Parker, D., & Stradling, S. (1998). Dimensions of driving anger, aggressive and highway code violations and their mediation by safety orientation in UK drivers. *Transportation Research Part F: Traffic Psychology and Behaviour, 1,* 107–121.

Langer, E.J. (1975). The illusion of control. *Journal of Personality and Social Psychology, 32,* 311–328.

Lerner, J.S., & Keltner, D. (2001). Fear, anger and risk. *Journal of Personality and Social Psychology, 81,* 146–159.

Lerner, J.S., Gonzalez, R.M., Small, D.A., & Fischhoff, B. (2003). Effects of fear and anger on perceived risks of terrorism: a national field experiment. *Psychological Science, 14,* 144–150.

McKenna, F.P. (1993). It won't happen to me: unrealistic optimism or illusion of control? *British Journal of Psychology, 84,* 39–50.

Parker, D., Lajunen, T., & Summala, H. (2002). Anger and aggression in three European countries. *Accident Analysis and Prevention, 34,* 229–235.

Parrot, W.G., & Spackman, M.P. (2000). Emotion and memory. In Lewis, M., & Haviland-Jones, J.M. (Eds.), *Handbook of Emotions* (pp. 59–74). New York: The Guilford Press.

Roberti, J.W. (2004). A review of behavioral and biological correlates of sensation seeking. *Journal of Research in Personality, 38,* 256–279.

Svensson, O. (1981). Are we all less risky and more skillful than our fellow drivers? *Acta Psychologica, 47,* 143–148.

Svensson, O., Fischhof, B., & MacGregor, D. (1985). Perceived driving safety and seatbelt usage. *Accident Analysis and Prevention, 17,* 119–133.

Weinstein, N.D. (1980). Unrealistic optimism about future life events. *Journal of Personality and Social Psychology, 39,* 806–820.

Zuckerman, M. (1994). *Behavioral Expressions and Biosocial Bases of Sensation Seeking.* Cambridge: Cambridge University Press.

Traffic and Transport Psychology
G. Underwood (Editor)
© 2005 Elsevier Ltd. All rights reserved.

18

BIG FIVE PERSONALITY TRAITS AS THE DISTAL PREDICTORS OF ROAD ACCIDENT INVOLVEMENT

Nebi Sümer[1], Timo Lajunen and Türker Özkan

INTRODUCTION

Personality characteristics are believed to play a critical role in accident involvement. Although a number of studies have shown that certain personality characteristics, such as sensation seeking and conscientiousness, are consistently associated with risky driving and/or high accident rate (e.g. Arthur & Graziano, 1996; Jonah, 1997), past research evidence relating personality characteristics to accident involvement has been equivocal. As suggested by Elander, West and French (1993), some methodological limitations and lack of well-established models examining the mediational links between personality variables and accident involvement play a role in the documented weak links. In this study, using the Five Factor Model (FFM) as the overarching representatives of personality characteristics, we tested a mediational model in predicting aberrant driving behaviours and accident involvement.

The FFM has been shown as a superordinate typology of "Big Five" stable, relatively orthogonal, and overarching personality dimensions (Goldberg, 1993; Costa & McCrae, 1995), each consisting of a number of sub-facets: (1) Neuroticism (i.e. tendency to experience negative affect and anxiety); (2) Extraversion (i.e. warmth, excitement-seeking); (3) Agreeableness (i.e. helpfulness, trust); (4) Conscientiousness (i.e. dependability, responsibility, self-discipline); and (5) Openness (i.e. adventurousness, broad-mindedness). As a comprehensive trait model of personality, the FFM has been widely applied in predicting various outcome variables from

[1] Department of Psychology, Middle East Technical University, 06531 Ankara, Turkey. *E-mail:* nsumer@metu.edu.tr (N. Sümer).

organizational behaviours (e.g. Salgado, 2002) to accident involvement (e.g. Clarke & Robertson, In press).

Personality characteristics and road-traffic accident

It is commonly accepted that personality characteristics underlie drivers' motivation to take risk on the road and they are closely linked with the driving style that they choose (see Elander et al., 1993; Lester, 1991). Past research on the personality correlates of accident involvement has documented a number of personality characteristics associated with accident risk. However, because of the extensiveness of these personality correlates and the mixed results obtained from these studies, it seems difficult to understand the pattern of assumed "causal" links between personality and road-accident risk. Using the trait approach in personality may help researchers better understand the links between personality and accident involvement.

From the trait perspective, initial studies using the Eysenck Personality Inventory showed that high levels of Extraversion and Neuroticism were associated with accident involvement (e.g. Fine, 1963). However, later studies either failed to show significant associations or yielded mixed results. For example, Lester (1991, p. 7) reviewed nine studies examining the relationship between Extraversion, Neuroticism, and accident and he concluded that, "...most commonly occurring results is that neither measure has been shown to be significantly related to accidents". Similarly, Elander et al. (1993) argued that the evidence on Extraversion and Neuroticism is inconclusive because differential crash involvement, especially exposure has been controlled for in these studies investigating the effect of personality variables.

A few studies directly examined the associations between the FFM and accidents. Arthur and Graziano (1996) demonstrated that Conscientiousness and road accident involvement were negatively and significantly correlated. Cellar, Nelson and York (2000) showed that Agreeableness was negatively correlated with both the total number of driving tickets and the number of accidents. In a recent study, Ulleberg and Rundmo (2003) tested a mediated model in which personality traits predict risky driving behaviours via risk perception and attitudes toward traffic safety. These researchers found that specific facets of the "Big Five" dimensions, such as altruism representing Agreeableness, anxiety representing Neuroticism, and sensation-seeking representing Extraversion, predicted both mediators and outcome variables suggesting that personality traits had an impact on risky driving behaviour via their effects on attitudinal determinants of these behaviours.

Recently, Clarke and Robertson (In press) conducted a comprehensive meta-analytic review on the effects of the Big Five personality factors and accident involvement in both occupational and non-occupational (i.e. traffic accidents) settings. These researchers used a coding method for different personality characteristics to classify them into the Big Five categories. They included 47 empirical studies examining the link between personality and accident involvement. Their findings in relation to traffic accidents revealed that three of the Big Five personality dimensions, namely Extraversion, low Conscientiousness, and low Agreeableness, were consistently associated with high accident involvement. Although Clarke and Robertson found mixed findings regarding Neuroticism and Openness and suggested a potential role of the moderator relationships between personality and accident involvement depending on the context, Conscientiousness and Agreeableness seemed to be the strongest predictors of traffic accident involvement.

Although personality variables including the Big Five factors seemed to be correlated with risky driving or accidents, as suggested by Elander et al. (1993) and Lajunen (1997), more comprehensive models are needed to systematically examine the causal links between these variables. Elander and his colleagues argued that personality variables influence crash risk through driving behaviour. These authors also suggested that personality variables as the more stable and distal elements of accident causation should be separated from the unstable and transient elements of accidents. Consistent with these suggestions, in a recent study, Sümer (2003) proposed a contextual model distinguishing personality variables as distal contextual factors and aberrant driving behaviours as proximal contextual factors in predicting accidents. Using latent variable analyses, Sümer demonstrated that three constructs in the distal context (i.e. psychological symptoms, sensation-seeking, and aggression) strongly predicted proximal constructs including aberrant driving behaviours, and in turn, these proximal variables predicted accident involvement.

Present study

The purpose of this study is to examine the contextual-mediated-model more systematically by using the Big Five factors as the distal contextual elements and aberrant driving behaviours as the proximal mediating elements in predicting accidents and accident risk. As seen in Figure 1,

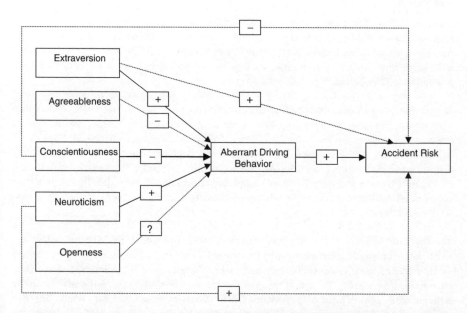

Figure 1. Proposed model linking personality variables to accident involvement via aberrant driving behaviours.

we expected that Agreeableness and Conscientiousness would have relatively strong negative effects, whereas Neuroticism and Extraversion would have relative strong positive effects on aberrant driving behaviours. In addition to their indirect effects via aberrant driving behaviours, we also expected that personality factors, especially Neuroticism, Extraversion, and Conscientiousness would have weak direct effects on accident risk (illustrated by the broken lines). The Openness factor yielded unequivocal findings in past studies (e.g. Clarke & Robertson, In press; Salgado, 2002) and conceptually it seems to have links to both negative driving style (such as sensation and excitement seeking) and positive styles (such as having a value and positive attitude). Therefore, we did not have a specific prediction regarding this factor.

METHOD

Participants and procedure

The sample initially consisted of 1001 drivers (705 male and 296 female) from three cities in Turkey (Ankara, İstanbul, and İzmir) across different age groups. Drivers were approached by a group of university students who were trained on data collection and interview techniques, and only those who agreed to fill out the questionnaire and had a driving license were included in the study. The participants were assured about anonymity and confidentiality of their responses.

Instruments

Aberrant driving behaviours. The Turkish version of the Driver Behaviour Questionnaire (DBQ) (Lawton, Parker, Manstead & Stradling, 1997) with seven additional items was used to measure aberrant driver behaviours (Sümer, Özkan & Lajunen, 2002). Participants were asked to indicate how often they committed each of the 35 behaviours in the previous year on a 6-point scale (0 = Never, 5 = Nearly all the time).

A principle component analysis with promax rotation on the 35 items of the DBQ yielded three interpretable components explaining 42% of the total variance. First component included 14 items characterizing drivers' violations. Thus, this component was labelled as "violations" explaining 29% of the variance. The second component consisted of 10 items reflecting drivers' errors that mostly include an inattention component, labelled "inattention errors" and it explained 9% of the variance. The third component consisted of 8 items, labelled "lapses" and it explained 4% of the variance. Reliability coefficients were acceptable ($\alpha = 0.87$, 0.85, and 0.64, respectively).

The Big Five measure. The Big Five Inventory (BFI: Benet-Martínez & John, 1998) was employed to measure the five personality traits. The BFI consists 44 items, allowing researchers quickly and efficiently assess the five personality dimensions—Neuroticism, Extraversion, Openness, Agreeableness, and Conscientiousness—when there is no need for more differentiated measurement of personality facets (Benet-Martínez & John, 1998). The BFI was adapted to Turkish Language by the first author following the standard translation and back translation procedure for an international project. The BFI was chosen because of its brevity and because it has proven useful for cross-cultural research (Benet-Martínez & John, 1998).

Ratings on the BFI items were made on a scale from 1 (disagree strongly) to 5 (agree strongly) for each item. Agreeableness, Conscientiousness, and Openness are represented by 9 items each and Extraversion and Neuroticism are represented by 8 items each. The Cronbach's alpha reliabilities for the 5 subscales were moderate ranging from 0.64 to 0.77 in this sample.

Demographics and accident history. Participants were asked to indicate their age, gender, frequency of driving, the number of accidents and offences during the last 3 years, the number of years a full driving license is held, and annual kilometres. Participants had a mean age of 36.28 years (SD = 11.08) and had held a driver's license for a mean period of 12.95 years (SD = 8.97). The mean kilometres driven per year was 19.142 km (SD = 25.469).

Statistical analyses

We tested the mediational model proposing that the Big Five traits predict accident risk via aberrant driving behaviours by employing the latent variable model using LISREL 8 program (Jöreskog & Sörbom, 1993). The traditional strategy among traffic psychology has been to investigate the associations between single measures of personality variables and various outcome measures including accident involvement. Unfortunately, correlations between variables may be exaggerated by common-method variance or attenuated by random error of measurement when single indicators are employed in measuring constructs (Hoyle, 1995). The current study sought to minimize these problems by using Structural Equation Modelling (SEM) with multiple indicators for two constructs: driver behaviours and accident risk.

In testing the proposed model, conventional cut-off criteria and fit indices were used (Hu & Bentler, 1999). These indices involved χ^2 goodness-of-fit index (GFI), adjusted goodness-of-fit (AGFI), χ^2: DF ratio, root mean square error of approximation (RMSEA), and comparative fit index (see Bollen, 1989; Hu & Bentler, 1999).

RESULTS

Prior to the analysis, data were checked for the missing cases and assumptions of multivariate statistics. The missing cases on major variables, which varied between 4 and 35 cases, were replaced with series means. Severe outliers that varied from 1 to 5 cases in certain variables, such as annual mileage and number of accidents, were removed and replaced with the mean of the variable. For example, the drivers reporting more than 500,000 km/year and more than six accidents were removed. Thus, the number of accidents ranged from 0 to 6, with a mean of 0.88 (SD = 1.25). Of the participants, 23% reported having only one accident, 24% reported two or more accidents, whereas 53% reported that they did not have an accident in the last 3 years. Total number of tickets taken because of various traffic offences and violations ranged from 0 to 14, with a mean of 1.49 (SD = 2.28).

Correlations among the major variables including demographics and the other descriptive statistics can be seen in Table 1. Demographic characteristics significantly correlated with

Table 1. Intercorrelations, means, and standard deviations of major variables ($N = 1001$).

Variables	1	2	3	4	5	6	7	8	9	10	11	12	13
(1) Gender (1 = M, 2 = F)	—												
(2) Age	−0.08**	—											
(3) Mileage	−0.18***	0.07*	—										
(4) Extraversion	0.10**	−0.12***	−0.01	(0.66)									
(5) Agreeableness	0.04	0.21***	0.01	0.06	(0.64)								
(6) Conscientiousness	0.05	0.31***	0.12***	0.16***	0.38***	(0.75)							
(7) Neuroticism	0.07*	−0.18***	−0.08*	−0.05	−0.42***	−0.37***	(0.72)						
(8) Openness	0.15***	−0.01	−0.04	0.38***	0.25***	0.31***	−0.15***	(0.77)					
(9) Inattention errors	0.09**	−0.12***	−0.08*	−0.13***	−0.30***	−0.38***	0.26***	−0.24***	(0.85)				
(10) Violation	−0.18***	−0.25***	0.07*	0.06	−0.32***	−0.38***	0.29***	−0.21***	0.49***	(0.87)			
(11) Lapses	0.03	−0.16***	−0.04	−0.07*	−0.27***	−0.37***	0.23***	−0.15***	0.60***	0.46***	(0.64)		
(12) Total tickets	−0.13***	−0.11***	0.14***	0.09**	−0.11**	−0.10**	0.07*	0.01	0.10**	0.29***	0.13***	—	
(13) Number of accidents	−0.03	−0.15***	0.08*	0.01	−.12***	−0.18***	0.08*	−0.05	0.12***	0.22***	0.16***	0.30***	—
M	1.30	36.29	19,143	3.42	3.74	3.94	2.53	3.74	0.42	0.95	0.85	1.49	0.88
SD	0.46	11.08	25,469	0.69	0.58	0.67	0.73	0.69	0.49	0.73	0.59	2.28	1.25

* $p < 0.05$, ** $p < 0.01$, *** $p < 0.001$. Note: Values in the parentheses represent Cronbach's alpha reliabilities. The range for the Big Five personality variables varies between 1 and 5; for the three driver behaviours 0 and 5; for total number of tickets 0 and 14; and for the number of accidents 0 and 6, with higher scores representing higher levels of these variables.

a number of variables. As can be expected, there were significant correlations between gender and driving behaviours as well as outcome variables.[2]

As presented in Table 1, examination of the correlations between the Big Five traits, driving behaviours and outcome variables revealed that personality traits had relatively stronger correlations with the three driving behaviour variables than the two outcome variables. Extraversion correlated significantly and negatively with inattention errors and lapses and correlated significantly and positively with total tickets. Both Agreeableness and Conscientiousness correlated negatively and significantly with all of the driving behaviour measures and outcome variables. This pattern was reversed for Neuroticism. Finally, Openness correlated significantly and positively with the three driving behaviours but its correlations with the outcome variables were insignificant. The three aberrant driving behaviours correlated significantly with the outcome variables.

In testing the proposed model, we used a partial correlation matrix as the input by controlling for annual km (exposure) and gender. First, we created two latent variables representing aberrant driving behaviours and accident risk. The three factors of the DBQ (i.e. inattention errors, violations, and lapses) were used as the indicators of the latent variable representing aberrant driving behaviours and the two behavioural outcomes; the number of accidents and tickets (offences) were used as indicators of the latent variable representing accident risk. The five personality traits were used as the separate independent (exogenous) variables.

Initially, a measurement model was tested to examine whether the indicators represented the assumed latent variables. As seen in Figure 2, the loadings of the indicators on both latent variables were high, ranging from 0.79 (violations) to 0.50 (number of accidents). Inspection of the modification indices suggested that the error term between the inattention errors and lapses was highly correlated, so this correlated error was added to the model. The magnitude of the correlated error between these two closely linked driving behaviours was in moderate size (0.20). All of the indicators were strongly loaded on the assumed latent variables suggesting that latent variables for aberrant driving behaviours and accident risk were sufficiently represented by the observed variables.

In testing the proposed model presented in Figure 1, we first estimated all of the possible direct and indirect paths between independent variables (i.e. the five personality variables) and mediator (i.e. aberrant driving behaviours), and dependent variable (i.e. accident risk). Following the examination of the path coefficients in this full-saturated model, in the second step, we re-run the analyses by eliminating the paths, which were not significant in the initial analyses (i.e. direct effects of the Big Five on accident risk with the exception

---

[2] We also compared male and female drivers by conducting a series of one-way ANOVAs on the major variables. Female drivers reported significantly less annual mileage ($F(1, 999) = 32.66, p < 0.001$), inattention errors ($F(1, 999) = 7.47, p < 0.01$), violations ($F(1, 999) = 35.20, p < 0.001$), overtaking tendency ($F(1, 999) = 29.27, p < 0.001$), and total number of tickets ($F(1, 999) = 6.13, p < 0.01$) than male drivers. However, they reported higher levels of Extraversion ($F(1, 999) = 9.95, p < 0.001$), Neuroticism ($F(1, 999) = 4.19, p < 0.05$), and Openness ($F(1, 999) = 22.46, p < 0.001$) than male drivers.

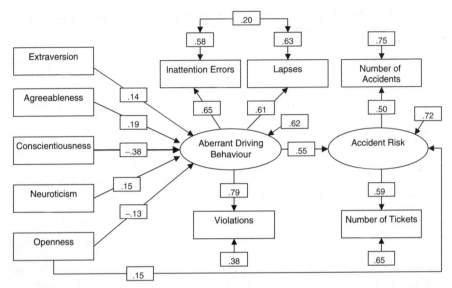

Figure 2. Proposed model linking personality variables to accident risk via aberrant driving behaviours.

of Openness). The difference between the two models with and without the eliminated paths was not statistically significant ($\chi^2\Delta(4, N = 997) = 3.2$).

Figure 2 illustrates the paths coefficients of the model with one correlated error and eliminated insignificant paths. Although Chi Square test was significant probably because of large sample size, this model yielded a good fit to data ($\chi^2(22, N = 997) = 98.61$, $p < 0.001$, GFI = 0.98, AGFI = 0.95, RMSEA = 0.06). As seen in Figure 2, all of the Big Five traits had significant effects on the latent mediator, path coefficients ranging from -0.36 (Conscientiousness) to -0.13 (Openness). As predicted, the effects of Conscientiousness and Agreeableness were negative and the effects of Extraversion and Neuroticism were positive. Openness had also weak but significant direct effects on both mediator and outcome variable (Path Coefficients = -0.13 and 0.15, respectively). As expected, latent variable for accident risk was relatively strongly and significantly predicted by the latent mediator variable (Path Coefficients = 0.55).

Supporting the mediated associations, LISREL analyses revealed that all of the indirect effects of the Big Five traits on accident risk via aberrant driving behaviours were statistically significant. Conscientiousness and Agreeableness had stronger indirect effects (indirect effects = -0.21, -0.11, respectively) than Neuroticism, Extraversion, and Openness (indirect effects = 0.08, 0.08, and -0.07, respectively). Finally, the five personality traits accounted for the 38% of the unique variance in aberrant driving behaviours. These driving behaviours and the direct effect of Openness accounted for 28% of the variance in accident risk.[3]

DISCUSSION

This study aimed to examine the mediated relationships between the Big Five personality factors and accident risk. Results indicated that all of the five personality factors had indirect effects on accident risk through their effects on aberrant driving behaviours. Predictive power of the personality variables and variances explained were moderately strong and consistent with our expectations. Consistent with previous studies (e.g. Arthur & Graziano, 1996), Conscientious-ness had stronger correlation with number of accidents than the other personality traits. Furthermore, consistent with the previous studies (e.g. Parker, West, Stradling & Manstead, 1995; Rimmö & Aberg, 1999), violations had stronger correlations with the outcome variables taping accident risk than did both inexperience errors and lapses.

Overall, supporting our hypotheses, results demonstrated that Conscientiousness had stronger predictive power than the other personality dimensions. Consistent with the previous studies (e.g. Arthur & Graziano, 1996; Clarke & Robertson, In press), as compared to the other personality factors, Conscientiousness had both a stronger direct effect on aberrant driving behaviours and an indirect effect on accident risk in this study. Low level of Conscientiousness seemed to make drivers prone to a host of aberrant driving behaviours, and these behaviours in turn lead to accident risk. In their meta-analyses, Clarke and Robertson found that Conscientiousness was significantly related with traffic accidents, but not with occupational accidents. These authors argued that "...because Conscientiousness plays a more important role where volitional control is higher, it may have greater influence over involvement in traffic accidents, where individuals have more direct control over their actions (e.g. driving recklessly or too fast for the road conditions), compared to work-related accidents" (p. 24). Similarly, Arthur and Graziano (1996) concluded that responsiveness of conscientious individuals to social responsibility and performance norms makes them engage in less risky behaviours and hence they avoid dangerous situations leading to road crashes.

Agreeableness also had a negative effect on aberrant driving behaviours and an indirect effect on accident risk. Similar to our findings, Clarke and Robertson (In press) found that Agreeableness is consistently associated with accident involvement in both occupational and traffic settings. Low levels of Agreeableness may be a risk factor in traffic environment because of its association with deviant behaviours and rule breaking (Salgado, 2002). It is plausible to suggest that those low on Agreeableness may be more likely to involve in aggressive driving and road rage, have communication problems with other road users, and break safety rules than those high on Agreeableness. Future studies should specifically examine the effects of low Agreeableness on driving aggression and its general impact on traffic climate.

---

[3] Traditionally, there are some methodological and statistical problems in analyzing accident data. One of the serious problems is that these types of data are non-normal and have a Poisson distribution. Considering that normal theory method (including ML) used in LISREL analyses has a disadvantage when data with non-normal distributions are used, we also tested the proposed model with EQS program that has the Satorra-Bentler scaled test statistic TSB to correct non-normal distributions. Results of the EQS analyses with normalization option yielded fit indices and structural coefficients very similar to the LISREL outputs reported in this study.

As predicted, both Extraversion and Neuroticism had weak but positive effects on aberrant driving behaviour and indirect effects on accident risk. This is consistent with previous research using both international data (Lajunen, 2001) and meta-analyses (Clarke & Robertson, In press). In Clarke and Robertson's review, Extraversion did not have an association with work related accidents but had a consistent link with traffic accidents. Regarding transport setting, these authors argued that extraverts would be especially vulnerable to accidents when undertaking work task involving monotonous working conditions and requiring sustained attention. However, past studies have not examined which dimensions of Extraversion make drivers more prone to accident involvement. On the basis of past findings on Extraversion, Elander et al. (1993) argued that when two dimensions of Extraversion, impulsivity and sociability, are considered, impulsivity dimension might be more associated with the number of crashes because of its connection with sensation seeking.

Neuroticism that is characterized by emotional instability, hostility, anxiety, and depression is systematically related to counterproductive behaviours (Salgado, 2002) and occupational accidents (Clarke & Robertson, In press). Previous findings regarding the associations between personality and traffic accidents have yielded either weak associations or a mixed pattern. In this study, Neuroticism was associated with more aberrant driving behaviours and accident risk. Clarke and Robertson (2005) argued that Neuroticism might be related to accident involvement because of its strong association with stress. Supporting this claim, Matthews, Dorn and Glendon (1991) found that general driver stress was positively correlated with Neuroticism and with minor accident involvement. Given the wide spectrum and multidimensional aspects of Neuroticism, it is very difficult to speculate how those with high Neuroticism act in driving environment. Future studies should examine more specific dimensions of Neuroticism in relation to road accident involvement.

Openness is one of the least studied traits in relation to accident involvement. Considering its sub-facets, we did not have a specific prediction for Openness. Our results showed that Openness was the only personality trait that had a direct effect on both latent variables for driving behaviours and accident risk. Openness had a negative effect on aberrant driving behaviours and a positive effect on accident risk. These contradictory results might be related to its multifaceted nature taping both positive and negative aspects regarding accident involvement. Clarke and Robertson (In press) proposed that high Openness might be positively associated with training proficiency so that it might be desirable for organizational productivity. Low Openness, however, would be related to an enhanced ability to focus on the task at hand. Therefore, those with low Openness were expected to be less likely to involve in accidents. Both Clarke and Robertson and Arthur and Graziano (1996) found very weak or insignificant links between Openness and accident involvement. Further research is needed to clarify the association between Openness and accident risk.

Relatively strong mediational links that were obtained between personality factors and accident risk via driver behaviours yielded support for the contextual mediated model (Sümer, 2003), suggesting that stable personality factors are the distal contextual elements whereas driver behaviours are the proximal predictors, mediating the effects of distal context on accident involvement. Furthermore, predictive power of the personality variables on the mediator and outcome variables vary depending on their contextual closure. The contextual model should be refined considering other potential mediators, moderators, and bidirectional associations between personality and accident involvement to better understand the underlying mechanisms.

Although the results of this study were generally consistent with previous research there are potential limitations that should be addressed in future studies. First, we estimated latent variables only for the two endogenous variables (i.e. aberrant driving behaviours and accident risk). However, single indicators were used for the exogenous variables (i.e. Big Five traits) without controlling for their unreliability. This might have resulted in attenuation of the path coefficients between personality traits and other variables.

Second, the number of accidents involved and offences were used as the indicators of outcome variable representing accident risk. Although factor loadings and the indices in the measurement model indicated that these two variables statistically captured the same construct, the latent variable does not directly represent accident involvement. Third, we collapsed all of the reported accidents into the same accident category ignoring the type of accidents. However, past studies showed that accident types, such as active and passive accidents, may be differentially associated with aberrant driving behaviours and personality traits (Parker et al., 1995). Type of accidents should be included in testing comprehensive models.

Fourth, although we used a large sample in this study, the sample is not representative of the Turkish drivers as a whole. The majority of drivers had high levels of education and were male and relatively young. Although we controlled for the effects of annual kilometres driven and gender in testing the proposed model, overall some of the demographic characteristics were very heterogeneous in this sample.

In general, the findings of the present study suggest that higher order personality factors have an effect on driving style that is reflected on aberrant driving behaviours with varying predictive power. These driving behaviours, in turn, have consistent effects on accident risk. Conscientious and agreeable individuals seemed to have the ability to regulate their driving behaviours and take safety cautions to avoid accidents. Extraverts and emotionally unstable individuals may be under risk especially when they fail to control their thrill seeking motives and when they drive under stress.

ACKNOWLEDGEMENTS

This study was supported by the Research Foundation of Middle East Technical University, Turkey. Grant No: AFP-2001.01.04.02.

REFERENCES

Arthur, W., & Graziano, W.G. (1996). The five-factor model, conscientiousness, and driving accident involvement. *Journal of Personality*, *63*, 593–618.
Benet-Martinez, V., & John, O.P. (1998). Los Cinco Grandes across cultures and ethnic groups: multitrait–multimethod analyses of the Big Five in Spanish and English. *Journal of Personality and Social Psychology*, *75*, 729–750.

Bollen, K.A. (1989). *Structural equations with latent variables.* New York: Wiley.

Cellar, D.F., Nelson, Z.C., & York, C.M. (2000). The five-factor model and driving behaviour: personality and involvement in vehicular accidents. *Psychological Reports, 86,* 454–456.

Clarke, D., & Robertson, I.T. A meta-analytic review of the big five personality factors and accident involvement in occupational and non-occupational settings. *Journal of Occupational and Organizational Psychology,* in press.

Costa, P.T., & McCrae, R.R. (1995). Domains and facets: hierarchical personality assessment using the Revised NEO Personality Inventory. *Journal of Personality Assessment, 64,* 21–50.

Elander, J., West, R., & French, D. (1993). Behavioural correlates of individual differences in road traffic crash risk: an examination of methods and findings. *Psychological Bulletin, 113,* 269–294.

Goldberg, L.R. (1993). The structure of phenotypic personality traits. *American Psychologist, 48,* 26–34.

Fine, B.J. (1963). Introversion-extraversion and motor vehicle driver behaviour. *Perceptual and Motor Skills, 16,* 95–100.

Hoyle, R.H. (1995). *Structural Equation Modelling: Concepts, Issues, and Application.* London: Sage.

Hu, L., & Bentler, P.M. (1999). Cutoff criteria for fit indexes in covariance structure analysis: conventional criteria versus new alternatives. *Structural Equation Modelling, 6,* 1–55.

Jonah, B.A. (1997). Sensation seeking and risky driving: a review and synthesis of the literature. *Accident Analysis and Prevention, 29,* 651–665.

Jöreskog, K.G., & Sörbom, D. (1993). *LISREL 8: Structural Equation Modelling with the SIMPLIS Command Language.* Hillsdale, NJ: Lawrence Erlbaum Associates Publishers.

Lajunen, T. (1997). *Personality factors, driving style, and traffic safety.* (Rep. No. 31.) Helsinki: Traffic Research Unit, Department of Psychology, University of Helsinki.

Lajunen, T. (2001). Personality and accident liability: are extraversion, neuroticism, and psychoticism related to traffic and occupational fatalities? *Personality and Individual Differences, 31,* 1365–1373.

Lawton, R., Parker, D., Manstead, A.S.R., & Stradling, S.G. (1997). The role of affect in predicting social behaviours: the case of road traffic violations. *Journal of Applied Social Psychology, 27,* 1258–1276.

Lester, J. (1991). *Individual differences in accident liability: a review of the literature, Research Report 306.* Crowthorne, Berkshire, UK: Transport and Road Research Laboratory.

Matthews, G., Dorn, L., & Glendon, A.I. (1991). Personality correlates of driver stress. *Personality and Individual Differences, 12,* 535–549.

Parker, D., West, R., Stradling, S., & Manstead, A.S.R. (1995). Behavioural characteristics and involvement in different types of traffic accident. *Accident Analysis and Prevention, 27,* 571–581.

Rimmö, P., & Aberg, L. (1999). On the distinction between violations and errors: sensation seeking associations. *Transportation Research Part F, 2,* 151–166.

Salgado, J.F. (2002). The Big Five personality dimensions and counterproductive behaviours. *International Journal of Selection and Assessment, 10,* 117–125.

Sümer, N., Özkan, T., & Lajunen, T., (2002, September). Construct validity of Driver Behaviour Questionnaire and its predictive power. In Sümer N. (Chair), *Measurement of driver behaviours*. Panel conducted at the XII. National Psychology Congress, Ankara, Turkey.

Sümer, N. (2003). Personality and behavioural predictors of traffic accidents: testing a contextual mediated model. *Accident Analysis and Prevention*, *35*, 949–964.

Ulleberg, U., & Rundmo, T. (2003). Personality, attitudes, and risk perception as predictors of risky driving behaviour among young drivers. *Safety Science*, *41*, 427–443.

AUTOMATION AND INFORMATION SYSTEMS

Traffic and Transport Psychology
G. Underwood (Editor)
© 2005 Elsevier Ltd. All rights reserved.

19

MIND OVER MATTER: WHO'S CONTROLLING THE VEHICLE AND HOW DO WE KNOW

Oliver Carsten[1]

INTRODUCTION

The vehicle manufacturers have revealed their long-term vision for the deployment of advanced driver assistance systems (ADAS). That deployment has already begun with the availability on the market of adaptive cruise control (ACC). ACC extends traditional cruise control by adding a headway function, so that the vehicle accelerates to and keeps its set speed unless time headway will go below a preset minimum in which case the minimum headway is maintained by automatically reducing speed. Acceleration of the lead car is mimicked up to the maximum set speed. The function of ACC is thus to replace the driver in the task of car following particularly on motorways and other high-speed roads. But ACC is just the first step in a planned path towards fully automated driving, at least on some roads and in some situations (Zwaneveld et al., 1999). This path or road map is shown in Figure 1, which is taken from an industry-led research project on ADAS. The next stage is for ACC to be extended to driving down to 0 km/h (so-called Stop&Go) and then to be supplemented by forward collision avoidance. At this point the car will be able to handle all car following situations and essentially we will have automated longitudinal control. The next stage is to add assistance systems for lateral control, including lane changes. Once a vehicle is capable of making autonomous decisions for both longitudinal and lateral control, most driving is automated. Full "autonomous" (i.e. automated) driving is achieved with the addition of a "Crossing Assistant" to aid drivers at intersections and predictive trajectory calculation.

These systems have profound implications for the human factor aspects of the driving task and great potential to modify driver behaviour, including in unexpected ways. Two immediate

---

[1] Institute for Transport Studies, University of Leeds, UK. *E-mail:* o.m.j.carsten@its.leeds.ac.uk (O. Carsten).

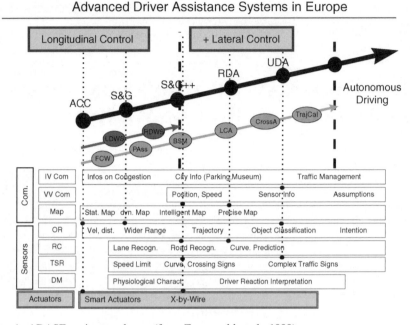

Figure 1. ADASE project road map (from Zwaneveld et al., 1999).

questions arise:

(1) How will drivers react to and respond with such systems (indeed will they respond at all)?

(2) How can we know in real time whether the driver will respond and therefore provide appropriate feedback or adapt to the predicted non-response?

In addition, a number of specific concerns about these systems can be raised:

• Will drivers understand the functionality and technical limitations of these systems?

• How will drivers respond when confronted with failures?

• How will drivers maintain their alertness and awareness when load from the driving task is very low?

• How will drivers handle the transition from virtually automated or fully automated driving on equipped roads to manual driving on non-equipped roads?

• How will driver attitudes and preconceptions influence their use or non-use of these systems?

Some, but by no means all, of these issues have been investigated in various studies (e.g. Stanton & Young, 2001), but there is a lack of systematic investigation and, influenced by lack of system availability, little study of how drivers use such systems over the long term (Saad, 2004).

WORKLOAD AND VIGILANCE EFFECTS OF SEMI-AUTOMATED SYSTEMS

With many of the ADAS systems proposed, we are likely to have underload in normal driving conditions and hence loss of vigilance and situation awareness by the driver (Endsley, 1995; Parasuraman, Molloy & Singh, 1993). With the ADAS in operation, particularly when the systems can perform both longitudinal and lateral control simultaneously, the driver's task becomes one of monitoring that the system is functioning properly. It is well known that humans are poor at monitoring, where there is a low demand for action but high demand for cognition. Lisanne Bainbridge (1987) called this as one of the "Ironies of Automation". Perhaps most dangerously, there is a potential rapid switch from underload to overload with failures and with emergency situations.

Given the potential for the driver to be out of the loop, it could be vital for an intelligent driver support system to "know" whether the driver is being attentive, particularly in situations that the system cannot handle and in the handover to manual driving. Observing that the driver is not attentive could result in a warning to the driver. Such observation could also be used to reinstate manual driving from time to time in order to increase vigilance. Ideally, the system should be able to assess all three levels of situation awareness, namely (1) driver perception of elements in the current situation, (2) driver comprehension of the current situation, and (3) driver projection of future status (Endsley, 1995). Conceding that (3) may be impossible, (2) extremely difficult, it is reasonable to look at current tools for assessing situation awareness to ascertain whether they can be applied for such real-time assessment.

There are a number of tools in the human factors cupboard for assessing situation awareness. One such tool is the Situation Awareness Global Assessment Technique (SAGAT; Endsley, 2000; Taylor, Selcon & Swinden, 1995). With the SAGAT technique, the simulation experiment is frozen at a predetermined or randomly selected time, the displays are blanked, and the operators (or drivers) are queried about their knowledge of the three levels of situation awareness. Another method is the Situation Awareness Rating Technique (SART; Jones, 2000) which uses a 10-dimensional or three-dimensional subjective self-rating. The three-dimensional scale can be converted into a single numeric value. Interestingly, one study has concluded that there is little correlation between SAGAT and SART and that subjective self-ratings of situation awareness "should be treated with caution" (Endsley, Selcon, Hardiman & Croft, 1998). But more to the point here, none of these techniques, whether direct measurement (SAGAT) or subjective rating (SART and others) is appropriate to real life driving as opposed to experimental situations using simulation.

So how could driver situation awareness be measured in real life and real time? One potential approach would be to use psychophysiological measures, provided of course it was possible to devise measures that could be collected non-intrusively. However, the state of the art here is not very promising. A recent review stated: "Very few studies have been conducted using psychophysiological measures to study *situation awareness* (SA). In fact, at this time only one such study is known" (Wilson, 2000). The sole exception is a study by Vidulich, Stratton, Crabtree and Wilson (1994) which reported that both EEG activity and eyeblinks showed effects that could be related to subjects' maintenance of situation awareness. And this study too was carried out on a simulator with the task being an air-to-ground combat mission in which the format of information was manipulated—some formats were conducive to good situation awareness, others were not. Wilson (2000) concludes: "It is not clear that psychophysiological measures can directly tap the high-level cognitive processes involved in SA…However, it is possible to use psychophysiological activity to determine whether a relevant stimulus was detected and ascertained to be important to the task at hand. Whether the information was *correctly* processed to maintain SA is not clear." In other words, such measures can be applied to identify level 1 situation awareness and to hint at level 2, but certainly not to investigate level 3. And there is no evidence of such techniques being applied in real time to driver observation.

THE NEED FOR REAL-TIME INFORMATION

In the brave new world of assisted driving, with a host of systems supplanting the driver in aspects of the driving task and responding to the current situation, there is a pressing need for the systems to have knowledge about the crucial aspects of the road and traffic environment, the vehicle's performance and the driver's skill, capacity and intentions. This knowledge should be used to understand the current situation and to project future status over the next few milliseconds and seconds. Rather than a cacophony of separate driver assistance systems operating separately, there is a need for a single coordinator or supervisor gathering information from the driver, from the vehicle and its systems and from the road and traffic environment. This is by no means a new vision. It was the guiding force of the Generic Intelligent Driver Support (GIDS) project of 1989–1991 (Michon, 1993). The GIDS architecture, as developed in the project, is shown in Figure 2.

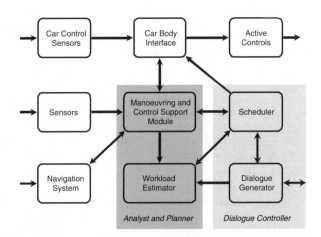

Figure 2. The overall GIDS architecture (Piersma, Burry, Verwey & van Winsum, 1993).

An extended version of the same architecture is shown in Figure 3. The extended version incorporates a "Personalized Support and Learning Module" (PSALM) which provides for support tailored to the individual driver. The version incorporating PSALM was not implemented in the original GIDS project, but was intended for development in the successor project ARIADNE. But, advanced though it was, the GIDS system was not really intended to manage interaction between the driver and various driver assistance systems. Rather, it was intended as the channel between the driver and a number of information and warning systems. Information and warnings could be provided to the driver through a variety of modes including a haptic throttle, but the driver was always to be in full control of the vehicle. The concept of PSALM itself was one of a tutoring and feedback system rather than a generalised observer of drivers' performance and behaviour interacting with a range of driver assistance systems.

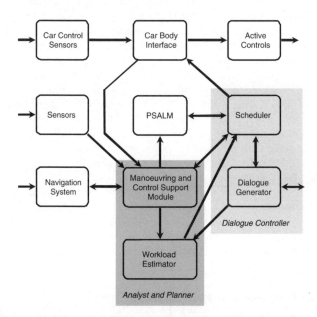

Figure 3. The extended GIDS architecture (Piersma et al., 1993).

Thus, GIDS did not really address the question of how much assistance to give the driver and how far the driver should be superseded in the driving task or the question of when to withdraw that support to increase driver attention. To address those questions, real-time information on driver vigilance is required.

There has been a considerable line of work on driver vigilance and fatigue starting with the DREAM project in the late 1980s through DETER, SAVE (De Waard, Van der Hulst & Brookhuis, 1997) and finally AWAKE (Bekiaris, Amditis & Wevers, 2001). The objective has been to create a real-time system to detect driver impairment (lack of vigilance) either using vehicle parameters alone or using a combination of driver physiological parameters, such as eyeblink patterns, and vehicle parameters. Early work showed that there was correspondence between lateral deviation and the alpha band of EEG, in that both lateral deviation and alpha grew substantially in amplitude with time on task, indicating the promise of detecting loss of vigilance from purely vehicle-based parameters (Brookhuis, Schrievers, Tarriere, Petit & Chaput, 1991). However, 13 years later we still do not have a vigilance warning system on the market. Karel Brookhuis, one of the prime movers in this research, has recently observed that "a valid framework for the evaluation of driver impairment is still lacking" (Brookhuis & De Waard, 2003). The problem of likely false alarms with systems that use vehicle parameters to detect impairment has also been highlighted (Brookhuis, De Waard & Fairclough, 2003).

Brain imaging is another promising technique. Functional Magnetic Resonance Imaging (fMRI) uses detection of blood oxygen level in the brain to provide high-resolution maps of neural activity. fMRI images can show when an image is detected in the brain's temporal cortex and when a decision on response to the image is made in the prefrontal cortex (Zimmer, 2004). One study has shown that fMRI can explain why so many people buy Coke rather than Pepsi, even though in blind taste tests Pepsi is more often preferred. In the blind test, those who prefer Pepsi showed a much stronger response in the ventromedial region of the prefrontal cortex, an area of the brain associated with reward of appetite. But in the open test, most subjects responded that they preferred Coke and this response was linked to activation of the hippocampus and the dorsolateral region of the prefrontal cortex, associated with emotion and affect. In other words, subjects were associating Coke with the brand's image (McClure et al., 2004). In studies of language ability, neuroimaging is capable of indicating the acquisition in language learning of the skills necessary to understand Mandarin Chinese (e.g. Wang, Sereno, Jongman & Hirsch, 2003) The imaging shows that the superior temporal gyrus is activated in order to interpret the complex intonations of Mandarin.

fMRI analysis has been proposed for the study of driving (DaimlerChrysler, 2001) and has even been applied, in spite of the difficulty of carrying out even limited simulated driving inside an fMRI chamber, in at least one study (Calhoun et al., 2002). However, there is no realistic prospect of collecting such data in a real vehicle being driven on a real road.

CAN WE IDENTIFY DISTRACTION IN REAL TIME?

The European HASTE (Human Machine Interface and the Safety of Traffic in Europe) project has been carrying out a systematic set of studies examining the effect of distraction on driving performance (Carsten & Nilsson, 2001). These studies have been carried out on a variety of driving simulators and instrumented cars, and have looked at driving on motorways, rural roads and urban roads. Two kinds of distraction have been considered, visual load and cognitive load, and both the amount of load in the secondary task and the difficulty of the primary driving task have been varied. The aim of HASTE is to develop methodologies and guidelines for the assessment of In-Vehicle Information Systems (IVIS).

The broad questions that HASTE is asking are how much distraction is too much (at what point can we identify significant deterioration in safe driving performance) and how do real IVIS map on to the scales of distraction and driving performance that have been determined by creating artificial or "surrogate" distraction tasks. Only the first part of the work—that assessing performance with the surrogate tasks—has been completed to date.

A large set of experiments, both on a variety of simulators and in instrumented cars on real roads, has been conducted. The approach adopted to examine driver behaviour was to require drivers to interact with the surrogate IVIS (S-IVIS) at various points in their driving.

Two different S-IVISs were used, one visual in the form of an arrows search task, and one cognitive in the form of an auditory memory task. Each task had three levels of difficulty, although for the on-road driving the hardest level of the visual task, level 3, was less difficult than it was in the simulator driving. This was because of concerns about maintaining safe driving. S-IVIS level was a within-subject factor, but S-IVIS type was a between-subject factor (except for the on-road-study in Helsinki where subjects drove with both types of S-IVIS). Timing and pacing of the S-IVIS was fixed, i.e. the tasks were system paced rather than driver paced. This was so that the "dose" of IVIS would always be known. In addition to "average" drivers, defined as being aged 25–50, older drivers aged 60 and above were used in some of the experiments.

For the simulator experiments, three different road layouts were created: an urban road, a rural road and a motorway. Within each of these roads and within a single drive, there were two levels of difficulty for the urban and motorway roads (level 1 without and level 2 with scripted events). In the rural road there were three levels of difficulty: straight sections (level 1), curved sections (level 2) and sections with events such as the car in front braking (level 3). All the three S-IVIS levels were encountered in each road level. In addition to driving with an S-IVIS, subjects also drove the road in baseline condition without an S-IVIS. The S-IVIS drives and baseline drives were counterbalanced.

The visual task was one in which the subject had to identify whether or not an up arrow was present on a screen in which both ease of distinguishing an up arrow from other distractor arrows and matrix size were manipulated to create the three levels of visual task (S-IVIS) difficulty. Overall, the findings were that increased visual distraction led to degradation of steering behaviour and of lateral control of the vehicle. Figure 4 shows the standard deviation of lateral position (SDLP) for average drivers, driving a rural road in the Leeds simulator. SDLP is averaged across all three levels of road difficulty and performance in the baseline (no S-IVIS) condition is compared with performance with each of the three levels of S-IVIS difficulty

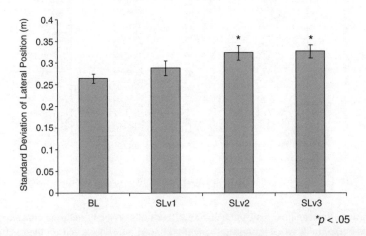

Figure 4. Effect of arrows task on standard deviation of lateral position (Leeds simulator).

(where SLv1 is the easiest and SLv3 the hardest). Performance at the two harder levels was reliably different from that in the baseline.

The HASTE experiments were intended to identify how far performance deteriorated as the driver became more distracted by a secondary task. But it is also possible to look at them in reverse: to ask if, when we observe the type of driving behaviour elicited by the visual distraction, we can conclude that the driver is in fact visually distracted such that he has his eyes off the road. It is too early to jump to such a conclusion, but it is possible that the HASTE work indicates a way of diagnosing visual distraction through vehicle performance data.

The cognitive task devised by HASTE consisted of an Auditory Continuous Memory Task (aCMT) in which the subject had to count the number of target sounds within a sequence of 15 sounds, some of which would be target sounds and others of which would be non-target (noise) sounds. Each sound was played for a maximum of 2 s, and the overall sequence took 45 s. Once again there were three difficulty levels: the subjects had to keep a separate tally of two, three or four target sounds.

The effects of the cognitive task on driving performance were very different from those of the visual task. Distraction from the cognitive task produced what at first sight appear to be *improvements* in steering behaviour. Cognitive distraction resulted in lower steering reversal rates and reductions in lateral deviation, as can been seen from Figure 5, which shows lateral deviation when driving on the rural road in the Leeds simulator. Deviation is reduced with increasing task load.

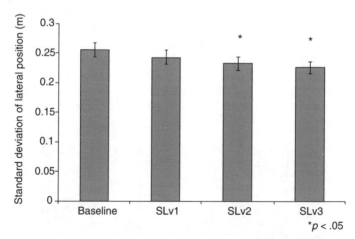

Figure 5. Effect of the auditory task on standard deviation of lateral position (Leeds simulator).

Accompanying the change in steering behaviour, there was an increased gaze concentration or visual funnelling, with gazes far less dispersed and much more focussed on the road straight ahead. This effect can be seen in Figure 6.

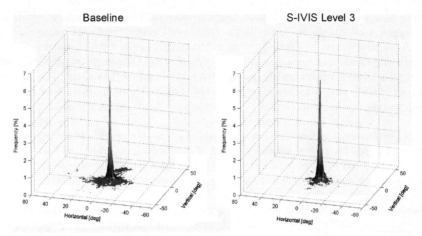

Figure 6. Spectral density plot of gaze angle, comparing cognitive distraction with baseline (Volvo simulator).

One set of field drives, carried out by VTT in Helsinki, captured interaction with pedestrians at a zebra crossing (see Figure 7). With the visual task, there are some signs of poorer interaction but with the cognitive task there is a striking deterioration. Drivers seem to be losing situation awareness, i.e. their understanding and prediction of pedestrian behaviour is affected. We do not know, since glance behaviour was not measured in this study, whether the gaze concentration effect of the cognitive task that has been noted above provides a partial explanation. But the capacity to interpret the situation and to act on that interpretation has been reduced. So the drivers may be looking, but they are failing to interpret.

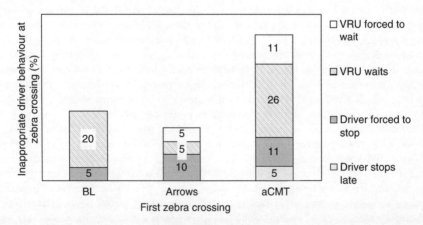

Figure 7. Interaction with pedestrians at zebra in Helsinki.

Brown (2002) has reviewed the accident causation factor of "looked but failed to see". One of his suggestions is that the factor may be associated with "limited capacity of an individual for processing information, which means there will be competition between visual stimuli for the viewer's attention". This is consistent with the effect observed at the zebra crossing in Helsinki, when some of the driver's capacity was diverted to the cognitive S-IVIS task. Perhaps fMRI analysis under these conditions might reveal whether the visual information from the scene is being processed.

As for visual distraction, the HASTE results on driving performance while under cognitive load can be reversed. The results can be conceived of as providing an indication of a method for identifying when drivers are cognitively distracted. Symptoms would be reductions in steering wheel reversals, combined with increased gaze concentration.

Of course an appropriate sensor suite for the detection of visual and cognitive distraction would have to be devised. For the vehicle-related parameters, such as steering behaviour, this is not problematic. Steering sensors are commonplace in instrumented cars. For lateral position, it would be possible to adapt the sensor systems for tracking lane markings which are the basis for lane departure warning systems, such as that available on the new Citroen C5. But what about eye movement analysis in real time? Seeing Machines' new faceLAB version 4 eye tracker, according to its product literature "enables analysis of completely naturalistic behaviour—including head pose, eyelid movement and gaze direction—in real time, under real-world conditions" (Seeing Machines, 2004). So now there is a real potential for the non-intrusive observation and analysis of driver eye movements. Whether the required accuracy of gaze direction is available without pre-calibration of the equipment is open to question, but the pace of product improvement is very rapid.

How Might we Use Information on Driver Distraction?

Of course, information on driver overload could be used to provide feedback to the driver in an effort to return focus to the road scene in the case of visual distraction and to switch attentional resources back to the primary task in the case of undue cognitive load from a secondary task. Whether such feedback would be effective requires further research. But there are also other more indirect applications for such diagnostic tools. Referring back to the manufacturers' roadmap in Figure 1, the next system for rollout is forward collision warning (FCW). One of the problems with FCW could be the perception by the driver that warnings are false, which may lead to ignoring critical warnings. False warnings are not just a problem of system reliability; they are also a problem of perceived appropriateness. A warning that occurs when the driver has his or her eyes on the road and when that driver has fully absorbed the seriousness of the situation may be treated as inappropriate because that driver is confident of being able to handle the situation. The same warning may be welcomed when that driver has his or her eyes off the road for whatever reason or when the driver's eyes are on the road but the situation is not being processed because of cognitive distraction. Thus, appropriate sensing systems for detecting visual or cognitive distraction could be of great utility in developing adaptive FCW systems. Such adaptive systems would warn the driver only when he or she truly required the warning.

CONCLUSIONS

We may not yet be able to use brain imaging inside a car being driven on a real road, but there are other ways to interpret not what the driver is thinking but at least how much the driver is seeing and thinking and whether those processes are related to the road scene or to something extraneous. In other words, we can use inference to determine, perhaps not what the driver is thinking, but at least how much the driver is thinking and whether the driver is concentrating on the road scene. We are very close to being able to apply sensor systems to assess loss of situation awareness in driving, and therefore being able to deploy strategies to maintain situation awareness, including perhaps warnings to the driver. Knowledge of driver vigilance could also be used to create adaptive automation in which drivers were brought back into the loop from time to time in order to maintain arousal. The HASTE results on driver distraction offer the promise of sensor systems that can identify when the driver is visually or cognitively distracted and that sensor information could be applied to tune collision warnings, so that they occur when truly needed and not when they are likely to be perceived as an annoyance.

REFERENCES

Bainbridge, L. (1987). Ironies of automation. In Rasmussen, J., Duncan, K., & Leplat, J. (Eds.), *New Technology and Human Error*. New York: Wiley.

Bekiaris, E., Amditis, A., & Wevers, K. (2001). *Advanced driver monitoring: the AWAKE project, Proceedings of the Eighth World Congress on Intelligent Transport Systems, Sydney, Australia.*

Brookhuis, K.A., & De Waard, D. (2003). On the assessment of criteria for driver impairment: in search of the golden yardstick for driving performance. *Proceedings of Driving Assessment 2003, the 2nd International Driving Symposium on Human Factors in Driver Assessment, Training and Vehicle Design*, Park City, Utah.

Brookhuis, K.A., Schrievers, G., Tarriere, C., Petit, C., & Chaput, D. (1991). *Monitoring driver status through in-vehicle parameters, Advanced Telematics in Road Transport: Proceedings of the DRIVE Conference*. Amsterdam: Elsevier.

Brookhuis, K.A., De Waard, D., & Fairclough, S.H. (2003). Criteria for driver impairment. *Ergonomics, 46* (5), 433–445.

Brown, I.D. (2002). *A review of the "looked but failed to see" accident causation factor, Behavioural Research in Road Safety: Eleventh Seminar*. London: Department for Transport, Local Government and the Regions.

Calhoun, V.D., Pekar, J.J., McGinty, V.B., Adali, T., Watson, T.D., & Pearlson, G.D. (2002). Different activation dynamics in multiple neural systems during simulated driving. *Human Brain Mapping, 16*, 158–167.

Carsten, O.M.J., & Nilsson, L. (2001). Safety assessment of driver assistance systems. *European Journal of Transport and Infrastructure Research, 1* (3), 225–243.

DaimlerChrysler (2001). Keeping an eye on the brain. *Hightech Report 2001*, 44–47.

De Waard, D., Van der Hulst, M., & Brookhuis, K. (1997). The detection of driver inattention and breakdown. In Albuquerque, P., Santos, J.A., Rodrigues, C., & Pires da Costa, A.H. (Eds.), *Human Factors in Road Traffic II: Traffic Psychology and Engineering*. Braga, Portugal: Universidade do Minho.

Endsley, M.R. (1995). Toward a theory of situation awareness in dynamic systems. *Human Factors, 37* (1), 65–84.

Endsley, M.R. (2000). Direct measurement of situation awareness: validity and use of SAGAT. In Endsley, M.R., & Garland, D.R. (Eds.), *Situation Awareness Analysis and Measurement*. Mahwah, NJ: Lawrence Erlbaum Associates.

Endsley, M.R., Selcon, S.J., Hardiman, T.D., & Croft, D.G. (1998). A comparative analysis of SAGAT and SART for evaluations of situation awareness. *Human Factors and Ergonomics Society 42nd Annual Meeting*, October, Chicago.

Jones, D.G. (2000). Subjective measures of situation awareness. In Endsley, M.R., & Garland, D.R. (Eds.), *Situation Awareness Analysis and Measurement*. Mahwah, NJ: Lawrence Erlbaum Associates.

McClure, S.M., Li, J., Tomlin, D., Cypert, K.S., Montague, L.M., & Montague, P.R. (2004). Neural correlates of behavioral preference for culturally familiar drinks. *Neuron, 44* (2), 379–387.

Michon, J.A. (Ed.) (1993). *Generic Intelligent Driver Support: A Comprehensive Report on the GIDS Project*. London: Taylor & Francis.

Parasuraman, R., Molloy, R., & Singh, I.L. (1993). Performance consequences of automation-induced "complacency". *International Journal of Aviation Psychology, 3* (1), 1–23.

Piersma, E.H., Burry, S., Verwey, W.B., & van Winsum, W. (1993). GIDS architecture. In Michon, J.A. (Ed.), *Generic Intelligent Driver Support: A Comprehensive Report on the GIDS Project*. London: Taylor & Francis.

Saad, F. (2004). Behavioural adaptations to new driver support systems: some critical issues. *International Conference on Systems, Man and Cybernetics* (IEEE SMC 2004), October 10–13, The Hague.

Seeing Machines (2004). http://www.seeingmachines.com/facelab.htm. Accessed 23 November 2004.

Stanton, N.A., & Young, M.S. (2001). *Developing a psychological model of the driver*, *Behavioural Research in Road Safety: Tenth Seminar*. London: Department for Transport, Local Government and the Regions.

Taylor, R.M., Selcon, S.J., & Swinden, A.D. (1995). Measurement of situational awareness and performance. In Fuller, R., Johnston, N., & McDonald, N. (Eds.), *Human Factors in Aviation Operations*. Aldershot: Avebury.

Vidulich, M.A., Stratton, M., Crabtree, M., & Wilson, G. (1994). Performance-based and physiological measures of situational awareness. *Aviation, Space and Environmental Medicine, 65* (5 Suppl.), A7–A12.

Wang, Y., Sereno, J.A., Jongman, A., & Hirsch, J. (2003). fMRI evidence for cortical modification during learning of mandarin lexical tone. *Journal of Cognitive Neuroscience, 15* (7), 1019–1027.

Wilson, G.F. (2000). Strategies for psychophysiological assessment of situation awareness. In Endsley, M.R., & Garland, D.R. (Eds.), *Situation Awareness Analysis and Measurement*. Mahwah, NJ: Lawrence Erlbaum Associates.

Zimmer, C. (2004). *Thomas Willis, The English Civil War and The Mapping of the Mind*. London: William Heinemann.

Zwaneveld, P.J., van Arem, B., Bastiaensen, E.G.H.J., Soeteman, J.J., Frémont, G., Bélarbi, F., Ulmer, B., Bonnet, C., & Gölliger, H. (1999). *Deployment Scenarios for Advanced Driver Assistance Systems*. Report Inro/VK 1999-07. TNO Inro, Delft, The Netherlands.

Traffic and Transport Psychology
G. Underwood (Editor)
© 2005 Elsevier Ltd. All rights reserved.

20

ADAPTATION EFFECTS IN AN AUTOMATED CAR-FOLLOWING SCENARIO

Eva-Maria Eick[1] and Guenter Debus[1]

INTRODUCTION

Full vehicle automation is predicted to be on British roads by 2030 (Walker, Stanton, & Young, 2001). Systems that support or automate parts of the driving task already appeared on the market. Automation of road traffic, in particular truck convoys, has the potential to greatly improve the performance of traffic systems. Benefits of an automated highway system (AHS) which is defined in general as "a system that combines vehicle and roadway instrumentation to provide some level of automated ("hands-off/feet-off") driving" (Levitan & Bloomfield, 1998) include, for example: increased efficiency, predictable journey times or reduced environmental pollution due to a decrease in fossil fuel consumption and emission. In contrast, there may be also some concerns regarding the driver's behaviour and his acceptance for such systems. Behavioural aspects of automatic vehicle guidance are the main focus of this chapter addressing in particular the small headway (THW) during automated driving periods and the effects on post-automated manual driving.

INITIAL POINT

The effects of automated traffic in Germany are analysed by departments of the Aachen University within several projects (e.g. EFAS[2]). The research group deals with the possibility of an automated convoy system in Germany. The idea is to couple two or more trucks with systems that allow automated driving. The vehicle in the leading position will be followed by other vehicles at a very small distance of less than 10 m. In terms of estimation of technological consequences and on the basis of a wide range of previous research on driving assistance,

---

[1] Institut für Psychologie Der RWTH-Aachen, Jägerstraße 17–19, 52066 Aachen, Germany. *E-mail:* evamaria. eick@post.rwth-aachen.de (E.-M. Eick).
[2] EFAS = Einsatzszenarien für Fahrerassistenzsysteme im Güterverkehr und deren Bewertung.

insights in the framework were gained from the initial project EFAS (see Henning & Preuschoff, 2003). The project assessed the potential of both positive and negative effects of automated traffic for truck convoys in the whole transport system. A following project (KONVOI[3]) is in progress and aims at testing and evaluating automated truck traffic in several field and simulator experiments. As Program for a European Traffic with Highest Efficiency and Unprecedented Safety (PROMETHEUS) and CHAUFFEUR (Schulze, 1997) are two of the industrial precursor projects, cooperation with these research groups is in progress as well.

QUESTION

In case of realization of those traffic scenarios the role of the driver will be completely different from what it is now. The question we took up was whether the small gaps during automated driving periods cause carry-over effects in form of too small THW (distance/velocity) during subsequent manual driving. What will the effects be on manual driving following an extended period of automated travelling with gaps considerably smaller than usual? THW during automated coupling is declared by less than 10 m which is 0.3 s time headway while driving with 100 km/h. Common THW are 1.0 s; the German law recommends THW of 1.8 s. Carry-over effects after driving on German highways with high speed are a well-established phenomenon: people get used to the high speed and are not aware of the hazard of high-speed driving after leaving the highway. Our point of interest was whether similar adaptation effects can be observed concerning the distance to the vehicle in front after driving in the automated modus.

Different phenomena are subsumed under the term of behavioural adaptation and will be illustrated in Chapter 21.

BEHAVIOURAL ADAPTATION AND AUTOMATED DRIVING — EMPIRICAL FINDINGS

In the current literature, behavioural adaptation is picked out as a central theme in the context of driver assistance systems. A brief overview is given by Dragutinovic, Brookhuis, Hagenzieker, and Marchau (2004). Studies from Heino, Rothengatter, and Van der Hulst (1995), for example, found that driving with an ACC decreased THW and variability in headway. Ward, Fairclough, and Humphreys (1995) found evidence for behavioural adaptation in form that drivers set the ACC at higher speeds and at shorter headways compared to unsupported driving. De Waard, Van der Hulst, Hoedemaker, and Brookhuis (1999) found large complacency within the AHS: in an emergency condition where the automated system failed to function properly and the driver had to take over speed control to avoid uncomfortable short headways only half of the participants took over control. This defaulted behaviour may be interpreted as a form of behavioural adaptation. Levitan and Bloomfield (1998) determined human factor aspects of the transfer of control from the AHS to the driver. They conclude that there may be carry-over effects on speed if drivers are given control over their vehicles at relatively high speeds (153 km/h in their study) in the automated lane: drivers may drive much faster than the

---

[3] KONVOI = Einsatz und Evaluierung von Lkw-Konvois im Straßengüterverkehr.

indicated speed limit when they enter the unautomated lane. Grayson (1996) published a report in the form of a commentary on behavioural response to safety measures, based on an extensive review of the literature. Grayson concludes that there is little evidence to support the contention that adaptation processes routinely act to reduce or nullify the effect of safety measures. All these findings are consistent with the definition for behavioural adaptation published by the OECD Research Group in 1990:

Behavioural adaptations are those behaviours which may occur following the introduction of changes to the road–vehicle–user system and which were not intended by the initiators of the change; behavioural adaptations occur as road users respond to changes in the road transport system such that their personal needs are achieved as a result; they create a continuum of effects ranging from a positive increase in safety to a decrease in safety.   (OECD, 1990).

THEORETICAL APPROACHES FOR BEHAVIOURAL ADAPTATION AND AUTOMATED DRIVING

Theoretical explanations of changes in road-user behaviour following the introduction of new measures have been proposed by Fuller, Summala or Wilde (for references see Grayson (1996)). The following remarks are not responsive to these theories but will suggest two approaches in Chapter 21. The two approaches are able to take into account the input and output of driving operations. Adaptation effects may be caused by *perception*, for example, through changing the frame of reference or through a more *action*-based component, for example through a situation-dependent inertia of the human system.

The first approach, focusing on *perception* follows from psychophysics and explains adaptation as a context effect through changing ones frame of reference (e.g. Helson, 1947, 1964). An important factor affecting perception is the external context in which a stimulus is judged. For example, a man 6 ft in height will look "tall" when surrounded by others of average height, and "short" among a group of professional basketball players. Context alters apparent size. In addition to external contexts, we all have internal frames of reference or standards by which stimuli are judged. The approach of adaptation-level theory and frame-of-reference effects is much broader and more detailed than illustrated above. Detailed mathematical models exist, but the remarks above will only give an idea of how to explain adaptation phenomena. Sensory adaptation may be caused by a continuous confrontation with one stimulus pattern ("lack of stimulus change") that leads to reduction in perceptual abilities. Many studies in the context of psychoacustic or haptic stimuli have been performed also in applied settings (Lauterbach & Sarris, 1980) but a transmission to the traffic context is yet missing. In the terminology of research on adaptation and driver assistance systems subjects may change their frame of reference during the automated mode and thus show different distance behaviour afterwards. In detail, subjects change their judgement of, for example, speed after long fast driving periods on highways. The "wrong" speed estimation leads to risky fast driving on highway exits and on connected country roads. High accident rate on these traffic points is one consequence.

The second approach is more *action*-oriented and follows task-switching theories (e.g. Allport, Styles, & Hsieh, 1994). Very often, experiments require the subject to maintain a given task over many trials, in which the same cognitive operations are to be performed repeatedly.

The term "task set" refers to the "effective intention to perform a particular task, regardless of which out of the range of task-relevant stimuli will occur" (Rogers & Monsell, 1995, p. 207). In everyday activity, on the contrary, subjects often shift rapidly, and repeatedly, from one intended cognitive operation to another, for example when driving a car. One question Allport and collegues and many other researchers (e.g. Mayr & Keele, 2000) took up was how the cognitive system is reconfigured to enable now one task to be performed, now another. Allport et al. demonstrate with series of experiments that shift costs appear during shifting from one task set to another, and that the shift costs represent a form of proactive inference from features of the task set implemented in preceding tasks. Mayr & Keele (2000) show that to implement a new task set, the previous task set must be inhibited and call that "backward inhibition". As an expression of backward inhibition the authors predicted increased response times when shifting to a task set that had to be abandoned recently and, thus, suffers residual inhibition. The critical backward inhibition effect on the level of abstractly defined perceptual task sets was obtained across several different experiments. Those reaction time based experiments are of course not comparable with those complex actions required during car driving. But the processes may be identical and thus the idea is transferable from the micro level to the macro level of car driving: during post-manual driving periods subjects still have activated their "old" task set. After turning into the manual modus, they carry on with their behavioural patterns from the automated modus. It is assumed that subjects adopt the task set even though it is from an automated modus and, therefore, a passive control of the car.

THREE STUDIES ABOUT THE EFFECTS OF VEHICLE AUTOMATION UPON DRIVING PERFORMANCE

Three studies have been accomplished to analyse the risks of automated traffic. The objective of the *first study* was to identify the effect of small gaps during automated driving on subsequent manual driving. In driving simulations subjects were confronted with automated and non-automated driving periods within a convoy. During automated phases the cars were coupled with extremely short time headways up to 0.3 s (8 m while driving with 100 km/h). Our interest was to identify whether subjects change their distance behaviour after having been confronted with those small gaps, which are realistic for automated driving. The interest was further to replicate the effect in successive driving sessions. Therefore, the habitual distance behaviour shown in the baseline was compared with post-automated distance behaviour in three driving blocks.

METHOD

As the method is comparable for all three studies the main characteristics will be described only once: in each of the three studies male and female students from the University of Wuerzburg took part. The number varied between 12 and 16 subjects. They were all trained simulator drivers. None of the *subjects* had taken part in a distance experiment in the past. Subjects were paid for their participation. The *simulator* experiment was conducted at the Center for Traffic Sciences Wuerzburg (IZVW). The internal space of the used driving simulator was identical to a BMW. The simulator consists of 11 personal computers with a 180° front projection system, 3 rear projections and a 6–6 Stewart platform. The moving system is of high importance because the studies aim at observing perceptual components of the driving task.

The automated driving task

The two systems that were used during automated driving are ACC and Heading Control (HC). An ACC is a system that is capable of maintaining a fixed time headway behind slower vehicles, as an added value to the conventional Cruise Control function of controlling a vehicle's speed at a driver-chosen level. The time headway is kept by adjusting the speed of the car to prevent exceeding a programmed headway of the system dependent on speed. An HC system is a system that assists the driver in his tracking task. The driver is moved back in the centre of the lane by the system in case of breaking out of the lane. The two systems were activated together to reach an acceptable level of automation during automated driving periods. Subjects had to absolve a minimal rest-task of steering. Realizing a full-automated driving task with not only "feet-off" but also "hands-off" was not possible because of technical restrictions of the simulator software. The automated driving period ended by deactivation of both systems step by step. During this decoupling the velocity of the following car was diminished and, therefore, the distance to the front car (which drove with constant speed) was enlarged. After ensuring that subjects had taken over the control they were reminded to follow the car in the front with free chosen distance and velocity. Measurement of THW first started at the point subjects accelerated autonomously to reach the car in the front. According to Endsley (1997) the degree of automation was in the middle of the 10-step scale because subject's tasks were monitoring and also minimal steering. They were always able to overtake the control of the car by over-ruling the systems.

The manual driving task

Subjects were instructed to follow the car in front of them in order to reach a destination, which was the same for all convoy-participants. The subjects were told, that the only person who knows the way would be the driver in the front. Overtaking was not allowed. The roadway had a few curves but headways of 4–5 s were sufficient to perform the instructed car-following. Thus, the driver was almost free in his choice of distance and velocity. As in the automated period, the driver has to follow a car but now regulating THW by himself. THW measures in post-automated driving periods should be ascertained not before the driver produces his autonomous distance in form of accelerating or decelerating up to the front car. The distance to the front car is enlarged to a multiple if the front car keeps on driving with his constant speed. Hence, measurement of THW in the manual driving period does not start before the following car tries to close on the front car. The first acceleration act marks the beginning of the measurement.

Experimental design

The experimental design varied in the three studies but the main course of action was comparable (see Figure 1): in the beginning of each block the subjects were following a car that drove with constant speed (100 km/h), choosing their individual time headways: the measured time headway is the baseline of each driver. After 12 km the two cars were coupled and the automated driving period was initiated with time headways of 0.3 s. The automated coupling period lasted for 33 km. During a decoupling period the gap between the cars was enlarged and free manual car-following took place the end of each block. Our interest was the difference of the free chosen time headway before and after automated driving periods. In the first study, all subjects had to complete three driving blocks in the described course of action, in the second study the automated driving period was experimentally varied between three blocks, in the third study subjects drove one large block with variations.

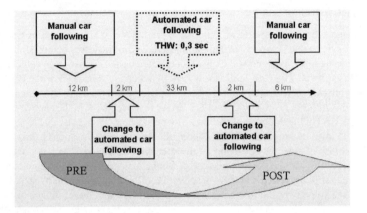

Figure 1. The experimental design of the studies.

Data collection and relevant variables

Variables recorded by the simulator-software were traffic variables (e.g. oncoming traffic) and behavioural parameters (e.g. distance, speed, gas pedal movements). For the main question, the most important variables were distance and velocity. Distance and velocity data were collected with a frequency of 100 Hz. The first two kilometres of each manual driving period in the beginning of each block were predefined as exercising driving periods.

Distance and velocity during driving is never constant (Wille & Debus, 2004). The graphic below exemplifies the variability that exists during normal car-following; the front car drives at constant speed (Figure 2).

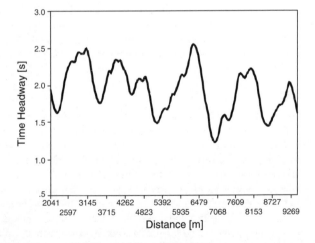

Figure 2. Time headway variability during car-following.

Even though the front car drives at constant speed (100 km/h) continuous acceleration and deceleration of the following car is observable. The results presented below demonstrate the minima and the lowest tercil of time headway variation as they illustrate the sphere of interest for reference of application. For each block and study independent variables were represented by the measuring period (pre-automated—post-automated), the dependent variable was THW.

The main result of the first study was that subjects drove with significantly smaller gaps after having been coupled (Figure 3).

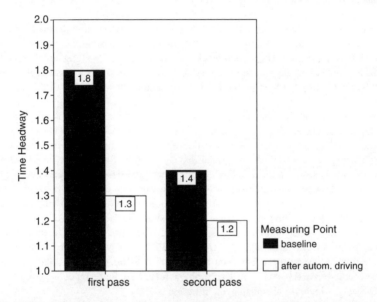

Figure 3. THW during pre- and post-automated driving (from Eick & Debus, 2004).

Analyses of the subjects' minimum time headway demonstrate even more risky driving during car-following in general and also a comparable reduction of the chosen time headway after automated driving. Minima in the pre-automated driving periods range from 0.3 to 2.4 s whereas minima in the post-automated driving period range from 0.17 to 1.96 s (for details see Eick, Wille, and Debus (2003)).

At this point there is evidence for risky time headway when driving with small gaps, but we are not able yet to conclude which factors caused the demonstrated effects. Driving with small gaps as a consequence of the coupling period may be mediated by several factors and may involve different psychological processes: the coupling and decoupling procedure itself may have a short-term effect. In addition, coupling per se and in difference, coupling with short gaps over time may have own effects. The nature of the effects is of great interest: are the effects short-lived and transient or stable, are they rather perceptually based or rather response-based? Answers to these questions are necessary for implementing adequate risk-preventing solutions within the man–machine interaction (MMI). Brookhuis & de Waard (1991) detected significant reduced time headways after long periods of driving. Therefore, "time-on-task" is another factor that must be verified. Consequently, a second simulator experiment was designed and executed in consideration of the mentioned factors.

The *second study*, therefore, aims at the characteristic of the adaptation phenomenon observed in the first study. Within the experimental design we tried to operationalize the three main questions of the causation of the observed adaptation effect: which role does time on task play? Is the degree of coupling distance of importance? Is the duration of the coupling period of importance? In addition, a replication of the data of the first study was aimed at.

The mean driving period (in the first study always automated driving with small gaps) differed between the three blocks. In the first block, two coupling-demonstrations framed a long period of manual driving (33 km). The second block was characterized by a long coupling period with individually convenient gaps (ascertained in block 1). The third block was a replication of the first study: people drove a long period (33 km) automatically with THW of 0.3 s.

Observing a replication of the results of the first experiment the data displays that people reduced their distance to the car in the front after driving automatically ($F[1] = 4.9; p < 0.06$). Comparable reduction of THW as in the first study was found. Driving with individually comfortable gaps had no effect on manual driving periods. Subjects indicated a diminutive increase of time headway after coupling periods. This condition explicitly shows that subjects do not always show reduced time headways after having been coupled. The results of block 1 confirmed the alternative hypothesis that it is not necessarily the long-lasting driving period with short THW but the coupling per se: subjects show significantly smaller time headways after the first and second short coupling demonstration. The first coupling demonstration led to time headway values around 1.2 s ($F[1] = 5.852; p < 0.05$) (Figure 4a), the second demonstration increased the effect even more ($F[1] = 9.160; p < 0.05$). The time headway decreased again (up to 0.9 s) (Figure 4b). Similar effects were found by considering the minima of the subjects, which are also displayed in Figure 4.

When successively analysing the extensive manual driving period in block 1, time-on-task effects were not found.

The results of the second study affirm the effects found in experiment one. In addition to long-term adaptation effects, a short-term responsiveness to coupling was found. It is yet to be proven how long the observed effects last while driving in the manual modus. No time-on-task effect was identified in our studies, but we are not able to obviate such effects in more expanded (manual) driving periods than used in our experimental design.

The results of the first and the second study still leave some answers open about the causing factors: is the effect caused by perception, for example, through changing the frame of reference? Or is the effect more action-based, for example, through a situation-dependent inertia of the human system. The *third study* addressed the question of the frame of reference. Subject's judgement about different distances was observed and evaluated by coupling them with low or high series of distances. One question was whether the frame of reference is fixed or manipulable. The expectation was that the treatment group confronted with the low series rates small distances less aversive than the treatment group confronted with the high

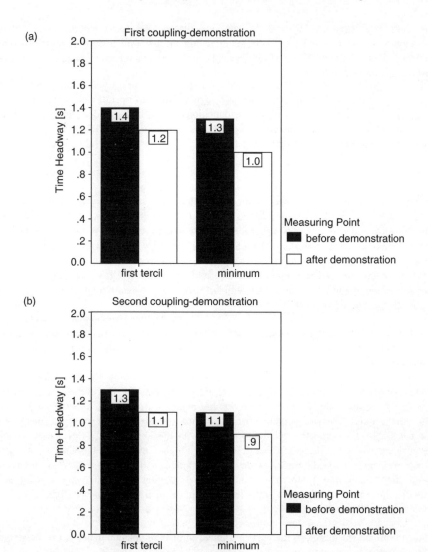

Figure 4. (a,b) THW after first and second coupling-demonstration (Eick et al., 2003).

series. Of interest was also the time headway behaviour after the confrontation with the series. The expectation was that the different judgements of the treatment groups do have an effect on the driving behaviour. The free chosen distance after having been confronted is probably influenced by the subject's judgement.

We tried to induce a certain frame of reference by coupling subjects in series: one subject group was coupled with very small distances, 0.3 s up to 1.2 s and another group with larger distances, 0.9 s up to 1.8 s. Each group was coupled with four different distances for a short period and the rating was surveyed during each coupling situation. We compared the ratings in the overlapping stimuli (0.9 and 1.2 s)—the manipulation check within the judgement to observe if subjects adopt a different frame of reference and if the reference frame has an effect on their distance rating (see Table 1).

Table 1. Serial stimuli for the two subject groups.

Group 1 (low series) (in seconds)	0.3	0.6	0.9	1.2		
Group 2 (high series) (in seconds)			0.9	1.2	1.5	1.8
			overlapping stimuli, rated by subjects			

On a seven-tiered scale subjects had to evaluate the actual distance by rating the comfort and the subjective distance (close/far). The scale ranged from very close or very uncomfortable (1) to very far or very comfortable (7). The rating of the headways of 0.9 and 1.2 s (the overlapping field) has been averaged and represents the manipulation check. Again, we expected a more aversive rating by the group confronted with larger distances because their generated frame of reference is on a higher level.

No significant differences in the *judgement* between the two groups with the different treatment were found in both rating categories. In tendency, the group with the higher distances rated more aversive, as expected.

The expectation was that the *driving behaviour* changes in consequence of the subject's rating. The freely chosen distance should, therefore, be smaller within the treatment group with the low-stimuli series. The interaction measuring-point $\times$ treatment group is significant ($F[1] = 6.4; p < 0.024$). As expected, the subject-group with the low-stimuli series shows reduced distance behaviour, but the group also shows a much higher level in the baseline as the second group even though the difference in the baseline value of 0.3 s between the groups is not significant. The second group shows no pre- and post-effect. The first group with the low-stimuli series reduced its headway after having been coupled with distances from 0.3 to 1.2 s from averaged 2.4 to 1.9 s (Figure 5).

Thus, the treatment produced the expected effect in driving behaviour but not in judgement behaviour of the subjects.

The expected interaction between the two treatment-groups was found in subject's driving behaviour, not in their adjudgement: the subject group confronted with low distances reduced their own distance after the confrontation significantly. The subject group confronted with distances in the range of their habitual distance behaviour shows no treatment effect. The adjudgement (near/far and comfortable/uncomfortable) on the serial coupling distances does not change after the series of coupling periods.

In conclusion, there is evidence that the perception is not influenced during and after automated driving with small gaps. Subject's estimation of distance is not distorted by confrontation

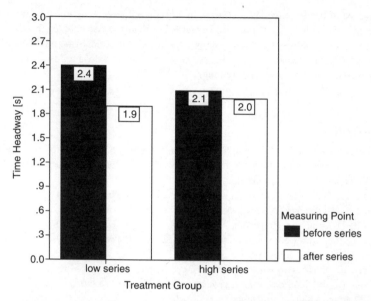

Figure 5. Driving behaviour of the two treatment groups before and after the confrontation with the distance series.

with very small or very large distances. The reference frame is obviously not manipulable. The operation level, on the other hand, changes significantly after automated driving periods, even if the confrontation with coupling periods (the series) is very short. These findings give an idea that the human system is liable to a system-inertia and that task switching causes so-called switch costs. But the presented data is not strong enough to give evidence on this presumption yet.

RÉSUMÉ AND RECOMMENDATIONS

The data of the studies show that adaptation effects occur. Usually we think about long-lasting conditions under which adaptation develops. But as the data shows, a short task switch (e.g. the active to passive role of the driver during coupling demonstrations) is sufficient to bring about adaptation behaviour. Whether different factors—coupling experience, duration of automatic driving and the deviation of coupling THW from manual THW—have combined effects is not clear until now. Further studies with respect to this point have to be accomplished. The processes, which mediate the adaptation effects, have to be clarified in further research. The present data on perceptual processes give only a first impression. The idea that the causation is settled on the operation level and that the observed behaviour is one form of so-called switch costs has to be proven. Those switch costs may represent a form of proactive interference from features of the task set implemented in preceding tasks (Allport et al., 1994). In all three mentioned studies the context is consistent throughout the different driving situations. We assume that adaptation effects disappear in case of changing the context analogous to the driving task (manual–automated).

The presence of headway feedback systems in vehicles achieved a significant reduction of the percentage of time following at low headways (i.e. less than 1 s) (see Fairclough, May & Carter, 1997). Thus, time headway feedback systems should be implemented and finally re-adaptation systems are highly recommended. In addition, drivers should be instructed about the phenomenon and receive a special training.

REFERENCES

Allport, D.A., Styles, E.A., & Hsieh, S. (1994). Shifting intentional set: exploring the dynamic control of tasks. In Umitta, M.C., & Moscovitch, M. (Eds.), *Attention and Performance XV* (pp. 421–452). Cambridge, MA: MIT Press.

Brookhuis, K., & de Waard, D. (1991). Assessing driver status: a demonstration experiment on the road. *Accident, Analysis and Prevention, 23*, 297–307.

De Waard, D., Van der Hulst, M., Hoedemaeker, M., & Brookhuis, K.A. (1999). Driver behaviour in an emergency-situation in the Automated Highway System. *Transportation Human Factor, 89.*

Dragutinovic, N.M., Brookhuis, K.A., Hagenzieker, M.P., & Marchau, V.A. (2004). *Behavioural adaptation in response to ADAS.* [www-Document]. URL: http://www. psychology.nottingham.ac.uk/IAAPdiv13/

Eick, E.-M., & Debus, G. (2004). Research on automation in automotive traffic: what we can give to and what we need from aeronautics. *Proceedings of HCI-Aeronautics 2004*, Toulouse, France.

Eick, E.-M., Wille, M., & Debus, G. (2003). Effects of driving in electronic coupled convoys of motor vehicles: empirical evidence of risky time-headway-adaptation and strategies of prevention. *Proceedings of the XV Triennial Congress of the International Ergonomics Association. Human performance and aging, 4*, 204–207.

Endsley, M.R. (1997). *Automation, situation awareness and free flight.* [www-Document]. URL: http://atm-seminar-97.eurocontrol.fr/endsley.htm

Fairclough, S.H., May, A., & Carter, C. (1997). The effect of time headway feedback on following behaviour. *Accident, Analysis and Prevention, 29* (3), 387–397.

Grayson, G.B. (1996). Behavioural adaptation: a review of the literature. *TRL Report 254.*

Heino, A., Rothengatter, J.A., Van der Hulst, M. (1995). *Collision avoidance systems safety evaluation.* DRIVE II Project V2002, Deliverable Report 33, Workpackage 0016, Groningen: University of Groningen.

Henning, K., & Preuschoff, E. Hrsg. (2003). *Einsatzszenarien für Fahrerassistenzsysteme im Güterverkehr und deren Bewertung, VDI Fortschrittsberichte, Reihe 12.* Düsseldorf: VDI-Verlag, pp. 193–201.

Helson, H. (1947). Adaptation-level as frame of reference for prediction of psychophysical data. *American Journal of Psychology, 60*, 1–29.

Helson, H. (1964). *Adaptation level theory.* New York: Harper & Row.

Lauterbach, W., & Sarris, V. (1980). *Beiträge zur psychologischen Bezugssystemforschung.* Bern: Verlag Hans Huber.

Levitan, L., & Bloomfield, J.R. (1998). Human factors design of automated highway systems. In Barfield, W., & Dingus, T.A. (Eds.), *Human Factors in Intelligent Transportation Systems* (pp. 131–163). Mahwah: Lawrence Erlbaum Associates.

Mayr, U., & Keele, S. (2000). Changing internal constraints on action: the role of backward inhibition. *Journal of Experimental Psychology: General, 129*, 4–26.

OECD (1990). *Behavioural adaptations to changes in the road transport system.* Paris: Organisation for Economic Cooperation and Development.

Rogers, R.D., & Monsell, S. (1995). Costs of a predictable switch between simple cognitive tasks. *Journal of Experimental Psychology: General, 124*, 207–231.

Schulze, M. (1997). CHAUFFEUR—electronic coupling of heavy trucks on European motorways; the project and its actual status. *Proceedings of the workshop on Intelligent Cars and Automated Highway Systems* (pp. 15–19). IROS 97, Grenoble France.

Walker, G.H., Stanton, N.A., & Young, M.S. (2001). Where is computing driving cars? A technology trajectory of vehicle design. *International Journal of Cognitive Ergonomics, 5*, 21–33.

Ward, N.J., Fairclough, S., & Humphreys, M. (1995). The effect of task automatisation in the automotive context, a field study of an AICC system. *Paper presented at the International Conference on Experimental Analysis and Measurement of Situation Awareness*, Florida.

Wille, M., & Debus, G. (2004). Regulation of time headway in a car following task. *Presentation on the Third International Conference on Traffic and Transport Psychology*, Nottingham, UK.

Traffic and Transport Psychology
G. Underwood (Editor)
© 2005 Elsevier Ltd. All rights reserved.

21

EVALUATION OF A DGPS DRIVER ASSISTIVE SYSTEM FOR SNOWPLOWS AND EMERGENCY VEHICLES

Michael E. Rakauskas[1,2], Nicholas J. Ward[1], Alec R. Gorjestani[3], Craig R. Shankwitz[3] and Max Donath[4]

Data maintained by NHTSA (Goodwin, 2002) from 1995 through 2001 show that 21% of all fatal and injury crashes occur on wet, slushy, or icy pavement; two-thirds of these crashes occur during low-visibility (rain, sleet, snow, or fog) conditions. Maintenance and emergency vehicles are often required to safely navigate through heavy snow, fog, and rain. These dangers are exacerbated by the need to quickly clear roads of snow or respond to incidents. In Minnesota, the annual snowfall is at minimum between 18 and 36 in. and the average wind speed can reach 12 mph (Nelson & Donath, 2002); this combination leads to low-visibility conditions, especially on roads lacking protection from the wind. Keeping emergency response vehicles safely in their lane is a priority during bad weather conditions to (1) avoid crashes by emergency response and road maintenance vehicles (crash risk) and (2) sustain rapid emergency responses during periods when roads are blocked or closed (traffic mobility).

In terms of crash risk, there are 131 snowplow crashes, on average, each year in Minnesota with 20 involving personal injuries (Bahler, 1999). The majority of these crashes were rear-end collisions, sideswipes, collisions with fixed objects, and sliding off of the road. These crash and weather-related winter incidents result in $1.8 million (US dollars) in snowplow

---

[1] HumanFIRST Program, University of Minnesota, Minneapolis, MN, USA.
[2] Correspondence to Michael Rakauskas, 1100 Mechanical Engineering, 111 Church Street S.E., Minneapolis, MN 55455, USA. *E-mail:* MickR@me.umn.edu (M.E. Rakauskas).
[3] Intelligent Vehicle Laboratory, University of Minnesota, Minneapolis, MN, USA.
[4] Intelligent Transportation Systems Institute, University of Minnesota, Minneapolis, MN, USA.

property damage, $3 million in other property damage, and $4.1 million in commercial vehicle delay annually. In terms of traffic mobility, road closures are costly with a projected $1.4 billion in lost wages and $0.6 billion in lost retail sales over the course of a day (The Salt Institute, 1999). Moreover, given that the delay in response time for medical treatment is a significant determinant of the outcome of a traumatic crash (Champion, 1999), the delay for emergency response vehicles can also impact the survivability of crashes during road closures.

Vision enhancement systems (VESs) can be used to reduce crash risk and increase traffic mobility during conditions of low visibility (Parkes, Ward & Bossi, 1995). Such systems can provide either (1) an enhanced image of the entire (forward) driving scene or (2) an augmentation of only selected critical features of the driving scene (Stapleton, Ward & Parkes, 1995). Scene enhancement may use processed sensor information such as infrared images superimposed in the forward view with a head up display (HUD) or on a standard display mounted in the dashboard. Scene augmentation may use sensor information to isolate and emphasize relevant elements using similar display formats. This augmentation may be in the form of icons and symbols, or as superimposed virtual analogues of the actual scene element.

Both these approaches have benefits and disadvantages. For example, an enhancement of the entire scene using infrared imaging can provide a full range of information to support the driving task. However, this large amount and form of imagery can produce cognitive tunneling whereby attention is focused on the enhanced image with reduced awareness of peripheral areas of the (non-enhanced) driving scene (Bossi, Ward, Parkes & Howarth, 1997). Conversely, whereas the selective augmentation of a restricted number of scene elements (such as lane boundaries or road hazards) reduces the amount of information, it may falsely presume which elements are currently relevant to the driver. However, if the function of the VES is limited to support a specific driving task, the augmentation approach may be supportive for that task domain. The potential for an augmented VES to support the specific driving task of lane keeping is evaluated in this test track study.

Researchers at the University of Minnesota's Intelligent Vehicles Laboratory (IV Lab) have developed a driver assistive system (DAS) to assist the drivers of highway maintenance (e.g. snowplow) and emergency response vehicles (e.g. ambulance, state patrol) to perform critical safety tasks under low-visibility conditions. The DAS includes a HUD to provide vision augmentation of lane boundaries (lane keeping) and radar to locate ambient traffic (collision avoidance). In addition, lateral support is also provided through tactile and audio warnings. For more than 5 years, the IV Lab has been iteratively designing and testing the DAS under simulated track-test and field-test conditions through cooperation with Mn/DOT and the Federal Highway Administration (FHWA).

In this study, snowplow operators drove a DAS-equipped truck on a test track in nighttime low-visibility conditions, similar to what drivers might encounter during normal snowplow operations. We hypothesized that driving in low visibility with the assistance of HUD conformal imagery along with tactile and audio lateral warnings would show safer driving performance and be perceived as safer.

METHODS

This experiment created a set of low-visibility conditions in which to test the DAS lateral warning and vision augmentation technology. Our research questions included:

(1) Does the system support driver performance in a manner consistent with reduced crash risk and improved productivity (mobility)?

(2) Do drivers find value in using the system?

Participants

The experimental sample was comprised of nine Mn/DOT snowplow operators assigned to routes along a rural Minnesota highway (MN TH7) that typically has poor visibility conditions and high snow accumulation in winter. The average age of the drivers studied was 39 years (range = 26–60). On average, these drivers had 9 years of plowing experience (range = 1–36). One driver was female.

Test environment

The track testing took place on the Minnesota Road Research Project's Low Volume Roadway (Mn/ROAD) outside Otsego, MN. The track is a 2.5-mile long, two-lane, elongated-oval track where both straights are approximately 1 mile in length (see Figure 1).

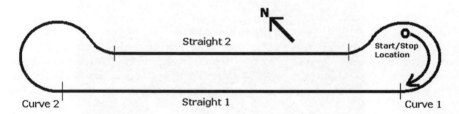

Figure 1. Schematic diagram (not to scale) of Mn/ROAD.

Test vehicle

The vehicle used was a MY1999 2540 International single-axle dump truck owned, operated, and maintained by Mn/DOT. It was outfitted with the same DAS used in previous phases of this project. The truck was configured with a front plow in order to simulate the truck weight distribution experienced during normal plow operations. A color LCD touch panel display was mounted near the dashboard for controlling the DAS. The display also presented a continuous choice reaction time task during the straight sections of the route to increase driver workload so that the combined driving task was more indicative of actual driving demands.

The driving assistive system. This comprehensive DAS utilizes dual frequency, carrier phase RTK DGPS integrated with a high-accuracy digital geospatial database, advanced automotive radar, and a driver interface comprised of visual, haptic, and audible components. The system provides high-fidelity representations of the ambient landscape through a HUD (Lim, Newstrom, Shankwitz & Donath, 2000), as shown in Figure 2.

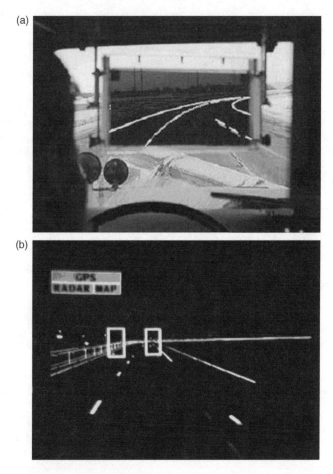

Figure 2. Views through the HUD: (a) first person view of road lines as seen during a curve in the road and (b) HUD image of two radar targets.

This VES system used an in-vehicle geospatial database combined with a query processor to extract the geospatial data in real time. As the vehicle moves along a stretch of highway, the vehicle's DGPS-derived position (and orientation) is used to query the centimeter accurate "digital map" and provide it to the HUD's graphics processor, which, in turn, computes the projection perspective needed for registration with the driver's eyes. In order to avoid eye fatigue, the optical properties of the HUD were designed with a virtual focus located approximately 12 m in front of the vehicle. The physical display of the HUD assembly occupies a subtended visual angle of approximately 21° from the driver's eye point and presents an image for the forward scene with a field of view of almost 19°. The HUD combiner is partially reflective and partially transmissive. Given that the position of the eye point can affect the alignment of presented objects with respect to the external scene (veridicality), the HUD mounting is adjustable so that its position can be adjusted to accommodate each individual driver.

The purpose of the HUD was to assist the driver in consistently seeing the lane boundaries and in heightening awareness of lane position. To the driver, analogues of painted road striping (in matching white or yellow color) and road furniture appear to overlay the true items when projected on the HUD. Lateral warnings were provided by haptic, audio, and visual lane "warnings" when the truck was determined to be departing the lane boundaries. On the HUD, the lane boundary about to be crossed would change color from white or yellow to red. The haptic warning was a directional vibration of the driver's seat to indicate departures to either the left or right. The audio warning was a rumble strip sound presented on either the left or right. In addition, radar was used to detect non-mapped objects and display the location of these hazards on the HUD (Figure 2b), though this feature was not analyzed here.

Validation of simulated weather conditions

This study was not conducted in low visibility (snow) conditions due to the unpredictability of weather during the study period. Instead, the study was conducted under "artificial" visibility restrictions and at night so that there were fewer visual cues to aid the drivers. The truck was further equipped with movable headlight and window tinting for the low-visibility (LV) and low-visibility with DAS (DAS) conditions. The window tinting was of the static-cling variety for ease in application and removal between conditions. The headlight blinders were constructed from shaded Plexiglas® and attached to a pivoting base. All exterior lights aside from the two front headlights were covered.

To verify the validity of this attempt to simulate restricted visibility conditions, several manipulation checks were performed, as listed below. Performance during the LV condition as compared to performance in the control (C) condition is depicted in Figure 3.

- *Illumination ahead of the vehicle*. The brightness of each headlight was measured by using a lux meter with and without the blinder installed. On average, with the blinders in place the headlights produced 44.4% of the illumination produced during clear visibility (a 55.6% reduction in illumination).

- *Visibility distance from the driver position*. An object was placed at an undisclosed location on the track and a driver slowly drove until he could see the object. For consistency the same driver (non-participant) was used each night. The visibility decrement suggests that participants in the LV condition could see 63.2% as far as they could in the C condition (a 36.8% reduction in viewing distance).

- *Observed impairment of driving performance*. Drivers drove significantly slower on straight road sections during the LV condition than they did in clear visibility ($Z_W = 2.38$, $p = 0.017$). This equates to average LV speeds being 89% of those in the C condition (an 11% mean decrease in speed).

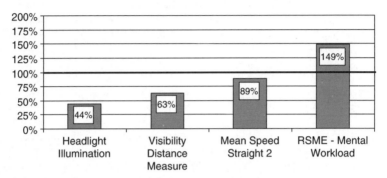

Figure 3. Low-visibility (LV) condition verification expressed as a percentage of the control (C) condition.

- *Subjective effort to cope with visibility restriction.* Drivers expressed being exposed to significantly more mental workload after the low visibility driving than after the clear visibility driving ($Z_W = 2.55$, $p = 0.011$). This equates to a 49% mean increase in mental workload during the LV condition.

Independent variables

This study used a within subjects design, where each of three circuits was driven under a different condition. The three conditions were: control (C), where there was no visual hindrance; low visibility (LV), where visibility is hindered by window tint and headlight filters; and low visibility with DAS (DAS), which had the same visibility limitations as the LV condition but drivers were given assistance the DAS. For this test, drivers were not given the option to turn off or adjust any of the components (e.g. haptic seat and audio warnings, or the HUD).

Dependent measures

Data were collected to measure driving performance and subjective workload for all conditions. Driving performance measures were continuously sampled throughout each circuit for each condition at a rate of 10 Hz, though only data from Straight 2 are presented here. Subjective measures were collected after each trial and at the end of the experiment.

Steering. Steering was measured in degrees the wheel moved from the top-center point. Smaller standard deviation (variation) of steering wheel position and larger mean time intervals between steering wheel reversals indicate safer driving performance. A steering wheel reversal was measured as a time when the wheel stopped traveling in one direction and began to move in the opposite direction (as defined in Verwey & Veltman, 1996).

Speed. The mean and standard deviation of speed were measured in miles per hour (mph). Larger mean speeds indicate that the driver feels more able to control the truck under the current road conditions. Smaller standard deviation of speed indicates safer driving performance.

Lane position. The position of the center of the truck was measured in meters from the mapped center of the lane. The vehicle position was then converted to a time-to-line crossing (TLC) value based on this distance from the outside of the tire to the nearest lane boundary divided by lateral speed. TLC tells us how long it would take to reach the lane boundaries if no changes in steering were made. Using the inverse of TLC, larger values represent a shorter time-based safety margin, so smaller 1/TLCs indicate safer driving performance. The 85th percentile of 1/TLC was used to represent the "typical" safety margin with respect to lateral control in the lane.

Lane departures. A truck was considered outside of the lane (i.e. a lane departure) when the outside of the tire crossed over the lane boundary. Median response times were collected and smaller times indicate safer driving performance. To consider the safety effect of outlier reactions, the maximum response time was also considered. Finally, in terms of the response outcome, the percentage of total time spent outside the lane boundary was also collected where smaller times indicate safer driving performance.

Subjective mental workload. Drivers were given the rating scale of mental effort (RSME) after each circuit. The RSME is a univariate scale for rating mental effort (Zijlstra, 1993) presented as a single continuum with specific points marked with workload descriptions. It has been shown to be a good measure of mental effort in cases where a secondary task is presented (Verwey & Veltman, 1996). Larger values indicate the participant felt they exerted a higher level of mental effort.

Usability. The acceptance scale developed by Van der Laan, Heino and de Waard (1997) was used to measure drivers' ratings of satisfaction and perceived usefulness of the DAS. This scale is presented to the driver as nine 5-category continuums (scored from -2 to $+2$) on various dimensions relating to the usefulness and satisfaction of the system.

Procedure

Prior to the study, a separate formal training session was held for drivers to learn and use the system on their normal routes during the winter. These drivers were then assigned to use one of these vehicles during normal winter operations. During low visibility these drivers reported using the DAS 44% of the time and, on average, used it 10 times during the winter season (range $= 3-20$ times) for a duration of 3 h (range $= 2-6$ h) each time.

Participants drove five practice laps. The first few laps allowed drivers to become familiar with the layout and particulars of the track. The remaining laps let them drive the track in the low-visibility condition with and without the DAS. These laps allowed drivers to be re-familiarized with the DAS and also demonstrate the test procedures and questionnaires to be used in the study.

Participants drove one circuit per condition and were told to maintain a speed that would allow them to keep the truck under control. In all three conditions, participants were also asked to complete a forced-choice secondary task while driving on the straight sections of track.

Analysis

For the performance and mental workload measures, two comparisons were made to assess specific trends:

- baseline comparison—comparing the C and DAS conditions (seeing if the DAS returns performance to a level of optimal visibility conditions)

- system comparison—comparing the LV and DAS conditions (seeing if the DAS improves performance to a level greater than unassisted low-visibility conditions)

Analyses were performed using the Wilcoxon signed ranks test (Z_W), and referencing of confidence intervals (CIs) to scale midpoints. All significance testing was done with an alpha of $p < 0.05$. Since the usability and interview results pertain only to the DAS condition, only descriptive statistics are presented.

RESULTS

Steering

There were marginally significant differences for steering variation on the system effect ($Z_W = 1.86$, $p = 0.063$) as well as significant differences on the baseline comparison ($Z_W = 2.37$, $p = 0.018$) (Figure 4). During low-visibility conditions, the DAS produced

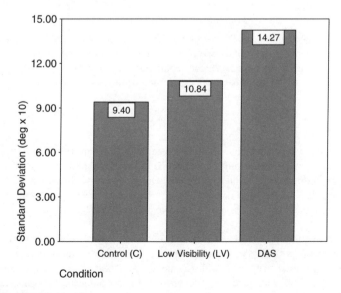

Figure 4. Variation in steering.

more steering position variability compared to unassisted driving. Moreover, there was more steering position variability with the DAS during poor-visibility conditions than without the system during optimal visibility. This suggests that drivers made more frequent steering responses in the DAS condition. This may be expected since only the DAS condition provided feedback indicating the need to make steering corrections with respect to lane position.

Significant findings were also present for steering reversal intervals as seen in Figure 5, where drivers show significantly shorter intervals between steering responses during the DAS-assisted condition than during the LV condition (system comparison: $Z_W = 2.37$, $p = 0.018$) and marginally shorter intervals during the C condition (baseline comparison: $Z_W = 1.86$, $p = 0.063$). Drivers using DAS exhibited shorter intervals between steering reversals than while driving in low visibility. Though not significant, the trend indicates that drivers in clear conditions exhibited shorter intervals than those in low visibility. This suggests that in our study drivers made more steering corrections when they were presented with more information about ambient driving conditions.

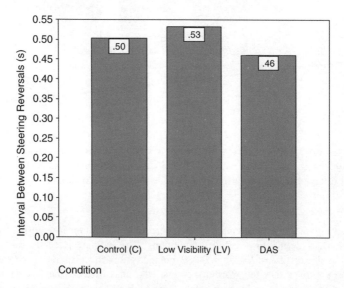

Figure 5. Intervals between steering reversals.

In summary, the DAS resulted in more steering activity. Since the system provided lane position information, it was expected that there would be more steering input if the information was utilized. Therefore, it appears that the drivers were using or responding to this information.

Speed

For mean speed, only the baseline comparison was significant ($Z_W = 2.20$, $p = 0.028$) as shown in Figure 6. Using the DAS during low visibility resulted in a significantly slower speed than normal driving during good visibility. During low-visibility conditions, the DAS did not significantly influence speed. There were no significant effects for speed variability.

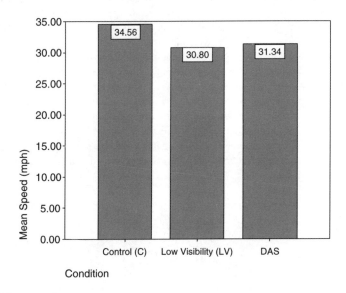

Figure 6. Mean speed.

In summary, mean speed was affected by the low-visibility manipulation, but variation in speed was not, suggesting that driving with the DAS does not cause drivers to significantly change their speed behavior from that during unassisted low-visibility conditions.

Lane position

As shown in Figure 7, the safety margin (85th percentile 1/TLC) for lane position was lowest without the DAS during low-visibility conditions. The baseline effect in this figure was marginally significant ($Z_W = 1.75, p = 0.080$) but the system effect was not. The trend indicates that the DAS improves the safety margin as compared to unassisted driving during low-visibility conditions, though the margin is not as safe as normal driving with good visibility.

Lane departures

Figure 8a shows the median response time to a lane boundary violation. Consistent with data for the lane position safety margin (Figure 7), response times during DAS-assisted low visibility tended to be much lower than unassisted low visibility though not as low as in clear conditions.

Clearly, there is a trend for the DAS to improve response time to lane boundary violations during low-visibility conditions, suggesting that the DAS can support reaction times as fast or faster than normal driving during good visibility. The trends here and for 1/TLC results appear to show that driving while assisted by the DAS allows drivers to have equivalent response times to the C condition and lower than unassisted LV. As a result, the vehicle was

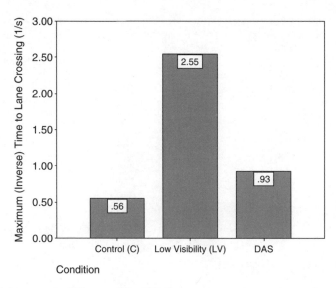

Figure 7. Safety margin 85th percentile 1/TLC.

outside the lane boundary less than with the DAS in comparison to the LV condition (Figure 9). The total duration of these lane boundary departures was reduced with the DAS. However, these trends were not statistically significant due to the low power of the analyses resulting from the small sample size ($E^2 < 12$).

In summary, these results suggest that using the DAS during (simulated) low-visibility conditions can improve lane control and safety margins.

Subjective mental workload

The baseline and system effects were statistically significant for subjective mental effort as shown in Figure 10. The DAS actually resulted in a significantly higher level of mental effort (system comparison: $Z_W = 2.52$, $p = 0.012$), presumably as a result of processing the system information presented in the HUD to support the driving task. This suggests that system processed information presented to drivers may require more effort to process in conjunction with low-visibility conditions than actual information when it is visibility in the driving scene.

Subjective usability

Figure 11 shows the participants' average usefulness and satisfaction scores, as calculated from responses on the Van der Laan et al. (1997) acceptance scale. Participants felt the DAS was useful and somewhat satisfying in its current implementation.

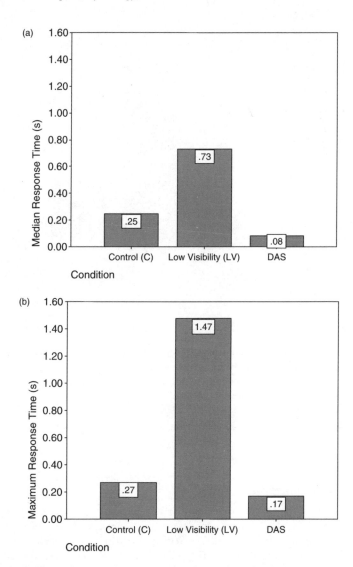

Figure 8. (a) Median and (b) maximum response time to lane departures.

Participants were asked what components they found most useful and subsequently what would be their ideal configuration. Over half of the drivers (6/9) thought that the ideal configuration would be using both the haptic seat lateral warnings and the HUD, followed by the HUD alone (2/9) or haptic seat alone (1/9). Drivers had a less favorable opinion of the audio warnings: none of the drivers found these to be favorable and one wished them removed.

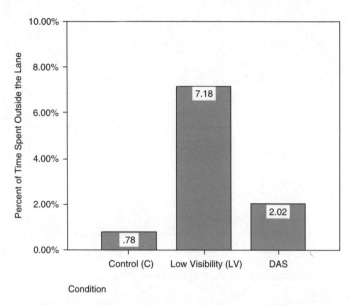

Figure 9. Percentage of time spent outside the lane boundaries.

When asked what could be improved, they requested that the system be less intrusive or bulky. Even though the HUD presents a minimal amount of conformal information, some wished for the clutter to be reduced in some way, possibly by eliminating images of roadside furniture. Just over half (5/9) of the drivers said they would like to have the final version of the DAS permanently installed in their vehicle and would use it if it were installed. All but one of the drivers (8/9) reported that they would recommend the DAS to other drivers.

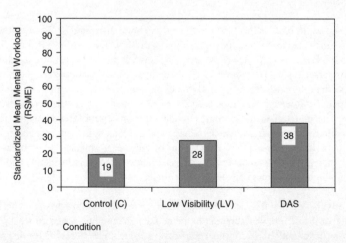

Figure 10. Graph of the mean RSME subjective mental workload scores (means were standardized to 100-point scale for graphing purposes).

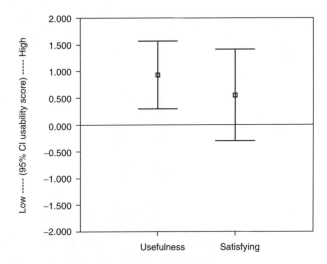

Figure 11. Mean usefulness and satisfaction scores for the DAS.

DISCUSSION

Results from the driving performance and lane position measures indicate that using the DAS during low-visibility conditions helped drivers maintain their lane position as well as during clear-visibility conditions. In this way, drivers spent less time outside the lane, and when they did leave the lane they were able to respond more quickly to the situation, thus reducing crash risk. It follows that if drivers are able to maintain their lane position while plowing, they are also more effective at clearing the road and increasing their overall productivity in regaining bare pavement.

It has been shown, in past studies, that the more drivers are distracted or the more they have to deal with in their environment, the more they will slow their speed (Brown, Tickner & Simmonds, 1969; Haigney, Taylor & Westerman, 2000; Waugh et al., 2000). As expected, we found that drivers using the DAS drove at a level comparable to that of the LV condition with an expected rise in effort while attending and processing information presented by the DAS. This additional mental effort supported increased driver performance and awareness as evidenced by the higher speeds maintained and increases in lane position control. Trends suggest that drivers were assisted in recovering from lane departures and in maintaining safer lane keeping. These results support the desired DAS effects on driving performance by decreasing crash potentiality, increasing the responsiveness of emergency vehicles to incidents, and increasing the speed at which snowplows can safely clear roads.

Almost all drivers said that they would recommend the system to other drivers, which suggests that the value of the system was apparent to them. Though opinions varied on what parts of the DAS were useful and satisfying, most participants tended to prefer the HUD for displaying lane assist information or the haptic seat for lateral warning information. Care should be taken to minimize what is displayed on the HUD and to place a system-wide focus on making less information more intuitive. It seemed that all drivers found benefit from some part of the DAS and that they trusted it, aside from the audio rumble strip warnings. This finding is supported by the findings of Dingus et al. (1997) who showed that there was no additional benefit when using additional audio warnings in tandem to a visual collision warning, though they may be useful to warn of unexpected and imminent dangers.

Many of the trends presented in these analyses were consistent with our expectations, but were not statistically significant. In this context, we should reiterate that all of our findings are based on a relatively small sample from which the analytic power was low. For the purposes of this evaluation we felt that the significant findings and trends were adequate to anticipate the operability, safety, and usability of the DAS in this context. Strong trends found in the data should be confirmed for reliability through larger samples of drivers before they are discussed as trends for all snowplow operators.

CONCLUSIONS

Overall, results support the desired effects of the DAS on driving performance by decreasing crash potentiality, increasing the responsiveness of emergency vehicles to incidents, and increasing the speed at which snowplows can safely clear roads. It seems the DAS is beneficial for those in situations warranting low-cost, visibility-enhancement solutions, with further cost benefits likely as the technology becomes more common and affordable. Areas experiencing high turnover, and thus large numbers of drivers inexperienced with particular routes, may also benefit from DGPS technology utilizing extensive digital maps. With some adjustments and through further testing of the current implementation, the DAS design will move closer toward these aspirations by making changes not only in how the system functions but also how it is implemented.

In addition, the practical importance of the DAS also extends to other emergency vehicles that have the need to be on the road during low-visibility conditions. Ambulances, fire trucks, and police vehicles need to use roadways during these critical times to aid other drivers who have fallen victim to inclement weather, or to respond to urgent situations. If not following a DAS-equipped plow, then enabling such vehicles with their own DAS would allow them to be more responsive while navigating low-visibility conditions.

Related applications of this technology are numerous. The ability to detect obstacles in the vehicle's path may be adapted for general usage in low-visibility driving situations. Route navigation through DGPS is becoming more prevalent in hand-held units; allowing this guidance to be displayed in a head-up format could arguably save lives by presenting information in ways that conform to the driver's visual field. Other aspects of the DAS' warnings may be applied to inattentive or drowsy driver warnings to alert of impending lane excursions or hazardous road events.

REFERENCES

Bahler, S. (1999). IUI snowplow evaluation ITS-80. *Presentation for Minnesota Guidestar Program, Projects in Progress, Snowplow IVI—Highway 101*. Retrieved on June 18, 2004 from http://www.dot.state.mn.us/guidestar/pdf/its80.pdf

Bossi, L., Ward, N., Parkes, A., & Howarth, P. (1997). The effect of vision enhancement systems on driver peripheral visual performance. In Ian Noy, Y. (Ed.), *Ergonomics and Safety of Intelligent Driver Interface* (pp. 239–260). Mahwah, NJ: Lawrence Erlbaum Associates.

Brown, I.D., Tickner, A.H., & Simmonds, D.C.V. (1969). Interference between concurrent tasks of driving and telephoning. *Journal of Applied Psychology, 53* (5), 419–424.

Champion, H.R. (1999). Reducing highway deaths and disabilities with automatic wireless transmission of serious injury probability ratings from crash recorders to emergency medical services providers. *Proceedings of the International Symposium on Transportation Recorders,* Arlington, VA, May 3–5.

Dingus, T.A., McGehee, D.V., Manakkal, N., Jahns, S.K., Carney, C., & Hankey, J.M. (1997). Human factors field evaluation of automotive headway maintenance/collision warning devices. *Human Factors, 39* (2), 216–229.

Goodwin, L. (2002). Analysis of weather-related crashes on US highways. Mitretek Systems, Inc. Posted on FHWA Road Weather Management Program—Best Practices for Road Weather Management Version 2.0. Retrieved on July 8, 2004 from http://ops.fhwa.dot. gov/weather/best_practices/1024x768/transform_param2.asp?xslname=pub. xsl&xmlname=publications.xml&keyname=25

Haigney, D.E., Taylor, R.G., & Westerman, S.J. (2000). Concurrent mobile (cellular) phone use and driving performance: task demand characteristics and compensatory processes. *Transportation Research—Part F, 3,* 113–121.

Lim, H.L., Newstrom, B., Shankwitz, C., & Donathm, M. (2000). A conformal augmented heads up display for driving under low visibility conditions. *Proceedings of the 5th International Symposium on Advanced Vehicle Control,* Ann Arbor, MI.

Nelson, B., & Donath, M. (2002). Evaluation Report Volume 2: Benefit Analysis. Intelligent Vehicle Initiative, Specialty Vehicle Field Operational Test. Mn/DOT-US DOT Cooperative Agreement, Task 7.4 of Cooperative Agreement. DTFH61-99-X-00101, December 2002.

Parkes, A., Ward, N., & Bossi, L. (1995). The potential of vision enhancement systems to improve driver safety. *Le Travail Humain, 58* (2), 151–169.

Salt Institute (1999). Billion$ at risk during snow emergencies…snowfighting investment pays big dividends. Press release on September 10, 1999. Retrieved on September 17, 2004 from http://www.saltinstitute.org/pubstat/s-p-dri.html

Stapleton, L., Ward, N.J., & Parkes, A.M. (1995). Automotive contact analogue head-up-display images and distance estimation. *Vision in Vehicles 6.* Derby, UK (September 13–16).

Van der Laan, J.D., Heino, A., & de Waard, D. (1997). A simple procedure for the assessment of acceptance of advanced transport telematics. *Transportation Research—C, 5* (1), 1–10.

Verwey, W.B., & Veltman, H.A. (1996). Detecting short periods of elevated workload: a comparison of nine workload assessment techniques. *Journal of Experimental Psychology—Applied, 2* (3), 270–285.

Waugh, J.D., Glumm, M.M., Kilduff, P.W., Tauson, R.A., Symth, C.C., & Pillalamarri, R.S. (2000). Cognitive workload while driving and talking on a cellular phone or to a passenger. *Proceedings from the IEA 2000/HFES 2000 Congress.*

Zijlstra, F.R.H. (1993). Efficiency in work behaviour. Unpublished Doctoral Dissertation. Technical University, Delft, The Netherlands.

Traffic and Transport Psychology
G. Underwood (Editor)
© 2005 Elsevier Ltd. All rights reserved.

22

ADAS' ACCEPTANCE AND EFFECTS ON BEHAVIOUR: THE CONSEQUENCES OF AUTOMATION

Karel A. Brookhuis[1] and Dick de Waard[2]

INTRODUCTION

There are a number of reasons why in recent years electronic driving aids are developed and implemented at an increasing rate and speed. The first and foremost reason is safety (i.e. the unacceptable number of accidents), but also economic principles are a compelling motive (congestion is expensive), while bringing comfort to the driver population is obviously a good sales argument. Environmental arguments play a role of growing importance as well.

Accident causes

Safety is primarily a "human-factors" case. Driver impairment is the first cause of accidents on (European) motorways. Based on a literature survey, Smiley and Brookhuis (1987) stated that at least 90% of all traffic accidents are to be attributed to human failure, for instance, through errors, inattention, alcohol or drowsiness at the wheel. According to Vallet (1991) it is generally a loss of alertness, which is the principal cause of fatal accidents (34%), while it is suggested that alcohol and fatigue are in all these accidents "prime causative factors", certainly during the weekend. The costs of road traffic accidents for society are enormous in terms of both human suffering and economical loss. In Europe alone around 50,000 people are killed in traffic accidents each year, while more than 1,500,000 are injured. Traffic congestion, i.e. the "regular" and those following traffic accidents, is a daily nuisance, predominantly present in the economically most sensitive places. At least 70 Billion Euros are spent each year on medical

[1] Transport Policy and Management, Delft University of Technology, Delft, The Netherlands.
E-mail: K.A.BROOKHUIS@ppsw.rug.nl (K.A. Brookhuis).
[2] Department of Psychology, University of Groningen, Groningen, The Netherlands.

treatment of injured people, the cost of congestion is many times that amount, and many thousands of person-years of work are lost.

Accident causation and prevention

Tunbridge, Ward, Dye and Berghaus (2000) report that examination of accidents' most prevailing factors shows, perhaps not surprisingly, the two most common "What happened?" factors being loss of control and failing to avoid a vehicle in the carriageway (i.e. a collision). In line with this, Shinar (1998) argues that the contributory factors can be hierarchically categorised as representing driver (i.e. error and impairment), environment, and vehicle factors, in that order.

Thus, the prevention or reduction of traffic accidents requires countermeasures that are centred on the prevention of those driver behaviours contributing to accidents. In Europe, the USA and Japan, combined ergonomic and engineering approaches to both hazard assessment and the indication of drivers' performance limits have developed into research and development of new and relevant (primary) safety measures. Brookhuis and Brown (1992) argued that an ergonomic approach to behavioural change via engineering measures, in the form of electronic driving aids, could be adopted in order to improve road safety, transport efficiency and environmental quality.

However, driver comfort appears to be a strong impetus for the development of electronic driving aids as well, at least from a marketing point of view. Thus, car manufacturers are keen on selling driver comfort and invest considerable effort in the development and improvement of comfort enhancing electronic aids, even if they are originally devised with safety in mind. A well-known example of the latter is advanced cruise control (ACC) which is actually an addition of a safety feature to the original cruise control by keeping a safe distance, nevertheless sold as a comfort aspect, for liability reasons (Van Wees, 2004). Although still rather expensive, prototypes of this type of system passed a number of tests (and improvements) and were successfully placed on the consumer market recently. Before the actual marketing, user needs research (marketing research) is indispensable, but also studies on acceptance and certainly on safety effects are still necessary after implementation, whether the system is sold as a comfort system or as a safety system. Among others, consumer acceptance is dependent upon such requirements as system safety, validity (does the system function correctly) and benefit (is there a positive cost-benefit balance). Finally, environmental issues are not really decisive in this area yet, but will gain weight quickly in the future.

ADVANCED DRIVER ASSISTANCE SYSTEMS

What is now called ADAS (Advanced Driver Assistance Systems) is to be considered as the collection of systems and subsystems on the way to a full automation, if that is ever realised (ADASE project deliverables, 1998). For the time being, only when on a dedicated traffic lane, the vehicle can be operated under fully automated control, which is very similar to the automatic pilot in airplanes (Congress, 1994), bailing out the human factor. ADAS concepts include among others blind spot detectors, ACC, Autonomous Intelligent Cruise Control (AICC), platoon driving, etc. in general AVG (Automated Vehicle Guidance). Some of the technology is available on the market, or ready to be marketed, some is developed but as a prototype still under test.

Human supervision

The classic goal of automation is to replace human manual control, planning and problem solving by automatic devices. However, these systems still need human beings for supervision and adjustment. It has been suggested that the more advanced a control system, the more crucial is the contribution of the human operator (Bainbridge, 1983).

The point made by Bainbridge (1983) is as follows: normal operation is performed automatically; abnormal conditions are to be dealt with manually. Unfortunately, as a result of automation, experience is limited, while in case of abnormal conditions (i.e. something is wrong with the process) unusual actions will be required. Also, human problem solving is not optimal under time-pressure.

Monitoring of (present) automatic processes is based on skills that (formerly) manual operators have, and that future generations of operators (/drivers) cannot be expected to have (Bainbridge, 1983). Pilots have also indicated that although automation reduced workload, it also had a negative effect on flying skills. They considered manually flying of a part of every trip important to maintain these skills (McClumpha, James, Green & Belyavin, 1991). The fact is that human beings are poor "process monitors" (e.g. Molloy & Parasuraman, 1996), i.e. they are not good in supervising automated systems. Before introducing any driver support system, the consequences of system operation in this sense should be identified.

Functionality, benefits and problems

Nevertheless, the purpose of introducing ADAS is that driver error will be reduced or even eliminated and efficiency is enhanced. Thus the benefits of ADAS implementations are potentially great because of a significant decrease in human suffering, economical cost and pollution, since (cf. Congress, 1994):

- driving safety will be considerably enhanced;

- many more vehicles can be accommodated;

- high-performance driving can be conducted without regard to vision, weather and environmental conditions;

- drivers using ADAS can be safe and efficient drivers (cf. elderly, inexperienced drivers).

So, the primary functionality of ADAS is to facilitate the task performance of drivers by providing real-time driving aid. This type of systems is usually also described by the term "co-driver systems" or "driver support systems". Driver support systems may operate in advisory, semi-automatic or automatic mode (e.g. Rosengren, 1995), all of which may have different consequences for the driving task, and with that on traffic safety. Although the purpose of a driver support system is to have a positive effect on traffic safety, adverse effects have been shown on driver behaviour, indicative for negative effects on traffic safety (Hoedemaeker & Brookhuis, 1999; Van Winsum, 1997; Zwahlen, Adams & DeBald, 1988). Firstly, the provision of information potentially leads to a situation where the driver's attention is diverted from traffic. Secondly, taking over (part of) the driving task by a co-driver system may well produce behavioural adaptation (Dragutinovic, Brookhuis, Hagenzieker & Marchau, 2004). Thirdly, because of automation drivers may be less alert and attentive. As a result, either the driver might not (or too late) be aware of a sudden hazard, or, is not fit (anymore) c.q. not ready for an adequate reaction.

Several reservations that have consequences for acceptance by the relevant stakeholders hold for the automated operation modes. Automation may cause complacency and increase reaction time. A few studies found signs of complacency, i.e. unjustified over-reliance on ADAS (De Waard, Brookhuis, Fabriek & Van Wolffelaar, 2004; De Waard, Van der Hulst, Hoedemaeker & Brookhuis, 1999), others reported deterioration in driving performance. In a test of reaction time to a system failure cue, Knapp and Vardaman (1991) and Parasuraman, Mouloua and Molloy (1996) found support for complacency, i.e. the reaction time to this cue increased compared to normal task performance. Ward (1996) and Ward, Fairclough and Humphries (1995) also found evidence for complacency, poor lane position control and failure to yield to other traffic were more frequently observed in drivers driving a car with AICC compared to drivers driving a normal car. This and other forms of behavioural adaptation, or compensation as it is called in a wider field, are factors that should be taken into account when investigating the conditions for introduction of ADAS (Dragutinovic et al., 2004; Verwey, Brookhuis & Janssen, 1996).

A key question is whether drivers will trust automated vehicles, whether they actually will reclaim control if required, what driving mode they prefer, and whether they finally accept supervising an automated vehicle instead of driving. Studies performed in an Automatic Highway System have shown that drivers supervising a fully automated system very often do not reclaim control in critical situations (Desmond, Hancock & Monette, 1998; De Waard et al., 1999), while from a safety perspective this is crucial, in particular in a vehicle with passengers or dangerous goods.

In a recent simulator study (De Waard et al., 2004) concerning automating public transport on the road, bus-drivers could switch from full automatic control (underground/metro type) to semi-automatic control (tram, i.e. longitudinal control operated by driver, lateral control by vehicle) to manual (bus). The driver is supposed to supervise the performance of the vehicle when in (semi-)automatic mode and can/should reclaim control if required. The results show that drivers in the automatic mode, so in fact being supervisors, did not always respond adequately, i.e. in time to unexpectedly crossing traffic. Training for a brief while (couple of hours) turned out to be effective to teach strategies to the drivers how to stay-in-the-loop and respond properly.

Conclusion

Introduction of fully automated systems is technically feasible now, but public introduction on a large scale is at least waiting for the safety provisions and the public acceptance, and also on proper legislation that clearly establishes responsibility and liability. Taking the results of recent experimentation into account, it is clear that a driving license issued for conventional driving should not be applied to driving (semi-)automated vehicles unconditionally, at least not without thorough preparation for what may happen in such conditions. Combined simulator and on-the-job training and separate licensing for limited periods of time, in type-approved simulators should be mandatory, very similar to what is considered normal in the training of pilots.

REFERENCES

ADASE (1998). Advanced Driver Assistance Systems in Europe. Project reports D3.1, D3.2, D3.3 and D4.1 to the European Commission.

Bainbridge, L. (1983). Ironies of automation. *Automatica, 19*, 775–779.

Brookhuis, K.A., & Brown, I.D. (1992). Ergonomics and road safety. *Impact of Science on Society, 165*, 35–40.

Congress, N. (1994). The Automated Highway System: an idea whose time has come. *Public Roads On-Line, Summer 1994.* http://www.tfhrc.gov/pubrds/summer94/p94su1.htm

Desmond, P.A., Hancock, P.A., & Monette, J.L. (1998). Fatigue and automation-induced impairments in simulated driving performance. *Transportation Research Records, 1628*, 8–14.

De Waard, D., Van der Hulst, M., Hoedemaeker, M., & Brookhuis, K.A. (1999). Driver behavior in an emergency situation in the Automated Highway System. *Transportation Human Factors, 1*, 67–82.

De Waard, D., Brookhuis, K.A., Fabriek, E., & Van Wolffelaar, P.C. (2004). Driving the Phileas, a new automated public transport vehicle. Paper, ICTTP 2004.

Dragutinovic, N., Brookhuis, K.A., Hagenzieker, M., & Marchau, V.A.W.J. (2004). Behavioural adaptation in response to ADAS. Paper, ICTTP 2004.

Hoedemaeker, M., & Brookhuis, K.A. (1999). Driving with an adaptive cruise control (ACC). *Transportation Research, Part F, 3*, 95–106.

Knapp, R.K., & Vardaman, J.J. (1991). Response to an automated function failure cue: an operational measure of complacency, *Proceedings of the Human Factors Society 35th annual meeting.* HFES: Santa Monica, CA, USA, pp. 112–115.

McClumpha, A.J., James, M., Green, R.G., & Belyavin, A.J. (1991). Pilots' attitudes to cockpit automation, *Proceedings of the Human Factors Society 35th annual meeting.* HFES: Santa Monica, CA, USA, pp. 107–111.

Molloy, R., & Parasuraman, R. (1996). Monitoring an automated system for single failure: vigilance and task complexity effects. *Human Factors, 38*, 311–322.

Parasuraman, R., Mouloua, M., & Molloy, R. (1996). Effects of adaptive task allocation on monitoring of automated systems. *Human Factors, 38*, 665–679.

Rosengren, L.G. (1995). Driver assistance and co-operative driving. In ERTICO (Ed.), Towards an intelligent transport system. *Proceedings of the First World Congress on Advanced Transport Telematics and Intelligent Vehicle Highway Systems* (pp. 1613–1622). London: Artech House.

Smiley, A., & Brookhuis, K.A. (1987). Alcohol, drugs and traffic safety. In Rothengatter, J.A., & de Bruin, R.A. (Eds.), *Road users and traffic safety* (pp. 83–105). Assen: Van Gorcum.

Shinar, D. (1998). Psychology on the road; The human factor in traffic safety. New York: Wiley.

Tunbridge, R., Clark, A., Ward, N., Dye, L., & Berghaus, G. (2000). Prioritising drugs and medicines for development of roadside impairment testing. Report Certified DR1 to the European Commission.

Vallet, M. (1991). Les dispositifs de maintien de la vigilance des conducteurs de voiture. In Vallet, M. (Ed.), *Le maintien de la vigilance dans kes transports*. Caen: Paradigm.

Van Wees, K. (2004). Thesis. Delft University of Technology.

Van Winsum, W. (1997). A validation study of a PC-based test of safety aspects of in-vehicle information systems: a test of a map display version of a RDS-TMC task, Report TM-97-C057. Soesterberg: TNO Human Factors Research Institute.

Verwey, W.B., Brookhuis, K.A., & Janssen, W.H. (1996). *Safety effects of in-vehicle information systems*, Report TM-96-C002. Soesterberg, the Netherlands: TNO Human Factors Research Institute.

Ward, N.J. (1996). *Interactions with Intelligent Transport Systems (ITS): effects of task automation and behavioural adaptation*. ITS Focus Workshop 'Intelligent Transport Systems and Safety', Februari 29th 1996, London.

Ward, N.J., Fairclough, S.H., & Humphreys, M. (1995). *The effect of task automation in the automotive context: a field study of an autonomous intelligent cruise control system. International conference on experimental analysis and measurement of situation awareness*, November 1-3, Daytona Beach, Florida, USA.

Zwahlen, H.T., Adams, C.C., & DeBald, D.P. (1988). Safety aspects of CRT touch panel controls in automobiles. In Gale, A.G., Freeman, M.H., Haslegrave, C.M., Smith, P., & Taylor, S.H. (Eds.), *Vision in Vehicles - II* (pp. 335–344). Amsterdam: Elsevier, North-Holland.

Traffic and Transport Psychology
G. Underwood (Editor)
© 2005 Elsevier Ltd. All rights reserved.

23

AGE, PREVIOUS KNOWLEDGE, AND LEARNABILITY OF DRIVER INFORMATION SYSTEMS

Ingo Totzke[1], Michael Hofmann[1] and Hans-Peter Krüger[1]

INTRODUCTION

A growing number of assistance and information functions, so-called driver assistance and information systems, have been integrated into the car. Information systems comprise functions like board computers, Internet, e-mail, SMS, etc. It is generally assumed that the use of information systems while driving adds an extra source of driver distraction, which may lead to a decrease in the driver's security. Distraction effects may be most serious at the beginning of handling information systems while driving (e.g. Brown & Carr, 1989; Damos & Wickens, 1980; Hirst, Spelke, Reaves, Caharack, & Neisser, 1980; Lintern & Wickens, 1991).

Although several empirical approaches deal with learning and memory, there is only little activity in the domain of learnability of menu-driven systems. Most studies deal with learning effects in hypertexts, text processing or mobile phones (e.g. Mead, Spaulding, Sit, Meyer, & Walker, 1997; Mitta & Packebusch, 1995; Naumann, Waniek, & Krems, 2001; Nielsen, Freyr, & Nymand, 1991; Zaphiris, Kurniawan, & Ellis, 2004) but these findings cannot be generalized to driver information systems without problems. A broader overview of learning effects in driver information systems is given by Jahn, Oehme, Rösler, and Krems (2004) who report learning curves in handling these systems for different age groups.

As a part of the project "Learnability of driver information systems" (funded by the Bundesanstalt fuer Strassenwesen and Forschungsvereinigung Automobiltechnik, Germany) the Center for Traffic Sciences addressed the question how users form knowledge on and attain

---

[1] Center for Traffic Sciences (IZVW), University of Wuerzburg, Roentgenring 11, 97070 Wuerzburg, Germany.
E-mail: totzke@psychologie.uni-wuerzburg.de (I. Totzke).

proficiency in previously unknown menu systems (see Totzke, et al., 2004). One emphasis of the project was the influence of the user's age on the learnability of driver information systems. This study takes up this emphasis: the effects of practice and age were examined in a single-task situation (i.e. using the menu system while not moving) and in a dual-task situation (i.e. using the menu system while driving). At first, these results are presented before discussing the possibility to reduce possible age effects by enhancing the previous knowledge of the user.

THEORETICAL BACKGROUND

The background of this problem is the so-called "general slowing hypothesis" (Cepeda, Kramer, & Gonzalez de Sather, 2001; Crossley & Hiscock, 1992; Tsang & Shaner, 1998). This assumption postulates that the speed of information processing of a person reduces with increasing age. Age effects are typically found for complex tasks (McDowd & Craik, 1988) or tasks with a great amount of controlled processing whereas automated processing is not influenced by a person's age (Jennings & Jacoby, 1997). Additionally, elderly people have increasing problems in solving dual-task situations (Crossley & Hiscock, 1992; Salthouse, Rogan, & Prill, 1984; Tsang & Shaner, 1998).

Age effects have also been reported in the domain of car driving (for an overview see Kaiser & Oswald, 2000; Parkin, 1993). Particularly the aspect of attentional deficits in dual-task situations (e.g. usage of driver information systems while driving) is discussed. Dingus et al. (1997), for example, report greater problems for elderly drivers in both driving safety and performance in handling driver information systems while driving (see also Brouwer, Waterink, van Wolffelaar, & Rothengatter, 1991; Ponds, Brouwer, & van Wolffelaar, 1988). Additionally, Green (2001) and Mourant, Tsai, Al-Shihabi, and Jaeger (2000) show that age effects depend on the difficulty of the combined tasks: the more difficult the subsidiary task, the more pronounced the age effects in driving as well as in the secondary task.

Cognitive competences can be positively influenced by adequate intervention programmes up to the eighth decade of a person's lifetime. Correspondingly, age effects can be reduced nearly completely by sufficient practice (Tsang & Shaner, 1998). Moreover, it is assumed that previous knowledge may reduce age effects (Jenkins, Corritore, & Wiedenbeck, 2003). Therefore, deficits in cognitive functions of elderly people, like learning and memory, are rather age-correlated than age-caused deficits (Hasselhorn, 1995).

METHODS

In this study, two menu systems were introduced: a so-called "everyday menu" (which was used in a single-task situation at a usual computer workstation) and a so-called "prototypical menu" (which was used both in single-task and dual-task situation). The "everyday menu" was identical concerning menu structure, but differed relatively from the content of the "prototypical menu". The dual-task conditions were carried out in a driving simulator with movement system. In the following, the menu systems and the driving task are introduced as well as information about procedure and subjects are given.

MENU SYSTEMS

The "everyday menu" was solely used in a single-task situation. In this situation, the subjects had to operate a menu system at a usual computer workstation (see Figure 1 on the left). The "everyday menu" consisted of items from everyday life. This menu system presented terms like house, animal, plant or continents on superordinate levels that led to more specific terms on subordinate levels of the menu system, like, for example, "animal" on superordinate level and "mammal", "farm animal" and "cow" on subordinate levels. This menu system comprised altogether 155 menu functions. As the menu system had been tested in preliminary studies, no semantic ambiguities were expected. The subjects had to execute given tasks within the "everyday menu" as, for example, "Go to dog". They were to head for this target item as fast and precisely as possible. Both navigation within the menu system and choosing the target item were carried out by a commercially available joystick (see Figure 1 on the right). After having chosen the accurate target item a new task was given. If the wrong target item was chosen, a so-called "mistake-display" was shown and the former target item had to be headed for again. In the single-task situation, three blocks of 51 tasks each were conducted.

Figure 1. Computer workstation (left) and joystick (right).

Additionally, the subjects had to handle a prototypical driver information system (called "prototypical menu") in both single-task and dual-task situation. This menu system consisted of 64 menu functions pertaining to superordinate terms like telephone or navigation which are typical for driver information systems in the car (Totzke, Rauch, & Krüger, 2004). The subjects were to execute given tasks as, for example, "Go to Bayern 3" (a radio station in Bavaria). The menu system was presented on a display in the upper middle-console of the car. The joystick was fixed near the gear-change. In the dual-task situation, the subjects had to drive as correctly as possible. They were instructed to use the menu system only in situations that left sufficient cognitive capacity. Therefore, the number of completed tasks differed between subjects. In order to assess dual-task effects, the "prototypical menu" was additionally handled while not moving (single-task situation). The subjects had to head for target items as fast and precisely as possible. Two control blocks of 21 tasks each were conducted.

Both menu systems were presented over a PC which computed the system and recorded information of the actual position within the menu and type and speed of every performed operation with a frequency of 10 Hz. For describing the speed of handling the menu systems, the following data were measured: (a) mean navigation time: the time for heading to the correct target item, (b) mean step time: the time for a single step within the menu system. Additionally, the accuracy of performance was defined by the following data: (c) relative error frequency: the ratio between the number of actually performed steps within the menu system until a subject chose the right target item and the number of minimally required steps within the menu. Values above "1" mean that the subject needed more steps within the menu system than necessary to navigate to the correct target item, (d) frequency of "mistake-displays": the frequency of having chosen a wrong target item.

DRIVING TASK

Handling the "prototypical menu" took place within a driving simulator with movement system (see Figure 2). This simulator consists of a 180° front projection system and three rear projections. It also has a 6-DOF motion system and is controlled by personal computers (for further information visit www.izvw.de). Data are sampled with a frequency of 100 Hz. In order to describe driving, the following parameters reflecting the lateral and longitudinal control of the car are referred to: (a) standard deviation of speed (km/h) and (b) exceeding the lane (frequency).

Figure 2. The Wuerzburg Simulator.

The driving task consisted of rather easy highway-scenarios as, for example, free driving, car following with and without overtaking, a construction site with narrow lane or crossings. The subjects had to choose a mean velocity of 100 km/h. Safety critical situations were introduced in the driving task as well (e.g. sharp left curves in which driving speed had to be reduced to pass through this situation safely). In addition, local traffic situations with a mean velocity of 50 km/h were realized. The sequence of these scenarios was manipulated in order to control effects of succession. The driving task took about 25 min.

The subjects were instructed to drive as correctly as possible. In the dual-task situation, they were instructed to use the menu system only in the situations, which left sufficient cognitive capacity. In order to assess possible dual-task effects, a control drive was carried out in which the subjects had to drive the simulator track without a secondary task.

PROCEDURE

The study was carried out in two sessions within a few days. Figure 3 gives an overview about the experimental sessions. In session 1, the "everyday menu" consisting of items from everyday life was used at a computer workstation (single-task situation, three blocks of 51 tasks each). In session 2, the "prototypical menu" was used in a single-task situation (two blocks of 21 tasks each, called "test") as well as in a dual-task situation while driving (two drives of a varying number of completed tasks, called "drive").

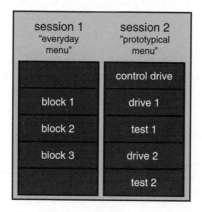

Figure 3. Schematic overview of the sessions.

In order to manipulate the previous knowledge, one half of the subjects only took part in session 2 with the "prototypical menu" whereas the second half of the subjects had already gathered experience with the "everyday menu" in session 1. It was assumed that experience in the "everyday menu" would have beneficial effects on handling the "prototypical menu" in the single-task as well as in the dual-task situation. All the subjects obtained a short introduction concerning structure and handling of the menu systems at their first participation. In this introduction, the subjects had to complete 12 tasks within a so-called "exemplary menu".

SUBJECTS AND DESIGN

In total, 24 subjects were examined in this study. In order to show possible age effects, half of the subjects were aged 55 and more ($m = 61.0$ years, sd $= 3.9$ years, three females, nine males), the other half aged 30 and less ($m = 24.1$ years, sd $= 2.1$ years, seven females, five males). All the subjects had a minimum driving experience of 10,000 km/year. In order to assess possible effects of previous knowledge, one half of each age group took part in both sessions (session 1: "everyday menu", session 2: "prototypical menu"), the other half participated only in session 2 ("prototypical menu").

This study used a mixed within-between design with the within-factor "practice" (blocks of tasks in menu system) and the between factors "age" (young vs. old), "situation" (single-task vs. dual-task situation) and "knowledge" (participation in session 1: yes vs. no).

RESULTS

Age and single-task situation

In a single-task situation (i.e. at a usual computer workplace), the performance of the older subjects in handling the "everyday menu" is lower than the performance of the younger subjects. As Figure 4 on the left shows older subjects take longer to head for the given target item in the menu system. While older subjects need about 10.5 s (sd = 3.4 s) on average to complete the task in block 1, younger subjects take only about 6.2 s (sd = 1.1 s). These age effects can be reduced with increasing practice so that the "mean navigation time" of older subjects averages about 9.7 s (sd = 2.4 s) in block 2 and 7.7 s (sd = 1.5 s) in block 3. Younger subjects take about 5.4 s (sd = 0.4 s) and 4.8 s (sd = 0.3 s) to complete the tasks.

This age-related difference in navigation speed can be attributed at least partially to differences in "mean step time" (see Figure 4 on the right). Older subjects constantly need more time to take another step in the menu system (block 1: m = 1.5 s, sd = 0.4 s; block 2: m = 1.3 s, sd = 0.3 s; block 3: m = 1.1 s, sd = 0.2 s) than young subjects (block 1: m = 0.9 s, sd = 0.2 s; block 2: m = 0.8 s; sd = 0.1 s   block 3: m = 0.7 s, sd = 0.1 s). Even after extensive practice, older subjects do not attain the speed level of the younger subjects.

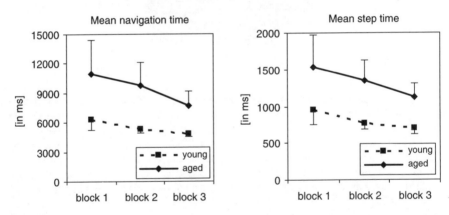

Figure 4. Mean navigation time (left) and mean step time (right) for each of the three trials in the "everyday menu" (N = 12 subjects). Means with standard deviations are displayed.

Particularly in block 1, older subjects make more mistakes in navigating the menu system (old: m = 1.40, sd = 0.12; young: m = 1.27, sd = 0.03; see Figure 5 on the left). Similar results can be found in block 2 (old: m = 1.35, sd = 0.14; young: m = 1.24, sd = 0.04). In block 3, these age effects disappear (old: m = 1.26, sd = 0.06; young: m = 1.24, sd = 0.06). Furthermore, older subjects make more mistakes in choosing the target item in block 1 (old: m = 0.14, sd = 0.19; young: m = 0.01, sd = 0.01) and block 2 (old: m = 0.09, sd = 0.10; young: m = 0.02, sd = 0.02) whereas no age-related effect exists in block 3 (old: m = 0.03, sd = 0.04; young: m = 0.01, sd = 0.02 see Figure 5 on the right). Older subjects seem to have more problems with remembering the target item they had to head for in block 1 and block 2.

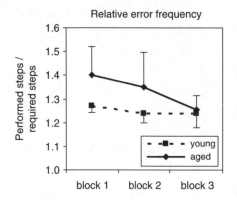
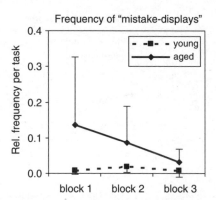

Figure 5. Relative error frequency (left) and relative frequency of "mistake-displays" (right) for each of the three trials in the "everyday menu" ($N = 12$ subjects). Means with standard deviations are displayed.

At last, the higher interpersonal variability of the older subjects both in speed and accuracy of handling the menu system has to be emphasized (see Figures 4 and 5).

All in all, this demonstrates that older subjects can achieve the level of accuracy of the younger subjects. Whereas significant age-related differences in speed have to be considered independently from practice in handling a menu system, young and old subjects are comparable concerning accuracy after extensive practice.

Age and transfer effects

Even with prior experience in handling the "everyday menu" in session 1, older subjects have greater problems in learning the "prototypical menu" in session 2 than younger subjects. While younger subjects can maintain their mean navigation time in both menu systems (session 1—block 3: $m = 4.7$ s, sd $= 0.2$ s, session 2—block 1: $m = 5.6$ s, sd $= 0.7$ s; block 2: $m = 4.4$ s, sd $= 0.4$ s), older subjects take longer to head for the target items in the "prototypical menu" (session 1—block 3: $m = 7.8$ s, sd $= 1.6$ s, session 2— block 1: $m = 14.0$ s, sd $= 5.8$ s; block 2: $m = 10.3$ s, sd $= 4.6$ s; see Figure 6 on the left). Similarly, older subjects make more mistakes in choosing the target item in the "prototypical menu" (parameter "frequency of 'mistake displays'", session 1—block 3: $m = 0.03$, sd $= 0.04$, session 2—block 1: $m = 0.33$, sd $= 0.25$; block 2: $m = 0.10$, sd $= 0.13$). An effect of the menu system on level of accuracy cannot be found for younger subjects (session 1—block 3: $m = 0.01$, sd $= 0.02$, session 2—block 1: $m = 0.04$, sd $= 0.05$; block 2: $m = 0.03$, sd $= 0.03$; Figure 6 on the right). Furthermore, interpersonal differences between older subjects are greater than between young subjects. Thus, older subjects have more problems in transferring knowledge from handling the "everyday menu" to the "prototypical menu".

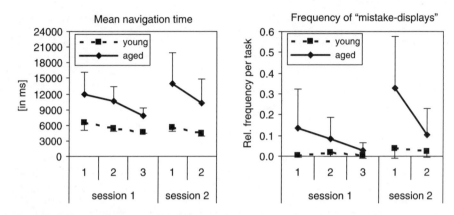

Figure 6. Mean navigation time (left) and relative frequency of "mistake-displays" (right) for each of the three trials in the "everyday menu" (session 1) and the "prototypical menu" (session 2; $N = 12$ subjects). Means with standard deviations are displayed.

Age and dual-task situation

The introduction of a dual-task situation leads to typical dual-task effects both in menu handling and in driving. At first, there are significant losses in speed and accuracy in the use of the menu system for young and old subjects in comparison to single-task situations. This effect can be attributed to the instruction that the subjects had to drive as correctly as possible and to use the menu system only in the situations, which left sufficient cognitive capacity. As expected, learning effects in using the menu system are found. With growing practice, the subjects head for the target item faster and make fewer mistakes within the menu system.

On average, older subjects complete fewer tasks in the menu system while driving than younger subjects (old—drive 1: $m = 18.9$, sd $= 7.8$; drive 2: $m = 35.2$, sd $= 13.7$; young—drive 1: $m = 37.6$, sd $= 8.9$; drive 2: $m = 50.0$, sd $= 12.4$; see Figure 7 on the left). This is caused by

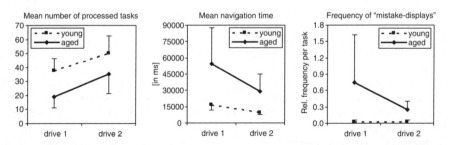

Figure 7. Mean number of processed tasks (left), mean navigation time (middle) and relative frequency of "mistake-displays" (right) for each of the two drives with secondary task ($N = 24$ subjects). Means with standard deviations are displayed.

higher mean navigation times for old subjects (old—drive 1: $m = 54.5$ s, sd $= 32.8$ s; drive 2: $m = 28.7$ s, sd $= 16.4$ s; young – drive 1: $m = 16.6$ s, sd $= 4.8$ s; drive 2: $m = 9.7$ s, sd $= 2.0$ s; see Figure 7 in the middle). Moreover, older subjects navigate less accurately within the menu system and make more mistakes in choosing the target item (old—drive 1: $m = 0.75$, sd $= 0.88$; drive 2: $m = 0.25$, sd $= 0.15$; young—drive 1: $m = 0.02$, sd $= 0.03$; drive 2: $m = 0.03$, sd $= 0.03$; see Figure 7 on the right). With increasing practice, these age effects diminish. Although older subjects do not achieve the performance level of younger subjects, age-related losses decrease significantly.

Additionally, detrimental effects of handling the "prototypical menu" can be found in driving. In the following, some results for free driving sections of the simulator track are presented. As can be seen in Figure 8 on the left, mean velocity in free driving is lower for the older subjects even in the control drive. Whereas older subjects drive with about 94.3 km/h (sd $= 7.9$ km/h), younger subjects choose a mean velocity of 100.3 km/h (sd $= 3.8$ km/h). The introduction of the secondary task strengthens this age effect: While the mean velocity of older subjects is about 81.0 km/h (sd $= 14.3$ km/h) in drive 1 and about 77.0 km/h (sd $= 13.4$ km/h) in drive 2, the mean velocity of the younger subjects is about 97.4 km/h (sd $= 6.1$ km/h) and 96.7 km/h (sd $= 7.3$ km/h). Hence, age-correlated differences in mean velocity are more prominent under dual-task conditions. There is no learning effect of using the menu system on driving. Learning effects of young and older subjects (for example: completing more tasks in the menu system while driving) take place only in the subsidiary task. As a consequence, the reduction of mean velocity is rather a dual-task effect than an effect of learnability.

Similar results can be shown for the variation of lateral position which is represented by the parameter "frequency of exceeding the lane", shown in Figure 8 on the right. At first, older subjects exceed the lane more often than young subjects in single-task as well as in dual-task conditions. Younger subjects leave this area about 0.25 times (sd $= 0.57$) in the control drive and about 0.90 times (sd $= 1.67$) in drive 1 and 1.12 times (sd $= 1.66$) in drive 2. On an average, older subjects leave this area about 0.78 times (sd $= 1.30$) in the control drive and

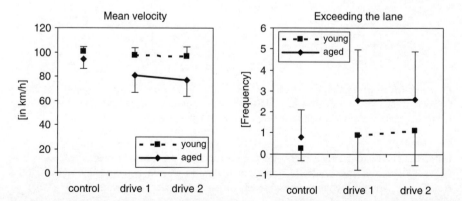

Figure 8. Mean velocity (left) and mean frequency of exceeding the lane (right) for each of the three drives ($N = 24$ subjects). Means with standard deviations are displayed.

about 2.53 times (sd = 2.43) in drive 1 and 2.58 times (sd = 2.29) in drive 2. Therefore, the age effect is more strengthened in the dual-task condition. At last, no influence of practice in using the menu system on driving can be found.

As a conclusion, particularly older subjects show problems in using a menu system while driving. Although older subjects generally drive more slowly and complete fewer tasks in the subsidiary task, these attempts to compensate age-related deficits are not sufficient for preventing the car from exceeding the lane.

Reduction of age effects

In order to reduce these age-related effects, a manipulation of the previous knowledge was introduced (i.e. participation in session 1). Figure 9 on the left shows the positive effect of the previous knowledge of older subjects on speed in using the menu system. Particularly in drive 1, there is an advantage of older subjects who have taken part in session 1 in which they encountered the "everyday menu" (knowledge: $m = 36.6$ s, sd = 18.0 s; no knowledge: $m = 69.5$ s, sd = 36.1 s). In drive 2, this knowledge effect decreases significantly for older subjects, but can still be shown (knowledge: $m = 23.4$ s, sd = 9.4 s; no knowledge: $m = 33.2$ s, sd = 20.3 s). For younger subjects, a knowledge effect cannot be found (drive 1— knowledge: $m = 16.5$ s, sd = 3.4 s; no knowledge: $m = 16.7$ s, sd = 6.2 s; drive 2— knowledge: $m = 10.7$ s, sd = 1.9 s; no knowledge: $m = 8.7$ s, sd = 1.6 s). Similar results were found for levels of accuracy in handling the menu system (see parameter "frequency of 'mistake-displays'" in Figure 9 on the right).

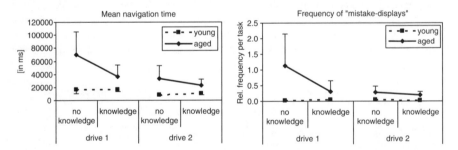

Figure 9. Mean navigation time (left) and relative frequency of "mistake-displays" (right) for each of the two drives with a secondary task. Means with standard deviations are displayed for participants with or without knowledge ($N = 24$ subjects).

Unfortunately, there is only a slight effect of previous knowledge on driving for old as well as for young subjects. Independently from participating in session 1, older subjects exceed the lane more often than young subjects (old—drive 1 knowledge: $m = 2.37$, sd = 2.65; no knowledge: $m = 2.70$, sd = 2.33; drive 2 knowledge: $m = 2.43$, sd = 2.47; no knowledge: $m = 2.73$, sd = 2.13; young—drive 1 knowledge: $m = 0.70$, sd = 1.37; no knowledge: $m = 1.10$, sd = 1.94; drive 2 knowledge: $m = 1.03$, sd = 1.38; no knowledge: $m = 1.20$, sd = 1.92;

see Figure 10). Experience in handling the "prototypical menu" while driving does not have a major effect on lateral control of the vehicle. Hence, previous knowledge in the domain of menu handling does not improve the driver's security with a subsidiary task.

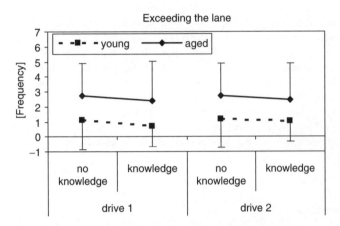

Figure 10. Mean frequency of exceeding the lane for each of the two drives. Means with standard deviations are displayed for participants with or without knowledge ($N = 24$ subjects).

CONCLUSIONS

All in all, this study demonstrates impressive age effects on the learnability of menu-driven information systems in single-task as well as in dual-task situations. Older users navigate menu systems with less speed irrespective of their degree of practice but these differences are reduced with increasing practice. Age-related differences in accuracy of using the menu system can only be shown at the beginning of practice. Generally, navigation speed and accuracy of older users differ more strongly between subjects. Therefore, older users can learn menu systems just like young users—they only have to invest more time at the beginning of practice.

Age effects are more prominent under dual-task conditions both in using the menu system and in driving. Although older users choose a lower mean velocity and complete less tasks in the menu system, these attempts to compensate age-related deficits do not prevent the driver from exceeding the lane. Therefore, older drivers seem to have more problems in integrating a secondary task (i.e. handling a driver information system) in driving. Effects of practice in the dual-task situation take place only on side of menu handling. Whereas age-related deficits in the secondary task are reduced with increasing practice, detrimental effects in driving remain constant.

Age effects in handling the menu system can be reduced by previous knowledge in single-task as well as in dual-task situations. Thus, active practicing a menu system may be recommended. On the other hand, a beneficial effect of previous knowledge was not found for vehicle handling of older users so that practice will not suffice to enhance driver's security. It is rather recommended for older drivers not to use driver information systems while driving. However, several older drivers are aware of these age-related risks in security as they revealed in an inquiry after the main study. They indicated that they usually would not use a driver information system while driving.

In the end, two methodological comments have to be added. At first, there are large differences between subjects concerning the total number of completed tasks in the menu system while driving. Younger subjects generally completed more tasks than older subjects so that conclusions of age-related effects based on drive 2 have to be taken with care as these effects may be overestimated. However, the direction of results remains the same. Second, previous knowledge for handling menu systems is largely age correlated (Kurniawan & Zaphiris, 2003). Younger subjects are more experienced in using mobile phones or personal computers than older subjects. Thus, the age effects presented in this study are not based on the biological age of the subjects alone but can also be attributed to age-correlated experience in handling menu systems.

REFERENCES

Brouwer, W.H., Waterink, W., Van Wolffelaar, P.C., & Rothengatter, T. (1991). Divided attention in experienced young and older drivers: lane tracking and visual analysis in a dynamic driving simulator. *Human Factors, 33* (5), 573–582.

Brown, T.L., & Carr, T.H. (1989). Automaticity in skill acquisition: mechanisms for reducing interference in concurrent performance. *Journal of Experimental Psychology: Human Perception and Performance, 15* (4), 686–700.

Cepeda, N.J., Kramer, A.F., & Gonzalez de Sather, J.C.M. (2001). Changes in executive control across the life span: examination of task-switching performance. *Developmental Psychology, 37* (5), 715–730.

Crossley, M., & Hiscock, M. (1992). Age-related differences in concurrent-task performance of normal adults: evidence for a decline in processing resources. *Psychology and Aging, 7*, 499–506.

Damos, D., & Wickens, C.D. (1980). The acquisition and transfer of time-sharing skills. *Acta Psychologica, 6*, 569–577.

Dingus, T.A., Hulse, M.C., Mollenhauer, M.A., Fleischman, R.N., McGehee, D.V., & Manakkal, N. (1997). Effects of age, system experience, and navigation technique on driving with an advanced traveler information system. *Human Factors, 39*, 177–199.

Green, P. (2001). *Variations in Task Performance between Younger and Older Drivers: UMTRI Research on Telematics.* Paper presented at the Association for the Advancement of Automotive Medicine Conference on Aging and Driving. Southfield, Michigan 19./20.02.2001.

Hasselhorn, M. (1995). Individuelle Differenzen im Bereich des Lernens und des Gedächtnisses [Individual differences in learning and memory]. In Amelang, M. (Ed.), *Verhaltens-und Leistungsunterschiede [Differences in Behaviour and Perform-ance], Enzyklopädie der Psychologie, Themenbereich C Theorie und Forschung, Serie VIII Differentielle Psychologie und Persönlichkeitsforschung Band 2*, (pp. 435–468). Göttingen: Hogrefe.

Hirst, W., Spelke, E.S., Reaves, C.C., Caharack, G., & Neisser, U. (1980). Dividing attention without alternation or automaticity. *Journal of Experimental Psychology: General, 109* (8), 98–117.

Jahn, G., Oehme, A., Rösler, D., & Krems, J.F. (2004). *Kompetenzerwerb im Umgang mit Fahrerinformationssystemen [Learnability in handling driver information systems], Berichte für Straßenwesen, Fahrzeugtechnik, Heft F 47.* Bergisch Gladbach: Wirtschaftsverlag NW.

Jenkins, C., Corritore, C.L., & Wiedenbeck, S. (2003). Patterns of information seeking on the web: a qualitative study of domain expertise and web expertise. *IT&Society, 1* (3), 64–89.

Jennings, J.M., & Jacoby, L.L. (1997). An opposition procedure for detecting age-related deficits in recollection: telling effects of repetition. *Psychology and Aging, 12,* 352–361.

Kaiser, H.J., & Oswald, W.D. (2000). Autofahren im Alter—eine Literaturanalyse [Driving and advanced age—a literature analysis]. *Zeitschrift für Gerontopsychologie & -Psychiatrie, 13,* 131–170.

Kurniawan, S.H., & Zaphiris, P. (2003). Web health information architecture for older users. *IT&Society, 1* (3), 42–63.

Lintern, G., & Wickens, C.D. (1991). Issues for acquisition and transfer of time-sharing and dual-task skills. In Damos, D.L. (Ed.), *Multiple-task Performance* (pp. S123–S138). London: Taylor & Francis Ltd.

McDowd, J.M., & Craik, F.I.M. (1988). Effects of aging and task difficulty on divided attention performance. *Journal of Experimental Psychology: Human Perception and Performance, 14,* 267–280.

Mead, S.E., Spaulding, V.A., Sit, R.A., Meyer, B., & Walker, N. (1997). Effects of age and training on world wide web navigation strategies, *Proceedings of the Human Factors and Ergonomics Society,* 41st Annual Meeting, pp. 152–156.

Mitta, D., & Packebusch, S.J. (1995). Improving interface quality: an investigation of human-computer interaction task learning. *Ergonomics, 38,* 1307–1325.

Mourant, R.R., Tsai, F., Al-Shihabi, T., & Jaeger, B.K. (2000). Divided attention ability of young and older drivers. *National Highway Traffic Safety Internet Forum,* 1–11.

Naumann, A., Waniek, J., & Krems, J. (2001). Knowledge acquisition, navigation and eye movements from text and hypertext. In Reips, U.-D., & Bosnjak, M. (Eds.), *Dimensions of Internet Science* (pp. 293–304). Lengerich: Pabst Science Publishers.

Nielsen, J., Freyr, I., & Nymand, H.O. (1991). The learnability of HyperCard as an object-oriented programming system. *Behaviour and Information Technology, 10,* 111–120.

Parkin, A.J. (1993). Getting old. In Parkin, A.J. (Ed.), *Memory—Phenomena, Experiment, and Theory* (pp. 172–195). Oxford, UK: Blackwell.

Ponds, R.W., Brouwer, W.H., & Van Wolffelaar, P.C. (1988). Age differences in divided attention in a simulated driving task. *Journals of Gerontology, 43* (6), 151–156.

Salthouse, T.A., Rogan, J.D., & Prill, K.A. (1984). Division of attention: age differences on a visually presented memory task. *Memory & Cognition, 12,* 613–620.

Totzke, I., Rauch, N., & Krüger, H.-P. (2004). Kompetenzerwerb und Struktur von Menüsystemen im Fahrzeug: "Breiter ist besser?" [Learnability and structure of menu systems in the car: "broad is better?"]. In Steffens, C., Thüring, M., & Urbas, L. (Eds.), *Entwerfen und Gestalten [Designing and Shaping], 5. Berliner Werkstatt für Mensch-Maschine-Systeme, ZMMS Spektrum, Band 18,* (pp. 226–249). Düsseldorf: VDI-Verlag.

Totzke, I., Hofmann, M., Meilinger, T., Rauch, N., Schmidt, G., & Krüger, H.-P. (2004). *Kompetenzerwerb für Informationssysteme—Einfluss des Lernprozesses auf die Interaktion mit Fahrerinformationssystemen [Learnability of information systems— influence of the learning process on the interaction with driver information systems].* FAT–Schriftenreihe Band 184. Offenbach: Berthold Druck.

Tsang, P.S., & Shaner, T.L. (1998). Age, attention, expertise, and time-sharing performance. *Psychology and Aging, 13*, 323–347.

Zaphiris, P., Kurniawan, S.H., & Ellis, R.D. (2004). Age related differences and the depth vs. breadth tradeoff in hierarchical online information systems. [Online-Resource]. Available: http://www.soi.city.ac.uk/~zaphiri/Papers/ERCIM02.pdf (12.04.2004).

Traffic and Transport Psychology
G. Underwood (Editor)
© 2005 Elsevier Ltd. All rights reserved.

24

AUTOMATED DRIVING DOES NOT WORK WITHOUT THE INVOLVEMENT OF THE DRIVER

Lena Nilsson[1]

INTRODUCTION

Technological progress has made automation of processes in various sectors of society possible. Reasons for introducing automation are, e.g. to increase effectiveness, to free human beings from unsuitable and dangerous tasks, and to eliminate what is usually called the (problem of the) "human factor". Automated systems can work with great strength and high precision, and all around the clock without showing signs of fatigue.

The development of Intelligent Transport Systems (ITS) enables bringing automation into the transport sector. The introduction of ITS in road transport started with the PROMETHEUS project about 20 years ago, and may turn out to be one of the most comprehensive and revolutionary transformations of the road traffic system. The general ITS objectives are to increase traffic efficiency, to improve traffic safety and to reduce traffic related pollution (Franzén, 1993; Perrett & Stevens, 1996). However, when it comes to how individual drivers are, or will be, influenced by the use of ITS there is still a lot more to wish for in spite of two decades of research. In this connection it is important to remember that the possibility to achieve the general social objectives is to a large extent controlled by changes at the individual level. It is obvious that the resulting impact depends on the type of ITS (driver assistance), the system design (HMI), implementation scenarios and strategies, etc. Considering the negative impact of human errors, and taking on the traditional view of human related factors as frequent causes of traffic accidents, replacement of as many human functions as possible with automated ones *may* appear as an attractive way of improving traffic safety. Thus, whether it is preferable to aim towards

[1] Swedish National Road and Transport Research Institute (VTI), Linköping, Sweden. *E-mail:*lena.nilsson@vti.se (L. Nilsson).

replacing the driver, or a number of driver functions, by automated driving is at least a reasonable question to ask.

THE DRIVING TASK AND TRAFFIC CONTEXT

Car driving can be described as performing a complex and dynamic control task (Rouse, 1981) within a "system", i.e. in traffic. Along with practising the driving task drivers increase their experience. They develop rules and schemas that control their behaviour in various (foreseen) situations. Thus, for experienced drivers the driving is a highly automated task.

When driving in traffic, drivers continuously meet a sequence of different situations. These situations are numerous, neither static nor similar, and very often they require that the drivers adapt their behaviour and interact with other road users. The road itself and the infrastructure remain relatively constant over time, but vary spatially. Adverse conditions may complicate the driving task further. Thus, the traffic context is characterised by continuously changing prerequisites and conditions. Therefore, car driving includes continuous *monitoring* of relevant parts of the environment. The driver has to know *where and when* to search (mainly look) for and acquire necessary information.

Secondly, today's traffic provides an enormous amount of potential information. However, during a specific journey only a small proportion of all available information is usually of importance, while most of it can be classified as "noise". The driver must be able to distinguish necessary and important information from information that is irrelevant for the task (trip) at hand. Therefore, car driving includes *selection* of relevant information from a "noisy" whole, meaning that the driver has to know *what* information is important and of relevance on different occasions and in various situations.

Finally, chance events and various degrees of uncertainty appear in traffic (Summala, 1986). The degree of uncertainty varies with how strongly the traffic and the traffic environment are regulated, and with how well road users obey and follow formal and informal rules and regulations. Therefore, car driving includes *readiness* for unexpected situations. Because situations not always develop accordingly and "as usual" the driver has to be prepared to *revise* and *change* planned actions, even if they result from "correct" predictions and interpretations based on previous knowledge and experience.

In summary, driving in the traffic context requires adapting to a continuously changing, complex and partly stochastic environment offering a certain amount of relevant information hidden in a large amount of "noise".

The demands from driving in the traffic context, as described above, require access to a number of human abilities and skills, which are more or less stable (or variable) over time and integrated together (Figure 1). The integrated total of perceptual, cognitive and motor abilities and skills are modified by experience, feedback, expectations and predictions as well as by the influence from motivation and attitudes. These mediating factors may also vary over time.

Figure 1. Human abilities and skills necessary to be possessed and integrated by the driver to meet the demands from the driving task.

The introduction of various types of driver assistance is intended to facilitate driving by *supporting* the described monitoring, selecting and (sometimes unpredicted) acting tasks demanded by the traffic context. An automated system, *replacing* the functions of the driver, thus has to possess a number of human qualities involved in driving. The system should for instance be able to predict, select, comprehend, integrate, adapt, execute, etc. Thus, in general, that is what an automated system has to fulfil! Is it a possible, reasonable or even wanted goal to aim for?

INTRODUCTION OF DRIVER ASSISTANCE

Introducing driver assistance based on new technology (ITS) can be seen as adding another component to the traditional driver–vehicle–environment interaction (Figure 2). It is reasonable to believe that adding this new component leads to increased complexity of the interaction. The foreseen increase of complexity can easily be imagined from the larger number of possible information and communication links when introducing an assistance system compared to the traditional interaction pattern (thick always bi-directional arrows compared to thin arrows in Figure 2).

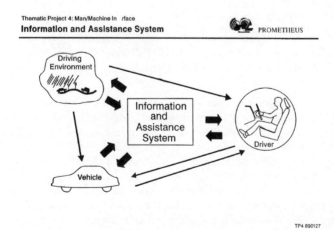

Figure 2. Adding driver information and assistance systems as a separate (fourth) component to the traditional three component driver–vehicle–environment interaction model (PROMETHEUS, 1989).

Along with the implementation of IT-based driver assistance, the driving task will gradually change as will the allocation of tasks between the human driver and the technical system. The changes include:

- *Transferring* certain human tasks to the technical system
- *Modifying* certain human tasks
- *Adding* new human tasks

TOWARDS HIGHER DEGREES OF AUTOMATION

The functionality of driver assistance systems can range from pure information to system intervention, i.e. it can represent varying levels of system automation, from the driver's perspective degrees of driver control. Five levels are usually distinguished:

Information. The driver assistance system presents a description of the "state of affairs" to the driver, who is in complete control ("in the loop"), and has to detect and interpret the information, take decisions and act.

Warning. The driver assistance system notifies the driver that a safety related limit/margin is reached (or passed) in situations where an immediate action is needed. The criterion for activation of a warning is set by "someone" else but the driver, usually the system designer. System designs that allow alternative criteria to be selected individually by drivers may be available.

Advise. Together with attracting the driver's attention, by informing or warning, the driver assistance system also recommends an action, e.g. a lane change, a speed reduction, a braking procedure.

Support. The driver assistance system starts an action, which the driver is supposed to continue, e.g. initiates a speed reduction by applying a counter force in the accelerator.

Intervention. Automated driving, where the driver assistance system takes over the control and acts automatically. The driver is "out of the loop". Full automation is (and probably will be) rarely used in driving, and most systems of this type can be overridden by the driver in certain circumstances.

If the driver is looked upon as being *unsafe*, i.e. as making errors that frequently cause accidents, while automated driving is looked upon as being *safe*, i.e. not causing such errors, then it may be possible that replacing the driver would lead to improved traffic safety with the driver playing a less critical role in future traffic—but only *if*. How factors with safety implications, like drivers' performance and condition, will be influenced by introducing automation of the task cannot be fully predicted from current knowledge. However, available research, for instance from the area of aviation, shows that human operators are very much needed in the control loop also in cases of high degrees of automation (Endsley & Kiris, 1995; Wickens, 1992). Technological assistance usually increases the demand on human cognition, while the demand on human action is reduced, as the operator's role changes from mainly manual to more supervisory control. Such a change may have negative consequences, as man is better at the first type of tasks. Besides, human performance of supervisory tasks has been shown to be impaired after a relatively short time on the task. The threat when placing the driver out of the loop may be diminished situation awareness (Endsley, 1995), incomplete understanding of the system's functional envelope and limitations, distrust or over-reliance on the assistance system, less or no practicing of the manual tasks, long periods of low workload with "nothing to do" interrupted by short periods of "critical" situations with very high workload. These deteriorations will have a negative impact on the driver's ability to take over when technology fails or conditions outside its functional envelope appear. When this happens, and it probably will, the impact of the driver's behaviour may become more rather than less important and crucial. Thus, in future traffic it is not unrealistic to assume that the traditional driver errors leading to accidents will decrease and new types of (technology induced) driver errors appear as accident causes. Also, the technical shortcomings will probably be rare, but combined with related new driver errors they may lead to severe consequences. Thus, automated systems still require humans and machines in interaction, making it impossible to eliminate the human driver. Instead the focus should be on optimising the interaction.

EMPIRICAL EXAMPLE

Adaptive cruise control (ACC) can be used as an example of a driver assistance system performing automated driving. It is designed to automatically keep a speed set by the driver as long as the time headway to vehicles ahead is longer than a preset minimum. In case the headway decreases to below the preset minimum, the ACC maintains the minimum headway by automatically reducing the speed. ACC systems are introduced as "comfort systems" and not primarily intended to improve safety. Their functional envelope is limited in terms of, for example, braking capacity and speed range, and fully automated driving can only be performed in certain traffic environments (road types and situations). Thus, the driver must have a correct understanding of the system limitations, supervise the automated driving, and intervene in case situations appear which cannot be handled by the ACC.

A study in the high fidelity driving simulator at VTI was undertaken to study ACC driving in situations requiring immediate manual intervention (Nilsson, 1995). The scenario used was a motorway with two lanes in each direction. Along the test route specifically designed "critical" traffic situations appeared (Figure 3). The two situations "cars ahead braking hard" with brake lights being lit (Figure 3, left) and "car pulling out from an overtaken queue" (Figure 3, middle) required more braking capacity than the ACC could generate. However, in these cases the ACC was able to detect the situation, knew its technical shortcomings, and presented a warning if necessary, i.e. when the driver had to intervene to avoid a collision. In the third situation, "stationary queues", the drivers approached standing-still vehicles in both lanes (Figure 3, right). Also in this case the braking capacity of the ACC was insufficient, but because the ACC was unable to detect stationary objects the drivers were not warned. They themselves had to detect the queues, interpret the situation (increased risk) and reduce the speed accordingly to avoid a collision.

Resulting TTC (time to collision) levels in the three "critical" situations are shown in Figure 4. In the situations with "cars ahead braking hard" and "car pulling out from an overtaken queue" ACC supported driving resulted in prolonged TTCs. A reasonable interpretation is that ACC supported driving leads to larger safety margins. This was *not* the case in the situation with the "stationary queues" where TTC decreased. The TTC result in a fourth situation, "out of range",

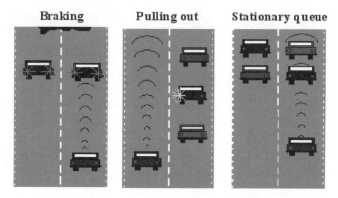

Figure 3. "Critical" traffic situations used to study situations where manual intervention is needed when driving with ACC.

is also presented in Figure 4. In this situation the speed dropped to outside the functional envelope of the ACC, i.e. to outside the lower speed limit of 30 km/h. Thus, the large TTC prolongation was a self-evident result in this case.

The strength of the driver interventions in the three "critical" situations is shown in Figure 5. Both the applied braking forces and the resulting deceleration levels are generally larger in the ACC supported condition compared with the unsupported condition.

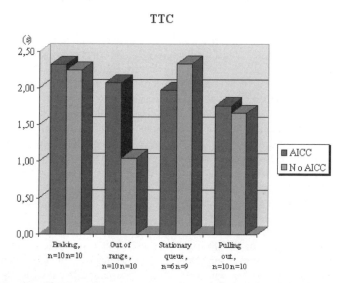

Figure 4. Resulting TTC values (means) for ACC supported and unsupported driving in "critical" situations, n = drivers managing the situations without having a collision.

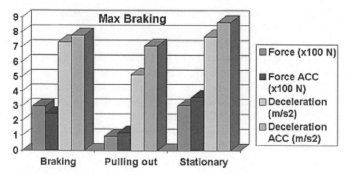

Figure 5. Resulting brake forces and deceleration values (means) for ACC supported and unsupported driving in "critical" situations.

The obtained results are summarised below for each "critical" situation separately, focusing on implications for the introduction of automated driving. In the situation with the *stationary queues* the ACC supported drivers reacted very late and abruptly when approaching the queue tails. Four out of 10 drivers could not manage the situation and had a collision, compared to one out of 10 drivers in the unsupported condition. The collisions could *not* be explained by increased workload or decreased alertness. The following can, at least partly, explain the result. During the driving session, and before the appearance of the stationary queues, the drivers had experienced several situations where the ACC acted and decreased speed automatically when approaching slower vehicles ahead. However, in the situation with the stationary queues the ACC did nothing, not even presented a warning. The drivers knew from the system description that the ACC could not handle stationary objects, but recognised too late that the situation they approached was such that they had to intervene and adapt the speed manually. Thus, in this situation the ACC had a negative impact on safety, probably to some extent because of the drivers' incorrect representation of the functional envelope and limitations of the ACC combined with (over-)reliance on the system and very little experience of ACC driving. A less negative impact on traffic safety can probably be achieved by improved system design and introduction as well as by training.

In the situation with a *car pulling out from an overtaken queue* immediate driver reactions were recorded for ACC supported *and* unsupported drivers. The reactions (interventions) were so quick that no warnings were activated in the ACC condition. However, in this situation ACC supported driving resulted in clearly larger braking forces and decelerations compared with unsupported driving. A reasonable explanation is that the situation with a car pulling out from an overtaken queue activated an over-learnt and automated behaviour no matter whether the drivers were driving with an ACC activated or not. The drivers had already developed rules and schemas to be applied in this type of situation, and the presence of the ACC did not influence this behaviour. The situation was in this respect "ACC neutral".

The situation with *cars ahead braking hard* resulted in rather strong but less immediate and timely driver actions (interventions). There were no large differences between the performance of ACC supported drivers and unsupported drivers, but their performance differed more than in the situation with a car pulling out from an overtaken queue. However, when cars ahead applied the brakes the ACC drivers did not intervene until after the warning was presented, leading to a more "homogenous" intervention pattern with less inter-individual variability. The basis for the somewhat delayed (re)action could be that situations with brake lights going on are common and frequent events in motorway driving, but usually not "that critical". For this reason, the drivers probably experienced the situation with cars ahead braking hard as less critical than for instance the situation with stationary queues. The behaviour was not automated in the sense that the activated brake lights on cars ahead immediately and automatically triggered a rule and initiated a predestined reaction. Instead, the drivers waited for the ACC to react (warn and "ask for" intervention), and thus used the warning onset as a control parameter.

DRIVER ASSISTANCE SYSTEMS AROUND THE CORNER

A number of driver assistance systems, representing different levels of automation, are already on the market or very close to enter. To reach a successful implementation and use of these systems and in a more long-term perspective the intended safety improvements, it has to be some guarantee that drivers can cope with the new task demands imposed. For this to be a reality human factors and traffic safety people, vehicle and system manufacturers have to co-operate in making driver assistance a help, not a hindrance creating "new" problems. In this process there are key issues that are important and necessary to keep in mind and work with towards an optimal system design. Some of them, focusing on automated driving but also applicable more generally, are

- Designing the systems based on human abilities, limitations and variability
- Ensuring that the driver remains in the control loop
- Making the system performance transparent (predictable, comprehensible, controllable)
- Making the system limitations and functional envelope clear and comprehensible (involves several "dimensions")
- Promoting correct and complete system representations (mental models) among the system users
- Clarifying who is doing what, driver and system
- Enabling timely driver interventions
- Promoting willingness to use as well as intended use
- Minimising (the possibility of) misuse

CONCLUSION

Driver assistance has been discussed all the way to replacing the driver, or certain driver functions, by automated driving. The discussion has emanated both from theoretical considerations and from using an empirical example, an investigation of possible effects of ACC driving in "critical" traffic situations. Both approaches result in the view that *automated driving does not work without the involvement of the driver, because also automated driving means interaction between humans/drivers and machines/vehicles.* The technical design of future driving assistance systems, also highly automated ones, are expected to be improved considerably. Therefore, some of the problems pointed out here, but not all, will most certainly be replaced by improved solutions and irrelevant. However, in the foreseeable time it will not be possible to design automated functions that work safely and appropriately in all possible traffic environments and conditions. The human driver with her specific qualities will be needed to intervene at certain occasions, and probably also to some extent decide and judge where and when to use what assistance. And even if automated systems can be designed to "know" their shortcomings, recognise situations they cannot handle, and communicate that knowledge by for example warnings, the human driver is very much needed to take care of these warnings and act accordingly.

REFERENCES

Endsley, M.R. (1995). Towards a theory of situation awareness in dynamic systems. *Human Factors, 37* (1), 65–84.

Endsley, M.R., & Kiris, E.O. (1995). The out-of-the-loop performance problem and level of control in automation. *Human Factors, 37* (2), 381–394.

Franzén, S. (1993). Introduction. In Franzén, S., & Parkes, A.M. (Eds.), *Driving future vehicles* (pp. 3–5). London: Taylor & Francis.

Nilsson, L. (1995). Safety effects of adaptive cruise controls in critical traffic situations. In VERTIS (Ed.), *Proceedings of "Steps Forward", the Second World Congress on Intelligent Transport Systems* (Vol. 3, pp. 1254–1259), Yokohama, Japan.

Perrett, K.E., & Stevens, A. (1996). *Review of the potential benefits of road transport telematics, TRL report 220.* Crowthorne, England: TRL.

PROMETHEUS. (1989). Introducing information and assistance systems in the driver–vehicle–environment interaction. Presentation material. PROMETHEUS HMI working group.

Rouse, W.B. (1981). Human–computer interaction in the control of dynamic systems. *Computer Surveys, 13* (1), 71–99.

Summala, H. (1986). The deterministic man in a stochastic world: Risk management on the road. In Brehmer, B., Jungerman, H., Lourens, P., & Sevon, G. (Eds.), *New directions in research on decision making.* Amsterdam: North-Holland.

Wickens, C.D. (1992). *Engineering psychology and human performance* (2nd ed.). New York: Harper Collins Publishers.

Traffic and Transport Psychology
G. Underwood (Editor)
© 2005 Elsevier Ltd. All rights reserved.

25

THE ROLE OF EXPECTATIONS IN INTERACTION BEHAVIOUR BETWEEN CAR DRIVERS

Maura Houtenbos[1,2], Marjan Hagenzieker[1], Peter Wieringa[2] and Andrew Hale[2]

INTRODUCTION

Background of the problem

Most of the research on traffic behaviour has focused on the individual road user, despite the fact that road users rarely encounter traffic situations in which they are not confronted with other road users. Most models of the driving task represent the driving task from the perspective of one individual road user. For example, in an overview article on driver behaviour models, Michon (1985) discusses models that primarily take only one active road user into account. Until now, models of driving behaviour focus on the interaction between road users and their impact on each other.

Take, for example, an intersection with two road users approaching each other from different directions. In this case, direct verbal communication with each other is not possible. Despite this, situations like these rarely develop into an accident. Michon (1985) points out that the interactions between road users are mediated by distinctive and frequently subtle cues. In the past, attempts to describe the relations between such cues and the road user's behaviour have been made, which have often taken the form of ethological models (Bliersbach & Dellen, 1980; Shor, 1964; van der Molen, 1983). In these models an attempt is made to determine specific behaviour, which elicits stimulus configurations. Unfortunately, as the focus is on the observable interaction situation, these models have not been able to describe the information processing of road users in interaction situations, which can be considered to drive the overt behaviour (e.g. paying attention to stimuli, interpreting them and deciding how to respond).

---

[1] SWOV Institute for Road Safety Research, Leidschendam, The Netherlands. *E-mail:* maura.houtenbos@swov.nl (M. Houtenbos).
[2] Delft University of Technology, Delft, The Netherlands.

It is remarkable that, with so many interactions in traffic, so few accidents actually occur, considering the limited communication possibilities between road users. Besides these communication limitations, other aspects contribute to the complexity of interactions in traffic. As Chauvin and Saad (2000) point out, the amount of experience of road users may differ, as may their goals, knowledge and strategies. They mention a number of measures in driving situations that support and organise interactions. First of all, the infrastructure and formal rules play an important role in organising the way in which interactions will develop. Also, means of communication such as the use of indicator, headlights and horn are mentioned by Chauvin and Saad. We could also add changes in approach-speed, gestures and eye contact to the list of means of communication.

Most accidents are currently attributed to the behaviour of the road users involved, which is often seen as deviating from some normative behaviour (Brookhuis, de Waard & Janssen, 2001). From this point of view, it is often assumed that the accident could only have been prevented by this same road user not exhibiting this behaviour. An aspect which is often neglected is that the accident could also have been prevented by the other road users involved performing some kind of behaviour which compensates for the behaviour of the first road user. As "deviating behaviour" occurs much more frequently than accidents, this could imply that this compensation mechanism must be quite robust. One should ask oneself when a particular action should actually be considered a "deviating behaviour", as these are often compensated for so smoothly that they are hard to recognise as deviating. Also, there is no easily definable boundary of "normal" or "correct" behaviour which can be defined if we take into account that normative traffic rules are often open to interpretation and even require that interpretation in order to make them applicable to the diversity of situations met in practice. Un till now, a detailed understanding of this compensatory mechanism has not yet been achieved.

Significance for ADAS

Development of Advanced Driver Assistance Systems (ADAS) has increased in recent years. Harbluk, Noy and Matthews (1999) mention three factors that have contributed to the increase in onboard ADAS. First of all, technological advances have enabled the integration of information and communication systems within cars. Second, the rapid increase in traffic intensity has made the driving environment more demanding. Third, they mention the increased demand of traffic participants to maximise driving efficiency and productivity of driving time through the use of in-vehicle technology.

Specific knowledge about the effects of these technological advances on driving behaviour is still lacking. However, this knowledge is essential to address the safety aspect of the new (due to ADAS) driving task, which is often neglected. Harbluk et al. (1999) remark that ADAS could result in fundamental changes in the nature of driving with possible adverse effects. Noy (1999) also stresses the need to evaluate the impact of new technologies on transportation safety prior to their implementation or commercialisation. According to Noy, an important risk of ADAS is behavioural adaptation, which is defined as a change in behaviour that occurs in response to a change in technology, but which was not intended by the designer (OECD Scientific Expert Group, 1990).

Current ADAS concepts have mostly neglected the interaction aspect of the driving task, which may lead to uncommon driver behaviour and to unforeseen and dangerous responses by surrounding road users. To be able to make any predictions about the impact of ADAS on driving behaviour, a deeper insight into interaction behaviour in traffic is needed to provide more extensive and safer design and use criteria. Chauvin and Saad (2000) also stress the importance of investigating the potential impact of new support systems being developed in car driving. As these systems are expected to have a special impact on driver behaviour in terms of, for example, the speed driven and/or the safety margins adopted in car-following situations, they will change drivers' behaviour and may thus alter the way they usually interact with other road users.

Objectives

The main objective of a study which is now being conducted in the Netherlands, is to achieve an understanding of the way road users are able to gear their behaviour to one another. This study will initially concentrate on the interaction between car drivers at urban intersections.

Expectancy in interaction behaviour

In interactions between car drivers at an intersection, time is usually limited. Therefore, car drivers need to anticipate the upcoming interaction situation by developing adequate ideas about what is about to happen in the near future, in order to be able to cross the intersection in the most efficient and safe manner. A model has been formulated that can be used to describe the interaction process. The model (Figures 1 and 2) that has been developed so far is based on models of information processing (Endsley, 1995; Wickens & Hollands, 2000) to which the concept of expectancy has been added. The model as shown here serves as a working model.

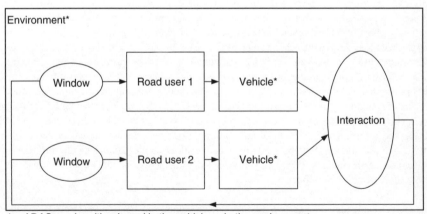

* = ADAS can be either based in the vehicle or in the environment

Figure 1. Interaction in driving.

This working model actually consists of two interdependent models, which initially serve to aid the hypothesis development. The first model (Figure 1) describes the entire interaction situation. The main idea of this model is that several road users perceive the environment

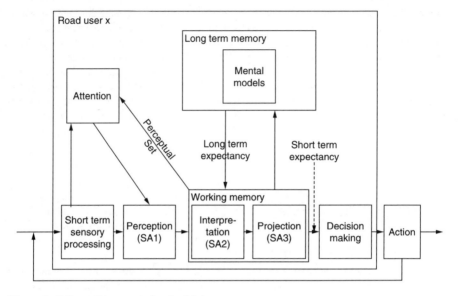

Figure 2. Information processing in driving.

through a "window", which produces a filtered perception of the environment, including any road users operating in it. Subsequently, the road users react through their vehicle to the situation they have perceived, producing an interaction with other relevant road users. Although only two road users are presented here, it is possible to add more road users. In this model ADAS is represented by an asterisk in the vehicle and environment boxes as ADAS may be present in either of the road users' vehicles or the environment (e.g. in the case of ISA[3]: which has parts of the system in the vehicle and parts in the environment). The second model (Figure 2) looks more closely at the road user in the first model. It describes the information processing of each road user involved in the interaction and includes aspects which are presumed to play an important role in interactions (e.g. expectancy). The model also contains the three fundamental aspects of situation awareness according to Endsley (1995) that are indicated by SA1, SA2 and SA3. The second model mainly serves to generate ideas about the role of expectancy and will be adapted according to the results of the studies performed in the developmental phase of this study. Also, an attempt will be made to generate ideas about parameters that influence the interactions. Subsequently, it will be assessed if the interaction model (Figure 1) can develop into a more quantitative model.

The distinction made in the second model between "long-term" and "short-term" expectancies is based on the distinction made by Knapp (1998/1999). He states that drivers bring two types of expectancy to their driving experience. Long-term (or a priori) expectancy is based on past experience, upbringing, culture and education. Short-term (or ad hoc) driver expectancy is based on local practices or situations encountered on a particular roadway during a

---

[3] ISA, intelligent speed adaptation.

particular trip. In this second model long-term expectancies are considered to be similar to "empty" scripts or schemata driven by information contained in mental models. For instance, anyone would know roughly what driving behaviour to expect when thinking of driving on a motorway. These expectations are referred to as long-term expectancies. Subsequently, short-term expectancies are considered to be the same scripts and schemata, but fed with information gathered through perception of the environment at a particular moment in time. Short-term expectancies can be considered similar to a situational model of the situation at hand, and could include such things as expectations about how busy certain intersections will be given the observed traffic flow.

Abelson (1981) also acknowledges a connection between scripts and expectancies. A script is seen as a structure of expectancies and defined by an event-focused schema that directs the activity in relation to knowledge that links action sequences to specific contexts. van Elslande and Fauncher-Alberton (1996) also mention studies which show that time constraints imposed on the cognitive processes implemented when driving require the acquisition of structured knowledge on which to base the expectancies specific to each journey (Alexander & Lunenfeld, 1986; Saad, Delhomme, & van Elslande, 1990; Theeuwes & Hagenzieker, 1993). This seems very relevant for interactions in traffic, as time constraints are definitely involved here. We could consider the structured knowledge mentioned above to correspond to the box in the working model containing "mental models", as the expectancies in the working model are based on the information in the mental models.

Theeuwes and Hagenzieker (1993) let subjects look at slides of traffic scenes in which target objects were either placed at an expected or at an unexpected location. They were asked to determine the presence of these target objects as fast as possible. The study indicated that the subjects strategically prepared for the upcoming stimulus and searched the scene based on the available contextual cues. These results also suggested that objects at an unexpected location are not seen too late, but not seen at all. The authors propose that the effect of contextual driven search might even be larger in a real driving task due to the relatively higher visual load. However, neither this, nor the range of parameters that play a role in expectations have been investigated.

The hypothesis that expectations must play a role in driving behaviour is confirmed by Russell (1998), who mentions that when a driver's expectancy is incorrect, either the driver takes longer to respond properly or he/she may respond poorly or wrongly. However, he does not provide any empirical evidence to back this up. Lunenfeld and Alexander (1984) also acknowledge the role of expectations. They illustrate this by mentioning a study by Johansson and Rumar (1971), who demonstrated in a study on brake reaction times that this was considerably longer when the signal was completely unexpected than when it was expected. Although both Russell and Lunenfeld and Alexander focus mainly on a road user interacting with the infrastructural aspect of the environment (like most research concerning driver expectancy), it is plausible that the same mechanism applies to road users interacting with other road users as well. One does not only have expectations of the infrastructure but also of the behaviour of other road users.

The concept of expectancy has often been used in previous traffic research (Dilich, Kopernik & Goebelbecker, 2002). Olson (1996), for example, defines expectancy as a predisposition of persons to believe that things will happen or be configured in certain ways. This definition is still relatively vague as to the effect of expectations on behaviour. Lunenfeld and Alexander (1990) on the other hand, do try to connect expectancy and behaviour. They state that expectancy relates to a driver's readiness to respond to situations, events and information in predictable and successful ways. The use of "predictable" in this definition can be taken in two ways: predictable to the experimenter, and/or to the other road users. If we take it in the latter sense it implies that expectancies are shared in some way between road users, which makes it even more plausible that expectations must play an important role in interactions.

Chauvin and Saad (2000) acknowledge the role of expectancy in particular in anticipating future (interaction) situations. According to them, managing interactions with other road users calls for a driver to understand the other road users' current behaviour and anticipate their intentions. This depends on the information other road users communicate explicitly, through the use of formal signs, or implicitly, through their behaviour. The understanding of communicated information also depends on one's body of knowledge, which structures expectations and enables one to formulate hypotheses about adjustments that other users may force the driver to make in his or her driving (Saad, Mundutéguy & Darses, 1999). This body of knowledge not only contains formal rules, but also informal rules, which can sometimes be free interpretations of formal rules. Informal rules are acquired through practice and experience with similar situations.

Although the literature seems to agree upon the notion that expectancy is an important concept in driving behaviour, empirical evidence to back this up is still missing. Empirical evidence concerning what expectations actually are and how they influence behaviour is especially lacking.

APPROACH: CONCEPT MAPPING

In order to investigate which parameters can be identified in (short-term) expectancies of interactions, an experiment using pictures and video fragments will be conducted. The approach to be used in this experiment will be based on a method discussed by Jackson and Trochim (2002), who believe this approach to be valuable to analyse open-ended survey responses. Although they use the approach of concept mapping in an organisational research background, it is considered useful to apply this approach in a different context.

Concept mapping consists of several stages. The first stage involves a survey in which responses in the format of a so-called "free list in context" are generated by the respondents triggered by a relevant situation or stimulus. Jackson and Trochim describe responses in this format as responses that typically vary from a few phrases to a couple of paragraphs and represent a wide variety of concepts with varying frequency. After the respondents have provided their "free lists in context", the next stage can commence: creating units of analysis. The authors describe a unit of analysis as consisting of a sentence or phrase containing only one concept. Unitising responses is done by breaking sentences into single concept phrases. All statements are then printed on cards, together with a random number to ensure that each statement is considered independently of other statements. The following stage consists of sorting the statements. This should be done by a group of at least 10 people, who sort the statements into piles of similar statements. The sorting respondents are allowed to make as many piles as they like. However, they are not allowed to make a pile with remaining cards that they feel are not similar to any of the other piles. Instead they should make a new pile for each "odd" statement. After sorting all statements, they are asked to give each pile a name that adequately reflects the statements in the pile.

In the next stage, the sorting results of each respondent are transferred into a binary square matrix. In such a matrix, where rows and columns represent statement numbers, each value represents whether statements are (1), or are not (0) sorted into the same pile. For each respondent, a matrix is made and after that, all matrices are added together to produce an overall result matrix, which contains an aggregation of similarity judgments made by all 10 respondents. This matrix is then used as input for Multidimensional Scaling Analysis. The results of this analysis should result in a final cluster solution map (for more information on this technique see Jackson & Trochim, 2002).

This method of concept mapping is thought to be a promising approach to generate a meaningful list of parameters that play a role in urban intersection interactions between car drivers. Therefore, the concept mapping technique has been somewhat adapted and is being used in an experiment that aims to answer the following question: which parameters can be identified in (short-term) expectancies of interactions?

Design

This experiment will consist of two sub experiments (1a and 1b) following exactly the same procedure. The only difference between the two is in the stimuli used. In Experiment 1a, the stimuli are still pictures of interaction situations, while in Experiment 1b the stimuli will be video clips of the same situations as the pictures. Comparison between the results of 1a and 1b will allow conclusions to be drawn about the importance of dynamic information as opposed to static information in determining the way in which people view interactions. Both sub experiments consist of two parts corresponding to the concept generation and concept sorting stages of "Concept Mapping".

Participants

Respondents are recruited by placing an advertisement in a local newspaper which includes the internet address of the experiment. There are no restrictions on the number of respondents that take part in the first section of the experiment (concept generation). For the second section (concept sorting), only 10 (paid) respondents will be selected based on several background variables.

Stimuli

The stimuli for both Experiment 1a and 1b were developed by recording video fragments from within a moving car using a video camera. These recordings were then extracted and searched for interaction situations, in which some kind of decision regarding the course of the situation needed to be made by any of the interaction partners. Eventually, 17 interaction situations were selected and still pictures were extracted from the video fragments for use in Experiment 1a.

In Experiment 1b the video fragments of the interaction situations will be used. The still pictures for Experiment 1a were then rated on six aspects in order to assess the complexity of the situation.

(1) Number of interaction partners, which is either rated "one" (less complex) or "more" (more complex).

(2) Number of different types of interaction partners, which is also rated "one" (less complex) or "more" (more complex). Examples of types include cyclists, pedestrians or car drivers.

(3) Number of branches of the intersection that interaction partners could possibly come from, which is rated "few" (less complex) or "many" (more complex). A T-junction would be an example of "few", whereas a 4-way intersection would be rated as "many".

(4) Is it an intersection with (less complex) or without (more complex) traffic lights or triangular stop markings?

(5) How many pieces of static information regarding right of way can be found in the still picture? Zebras, triangular stop markings and traffic signs would each be rated a piece of static information regarding right of way. It is assumed that the more pieces of information, the more complex the situation is.

(6) Should the "respondent's car" give right of way according to traffic rules? This last aspect is added to discriminate between situations that would otherwise be rated the same.

Finally, in order to achieve a collection of stimuli which vary in complexity, pictures were selected based on the above-mentioned aspects. Pictures of situations where a roundabout was involved were also excluded from the final set of pictures. This exclusion is based on the fact that a still picture made on a roundabout does not display the roundabout features clearly enough. Subsequently, respondents are not able to tell that the picture is made on a roundabout and will not be able to judge the situation in the correct context. The same problem occurs with pictures of a situation in which a traffic light is involved but not to be found in the still picture. This could lead to respondents judging the situation as if there were no traffic lights at all. Table 1 shows the way the final selection of stimuli was rated. See Figure 3 for an example of a selected stimulus.

Table 1. Rating of stimuli.

Situation	1	2	3	4	5	6
1	More	One	Many	No	0	Yes
2	One	One	Many	No	2	Yes
3	More	More	Many	No	0	Both
4	One	One	Many	Yes	3	No
5	One	One	Few	No	1	Yes
6	One	One	Many	No	0	No
7	More	One	Few	No	0	Yes
8	More	More	Few	Yes	5	Yes
9	One	One	Many	Yes	2	Yes
10	One	One	Many	Yes	3	No

Figure 3. Example of a stimulus used in the experiment.

The rating of stimuli for this study will eventually enable us to compose a complexity-score for future research by combining the ratings of each of these six aspects. This complexity-score will allow us to determine the effect of complexity on expectancy.

Procedure

Respondents are presented with 10 pictures (in random order) and are asked to answer the following two questions for each situation.

(1)   What do you expect will happen here?

(2)   Why do you expect that?

Respondents type their free text answers into a space below the picture which allows for an unlimited amount of words. These are transformed into "if... then..." statements. See Table 2 for an example.

Table 2. Example of a unit of analysis.

Response	"If... then..." statement
Decrease speed or even stop before the VW Golf crosses the road	*If* a car is starting to cross the road, *then* I will decrease speed or even stop

In the second phase of the experiment, 100 statements will be randomly selected for 10 respondents to sort and name. Multidimensional scaling will be performed to discover which are the important clusters of expectations and how they are categorised by the respondents.

Expected results

The results of the first experiment will tell us which aspects of the situation have an effect on a person's expectations and will allow us to formulate hypotheses concerning the expectations of drivers in interaction situations. These hypotheses can then be tested in a follow-up experiment.

The complete study should lead to a model, which describes the interaction process (initially on intersections). Also, an understanding of the impacts of ADAS on the interaction process should be achieved by the end of this study. Furthermore, a method will be developed to test the impact of a particular ADAS on the interaction process. The understanding of the impacts of ADAS will enable a list to be drawn up of requirements, ADAS must meet to support the interaction process as well as possible.

CONCLUSIONS

A review of the literature has shown that interaction behaviour is an important aspect of the driving task. Nevertheless, research on driving behaviour has included relatively few studies on interaction behaviour. In the light of upcoming technologies (ADAS), it is even more important to understand the interaction aspect of the driving task. The present study aims to create a better understanding of interaction behaviour. Expectancy seems to be a key in understanding how road users are able to interact with each other so well. Therefore, we will start the research with a focus on "expectancy". When a more detailed understanding has been achieved of the interaction process between road users at an intersection, a start can be made with identifying the impacts of ADAS on the interaction process.

ACKNOWLEDGEMENTS

This study is part of a PhD project, which is one of six sub projects of the BAMADAS research program and funded by NWO and CONNEKT. The research is performed at the TU Delft (Safety Science) as well as at the SWOV Institute for Road Safety Research.

REFERENCES

Abelson, R.P. (1981). Psychological status of the script concept. *American Psychologist, 36,* 715–729.

Alexander, G.J., & Lunenfeld, H. (1986). *Driver Expectancy in Highway Design and Traffic Operations (Publication No. FHWA-TO-86-1).* Washington, DC: Federal Highway Administration.

Bliersbach, G., & Dellen, R.G. (1980). Interaction conflicts and interaction patterns in traffic situations. *International Review of Applied Psychology, 29,* 475–490.

Brookhuis, K.A., de Waard, D., & Janssen, W.H. (2001). Behavioural impacts of advanced driver assistance systems: an overview. *European Journal of Transport and Infrastructure Research, 1* (3), 245–253.

Chauvin, C., & Saad, F. (2000). Interaction and communication in dynamic control tasks: ship handling and car driving. *International Conference on Traffic and Transport*

Psychology, 4–7 September 2000, Berne, Switzerland, Swiss Council for Accident Prevention, Berne.

Dilich, M.A., Kopernik, D., & Goebelbecker, J. (2002). Evaluating Driver Response to a Sudden Emergency: Issues of Expectancy, Emotional Arousal and Uncertainty (SAE 2002-01-0089), Warrendale.

Endsley, M.R. (1995). Measurement of situation awareness in dynamic-systems. *Human Factors*, *37* (1), 65–84.

Harbluk, J., Noy, Y.I., & Matthews, M.L. (1999). Situation awareness: what is it and why it matters for ITS, ITS: smarter, smoother, safer, sooner. *Proceedings of the Sixth World Congress on ITS*, 8–12 November 1999, Toronto.

Jackson, K.M., & Trochim, W.M.K. (2002). Concept mapping as an alternative approach for the analysis of open-ended survey responses. *Organizational Research Methods*, *5* (4), 307–336.

Johansson, G., & Rumar, K. (1971). Drivers brake reaction times. *Human Factors*, *13* (1), 22–27.

Knapp, K. (1998/1999). Driver expectancy, traffic control and roadway design. *Technology News*, 1–2.

Lunenfeld, H., & Alexander, G.J. (1984). Human factors in highway design and operations. *Journal of Transportation Engineering*, *110* (2), 149–158.

Lunenfeld, H., & Alexander, G.J. (1990). A Users' Guide to Positive Guidance. Report No. FHWA-SA-90-017. US DOT.

Michon, J.A. (1985). A critical view of driver behavior models: what do we know, what should we do? In Evans, L., & Schwing, R.C. (Eds.), *Human Behavior and Traffic Safety* (pp. 485–520). New York: Plenum Press.

Noy, Y.I. (1999). The need for integration of ergonomics in transportation policy, invited keynote address. *International Symposium on Automotive Technology and Automation, Proceedings of the 32nd ISATA*, June.

OECD Scientific Expert Group (1990). *Behavioural Adaptation to Changes in the Road Transport System*. Paris: OECD.

Olson, P.L. (1996). *Forensic Aspects of Driver Perception and Response*. Tucson, AZ: Lawyers & Judges Publishing Company, Inc.

Russell, E.R. (1998). Using concepts of driver expectancy, positive guidance and consistency for improved operation and safety. *Crossroads 2000, a Research Conference*, August 19–20 1998, Iowa State University, Ames, Iowa.

Saad, F., Delhomme, P., & van Elslande, P. (1990). Drivers' speed regulation when negotiating intersections. In Koshi, M. (Ed.), *Transportation and Traffic Theory* (pp. 193–212). Amsterdam: Elsevier.

Saad, F., Mundutéguy, C., & Darses, F. (1999). Managing interactions between car drivers: an essential dimension of reliable driving. *Proceedings of Seventh European Conference on Cognitive Science Approaches to Process Control (CSAPC '99)*, 21–24 September, Villeneuve d'Ascq, Presses Universitaires de Valenciennes.

Shor, R.E. (1964). Shared patterns of nonverbal expectations in automobile driving. *Journal of Social Psychology*, *62*, 155–163.

Theeuwes, J., & Hagenzieker, M.P. (1993). Visual search of traffic scenes: on the effect of location expectations. In Gale, A.G. (Ed.), *Vision in Vehicles IV* (pp. 149–158). Amsterdam: Elsevier.

van der Molen, H.H. (1983). *Pedestrian Ethology: Unobstrusive Observations of Child and Adult Road-Crossing Behaviour in the Framework of the Development of a Child Pedestrian Training Programme*. Haren, The Netherlands: Traffic Research Center, University of Groningen.

van Elslande, P., & Fauncher-Alberton, L. (1996). When expectancies become certainties: a potential adverse effect of experience, traffic and transport psychology: theory and application. *Proceedings of the International Conference on Traffic and Transport Psychology*, May, 22–25, Valencia, Spain.

Wickens, C.D., & Hollands, J.G. (2000). *Engineering Psychology and Human Performance* (3rd ed.). Upper Saddle River, NJ: Prentice Hall.

DRIVING PERFORMANCE I:

CONTROL AND WORKLOAD

Traffic and Transport Psychology
G. Underwood (Editor)
© 2005 Elsevier Ltd. All rights reserved.

26

CROSS MODAL EFFECTS IN TRANSPORTATION

John A. Groeger[1]

INTRODUCTION

Safe car driving and train driving both depend on enduring operator characteristics, such as having sufficient task competence and experience to deal with the demands of the task, and transitory fluctuations in cognition, such as having sufficient current attentional and working memory resources to ensure that appropriate task competencies are elicited and deployed. In both tasks the drivers have available a range of auditory and visual cues which might temporarily guide their behaviour. This chapter will consider how visual and auditory information are combined in order to (a) facilitate judgements and adjustments of speed, and (b) allow train drivers to respond to the signals they encounter. For both car and train drivers, this research will demonstrate how important it can be to integrate information across sensory modalities, showing that cross modal effects in transportation are both of considerable theoretical interest, and may have profound practical consequences.

The term "cross modal" has different meanings for different people. For those steeped in human experimental psychology, the term will be interpreted as referring to the sometimes-curious effects one sensory modality has on our perception of another, or how the resultant percept combines elements of two or more senses. For those concerned with individual and mass transportation, the term "cross modal" will suggest travel behaviour or travel choice, using some combination of bicycles, cars, buses, trains and perhaps even ships or planes. This difference in interpretation itself illustrates an important aspect of perception, i.e. that what we believe we experience depends on our knowledge and background, as well as the information detected by our senses. However, here I will concentrate on another aspect of perception—the effects of combining different sources of sensory information on our judgement and behaviour—and illustrate the importance of understanding these "cross modal" effects, in two different transport settings—car drivers' judgements of speed, and train drivers' detection of railway signals. Before doing so I offer a brief overview of the importance and interpretation of cross modal effects in the mainstream psychological literature.

---

[1] Department of Psychology, University of Surrey, Guildford GU2 7XH, UK. *E-mail:* j.groeger@surrey.ac.uk (J.A. Groeger).

CROSS MODAL EFFECTS IN PERCEPTION

A variety of findings illustrate the effects that two modalities may have on each other. For example, amplifying and distorting the sound made by our hands when they rub together influences the judgements we make about the texture of our own skin (Jousmäki & Hari, 1998), while changing the colour of the drinks or food we consume alters our assessment of their flavour (DuBose, Cardello, & Maller, 1980). Demonstrations of how audition and vision influence each other are more prevalent in the mainstream psychological literature. When attempting to localise a sound which would otherwise be difficult to place (e.g. pure tone), participants who see a light emanate from a particular location will tend to report the sound as also having come from that location (see Radeau, 1994; Spence & Driver, 2000). This so-called ventriloquism effect underlies our everyday experience of believing a wooden dummy, in the hands of a competent ventriloquist, is actually speaking. Another very striking effect of combining sound and moving visual stimuli was reported by Watanabe and Shimojo (2001). In this demonstration, two black spots move towards each other. A tone which is heard as the two spots touch strongly gives the impression that they have collided and bounced away from each other retracing their original paths. A sound heard at any other point, or witnessing the two spots travelling in silence, gives the impression that they pass through each other, and continue on their original trajectory.

Perhaps the cross modal effect that has had the most far reaching theoretical impact was discovered at the University of Surrey by McGurk and MacDonald (1976). The McGurk effect, as it has come to be known, is the result of what happens when people watch the silent film of someone saying /aga/, over which is dubbed the sound of someone saying /aba/. When these auditory and visual stimuli are presented simultaneously, people reliably report hearing /ada/, despite being able to lip read the silent film, and can say aloud the correct stimulus identity when either is encountered alone. This effect, demonstrating a fusion of information from separate senses, can yield a unique percept and is one of many accounted for by the Fuzzy Logic Model of Perception (FLMP), proposed by Massaro (1998, 1999). With the FLMP, perceivers are assumed to make use of multiple sources of information to enable their identification and interpretation of what they sense. Four successive, but overlapping, stages of information processing support this: Evaluation (where each source of information is continuously evaluated to give the degree to which that source specifies various alternatives), Integration (during which the sources are combined in a multiplicative fashion to provide an overall support for each source of information), Assessment (which specifies all viable response alternatives) and Response Selection (at which the response to be made is determined by its degree of match to the input). The result of progressing through these stages is that in the resultant judgement and behaviour, one modality will be weighted more heavily than another, to the extent that it produces a greater reduction in uncertainty (see also Driver & Spence, 1998). There is considerable support for this account at neural level, since as Stein and Meredith (1993) report, single cell recording in Superior Colliculus reveals multi-modal neurons which respond only when two modalities are simultaneously stimulated. Moreover, cell responses are multiplicative, compared with stimulation in either modality alone.

This all may seem very distant from and, superficially at least, irrelevant to the task of drivers and the researchers who would understand and predict drivers' behaviour. However, driving is, quintessentially, a multi-modal task (see Groeger, 2000, for extensive discussion). When we drive up to a set of traffic signals, we have some sense of the speed at which we are travelling, we may be aware of looking at the lights, of the vehicles ahead, the pedestrians crossing the junction, but seem to be less aware of the sound of our car's engine, of the resistance from the pedals our feet are pressing upon, and the resistance of the steering wheel as we grip it. Do some or any of these sensory experiences influence each other? Would our experience of speed from any single one of these direct/indirect indications differ from the impression we derive from the multi source information usually available? In the first of the sections below I consider these questions in the context of driving. However, it is important to acknowledge that in many instances drivers may not need to be aware of the sounds that emanate from their environment. Because of this I will, in penultimate section, address performance characteristics in transport mode—train driving—in which the auditory and visual environment are critically interdependent.

DRIVERS' JUDGEMENTS AND ADJUSTMENTS OF SPEED

Some years ago I carried out a study in the Leeds Driving Simulator in which drivers made judgements of, and then adjustments to, their current speed. The purpose of the study was to assess the validity speed and distance judgements made under simulated driving conditions, but the data are also very relevant to the above discussion of cross modal effects. I will only summarise the method and validation results here, because both are described in full in Groeger, Carsten, Blana, and Jamson (1999), and because I want to concentrate on a new analysis of the original data I completed recently.

Twenty experienced drivers sat in a full-size vehicle, surrounded on all sides by a screen that depicted a flat, featureless landscape and a flat, straight road. In the course of the study, each trial began with the vehicle in which the participant was travelling "moved" at a particular constant speed. After 10 s the participant was required to estimate their current speed, and enter this using adjustable paddles on the steering column—the number produced by doing so appeared on a dashboard LCD. Having confirmed their estimate, an instruction appeared on the LCD requiring the participant to either halve or double their current speed, using the car's brake and/or accelerator. Three trials at each speed were performed in a block, trial blocks requiring halving or doubling were fully counterbalanced. When required to reduce their current speed, participants saw speeds of 20, 30, 40, 50, 60, 70, 80 mph, and thereafter attempted to halve these before the next speed was encountered. When required to increase their speed participants saw speeds of 10, 15, 20, 25, 30, 35, 40 mph, and thereafter attempted to double these before the next speed was encountered. This arrangement of trials was completed three times in separate blocks: once with sound alone, once with vision alone, and once with both sound and vision. The order of these blocks was also counterbalanced.

Figure 1 shows the estimated speeds from each condition. As might be expected the estimates drivers give depend on what speed it is they see ($F(10, 190) = 37.81, p < 0.001$). It is evident from Figure 1 that estimates depend on whether the speed is estimated on the basis of sound alone or whether there is visual information available ($F(20, 380) = 26.97, p < 0.001$). These data are broadly consistent with those reported by other authors. Thus, drivers underestimate speeds, particularly at higher speed (see also Recarte & Nunes, 1996), and providing sound has little effect on the estimates made with vision alone (see also Evans, 1970; Triggs & Berenyi,

1982). This latter result might seem, at first glance, to suggest that there is no evidence of cross modal integration of information. In other words, if there is cross modal integration, estimates made on the basis of vision and sound together might be expected to lie some place between those made for vision and sound alone. However, as discussed earlier, Massaro's FLMP model proposes that sources of information will influence the percept formed to the extent that the source serves to reduce uncertainty (i.e. provides information). Examining the standard errors shown for each estimate in Figure 1, speed estimates made on the basis of sound alone are far more variable than those made on the basis of vision alone. This impression is confirmed by comparing the variance (i.e. standard deviation squared) of the three estimates each participant made for each speed for sound alone and vision alone $(F(1, 19) = 13.38, p < 0.001)$. This analysis also indicated that for some speeds, the difference in variance in estimated speed in the sound-alone and vision-alone conditions is less than for others $(F(10, 190) = 2.75, p < 0.005)$, notably those between 30 and 50 mph. Since information is inversely proportional to variance, according to Massaro's model, estimates of speed based on sound alone should be less like those in the sound and vision condition for speeds for speeds 30 mph and below and for speeds 50 mph and above.

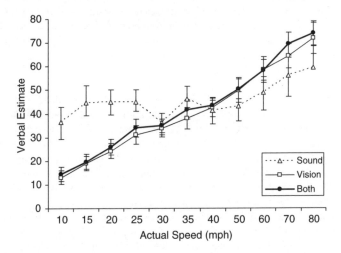

Figure 1. Mean and standard errors of speed estimated based on sound alone, vision alone and sound with vision.

Figure 2a,b shows the adjustments drivers made to speed when asked to halve or double the speed they saw initially. When required to halve the current speed, participants made reliably different adjustments $(F(6, 114) = 76.52, p < 0.001)$, but the size of the adjustment made depended on both the initial speed and whether participants were adjusting sound alone, vision alone or both $(F(12, 228) = 2.69, p < 0.005$; see Figure 2a). When required to double the current speed, participants again made reliably different adjustments $(F(6, 114) = 28.44, p < 0.001)$, but the size of the adjustment made depended on both the initial speed and whether participants were adjusting sound alone, vision alone or both $(F(12, 228) = 5.66, p < 0.001$;

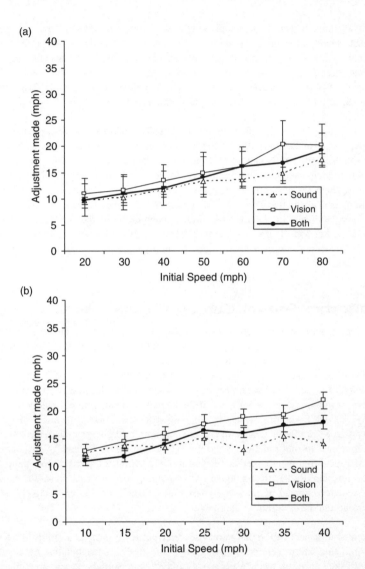

Figure 2. (a) Mean and standard errors of 50% downward speed adjustments based on sound alone, vision alone and sound with vision. (b) Mean and standard errors of 100% upward speed adjustments based on sound alone, vision alone and sound with vision (100% increase attempted).

see Figure 2b). Inspection of both figures suggests that adjustments made when both auditory and visual information are available are different to the adjustments made when either source of information is present in isolation, with the generally higher adjustments made on the basis of sound alone being tempered by the information available from visual information. Consistent with this apparent bisection of sound-alone and vision-alone adjustments, the variance in adjustments made when only sound or only vision are available do not differ reliably for overall, nor do they show any modality by speed interaction. This is the case for trials on which participants attempted to halve (Sound vs. Vision: $(F(1, 19) = 1.54$, n.s.; Sound vs. Vision by Speed: $(F(6, 114) = 1.17$, n.s.) or double (Sound vs. Vision: $(F(1, 19) = 1.12$, n.s.; Sound vs. Vision by Speed: $(F(6, 114) = 1.24$, n.s.) the initial speed.

In summary, this study shows that drivers are equally unable to increase or decrease speed accurately, (see also Denton, 1966). This is also consistent with the downward adjustment condition of Recarte and Nunes (1996) but not, it should be noted, with the conditions in which their participants attempted to increase speeds. Both for upward and downward speed adjustments, there is substantial evidence of cross modal integration of auditory and visual information, and again the extent and direction of adjustments made is largely consistent with Massaro's FLMP model of cross modal integration. In the next sections I want to illustrate a further aspect of cross modal integration, this time with reference to how train drivers' judgements of what a visual signal is implying may or may not be influenced by auditory warnings.

IDENTIFICATION TIMES OF CAUTIONARY RAILWAY SIGNALS

The differences in the kinetic energy of moving cars and trains are considerable, partly because of the respective weights of the vehicles involved, and partly because of differences in friction between their wheels and the surfaces over which they travel. For example, with a full application of the brakes along a flat dry track, a train travelling at 30 or 70 mph will require approximately 0.5 or 1.7 miles, respectively, to come to stop (Railtrack, 2002; GK/RT0034). In contrast, stopping distances for a car at the same speeds are approximately 50 and 250 ft (Highway, 2004). These differences in stopping distances effectively mean that the traffic control system we are familiar with on the road, i.e. a traffic-light system adjacent to a junction controlling access to that junction, could not safely stop trains. Instead, in Britain and many other countries, a four-aspect predictive system of signalling is typical of how the progress of trains is controlled. Rather than a signal telling the train driver that it is safe to proceed, the principle functions served by railway signals is to inform the driver of the likely state of the signal beyond that he is currently approaching.

The typical four-aspect rail signal comprises four vertically arranged lamps. Two of these, when illuminated, show yellow, the others red and green. When functioning correctly, the signal will show one of four "aspects", a solitary red, solitary green or solitary yellow illumination, and the simultaneous illumination of both yellow lamps. Each aspect uniquely specifies the state of the track between the signal ahead and the next signal that will be encountered, and requires a different action or level of caution from the driver. A single green signal permits the driver to maintain his current speed, knowing with certainty that the next signal he encounters will again be green, or two yellows. Two yellows require the driver to be more cautious, and to expect that the next signals will again be two yellows, green or, more seriously, a single yellow. Single yellow requires a lowering of speed, and increased caution since the next signal may be two yellows, a single yellow or, in the most serious case, red. Single red signals indicate a need to stop immediately, without passing the signal.

In conjunction with these visual signals, an on-board Automatic Warning System (AWS) sounds an alarm in the driver's cab, when his cab passes over a trackside magnet placed approximately 200 yards from the signals. A bell denotes that the signal ahead is green; a klaxon denotes that the signal ahead is displaying a cautionary aspect (i.e. two yellows, one yellow or red). The driver need do nothing on hearing the bell, but must press a button to cancel the klaxon. Failure to do so within a few seconds will result in the automatic application of brakes. It is worth noting that for the current recommended minimum distance of the AWS magnet from signals, no train travelling above a few miles per hour on a flat section of track would stop in the interval between the AWS sounding and reaching the signal. Because of this AWS is regarded by the rail industry as a secondary safety system, i.e. one that if defective does not preclude a train being brought into operation. The Southall rail crash (19/09/97), which resulted in the deaths of seven people and tens of millions of pounds of damage, occurred when a driver who had been driving a train for several hours without an operational AWS, passed a signal showing a red aspect.

In the course of attempting to understand the underlying causes of this and other rail crashes, two aspects of the ways train drivers are signalled gave me considerable cause for concern. The first, rather obviously, was that while the available auditory warnings distinguish between non-cautionary and cautionary signals, they do not distinguish between signals that require different levels of caution. In terms of Massaro's FLMP model of cross modal integration, since, in principle at least, the green signals and all others are readily distinguishable, the informational value of the AWS auditory warning should be negligible. The other, less obvious, concern arose from what seemed to be a reasonable deduction from attentional theory that not all of the four signalling aspects currently used should be equally easy to identify.

Consider the number of pieces of information one would need to discriminate between the four signals. Colour alone (i.e. red, green) is enough for one to identify the more and least restrictive aspects, but "yellowness" is not enough for one to discriminate between one and two yellow lights. To distinguish between these we need information regarding number, i.e. whether one or two illuminations are present. However, while "twoness" uniquely determines that the minimal cautionary signal is present (i.e. two yellows), determining that there is only one source of illumination present does not distinguish between red, green and single yellow. As already discussed, determining that a signal is red or green can be done on the basis of colour alone, but single yellow requires the integration of information about both colour and number. It seemed to me that the prediction one would have to make on the basis of theories of visual attention such as Feature Integration Theory (Treisman & Gelade, 1980; Treisman & Sato, 1990) and Guided Search Theory (Cave & Wolfe, 1990; Wolfe, 1994), was that identifying single yellow signals would take longer than all other signals.

We have recently tested this prediction, and the suggestion that the auditory warnings delivered by AWS do not aid signal identification, in two studies of undergraduates' signal detection and identification skills in a simple simulation of railway signals (see Groeger, Clegg, & O'Shea, in press, for full details). Participants in both studies were forewarned where on a screen a signal would appear, their task being simply to press one of four buttons depending on whether the signal was single yellow, two yellows, red or green. In the first study participants carried out the task without AWS-type warnings before the signal came into view, in the second study, a bell (Green) or klaxon (two yellows, yellow, red) sounded before the signal appeared. Figure 3 summarises the reaction times in both studies, for conditions in which a single four aspect signal was presented. In the first and second study, planned comparisons confirmed that reaction time for single yellow signals were reliably longer than for all other signal aspects ($p < 0.01$ and $p < 0.001$, respectively). Of greater relevance to this presentation is the striking effect of AWS warnings as indicated by the 95% confidence intervals plotted for each mean. These indicate that while warnings are associated with faster decisions overall, the greatest reduction in identification occurs where the auditory warning is unique, i.e. has least uncertainty about what the visual signal is. In contrast, each of the cautionary signals benefits to the same extent from the AWS warning they each share.

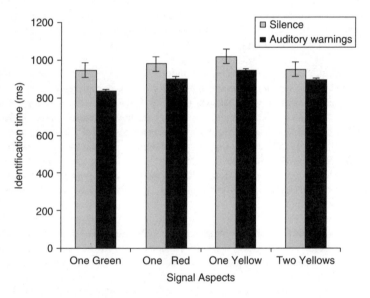

Figure 3. Mean time taken to identify railway signals with and without auditory warnings (error bars show 95% confidence intervals).

These findings, albeit arising from a simple laboratory simulation, suggest that four-aspect signalling has a temporal cost that has hitherto not been recognised: single yellow, probably because it can only be verified by deriving both colour and number information from the scene, takes longer to identify and respond to than other signals. Given the discussion earlier about the inherent difficulties of bringing a train to a stop, single yellow, because it invariably precedes a red signal, is of critical importance for the avoidance and mitigation of signals passed at danger (SPADS). I would argue that although train drivers are both more highly trained and more experienced than undergraduates at making such decisions, this temporal disadvantage of the single yellow signal reflects the operation of fundamental perceptual–attentional processes which are less likely to change with training and experience, and furthermore the complexity of the train drivers task is considerably more difficult than the task we have simulated. Because of this I would anticipate that a field study with real train drivers approaching real signals would show a still stronger effect. Furthermore, as this work shows, while the AWS signals may serve as an alerting function, the current warnings do not override the temporal disadvantage of single yellow. This alerting function was also noted in a unique study of train drivers' eye-movements as they drove in-service trains, where it was found that signals were sometimes not looked for until the AWS had sounded (Groeger, Bradshaw, Everatt, & Merat, in press). Without such a system in operation, these results imply that there is a far greater likelihood of misreading a signal because there is insufficient time to do so (e.g. because visual search for an upcoming signal has begun too late), or of missing a signal completely. The consequences of this will be immediately obvious for those who have studied the Southall rail crash.

SUMMARY AND CONCLUSIONS

In this presentation I have considered two aspects of how drivers might control their speed, or how they might be signalled that a speed change is required. While there are many differences between the car and the train driver's task, questions such as how different sources of information are combined to enable action, and what the relative weighting of different sources of information might be, are of considerable importance for both tasks. These considerations have, I suspect, barely concealed my grander purpose, to illustrate how a theoretical understanding of cognitive processes can allow us to make and test predictions that might not otherwise be obvious, but which—if supported—can have profound practical consequences.

ACKNOWLEDGEMENTS

Thanks are due to Paul Sowden and Helen Payne, colleagues at the University of Surrey, for the demonstration of bouncing and streaming balls (after Watanabe and Shimojo, 2001) that so entertained the audience at this keynote address.

REFERENCES

Cave, K.R., & Wolfe, J.M. (1990). Modeling the role of parallel processing in visual search. *Cognitive Psychology*, 22, 225–271.

Denton, G.G. (1966). A subjective scale of speed when driving a motor vehicle. *Ergonomics, 9*, 203–210.

Driver, J., & Spence, C. (1998). Attention and the crossmodal construction of space. *Trends Cognitive Science*, 2, 254–262.

DuBose, C.N., Cardello, A.V., & Maller, O. (1980). Effects of colorants and flavorants on identification, perceived flavor intensity, and hedonic quality of fruit-flavored beverages and cake. *Journal of Food Science*, 45, 1393–1399.

Evans, L. (1970). Speed estimation from a moving vehicle. *Ergonomics, 13* (2), 219–230.

Groeger, J.A. (2000). *Understanding Driving: Applying Cognitive Psychology to a Complex Everyday Task*. Hove, UK: Psychology Press.

Groeger, J.A., Carsten, O., Blana, E., & Jamson, H. (1999). Speed and distance estimation under simulated conditions. In Gale, A. (Ed.), *Vision in Vehicles VII* (pp. 291–300). Oxford: Elsevier.

Groeger, J.A., Bradshaw, M.F., Everatt, J., & Merat, N. (in press). Allocation of visual attention among train drivers. In Gale A.G. (Ed.), *Vision in Vehicles: IX*. Amsterdam: Elsevier.

Groeger, J.A., Clegg, B.A., & O'Shea, G. (in press). Conjunction in simulated railway signals: a cautionary note. *Applied Cognitive Psychology*.

Highway Code, (2004). Department of Transport. http://www.highwaycode.gov.uk/09.shtml

Jousmäki, V., & Hari, R. (1998). Parchment-skin illusion: sound-biased touch. *Current Biology, 8,* R190.

Massaro, D.W. (1998). *Perceiving Talking Faces: From Speech Perception to a Behavioral Principle.* Cambridge, MA: MIT Press.

Massaro, D.W. (1999). Speechreading: illusion or window into pattern recognition. *Trends Cognitive Science, 3,* 310–317.

McGurk, H., & MacDonald, J. (1976). Hearing lips and seeing voices. *Nature, 264,* 746–748.

Radeau, M. (1994). Auditory–visual spatial interaction and modularity. *Current Psychology of Cognition, 13,* 3–51.

Railtrack PLC (Safety & Standards Directorate) (2002). Signal Sighting, GK/RT0037, Issue 4.0, October 2002, London.

Recarte, M.A., & Nunes, L.M. (1996). Perception of speed in an automobile: estimation and production. *Journal of Experimental Psychology: Applied, 2,* 291–304.

Spence, C., & Driver, J. (2000). Attracting attention to the illusory location of a sound: reflexive crossmodal orienting and ventriloquism. *NeuroReport, 11,* 2057–2061.

Stein, B.E., & Meredith, M.A. (1993). *The Merging of the Senses.* Cambridge, MA: MIT Press.

Treisman, A.M., & Gelade, G. (1980). A feature-integration theory of attention. *Cognitive Psychology, 12,* 97–136.

Treisman, A., & Sato, S. (1990). Conjunction search revisited. *Journal of Experimental Psychology: Human Perception and Performance, 16,* 459–478.

Triggs, T.J., & Berenyi, J.S. (1982). Estimation of automobile speed under day and night conditions. *Human Factors, 24* (1), 111–114.

Watanabe, K., & Shimojo, S. (2001). When sound affects vision: effects of auditory grouping on visual motion perception. *Psychological Science, 12* (2), 109–116.

Wolfe, J.M. (1994). Guided search 2.0: a revised model of visual search. *Psychonomic Bulletin & Review, 1,* 202–238.

Traffic and Transport Psychology
G. Underwood (Editor)
© 2005 Elsevier Ltd. All rights reserved.

27

REGULATION OF SPEED AND TIME-HEADWAY IN TRAFFIC

Matthias Wille[1] and Guenter Debus[1]

INTRODUCTION

Driving behaviour and car-following

From different points of view, it is of interest, how drivers behave in traffic regarding the preceding vehicle, i.e. with which distance and at which speed they drive. Both parameters are included in the time-headway (THW), which marks the time until the driver reaches the actual position of the preceding car. Regarding aspects of accident prevention, a THW is required big enough for the driver to react to manoeuvres of the leading car and to stop the car if necessary before crashing into the rear end of the preceding vehicle. If the optimisation of the traffic flow is focussed, then the speed variation is of interest and a stable speed with less variation is advantageous. Regarding the behaviour from the perspectives of basic research, then the question arises, how the driver regulates his THW behaviour. Here, perception factors, learning factors and motivational factors are important.

In real traffic, the complexity of the THW regulation can hardly be examined. Because the front driver has no constant speed and regulates likewise the distance to the next preceding vehicle. To that extent it is of highest interest to find standardised conditions on which the behaviour regulation can be examined systematically. Driving simulators, in which the handling of preceding vehicles is under control, are a great opportunity. Such investigations were the starting point for the findings reported here.

Observation in simulation studies

We carried out several experiments in a project on accidents under foggy weather conditions (Debus et al., 2004). We tested the hypothesis that under foggy conditions drivers keep closer

---

[1] Department of Psychology, Aachen University, D-52066 Aachen, Germany. *E-mail:* wille@psych.rwth-aachen. de (M. Wille); debus@psych.rwth-aachen.de (G. Debus).

to the car ahead in order to keep it in sight as a point of orientation—in terms of THW, they drive with less THW. Furthermore, the hypothesis means that drivers also attach themselves if the preceding vehicle accelerates and therefore threatens to go out of sight. For the examination of these hypotheses a set of conditions was studied: the drivers drove with misty and with clear sight, alone or behind a preceding vehicle. The preceding vehicle drove at a constant speed or accelerated in certain distance sections.

Remarkably, the finding was that the drivers did not exhibit a constant speed under any test conditions and while driving in convoys no constant distance was held, even if the vehicle in front of them held a constant speed. If the drivers were asked about their handling, they made the preceding vehicle (with constant speed) responsible for variations of the distance. Therefore, we looked at the variation of speed and THW behaviour more closely.

Oscillations in speed and time-headway

The variations show regular changes of approximation towards and gaining distance from the preceding vehicle apart of slow long-term trends. The data speaks for a repeated change of gradual approximation up to the point of threshold of the closest THW the individual driver tolerates and where he starts to decelerate (a local minimum THW). Consequently an enlargement of the THW takes place until the reversal point of the farthest THW where the driver decides to accelerate again (a local maximum THW). Even without a preceding car the speed varies between these reversal points of tolerated speed.

The data of such THW variations has to be analysed regarding its frequency components. At first sight it seemed correct to characterise the oscillation in speed and THW behaviour by mean amplitude and period of the speed curve. While the amplitude stands for the extension of the speed variation, the period describes the duration of the speed change. But regarding driving at different speeds, the question arises by which dimension the period is to be parameterised: the period could be described by the distance or the time axis. We decided to use the time axis for two reasons. First, the description of the period by the distance axis would render the period highly speed dependent. And second, the perception of the dynamic traffic situation is based on time-components as shown in the theory of "time to collision" by Lee (1976).

Comparing the testing conditions on the basis of these parameters, we found empirical evidence for the hypothesis that the speed oscillation implies shorter periods under foggy conditions and is therefore faster than under clear sight. It turned out that this fast speed oscillation could be a critical factor in traffic flow. As the experiments were not designed to study oscillation behaviour and the travelling time was too short under some conditions to analyse the speed variation in a proper way, we carried out a new study.

Theoretical background

Oscillation behaviour in longitudinal vehicle control has been considered by several authors (e.g. Chen, 1992; Herman, Montroll, Potts, & Rothery, 1959; Wiedeman, 1974). On the basis of theoretical assumptions about behaviour regulation predictions on accidents can be made, e.g. for driving in convoys. We carried out a traffic flow simulation and could convincingly show that the probability of accidents under foggy weather conditions increases when drivers in a convoy vary their headway too much and drive in an unstable manner. Several factors seem to be relevant, in particular speed and THW perception (e.g. Recarte & Nunes, 1996). Keeping these theoretical points in mind, we carried out our new study as a replication of our former experiments to improve data collection over time.

METHOD

Apparatus

To investigate the speed and THW variation under different conditions, research was carried out by means of a driving simulator. We used the driving simulator at the IZVW (interdisciplinary centre for traffic science) at the University of Wuerzburg/Germany shown in Figure 1. This simulator has a motion system which can provide acceleration forces up to 5 m/s in a linear way and up to $100°/s^2$ in a rotational way.

Figure 1. The driving simulator at the IZVW.

The simulator contains the front cabin of a BMW type 5 with a fully instrumented console which corresponds to that of the series-manufactured vehicle with automatic transmission. For the realistic representation of the steering moment a servo actuator steered on the basis of a steering model. The projection was effectuated by three tube projectors (CRT—Cathode Ray tube) which were attached in the dome. By these three channels a screen section was given at an angle of 180° in front of the vehicle. LCD displays were used as outside and inside mirrors. The simulator consisted of 11 personal computers and the data exchange between the computers was effectuated by a 100 Mbit Ethernet.

The system was handled from a control position, from which the drivers could be observed by a video plant and the investigator was able to stay in contact with the participant by an intercom system.

Participants

Twelve participants (7 male and 5 female) took part in the experiment. They were all trained simulator drivers from a pool of participants which the simulator team often invite for their investigations. It is very important to highlight that these subjects were used to driving in a simulator and had some hours of training in the past and took part in further experiments. Otherwise the main purpose of the investigation may be masked by the effect of habituation. The age of the participants was between 21 and 59 years and they all had a driving license throughout a minimum of 2 years. They all drove between 10,000 and 20,000 km a year, thus their driving experience was quite high. No driving beginners took part in the study. The profession of the participants varied from student to housewife and travelling agent.

Experimental design and procedure

In our research, we had two variation factors: sight and the driving task itself. The factor "Sight" consisted of two conditions: one foggy condition with a sight of only 50 m ahead and one clear sight condition. The factor "Driving task" had three conditions: a simple driving condition, a car-following condition with the leading car driving 74 km/h (slow car-following) and a car-following condition with the leading car driving 141 km/h (fast car-following). The fast car-following condition was only carried out at clear sight as no one would be inclined to follow a leading car as fast as under the foggy condition. So overall there were five driving situations the participants had to accomplish:

- driving alone at clear sight,
- driving alone through fog,
- following the slow leading car (74 km/h) at clear sight,
- following the slow leading car (74 km/h) through fog, and
- following the fast leading car (141 km/h) at clear sight.

The velocity of the leading car is based on an earlier study which showed the mean velocity people chose to drive under different sight conditions while following a leading car (Debus et al., 2005). Within the three car-following conditions, the leading car drove with a constant speed at the velocity mentioned above. Thus, every speed variation can be addressed to the subjects and is not induced by the leading car.

The participants had to drive 20 min under each condition, whereas the first 5 min under each condition was not included into data analysis and rejected as "run-in-phase". We specially based the length of the condition on the time factor and not on a distance factor, as we related the speed variation values also to the timing factor and thus it seemed more important that the condition conveyed the same time.

The type of road presented in the simulator was a highway with gentle curves. The landscape was flat and wide open with some trees in the surrounding. The subjects drove on the right lane of a two-lane highway with no other traffic in the direction of motion, while there was light traffic on the opposite lane.

The instruction was to drive as usual within the driving alone conditions and to simply follow the leading car in the car-following condition. Between the conditions there was a short brake for the participants.

Data

Data was collected by the simulator software with a frequency of 100 Hz, which includes traffic variables and behavioural parameters like driven speed and distance to the preceding car.

In a first step, the frequency of the data collection was reduced from 100 to 2 Hz, which means two data strings per second, which would be enough for analysing human-based speed variation. Consequently the minimum, mean and maximum values of speed and THW were established for every subject and condition.

We calculated the oscillation parameters only for the speed variation as speed regulation is the underlying criteria for the driven THW. As long as the leading car drives with a static speed no additional information can be drawn by the THW variation parameter. The design of the speed variation parameters is shown in Figure 2 which presents the variation of speed over time, exemplified for one person in one condition. At first, we marked the reversal points of the velocity—the points where an acceleration or a deceleration begins. In Figure 2, two of these reversal points were exemplarily marked with a circle. In order to mark all of them, a mathematical method was used based on the "seasonal difference" of the speed values. Because the seasonal difference is always positive in the acceleration phase and negative in the deceleration phase the reversal points of speed are easy to detect by identifying the point where the algebraic sign of the seasonal difference flips.

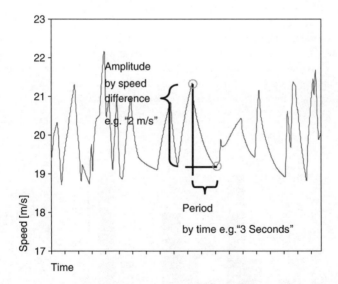

Figure 2. The variation of speed over time and the building of the speed variation values "Amplitude" and "Period" of speed changes.

The speed reversal point at the beginning of a deceleration phase (and therefore the ending of an acceleration phase) is furthermore called a "local maximum" because the speed reaches a local height and from thereon decreases. The speed reversal point at the beginning of an acceleration phase (and therefore the ending of a deceleration phase) is called a "local minimum" because the speed here reached a local minimum and from thereon starts to gain height again.

By building the seasonal difference from these local maxima and minima the speed variation parameters are generated. The "amplitude" is established while taking the magnitude of the speed variation from one local maximum to the next local minimum, or vice versa, into account. If the seasonal difference from an ongoing timing-component is calculated, the duration of a speed change from one local maximum to the next local minimum or vice versa is identified by time—the "period" of a speed change. Please notice, that the term period, in fact, marks a half period because it is an acceleration or a deceleration phase and a period in physical terms marks an acceleration and a deceleration taken together. The advantage of this semi-period is, that the possibility is given to distinguish between acceleration and deceleration and analyse it separately if necessary.

For the statistical analysis we decided to use nonparametric tests (Friedman and Kendall-W) as long as the distribution form of the new parameters is not yet clear.

RESULTS

First, an overview on the traditional parameters is given.

In Figure 3 you see the minimum, the overall mean and the maximum of the driven speed under each condition. In the car-following condition, the mean speed is given by the speed of the preceding car. As you can see for example, the speed parameters look the same under the car-following condition with 74 km/h under clear sight as well as under the foggy condition. But they do not represent the same driving behaviour as will be pointed out later.

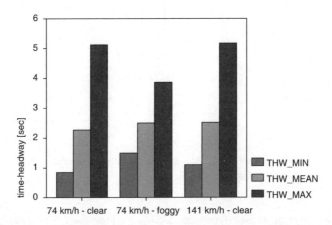

Figure 3. The minimum, overall mean and maximum speed under each condition.

In Figure 4 you see the minimum, the overall mean and the maximum of the THW to the preceding car in the three car-following conditions. The mean THW is indicated with a value above 2 s, quite comfortable under all conditions. Interestingly, the minimum THW while driving through fog is larger than the other minimum THWs. This stands in contrast with many well-known theories on driving in foggy conditions which stated that the main reason for accidents under foggy conditions is a shorter THW. This will be discussed in detail later, but it leads us to the question, what happens in foggy conditions or how do we regulate our speed? And therefore we proceed directly to our new parameters: the amplitude and the period of speed variation.

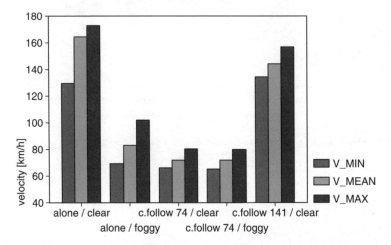

Figure 4. The minimum, overall mean and maximum of THW under the three car-following conditions.

Figure 5 shows an overview on the amplitude of the speed variation. Throughout all conditions the amplitude seems to be stable and no significant differences can be found.

The amplitude is about 1 m/s which means that the extension of the speed variation is about 3 km/h. Only the dispersion of the amplitude under the driving alone condition at clear sight is much larger than under the other conditions. But it is quite clear that this is based on the high degree of freedom in driving that the participants had under this condition. So furthermore, we will focus on the period—the duration of the speed changes.

In Figure 6 you see the period for each condition. It is outstanding that there is much variation in the period of speed oscillation under the different conditions and an overall analysis shows highly significant effects on the period with a $p < 0.001$ (Chi^2 = 32.200, df = 4). Thus, the duration of speed changes differs between the driving conditions.

The longest period of speed variation lies within the driving alone condition under clear sight. It takes about 145 s for an acceleration or a deceleration (please remember that these are both

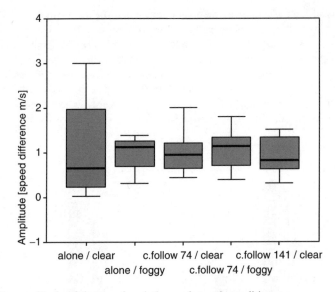

Figure 5. The amplitude of the speed variation under each condition.

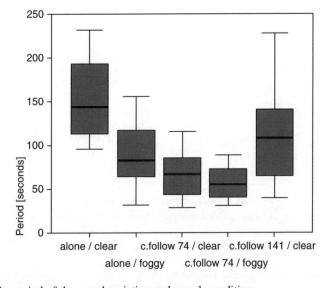

Figure 6. The period of the speed variation under each condition.

reported in combination as the "period"). The shortest period is given under the car-following condition in fog with the leading car driving 74 km/h. The duration of a speed change is here only about 55 s—that is nearly a third of the period while driving alone at clear sight.

To go more into detail we analysed the period by comparing the conditions pairwise for our two factors first, sight and driving task and second, speed dependency.

First of all, let us have a look at the effect of car-following. To do so, we compared the driving alone condition at clear sight with the car-following condition at clear sight while the leading car was driving 141 km/h. While driving alone, the period was significantly larger (about 145 s) than whilst following a leading car (about 110 s) ($p = 0.004$, $\text{Chi}^2 = 8.333$, df = 1). To see if this effect still comes through under the foggy sight condition, we compared the driving alone condition in fog with the car-following condition in fog with the leading car driving 74 km/h. Again the period is significantly larger when driving alone (about 80 s) than whilst following a leading car (about 55 s) ($p = 0.021$, $\text{Chi}^2 = 5.333$, df = 1). Thus, there is more speed variation while following a leading car than whilst driving alone. This is easy to understand, as whilst following a leading car freedom of driving is limited. The safety drivers like to keep limits their acceleration and the fact that drivers do not want to loose the preceding car out of sight limits their freedom of deceleration and therefore regulation. Thus, drivers effectuate more frequent speed variations which results in a shorter duration of the speed variation.

But there is a problem with these findings: mean speed was not constant over all conditions, so the effect could be based on mean speed as well. The mean speed under the driving alone condition under clear sight is 163 km/h whereas the mean speed of the car-following condition at clear sight was 141 km/h (the speed of the leading car). Under the foggy conditions the mean speed while driving alone was 83 km/h whereas the mean speed while following another car was 74 km/h. So in both sight conditions the participants drove faster while just driving alone. We will keep this possible mean speed effect in mind while going to the next point of interest: the effect of sight.

To investigate the effect of sight on the period of speed variation, we compared the driving alone condition under both sight variations and car-following conditions with the leading car driving 74 km/h under both sight conditions. While driving alone under clear sight the period is significantly larger than while driving alone in the fog (about 145 s vs. about 80 s) ($p < 0.021$, $\text{Chi}^2 = 5.333$, df = 1). But again the data on period are confounded with speed because under clear sight the participants drove a mean speed of 163 km/h whilst through fog they only drove 83 km/h. So again it is not quite clear if the effect is based on mean speed in the way that an increased fastness provokes a larger period.

But now we are going to look at a situation where the people drove the same speed under different sight. It is the effect of sight while drivers in both conditions followed a leading car with 74 km/h: under clear sight the duration of the period was about 70 s and in foggy conditions the duration of the period was about 55 s. Unfortunately these findings passed significance closely ($p < 0.083$, $\text{Chi}^2 = 3.000$, df = 1). Nevertheless, they are an indicator that the period is also influenced by sight.

At last, we take a look at the effect of speed while comparing the two car-following conditions at clear sight: when following a leading car with 141 km/h the period is significantly larger (about 110 s) than while following a leading car with 74 km/h (about 70 s) ($p < 0.004$, $Chi^2 = 8.333$, df = 1). Thus, the period depends clearly on speed and is larger when driving faster. In this context that means that there is less speed variation when driving faster over the same time.

In summary, we can say that the period of the speed variation depends on the driven speed. But the findings also indicate that the period depends on sight and is smaller when driving through fog than while driving at clear sight. And furthermore, the period is smaller when following a leading car than when driving alone. The amplitude of the speed variation turned out to be a stable parameter which is not affected by different driving situations.

CONCLUSION

To understand the accidents under foggy weather conditions, where many cars on a highway crash into the rear end of each other, it is important to investigate beneath the static parameters of speed and THW the variation of the speeding-behaviour as well.

As pointed out earlier, the minimum THW is not reduced while driving in fog as many theories on accidents in foggy conditions suggest (e.g. Richter, 2002; Schönbach, 1996). The mean THW is nearly the same as while driving under clear sight but the minimum THW is even enlarged. But from our speed variation data we know a little more about driving behaviour in fog: the speed variation is the highest in all conditions. This may be based on the low velocity people drive in fog but there must be another point that leads to more speed variation under fog than in clear sight. As can be seen by comparing both car-following studies with the leading car driving 74 km/h under different sight, the period is shortened in the foggy condition. We also know about driving in fog, that people tend to build long car convoys. Furthermore, car-following leads to more speed variation as well. So we have three reasons why the speed variation is very high under foggy conditions: bad sight, slow speed and car-following. And if you imagine the long car chains it is quite clear that these speed variations will disturb the traffic flow and even cause traffic jams. Taking into account that in addition most drivers drive too fast in the fog to stop within their sight and that these drivers do not expect a traffic jam as long as they are driving alone in the fog with no car to follow, then the accident is easy to imagine. A fast driver who is unable to stop within his sight crashes in a rear end of a car convoy that nearly stops because of the speed variation.

These findings could be shown after entering our speed variation data into a traffic-flow simulation. But before entering our speed variation data and while the programme had only been working with the static parameters of speed and THW accidents under foggy conditions could never been shown.

The oscillations of THW documented in our experimental settings are worth a more detailed study. Reviewing the literature we do only sparsely find systematic empirical studies and theoretical concepts. A driver regulation model is needed as basis for delivering empirical testable hypotheses. Several aspects have to be considered, among other things, the question whether time instead of distance—in all cases—is the psychologically meaningful basis for parameterising oscillation, the challenge to clarify the relation between oscillation parameters and driving speed, the task to disentangle the role of perceptual (speed and headway perception) and operational, automatical and intentional processes.

It is not the aim of the present chapter to start a full theoretical discussion. We are interested in focussing our attention on the phenomenon. Further research is in progress.

REFERENCES

Chen, Z. (1992). *Menschliche und Automatische Regelung der Längsbewegung von Personenkraftwagen, Fortschrittsbericht, VDI-Reihe 12,168*. Düsseldorf: VDI-Verlag.

Debus, G., Heller, D., Wille, M., Dütschke, E., Normann, M., & Placke, L. (2005). Risikoanalyse zu Massenunfaellen im Nebel, *Bericht der Bundesanstalt für Straßenwesen*. In press.

Herman, R., Montroll, E.W., Potts, R.B., & Rothery, R.W. (1959). Traffic dynamics: analysis of stability in car following. *Operations Research, 7*, 86–106.

Lee, D.N. (1976). A theory of visual control of braking based on information about time-to-collision. *Perception, 5*, 437–459.

Recarte, M.A., & Nunes, L.M. (1996). Perception of speed in an automobile: estimation and production. *Journal of Experimental Psychology/Applied, 2*, 291–304.

Richter, S. (2002). *Einstellungen und Verhalten beim Fahren im Nebel*. Aachen: Shaker.

Schönbach, P. (1996). Massenunfälle bei Nebel. *Zeitschrift für Sozialpsychologie, 27*, 109–125.

Wiedeman, R. (1974). Simulation des Straßenverkehrsflusses, *Schriftenreihe des Instituts für Verkehrswesen der Universität Karlsruhe*, Heft 8.

Traffic and Transport Psychology
G. Underwood (Editor)
© 2005 Elsevier Ltd. All rights reserved.

28

SPEED, TRAFFIC COMPLEXITY AND VISUAL PERFORMANCE: A STUDY ON OPEN ROAD

Luis M. Nunes[1] and Miguel A. Recarte[2]

INTRODUCTION

Speed control is one of the main tasks that a driver must fulfil, and the relevance of an appropriate speed choice regarding road safety is obvious. But the concept of appropriate speed is ambiguous and controversial: physical laws, psychological knowledge and legal restrictions do not converge in an integrated model. Once engineering provides roads and vehicles that can tolerate fairly high speeds, the human limits of the driver seem to be the major constraint of speed. A driver should manage speed so that the tolerance thresholds of road and vehicle are not exceeded and considering each particular traffic situation. The perception of road surface adherence, braking distances, headways, etc. is difficult, requires expertise, and because of this, it is inaccurate. Anticipating trajectories and actions of other users increases complexity. Perceptual or decisional errors (omissions, wrong decisions), self-assessment errors (lack of awareness, overconfidence) and strategic errors (risk acceptance or risk blindness) suggest a complex framework in which the risk of speed may involve quite different dimensions. But if speed is a suitable variable to predict vehicle–road interactions, we wonder about its psychological value to explain driver–vehicle–road interactions concerning risk of human failure. The contribution of this chapter is to provide empirical evidence of a psychological perspective in which the attentional variables are crucial to understand the risk of speed: we will analyse and discuss the relation between speed, traffic demands, assignment of visual resources and probability of human error.

Given that the driver has to take appropriate decisions in time, higher speeds presumably imply higher visual processing demands (more things to perceive and more decisions per unit of time). Assuming the limited capacity of the human cognitive system, it seems logical to hypothesize

---

[1] Dirección General de Tráfico, Madrid, Spain. *E-mail:* argos@dgt.es (L.M. Nunes).
[2] Faculty of Psychology, Universidad Complutense, Madrid, Spain.

about the existence of psychological constraints for speed, perhaps leading to perceptual or decision impairment. In general terms, two main questions have to be addressed: does increased speed mean increased processing demands? And if this is the case, do higher speeds lead to a simple reassignment of resources or to an increased probability of information processing errors?

Bartmann, Spijkers and Hess (1991), when studying the effects of driving speed and road characteristics on the field of vision, found that the effect of speed cannot be considered independently of the road type and traffic intensity. The higher proportion of glances rated as relevant for driving with higher speeds led the authors to suggest that the classical phenomenon called "tunnel vision" (Ikeda & Takeuchi, 1975; Mackworth, 1965), often invoked as an example of a speed-induced perceptual impairment (Lejeune, 1959; Lorenz, 1971), should be reinterpreted as an optimization strategy: a simple consequence of attending relevant objects such as cars or the road itself, a shift of attention towards the driving task. Kayser and Hess (1991) supported the same interpretation of tunnel vision and remarked that higher speeds are not constrained by psychological limitations imposed by the field of vision.

Miura (1990), in a real traffic experiment, found a decrease in peripheral visual performance attributable to increased situational demands and, along the same line, rejected the deterioration hypothesis in favour of an optimization strategy to cope with higher demands. However, it turned out that the observed effects came from the complexity of traffic environment but not from increased speed: the author suggested that the determinant is the temporal density of information acquisition and processing but not the temporal density of available information per se.

In summary, the aforementioned examples suggest that some resource reallocation response has been identified as a response to traffic complexity (in terms of traffic intensity and road design), although, the extent to which speed contributes to making the driving task more demanding seems less clear. To some extent, the attentional shift towards the driving task may result in visual search changes, some of them hypothetically related to reduced peripheral visual performance, classically interpreted as "tunnel vision". Nevertheless, such interpretation is controversial and there is some evidence to reject the idea of visual impairment. Instead of tunnel vision, there may be just a spatial gaze concentration effect, reflecting optimization of visual resources: more time scanning the road ahead and less time looking at irrelevant objects in the landscape.

Although not caused by speed, a case of perceptual impairment combined with spatial gaze concentration was also found in actual driving conditions as a consequence of increased mental load imposed by secondary cognitive tasks (Recarte & Nunes, 2003). But the visual performance impairment did not selectively affect the periheral field of view. Following Holmes, Cohen, Heith and Morrison (1977), we rejected the "tunnel vision" hypothesis. Analogous results and interpretation were obtained by Van der Weijgert and Van der Klok (1999). Here, the spatial gaze concentration effect was also interpreted as a plausible adaptive response to optimize the visual information acquisition.

What could we infer if a similar pattern of gaze concentration occured with speed? Should we also interpret it as optimization strategy to cope with a hypothetical increased workload induced by speed? Should the same effect have the same functional meaning at a psychological level? And what about other visual changes caused by increased mental workload, such as pupil dilatation and reduced mirror inspection? Should they also occur with increased speed or traffic complexity and have the same meaning?

A further reanalysis of the results of Recarte and Nunes (2003) suggested that, like mental tasks, speed could also contribute to spatial gaze concentration, although with no apparent signs of visual impairment in terms of detection and discrimination capacities. But when considering speed as an independent variable, an unexpected effect emerged: pupil size, instead of increasing, tended to decrease with increasing speed. The lack of visual impairment effects on detection and discrimination together with the pupil results was inconsistent with a hypothetical increased load attributable to speed.

A previous research on the attentional demands of speed control (Recarte & Nunes, 2002) demonstrated that explicit speed restrictions imposed additional workload, both at the visual and at the cognitive level. However, under free speed choice, although the preferred speed was higher, it remained unaffected by the additional load of mental tasks, and speed control was equally achieved with much less visual resources dedicated to the speedometer.

We decided to address the visual demands imposed by speed within and across different traffic conditions in a specific experiment. Its objective is to describe driver's visual response to speed and traffic complexity and to provide an interpretation of the observed visual changes in attentional terms, including the comparison with the effects produced by increased mental load. In order to allow a more conclusive interpretation of visual changes, we included a dual task imposing additional visual load, and we expected that the visual load that could be derived from speed, traffic complexity or its combination would interfere with the visual detection and discrimination task. The analysis of visual performance regarding eccentricity would allow us to draw some conclusions about the eventual effects on peripheral visual performance.

Moreover, we considered that the most adequate approach to study the genuine effects of speed should be a condition of free speed choice and a low-restrictive road environment. So the experimental design and procedure to "manipulate" speed as independent variable should take into account the drawback of direct experimental manipulation by means of explicit speed instructions such as target speed or speed restrictions. In accordance with the individual speed choice and in order to study the speed effect, we considered that a relative speed scale referred to the individual level would have more psychological meaning: the same speed value in km/h can be high for one individual and low for another. Consequently, speed as independent variable, represents a category of the individual speed along the individual speed range.

METHOD

Participants

Fourteen drivers of both sexes (7 + 7), with an age range of 23–35 years, all with more than 4 years of driving experience and normal visual acuity (uncorrected) participated in the experiment. They were paid for their participation.

Experimental conditions and design

Speed and traffic complexity were the main independent variables. A visual detection and discrimination test was used and a control condition of ordinary driving was included. As speed and traffic complexity do not vary independently in real traffic, we decided to make the experiment long enough to collect a large amount of data. In order to minimize the undesirable bias derived from instructions affecting numerical representations of speed (Recarte & Nunes, 2002), no explicit target speed instructions were given, the speedometer was concealed, and the experiment was run in the least restrictive road type as possible: the motorway. The drivers were encouraged to choose their speed and make it vary along a range they felt was appropriate to drive safely according to their own criteria and relying more on their subjective appreciation than on numerical representations in km/h.

The route included two stretches of motorways (AP6 and AP51), which mean hourly traffic flow ranged from 2529 to 195 vehicles/hour. Traffic complexity should be rated in a further analysis of video recordings on a three-point scale: 0 means *no vehicles at all* or *one vehicle visible but very far away*; 1 means *one vehicle is visible ahead, but no significant action is involved such as being overtaken or overtaking with no lane change*; 2 means when *two or more vehicles are visible or when changing lanes or other more complex manoeuvres are involved*. The individual speed scale was built by categorizing the particular range of measured speeds of each participant on a three-point scale (low, medium, high) and equalizing the number of observations for each category. In summary, on two motorways, a visual detection and discrimination test was performed and compared with a control condition of ordinary driving. For the analysis of detection regarding speed and traffic complexity, the data of both motorways were collapsed and resulting in a design of 3 speeds (low, medium, high) × 3 levels of traffic complexity (0, 1, 2).

Instruments

The participants drove an instrumented car and were accompanied by the experimenter in the rear right seat. The car is a standard Citröen BX-GTI and is equipped with an unobtrusive eye-tracking system (Dornier) that provides online gaze coordinates, and their correspondence on a video-recorded road scene. More details can be seen in Gottlieb, Scherbarth and Guse (1996). The vehicle includes a system for automatic presentation of visual targets to perform an in-vehicle visual detection and discrimination test consisting of a set of 10 flashing spotlights of approximately 30 min/arc of visual angle that can appear in the driver's visual field in a spatial range of approximately 60° horizontally by 25° vertically, the same used in Recarte and Nunes (2003). Four of these targets (virtual targets) were obtained by reflection of light beams on the windshield surface whereas the other six targets (real targets) were high-luminance electronic light-emitting diodes (LEDs). Two response buttons, one for each hand, were ergonomically installed near the steering wheel (Figure 1). The flashing rate of the spotlights could be high or low (high rate = 0.2 s on/0.2 s off; low = 0.3 s on/0.3 s off). Each flashing target remained activated for 3 s and the ISI varied between 12 and 30 s. More details of the vehicle and of the discrimination test can be seen in Nunes and Recarte (1997) and in Recarte and Nunes (2003), respectively.

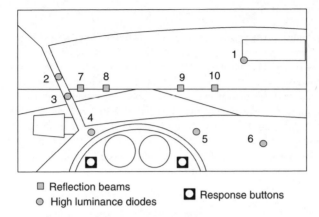

Figure 1. Targets and response buttons location.

Procedure

Participants received general information about the purpose of the study and an appropriate training period to drive the car and to perform the discrimination test. Afterwards, the experimenter warned the participant that, except for some periods that he would indicate, any target could appear at any time. The experiments were run in normal daylight conditions; the participants drove for about 350 km with a short break in the middle of the experiment. Particular events such as traffic jams or road construction works were excluded as invalid conditions for the experiment.

Dependent measures

All dependent measures were obtained from a few primary data: pupil size, gaze coordinates, target activation and discrimination responses were automatically recorded in data files. Pupil diameter was expressed in internal units of the eye-tracking system (pixels). Gaze coordinates were expressed in horizontal and vertical degrees of visual angle. An algorithm was used to calculate ocular fixations, the same as used in Recarte and Nunes (2000). Saccadic amplitude was inferred from consecutive fixations. Spatial gaze variability, as dependent measure, was a score obtained for each participant and condition resulting from the product of vertical and horizontal variability (the standard deviation of X and Y gaze coordinates). Regarding the detection and discrimination test, we measured the percentages of detected targets, correct responses and response times. When the targets were glanced at (which was the predominant visual response to the targets), a subdivision of the total response times in three time stages was considered: (a) *detection time*: from target activation until the beginning of a saccade towards the target; (b) *inspection time*: time spent looking at the target; (c) *decision time*: from the instant the participant's eyes left the target until the he/she pressed the response button. This subdivision of time based on ocular behaviour is a method for making plausible inferences about how information processing stages underlying gaze control and action are affected by the independent variables.

RESULTS

This section includes: (a) categorization of speed and traffic complexity; (b) general analysis of ocular behaviour; (c) performance on the detection test; and (d) eccentricity analysis. With some exceptions that will be specified below, the following results are based in an ANOVA of 3 speed × 3 traffic complexity × 14 participants for each dependent measure, although we will not inform about the differences between participants. Regarding the differences between the control condition (just driving with no visual detection task) versus the detection condition, no relevant effects were found, except the obviously expected higher gaze dispersion caused by the glances towards the targets, as in Recarte and Nunes (2003). However, as detection did not interact with the independent variables, we could collapse the data of detection and control conditions with no loss of relevant information.

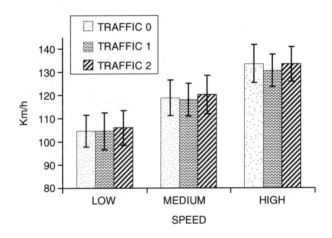

Figure 2. Mean speed values for each category of speed and traffic complexity.

Speed and traffic complexity

Figure 2 represents mean speed values for each combination of speed and traffic complexity. The percentage of observations for each traffic complexity level was: traffic 0 = 47%, traffic 1 = 30%, traffic 2 = 23%.

General analysis of ocular behaviour

Pupil size. As expected, increased traffic complexity produced a linearly significant increase in pupil size, $F(2, 26) = 29.10$, $p < 0.001$. On other hand, the opposite effect (pupil contraction) was due to speed, $F(2, 26) = 43.39$, $p < 0.001$. Although this result was in accordance with previous tendencies observed in the reanalysis of data from the past experiments, it was still unexpected because it goes against the hypothesis of increased effort due to speed and because it had never been reported in literature. A significant interaction showed that the pupil increase due to traffic was more pronounced for lower speeds, $F(4, 53) = 6.07$, $p < 0.001$. Data can be seen in Figure 3.

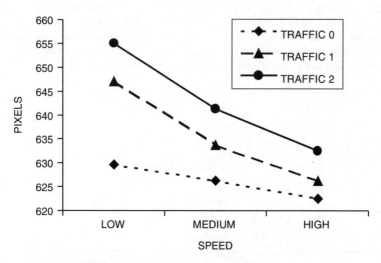

Figure 3. Pupil diameter (in pixels of eye image) by speed and traffic complexity.

Fixation duration. Figure 4 displays the data of fixation duration. Fixations became significantly longer with speed, $F(2, 26) = 6.20$, $p < 0.01$, and shorter with increasing traffic complexity, $F(2, 26) = 6.20$, $p < 0.05$. No interactions were found. The effect of traffic complexity suggests the need to explore more things in the same time, and the longer fixations due to speed seem to reflect glances in which the eyes keep fixating the road ahead. In fact, a correlational analysis of fixation duration and gaze coordinates indicated that longer fixations occur in the most central area of the visual field ($r = -0.18$).

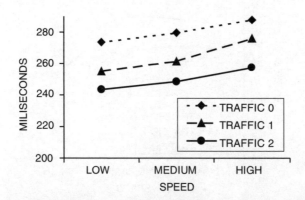

Figure 4. Fixation duration by speed and traffic complexity.

Spatial gaze variability. A spatial gaze variability score was defined for each participant and condition in order to perform the analysis of spatial gaze distribution, and a repeated measures analysis (3 speed × 3 traffic complexity) was performed in this case. The variability score consists of the product of one standard deviation of horizontal gaze coordinates × one standard deviation of vertical gaze coordinates, the units are square degrees of visual angle, and it represents the size of the area of interest. The results revealed that the scanned area was significantly reduced with increasing speeds, $F(1, 13) = 7.91$, $p < 0.05$ (see Figure 5). No effects were found due to traffic complexity or its interaction with speed.

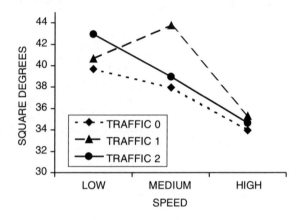

Figure 5. Spatial gaze variability by speed and traffic complexity.

Saccadic amplitude. Although there is some redundancy between saccadic amplitude and spatial gaze variability, the same fixation distribution can also be achieved with different saccadic amplitudes. Higher speeds produce shorter saccadic amplitude, $F(2, 36) = 3.93$, $p < 0.05$, whereas traffic complexity produces the opposite effect, $F(2, 31) = 3.46$, $p < 0.05$ (see Figure 6). No interaction was found. The results regarding speed were as expected from

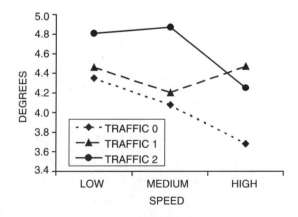

Figure 6. Saccadic amplitude by speed and traffic complexity.

the reduced spatial gaze variability. The effect of traffic complexity reflects the higher ocular activity coming from the need to fixate other vehicles, even though spatial variability was not affected, as seen in the previous section.

Blink rate. A blink inhibition effect due to traffic complexity can be inferred from the reduced blink rate (see Figure 7): this variable was significantly affected by traffic complexity only, $F(2, 35) = 5.34$, $p < 0.01$. No effects of speed or interaction were found. Such effect is consistent with the increased processing demands imposed by the traffic conditions.

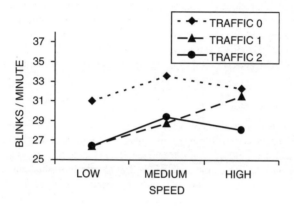

Figure 7. Blink rate by speed and traffic complexity.

Rear-view mirrors inspection. Figure 8 represents the percentage of fixations made on any of the rear-view mirrors (the interior mirror and the offside mirror), and reflect a significant decrease in mirror inspection attributable to speed, $F(2, 27) = 4.67$, $p < 0.05$, and an increase in their inspection with increasing traffic complexity, $F(2, 27) = 8.24$, $p < 0.05$. No interaction was found. The lower mirror inspection with higher speeds seems consistent with the lower

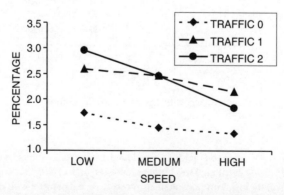

Figure 8. Percentage of fixations on rear-view mirrors by speed and traffic complexity.

probability of being overtaken and with the higher need to attend to the road ahead. The effect of traffic complexity seems obvious, as higher complexity levels include lane changes and overtaking manoeuvres.

Discussion of ocular behaviour results. Speed and traffic complexity produce observable changes in driver's visual behaviour that are meaningful from an attentional perspective. The effects of traffic complexity are consistent with physiological signs of higher effort (pupil dilation) and with increased visual demands: shorter fixations, increased saccadic amplitude, blink inhibition and increased mirror inspection. With regard to speed, although we cannot provide an explanation for the pupil contraction effect, this response is contrary to an increased workload. The spatial gaze concentration effect combined with less frequent mirrors inspection, reduced saccadic amplitude and longer fixations on the central area of the visual field suggests that attention is predominantly focused on the road ahead. Higher speed is achieved with an adaptive reallocation of visual resources on the more relevant areas of the visual field.

Performance on the detection test

Detected targets. The percentage of detected targets was unaffected by speed and dropped significantly with increasing traffic complexity, from 70% with no traffic to 55% in the case of complexity 2, $F(2, 40) = 23.05, p < 0.001$ (Figure 9). No interaction was found. The existence of interference between the detection test and the driving task is attributable to the presence of other vehicles to attend to or interact with. Regarding speed, no signs of interference appeared.

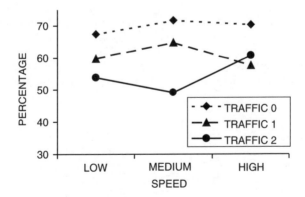

Figure 9. Percentage of detected targets by speed and traffic complexity.

Correct responses. An analogous pattern was found for the discrimination capacity: traffic complexity but not speed contributed to a higher proportion of decision errors. As can be seen in Figure 10, a significantly lower proportion of correct responses occurred with the highest traffic complexity level, $F(2, 40) = 3.31, p < 0.05$.

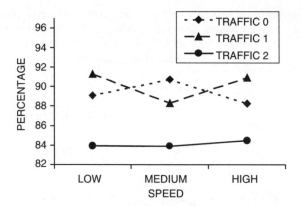

Figure 10. Percentage of correct discrimination responses among the detected targets by speed and traffic complexity.

Response times. With respect to the timing of the discrimination responses, we analysed not only the total response time but also the partial times based on the ocular responses to the activated targets according to the above-mentioned criteria (Methods section, Dependent measures subsection).

Total response time. The results (see Figure 11) indicate that higher speeds led to faster responses, $F(2, 33) = 4.66$, $p < 0.05$, whereas traffic complexity contributed to increase the response times, $F(2, 34) = 3.25$, $p < 0.05$. No interactions were found between speed and traffic complexity.

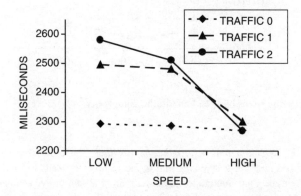

Figure 11. Total response time by speed and traffic complexity.

Partial times. The analysis of partial times (detection, inspection and decision) was based on those targets that were glanced at prior to giving a response (67% of cases). The other 33%

represents responses given without glancing at the targets or lack of ocular data. Traffic complexity, but not speed, altered the ocular response to the targets, causing late detection, $F(2, 47) = 3.19$, $p < 0.05$, and reduced inspection time, $F(2, 39) = 12.16$, $p < 0.001$, (see Figures 12 and 13). No differences were found in decision times.

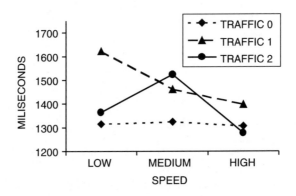

Figure 12. Detection times by speed and traffic complexity.

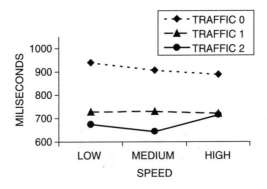

Figure 13. Inspection times by speed and traffic complexity.

Discussion of the detection and discrimination results. The reduced performance in the detection and discrimination test proves that traffic complexity leads to increased effort and interference. The effects attributable to speed were either absent or even showed an increased performance, perhaps attributable to heightened arousal, if one examines the reduced response times with no negative effects on the percentage of correct responses. Partial times show that late detection and lower inspection times are the cause of the poorer discrimination performance. The presence of other vehicles, but not speed, is what contributes to an increased workload and information processing impairment.

Eccentricity analysis

As in Recarte and Nunes (2003), the subset of four virtual targets (those that appeared by reflection on the windshield) was more appropriate for this analysis. Eccentricity, here as independent variable, was measured with regard to the actual eye coordinates at the moment of stimulus onset. Here, we inform about the detection probability in two separate analyses: detected targets as a function of eccentricity and speed, and as a function of traffic complexity, respectively. The results followed the expected gradient: lower detection rate appeared with higher eccentricities. But neither speed (Figure 14) nor traffic complexity (Figure 15) interacted with eccentricity, that is to say, the detection gradient was unaffected by speed or traffic complexity.

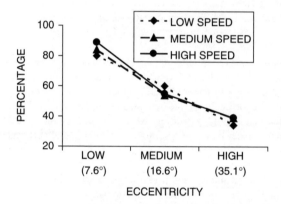

Figure 14. Percentage of detected targets by eccentricity and speed.

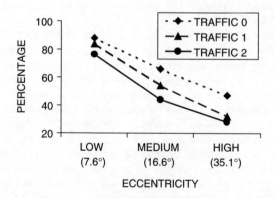

Figure 15. Percentage of detected targets by eccentricity and traffic complexity.

Discussion of eccentricity results. The results do not provide support for a selective detrimental effect on peripheral visual performance due to speed or traffic complexity. Although only the data on detection are displayed, the same absence of interaction was obtained with regard to discrimination errors or response times.

GENERAL DISCUSSION

The observed effects provide evidence of adaptive attentional responses to speed and traffic complexity. Regarding traffic versus speed, if the presence of traffic involves relevant objects that must be attended to, speed does not contribute to an additive effect of increased workload, at least within the range of speeds that were tested. Theoretically, the human brain can process all the information contained in a fixation, as the fovea imposes strong limits at the input level (Van der Heijden, 2004). As fixation is a static (stabilized) sample of a scenario, motion or speed cannot increment its information content. If more information must be extracted, the eye may scan the environment more efficiently (fixation duration and distribution, saccadic activity), although within some limits: a fixation must have a minimum duration and a saccade cannot exceed a maximum speed. This suggests that although there is no opportunity to be overloaded by a visual input, the best visual scanning strategy may fail to extract all the information needed to drive safely.

Whereas the demands of traffic explicitly require targets to be processed, the effect of speed has a different nature. Speed seems to produce a change in the mental set with an effective visual resource reallocation, with no increased workload, and may be accompanied by heightened arousal (drivers often report feeling more activated at higher speeds). The results of detection together with eccentricity analysis and spatial gaze concentration constitute an additional example of the independence of gaze concentration and peripheral performance, as in Recarte and Nunes (2003).

The common assumption of the relation between speed and workload seems to be false as a general statement. This is in conflict with the interpretation of Jordan and Johnson (1993) of a speed reduction caused by increased cognitive workload. We suggest that such speed reduction may not be of an attentional nature but a means to reduce the threat of the perceived risk, a preventive measure to reduce the consequences of an eventual accident.

The unidimensionality of speed may be the cause of the weakness of its relation with the complexity of attentional processes, and thus the weakness of its predictive value regarding information processing failure. The general tendency to isolate speed as a significant risk predictor, although very popular among descriptive studies based on accident statistics, has low psychological content, as it provides no comprehension of how speed affects driving behaviour. Psychosocial studies addressing speeding behaviour and violations may contribute to improve the rule compliance policies, but are unsuitable to evaluate the rules themselves. The relative success of speed reduction policies may obscure the need of a comprehensive approach at performance level. But a genuine psychological approach to speed should go beyond correlational analyses of speed and accidents or physical arguments such as increased braking distances or higher severity of crashes. A description of how the probability of human error is affected by speed is crucial, otherwise, the term "risk of speed" becomes fallacious in behavioural science because it tells more about physics than about behaviour. Paradoxically, generic studies on the risk of speed are widespread, whereas behavioural studies on speed and performance are scarce.

The range of speeds studied here is quite representative of current speeds in Spanish motorways, being traffic congestion out of the scope of the study. Probably, for higher speeds and under high pressure, speed should interact with traffic complexity. However, if it was the case, the contribution of speed to increased workload should be closely related with the complexity of each situation. In order to develop an intelligent alternative for speed control and more effective safety measures, generic considerations about the risk of speed should be discouraged: speed should be considered together with attention and in specific traffic conditions.

REFERENCES

Bartmann, A., Spijkers, W., & Hess, M. (1991). Street environment, driving speed and field of vision. In Gale, A.G., Brown, I.D., Haslegrave, C.M., Moorhead, I., & Taylor, S. (Eds.), *Vision in Vehicles III* (pp. 381–390). Amsterdam: Elsevier.

Gottlieb, W., Scherbarth, S., & Guse, K. (1996). New scientific instrument for vision in vehicles research. In Gale, A.G., & Haslegrave, C.M. (Eds.), *Vision in Vehicles V* (pp. 203–210). Amsterdam: Elsevier.

Holmes, D.L., Cohen, K.M., Heith, M.M., & Morrison, F.J. (1977). Peripheral visual processing. *Perception and Psychophysics, 22*, 571–577.

Ikeda, M., & Takeuchi, T. (1975). Influence of foveal load on the functional visual field. *Perception and Psychophysics, 18* (4), 255–260.

Jordan, P.W., & Johnson, G.I. (1993). Exploring mental workload via TLX: the case of operating a car stereo whilst driving. In Gale, A.G., Brown, I.D., Haslegrave, C.M., Kruysse, H.W., & Taylor, S.P. (Eds.), *Vision in Vehicles-IV* (pp. 255–262). Amsterdam: Elsevier.

Kayser, H.J., & Hess, M. (1991). The dependency of drivers' viewing behaviour on speed and street environment structure. In Gale, A.G. Brown, I.D., Haslegrave, C.M., Moorhead, I., & Taylor, S. (Eds.), *Vision in Vehicles III* (pp. 89–94). Amsterdam: Elsevier.

Lejeune, W. (1959). Wahrnehmunggsproleme bei hoerer Geschwindikeit. *Verkehrs-Medizin, 5*, 45.

Lorenz, E.H. (1971). *Trassierung und Gestaltung von Strassen und Autobahnen*. Wiesbaden: Bauverlag GmbH.

Mackworth, N.H. (1965). Visual noise causes tunnel vision. *Psychonmomic Science, 3*, 67–68.

Miura, T. (1990). Active function of eye movement and useful field of view in a realistic setting. In Groner, R., d'Ydewalle, G., & Parham, R. (Eds.), *From Eye to Mind: Information Acquisition in Perception, Search and Reading* (pp. 117–129). Amsterdam: Elsevier.

Nunes, L.M., & Recarte, M.A. (1997). Argos program: development of technological systems and research programs for driver behaviour analysis under real traffic conditions (ISHFRT 2). In Alburquerque, P.A., Santos, J.A., Rodrigues, C., & Pires da Costa, A.H. (Eds.), *Human Factors in Road Traffic II* (pp. 154–159). Braga, Portugal: Universidade do Minho.

Recarte, M.A., & Nunes, L.M. (2000). Effects of verbal and spatial-imagery task on eye fixations while driving. *Journal of Experimental Psychology: Applied, 6*, 31–43.

Recarte, M.A., & Nunes, L.M. (2002). Mental load and loss of control over speed in real driving: towards a theory of attentional speed control. *Transportation Research, Part F: Traffic Psychology and Behaviour, 5F* (2), 111–122.

Recarte, M.A., & Nunes, L.M. (2003). Mental workload while driving: effects on visual search, discrimination and decision making. *Journal of Experimental Psychology: Applied, 9,* 119–137.

Van der Heijden, A.H.C. (2004). *Attention in vision. Perception, Communication and Action.* Hove, UK: Psychology Press.

Van der Weijgert, E.C.M., & Van der Klok, G.M.J. (1999). Parallel processing and interference in simultaneous foveal and peripheral task performance. In Gale, A.G., Brown, I.D., Haslegrave, C.M., & Taylor, S.R. (Eds.), *Vision in Vehicles VII* (pp. 73–81). Amsterdam: Elsevier.

Traffic and Transport Psychology
G. Underwood (Editor)
© 2005 Elsevier Ltd. All rights reserved.

29

EFFECTS OF MOTORWAY LIGHTING ON WORKLOAD AND DRIVING BEHAVIOUR

Jeroen H. Hogema[1], Hans A. Veltman[1] and Annelies van 't Hof[2]

INTRODUCTION

In order to make decisions concerning the installation or replacement of public lighting along roadways, knowledge is needed on the advantages and disadvantages of lighting. Over the years, the ideas about the function of lighting change. The current Dutch design guidelines for motorways include criteria for roadway lighting. The Ministry of Transport, Public Works and Water Management continues to search for the appropriate use of lighting, taking into account traffic safety as well as energy consumption and the environment.

Traffic safety has always played a major role in the roadway lighting discussion. Since a reduction in accidents is expected due to lighting, the traditional policy has been to install lighting as soon as the mean traffic flow exceeded a certain threshold. However, over the years environmental and energy consumption issues have gained importance. For example, in 1998, a test with dynamic public lighting was conducted: the amount of lighting was adapted to the traffic and weather conditions in such a manner that the amount of lighting was sufficient to ensure safe and efficient traffic flow, while avoiding unnecessarily high levels of illumination (Folles, IJsselstijn, Hogema & Van der Horst, 1999). Besides the normal level of illumination ($100\% = 1$ cd/m^2), a reduced (20%) and an increased level (200%) was employed. The test results showed that under favourable conditions, the lower lighting level can be safely used, whereas under other conditions (rain), the normal level is to be preferred. Advantages of the 200% level over the normal level were not found.

---

[1] TNO Human Factors, Soesterberg, The Netherlands. *E-mail:* hogema@tm.tno.nl (J.H. Hogema); veltman@tm.tno.nl (J.A. Veltman).
[2] Ministry of Transport, Public Works and Water Management, Rotterdam, The Netherlands. *E-mail:* a.vthof@avv.rws.minvenw.nl (A. van 't Hof).

This project showed that there were margins in which the motorway lighting could be safely varied. This triggered further questions concerning the relationships among roadway illumination levels, driving behaviour and driver workload. Therefore, the Dutch Ministry of Transport, Public Works and Water Management initiated a project that had two goals:

(1) to identify which measures are suitable for measuring workload in relation to lighting and

(2) to investigate whether traffic flow data can be used to estimate workload, thus enabling a lighting adaptation mechanism based on workload.

Based on a literature survey, an inventory was made of indicators and methods to quantify effects on driving behaviour and workload effects due to motorway illumination (Hogema & Veltman, 2002). Based on this study, a set of measures and methods was selected, including a mentally loading secondary task.

METHOD

The project consisted of two separate phases. In the first phase, executed between February and March 2002, runs were conducted after the evening rush hour: approximately between 8 and 11 o'clock in the evening (Hogema & Veltman, 2002). In the second phase, executed in November and December 2002, runs were started when the evening rush hour was near its end. Thus, measurements were conducted between 6 and 9 o'clock in the evening (Hogema & Veltman, 2003). The main difference between the two phases, therefore, was the traffic volume: relatively low in the first, and relatively high in the second phase. Otherwise, the research method was practically identical in both phases.

The experiment was conducted using one of the instrumented vehicles of TNO Human Factors: an Opel Vectra. All runs were conducted well after sunset. A comparison was made between conditions with and without public lighting. The second main independent variable was a secondary task. Both variables were varied within subjects.

All runs were conducted under favourable weather and road conditions, on the A50 motorway in The Netherlands. The route was from Grijsoord Junction in southern direction to Exit Renkum, and then back in northern direction to Grijsoord. Normally, a dynamic public lighting system is operational on this stretch of motorway. For the purpose of this study, the lighting was switched manually to 100 or 0%.

This experimental set-up had the advantage that behaviour and workload could be measured on one single location, under different levels of illumination. In order to control for variations on traffic volume and composition, measurements were only conducted on weekdays and started around the same time on each evening.

Participants

In each phase, a group of 32 subjects participated, yielding a total of 64 participants in the entire study. Criteria for selection were: a driving experience of at least 10,000 km/year, in possession of a driving licence during at least the last 5 years, and aged between 25 and 55 years.

Secondary task

When the driving task is mentally loading, the driver can compensate by reducing the attention paid to other tasks. This mechanism is the basis of the secondary task paradigm. By introducing an extra task that is not related to the driving task, the performance on this secondary task is an indicator of the "spare capacity" the driver has available. A secondary task can also be applied to increase the overall task load. With such a loading secondary task, effects of independent variables on workload can occur that are not found in the absence of this secondary task.

The secondary task applied in this project was a new version of the continuous memory task (CMT) that was successfully applied in earlier research (Van Breda & Veltman, 1998). The new version used three separate auditory stimuli: a low-pitched, a medium-pitched and a high-pitched tone (L, M and H), with a fixed duration of 0.5 s. The interval between two subsequent stimuli had a uniform random distribution between 3 and 5 s.

The subject could react to the stimuli by pressing a small finger switch attached to the index finger of the left hand. The switch could be pressed by tapping it on the steering wheel. The medium-pitched tone had to be ignored. When hearing a low or high-pitched tone, the subject had to respond and in addition had to keep track of how often these tones were heard: a single "click" had to be given after each first presentation, and a "double click" after each second presentation.

Audio feedback was given of errors on the memory task (misses as well as false alarms on double clicks). On this error signal, all counters were reset.

Procedure

Subjects participated in pairs: when one drove, the other could rest. The experiment was run from the regional motorway road authority office, near the start of the experimental route. Subjects received a written instruction. The general driving instruction was to drive swiftly, without breaking any traffic laws. Concerning the secondary task, it was emphasised that the driving task (driving safely and swiftly) had the highest priority: the driving task should not suffer from the secondary task.

Next, electrodes for physiological measures (electrocardiogram (ECG) and eye blinks) and respiration belts (Phase 1 only) were attached.

During runs, an experimenter was seated on the passenger's seat to monitor the data acquisition and to give route directions. Before the first experimental run, the subject practiced the secondary task with the vehicle stationary on a parking place.

In the analysis, only data gathered on the main carriageway of the A50 motorway were used. This is a two-lane motorway. Each run yielded two stretches of 6 km each.

On each evening, both lighting conditions were applied. The lighting condition was only changed once on each evening: first all measurements were done under one condition, and then they were done in the other condition. After the measurements were finished, the normal lighting schedule was activated. In both lighting conditions, each participant completed two runs: one with and one without the secondary task.

After each run, the subject indicated the experienced mental effort on a subjective rating scale, the Dutch Rating Scale of Mental Effort (RSME) (Zijlstra & Van Doorn, 1985).

Data collection and analysis

During runs, the following data were collected:

- the steering wheel angle (sampled at 10 Hz),
- the following distance (measured with a ControLaser mounted on the dash board; 0.1 m resolution, 10 Hz sampling rate) and
- speed, position and time based on GPS (update frequency 0.5 Hz).

Two forward-looking CCD video cameras were mounted in the vehicle. The video images were used to measure the lateral position of the vehicle with respect to the lane boundaries.

The following driving behaviour variables were analysed:

- the average and standard deviation of speed,
- car-following behaviour, expressed as the mean time headway, and the percentage of time with a headway below 1, 2, 3 and 4 s,
- lane change behaviour, expressed as the lane change frequency (changes per minute),
- lane keeping behaviour, expressed as the mean and standard deviation of the lateral position,
- time-to-line crossing (TLC) and
- various measures that express steering effort.

Measures derived from the secondary task were:

- the mean reaction time and
- the error rate (number of error per minute).

The following physiological data were gathered and analysed.

- The ECG was measured using three Ag/AgCl electrodes. From the ECG data, the R-peaks were determined off-line to obtain the heart rate and the heart rate variability.
- Respiration was measured using two elastic belts (one for the chest and one for the abdomen). From the combined signal, the breathing frequency was determined.
- The electro-oculogram (EOG) was measured using two electrodes, one above and one below the driver's right eye. From these data, the eye blink frequency, blink duration and blink amplitude were analysed.

The aim of the analysis was to investigate how the dependent variables were influenced by the independent variables "lighting" (on or off) and secondary task (with or without). In this process, it should be taken into account that other factors influence the same dependent variable simultaneously. One such factor is the traffic condition, which can be quantified as the traffic volume (vehicles/hour). Inductive loop detector data from the traffic signalling system on this stretch of motorway were used for this purpose. One-minute averages (i.e. averaged over both lanes of the motorway) were available from loop detectors in each carriageway. Based on these data, the traffic speed and volume could be incorporated into the analysis.

RESULTS

In this chapter, a limited selection of the results is presented. For a full overview, the reader is referred to the original research reports (Hogema & Veltman, 2002, 2003).

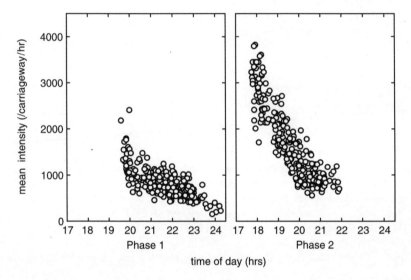

Figure 1. Traffic volume during the measurements as a function of time: Phase 1 versus Phase 2 inductive loop detector data.

The traffic volume and traffic speed were determined from the inductive loop detector data. Using GPS data, the time at which the instrumented vehicle passed the loop detectors was obtained. Next, to characterise the traffic state during this run, a 3 min average of the loop detector data was determined around the time the loop detectors were passed. The resulting mean traffic volume during the test runs is shown as a function of time in Figure 1. In agreement with our expectations, the traffic volume reduces during the evening, and volumes in Phase 2 were considerably higher than in Phase 1.

A first analysis revealed that several of the dependent variables were strongly correlated with traffic volume in Phase 2 (see Table 1). Therefore, the Phase 2 data were analysed with analysis of covariance, using public lighting and secondary task as the independent variables, and the mean traffic volume as a co-variate. In Phase 1, these correlations between the dependent variables and the traffic volume were not found. Therefore, the Phase 1 results were analysed with analysis of variance, using public lighting and secondary task as the independent variables.

Table 1. Correlations between dependent variables and traffic volume (all significant at $p < 0.05$) (Phase 2).

Variable	Correlation coefficient
Mean speed	−0.52
Standard deviation speed	0.28
Lane change frequency	−0.17
% time headway < 1 s	0.28
% time headway < 2 s	0.47
% time headway < 3 s	0.50
% time headway < 4 s	0.52
% of time in right lane	−0.19
CMT error frequency	0.27
Eye blink amplitude	0.15
Eye blink rate	−0.30

Mean speed

The mean speed as a function of lighting and secondary task, as found in Phase 1, is shown in Figure 2. The results showed a main effect of public lighting ($F(1, 22) = 7.5$; $p < 0.05$): without lighting, the mean speed was lower than with lighting (110.8 and 112.9 km/h, respectively). Next, there was a significant effect of the secondary task ($F(1, 22) = 11.0$; $p < 0.01$): without CMT, the mean speed was higher than with CMT (113.1 and 110.6 km/h, respectively).

In Phase 2 a similar effect of the secondary task was found, but no effect of public lighting.

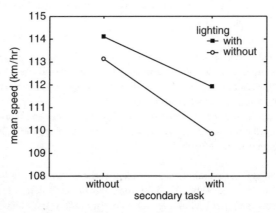

Figure 2. Mean speed as a function of lighting and secondary task (Phase 1).

Time headway distribution

The percentages of time with a headway below 1, 2, 3 and 4 s were analysed. In neither of the phases, an effect of lighting or secondary task was found. The means are shown in Figure 3. The means in Phase 2 are higher than in Phase 1, which is in line with the higher traffic volume in Phase 2.

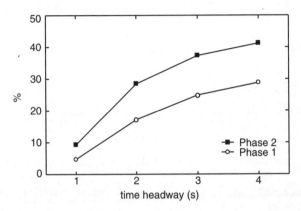

Figure 3. Percentage of time with headway below 1, 2, 3 and 4 s, as a function of phase.

Lane change and lane choice behaviour

In Phase 1 results showed that with the secondary task, fewer lane changes were carried out than without the secondary task. Expressed as the number of lane changes per minute, the means were 1.08 changes per minute with, and 1.33 changes per minute without the secondary task.

The percentage of time spent in the right lane was also analysed. Phase 1 results revealed an effect of the secondary task ($F(1, 19) = 13.4$; $p < 0.01$), showing that with secondary task, a larger proportion of time was spent in the right lane (79.7 and 73.7%, respectively).

In the second phase, qualitatively similar effects of the secondary task were found. Effects of lighting on the lane change or lane choice behaviour were not found in either of the phases.

Steering effort

One of the measures for steering effort is the steering reversal rate (SRR): the number of times per unit of time that the steering wheel is reversed through a certain gap. A higher SRR is indicative for a higher steering effort. The results of Phase 2 for a 1° gap are shown in Figure 4.

There were significant effects of lighting and of the secondary task. Without lighting, the SRR was higher than with lighting ($F(1, 32) = 4.7$; $p < 0.05$), and with the secondary task the SRR was higher than without the secondary task ($F(1, 32) = 5.2$; $p < 0.05$). Compared against the baseline condition (with lighting, no secondary task), removing lighting and adding

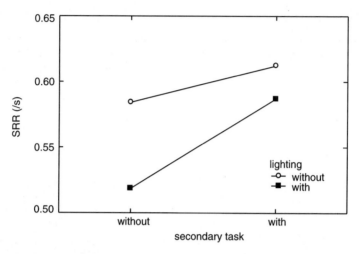

Figure 4. Steering reversal rate as a function of van lighting and secondary task (Phase 2).

the secondary task have highly similar effects on steering effort in terms of SRR effect size. Phase 1 showed similar results.

The steering effort was also analysed in terms of the high-frequency area (HFA) measure. This variable is derived from the steering wheel signal by determining the power spectral density function using a Fast Fourier Transformation. Next, the HFA-measure is calculated as the energy in the frequency band 0.3–0.6 Hz divided by the energy in the frequency band 0.0–0.6 Hz. The choice of these frequency bands is based on the finding that extra steering effort due to a more difficult steering task is especially seen in the higher frequency band (Blaauw, 1984).

In Phase 1, a marginally significant effect of lighting was found ($F(1, 22) = 3.8; p < 0.1$): with lighting on, the HFA was slightly smaller than with lighting off (0.28 and 0.29, respectively). In Phase 2, no significant effects or interactions on HFA were found.

As a third and last measure for steering effort, the standard deviation of the steering wheel angle was analysed. The Phase 1 results showed a significant effect of lighting ($F(1, 22) = 10.9$; $p < 0.01$): without lighting, the standard deviation was higher (1.84°) than with lighting (1.72°). In Phase 2, no significant effects or interactions were found.

Lane keeping

Lane keeping behaviour was analysed in terms of the standard deviation of the lateral position (SDLP). In this analysis the lane, the vehicle was driving in (left lane or right lane), was also included as an independent variable.

The Phase 2 results showed an effect of lane ($F(1, 32) = 170; p < 0.001$): in the left lane, the SDLP was smaller than in the right lane (0.20 and 0.27 m, respectively). Furthermore, there was a marginally significant effect of secondary task ($F(1, 32) = 4.0; p < 0.1$): without secondary task, the SDLP was higher (0.24 m) than with secondary task (0.23 m). Also the interaction between these variables was significant ($F(1, 32) = 4.7; p < 0.05$). All these effects are shown in Figure 5. A Tukey test revealed that the effect of secondary task was significant only in the left lane ($p < 0.01$).

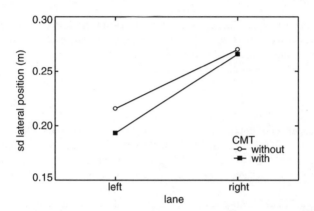

Figure 5. Standard deviation of the lateral position as a function of lane and secondary task (Phase 2).

The Phase 1 results revealed a similar effect of lane, but no effects of lighting or secondary task.

Eye blink frequency

From the EOG measurements, the eye blink frequency was derived. As Figure 6 shows for Phase 1, the blink frequency was somewhat higher with road lighting than without lighting ($F(1, 22) = 8.5; p < 0.01$), which indicates a lower visual effort due to road lighting.

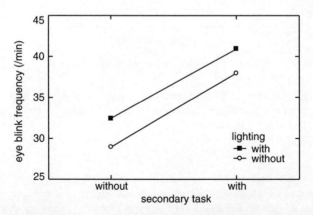

Figure 6. Eye blink frequency as a function of lighting and secondary task (Phase 1).

Furthermore, with the secondary task, the blink frequency was higher than without the secondary task $(F(1, 22) = 21.4; p < 0.001)$.

In Phase 2, a similar effect of the secondary task on the blink frequency was found, but no main effect of lighting.

In general, the direction of an effect of a secondary task on eye blink frequency depends on the type of task. In experiments with memory tasks, usually an increase of the eye blink frequency is found with increasing mental effort (Veltman & Gaillard, 1998). This is in line with the effect of the secondary task found in the current project.

Heart rate

In Phase 1, a main effect of lighting was found $(F(1, 22) = 5.6; p < 0.05)$: the mean heart rate was higher without than with lighting (75.3 and 72.8 min^{-1}, respectively). There was also an effect of the secondary task $(F(1, 22) = 10.1; p < 0.01)$: the heart rate was higher with than without secondary task (75.3 and 72.9 min^{-1}, respectively). Both effects are shown in Figure 7.

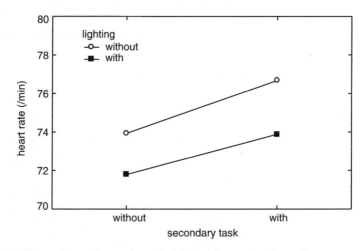

Figure 7. Effects of secondary task and lighting on heart rate (Phase 1).

In Phase 2, a similar effect was found for the secondary task $(F(1, 32) = 5.6; p < 0.05)$: with CMT, the mean heart rate was higher than without CMT (75.2 and 73.3 min^{-1}, respectively). An effect of lighting was not found here.

Mental effort

The subjective mental effort (RSME) showed a main effect $(F(1, 32) = 51; p < 0.001)$: there was a higher mental workload with the secondary task present. Furthermore, a marginally significant effect of lighting was found $(F(1, 32) = 4.1; p < 0.1)$ showing that with public lighting the mental effort was lower than without lighting (see Figure 8).

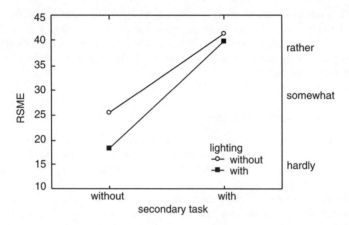

Figure 8. Subjective mental effort (RSME) as a function of lighting and secondary task (Phase 2).

Effects of traffic volume

The previous sections presented results concerning effects of roadway lighting and a secondary task, taking into account possible effects of traffic volume.

However, this does not show how effects of traffic volume on behaviour and workload relate to the effects of lighting and the secondary task (in direction and magnitude). Therefore, an additional analysis was carried out using traffic volume as an independent variable. To enable this, the traffic volumes were first categorised into *low* or *high*. A selection of the results is shown in Table 2.

Table 2. Some effects of traffic volume (means and significance).

Variable	Low volume	High volume	Significance
Mean speed (km/u)	113.1	107.9	$p < 0.01$
% of time with headway < 1 s	6.37	11.48	$p < 0.01$
% of time with headway < 4 s	32.0	49.9	$p < 0.01$
Secondary task error frequency (errors/min)	1.01	1.32	$p < 0.01$
Eye blink duration (ms)	82.8	78.4	$p < 0.01$
RSME $(-)$	29.9	33.2	$p < 0.1$

Several effects of traffic volume were found in line with the expectations. Higher traffic volumes yield a lower mean speed, more frequent car-following situations (headway < 4 s) and more frequent "short" following (<1 s headway). These results, found here by measuring within a single vehicle over a certain stretch of road, correspond with results reported elsewhere, where inductive loop detectors were used to measure many vehicles on one cross section of a motorway (Hogema, 1996).

When an effect was found of both the secondary task and the traffic volume, the direction of the effect was the same, and consistent with the interpretation in terms of workload: adding the secondary task and increasing the traffic volume results in a higher workload. Traffic volume also appeared to have an effect on the error frequency of the secondary task: more errors were made under high traffic volume.

Discussion and Conclusions

From the literature, it is known that public lighting has only minor effects on driving behaviour when road and weather conditions are favourable. When effects are reported at all, their size is typically small (Hogema & Veltman, 2002). The results from the current project are in line with these results. In the first phase (with relatively low traffic volumes) a slightly higher mean speed was found in the presence of public lighting. In the second Phase (with relatively high traffic volumes) this effect was not found. Possibly, traffic volume influenced workload differently than expected. When more traffic is present, the road illumination is better and the direction of the road can be perceived better due to the lights of the other vehicles. A higher traffic volume yields a higher workload, but an additional workload effect of roadway lighting is relatively small.

When drivers have to deal with higher workload, they often have two options: they can increase their effort expenditure or they can try to reduce the task load. A reduction of speed is an example of a reduction of the task load. With a lower speed, drivers have more time available to anticipate and this reduces the workload. The present experiment showed a combination of the two options. In Phase 1, the speed was reduced when the lighting was switched off and the mental effort was increased (higher heart rate and fewer eye blinks). In Phase 2, the blink duration was shorter when the lighting was switched off and the drivers increased the number steering reversals. Speed changes due to lighting were not found in Phase 2, most probably because the drivers could not easily adapt the speed to the workload level because of the high traffic density.

The effects that were found were rather small. It should be noted, however, that these results were found under favourable circumstances:

- data were only collected under favourable weather conditions and with an unrestricted traffic flow,

- data were only collected on a homogenous stretch of motorway (no merging or weaving sections),

- the participants were a fairly homogeneous group, without, e.g. inexperienced or elderly drivers and

- the experiment was organised such that driver state affecting factors (fatigue or persisting monotony) did not play a role.

Under less ideal conditions, stronger effects of lighting can be expected. For example, it is known that weather conditions influence driving behaviour and workload (Hogema, 1996; Hogema & Kaptein, 1998), and especially during rain, mental workload is strongly affected by public lighting. In contrast, in the current research emphasis was on the sensitivity of the various workload measures to distinguish among lighting conditions when road and weather conditions are favourable.

Focussing on the various steering effort measures that were used, the SRR was more sensitive than the HFA or the standard deviation of the steering wheel angle. Only the SRR showed effects of lighting as well as effects of the secondary task in both phases.

Secondary tasks can be applied for two purposes. The first is as a measure for workload: the higher the workload induced by the driving task, the worse the performance on the secondary task. In the current study, this approach did not succeed: lighting did not influence the secondary task performance. The influence of traffic volume on workload on the other hand could be measured with the secondary task: more errors were made under higher traffic volumes.

A secondary task can also be applied to increase the overall task load. The secondary task indeed increased the workload, as shown in the mean speed, lane change behaviour, SRR, eye blinks and the subjective mental effort. However, this additional workload did *not* make effects of public lighting visible on other variables.

It must be concluded that secondary tasks were not successful in measuring workload effects of public lighting.

A further question in this project was how workload relates to traffic flow variables such as traffic volume and speed. Effects of lighting that are robust enough to be found in both project phases were the SRR, the eye blink frequency and the RSME. These are all variables that can be measured within a vehicle or on a driver, but not through roadside sensors such as inductive loop detectors or video systems. On the other hand, factors that can be adequately measured in the traffic flow (speed, volume, headways, etc.) were not suitable to measure workload effects of lighting. Therefore, it must be concluded that switching criteria for public lighting based on workload criteria are not feasible.

Traffic lighting generates a lot of interest. The current project has been followed closely by the media as well as by people living nearby the test route. Also in the Ministry of Transport, Public Works and Water Management the study has been closely monitored. For now, there are two main areas of application of the project results. The first is a follow-up project focussing on the relation between workload and all elements a driver encounters during a trip, such as the workload effects of road elements on, along or above the road. Second, the results are used in the further policy development concerning public lighting of the Ministry of Transport, Public Works and Water Management. The results have further strengthened the policy to look beyond merely traffic volumes, and also take into account energy consumption and environmental issues.

REFERENCES

Blaauw, G.J. (1984). Car driving as a supervisory control task. PhD Thesis. Soesterberg: Instituut voor Zintuigfysiologie TNO.

Folles, E., IJsselstijn, J., Hogema, J.H., & Van der Horst, A.R.A. (1999). Dynamic public lighting (cover report). Rotterdam, The Netherlands: Ministry of Transport, Public Works and Water Management, Transport Research Centre.

Hogema, J.H. (1996). Effects of rain on daily traffic volume and on driving behaviour. Report TM-96-B019. Soesterberg: TNO Human Factors Research Institute.

Hogema, J.H., & Kaptein, N.A. (1998). Dynamische Openbare Verlichting (DYNO). Fase 3: Praktijkevaluatie. Rapport TM-98-C038. Soesterberg: TNO Technische Menskunde.

Hogema, J.H., & Veltman, J.A. (2002). Werkbelasting en rijgedrag tijdens duisternis: eerste veldexperiment. TNO-rapport TM-02-C046. Soesterberg: TNO Technische Menskunde.

Hogema, J.H., & Veltman, J.A. (2003). Werkbelasting en rijgedrag tijdens duisternis: tweede veldexperiment. TNO-rapport TM-03-C018. Soesterberg: TNO Technische Menskunde.

Van Breda, L., & Veltman, J.A. (1998). Perspective information in the cockpit as a target tracking aid. *Journal of Experimental Psychology—Applied*, *4*, 55–68.

Veltman, J.A., & Gaillard, A.W.K. (1998). Physiological workload reactions to increasing levels of task difficulty. *Ergonomics*, *5*, 656–669.

Zijlstra, F.R.H., & Van Doorn, L. (1985). The construction of a subjective effort scale (Report). Delft: Department of Social Sciences & Philosophy, Delft University of Technology.

Traffic and Transport Psychology
G. Underwood (Editor)
© 2005 Elsevier Ltd. All rights reserved.

30

A STUDY OF CONVERSATION PERFORMANCE USING MOBILE PHONES WHILE DRIVING

Toni Luke[1], Rachel Smith[1], Andrew M. Parkes[1] and Peter C. Burns[2]

INTRODUCTION

The use of hand-held mobile phones while driving was banned in the UK from the 1st December 2003. This legislation was passed in response to growing concern about the negative impact of mobile phone use on road safety. It is still legal to talk on a mobile phone while driving if using certain types of hands-free equipment. This is because there is a perception that the primary risk associated with phone use is the manual manipulation of the phone, which may impair the driver's physical control of the vehicle. However, there is a growing body of evidence to suggest that it may be holding a conversation itself that causes driver distraction (Burns, Parkes, Burton, Smith, & Burch, 2002; Consiglio, Driscoll, Witte, & Berg, 2003; Fairclough, Ross, Ashby, & Parkes, 1991; McKnight & McKnight, 1993; Parkes, 1993; Parkes & Burns, 2004; Parkes & Hooijmeijer, 2000; Strayer, Drews, & Johnston, 2003; Strayer & Johnston, 2001).

Strayer et al. (2003) suggest that participation in a mobile phone call disrupts driving performance because it diverts attention away from the driving task to another cognitively engaging task: the conversation. Conversation has a number of different cognitive elements including: comprehension of the other speaker; memory of various conversational elements; decision making and monitoring spoken output. There are a large number of studies that examine the cognitive interference of conversation on driving. However, there are fewer studies that reverse this question to examine the impact of driving on conversation performance.

Studies that have examined verbal performance in relation to driving have typically used standardised verbal tasks in a simulated environment. The primary focus of these studies has

---

[1] TRL Limited, UK. *E-mail:* tluke@trl.co.uk (T. Luke).
[2] Transport Canada, Canada.

been to examine the effect of the cognitive distraction on driving. However, performance measures on the secondary verbal task have also been reported, (Fox & Parkes, 1989; Parkes, 1991a,b).

Horswill and McKenna (1999) used a verbal recognition task to investigate the effect of interference on risk taking judgements. Results indicated that participants made more errors on the verbal task when performing simulated driving tasks than when performing the verbal task alone. In addition, the number of errors varied according to the particular task the participants did.

Spence and Read (2003) investigated the effect of a verbal shadowing task on a simulated driving task. The effects of the dual task on the shadowing performance were also reported. Participants reported more relevant words when performing the shadowing task alone compared to while driving.

These studies provide evidence that driving can impact performance on a verbal task. However, they are not directly related to performance when using a mobile phone. A study which did examine mobile phone conversation specifically was Radeborg, Briem, and Hedman (1999). Radeborg et al. examined performance on a verbal working memory task during simulated driving tasks. Participants were required to differentiate between semantically meaningful and nonsensical questions and to remember words from sets of these sentences. Auditory material was presented via a hands-free mobile phone. Performance on the task was better when not driving.

Parkes (1991a) reported a significant decrease in scores on different kinds of verbal task during a mobile phone conversation while driving compared to a driver passenger conversation or a normal telephone conversation without driving. The verbal tasks used measured verbal and numerical memory and interpretation.

Burns et al. (2002) used the Rosenbaum Verbal Cognitive Test Battery (RVCB) to facilitate mobile phone conversations via both hand-held and hands-free equipment. Performance on conversations conducted while driving was uniformly worse than conversations conducted without a concurrent task. There were some differences between hand-held and hands-free phones. Hands-free performance was worse for sentence repetition tasks but was better than hand-held performance for the number of pauses in the monologue and the number of errors made on verbal puzzles. These results support the notion of interference of driving with conversation performance and suggest that there may be some qualitative differences between different conversation media.

Parkes (1991b) examined the effect of driving on the structure and style of a more natural negotiation task. Participants took part in a series of role-playing exercises, which involved a negotiation dialogue with an experimenter. These conversations were conducted in several different conditions: face to face; via a telephone while driving; with a passenger while driving and via a hands-free phone while driving. Performance was scored according to efficiency (number of words used and time taken), outcome and perceived difficulty. Conversations conducted by mobile phone while driving were of average efficiency. However, they resulted in less satisfactory outcomes and greater perceived difficulty.

This chapter presents the results of a study that further examines the difference between conversation performance via different media. The aim is to compare performance on verbal tasks for different types of conversations: face to face; with a passenger while driving and via hands-free equipment while driving. This research was undertaken as part of a larger study on the distraction effects of mobile phone use and other in-vehicle tasks. Only aspects relevant to the conversation performance will be discussed in this chapter.

METHOD

Participants

Thirty drivers aged between 21 and 64 ($M = 40.9$, SD $= 12.39$) participated in this study. They all had experience of using mobile phones. The sample was split evenly by gender. The sample of mobile phone users was randomly selected from the TRL volunteer database, a pool of over 1300 drivers representing a cross-section of the driving population of Hampshire, Berkshire and Surrey.

Procedure

Participants initially completed a warm-up drive to familiarise them with the driving simulator.

The experimental conditions relevant to conversation performance were as follows:

- *Conversation control*—Face to face conversation, without driving

- *Passenger*—Conversation with the experimenter as a passenger while driving

- *Hands-free*—Conversation with the experimenter through a hands-free mobile phone system while driving

The order of conditions was balanced. Video and audio recordings were taken of the conversations and tasks.

Equipment

The TRL driving simulator consists of a medium size saloon car surrounded by 3×4 m projection screens giving 210° front vision and 60° rear vision, enabling the normal use of vehicle mirrors. The car body shell is mounted on hydraulic rams that supply motion to simulate the heave, pitch and roll experienced in normal braking, accelerating and cornering. When negotiating curves, the simulator provides realistic forces experienced by the driver through the steering wheel. The provision of car engine noise, external road noise and the sounds of passing traffic further enhance the realism of the driving experience.

A professionally fitted Nokia hands-free phone kit was used with a Nokia 3310 phone in this study. The phone bracket was mounted on the upper left side of the centre stack within easy reach and view from the driving position.

Route and traffic scenarios

In the driving conditions of this study participants drove a 17-km route that was composed of four different segments. The route started with a car-following task on a motorway.

Drivers were instructed to maintain their initial distance from the lead vehicle, which oscillated in speed between 50 and 70 mph (80–113 km/h). The next section consisted of normal motorway driving. The participants next navigated a section of curved road where they were instructed to maintain a constant speed of 60 mph (96.6 km/h) and position in the centre of the lane. Finally, participants drove a section of dual-carriageway where they were instructed to selectively respond to four different warning signs.

Conversation tasks

Hands-free conversation. Questions from the RVCB were given by the experimenter over the hands-free phone while the participant drove the route. The RVCB measures judgement, flexible thinking and response times (Waugh et al., 2000). The battery is composed of a 30 item remembering sentences task (e.g. repeat the sentence: "Undetected by the sleeping dog, the thief broke into Jane's apartment") and 30 verbal puzzle tasks (e.g. Answer the question: "Felix is darker than Antoine. Who is the lighter of the two?"). The test battery has five levels of difficulty with six items within each level for both sentence repetition and verbal and numerical puzzles. These questions were split across the conditions and also included short monologues on familiar topics (e.g. 40 s describing a recent holiday). Questions were presented at fixed points on the route regardless of the traffic conditions.

Passenger conversation. In the passenger condition the conversation took place with the experimenter occupying the front passenger seat of the vehicle alongside the driver while they drove the route. Questions in this condition were also drawn from the RCVB and were matched for difficulty with the other two conversation conditions. Questions were presented at approximately the same point in the route as in the hands-free condition. However the experimenter made some allowance for the traffic situation. For example, if the participant was being overtaken then the experimenter would pause and allow them to finish before asking the question.

Conversation control. In order to provide a baseline for both of the conversation conditions (hands-free and passenger), data was collected for a similar standardised conversation conducted away from the vehicle in a relaxed seating area. The experimenter sat opposite to the participant. This enabled an assessment of the effect of driving the simulated vehicle on the quality of the conversation itself. The questions were paced in a normal face to face conversation, when the participant had finished the response the experimenter proceeded with the next question.

RESULTS

Data analysis

The data was analysed to determine the impact of driving and conversation medium (hands-free phone, car passenger or face to face) on conversation performance. Descriptive analyses were performed on all of the data from the experiment (central tendencies and distributions). The data was screened for anomalies and violations of parametric assumptions. This was followed by inferential analyses. The main analysis was a repeated measures analysis of variance (ANOVA). Post-hoc t-tests were used to further examine the main effects of condition.

Using a similar approach to Chapanis, Ochsman, Parrish, and Weeks (1972) a number of measures were used to examine the quality of the conversations in each condition:

- Correct sentence repetition

- Response time to sentence repetition

- Pauses in monologue

- Rate of talking in monologue

- Correct answers to verbal and numerical reasoning puzzles

- Question response times

The general experimental hypothesis was that conversation performance would be worst in the hands-free condition, better in the passenger condition and best of all in the conversation control condition. Better performance would be reflected by fewer pauses, more correct responses and a higher rate of speech.

Sentence repetition

A one-way repeated measures ANOVA was calculated for the mean number of sentences repeated correctly for the three different conditions. There was a significant main affect for the total number of sentences repeated correctly by condition $\{F(1.9, 53.3) = 68.14, p < 0.001, MSE = 0.71\}$. There was no significant difference between the mean number of correctly repeated sentences in the control and the passenger conditions. There was a significant difference between the number of sentences answered correctly in the control condition and the hands-free condition ($p < 0.001$) and between the passenger condition and the hands-free condition ($p < 0.001$) (Figure 1).

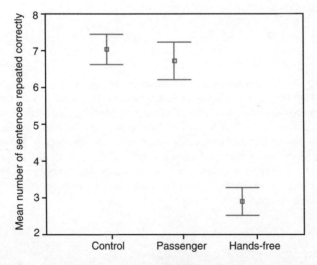

Figure 1. Mean number of sentences repeated correctly (± 1 SD).

Mean response time for sentence repetition. A one-way repeated measures ANOVA was calculated for the mean response time for sentences repeated for the three different conditions. There was a significant main effect for time by condition $\{F(1.6, 44.3) = 88.87, p < 0.001,$ MSE $= 0.76\}$. The time taken to repeat back sentences was significantly less during the control condition than either the passenger ($p < 0.05$) or the hands-free condition ($p < 0.001$). There was also a significant difference between the passenger condition and the hands-free condition ($p < 0.001$) (Figure 2).

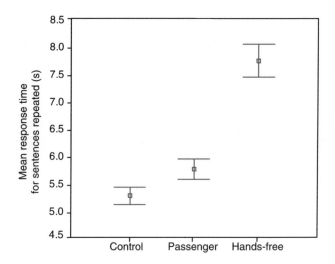

Figure 2. Mean response time for sentence repetition (± 1 SD).

Monologue

Mean number of pauses in monologue. The number of pauses during the monologue section was calculated. A one-way repeated measures ANOVA was calculated for the number of pauses across the three conversation conditions. There was a significant main effect for the number of pauses by condition $\{F(1.6, 47.8) = 22.67, p < 0.001,$ MSE $= 0.45\}$. Post-hoc tests were run to compare the conditions. The number of pauses was significantly less in the control condition than in the hands-free condition ($p < 0.001$). There were also significantly fewer pauses during the passenger conversation than the hands-free conversation. There was no significant difference between the number of pauses during the control condition and the passenger condition (Figure 3).

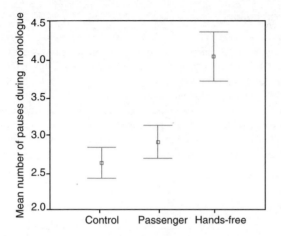

Figure 3. Mean number of pauses in monologue (± 1 SD).

Rate of talking

The rate of talking was calculated for the conversations by counting the number of words spoken and dividing it by the duration of the monologue. A one-way repeated measures ANOVA was calculated for the rate of talking across the three conversation conditions. There was a significant main effect of condition on the mean rate of talking $\{F(2, 56) = 48.28, p < 0.001, \text{MSE} = 0.63\}$. Post-hoc tests were run to identify the differences. The rate of talking was significantly faster during the control conditions than either the passenger or hands-free ($p < 0.001$). There was also a significant difference between the passenger conversations and the hands-free conversations (Figure 4).

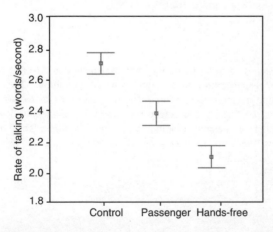

Figure 4. Mean rate of talking (± 1 SD).

Verbal and numerical puzzles

Mean total number of correct answers. A one-way repeated measures ANOVA was calculated for the mean total number of questions answered correctly for the three different conditions. There was a significant main affect for the total number of questions answered correctly by condition $\{F(1.9, 53.8) = 3.74, p < 0.05, \text{MSE} = 0.12\}$. The number of correct answers was significantly higher in the control condition than in the hands-free condition ($p < 0.001$). There was no significant difference between the number of correct answers in the control condition and the passenger condition, or between the passenger and hands-free conditions, though the trend in the results towards worse performance in the hands-free condition is repeated (Figure 5).

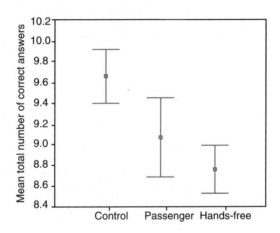

Figure 5. Total number of correct answers (± 1 SD).

Mean question response time. A one-way repeated measures ANOVA was calculated for the mean question response time for the three different conditions. There was a significant main affect for the mean response time for the questions answered $\{F(2, 56) = 6.74, p < 0.05, \text{MSE} = 0.19\}$. The question response time was significantly lower for the control condition than either the passenger or the hands-free condition. There was no significant difference between the response times of the passenger and the hands-free conditions (Figure 6).

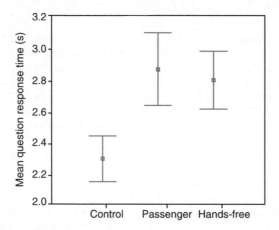

Figure 6. Question response time ($\pm$ 1 SD).

SUMMARY

In general conversation performance was worse in the driving conditions, both with a passenger or using a hands-free kit. The worst performance was observed when talking on a hands-free kit. The conversation performance when driving and talking to a passenger was generally worse than the control condition although the worst performance was observed when talking on the hands-free kit. For some of the performance measures there was no difference between talking to a passenger and talking when not driving.

There were three main conversation tasks, monologue, verbal puzzles and sentence repetition. The overall rate of talking in the monologue was slower when driving than when not driving. The slowest rate of talking was observed when using the hands-free kit. There were also a greater number of pauses in the monologue when driving and using the hands-free kit. There was little difference in the number of pauses between the passenger and conversation control conditions.

Fewer sentences were repeated correctly in the hands-free condition than in either the passenger or the control condition. The mean response time for sentence repetition was higher in the hands-free condition than the passenger and control conditions. Finally, the response times for sentence repetition in the passenger condition were also significantly higher than the control condition.

In the hands-free and passenger conditions less verbal puzzle questions were answered correctly than in the control condition. Mean question response times were also higher in the hands-free and passenger conditions than in the control condition. There was no difference between the number of correct answers or response times in the passenger and hands-free conditions. Overall, this indicates much worse performance on verbal puzzles when driving than when not driving.

DISCUSSION

The fact that conversation performance is generally worse while driving and talking, either to a passenger or on a hands-free kit, suggests that driving interferes with conversation. This is supported by the finding that all drivers rated the conversation tasks as more difficult when driving than when not. It is also consistent with research, which indicates that driving performance is impaired by phone conversations. This is not surprising given that conversation and driving both make cognitive demands. When driving, both the style of the conversation (pace, pauses), and the ability to reproduce and interpret information decline.

The most interesting findings are those that demonstrate a difference between the passenger and the hands-free conditions. Both of these tasks allow the driver to retain full physical control of the vehicle, unlike when using a hand-held phone, and the conversation tasks were the same in both conditions. Therefore, differences must be a function of some attributes of the hands-free conversation. Difficulty using the hands-free system could be caused by the system operation or the technical performance of the system in terms of sound quality. Either of these factors might be expected to impact on the conversation task. However, such factors did not feature in this study. The cellphone calls were initiated and terminated by the experimenter, removing the need for the participant to do anything other than engage in the conversation. The technical quality of the phone line was clear, and there were no problems of intelligibility.

Therefore, it must be some aspect of the situation, apart from the driving and performance of a verbal task, which affects conversation performance. Not only is the passenger physically close to the driver, adjustments to the pacing of the conversation by the passenger, in response to the driving situation, may have an effect on the workload and consequent quality of the conversation by the driver.

Differences between passenger and hands-free may also be accounted for, in part, by social aspects of the conversations. From a theoretical viewpoint support comes from the *formality* model (Morley & Stephenson, 1969), the *social presence* model (Short, Williams, & Christie, 1976) and the *cuelessness* model (Rutter, Stephensen, & Dewey, 1981). These models make similar assumptions about the way that a conversation may be influenced by the medium in which it is conducted. The thrust of the argument being that a lack of natural cues when the participants are separated visually, leads to a more impersonal style of conversation, with consequences for the pacing and turn-taking exhibited.

However, it should be remembered that the conversation tasks used in this study were highly structured, and far removed from natural discourse. The measures used relate more to the verbal and cognitive ability of the participants under conflicting workload conditions than to the style of the conversations. *Social impact theory* (Latané, 1981) states that the likelihood that a person will respond to social influence is mediated by the strength, immediacy and number of sources of influence. In the passenger condition the experimenter was physically close to the participant, resulting in greater immediacy. The participant could have been influenced to devote more resources to the conversation tasks, than they did with the remote experimenter, and consequently show behaviour closer to that seen in the non-driving control.

The comparison between the conversation conditions is strengthened by the use of a standardised conversation script. The RVCB provides test items that are matched for difficulty. This means that differences in performance between conditions can be attributed to factors other than the test material. However, a drawback is that the verbal cognitive test battery is not equivalent to normal conversation.

The element of the participant's task that was closest to the natural flow of a conversation was the short monologue, where the participant was free to express their ideas as they wished. The pattern of results for performance of the monologue task can also be attributed to the cognitive demands of the simultaneous tasks. The control condition was least demanding, and this was reflected in the least number of pauses and the highest rate of talking. Performance on the hands-free mobile phone was the slowest, and included the most pauses. Again, there was a clear difference in pattern between the passenger and hands-free conditions.

This study demonstrates that using a mobile phone via hands-free kit while driving is not equivalent to talking to a passenger. It is a more difficult task. The results of this study imply that performing a complex or demanding conversation while driving is difficult and that the quality of the information exchange could be compromised under these circumstances. This research may be particularly relevant to companies where employees use mobile phones for work, and may wish to develop policies regarding phone use. It is also of relevance in situations where important information needs to be exchanged accurately by other means while driving such as in the ambulance service or police force.

In this study the control conversation took place in a different environment to the driving conditions. The conversation was also conducted face to face, away from the vehicle, rather than in the simulator vehicle, similar to the passenger or hands-free conversations. For a complete design, two non-driving conditions would have been required, replicating the passenger and hands-free driving conditions, but with the driving simulation task removed. In spite of these limitations it is clear that the major influence of performance is the presence of the dual-task element.

The conversation scripts based on the verbal test battery used in this study were highly appropriate from an experimental point of view. Nevertheless, they may not be representative of realistic conversation. Future research should attempt to extend the approach of Parkes (1991b) who used a role-playing negotiation task and examine the effect of driving on different types of natural conversation. Potential studies could look at different types of natural exchange that vary in complexity and importance. For example, a study could compare general idle conversation, making arrangements, discussing business and having a debate or argument.

ACKNOWLEDGEMENTS

This research was funded by the UK Department of Health as part of the Mobile Tele-communications and Health Risks Research Programme (MTHR).

REFERENCES

Burns, P.C., Parkes, A.M., Burton, S., Smith, R.K., & Burch, D. (2002). How dangerous is driving with a mobile phone? Benchmarking the impairment to alcohol. *TRL report 547*. Transport Research Laboratory, Crowthorne, UK.

Chapanis, A., Ochsman, R.B., Parrish, R.N., & Weeks, G.D. (1972). Studies on interactive communication I. Effects of four communication modes on the behaviour of teams during co-operative problem solving. *Human Factors, 4*, 487–510.

Consiglio, W., Driscoll, P., Witte, M., & Berg, W.P. (2003). Effect of cellular telephone conversation and other potential interference in reaction time and braking response. *Accident Analysis and Prevention, 35*, 495–500.

Fairclough, S.H., Ross, T., Ashby, M.C., & Parkes, A.M. (1991). Effects of handsfree cellphone use on driver behaviour. *Proceedings of the ISATA Conference*, Florence, Italy, 403–410.

Fox, S., & Parkes, A.M. (1989). The effects of driving and handsfree telephone use on conversation style and decision making ability. *HUSAT Memo. No. 434R*. HUSAT Research Centre, Loughborough University of Technology, UK.

Latané, B. (1981). The psychology of social impact. *American Psychologist, 36*, 343–356.

Horswill, M.S., & McKenna, F.P. (1999). The effect of interference on dynamic risk taking judgements. *British Journal of Psychology, 90*, 189–199.

McKnight, J., & McKnight, S. (1993). The effect of cellular phone use upon driver attention. *Accident Analysis and Prevention, 25* (3), 259–265.

Morley, I.E., & Stephenson, G.M. (1969). Interpersonal and interparty exchange: a laboratory simulation of an industrial negotiation at the plant level. *British Journal of Psychology, 60*, 543–545.

Parkes, A.M. (1991a). Drivers' decision making ability whilst using carphones. In Lovesey, T. (Ed.), *Contemporary Ergonomics* (pp. 427–432). London: Taylor & Francis.

Parkes, A.M. (1991b). The effects of driving and handsfree telephone use on conversation structure and style. *Proceedings of the Human Factors Association of Canada Conference* (pp. 141–147), Canada: Vancouver.

Parkes, A.M. (1993). Voice communications in vehicles. In Parkes, A.M., & Franzen, S. (Eds.), *Driving Future Vehicles* (pp. 219–228). London: Taylor & Francis.

Parkes, A.M., & Burns, P.C. (2004). Mobile phones and car driving: cause for concern or action? *Behavioural Research in Road Safety: 14th Seminar* (pp. 87–89). Department for Transport, UK.

Parkes, A.M., & Hooijmeijer, V. (2000). The influence of the use of mobile phones on driver situation awareness. National Highway Traffic Safety Administration (NHSTA). Internet Forum on "The safety impact of driver distraction using in-vehicle devices." July 5th 2000, [www.driverdistraction.org].

Radeborg, K., Briem, V., & Hedman, L.R. (1999). The effect of concurrent task difficulty on working memory during simulated driving. *Ergonomics, 42*, 767–777.

Rutter, D.T., Stephenson, G.M., & Dewey, M.E. (1981). Visual communication and the content and style of conversation. *British Journal of Psychology, 20*, 41–52.

Short, J., Williams, E., & Christie, H. (1976). *The Social Psychology of Telecommunications*. Chichester: Wiley.

Spence, C., & Read, L. (2003). Speech shadowing while driving: on the difficulty of splitting attention between eye and ear. *Psychological Science, 14* (3), 251–256.

Strayer, D.L., & Johnston, W.A. (2001). Dual-task studies of simulated driving and conversing on a cellular telephone. *Psychological Science*, *12* (6), 462–466.

Strayer, D.L., Drews, F.A., & Johnston, W.A. (2003). Cell phone-induced failures of visual attention during simulated driving. *Journal of Experimental Psychology: Applied*, *9* (1), 23–32.

Waugh, J.D., Glumm, M.M., Kilduff, P.W., Tauson, R.A., Smyth, C.C., & Pillalamarri, R.S. (2000). Cognitive workload while driving and talking on a cellular phone or to a passenger. *International Ergonomics Association Conference*, San Diego, USA.

Traffic and Transport Psychology
G. Underwood (Editor)
© 2005 Elsevier Ltd. All rights reserved.

31

TRAFFIC PSYCHOLOGY THEORIES: TOWARDS UNDERSTANDING DRIVING BEHAVIOUR AND SAFETY EFFORTS

Heikki Summala[1]

INTRODUCTION

It is an often presented view that the theory development in traffic psychology has not proceeded very well during recent decades. Especially, testable (falsifiable) hypotheses have not been drawn from theories, which also means that alternative theories cannot be put into test.

Useful taxonomies have been presented, however. Among the most influential ones, the hierarchical structure of driving task is now generally understood, being helpful in structuring driver skills and mechanisms that affect exposure to risk and accident output of the system. Allen, Lunenfeld and Alexander (1971) were among the first to present such a hierarchy more than 30 years ago in their analysis of drivers' information needs, and it was after the meeting held in Gieten, Netherlands, in May 1978 (Michon, 1979), that this basic hierarchical structure was soon adopted by researchers in the field. As combined with Rasmussen's (1983) knowledge–rule–skill categorization, it gives a good framework for task descriptions (e.g. Hale, Stoop & Hommels, 1990). Driver education is one field which has obviously benefited from better structured taxonomies (Hatakka, Keskinen, Gregersen, Glad & Hernetkoski, 2002; Keskinen, Hatakka, Laapotti, Katila & Peräaho, 2004). Such a hierarchical structure, together with a detailed taxonomy of on-road control tasks and respective exposure, is also a necessary tool for understanding accident loss as related to exposure to risk (see "multiple sieve model"; Summala, 1997).

What is needed, however, is truly functional models which predict dynamic road user behaviour on road. Good progress has been made in modelling certain partial tasks. It has been shown,

---

[1] Department of Psychology, University of Helsinki, Helsinki, Finland. *E-mail:* heikki.summala@helsinki.fi (H. Summala).

for example, that drivers are not simple servomechanisms who keep the car in the middle of lane and continually correct smallest deviations. A two-level model of Donges (1978), followed by time-based models of Godthelp, Milgram and Blaauw (1984), helped explain the active, dynamic role of the driver, and the degrees of freedom he/she has in one basic driving task, lane keeping.

The present work, a conclusion of the Symposium on Traffic psychology theories in ICTTP 2004, takes a challenging task in searching for more general mechanisms which explain drivers' dynamic behaviour. We focus on the question of primary interest in traffic psychology: what actually guides a driver in traffic? What are the basic mechanisms that, for example, determine drivers' moment-to-moment speed control, in different environments, as restricted by speed limits or not. In other words, we are searching for general psychological pacing factors in driver's behaviour.

This chapter is not all-inclusive. Many popular models are excluded that have been applied in traffic psychology. For example, social psychological models (e.g. Ajzen, 1991) are not considered here, although we agree with Rothengatter's (2002) conclusion that (one) focal point in traffic psychology is where performance theory and social–psychological theory meet. We exclude—almost totally—discussion on individual differences. We concentrate on motor vehicle drivers, well knowing that the same brains, and largely the same cognition and emotions guide us as a pedestrian and bicyclist.

However, as related to the taxonomies mentioned above, we should be able to predict how different hierarchical levels influence each other; how on-road driving experiences translate to travel choices, e.g. when older people reduce driving at night or in impaired weather conditions. This, and the search for general pacing factors, is very much related to a challenge for traffic psychology: what actually determines the effectiveness of transport system modifications?

Gibson and Crooks (1938) were among the first who referred to behavioural feedback, or behavioural adaptation, the driver's offsetting response to technical safety measures. They noted that when provided with better brakes, drivers delay braking accordingly. This effect has been shown in research on antilock brake system (Aschenbrenner & Biehl, 1994; Evans & Gerrish, 1996; Sagberg, Fosser & Saetermo, 1997). Trade-off between safety and other goals and motives of driving is a fundamental feature of the road user and the traffic system. One of the big challenges is to explain the mechanisms and predict the existence and size of such behavioural adaptation, given any change in the system.

This chapter traces two important lines of thinking in traffic psychology and presents a synthesis, a "multiple comfort model" to explain normal driving and its limits.

SEARCH FOR PSYCHOLOGICAL PACING MECHANISMS IN DRIVING

Emotional tension

One important line of thinking starts from the work of Taylor (1964). Based on his on-road study with galvanic skin response measurements, he proposed that level of emotional tension or anxiety guides the driver: "Driving is a self-paced task governed by the level of emotional tension or anxiety which the driver wishes to tolerate".

Wilde (1982), in his well-known and much debated model, proposed that drivers tend to target a certain level of risk. The actual model is a simple homeostatic (thermostatic) system with a traditional optimizing decision model included in it, but the model is best known from its safety prediction: should any changes be made in the traffic system, road users tend to maintain a certain target level of risk and, therefore, safety level keeps approximately constant. It is obvious that this is not the case, as already predicted by Smeed (1949) and confirmed by many big successes in safety developments (see, e.g. Evans, 1991; Robertson & Pless, 2002).

All theorists do not abandon Wilde's idea of target risk, however. Fuller (2000, 2004), in his task–capability interface model, incorporates it when combining risk homeostasis and zero-risk (see below) models, referring to task difficulty as a control measure. Fuller claims that drivers are sensitive to task difficulty and try to keep experienced difficulty within a certain margin. Vaa (2004) takes a good step forward when searching for other options. He lists several candidates for drivers' targets. Drivers may target for a certain arousal level, in all of its varieties, and sensation, pleasure, security, workload, avoiding violations, or even non-compliance of the rules. Finally, while applying Damasio's (1994) model of emotions and feelings, he proposes that the pacing factor is target feeling or best feeling, and the body is the risk monitor.

Näätänen and Summala (1974, 1976), who also studied Taylor's (1964) work thoroughly, adopted quite a different position. In line with Taylor they claimed that driving is a self-paced task, the level of task difficulty is determined by the driver according to their motives. (This is the prerequisite for the fact that many safety measures have not led to expected results.) In sharp contrast to Wilde's model they proposed a threshold model with three major starting points:

(1) Subjective risk monitor for present or anticipated fear is the inhibitory mechanism in driver behaviour.

(2) Drivers' goals and excitatory motives push them towards the limits, e.g. towards higher speed if not otherwise restricted.

(3) Safety margins are in a key position in driver's task control (see the next section).

In their control flow model, Näätänen and Summala (1974) postulated a motivation module which produces desired actions or tends to keep pace (to maintain progress). Action is continuously monitored by the subjective risk (fear) monitor which, given a certain threshold is exceeded, takes a role in decisions. Groeger (2000, 2004), in his differential analysis, gives a related, detailed model of how drivers manage with implied goal interruptions, appraising them, and planning and implementing actions to handle them, along with a multitude of factors that explain interindividual variance in these performances.

Drivers' goals and the so-called extra motives, both those arisen in traffic and the other brought from outside it, get an important role in Näätänen and Summala model. For example, maintaining progress—and target speed level especially—is an important motivating factor (Summala, 1988). Unexpected delays or even momentary decelerations are felt punishing and, especially if interpreted as caused by another driver, may cause aggressive reactions (e.g. Shinar, 1998). Most of the time, driving is quite habitual activity with no concern of risk (hence the "zero-risk model") but excitatory and inhibitory motives may also compete in certain situations. Thus, for example, if one is waiting for a gap in oncoming flow to overtake a slower vehicle on a two-lane road, while being at risk of missing an important appointment, there are two motives that compete in decision making rather than rational risk calculation, and it is emotions rather than pure cognition that takes a leading role (Summala & Näätänen, 1988).

Safety/comfort zone

Another line of thinking comes from two sources, from the so-called proxemics approach (Hall, 1966) and from an early work of Gibson and Crooks (1938) on safety zone.

Hall (1966) described people having different zones around them, depending on who is approaching. The intimate zone, with full contact, is reserved only for closest people—family members and best friends—while personal, social, and public zones are applied for less familiar people and social situations. These zones translate to critical distances, thresholds which trigger approach or avoidance response, or flight or fight response. In public space an approaching person's appearance and his/her perceived or interpreted intentions influence on feelings of comfort and safety, i.e. the threat the approaching person represents. In that sense, humans have safety or comfort zone around them in all environments, with strong emotional characteristics.

When a human being is in motion, he/she must reserve additional margins, especially ahead of him/her, to avoid colliding with obstacles: the faster the self-motion the more space is needed in front. Gibson and Crooks (1938), in their excellent analysis and series of drawings, demonstrate how roadway, obstacles, and other road users modify this space—safety zone.

The safety zone, or safety margins which road users must keep around them, can be expressed (and are functional) both in space and time. We have to drive a car through narrow gaps, keep distance to other vehicles and to pedestrians, bicyclists and roadside obstacles. This is essential metrics in everyday control of safety. On a two-lane road, for example, an almost certain death lurks at a distance of 2–3 m when one meets a heavy vehicle (even a car) and every driver must take care of keeping a sufficient margin (Figure 1).

However, car control is also extensively based on time margins, as proposed by Lee (1976) for car following and by Godthelp et al. (1984) for lane keeping. Time-to-collision is a central control measure when we keep distance to a vehicle in front which changes speed. It is also essential when drivers prepare to stop in front of an obstacle. Time-to-lane-crossing sets limits to lane control and determines steering behaviour.

It is essential to note that time safety margins have an important feature: they also imply a concept of available time. Available time determines brake reaction latencies and time sharing, among other things. The detection of an obstacle often triggers nothing more than gas pedal response (lifting a foot off the pedal) and steering response, but if the obstacle cannot be passed, braking takes place at the threshold determined by time-to-collision (Summala, 2000). On the other hand, a wider road and lower speed mean more time in terms of time-to-lane-crossing and, accordingly, drivers allow more time to secondary tasks.

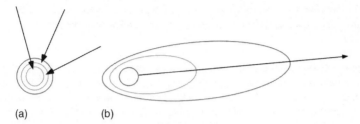

(a)   (b)

Figure 1. (a) Humans can be seen as having different zones (intimate, personal, social) around them (Hall, 1966), with thresholds which trigger approach or avoidance response, depending on the approaching person (or animal or object). (b) When in motion, more space is needed in front to avoid collisions with objects. The safety zone (Gibson & Crooks, 1938), whether in motion or not, can also be seen as a comfort zone, with no threat or risk felt (cf. "zero-risk model", Näätänen & Summala, 1976; Summala, 1988).

On a curvy road at high speed instead they have to attend to the road and steering entirely (Wikman, Laakso & Summala, 1997).

This is one basis for the behavioural adaptation phenomenon. Goals and motives push drivers so that they tend to take all space and time available to maintain and promote progress, up to their safety margin thresholds, if not restricted by speed limits for example. Elvik (2004) also defines behavioural adaptation such that it refers to how road users assess their safety margins when travelling, in contrast to engineering effects that change structural safety margins. A good example of truly structural safety margins is a median guardrail now also installed on one-carriageway roads in Sweden and Finland. It does not give many chances for drivers to compensate, and cuts as many as 60% of fatalities on ordinary roads (Carlsson, 2002; Näätänen & Summala, 1973). In marked contrast, the so-called wide-lane road (one lane of 5.25 m in width in each direction without median guardrails) is an extreme example of a structural change that trusts on drivers' behavioural safety margins, with little effect on safety: drivers take additional lateral space into effective use to serve faster progress.

Elvik (2004) gives a list of nine basic risk factors to describe the engineering effects of any road safety measure. The list includes a few factors that come close to the variables that drivers appear to use in controlling the difficulty of their task, therefore, being highly susceptible to offsetting behavioural adaptation. Visibility improvement by road lighting, for example, changes detection distances, time margins, and available time, which drivers tend to use in line with their motives. And as we see below, complexity, as defined by Elvik as the amount of new information a road user has to process per unit of time, can also be seen as an important variable which drivers can and do easily adjust, and which is closely connected to the concepts of time margin and available time.

Time margins and mental load

The concept of available time is directly related to workload felt by drivers. It is the other side of task complexity, the information to be processed in a time unit. The more complex the task (e.g. traffic environment), given same speed, the higher the workload. By adjusting speed drivers can easily reduce the information processing rate and provide themselves more time and less workload.

Time pressure is not the only determinant of workload which is usually understood as a multidimensional concept. For example, the NASA-TLX instrument for workload assessment includes nine subscales (Hart & Staveland, 1988). In motion, however, and especially at speeds of vehicular traffic, time is critical and time-based workload essential. This is in line with Hancock and Caird's (1993) model which predicted that mental load grows as effective time for action decreases. On the other side, sufficient time and adequate time margins imply the feeling of comfort and safety (Figure 2).

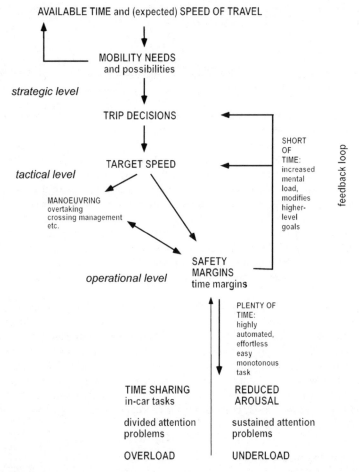

Figure 2. Time margins and available time for action, through mental load, mediate between different levels of driving. Adapted from Summala (1997).

Accordingly, the hierarchical model of behavioural adaptation (Summala, 1997) also predicts that available time and related workload mediate between operational and tactical, even strategic levels of driving.

Given a certain speed and certain complexity of the environment,

(a) if a driver cannot complete all operational subtasks (in the control of car and traffic) at this speed (within available time margins) he/she feels increased mental load and

  – either slows down to get more time, to reach the feeling of control and acceptable or comfortable level of workload; or

  – continues in the instable zone and may experience overload problems.

(b) Or, if a driver has plenty of time, like on a high-standard road at fairly low speed, he/she

  – is inclined to perform secondary tasks; or

  – gets bored and tired,

  both of which mean instable performance of the driver/vehicle system. Secondary tasks lead to inferior primary task performance, overload and increased risk, while underload and lowered arousal level may result in delayed responses and attention lapses, if not falling asleep.

Available time thus incorporates many essential features like complexity, mental load, and stress. It is, by definition, always a factor when humans are in motion. It is also a factor when road users are doing decisions while stopped in traffic, in gap acceptance for example, when drivers are crossing or entering a priority road. In that case, the traffic flow on a main road actually means making a selection from a number of closing time margins, and the situation may be very loading.

Task workload has sometimes been described as a margin between task demands (or task results), on one hand, and physiological or motivated capacity, on the other hand, such that physiological capacity sets the absolute limits while motivated capacity may vary considerably below the physiological capacity (Jex, 1988). Similarly, drivers may choose more relaxed pace but it may mean, at least during a recreational trip, more sightseeing and more attentive resources allocated to other than driving tasks. Fuller (2000), in his task–capability interface model, defines task difficulty arising from the difference between what is demanded and what capabilities are available. Task difficulty—and perceived risk—will increase as the threshold of being unable to meet the demands of the task approaches.

Hancock and Warm (1989), in their stress model, describe both physiological and psychological adaptability (attentional resource capacity) as a function of stress level. Adaptability follows an inverted (flat-bottom) U-shaped function, with wide physiological zone of maximal (quite constant) adaptability at intermediate stress levels, surrounded by dynamic instability areas on both sides, in hypostress and hyperstress conditions. Psychological zone of maximal adaptability is somewhat narrower, and attentional resources drop sooner when stress decreases or increases. At medium stress level, within maximal psychological (and physiological) adaptability zone, the authors place a comfort zone. This comfort zone, when applied to driving, should provide maximal attentional resources and maximal adaptability to new situations, as well as a feeling of full control and comfort.

DETERMINANTS FOR THE "BEST FEELING": MULTIPLE COMFORT ZONE MODEL

The theoretical approaches presented above are schematically outlined in Table 1. To combine the two main lines, the tension approach (especially Vaa's best feeling concept) and the safety margin approach, a "multiple comfort zone" model is suggested to explain normal everyday driving, like speed control or a decision whether to overtake a slower car. It is not only safety margins of course, which determine drivers' (and other road users') comfort in traffic. Trip-related goals, obedience to the rules and social norms, comfort of the car and roadway, and pleasure drawn from driving, all contribute to it. Therefore, a set of functional control variables is proposed which drivers are assumed to keep within an acceptable range, in the "comfort zone", such that this process determines the speed level in normal routine driving. It is a satisficing model in the sense of Simon (1955).

The proposed variables to be kept within the comfort zone, to exemplify normal driving situations, are the following:

(1) *Safety margins (to survive)*. The comfort zone implies sufficient space and time margins. Safety margins are understood as being the major tool for survival. Sufficient margins are needed by drivers to feel safe and comfortable while driving.

(2) *Good or expected progress of trip*. Keeping in the comfort zone implies that travel progresses as expected; normal, expected traffic congestions are being tolerated. Feelings of good progress are influenced by goals and motives. Sensory and cognitive adaptation to speed may easily increase the speed level which is felt comfortable, and maintaining speed (target speed) becomes a strong motivating factor.

Table 1. Different converging approaches in search of psychological pacing factors in car driving. (a) From emotional tension to best feeling, and (risk) monitor; (b) from safety zone to comfort zone; and, as an extension of safety margins, (c) from time-based margins to task load and, as a synthesis here presented, a "multiple comfort zone" model.

Level of emotional tension or anxiety (Taylor, 1964)	Subjective risk monitor, Fear monitor, Motives (Näätänen & Summala, 1974, 1976)	Target risk (Wilde, 1982)	Target feeling, best feeling, *monitor* (Vaa, 2004)
Safety zone (Gibson & Crooks, 1938); Proxemics (Hall, 1966)	Safety margins (Näätänen & Summala, 1976; Summala & Näätänen, 1988)		Comfort zone (Hancock & Warm stress model, 1989)
Time-to-contact (Lee, 1976); Time-to-line-crossing (Godthelp et al., 1984)	Time margins, available time (Summala, 1988, 1997)	Task difficulty (Fuller, 2000, 2004)	"Multiple comfort zone" in routine driving

(3) *Rule following.* Rule following (see *avoiding violations* in Vaa, 2004) is a major pacing factor when speed limits restrict speed rather than infrastructure. The comfort zone implies no concern of getting fined. The critical limits are usually well known by drivers. For example, in Finland drivers generally know that police applies an approximate 10% tolerance in speed enforcement, and police even make this public knowledge. Compliance with rules does not only mean the law but also social rules, which may differ a lot from what is defined in the law.

(4) *Vehicle/road system.* The modern cars are silent and go smoothly at speeds normally used. Poorly balanced tires make the car shaking at high speeds, however, and gravel, snow, or ice on road makes control much less confident and comfortable. The comfort zone implies smooth car/road performance but also acceptable lateral forces and friction which contribute to the feeling of control. Actually, available friction can also be expressed as a safety margin type measure (Rumar, Berggrund, Jernberg & Ytterbom, 1976; Summala & Merisalo, 1980; Wong & Nicholson, 1992).

It is obvious that all drivers do not (always) want to keep in the comfort zone but search for other feelings from driving. Drivers always have other motives and goals, "extra or additional motives" (Näätänen & Summala, 1976) which are related to age, gender, driving experience, life situation, life style, personality, health, and many trip-centred factors. Hence, pleasure of driving is an important determinant, the fifth in our list (see also, e.g. Rothengatter, 1988).

(5) *Pleasure of driving.* A driver can experience pleasurable feelings in normal, safe, rule-following driving, e.g. due to feeling of control. But driving for pleasure may mean sensation seeking and "high" from speed, acceleration, and close margins.

Other extra motives, and respective feelings, such as hurry, social pressure (in car and by other drivers), self-enhancement, competition, anger and aggressiveness, thrill seeking, may also take control.

CONCLUSION

Emotions and feelings, task difficulty, and mental load are important determinants of driving. But we also need something else to explain moment-to-moment control of driving. It is presented here that the basic control measures that serve survival are safety margins, both in space and time, which always matter when a human being is controlling his/her motion. Time margins, through the concept of available time, have a close connection to workload and feeling of comfort, and they mediate between different levels of the driving task. Routine driving can be seen as a set of factors to be kept within the "comfort zone", including safety margins, progress of travel, rule following, and smooth operation of car (and roadway). Pleasure and other "extra motives" and related feelings and emotions can take place among the factors, modify the effects and even take a leading role every now and then.

This model gives a framework for explaining and evaluating behavioural adaptation effects. If not restricted, drivers' behaviour tends to follow task demands at a certain margin, according to their prevailing goals and motives, so that they make use of all available space and time. The traffic code and social rules, as well as habits that build upon them, are limiting factors, while hard insurmountable structures are often needed to resist offsetting tendencies.

REFERENCES

Ajzen, I. (1991). The theory of planned action. *Organizational Behavior and Human Decision Processes, 50,* 179–211.

Allen, T.M., Lunenfeld, H., & Alexander, G.J. (1971). Driver information needs. *Highway Research Record, 366,* 102–115.

Aschenbrenner, K.M., & Biehl, B. (1994). Improved safety with technical measures? Empirical studies regarding risk compensation processes in relation to anti-lock braking systems. In Trimpop, R.M., & Wilde, G.J.S. (Eds.), *Challenges to Accident Prevention. The Issue of Risk Compensation Behaviour.* Groningen: Styx.

Carlsson, A. (2002). *Uppföljning av mötesfria vägar, VTI notat 29-2002,* VTI.

Damasio, A.R. (1994). *Descartes' Error: Emotion, Reason, and the Human Brain.* New York: G.P. Putnam's Sons.

Donges, E. (1978). A two-level model of driver steering behavior. *Human Factors, 20,* 691–707.

Elvik, R. (2004). To what extent can theory account for the findings of road safety evaluation studies? *Accident Analysis & Prevention, 36,* 841–849, Also presented at the 3rd International Conference on Traffic and Transport Psychology 2004, Symposium on Traffic Psychology Theories, Nottingham, UK.

Evans, L. (1991). *Traffic Safety and the Driver.* New York: Van Nostrand Reinhold.

Evans, L., & Gerrish, P.H. (1996). Antilock Brakes and Risk of Front and Rear Impact in 2-Vehicle Crashes. *Accident Analysis & Prevention, 28* (3), 315–323.

Fuller, R. (2000). The task–capability interface model of the driving process. *Journal Recherche-Transport-Sécurité (RTS), 66,* 47–59.

Fuller, R. (2004). Zero risk versus target risk: can they both be right? *Paper presented at the 3rd International Conference on Traffic and Transport Psychology 2004, Symposium on Traffic Psychology Theories,* Nottingham, UK.

Gibson, J.J., & Crooks, L.E. (1938). A theoretical field-analysis of automobile driving. *American Journal of Psychology, 51,* 453–471.

Godthelp, H., Milgram, P., & Blaauw, G.J. (1984). The development of a time-related measure to describe driving strategy. *Human Factors, 26,* 257–268.

Groeger, J.A. (2000). *Understanding Driving.* Hove, East Sussex: Psychology Press.

Groeger, J.A. (2004). Modelling driver behaviour: psychological plausibility and prediction, *Paper presented at the 3rd International Conference on Traffic and Transport Psychology 2004, Symposium on Traffic Psychology Theories,* Nottingham, UK.

Hale, A.R., Stoop, J., & Hommels, J.G. (1990). Human error models as predictors of accident scenarios for designers in road transport systems. *Ergonomics, 33,* 1377–1387.

Hall, E.T. (1966). *The Hidden Dimension.* Garden City: Doubleday.

Hancock, P.A., & Caird, J.K. (1993). Experimental evaluation of a model of mental workload. *Human Factors, 35,* 413–429.

Hancock, P.A., & Warm, J.S. (1989). A dynamic model of stress and sustained attention. *Human Factors, 31,* 519–537.

Hart, S.G., & Staveland, L.E. (1988). Development of the NASA-TLX (Task Load Index): results of empirical and theoretical research. In Hancock, P.A., & Meshkati, N. (Eds.), *Human Mental Workload* (pp. 139–183). Amsterdam: Elsevier.

Hatakka, M., Keskinen, E., Gregersen, N.P., Glad, A., & Hernetkoski, K. (2002). From control of the vehicle to personal self-control: broadening the perspectives to driver education. *Transportation Research F: Psychology and Behaviour, 5,* 201–215.

Jex, H.R. (1988). Measuring mental workload: problems, progress, and promises. In Hancock, P.A., & Meshkati, N. (Eds.), *Human Mental Workload* (pp. 5–39). Amsterdam: Elsevier.

Keskinen, E., Hatakka, M., Laapotti, S., Katila, A., & Peräaho, M. (2004). Driver behaviour as a hierarchical system. In Rothengatter, T., & Huguenin, R.D. (Eds.), *Traffic & Transport Psychology*. Amsterdam: Elsevier.

Lee, D.N. (1976). A theory of visual control of braking based on information about time-to-collision. *Perception, 5*, 437–459.

Michon, J.A. (1979). *Dealing with danger. Report of the European Commission MRC Workshop on Physiological and Psychological Performance Under Hazardous Conditions*, Gieten, The Netherlands, 23–25 May, 1978, Report VK 79-01, Traffic Research Center, University of Groningen.

Näätänen, R., & Summala, H. (1973). Physical and psychological aspects of crash barriers. *Accident Analysis and Prevention, 5*, 247–251.

Näätänen, R., & Summala, H. (1974). A model for the role of motivational factors in drivers' decision-making. *Accident Analysis and Prevention, 6*, 243–261.

Näätänen, R., & Summala, H. (1976). *Road-User Behavior and Traffic Accidents*. Amsterdam/New York: North-Holland/American Elsevier.

Rasmussen, J. (1983). Skills, rules, and knowledge; signals, signs, and symbols, and other distinctions in human performance models. *IEEE Transactions on Systems, Man, and Cybernetics, SMC-13*, 257–266.

Robertson, L.S., & Pless, I.B. (2002). For and against: does risk homoeostasis theory have implications for road safety. *British Medical Journal, 324*, 1151–1152.

Rothengatter, T. (1988). Risk and the absence of pleasure: a motivational approach to modelling road user behaviour. *Ergonomics, 31*, 599–607.

Rothengatter, T. (2002). Drivers' illusions—no more risk. *Transportation Research Part F: Traffic Psychology and Behaviour, 5* (4), 249–258.

Rumar, K., Berggrund, U., Jernberg, P., & Ytterbom, U. (1976). Driver reaction to a technical safety measure: studded tires. *Human Factors, 18*, 443–454.

Sagberg, F., Fosser, S., & Saetermo, I.A.F. (1997). An investigation of behavioural adaptation to airbags and antilock brakes among taxi drivers. *Accident Analysis and Prevention, 29* (3), 293–302.

Shinar, D. (1998). Aggressive driving: the contribution of the drivers and the situation. *Transportation Research Part F: Traffic Psychology and Behaviour, 1* (2), 137–159.

Simon, H. (1955). A behavioral model of rational choice. *Quarterly Journal of Economics, 69*, 99–118.

Smeed, R.J. (1949). Some statistical aspects of road safety research. *Journal of the Royal Statistical Society, Series A (General), 112*, 1–34.

Summala, H. (1988). Risk control is not risk adjustment: the zero-risk theory of driver behaviour and its implications. *Ergonomics, 31*, 491–506.

Summala, H. (1997). Hierarchical model of behavioural adaptation and traffic accidents. In Rothengatter, T., & Carbonell Vaya, E. (Eds.), *Traffic and Transport Psychology* (pp. 41–52). Amsterdam: Pergamon.

Summala, H. (2000). Brake reaction times and driver behavior analysis. *Transportation Human Factors, 2*, 217–226.

Summala, H., & Merisalo, A. (1980). A psychophysical method for determining the effect of studded tires on safety. *Scandinavian Journal of Psychology, 21*, 193–199.

Summala, H., & Näätänen, R. (1988). The zero-risk theory and overtaking decisions. In Rothengatter, T., & de Bruin, R. (Eds.), *Road User Behaviour: Theory and Research* (pp. 82–92). Assen/Maastricht: Van Gorcum.

Taylor, D.H. (1964). Drivers' galvanic skin response and the risk of accident. *Ergonomics, 7,* 253–262.

Vaa, T. (2004). Developing a driver behaviour model based on emotions and feelings: proposing building blocks and interrelationships, *Paper presented at the 3rd International Conference on Traffic and Transport Psychology 2004, Symposium on Traffic Psychology Theories*, Nottingham, UK.

Wikman, A.-S., Laakso, M., & Summala, H. (1997). *Time sharing of car drivers as a function of driving speed and task eccentricity*, The 13th Triennial Congress of International Ergonomics Association, Tampere, Finland, June 29–July 4, 1997.

Wilde, G.J.S. (1982). The theory of risk homeostasis: implications for safety and health. *Risk Analysis, 2,* 209–225.

Wong, Y.D., & Nicholson, A. (1992). Driver behavior at horizontal curves—risk compensation and the margin of safety. *Accident Analysis and Prevention, 24* (4), 425–436.

DRIVING PERFORMANCE II:

PERCEPTION AND AWARENESS

Traffic and Transport Psychology
G. Underwood (Editor)
© 2005 Elsevier Ltd. All rights reserved.

397

32

DRIVER'S PERCEPTION OF SELF-EXPLAINED ROAD INFRASTRUCTURE AND ARCHITECTURE

Oliver Carsten[1], Lidia Zakowska[2] and Hamish Jamson[1]

INTRODUCTION

Theoretical studies of the current knowledge on self-explaining road (SER) (Thewues & Godthelp, 1993) concept and its implementation into road design research and design practices (Wilde, 1995; Cohen, 1998; Krammes, 2000), as well as analysis of questionnaire research conducted in Poland (Zakowska, 2001), led the authors to design a study in which SER markings on the road surface were used to alert drivers of hazardous locations.

The first steps were the graphical modelling of virtual road and road environment and the designing of graphic information system (horizontal markings to indicate road geometry) in line with the SER concept. In addition, the perceptual properties of architectural objects were tested, based on graphical modelling of objects observed by drivers along the road. This interdisciplinary experimental design required experts from traffic psychology, road design, architecture and computer graphics.

Pilot study results obtained in a simple simulation environment in Poland (Zakowska & Carsten, 2002) allowed the authors to select the database for the main experiment to be conducted in driving simulator.

The presented experiment was made in Britain (ITS, Leeds) in the fully simulated environment of the Leeds driving simulator (Carsten & Gallimore, 1996). During the experiment, the safety effects of applying the SER concept to road design were tested. The evaluation tests the driver performance in simulated road environments, comparing SER with non-SER road scenes. The evaluation is dual: a subjective assessment of the visual road environment and also objective evaluation of driving performance in the fully animated environment in a high fidelity driving simulator.

---

[1] Institute for Transport Studies, University of Leeds, Leeds, UK.
[2] Department of Architecture A-9, Cracow University of Technology, Cracow, Poland. *E-mail:* lzakowsk@usk.
pk.edu.pl (L. Zakowska).

EXPERIMENTAL SCENARIOS

The virtual drive took place in a rural setting, marked consistently with standard UK road markings. The posted speed limit was 60 mph. At the start of the run, a lead vehicle maintained a steady 3 s headway in front of the simulator driver. Every 6 km of the virtual network, the simulator driver experienced an intersection. Four separate intersections, marked with and without *SER markings* were investigated.

The first intersection was a minor road merging road from the left (Figure 1). On the approach to the junction, the road markings were standard UK, i.e. 2 m mark, 7 m gap with solid edge lines. 150 m before the intersection, the edge lines were replaced with the "junction left" edge line. This line was 2 m in length.

Figure 1. Minor road from left with self-explaining markings.

The second intersection was similar to the first intersection, but the minor road merged to the right. Again, 150 m before the junction, SER markings showed the upcoming intersection. At this intersection the lead vehicle slowed to turn right off the main road. The third intersection was identical to the first intersection, but on this occasion there was no lead vehicle for the simulator driver to follow.

The fourth and final intersection was a crossroad. A vehicle was waiting on the left-hand arm of the junction and emerged in front of the simulator driver when the simulator driver was 3 s away from the intersection (Figure 2). This critical event required a braking response in order to avoid a collision.

Figure 2. Critical event at cross-roads intersection.

PARTICIPANTS

A between-subjects design was employed, such that 10 participants experienced the four intersections with the *SER markings* and half with the same vehicle scenarios and same four junctions marked in a standard UK style. Ten drivers performed in the baseline condition, of which four were males and six females; their mean age was 37 (SD = 9.2). Eight drivers participated in the *SER markings* condition (three males, five females, mean age = 36, SD = 6.4).

APPARATUS

Figure 3 was used for the study. The simulator is based on a complete Rover 216GTi, with all of its driver controls and dashboard instrumentation still fully operational. A real-time, fully textured and anti-aliased, 3D graphical scene of the virtual world is projected on a 2.5 m radius cylindrical screen in front of the driver. This scene is generated by an SGI Onyx2® Infinite Reality2 graphical workstation. A Roland digital sound sampler creates realistic sounds of engine and other noises via two speakers mounted close to each forward road wheel. The projection system consists of five forward channels, the front three at a resolution of 1280 × 1024 pixels. The images are edge-blended to provide a near seamless total image, and along with two peripheral channels (640 × 480 each), the total horizontal field of view is 230°. The vertical field of view is 39°. A rear view (60°) is back-projected onto a screen behind the car to provide an image seen through the vehicle's rear-view mirror. The frame rate is fixed to a constant 30 Hz. Although the simulator is fixed-base, torque feedback at the steering wheel is provided via a motor fixed at the end of the steering column and a vacuum motor provides the brake pedal booster assistance. Data are collected at the frame rate.

Figure 3. The Leeds driving simulator.

RESULTS

First intersection (exit left)

Data were recorded at two separate locations associated with the first intersection. Point A was defined where the *SER markings* began at 150 m before the intersection. Point B was defined at the intersection itself. *Speed* and *lateral position* at points A and B were recorded as was the *minimum time-to-line crossing* to the lead vehicle during the negotiation of the 150 m approach to the intersection. Independent sample *t*-tests were performed to assess the impact of the SER on driving performance.

Lateral position was defined at the distance from the left-hand edge of the road surface to the centre of gravity of the vehicle.

Imagine the car driving on the left-hand side of the road performing a right-hand turn. The time-to-edge line crossing (Godthelp, 1981), describes the instantaneous time for the outside edge of the front, kerbside wheel to cross the edge line, should the vehicle remain on its current course with the same speed. Similarly, the time-to-centre line crossing is the instantaneous time for the outside of the offside wheel to cross the centre line (Figure 4). As the vehicle approaches the edge or centre line, time-to-line crossing (TLC) decreases until it reaches a minimum. TLC reflects the time available for error neglecting, assuming a fixed steering strategy. In other words, TLC reflects a lateral control safety margin. The distribution of TLC is not normal, so in order to determine the safety margins, minimum TLC to either edge or centre line is normally used. The *minimum TLC* was defined as the minimum value achieved between points A and B.

$$TLC = \frac{DLC}{v}$$

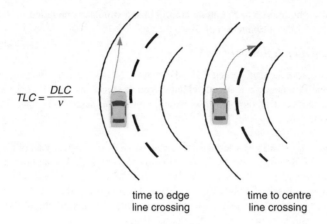

$$TLC = \frac{DLC}{v}$$

time to edge   time to centre
line crossing   line crossing

Figure 4. Time-to-line crossing.

where

TLC = time-to-line crossing

DLC = distance-to-line crossing (length of arc segment of vehicle path)

v = vehicle forward speed

Table 1 shows the driving performance recorded at the approach to and at the first intersection. All data were normally distributed and showed equality of variance using the Levene test. No results were significant, however, the strongest trend was that on the approach to the intersection, both groups of drivers tended to move towards the centre of their lane, away from

Table 1. Driving performance at the first intersection.

Dependent variable	Baseline		SER		t	p (2-tailed)
	Mean	SE	Mean	SE		
Speed at A (mph)	53.3	1.33	51.4	1.66	0.891	0.386
Speed at B (mph)	51.6	2.33	51.2	0.924	0.124	0.903
Speed change (B − A)	−1.72	1.31	−0.243	0.454	−0.854	0.406
Lat pos at A (m)	2.07	0.0630	2.19	0.0573	−1.46	0.165
Lat pos at B (m)	2.29	0.0870	2.35	0.0805	−0.516	0.613
Lat pos change (B − A)	0.221	0.0563	0.157	0.0454	0.857	0.404
Min TLC (s)	0.884	0.273	0.754	0.262	0.339	0.739

the intersecting road of the junction. Drivers in the SER condition tended to drive about 200 mm closer the centre line on the approach to the intersection, whilst drivers in the baseline condition adopted this lane position much later. It was also apparent that SER tended to reduce driving speed 150 m before the intersection and drivers adopted a more consistent speed over the approach to the intersection. Lateral control of the simulator, recorded by *minimum TLC*, was unaffected by the introduction of SER.

Second intersection (exit right)

During this scenario, the lead vehicle slowed to exit the main road at the intersection. Data were recorded at the instant when the lead vehicle began to slow down, 4 s before the intersection itself. Again, independent sample *t*-tests were performed to assess the impact of the SER on driving performance.

Brake reaction time (BRT) was defined at the time between the first slowing of the lead vehicle, indicated to the following driver by the illumination of its brake lights, and the first subsequent brake pedal effort recorded of the simulator driver. *Minimum headway* was defined as the minimum time headway achieved by the simulator driver between the initial braking of the lead vehicle and its turning off the main route. Minimum headway, like minimum TTC, reflects risk margin: small minimum headways indicate high risk.

Time to collision (TTC) in a car following scenario was defined as the instantaneous time that, with both the simulator car and lead car travelling at their current speeds, would elapse before a collision between them. TTC reflects risk margin: the less TTC, the less margin.

$$TTC = \frac{s}{\Delta v}$$

where

TTC = time to collision

s = distance between the two vehicles

Δv = difference between the speeds of the two vehicles

Table 2. Driving performance at the second intersection.

Dependent variable	Baseline		SER		t	p (2-tailed)
	Mean	SE	Mean	SE		
Speed (mph)	55.1	1.376	47.6	3.59	2.102	0.052
Lat pos (m)	2.15	0.0826	2.07	0.104	0.567	0.579
BRT (s)	1.83	0.150	1.88	0.262	−0.145	0.887
Min headway (s)	2.26	0.0888	2.94	0.535	−1.395	0.182
Min TTC (s)	3.60	0.133	6.34	2.620	−1.177	0.257
Min TLC (s)	1.58	0.433	1.81	0.484	−0.354	0.728

Table 2 shows the driving performance recorded at the second intersection. All data were normally distributed and showed equality of variance using the Levene test. Speed at lead vehicle braking, essentially mid-way throughout the intersection approach, was significantly slower for drivers experiencing SER. Whilst the change in BRT between the two conditions was not significant, there was a trend that the drivers experiencing SER responded around

0.05 s quicker to the lead vehicle's braking that in turn lead to a greater safety margin, shown by longer *minimum TTC* and *minimum headway* during the event. Lateral control of the simulator vehicle, recorded by *minimum TLC*, was unaffected by the introduction of SER.

Third intersection (exit left)

The third intersection was identical to the first intersection, the only difference being in the scenario: there was no lead vehicle present since it had turned off the main route at the second intersection. Data were recorded at the same two separate locations associated with the first intersection. Point C was defined where the *SER markings* began at 150 m before the intersection. Point D was defined at the intersection itself. *Speed* and *lateral position* at points C and D were recorded as was the *minimum TTC* to the lead vehicle during the 150 m approach to the intersection. Independent sample *t*-tests were performed to assess the impact of the SER on driving performance.

Table 3. Driving performance at the third intersection.

Dependent variable	Baseline		SER		t	p (2-tailed)
	Mean	SE	Mean	SE		
Speed at A (mph)	55.8	1.32	53.1	2.88	0.906	0.378
Speed at B (mph)	53.2	1.60	52.1	1.23	0.377	0.711
Speed change (B − A)	− 2.56	1.01	− 1.02	0.335	− 1.17	0.258
Lat pos at A (m)	2.14	0.0908	2.25	0.0865	− 0.810	0.430
Lat pos at B (m)	2.18	0.0764	2.15	0.0980	0.252	0.804
Lat pos change (B − A)	0.0382	0.0635	− 0.0961	0.140	0.937	0.363
Min TLC (s)	0.393	0.209	0.641	0.307	− 0.690	0.500

Table 3 shows the driving performance recorded at the approach to and at the first intersection. All data were normally distributed and showed equality of variance using the Levene test. No results were significant, however, the same trends in speed were apparent as observed at the first intersection. Drivers in the SER condition tended to drive marginally slower than those in the baseline condition strongest trend and adopted a more consistent speed throughout the approach to the intersection. The trend that drivers in the SER condition tended to drive closer the centre line on the approach to the intersection was again seen. Drivers in the baseline condition again adopted this lane position only at the intersection itself. Lateral control of the simulator, recorded by *minimum TLC*, tended to show a more accurate lateral control of the vehicle in the SER condition.

Fourth intersection (crossroads)

This scenario included the emerging vehicle as described earlier and data were collected as this vehicle began to pull out into the path of the simulator vehicle. An additional measure

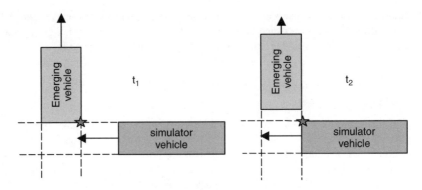

Figure 5. Definition of post-encroachment time (PET) as the time between t_1 and t_2.

Table 4. Driving performance at the fourth intersection.

Dependent variable	Baseline		SER		t	p (2-tailed)
	Mean	SE	Mean	SE		
Speed (mph)	51.9	1.83	49.1	2.28	0.977	0.343
Lat pos (m)	2.09	0.110	2.04	0.0841	0.358	0.725
BRT (s)	1.77	0.114	1.699	0.148	0.372	0.716
Min TLC (s)	1.25	0.375	0.606	0.233	1.360	0.193
PET (s)	1.84	0.301	2.62	0.451	−1.48	0.158

for this analysis was *post-encroachment time* (PET). PET was defined as the time between the rear of emerging vehicle fully clearing the path of the simulator vehicle and the simulator arriving at this same point. The shorter the PET the closer the two vehicles came to a collision, hence the longer the PET the greater the safety margin. Figure 5 shows the definition of PET.

Table 4 shows the driving performance data recorded at the fourth intersection. The same trend of lowered speed in the SER condition was seen. In addition, PET approached one-tailed significance that PET was longer and hence safer in the SER condition. This is probably due to the slower speed and that brake reaction to the emerging vehicle was quicker in the SER condition. The effect on lateral control was in the opposite direction than the effect observed at previous intersections.

CONCLUSIONS

The main goal of this project was to test the safety effects of applying the SER concept to road design. The results presented below shows the potential capabilities of applying simulation and visualisation of the designed road view as a way of making improvements in traffic safety.

The nature of the study (i.e. one with quite severe events) required a more inefficient between-subjects design. As a result we did not obtain significance with the 10 drivers in the baseline condition and 8 drivers in the experimental condition. However, the results in terms of indicators such as TTC and PET, which are closely related to accident risk, are very encouraging. The speed and TLC results also show the drivers adopting a more cautious approach with SER. Therefore, further exploration of the SER concepts for warning drivers about junctions is warranted.

ACKNOWLEDGEMENTS

This work presents results of the project (WAR/341/207) conducted in cooperation of British and Polish researchers in frame of the BPRPP, British–Polish Research Partnership Programme 2001–2003.

REFERENCES

Carsten, O.M.J., & Gallimore, S. (1996). The Leeds driving simulator: a new tool for research in driver behaviour. In Gale, A.G. (Ed.), *Vision in Vehicles—V*. Amsterdam: Elsevier.

Cohen, A.S. (1998). Visuelle Orientierung im Strassenverkehr. Eine empirische Untersuchung zur Theorie des visuellen Abstattens. BFU—Report 34.

Godthelp, J. (1981). Vehicle control during curve driving. *Human Factors, 28* (2), 211–221.

Krammes, R.A. (2000). Interactive highway safety design model for safety evaluation if highway. *2nd International Symposium on Highway Geometric Design* (pp. 571–576). Köln: TRB & FGSV, Mainz, Road and Transportation Research Association.

Thewues, J., & Godthelp, J. (1993). Self-explaining roads. In de Kroes, J.I., & Stoop, J.A. (Eds.), *Proceedings of the First World Congress on Safety of Transportation* (pp. 56–66). Delft, The Netherlands: Delft University Press.

Wilde, G.J.S. (1995). *Target Risk*. Toronto: PDE Publications.

Zakowska, L. (2001). Wizualizacja w projektowaniu dróg. Aspekty bezpieczeństwa i estetyki. *Zeszyty Naukowe Politechniki Krakowskiej, Seria Architektura nr 44*, 1–208.

Zakowska, L., & Carsten, O. (2002). Poprawa bezpieczeństwa ruchu w efekcie stosowania koncepcji SER w projektowaniu drogowym. *BRD 2002, GDDKiA*, 227–235.

Traffic and Transport Psychology
G. Underwood (Editor)
© 2005 Elsevier Ltd. All rights reserved.

33

THE EFFECT OF VEHICLE NAVIGATION SYSTEMS ON THE FORMATION OF COGNITIVE MAPS

Gary E. Burnett[1] and Kate Lee[1]

INTRODUCTION

Tolman (1948) is generally considered to be the first to propose that, following a sufficient period of environmental learning, animals (including humans) form a mental representation of space that is the analogy of a real map, a *cognitive map*, as he called it. Although authors have questioned whether the map metaphor is indeed valid (see Kitchin (1994) for a review of this issue), the term still commonly appears in the environmental psychology and human geography literature.

A popular area of study concerns how cognitive maps support individuals in "spatial problem solving" (Arthur & Passini, 1992), notably relating to navigation. An individual who possesses a well-formed cognitive map is able to accomplish navigation tasks based on their own internal knowledge with few cognitive demands. Indeed, in many situations (e.g. when travelling within a home town), the navigation task may involve automatic processing (Jackson, 1998). Informed individuals also have the flexibility to choose and then navigate numerous alternative routes to suit particular preferences (e.g. for a scenic versus efficient route), or in response to unanticipated situations, e.g. heavy traffic, poor weather. Finally, as noted by Hill (1987), a well-formed cognitive map provides a wider transport efficiency and social function, since it empowers a person to navigate for others, for example, by providing verbal directions as a passenger, pedestrian or over the phone, sketching maps to send in the post, and so on.

---

[1] School of Computer Science and IT, University of Nottingham, Nottingham, UK. *E-mail:* gary.burnett@ nottingham.ac.uk (G.E. Burnett).

Further issues of interest relate to the evolution of the content and accuracy of cognitive maps. In this respect, the acquisition of environmental spatial knowledge (commonly referred to as the cognitive mapping process) is generally agreed to progress through several developmental stages or levels. As noted by Gould (1989, p. 443), "levels are defined differently by nearly every author". Nevertheless, it is usually the case that three levels are described, and, for the purposes of this chapter, the following terms and definitions will be used (after Stern & Leiser, 1988):

(1) *Landmark* knowledge—memory for distinctive objects and/or views within the environment.

(2) *Route* knowledge—memory for procedural linking of landmarks, including order, inter-landmark distances and required actions.

(3) *Survey* knowledge—memory in which landmark and route knowledge are integrated into a configurational, map-like whole. Individuals with strong survey knowledge for an area are able accurately to estimate straight-line directions and distances to unseen locations, and plan routes between places which have not been visited before.

It is important to note that current thinking does not view these stages as discrete independent forms progressed through in order (Kitchin, 1994). Rather, the overriding assumption is that, as one's knowledge develops, there are qualitative (e.g. knowledge of routes versus distinct objects) as well as quantitative (e.g. knowledge of more landmarks) changes. In addition, it is widely recognised that the content and accuracy of a cognitive map is considerably affected by the means by which it is developed (Richardson, Montello, & Hegarty, 1999). In this respect, people have traditionally acquired environmental spatial knowledge through direct exploration of an environment, and/or through indirect methods, such as the study of formal maps, informal sketch maps, verbal instructions, and so on.

Vehicle navigation systems aim to support drivers in strategic (e.g. route choice) and tactical (e.g. turn decisions) components of the overall driving task, and, as such, they provide a relatively novel means by which individuals acquire and use spatial information. There has been considerable interest from researchers and practitioners in the design and evaluation of user-interfaces for vehicle navigation systems (see Burnett, 2000a; Srinivisan 1999 for reviews). This emphasis is to be expected given that this technology is arguably the most sophisticated with which drivers have had to interact within vehicles. Furthermore, in contrast with the vast majority of computing applications, vehicle navigation systems will inevitably be used within a dual-task, divided attention context, in which there are considerable safety implications for poor performance.

Of the large number of empirical studies concerning vehicle navigation systems, the vast majority have addressed specific user-interface design questions, such as whether an interface should employ voice and/or visual information, utilising methodologies that have focused on the initial experiences of a driver with a system—typically, the exposure to a system has been limited to less than half a day. Furthermore, methods have commonly incorporated measures relating to the effects of a system on drivers' navigational effectiveness (assessed by measuring the frequency of wrong turnings, journey time, etc.) and overall driving performance (assessed either directly, by means such as vehicle control parameters, or indirectly, through visual demand metrics, workload indicators, and so on). As a result of this research focus, numerous design guidelines and principles have been produced emphasising the need for user-interfaces for vehicle navigation systems, which minimise the demands (predominately visual and cognitive) of the navigation task, particularly when systems are used within wholly unfamiliar areas. (e.g. Green, Levison, Paelke, & Serafin, 1995; Ross et al., 1995).

Unfortunately, this emphasis neglects some fundamental longer term issues, and more recently authors (e.g. Adler, 2001; Smiley, 2000) have noted that the ultimate safety and efficiency gain (or loss) associated with drivers' use of this technology will be affected by a wider range of behavioural questions concerning system use over time. In particular, it will be critical to understand how users of navigation systems might adapt their overall travelling patterns. In this respect, it has been hypothesised by several researchers (e.g. Burns, 1997; Smiley, 2000) that the use of vehicle navigation systems may increase drivers' exposure to navigational uncertainty, as a result of additional journeys being made within unfamiliar areas. Furthermore, it has been predicted (Van Winsum, 1993) that route choice behaviour will change as drivers increasingly make use of computer, rather than human, generated routes. Presently, no empirical research exists to support or refute such claims.

A mediating factor critical to these issues concerns the extent to which drivers develop a cognitive map when using a vehicle navigation system. The level of such internal knowledge will inevitably affect dependency on an external source of navigation information. Despite the fact that numerous authors have commented on the importance of this issue (Adler, 2001; Gould, 1989; Jackson, 1998), remarkably few empirical studies have been undertaken. Furthermore, existing studies have been limited in three key aspects:

(1) Requiring drivers passively to watch videos of interconnected routes whilst listening to navigation decisions, rather than actively partaking in navigation tasks (e.g. turn decisions)—as for Jackson (1996, 1998).

(2) Artificially motivating participants to learn the area in which they are travelling, by continually testing cognitive map development—as for Jackson (1996, 1998).

(3) Utilising indirect (i.e. travel times), rather than direct measures of cognitive map development—as for Adler (2001).

The study reported in this chapter, aims to provide some preliminary data related to the impact of vehicle navigation system use on the formation of drivers' cognitive maps. A methodology is utilised which intends to overcome the limitations of previous research on this topic.

METHOD

In a factorial (between subjects) design experiment, 12 people (6 male and 6 female) drove a series of routes within a STISIM fixed-base driving simulator using either a traditional method for navigation (based on viewing a paper map) or simple turn-by-turn guidance. The majority of participants were young (mean age 27, range 22–56). All participants had possessed a full driving licence for at least 2 years and drove every day. In addition, the majority of participants (10 of 12) considered themselves to be "good" navigators.

The simulator includes primary driving controls (steering wheel, brake, accelerator) and a 60° horizontal field of view driving scene is projected on to a large curved screen. The virtual town used for this study was programmed within the simulator utilising 3D StudioMax™, and was approximately 1200 m × 1200 m in area. In detail, it comprised 37 separate roads (paths), 40 junctions (nodes/intersecting paths) and a number of external objects (landmarks—including 26 buildings, a roundabout, 2 stationary pedestrians, 29 road signs, and 28 trees). See Figure 1 for example screen shots from the virtual town.

Figure 1. Example screen shots from virtual town.

At the beginning of the study, participants were given a brief description of the task to be completed, but were not informed as to what specifically would be included in the tests at the end of the navigation task. This was purposely left unclear to increase the validity of the experiment, that is, to reduce the likelihood of participants actively trying to remember landmarks, roads and junctions during the study. Each participant was then allowed a 5-min practice run in the driving simulator. For the experimental period, all participants completed four separate routes in the same order (route 1 through to route 4). Each route took approximately 5 min to drive (with no navigational errors), had some degree of overlap, and followed on from the previous route, with the car facing in the same direction as it had at the end of the previous route. Furthermore, each route had a specific landmark at its start and end point.

Before the start of each route, all participants were shown the relevant route map, with the route they should take outlined (see Figure 2 for an illustration of each route map). All participants were informed when they had reached their destination for each route and told to stop in an appropriate place. Participants were videoed during their journeys in order to analyse if any navigational mistakes were made. Participants in the traditional group were allowed to look at the map for as long as they needed before starting to drive. They were also able to make any notes including directions to be used whilst driving. If they so wished, these participants could use the directions they had written prior to the start of each route, as well as using the map, during their journey. They were then required to navigate themselves from the start to end point, attempting to take the route highlighted on the map, rather than choosing their own route. Conversely, those in the guidance group were only allowed to view the relevant map for 20 s prior to starting each route. Simple voice guidance instructions were read out to the guidance participants at specific points in each route, for the purpose of simulating a vehicle

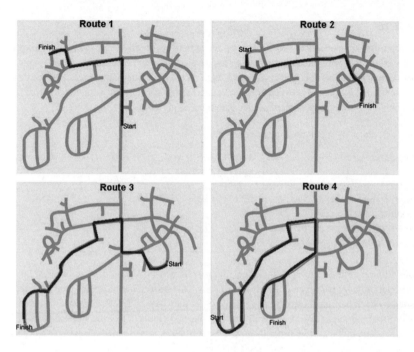

Figure 2. Recommended routes to be travelled through virtual town.

navigation system. These instructions were based on a review conducted by Burnett (2000a) of the user-interfaces for current vehicle navigation systems, and included references to ego-centred directions (left, right, straight ahead), junction type (cross roads, roundabout), and side turn counting (next turn, second turning). If the participants did not understand an instruction, they were informed to say "repeat", for the instruction to be read out again. If they became lost, the guidance instructions were adapted to take them to their destination, using a route as similar to the original as possible.

Following the experimental period, the participants' spatial knowledge was tested utilising measures appropriate to the three stages of development: landmark, route and survey knowledge. Firstly, landmark and route knowledge were tested using a set of screen shots of scenes from the driving simulator. For each route in turn, participants were asked to pick out scenes that they remembered seeing on that route. In each route's set of screen shots there were two "dummy" scenes that were not present in the virtual town. They were then asked to place the remembered scenes in the order that they believed they encountered them along the route. Survey knowledge was tested by asking the participants to draw a sketch map (on a blank piece of A4 paper) of what they remembered seeing in the environment, including any roads, buildings or other landmarks. They were asked to put roads or landmarks in relation to other roads or landmarks as best they could remember. Participants were asked to label any landmarks they drew.

RESULTS

The proportion of scenes that were correctly recognised as having been seen before provided a measure of the extent to which participants remembered discrete components of the journeys they had made, that is, landmark knowledge—see Table 1. A one-tailed un-paired t-test revealed that there was a significant difference between conditions, that is, that participants using a traditional method remembered a greater proportion of scenes than those using guidance ($t(10) = 2.77; p < 0.05$).

Table 1. Results of scene recognition/ordering tests.

Dependent variables	Traditional (n = 6)				Guidance (n = 6)			
	Mean	S.D.	Max	Min	Mean	S.D.	Max	Min
Proportion of scenes correctly recognised (%)	59.8	12.57	70.6	35.3	34.3	18.76	58.8	5.9
Proportion of scenes recognised in correct order location (%)	21.7	19.87	47	0	5.0	5.90	12	0

To provide a measure of route knowledge, an analysis was conducted for the ordering of screen shots undertaken by participants. Table 1 also shows the proportion of scenes that were correctly reported by each participant as occurring in the order they would have been viewed when driving. It is clear that participants were generally poor at this task (indeed, 5 of the 12 participants did not place any scene in the correct order location). Nevertheless, a one-tailed un-paired t-test revealed that participants using a traditional method remembered a greater proportion of scenes in the correct order location than those using guidance ($t(10) = 1.97; p < 0.05$).

A range of analyses were conducted on the sketch maps provided by participants (see Table 2), primarily using methods proposed by Rovine and Weisman (1989). This included an assessment of the following characteristics:

(1) absolute number of landmarks contained within the maps,

(2) absolute number of path segments (pre-defined groupings of roads and junctions within the overall area),

(3) the accuracy of placement of landmarks—number of landmarks within a sketch map placed correctly, either in relation to other landmarks, or to a path segment.

One tailed un-paired t-tests revealed a significant difference between conditions for the number of landmarks drawn variable ($t(10) = 2.71; p < 0.05$). Whilst there was a trend for differences in

Table 2. Descriptive statistics for sketch maps provided by participants.

Dependent variables	Traditional (n = 6)				Guidance (n = 6)			
	Mean	S.D.	Max	Min	Mean	S.D.	Max	Min
Number of landmarks drawn	14.0	5.06	19	5	7.3	3.27	12	4
Number of path segments drawn	2.5	1.05	4	1	1.3	1.86	5	0
Number of landmarks drawn in correct location	5.5	3.27	11	2	3.0	3.10	9	1

favour of the traditional method for the number of path segments and landmark placement accuracy variables, these differences did not reach significance ($p = 0.16$ and 0.13, respectively).

In addition, the complexity of maps were classified using the categorisation scheme first proposed by Appleyard (1970). In this method, maps are considered to be either "sequentially dominant" (primarily roads) or "spatially dominant" (primarily landmarks). These broad categories are then broken down into sub-categories in which there is a progression from simple maps with no integration of elements (e.g. spatial scattered) through to more complex maps in which landmarks and routes are integrated into a whole view (e.g. sequential netted). Table 3 shows the categories of maps drawn by participants, and reveals that the majority of drivers for the guidance condition (five out of six) drew the simplest category maps (i.e. spatial scattered and sequential fragmented), whereas for the traditional condition, a wider range of map types were drawn. Example maps sketched by participants in the two conditions are also shown in Figure 3.

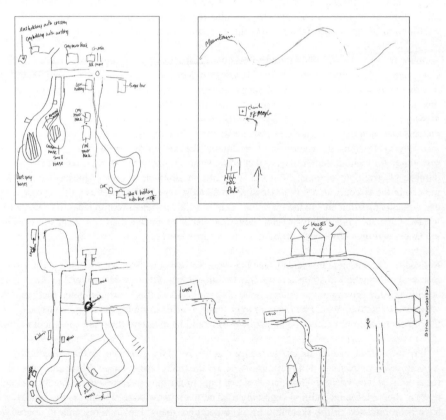

Figure 3. Examples of maps drawn by participants: (left) traditional condition, (right) guidance condition.

Table 3. Number of participants who drew particular categories of map.

Map types	Traditional (n = 6)	Guidance (n = 6)
Spatial scattered	1	2
Sequential fragmented	1	3
Sequential branch and loop	2	0
Sequential netted	2	1

DISCUSSION

The results of this initial study provide strong evidence that the use of a vehicle navigation system will impact negatively on the formation of drivers' cognitive maps. Specifically, drivers who received typical vehicle navigation system instructions remembered fewer scenes, were less accurate in their ordering of images seen along routes and drew simpler maps, which included a smaller number of landmarks, when compared to those using traditional methods. A large number of reasons can be hypothesised as to why such a large effect was found, despite the obvious limitations in sample size. Further research must aim to ascertain the relative contribution of the various factors using a larger, wider range of participants.

A major factor is clearly the nature of decision making involved in the two situations. When using turn-by-turn instructions, drivers' navigation decisions are essentially simple, requiring few mental resources. In essence, for each manoeuvre, the driver must process an ego-centred direction (left, right, straight on), together with information concerning the proximity of an associated action (next turn, 3rd exit). Furthermore, the pacing of the guidance instructions dictates that such decisions are undertaken over short time periods (just over the approach to a manoeuvre). In contrast, when using a traditional method a driver must maintain a sense of orientation throughout the journey, as well as make specific turn decisions, often with a greater number of available options. There is a wealth of research within cognitive psychology indicating the effect of depth of processing on memory (see Eysenck, 1993). In this case, one can argue that participants in the traditional condition had a greater requirement to evaluate the worth of the navigation information they were using or intended to use, than those using guidance, and thus processed information at a deeper level.

Related to this variance in decision-making processes was the evidence (through participants' post-trial comments) that drivers in the traditional condition were actively paying more attention to the driving environment. Several participants in this condition noted that, as they were aware that they would be required to navigate a series of routes through the virtual town, they had sought to remember landmarks which would be of use to them in subsequent routes.

A third factor concerns the time required for map study. In the guidance condition, participants were only shown the map for a short time, whereas the traditionalists were able to study the map for as long as they wished. This increased exposure to the map overview undoubtedly assisted those in the traditional condition in gaining road network knowledge, which, in turn, is likely to have been reflected in the sketching of more complex maps. Previous research in cognitive mapping (e.g. Thorndyke & Hayes-Roth, 1982) has demonstrated how the study of maps can greatly aid in the development of survey knowledge.

Temporal differences also existed between conditions relating to the overall exposure to the environment. Five of the six participants using a traditional method deviated from the recommended route for at least one of their four journeys. In the guidance condition, only one person deviated from a recommended route. As a result, traditionalists generally spent longer in the virtual town, subsequently covering a greater geographical area.

Finally, there was some anecdotal evidence (through participants' comments) that the traditional methods were associated with increased stress in the navigation task. This is to be expected given the likely increase in the demands of navigating, plus the occurrence of several navigational errors, as mentioned above. Studies in the environmental psychology field (see for instance, Evans, Skorpanich, Garling, Bryant, & Bresolin, 1984) have shown that stress can have a positive effect on cognitive map formation. Evans et al. hypothesise that such an effect may arise because individuals under conditions of stress are resource-limited with respect to working memory capacity, and thus focus on the most apparent aspects of the situation (such as the order of events), rather than qualities which require more processing.

In this study, drivers experienced tactical aspects of the navigation task (i.e. turn decisions), but did not have to make strategic decisions concerning which route to take. Our intention was to maintain a degree of control over the drivers' exposure to the virtual town (although as noted above, the occurrence of navigational errors negated this control). With a navigation system, a driver's involvement in strategic aspects of the overall navigation task is fairly limited, as a driver typically has to confirm, rather than choose a route. Consequently, it is hypothesised that drivers using traditional navigation methods, who were also active in route choice decisions, would ultimately possess cognitive maps considerably more enhanced than those resulting from the use of a navigation system.

The current study did not seek directly to address the implications of cognitive map development (or lack of) on the wider issues of safety and efficiency. Clearly though, there is an urgent need to understand the various trade-offs that are likely to result between cognitive map development, and a range of wider variables, notably navigation demands and performance. In this respect, Figure 4 hypothesises relationships between spatial knowledge and navigation task demands. The figure makes it clear that with traditional methods task demands are initially high, but as exposure to the environment continues and spatial knowledge develops, demands are likely to drop markedly, such that there is no longer a requirement for the use of external information (the "point of independence"). In contrast, with guidance, whilst task demands are relatively low, spatial knowledge does not develop and there is a constant need to use the external information source. Furthermore, it is predicted that task demands do not reach the low levels ultimately achieved when using more active forms of navigation.

Following on from these points, it is argued that future work should consider the design and evaluation of adaptive *learning-oriented* user-interfaces for vehicle navigation systems, as an alternative to the current *uncertainty minimising* styles. Such interfaces would aim to provide navigation information in a form, which ensures that the demands of the navigation task in wholly unfamiliar areas are at an acceptable, low level, whilst aiming to support drivers in the cognitive mapping process. In essence, they would aspire to move people onwards through the various development stages, ultimately to a level in which they are able to navigate effectively for themselves and others, independent of any external information.

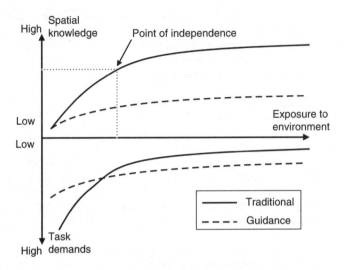

Figure 4. Hypothesised relationships between navigation task demands and cognitive map development.

Theories and empirical research from the environmental psychology and human geography fields on human navigation and way-finding strategies would be of relevance to this topic. In particular, it is well known that distinctive features of the environment (i.e. landmarks, such as restaurants, churches, petrol stations, etc.) are of great importance in the development of a cognitive map. Landmarks are known to form the skeletal frame of reference around which to build other levels of knowledge (Sadalla, Burroughs, & Staplin, 1980), and, as such, can serve a number of different functions within the cognitive mapping process (Hirtle & Hudson, 1991). For instance, a landmark may originally operate as an object on its own in space. At a later time, the same landmark may act as a place on a route, and then later still the landmark may serve as a point where a number of routes cross.

A number of authors have noted the requirement to include landmarks within the user-interfaces for vehicle navigation systems (e.g. Alm, 1993; Burnett, 2000b). Indeed, attempts have been made recently to identify and prioritise the characteristics of "good" landmarks for navigation (Burnett, Smith, & May, 2001; Ross, May, & Grimsley, 2004). Nevertheless, the focus in this human factors work has been on the development of user-interfaces incorporating specific landmarks, which aim to minimise navigational uncertainty in unfamiliar areas, rather than aid in cognitive map development. In this respect, there is a need to revisit the fundamental work conducted by notable authors such as Appleyard (1969), Kaplan (1976) and Lynch (1960), in which they defined the attributes of a distinctive landmark within an individual's mental representation.

CONCLUSIONS

The results of this study, together with data from previous research, provide clear evidence that the "normal" development of a driver's spatial knowledge (their cognitive map) will be affected negatively by the use of vehicle navigation systems. This chapter, proposes a range of reasons as to why such an effect arises: the simplicity and shortened timescales of navigational decision making; the low level of attention given to the environment; the reduced time taken to study map configurations; and the limited stress incurred through navigation.

Research must now investigate the wider picture, that is, how cognitive map development relates to the measures traditionally utilised in this domain, such as task demands and performance. Whilst the use of a vehicle navigation system may result in short-term benefits, such as low workload and high levels of navigational performance in unfamiliar areas, the longer term situation is less clear.

As part of this research agenda, it is believed that there is considerable potential for a paradigm shift in user-interface design for vehicle navigation systems from an emphasis on minimising navigational uncertainty towards the use of learning-oriented systems. Future research must aim to develop such interfaces based on current knowledge within the environmental psychology and human geography fields, and subsequently to compare their effectiveness with the status quo.

REFERENCES

Adler, J.L. (2001). Investigating the learning effects of route guidance and traffic advisories on route choice behavior. *Transportation Research Part C, 9,* 1–14.

Alm, H. (1993). Human factors considerations in vehicle navigation aids. In Medyckyj-Scott, D., & Hearnshaw, H.M. (Eds.), *Human factors in geographical information systems* (pp. 148–157). London: Belhaven Press.

Appleyard, D.A. (1969). Why buildings are known—a predictive tool for architects and planners. *Environment and Behaviour, 1,* 131–156.

Appleyard, D.A. (1970). Styles and methods of structuring a city. *Environment and Behaviour, 2,* 100–116.

Arthur, P., & Passini, R. (1992). *Wayfinding: people, signs and architecture.* New York: McGraw-Hill.

Burnett, G.E. (2000a). *Usable vehicle navigation systems: are we there yet? Proceedings of Vehicle Electronic Systems 2000—European Conference and Exhibition.* Leatherhead, UK: ERA Technology Ltd, (pp. 3.1.1–3.1.11).

Burnett, G.E. (2000b). "Turn right at the traffic lights": the requirement for landmarks in vehicle navigation systems. *Journal of Navigation, 53* (3), 499–510.

Burnett, G.E., Smith, D., & May, A.J. (2001). Supporting the navigation task: characteristics of good landmarks. In Hanson, M.A. (Ed.), *Contemporary Ergonomics* (pp. 441–446). London: Taylor & Francis.

Burns, P.C. (1997). Navigation and the older driver. Unpublished PhD dissertation, Loughborough University, UK.

Evans, G.W., Skorpanich, A., Garling, T., Bryant, K.J., & Bresolin, B. (1984). The effects of pathway configuration, landmarks and stress on environmental cognition. *Journal of Environmental Psychology, 4,* 323–335.

Eysenck, M.W. (1993). *Principles of Cognitive Psychology.* Hove, UK: Lawrence Erlbaum Associates.

Gould, M.D. (1989). Considering individual cognitive ability in the provision of usable navigation assistance. In Reekie, D.H.M., Case, E.R., & Tsai, J. (Eds.), *Proceedings of Vehicle Navigation and Information Systems Conference* (pp. 443–447). Piscataway, NJ: Institute of Electrical and Electronics Engineers.

Green, P., Levison, W., Paelke, G., & Serafin, C. (1995). *Preliminary Human Factors Design Guidelines for Driver Information Systems, Technical Report No. FHWA-RD-94-087.* Washington, DC: US Government Printing Office.

Hill, M.R. (1987). "Asking directions" and pedestrian wayfinding. *Man–Environment Systems, 17* (4), 113–120.

Hirtle, S., & Hudson, J. (1991). Acquisition of spatial knowledge for routes. *Journal of Environmental Psychology, 11,* 335–345.

Jackson, P.G. (1996). How will route guidance information affect cognitive maps? *Journal of Navigation, 49,* 178–186.

Jackson, P.G. (1998). In search of better route guidance instructions. *Ergonomics, 41* (7), 1000–1013.

Kaplan, S. (1976). Adaptation, structure and knowledge. In Moore, G., & Golledge, R. (Eds.), *Environmental Knowing: Theories, Research and Methods* (pp. 32–45). Stroudsburg, PA: Dowden, Hutchinson and Ross.

Kitchin, R.M. (1994). Cognitive maps: what are they and why study them? *Journal of Environmental Psychology, 14,* 1–19.

Lynch, K. (1960). *The Image of the City.* Cambridge, MA: MIT Press.

Richardson, A.E., Montello, D.R., & Hegarty, M. (1999). Spatial knowledge acquisition from maps and from navigation in real and virtual environments. *Memory and Cognition, 27* (4), 741–750.

Ross, T., Vaughan, G., Engert, A., Peters, H., Burnett, G.E., & May, A.J. (1995). *Human Factors Guidelines for Information Presentation by Route Guidance and Navigation Systems.* Loughborough, UK: HUSAT Research Institute, DRIVE II V2008 HARDIE, Deliverable 19.

Ross, T., May, A.J., & Grimsley, P.J. (2004). Using traffic light information as navigation cues: implications for navigation system design. *Transportation Research Part F, 7* (2), 119–134.

Rovine, M.J., & Weisman, G.D. (1989). Sketch-map variables as predictors of way-finding performance. *Journal of Environmental Psychology, 9,* 217–232.

Sadalla, E.K., Burroughs, W.J., & Staplin, L.J. (1980). Reference points in spatial cognition. *Journal of Experimental Psychology: Human Learning and Memory, 6* (5), 516–528.

Smiley, A. (2000). Behavioural adaptation, safety, and intelligent transportation systems. *Transportation Research Record 1724* (Paper No. 00-1504), 47–51.

Srinivisan, R. (1999). Overview of some human factors design issues for in-vehicle navigation and route guidance systems. *Transportation Research Record 1694* (Paper no. 99-0884). Washington, DC: National Academy Press.

Stern, E., & Leiser, D. (1988). Levels of spatial knowledge and urban travel modelling. *Geographical Analysis, 20* (2), 140–155.

Thorndyke, P.A., & Hayes-Roth, B. (1982). Differences in spatial knowledge acquired from maps and navigation. *Cognitive Psychology, 14,* 560–589.

Tolman, E.C. (1948). Cognitive maps in mice and men. *Psychological Review, 55,* 189–208.

Van Winsum, W. (1993). Selection of routes in route navigation systems. In Parkes, A.M., & Franzen, S. (Eds.), *Driving Future Vehicles* (pp. 193–204). London: Taylor & Francis.

Traffic and Transport Psychology
G. Underwood (Editor)
© 2005 Elsevier Ltd. All rights reserved.

34

MENTAL REPRESENTATION OF TRAFFIC SIGNS: ROLE OF SIGN COMPLEXITY AND SEMANTIC INFORMATION

Cándida Castro[1], Francisco J. Tornay, Sergio Moreno-Ríos, Cristina Vargas and Enrique Molina

INTRODUCTION

Signs are a key element of the traffic environment. They inform, restrict, warn and admonish traffic users. It is indispensable for the latter to keep track on real time of the information that traffic signs provide in order to perceive it, understand it, remember it and combine it with other pieces of information and users' own goals, so that they can reach a right decision on what to do next. Oddly enough, most of the extensive body of literature about traffic sign has focused only on the perception or memory parts (see Castro & Horberry, 2004, for a thorough review). Little attention has been devoted to the way in which traffic users represent sign information internally and to the way such representations are combined with one another and with other pieces of information and users' goals.

The present work is an initial attempt to address such issues. The starting point is a closer inspection into what a traffic sign stands for. Indication and danger signs convey information about current traffic conditions. Ideally, they should always correspond to actual conditions, that is, they should be true. Even if they are not (which happens occasionally), they at least have a well-defined truth value. That is, indication and danger signs stand for *logical propositions*. On the other hand, no truth value can be attached to prohibition and obligation signs. They inform traffic users about rules they must comply with. Logic has also studied such pieces of information and has also considered them to be a kind of logical proposition, they are not be *alethic* (truth valued) but *deontic* or *normative* propositions (see, e.g. Hughes & Cresswell, 1996, for a complete discussion). Deontic logic supplements standard propositional or predicate

---

[1] Departamento de Psicologia Experimental. Facultad de Psicología, Universidad de Granada, Campus Cartuja S/N 18071, Granada, Spain. *E-mail:* candida@ugr.es (C. Castro); ftornay@ugr.es (F.J. Tornay).

logic with a set of modal operators such as *is-allowed* or *is-compulsory*. In both cases, such propositions may be combined to produce new information about traffic. Such a combination is an example of a deduction or, more generally, of a reasoning task.

This simple analysis shows a self-evident but usually overlooked fact about traffic: superimposed over traffic users' main task of moving around whilst avoiding accidents there is a reasoning task involving the inference of new propositions on the basis of information from traffic signs and representations from long-term memory. The present work takes this fact as a starting point for applying research and theories about human reasoning to traffic-sign understanding. This will allow us to address questions about how traffic-sign information is represented, how different representations are combined and, on the long term, may allow us to take a fresh look on ways of improving sign design.

We intend to present the main points of this on-going research by (a) reviewing the main rationale along with a previous finding from our laboratory (Tornay, Castro & Moreno-Ríos, in press); (b) presenting new data that elaborate and extend such a finding; (c) interpreting the new data and advancing possible developments. In keeping with the usual structure of an experimental report, part "a" will be dealt with in this introduction; the new experiment will be presented later in the work and part "c" will be included in the *general discussion* section. We hope this layout will allow readers to get a clear, though somewhat hasty, notion of the main points of this research line.

OBLIGATION VERSUS PROHIBITION

Literature about traffic signs has traditionally reported that performance is better when responding to obligation than to prohibition signs (e.g. Macdonald & Hoffmann, 1978). Usual interpretations seem to imply a motivational reason, in the sense that people are less willing to comply with a blunt prohibition than with a positive statement about what they are allowed to do. It is possible, however, to offer alternative explanations based on the internal representations that traffic signs may elicit. There are two general possible accounts that we may call *syntactical* and *semantical*.

According to the syntactical view, human beings can directly represent some logical information, other aspects must be restated in terms of these primitives, *obligation* might be a primitive, whereas *prohibition* would have to be represented as a kind of negated obligation (e.g. is-obligatory not-to...). This is similar to the traditional, syntactical explanation of why negative propositions are more difficult to understand than affirmative ones: an explicit representation of the negation operator would increase memory load and processing time as compared with positive propositions. However, Wason (1965) offered an alternative *semantical* account and supported it by showing that it is possible to reduce the difficulty of negations. Such a reduction occurs in so-called "contexts of plausible denial". A simple example would be a task in which a participant sees five circles all blue but for the fourth one, which is green. The negative sentence "the fourth circle is not..." can be completed fairly rapidly with the world blue. Wason suggested that negations are typically used to deny presuppositions and that the negated content is attended. In "She is not drinking coffee" attention is directed to "coffee" and the explicit negation is processed. In some circumstances people avoid the explicit negation thinking in the "positive" alternatives in the complementary set, e.g. other drinks that are not coffee and come into the mind. This is the so-called *contrast class* (see Oaskford, 2002). One factor implicated in the difficulty of accessing one of its elements is the size of the contrast class. It is easier with small classes such as in "it is not female" (Schroyens, Schaeken, Verschueren & d'Ydewalle, 2000).

This is a strong support for a semantic account of the effect. The key factor may be the amount of *semantic information* provided by the proposition. A premise contains more semantic information when it rules out more possibilities (e.g. Johnson-Laird & Byrne, 2002), that is, semantic information refers to how many situations a given sentence discards. The more incompatible situations, the more semantic information the sentence provides. According to this view, positive propositions are usually easier to process because they typically provide more semantic information, as one can easily observe by comparing the sentences *my car is white* and *my car is not white*. Eliminating this advantage is enough for cancelling (or even inverting) the effect.

The semantical account of negation can be easily extended to explain the advantage of obligation over prohibition signs because an obligation sign usually provides more semantic information than a prohibition sign. For instance, if there are three alternative roads, making it compulsory to follow one of them reduces the alternative to one, whereas prohibiting one road still allows a choice between two roads.

A previous experiment in our laboratory (Tornay et al., in press) tested whether a similar plausible deniability effect occurs in the representation of traffic signs. The design aimed at ensuring that prohibition and obligation signs provided the same amount of semantic information. The task consisted in evaluating whether a simulated turn was or not allowed by the present traffic signs (see the "Method" section and Figure 1 for a thorough explanation). In one condition (Figure 1a) there was a three-way junction with the car approaching through one of the roads. Therefore, there were two possible turns. In that case a "forbidden left turn" sign would be equivalent to a "mandatory right turn" sign. In another condition (Figure 1b) there were three roads in the intersection and, therefore, two possible turns. In that case the "forbidden left turn" sign would correspond to a "mandatory right turn or straight ahead movement". By choosing only equivalent signs in both conditions, it was possible to exactly match the amount of semantic information for both categories of sign. This design was comparable with Wason's plausible deniability contexts.

The results showed no overall advantage of mandatory signs. Instead, performance depended on whether the turn was or not allowed by the signal, resulting in a perfect interaction between sign category and kind of turn: with obligation signs, performance was better when reporting that a turn was legal than when declaring a turn was not allowed, whereas the opposite was true in the case of prohibition signs. This pattern is analogous to Wason's results in the field of negation research. It strongly favours a semantic account of sign representation, because (a) it is difficult to explain an inversion of the effect from a motivational or syntactical standpoint and (b) it shows the importance of semantic information. We will next present a new experiment that intends to extend these findings and find out to what extent they generalise to different stimuli and situations.

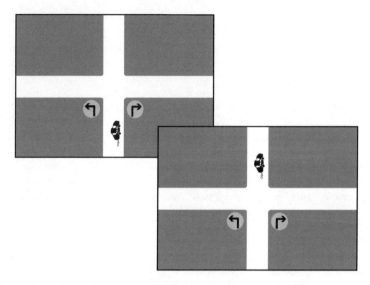

Figure 1. Example of two consequent traffic scenes of a four-way junction with prohibition sign.

EXPERIMENT

The experiment described in the introduction shows that it is possible to obtain an effect analogous to Wason's plausible denial in the context of traffic signs, which strongly supports a semantic account of traffic-sign understanding. However, there are some aspects of the experiment that demand a closer examination. In the four-way condition, matching the amount of semantic information provided by the two sign types involved using simple (one-headed, such as "no left turn") prohibition signs but complex (double-headed, such as "turn left or right") signs. The fact that the pattern of results was similar to that in the three-way condition, where signs were always single headed, suggests that such a difference was not as decisive as it may seem. However, it is still important to address the effect of sign complexity, not only for discarding alternative interpretations of the data but also because it is linked to the next stage in our research line: studying the combination of different pieces of information from traffic signs. A double headed sign stands for a complex proposition composed by two simple ones ("turn left or turn right"). In this experiment we will manipulate the number of independent simple propositions by changing the number of signs, presenting either only one or two one-headed signs.

We will only consider the four-way condition, in which a car approaches from a street and has three different alternatives to choose from (see Figure 1). The approach will be the opposite from the one taken in our previous experiment: we will match the number of signs presented in the obligation and in the prohibition conditions, thus allowing certain mismatch in the semantic information provided by them in each case. For instance, when only one simple sign is presented in the four-way condition prohibition signs provide less semantic information than obligation signs because in the former case there are two allowed possibilities and in the latter one only one is allowed (compare a "forbidden left turn" sign with a "turn left" sign when there are three alternative roads). The opposite is true when two signs are presented (compare a "do not turn left and do not turn right" sign with a "turn left or turn right" sign). Therefore, the amount of semantic information will be matched across all trials (with one and two signs) but not in each condition. This way, we will obtain a direct comparison with the previous experiment. By considering both of them we can assess the effect of the amount of semantic information and that of the number of simple deontic propositions independently.

There is another important difference between this experiment and the previous one. Standard obligation and prohibition signs do not only differ in their meaning but also in their appearance. An important perceptual difference between them is the fact that the arrows depicted in prohibition signs are crossed by a strikeout signal, which stands for some kind of negation operator. This, however, does not apply to the "forbidden direction" or "do not go forward" sign. In order to control this possibly confounding factor we will use new, non-standard signs that convey the information by means of a colour code without using differential operators (see Figure 2).

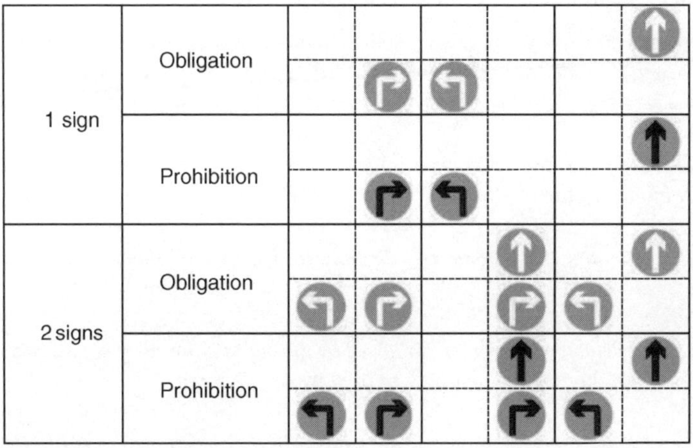

Figure 2. Experimental conditions.

To sum up, we expect that this experiment will provide a wealth of information about how different pieces of traffic-related information is combined (by assessing the effect of the number of signs independently from that of semantic information) and, at the same time, discard confounding perceptual factors and generalise the results to new signs.

Method

Participants. A total of 20 participants took part in the study. They were all psychology students at the University of Granada, Spain. Their ages ranged from 18 to 25. They all had normal or corrected-to-normal vision.

Stimuli. The material used in this experiment consisted of junction road traffic scenes (see Figure 1) with obligation and prohibition signs. Instead of the usual traffic signs, the signs were always grey circles with arrows pointing to different directions. The arrow colour was either white or black to denote obligation or prohibition. The meaning of each colour was counterbalanced across participants.

On half of the trials only one traffic sign was presented, on the others there were two different traffic signs. Figure 2 shows the different sign combinations.

Procedure. Each participant carried out the experiment individually. Every person sat on a chair in front of the computer screen and performed the task.

On each trial, two consecutive screens were always shown. The first scene was shown for 1000 ms. After that, a second scene was displayed for a maximum of 2000 ms or until the participant's response. Both the presentation of stimuli and the collection of responses were controlled by the E-Prime, Version 1.1. (Schneider, 2003) Software.

An example of the instructions given to the participants follows:

Your task consists in evaluating the events that are shown in consecutive traffic scenes. Two scenes will be displayed on each trial: The first screen will always show a car on the lower street plus some signs: The signs will always be grey circles with arrows pointing to the roads directions.

The white arrow denotes that it is compulsory to take that direction, the black arrow expresses that it is prohibited to turn in the corresponding direction.

The second screen shows the same car arriving to one of the other three pathways in the junction.

Please indicate whether the trajectory followed by the car is allowed or not allowed. Take into account the information offered by the sign to make the decision.

Press the key "P", "permissible" as fast as possible if the manoeuvre is allowed or press the key "N", "not permissible " if the manoeuvre made by the car is not allowed according to the signs.

The response was simple and involved pressing one of these two keys. The response hand was counterbalanced across subjects. The experiment consisted of one practice block and four experimental blocks with breaks in between. The presentation order for the stimuli was determined randomly for each block and for each subject, 48 experimental trials were carried out in each block. Twenty-four observations were collected for each experimental condition.

Results

In order to eliminate statistical outliers, we discarded the data from all trials on which reaction time was more than three standard deviations away from the mean, this criterion resulted in

1.17% of the trials being eliminated from analysis. We submitted the remaining reaction time measures for correct responses to a $2 \times 2 \times 2$ repeated-measures ANOVA. The variables were all manipulated within subjects and their values were randomly chosen on a trial-by-trial basis. They were the following: number of signs (1 or 2), regulatory sign (prohibition or obligation) and car manoeuvre (not-allowed or allowed). The following results were obtained (see Figure 3).

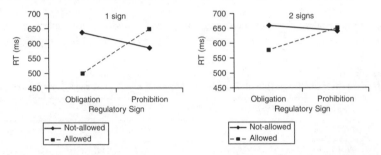

Figure 3. Mean reaction time for 1 sign in the 2×2 conditions manipulated: Regulatory sign (prohibition or obligation) X Manoeuvre (not-allowed or allowed) and mean reaction time for 2 signs in the 2×2 conditions manipulated: Regulatory sign (prohibition or obligation) X Manoeuvre (not-allowed or allowed).

The second-order interaction between the three factors was significant $F(1,19) = 7.015$, MSE $= 2782.55$, $p < 0.0158$. The first-order interaction between the factors regulatory sign and manoeuvre was also reliable, $F(1,19) = 28.41$, MSE $= 7549.98$, $p < 0.0001$.

Also significant were the main effect of number of signs, $F(1,19) = 13.93$, MSE $= 4053.38$, $p < 0.0014$, the main effect of regulatory sign, $F(1,19) = 11.60$, MSE $= 3732.32$, $p < 0.0029$, and that of manoeuvre, $F(1,19) = 18.15$, MSE $= 4598.98$, $p < 0.0004$.

In order to analyse the reliable three-way interaction further separate analysis were carried out for the one-sign and the two-sign conditions. The analysis of the one-sign experimental condition was as follows. The Regulatory sign X Manoeuvre interaction was significant, $F(1,19) = 44.12$, MSE $= 4118.02$, $p < 0.0001$. The main effect of regulatory sign was also significant, $F(1,19) = 15.27$, MSE $= 2869.23$, $p < 0.0009$. The main effect of manoeuvre was also reliable, $F(1,19) = 14.24$, MSE $= 3672.42$, $p < 0.0012$. This variable produced reliable results both in the obligation-sign condition, $F(1,19) = 59.25$, MSE $= 3619.17$, $p < 0.0001$, and in the prohibition-sign condition, $F(1,19) = 4.68$, MSE $= 4170.70$, $p < 0.0434$.

The analysis of simple effects for the two-sign experimental condition revealed a reliable effect of the Regulatory sign X Manoeuvre interaction, $F(1,19) = 8.41$, MSE $= 52298.58$, $p < 0.0091$. The main effect of manoeuvre was also reliable, $F(1,19) = 11.27$, MSE $= 32372.78$, $p < 0.0033$. The main effect of regulatory sign was not significant. This variable produced reliable results in the obligation-sign condition, $F(1,19) = 21.01$,

MSE $= 83482.38$, $p < 0.0002$, but not in the prohibition-sign condition, $F(1,19) < 1$. This latter result contrasts with the findings in the one-sign condition.

We can summarise the analysis of reaction-time data by indicating that obligation signs produce a similar pattern of results, regardless of whether one or two signs are presented. However, the improvement in performance for declaring that a turn is not allowed that appears when one prohibition sign is presented vanishes when two different signs must be taken into account. Such a difference explains the reliable three-way interaction found in the analysis.

The analysis of response accuracy (percentage of incorrect responses, see Table 1) only showed a reliable Regulatory sign X Manoeuvre interaction, $F(1,19) = 7.25$, MSE $= 66.72$, $p < 0.015$.

Table 1. Response accuracy (percentage of errors) for the different experimental conditions.

	Regulatory signs(%)			
	Obligation		Prohibition	
	Not-allowed turn	Allowed turn	Not-allowed turn	Allowed turn
1 sign	17.93	15.63	15.90	25.96
2 signs	21.75	17.40	17.05	29.34

There was a marginally reliable effect of manoeuvre both in the obligation-sign condition, $F(1,19) = 3.53$, MSE $= 29.08$, $p < 0.073$, and in the prohibition-sign condition, $F(1,19) = 4.30$, MSE $= 10.13$, $p < 0.052$ (see Table 1).

Discussion

The main feature of the pattern of results is the clear three-way interaction between the three factors. As noted in the introduction to the experiment, with only one sign, obligation signs provide more semantic information than prohibition signs. This mismatch results in a reliable main effect of regulatory sign, which shows that obligation signs produce faster responses in average. Such an effect was absent in our previous experiment, where the amount of semantic information provided by both sign types was carefully matched. This difference, however, does not alter the general pattern of results, which is similar to the one found in our previous experiment. That is, reaction times for responding that a turn is allowed are faster when obligation signs are presented and the reverse holds when prohibition signs are used. This is a *plausible denial* effect which suggests that it is possible to eliminate the advantage of obligation signs in some cases (when responding that an action is not allowed) as long as there is not a large mismatch in semantic information even if it is not exactly equal.

The results are strikingly different when two signs are used. Obligation signs still improve reaction times when an *allowed* response must be made but the advantage of prohibition signs in the case of *not-allowed* responses vanishes. This is especially interesting because, as noted in the introduction to the experiment, prohibition signs provide more semantic information in this condition than obligation signs. This result suggests that semantic information is not the only factor to take into account. The fact that this difference appears in the two-sign condition suggests that the difference between mental obligation and prohibition representations may lie more in the combination than in the understanding stage. One way of explaining and deriving predictions from these findings is by falling back on one of the most important accounts about human reasoning: the mental-model theory.

GENERAL DISCUSSION: MENTAL MODELS AND TRAFFIC SIGNS

According to mental-model theory (e.g. Johnson-Laird, 1983), human beings represent propositions as a set of states of the world compatible with the information provided by them. For example, reading or hearing the sentence "every time it rains, Mary gets wet" would not (or, at least, not only) result in an abstract representation of the underlying proposition. It would result in a series of mental images of Mary getting wet in the rain. As a matter of fact, the representations need not be, and probably are not, proper mental images, but they are assumed to be analogical representations processed by short-term memory and, at any rate, are concrete examples of situations compatible with the proposition. Not every situation is represented, at least initially, only those that the proposition directly suggests. The mental-model theory is a semantic account, in the sense that it proposes that representations take into account specific examples, rather than abstract logical rules. Note that semantic information is a key factor for the theory because the more semantic information a traffic sign provides the less mental models are generated and, thus, the less memory load is necessary, which would produce an improvement in performance.

Understanding a proposition would amount to generating this kind of representations. Every represented situation is a *mental model*. The theory goes on to propose that it is possible to combine the mental models elicited by a different proposition in order to come up with new information. For instance, if, after processing the aforementioned proposition, a person is told that "today, it is raining", a series of mental models depicting rain in the present day would appear in short-term memory. The representation of rain in both sets of mental models would be identified; producing combination mental models which would make it clear that today Mary must be wet. The theory considers other possible stages of deduction, which are beyond our present scope. Taken together the assumptions of the theory can generate predictions about actual performance in many deductive tasks. The mental model theory has had considerable success in explaining many reasoning effects (Johnson-Laird, 2001).

It is simple to explain the results of our first experiment in terms of the mental-model theory: observing a "turn left" sign elicits the representation of a car making a legal left turn; a "forbidden right turn" would produce the mental representation of a car making an illegal right turn. Although both signs are logically equivalent, they would result in completely different mental representations, which would explain the different results: in the first case it would be easier to respond that a left turn is legal than to indicate that a right turn was not because the first had already been represented, whereas the other must be constructed after the turn has already taken place. The opposite would hold for the prohibition sign.

The results in the two-sign condition may be related to another general finding in the reasoning literature is the difficulty of making deductions based on the knowledge that something is false.

In many cases people seem to have problems using representations of states of the world that they know are false. This result is known as the *principle of truth*.

However, most people have no difficulty understanding counterfactual propositions or, in general, imagining false situations and even supposing or pretending they are true. Goldbarg and Johnson-Laird (2001, see p. 567 for a discussion) reviewed the relevant literature and concluded that the difficulty was not related to the initial representation of false information, which could be carried out easily. What is difficult is to combine false states of the world in order to come up with new hypothetical information. In Goldbarg and Johnson-Laird's terms false *atomic beliefs* are easy to represent but drawing conclusions from a set of different pieces of information is a hard task if we know that information to be false. Goldbarg and Johnson-Laird tried to explain this result by assuming that mental footnotes cannot be combined.

The results obtained in the two-sign condition may be explained along the lines of Goldbarg and Johnson-Laird's argument. Representing deontic information may be akin to representing hypothetical information: representations may consist of a set of concrete mental models stored in short-term memory with attached mental footnotes, marking them as *false* or *forbidden*. Note that no specific mental footnotes are assumed to be attached to actual and allowed situations. Therefore, representing isolated simple prohibition signs would be similar to and not necessarily less efficient than representing obligation signs. However, combining the former would be impossible because of the necessity of including mental footnotes in the combination. In that case, it would be necessary to convert the representations to their obligation counterparts, which would reduce performance and eliminate the advantage of prohibition signs for declaring that a turn is not allowed, which is exactly the pattern found in the two-sign condition.

Clearly, this is a *post-hoc* explanation that must be submitted to further empirical tests. However, we think that the experiments and theoretical background that have been presented in this report may prove a powerful way of studying and analysing traffic signs and their impact on human performance.

REFERENCES

Castro, C., & Horberry, T. (2004). *The Human Factors of Transport Signs*. Boca Raton, FL: CRC Press.

Goldbarg, E., & Johnson-Laird, P.N. (2001). Naive causality: a mental model theory of causal meaning and reasoning. *Cognitive Science, 25*, 565–610.

Hughes, G.E., & Cresswell, M.J. (1996). *A New Introduction to Modal Logic*. London: Routledge.

Johnson-Laird, P.N. (1983). *Mental Models: Towards a Cognitive Science of Language, Inference and Consciousness*. Cambridge: Cambridge University.

Johnson-Laird, P.N. (2001). Mental models and deduction. *Trends in Cognitive Sciences, 10*, 434–442.

Johnson-Laird, P.N., & Byrne, R.M. (2002). Conditionals: a theory of meaning, pragmatics and inferences. *Psychological Review, 109*, 646–678.

Macdonald, W.A., & Hoffmann, E.R. (1978). Information coding on turn restriction signs. *Proceedings of the 9th ARRB Conference, 9* (5), 361–382.

Oaskford, M. (2002). Contrast classes and matching bias as explanations of the effects of negations on conditional reasoning. *Thinking and Reasoning, 8,* 135–151.

Schneider, W., (2003). *Psychology Software Tools,* Inc. Available: [Online] http://www. pstnet.com

Schroyens, W., Schaeken, W., Verschueren, N., & d'Ydewalle, G. (2000). Conditional reasoning with negations: implicit and explicit affirmation or denial and the role of contrast classes. *Thinking and Reasoning, 6,* 221–252.

Tornay, F.J., Castro, C., & Moreno-Ríos, S. (in press). Inferring from signs expressing obligation and prohibition. In Gale, A. et al. (Eds.), *Vision in Vehicles X.*

Wason, P.C. (1965). The contexts of plausible denial. *Journal of Verbal Learning and Verbal Behaviour, 4,* 7–11.

Traffic and Transport Psychology
G. Underwood (Editor)
© 2005 Elsevier Ltd. All rights reserved.

35

PROFESSIONAL DRIVER TRAINING AND DRIVER STRESS: EFFECTS ON SIMULATED DRIVING PERFORMANCE

Lisa Dorn[1]

INTRODUCTION

Professional drivers are at increased risk of accident involvement (Broughton, Baughan, Pearce, Smith & Buckle, 2003) and have work-related issues to deal with that are likely to increase driver stress and exposure to risk (Dorn & Brown, 2003). Well-designed training could upgrade driver abilities, yet literature reviews have asserted that driver training may be counterproductive in improving road safety (Christie, 2001; Mayhew & Simpson, 2002). But, studies tend to focus on an extremely unreliable criterion measure—accidents (af Wåhlberg, 2003). Perhaps, a more useful start to evaluating the effectiveness of driver training might be to consider whether driving performance is qualitatively improved and safer according to the level of training proficiency attained. In a study of real driving, Teffner, Barrett & Petersen (2002) show improved performance amongst trained driving instructors in cornering trajectory, emergency braking strategy and high speed swerve and recovery tasks compared with untrained experienced drivers. In a simulator-based task, Dorn & Barker (2005) report significant differences between trained experienced drivers and non-trained experienced drivers on speed choice in response to hazards, the initiation of safer overtaking and safer vehicle positioning compared with untrained drivers. There are methodological difficulties in using this kind of experimental design to investigate training effects. One might expect there to be driving performance differences between professionally trained and non-professionally trained drivers. This kind of design says little about what aspects of professional driver training could be improved upon to reduce accident risk. The purpose of the present study then is to consider whether there are driver group differences in driving performance between drivers trained to a standard professional level compared with those trained to an advanced professional level of

[1] Driving Research Unit, Department of Human Factors and Air Transport, Cranfield University, Cranfield, Bedfordshire MK43 0AL, UK. *E-mail:* l.dorn@cranfield.ac.uk (L. Dorn).

proficiency with a view to informing the content of professional driver training. By comparing two sets of professionally trained drivers but with different levels of proficiency, standard professional drivers operate as a control group for more advanced professional drivers.

Police driver training is a good model to use to investigate driver training effects due to clear differences between standard and advanced police driver training. In addition, generally police drivers receive similar driver training, and work under similar organisational policies and practises. In the UK, the content of standard police driver training broadly includes instruction in safe systematic driving techniques, highway code, protection at a road incident scene; attitudinal training, stopping vehicles; skid techniques and manoeuvrability; familiarisation and vehicle care, emergency response driving, night driving, and basic pursuit driving. Advanced police driver training includes all the elements of standard training but is enhanced with practical training in safe, systematic high speed driving techniques to a high degree of all round proficiency. Furthermore, advanced driver training places greater emphasis on hazard awareness and maintaining visual contact following a target vehicle whilst also refining observation skills to anticipate danger. The advanced course is longer than the standard course (about 3 weeks versus about 4–5 weeks but this varies across forces). Both courses instruct in safe overtaking in which trainees overtake by observing the road ahead for layout, road signs, hazards, etc. identify a safe gap and then pull out to initiate an overtake at speed. But, standard drivers do not get the opportunity to practise these manoeuvres during training to the same extent as advanced drivers do, nor do they have as many hours instruction in developing other driving skills. Given these driver training differences, it is expected that advanced drivers will demonstrate safer driving performance in comparison with standard drivers, especially with regard to speed, overtaking and driving behaviour at particular hazards.

There is a further rationale for this study that has not previously been considered in the literature with respect to driver training proficiency. Stress states can interfere with several distinct components of the driving task including psychomotor control and hazard detection (Matthews et al., 1993; Matthews, Sparkes & Bygrave, 1996) and not surprisingly, previous research has shown a link between driver stress and accident involvement amongst non-professionally trained (Matthews, Dorn & Glendon, 1991) and professionally trained drivers (Dorn & Garwood, 2005). There are a number of reasons why this relationship may exist. Firstly, stress might interfere with attention to driving by generating anxiety, worry and task-irrelevant thoughts that reduce the availability of attentional resources for the driving task. Second, stress could impair the driver's judgement in the selection of coping strategies to deal with a hazardous situation. The implication here is that vehicle-handling skills honed during training may not always be well executed under the pressure of day-to-day professional driving—despite superior driving skills. For police drivers, there is little debate that driving is stressful and at times life threatening. Driving in response or pursuit requires police officers to put themselves in unpredictable traffic situations. They frequently respond to calls where there is little information available about what is occurring at the scene, or chase a suspect at speed under dangerous circumstances. Responses to stress will vary according to individual differences but qualitative research (Dorn & Brown, 2003) reported that over 40% of police drivers interviewed felt that stress-related problems contributed to police collisions.

Driver stress can be conceptualised as a continual interaction of factors both intrinsic and extrinsic to driving, mediated by an individual's appraisal of the driving task (Gulian,

Matthews, Glendon, Davies & Debney, 1989). Matthews (2001) proposed that driver stress vulnerability relates to cognitive processes of appraisal and coping specified by transactional models of stress (Lazarus & Folkman, 1984). In this way, driver stress is generated by cognitive appraisals that demands of the driving task exceed the driver's capabilities and coping resources. The driver stress inventory (DSI; Gulian et al., 1989) aims to measure an individual's vulnerability to stress reactions during driving and is a reliable measure of driver stress (Glendon et al., 1993). The DSI includes five dimensions of driver stress, thrill seeking, aggression, dislike of driving, hazard monitoring, and fatigue proneness (Matthews et al., 1991; Dorn & Matthews, 1995; Matthews, Desmond, Joyner & Carcardy, 1997; Matthews, Tsuda, Xin & Ozeki, 1999).

The present research aimed to test the relationship between the DSI factors and driving performance. It is expected that different factors might relate to specific aspects of driving task performance amongst police drivers in the same way as that shown in previous studies with non-professionally trained drivers (Matthews et al., 1996, 1998; Matthews, 2001). There are several a priori reasons why established links might also be found amongst police drivers. Firstly, police drivers may be attracted to the thrill of driving so high scores on *thrill seeking* are expected to be associated with more risky decision-making to satisfy sensation seeking motivations whilst driving. Secondly, police drivers are trained to drive with confidence and maintain a "presence" on the road when the situation demands it. They are regularly exposed to other non-paced drivers who often respond inappropriately to the "Blues and Twos". Previous research has shown that *aggression* is characterised by negative appraisals of other drivers expressed through intimidation and is associated with tailgating, frequent overtaking, higher frequencies of driving errors and deliberate violations such as speeding (Matthews, 1993; Matthews et al., 1997). It is reasonable to suggest then that increased aggression may be associated with unsafe driving manoeuvres amongst police drivers as well. Thirdly, *dislike of driving* is associated with negative self-appraisal, and these cognitions generate negative mood states and worries which tend to interfere with task performance (Matthews, 2001). Given that personal safety is threatened during overtaking manoeuvres it is anticipated that high scores on dislike are associated with more risky overtaking. Fourthly, increased scores on *hazard monitoring* are associated with active attempts to anticipate danger that may in part be linked to visual search strategies. Crundall & Underwood (1998) found that experienced drivers adapt their visual search according to roadway demands whereas novice drivers adopt a less flexible strategy. In a study of police drivers, Crundall, Chapman, Phelps & Underwood (2003) reported that police drivers demonstrated greater visual sampling rate and spread of search and increased electrodermal activity when viewing pursuits compared with novice drivers and age-matched controls. It is hypothesised then that increased hazard monitoring scores may be associated with safer driving performance at hazards. Finally, police drivers drive for long periods and may suffer from fatigue (Matthews & Desmond, 1996). The *fatigue proneness* dimension measures an individual's vulnerability to experience driver fatigue after several hours of prolonged driving. It relates to drowsiness, day dreaming, boredom and may be correlated with slower reactions and reduced attention to components of the driving task.

The DSI also measures specific driver stress coping strategies based on cognitive appraisals of the driving task, including, emotion-focused coping, confrontive coping, task-focus coping, avoidance and reappraisal coping (Matthews, 1993). Poor driver stress coping strategies would not only fail to manage the experience of driver stress but also may intensify it. Taking these in turn, emotion-focused coping refers to self-criticism as a driver and may impair driving performance through distraction and self-focus, whereas confrontive coping involves mastery of the driving challenge through self-assertion or conflict and are clearly dangerous driver coping strategies. Task-focus coping refers to active attempts to change the external environment via a behavioural response, for example, reducing speed when driving conditions are dangerous and is, therefore, an effective coping strategy in the face of driver stress. Similarly, reappraisal coping is an attempt to deal with driver stress by re-appraising one's emotional and cognitive reactions and tends to have a more positive influence on driving behaviour. Avoidance coping, on the other hand, is the attempt to ignore the stressor often through self-distraction and diverting attention away from driving and in this way performance could be impaired. It is expected that these specific coping strategies are associated with components of driving task performance such that emotion-focused coping, confrontive coping and avoidance is expected to relate to risk taking whereas task focus and reappraisal is expected to relate to safer driving performance.

The purpose of the present study then is twofold. Firstly, to test the hypothesis that advanced police driver training leads to safer simulated driving performance compared with standard driver training. Secondly, to consider the hypothesis that driver stress factors are associated with specific components of simulated driving task performance amongst police drivers in an expected direction as that found for non-professionally trained drivers.

METHOD

Participants

Fifty-three police drivers were recruited as volunteers from two urban police services via newsletter, website and direct contact. Both police services used very similar driver training approaches for both advanced and standard courses and were operationally adjacent in the south-east of England. The average age was 36.7 (SD = 5.67). The police drivers had held a full driving licence on average for 18.37 years. Sixty-seven per cent of the sample reported driving over 15,000 miles per annum and all drivers reported driving everyday. There were 14 police officers trained to a standard level of driving proficiency and 39 officers trained to an advanced level of driving proficiency. Of the police drivers trained to an advanced level, 10 had undertaken specialist pursuit training and three had been trained on anti-surveillance/anti-ambush courses with 27 of the 39 having also completed other kinds of shorter courses such as driving specialist police vehicles and motorcycle training. The mean age for the advanced drivers was 37.28 and the mean age for the standard drivers was 33.93.

Design and procedure

All participants were asked to take part in a driving simulator-based experimental trial in which they were required to drive along a scenario partitioned into a "rural" section, representing single lane country roads with hills and bends with occasional traffic, a "link" section, representing a stretch of single-lane, fairly straight, open road, relatively free of traffic and finally an "urban" section representing driving through a built-up area, with traffic lights, pedestrians and a single and dual carriageway with occasional traffic. The participants were seated in the driving simulator at a distance of 1 m (39 in.) from the screen, resulting in an approximate eye-to-screen distance of 75 cm (25 in.). The participant viewed the road ahead on a 22-in. visual display unit. Participants were given a 10-min practice trial on the driving simulator to get used to the feel of the steering wheel and pedal controls. Next, participants took part in the experimental trial and were instructed to drive the way they would normally drive and deal with the conditions presented as if they are really happening. The scenario was 9.12 miles in length and took about 15 min to complete, depending on preferred speed. Vehicles behind the driver never overtook the driver, although they could be viewed in a rear-view mirror. All traffic lights were encountered during the urban section of the scenario. Traffic lights were always set to "go".

To test for risk taking propensity, the participants were given two main tasks to complete. Firstly, they were asked to overtake a slow-moving bus during the link section. Here, certain sections of the link roads had been programmed with hills and bends and double white lines (indicating in the UK that overtaken is prohibited) in the centre of the road. Oncoming traffic was relatively infrequent. Secondly, they were asked to maintain visual contact with a lead vehicle travelling at 55 mph in a 30 mph urban section without seriously compromising safety. An independent measures design was used with police driver group (standard and advanced drivers) as between subjects factors and dependent measures were scenario completion time (the total number of seconds taken to complete the entire simulation from beginning to end); speed (mph), overtaking risk (the number of occasions that the driver crossed the roadway division when there were double white lines indicating "no overtaking"); and lateral separation (the distance from the parked bus and the driver's vehicle measured in feet). Speed on approach to traffic signals was recorded on three occasions. Firstly, 450 ft, secondly 300 ft and finally 150 ft distance from the traffic lights. Speed was averaged at each of these distances and recorded and averaged over the 1500 ft before the traffic lights (the earliest point at which the traffic lights were visible to the participant) until passed. Speed at passing traffic signals was also measured. Participants completed the DSI either before or after the simulated driving task and were also asked to rate their chances of being involved in a road traffic accident in the next 12 months ranging from extremely unlikely (0) to extremely likely (10).

The driving simulator

The driving simulator was built using the STISIM PC-based interactive driving simulator model 100. The simulation included vehicle dynamics, visual and auditory feedback and performance measurement system, full sized driving controls including a modular accelerator and brake pedal unit, and speed sensitive steering feel provided by computer controlled torque motor (360° steering capability). The simulator incorporates a high-resolution digital-optical control input sensors, an audio amplified stereo speaker set and sound card (sound blaster Live PCI) and graphics card (3D voodoo2, 24 MB RAM; resolution: 1024 × 768). The scenario was presented on a 22 in. VGA colour monitor. The hardware and software were housed in a frame with a car seat built from the dimensions of a Ford Escort car. The screen update was set to produce between 10 and 30 frames per second depending on the complexity of the view, leading to a moderately smooth apparent motion. The road was represented within a rectangle that was 1024 pixels wide and 768 pixels high with the screen representing the sky above, a speedometer below, and a rear-view mirror in the top left-hand corner. The simulator displayed realistic three-dimensional scenes at 135° field view including pedestrians, buildings, road signs and oncoming traffic. The participant viewed objects up to 1500 ft away appropriately scaled in size and perspective. In accordance with the British Highway code, relevant road signs and markings were included in the scenario such as speed limit signs, signs warning of impending bends in the road approaching, and double/dashed white lines in the centre of the road.

RESULTS AND DISCUSSION

Age, experience and driver training differences

Advanced drivers report driving more miles annually and weekly and have been driving as a police officer for nearly twice as long as standard drivers. Standard drivers had received police driver training more recently than advanced drivers. However, Table 1 shows no significant differences for age, mileage and experience between the two police driver groups.

Table 1. Police driver group differences in age, experience and driver training.

Variable	Advanced drivers, mean and SD	Standard drivers, mean and SD	*t*-value	Significance level (one-tailed)
Age	37.28 (4.98)	33.93 (5.79)	0.552	ns
Annual (work and leisure) mileage	13,533 (6217)	10,970 (5834)	0.36	ns
Weekly mileage at work	333 (274)	231 (199)	0.493	ns
Number of years since gaining first police driving licence	13.74 (6.28)	7.36 (6.05)	0.011	ns
Number of years since last police driver training course attended	6.12 (5.76)	3.21 (3.20)	3.71	ns

Hypothesis 1: driver group difference in driving performance

Speed. Analysis revealed that standard drivers were faster on approach to Signal 1, 2 and 3 (Signal 1; $t = 2.20, p < 0.05$, Signal 2; $t = 2.00, p < 0.05$, Signal 3; $t = 2.21, p < 0.05$) and on passing Signal 1 ($t = 1.70, p < 0.05$) compared with advanced drivers. Results also showed that standard drivers were faster during both the rural ($t = 1.91$, $p < 0.05$) and the "link" sections ($t = 1.92, p < 0.05$) and faster overall, completing the driving simulator component of the study in less time than advanced drivers ($t = 1.95, p < 0.05$) (see Table 2). In comparison to standard drivers, advanced drivers exhibited lower speeds in both the rural and link sections and took longer to complete the simulated scenario overall.

The characteristic speed differentials between the police driver groups indicate a consistent pattern of speed choice with standard drivers adopting significantly higher speeds across a range of different road and traffic contexts compared with advanced drivers. These findings

Table 2. Police driver group differences in simulated driving performance.

Performance measure	Advanced drivers mean	Standard drivers mean	t-value	Significance level (one-tailed)
Mean speed approaching Signal 1	39.5 mph	45.4 mph	2.20	0.05
Speed passing Signal 1	41.9 mph	46.8 mph	1.70	0.05
Mean speed approaching Signal 2	48.2 mph	54.5 mph	2.00	0.05
Mean speed approaching Signal 3	48.8 mph	58.4 mph	2.21	0.05
Mean speed in rural section	34.1 mph	35.8 mph	1.91	0.05
Mean speed in link section	47.6 mph	49.3 mph	1.92	0.05
Total time	802.5 s	745.2 s	1.95	0.05

suggest that advanced driver training may indeed be influential in making safer speed choice decisions in comparison to drivers who have received training to a standard level of proficiency.

Overtaking. Analysis revealed that standard drivers were over five times ($n = 4, 26.4\%$) more likely to cross the roadway division at unsafe locations during the overtaking manoeuvre than advanced drivers ($n = 2, 5.1\%$) ($\chi^2 = 5.6$, DF $= 1, p < 0.05$). It should be noted that the total number of risky roadway crossings across the total driver sample was small ($n = 6$). Perhaps, additional advanced driver training in overtaking is exerting an influence on decision making when initiating an overtaking manoeuvre.

Risk perception. Interestingly, standard drivers rate their chances of being involved in an accident in the next 12 months significantly lower than advanced drivers do ($t = 9.53, p < 0.01$; $\bar{x} = 1.25$ vs. $\bar{x} = 2.50$) suggesting an illusory sense of control in comparison with advanced drivers. This may help explain differences between the police driver groups in risk taking. Perhaps, standard drivers drive at increased risk compared with advanced drivers because they believe they are unlikely to be involved in an accident.

With respect to the first hypothesis then, driver group differences in simulated driving performance were found in the expected direction. Advanced drivers showed greater caution in speed choice at traffic signal hazards and during overtaking compared with standard drivers. Standard drivers also rated their chances of being involved in an accident significantly lower than did advanced drivers.

Hypothesis 2: driver stress and driving performance

Hazard awareness and driver stress and coping. In the urban section, correlations between the DSI and driving performance revealed that increased scores for hazard monitoring ($r = -0.29, n = 53, p < 0.05$) were significantly associated with reduced speed when passing the parked bus hazard. Here, police drivers high in hazard monitoring appear to be aware of their hazardous surroundings and respond appropriately. Sensitivity to the parked bus hazard may have been due to increased visual sampling rate and spread of search as a function of police driver training (Crundall et al., 2003). There was also a significant correlation between speed at passing the bus and scores for confrontive coping ($r = 0.29, n = 53, p < 0.05$) with increased scores being correlated with increased speed at this particular hazard. Clearly, confrontive coping is associated with more risky driver decision-making as expected. Proximity to the parked bus was also significantly positively correlated with task focus ($r = 0.27, n = 53, p < 0.05$) with high task focus scores being associated with maintaining a greater distance from the parked bus hazard confirming that task focus has a beneficial effect on driving performance.

Overtaking and driver stress. The results for the overtaking task were found to yield significant differences between overtaking behaviour and elevated scores on the dislike of driving dimension of driver stress. Drivers who crossed the centre line at potentially unsafe locations scored higher on dislike of driving compared with police drivers who crossed the centre line at safer locations ($t = 2.46, p < 0.05$) (see Figure 1). This finding confirms previous research showing that high dislike drivers are more prone to stress when personal safety is threatened (Matthews, 1993).

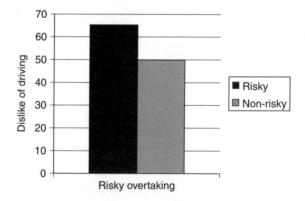

Figure 1. Mean dislike of driving differences between risky and non-risky overtaking manoeuvres. Note: unequal population variances were assumed in this instance.

Drivers who crossed the roadway division at potentially unsafe locations scored significantly higher on thrill seeking compared to those who did not cross the roadway division at unsafe locations. ($t = 1.8, p < 0.05$) and this finding confirms that thrill seeking is related to sensation seeking when driving amongst police drivers (see Figure 2) as well as amongst non-professional drivers (Matthews et al., 1996, 1998; Matthews, 2001).

There was no evidence that aggression was associated with unsafe driving performance and fatigue proneness was not associated with slower reactions to hazards as found in previous studies (Matthews et al., 1997). Perhaps, this can be explained by reference to the format of the simulated scenario used for this study. The traffic was fairly light, even in the urban section, and drivers high in aggression may not have mobilised their usual strategies of competing with

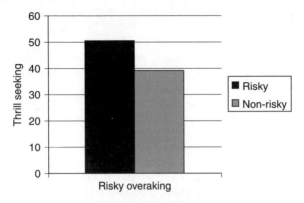

Figure 2. Mean thrill seeking differences between risky and non-risky overtaking manoeuvres. Note: unequal population variances were assumed in this instance.

other drivers under these less demanding driving situations. With regards to fatigue proneness, the scenario took about 15 min to complete and was, therefore, not particularly fatiguing (Matthews & Desmond, 1996).

CONCLUSION

The results show that advanced drivers demonstrate safer driving performance than standard drivers and suggest that perhaps advanced police driver training should be extended to include all police drivers, especially given that it is standard police drivers that appear to have an increased exposure to risk of collisions (Rix, Walker & Brown, 1997) compared with advanced police drivers. It also appears that extensive driver training may fail to protect police drivers from the potential deleterious effects of driver stress on driving performance. Differently trained police drivers do not seem to differ in the effect driver stress has on driving performance despite advanced driver training. Confrontive coping, thrill seeking and dislike are of particular concern. Yet to date, much driver training fails to consider the influence of driver stress and coping and neglects research for over a decade showing its impairing effects on driving performance. Driver stress management techniques could be trained as part of professional driver training. There are also implications for designing training interventions that aim to minimise potentially hazardous styles of driver appraisal and coping and improve hazard monitoring and task focus given the beneficial effects reported here. For example, stress management techniques directed towards high dislike drivers should aim to reduce negative effect without also generating an overly optimistic view of personal competence (Dorn & Brown, 2003). Police driver training should aim to combat an illusory sense of control amongst standard police drivers in particular given the present findings for police driver group differences in risk perception. Furthermore, police driver training should also aim to instruct the trainee in coping strategies for dealing safely with feelings of anger and frustration whilst on duty. Reacting in a confrontational manner is maladaptive and can lead to unsafe decision-making as in the link between confrontive coping and hazard awareness shown in the present study. Training in controlling thrill-seeking tendencies is also recommended. Better driver training can be ultimately evaluated in terms of its effect on accident reduction amongst an extremely vulnerable driver group.

However, it must be pointed out that advanced drivers experience post-training will also have undoubtedly influenced driving behaviour sampled for this study. Advanced drivers are likely to have had experience of following a vehicle at speed in a built-up area, whereas standard drivers may have had less experience of this kind of task. Further, research would need to examine more closely the effects of professional driving training and experience on driving performance. These findings provide initial support that whilst on the one hand police drivers trained to a higher level of proficiency demonstrate safer driving performance, on the other hand there is evidence that driver stress and coping is associated with increased risk taking. Perhaps, strategies that attempt to address appraisal and motivation and effects of emotional state on driving behaviour may be critical in improving police driver training.

ACKNOWLEDGEMENTS

I would like to thank the Police Scientific and Development Branch of the Home Office for their support for this research and all the participants for their assistance. I am also grateful to Cathy Birch for co-ordinating this study.

REFERENCES

af Wåhlberg, A.E. (2003). Some methodological deficiencies in studies on traffic accident predictors. *Accident Analysis and Prevention, 35*, 473–486.

Broughton, J., Baughan, C., Pearce, L., Smith, L., & Buckle, G. (2003). Work-related road accidents. *TRL Report, 582*.

Christie, R. (2001). *The Effectiveness of Driver Training as a Road Safety Measure: A Review of the Literature*. Noble Park, Victoria: Royal Automobile Club of Victoria (RACV) Ltd.

Crundall, D., & Underwood, G. (1998). Effects of experience and processing demands on visual information acquisition in drivers. *Ergonomics, 41*, 448–458.

Crundall, D., Chapman, P., Phelps, N., & Underwood, G. (2003). Eye movements and hazard perception in police pursuit and emergency response driving. *Journal of Experimental Psychology: Applied, 9* (3), 163–174.

Dorn, L., & Barker, D. (2005). The effects of driver training on simulated driving performance. *Accident Analysis and Prevention, 37*, 63–69.

Dorn, L., & Brown, B. (2003). Making sense of invulnerability in a qualitative study of police drivers. *Safety Science, 41* (10), 837–859.

Dorn, L., & Garwood, L. (2005). Development of a psychometric measure of bus driver behaviour. *Behavioural Research in Road Safety: 14th Seminar*. Department for Transport, London: HMSO.

Dorn, L., & Matthews, G. (1995). Prediction of mood and risk appraisal from trait measures: two studies of simulated driving. *European Journal of Personality, 9*, 25–42.

Glendon, A.I., Dorn, L., Matthews, G., Gulian, E., Davies, D.R., & Debney, L.M. (1993). Reliability of the driving behaviour inventory. *Ergonomics, 37*, 727–735.

Gulian, E., Matthews, G., Glendon, A.I., Davies, D.R., & Debney, L.M. (1989). Dimensions of driver stress. *Ergonomics*, *32*, 585–602.

Lazarus, R.S., & Folkman, S. (1984). *Stress, Appraisal and Coping*. New York: Springer.

Matthews, G. (1993). Cognitive processes in driver stress, *Proceedings of the 1993 International congress of Health Psychology*. Tokyo: ICHP, pp. 90–93.

Matthews, G. (2001). A transactional model of driver stress. In Hancock, P.A., & Desmond, P.A. (Eds.), *Stress, Workload and Fatigue*. New Jersey: Lawrence Erlbaum.

Matthews, G., & Desmond, P.A. (1996). Personality and multiple dimensions of task induced fatigue: a study of simulated driving. *Personality and Individual Differences*, *25*, 443–458.

Matthews, G., Dorn, L., & Glendon, A.I. (1991). Personality correlates of driver stress. *Personality and Individual Differences*, *12*, 535–549.

Matthews, G., Dorn, L., Hoyes, T.W., Glendon, A.I., Davies, D.R., & Taylor, R.G. (1993). Driver stress and simulated driving performance: studies of risk taking and attention. In Grayson, G.B. (Ed.), *Behavioural Research in Road Safety III* (pp. 1–10). Crowthorne: Transport Research Laboratory.

Matthews, G., Sparkes, T.J., & Bygrave, H.M. (1996). Stress, attention overload and simulated driving performance. In Gale, A.G., Brown, I.D., Haslegrave, C.M., & Taylor, S.P. (Eds.), *Vision in Vehicles* (pp. 33–40). Amsterdam: Elsevier.

Matthews, G., Desmond, P.A., Joyner, L.A., & Carcardy, B. (1997). A comprehensive questionnaire measure of driver stress and affect. In Carbonell Vaya, E., & Rothengatter, J.A. (Eds.), *Traffic and Transport Psychology: Theory and Application* (pp. 317–326). Amsterdam: Pergamon Press.

Matthews, G., Dorn, L., Hoyes, T.W., Davies, D.R., Glendon, A.I., & Taylor, R.G. (1998). Driver stress and performance on a driving simulator. *Human Factors*, *40* (1), 136–149.

Matthews, G., Tsuda, A., Xin, G., & Ozeki, Y. (1999). Individual differences in driver stress vulnerability in a Japanese sample. *Ergonomics*, *42*, 401–415.

Mayhew, D.R., & Simpson, H.M. (2002). The safety value of driver education and training. *Injury Prevention*, *8*, ii3–ii8.

Rix, B., Walker, D., & Brown, R. (1997). A study of deaths and serious injuries resulting from police vehicle accidents, *Police Research Group, Home Office*. London: HMSO.

Teffner, P., Barrett, R., & Petersen, A. (2002). Stability and skill in driving. *Human Movement Science*, *21*, 749–784.

Traffic and Transport Psychology
G. Underwood (Editor)
© 2005 Elsevier Ltd. All rights reserved.

36

DOES TIME SLOW DOWN IN A CAR CRASH? DANGER, TIME PERCEPTION AND SPEED ESTIMATES

Peter Chapman[1] and Geoffrey Underwood[1]

INTRODUCTION

People often report that time appears to slow down when they experience a stressful event, for example, a car crash. If time is systematically distorted in such situations there may well be important practical implications for both drivers' behaviour during dangerous situations, and their subsequent reporting from memory of details about such events. However, conducting experimental research into this phenomenon has proved surprisingly complex. Although there is a wealth of research on time perception and estimation, most research only addresses this phenomenon indirectly. Typical experimental tasks involve remote time estimates (e.g. Pedersen & Wright, 2002), a variety of prospective duration judgments (e.g. Zakay, 1993a,b, 1998), and tapping or musical timing tasks (e.g. Boltz, 1995). While many of these tasks suggest that stress may indeed affect time perception, the tasks that are used are often far removed from the actual distortion of subjective time in real-world stressful events. In this chapter, we introduce a new task that may shed light on distortions of subjective time when driving in dangerous situations, however, before describing the task it is worth briefly reviewing some of the past work on time perception generally, and related to emotional or stressful events in particular.

TIME PERCEPTION

The study of people's perception of time has a distinguished history in psychology. William James, often seen as the father of modern psychology devotes a full chapter of *The Principles of Psychology* (1890) to the perception of time, similar to the space given to topics such as

---

[1] Accident Research Unit, School of Psychology, University of Nottingham, Nottingham NG7 2RD, UK.
E-mail: peter.chapman@nottingham.ac.uk (P. Chapman).

attention or memory. James' basic observation on the perception of time lies at the heart of resolving contradictory results in the time perception literature:

In general, a time filled with varied and interesting experiences seems short in passing, but long as we look back. On the other hand, a tract of time empty of experiences seems long in passing but in retrospect short (James, 1890/1950, p. 624).

James here makes the distinction that is often drawn between prospective time estimates (those made while the time interval is being experienced) and retrospective time estimates (those made later, when looking back at a time interval in memory). This difference between prospective and retrospective tasks, or experienced duration vs. remembered duration (Block, 2003), turns out to be critical to understand before making any predictions about what might happen to subjective time during a dangerous driving situation. From James' observation we might predict that a driver in a dangerous situation would be experiencing "varied and interesting experiences" and hence would experience time to speed up prospectively, but slow down retrospectively. Plenty of subsequent research has supported and refined James' observation. Thus retrospective time estimates do seem to increase as a function of the amount of information stored (e.g. Ornstein, 1969), although subsequent theories have suggested that the particularly important types of information are those providing segmentation of the interval (e.g. Poynter, 1983) or changes in context (e.g. Block, 1978, 1982). The key thing about such retrospective judgments is that, the participant is not aware that they will be making time estimates at the time they experience the interval or event whose temporal extent will later be judged. One difficulty with using retrospective judgment tasks is that it is often only possible to obtain a single observation from each participant, since once they are alerted to the importance of time judgments they may attend to the passage of time in later tasks in an unnatural manner.

In contrast to retrospective tasks, in prospective tasks, the participant is encouraged to attend to the passage of time, making the presentation of multiple stimuli in complex within-subjects designs possible. A variety of different prospective tasks have been used ranging from simple numerical judgments to interval reproduction tasks in which participants might have to press a button when they felt a specific interval had passed. Although there is plenty of evidence that different prospective tasks produce quantitatively different results (e.g. Zakay, 1993a,b) there is broad agreement on some of the factors that influence prospective judgments, and notable similarities between most of the theories that have been used to explain these influences. As James (*op. cit.*) noted, filled intervals tend to result in the feeling that time is passing rapidly, and consequently people make short verbal estimates or reproduced time intervals (e.g. Hicks, Miller, & Kinsbourne, 1976; Zakay & Block, 1997) compared to unfilled intervals. However, it is not simply the nature of the interval that is important in this case, but the way in which attention is devoted to it (Underwood, 1975; Underwood & Swain, 1973). Many current theories assume that people have broadly accurate timing information available from some form of internal clock (e.g. Hoagland, 1933, 1935; Matell & Meck, 2000; Treisman, 1963). Although the clock is generally thought to be accurate it may be influenced to a small degree by factors such as body temperature (e.g. Hancock, 1993; Wearden & Penton-Voak, 1995). Nonetheless the ability to use information from any central pacemaker requires the allocation of attention to these timing signals. As attention to such signals increases, so may experienced duration, and when attention is removed from these signals timing becomes less accurate (e.g. Brown, 1998; Macar, Grondin, & Casini, 1994). The link between mental workload and prospective duration estimations has been found to be so direct in some circumstances that it has been proposed that prospective judgments can be used as a sensitive, practical and unobtrusive measure of mental workload (Zakay, Block, & Tsal, 1999).

The problem with typical prospective explanations and theories is that they intuitively predict that in a stressful driving situation time should appear to pass rapidly, either because of the speeding up of a biological clock, or because of a high mental workload removing attention from an internal timing signal. This is exactly the opposite of the real-world phenomenon that we were hoping to explain, but it does raise the possibility that the idea of time slowing down in a car crash is actually an illusion brought about memory. Perhaps subjective time as assessed by prospective tasks actually speeds up in dangerous situations, but people do not attend to the experience until later, at which point they erroneously conclude that it slowed down based on the amount of information, contextual change etc. available during the event. Of course, the amount of information and workload present in a car crash is not the only thing that is unusual about such events. One key issue that needs to be considered is the emotional and threatening nature of such a circumstance.

TIME AND EMOTION

Although a number of studies have explored aspects of time estimation with respect to emotional stimuli, there is one of particular interest in its exploration of arousal and valence of emotion and their effects of prospective time judgments. Angrilli, Cherubini, Pavese, and Manfredini (1997) had participants view a series of slides taken from the International Affective Picture System (IAPS; Centre for the Study of Emotion and Attention, 1995) for either 2, 4 or 6 s. The slides systematically differed in valence (positive or negative) and arousal (high and low) based on previous ratings of the slides (e.g. Lang, Greenwald, Bradley, & Hamm, 1993). One group of participants used an analogue scale (20 cm, graduated from 0 to 10 s) to rate the perceived duration of each slide, while a second group of participants used an interval reproduction method in which they had to hold down a button for as long as they felt the slide had been present. Both groups of participants made substantial underestimates of the true durations of slides (a mean underestimate of around 25% of the original stimulus presentation time), with the underestimates being larger in the reproduction task than in the analogue scale task. There was an interaction between arousal and valence, with the largest underestimates being made to high-arousal positive slides (described as an erotic couple, a naked couple and a kissing couple) and to low-arousal negative slides (described as a big spider on banana, rat in the dirt and dead cow). Less dramatic, but still significant underestimates were observed for high-arousal negative slides (showing mutilated bodies) and low-arousal positive slides (babies and animals), though these underestimates were no larger than those observed for neutral slides. They also found that for high-arousal slides (positive or negative) underestimates were greater when the original display time was longer. A similar pattern was observed for low-arousal slides, except that large underestimates were also obtained at the shortest (2 s) slide presentations.

Angrilli et al. (1997) concluded that their low-arousal results were consistent with the predictions of attentional theories of prospective time estimations. Thus, the greater attentional demands of the negative stimuli (as evidenced by electrodermal activity) caused subsequent underestimates of duration. However, they conclude that understanding the high-arousal results would require a different explanation, and propose that for high-arousal stimuli a physiological distinction between avoidance and approach reactions needs to be considered. However, one problem with the Angrilli et al. (1997) study is deciding how to interpret the results from their neutral condition. Angrilli et al. (1997) exclude the neutral condition from most of their analysis and discussion. In fact, neutral stimuli in their paper are actually reported to produce greater time underestimates than emotional ones ($M = -0.268$ for neutral slides, $M = -0.251$ for the average emotional slide). This suggests that their results might be better interpreted as showing relative overestimates of time for high-arousal negative stimuli and low-arousal positive stimuli rather than general time underestimates for emotional stimuli. It is also questionable whether the arousal dimension as assessed in positive stimuli is really the same thing as arousal in negative stimuli when IAPS stimuli are used. It is clear that assessments of erotic IAPS stimuli are gender specific (Lang, Bradley, & Cuthbert, 2001) and may be better considered a special case rather than part of a continuum of emotional reaction. The idea that high-arousal negative stimuli might produce prospective overestimates is exciting in that it would be consistent with the idea of time subjectively slowing down in a car crash. However, it is important to note that the results from this condition are still underestimates of duration, and no different to estimates made to low-arousal pleasant stimuli, or neutral. Another issue with this type of task is that the stimuli are static slides. It is difficult to be sure that results obtained when viewing a static slide will actually apply in real-world situations. More realistic studies have been performed, and although such studies have explored time estimates for emotional films, typically a retrospective paradigm has been used.

Loftus, Schooler, Boone, and Kline (1987) had participants watch a short film of a bank robbery and later answer a series of questions about the film including a retrospective duration estimate. Participants almost universally made dramatic overestimates of the film duration (thus a 30 s film received a mean duration estimate of 147 s in Experiment 1). In Experiment 3, two versions of the film were used, a high stress and low stress version. Large overestimations were observed in both cases, but were significantly higher for the stressful version than the low stress version. Loftus et al. (1987) set out to find evidence based on the storage size hypothesis (Ornstein, 1969) that these overestimates could be related to more information in memory for the stressful stimuli. They also predicted that gender differences in estimates could be explained by women finding the film more stressful than men and hence making longer estimates. However, neither of these specific hypotheses was supported. No overall correlation between time estimates and any of memory quantity, memory accuracy, or arousal ratings was observed. Thus, although the study demonstrates dramatic retrospective overestimates of a filmed stressful event the precise mechanism underlying the effect remains rather unclear.

DOES TIME SLOW DOWN IN A CAR CRASH?

The literature reviewed so far leaves little doubt that retrospective tasks are likely to produce large overestimates consistent with the idea that remembered dangerous events will appear to have passed slowly. However, the evidence from prospective studies is much less clear. We thus decided to use a novel type of prospective task to explore perception of time in filmed dangerous events. Our logic was that if time perception really is distorted at the moment a stressful event is experienced, participants should be systematically biased in their ability to judge the actual speed at which a film of such an event is playing. If time really slows down in stressful events, then a film watched at the correct speed, but without any subjective feeling of danger, should be judged as playing too fast. The following study was designed to explore this possibility by having drivers watch a series of driving events, some dangerous, some safer, whose speed had been systematically distorted and asking them to judge what distortion had been made. For this initial study, two sample populations were immediately available, a group of young recently qualified novice drivers, and a group of older, more experienced drivers. Theoretically, there are reasons to think that both age and driving experience might influence time estimates in this paradigm, thus despite the limited statistical power of between subjects comparisons with relatively small sample sizes, it was decided to take half the population from each group in order to gain some predictions about what might be found if larger better controlled populations took part in such a task.

METHOD

Participants

The participants were 20 drivers in two groups. Ten were young novice drivers with a mean age of 19.2 years, a mean driving experience of 1.4 years, and an average annual mileage of 910 miles. The other group consisted of 10 older more experienced drivers, with a mean age of 53.1 years, a mean driving experience of 29.9 years, and a mean annual mileage of 6400 miles.

Stimuli/apparatus

Twenty short sections of driving similar to that described by Chapman and Underwood (1998a,b) were selected. Each section showed 8 s of film recorded from a moving vehicle in traffic taken from the driver's point of view. These consisted of 10 pairs of stimuli, such that each item in a pair showed a section of driving on similar roads and traffic conditions, but in one of the pair a dangerous event occurred, while in the other item in the pair events were generally safe normal driving events. The safety of events was assessed by having a wide selection of previous participants view the full films and press a response button when they felt that a dangerous event was occurring. The films were then digitised and edited using Apple Final Cut Pro. Each clip was then sped up or slowed down using Final Cut. When the film was slowed down, footage was then removed from the end of the clip such that the total clip duration remained at 8 s. When the film was speeded up additional footage was added to the end of the clip to retain a total length of 8 s. Five versions of each clip were thus created, one at 80% of its true speed (slowed down), one at 90% (slightly slowed down) one at 100% (the original clip), one at 110% (slightly speeded up), and one at 120% (speeded up). The 20 films were then edited into a series stimulus tapes in which the order and presentation speed of individual films was counterbalanced such that each type of film was always displayed at a mean speed of 100%. Each tape contained 20 clips, half dangerous, half safe, and within each film type there were clips shown at each of the five possible speeds. Final tapes were output onto MiniDV tapes and played using a Sony DSR-11 digital tape deck connected to an LG television monitor with a $40 \times 30 \, cm^2$ screen at a distance of 70 cm (subtending a visual angle of approximately 30° horizontally).

Procedure

Participants were informed that they would be viewing a series of brief films of driving situations, some of which had been digitally sped up, some of which had been digitally slowed down, and some of which were playing at the correct speed. They first viewed a brief film of pedestrians walking through a shopping centre and were shown what this film looked like slowed down to 70, 80 and 90% of its true speed, played at the correct speed (100%) and sped up to 110, 120 and 130% of its true speed. They then viewed the series of 20 clips of driving situations and after viewing each clip circled a number on a seven point scale to indicate their estimate of the speed the current clip was being played at. The response alternatives were 70, 80, 90, 100, 110, 120 and 130%. The scale was labelled as much too slow (70%), correct (100%) and much too fast (130%).

RESULTS

Data were analysed in an analysis of variance with one between subjects factor with two levels (whether the drivers were older more experienced drivers, or younger novice drivers), and two within subjects factors, one with five levels (the true film speed being judged—80, 90, 100, 110 or 120%) and one with two levels (whether the driving situation was dangerous or relatively safe). There were significant main effects of both within subjects factors; driving situation, $F(4.72) = 38.67$, MSE $= 61.31$, $f = 1.47$, $p < 0.001$, and true film speed, $F(1, 18) = 35.20$, MSE $= 106.29$, $f = 1.40$, $p < 0.001$. The former effect simply demonstrates that participants were sensitive to the manipulations in film speed that were made, while the latter effect comes about because dangerous driving situations were generally rated as having been sped up

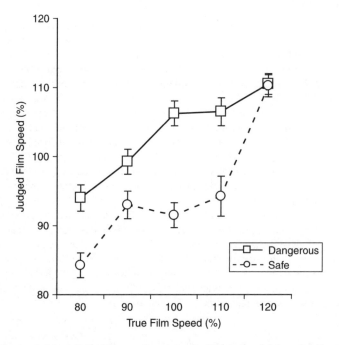

Figure 1. Mean rated speed of videos as function of whether the driving situation was dangerous or safe and of the true speed at which the film was being played. Error bars show the standard error above and below the mean.

(mean rating 103.3%), while safer situations were generally rated as having been slowed down (mean rating 94.65%). There was also a significant interaction between the two factors that is shown in Figure 1, $F(4,72) = 3.52$, MSE $= 90.74$, $f = 0.44$, $p = 0.011$. Analysis of simple main effects demonstrates that the difference in speed ratings between dangerous and safe situations is significant, $p < 0.05$ at all levels of true film speed except when the film was sped up to 120%.

Although the older, more experienced drivers did tend to give generally higher speed ratings than the younger, novice drivers, (100.2% vs. 97.75%), the main effect of driver experience was not significant, $F(1,18) = 2.53$, MSE $= 118.7$, $f = 0.37$, $p = 0.129$, and nor was the interaction between driver experience and situation type, $F(1,18) = 1.44$, MSE $= 196.3$, $f = 0.28$, $p = 0.246$. Although this main effect and interaction does not reach significance, the relatively small sample size and relatively large effect sizes as assessed by Cohen's f suggest that it might be worth exploring these effects with a larger sample. Analysis of simple main effects on this interaction does suggest that there is a marginally significant effect of driver experience in dangerous situations, $F(1,36) = 3.92$, MSE $= 112.5$, $f = 0.47$, $p = 0.055$. This is illustrated in Figure 2.

The interaction between driver experience and true film speed is plotted in Figure 3. Once again, this interaction does not reach significance, $F(4,72) = 1.705$, MSE $= 61.31$, $f = 0.31$, $p = 0.158$, although analysis of simple main effects does indicate a significant effect of driver

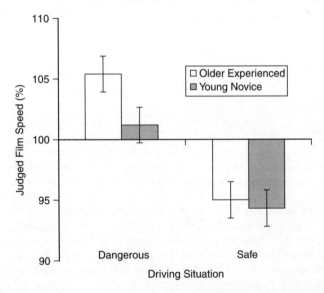

Figure 2. Mean rated speed of videos as function of whether the driving situation was dangerous or safe and whether the raters were relatively old experienced drivers, or younger novice drivers. In each case accurate responding would give a mean speed of 100%, numbers greater than 100 indicate that participants felt the video had been sped up, while those below 100 indicate that they felt the video had been slowed down. Error bars show the standard error above and below the mean.

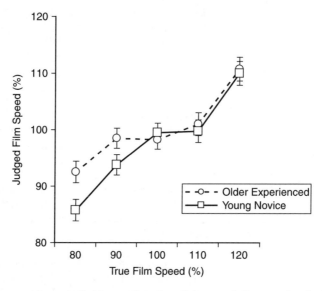

Figure 3. Mean rated speed of videos as function of the actual film speed and whether the raters were older more experienced drivers or younger novice drivers. Error bars show the standard error above and below the mean.

experience for true film speeds of 80%, $F(1,90) = 6.26$, MSE $= 72.79$, $f = 0.26$, $p = 0.014$, and a marginal effect at true speeds of 90%, $F(1,90) = 3.10$, MSE $= 72.79$, $f = 0.19$, $p = 0.082$.

DISCUSSION

The clearest aspect of the results is that, as predicted, there is a substantial main effect of danger, with the more dangerous films being judged as playing too fast, while the safer ones are generally judged to be playing too slowly. Our initial explanation for this effect is that time does subjectively slow down in dangerous circumstances—when a video of such an event is seen playing at normal speed, it will thus feel as if it is passing too quickly. Note that although the task can be seen as a prospective speed judgment task, part of this interpretation of the results is that a comparison is being made with some form of reference event. Thus, we are not assuming that the participants in our study are actually experiencing high levels of arousal, instead they are comparing the current stimulus with one that they recognise from actual events in which they were experiencing arousal. Unfortunately, a directly contrary explanation of these results is also possible. It is conceivable that participants are reacting to our stimuli exactly in the way they would if they were encountering the stimuli in the real world. The logic here would be that time in stressful situations actually speeds up, and this is why they judge stressful films to be playing too fast. This interpretation of our results is consistent with some other research using prospective tasks, but seems to provide the counterintuitive suggestion that time does not slow down in dangerous situations—it actually speeds up, but we are fooled by memory into thinking that it slowed down at the time. As in many other prospective time estimation tasks we have found a clear effect, but have to be extremely careful in how we interpret it. One way to resolve the debate might be to vary the task in such a way that it is more, or less realistic, measure physiological arousal and see whether induced arousal when performing the task was determining the degree of speed overestimation observed.

Another way to resolve the prospective vs. retrospective account of these results would be to explore variations in participants' previous exposure to such circumstances. If the first explanation is correct, then participants would have to have previously experienced similar dangerous events before any time distortion would occur—if we have not learned to expect time to slow down in dangerous driving situations, our speed judgments of these tapes should not be systematically biased in this way. The prediction would thus be that more experienced drivers would produce greater overestimates of speed in dangerous driving situations than novices with less experience of such situations. This is precisely the trend that is visible in Figure 2, although we need to be careful not to overinterpret an interaction that does not reach significance. It is also important to note that our participant groups differed dramatically in age as well as in driving experience. Many researchers have found time estimation differences as a function of age (e.g. Block, Zakay, & Hancock, 1998; see also, Draaisma, 2004), so it would be important to dissociate these variables as much as possible in future research.

The current results are interesting in that they imply that there are likely to be large differences in the temporal experience of dangerous and safer driving situations. The novel technique of assessing time perception leaves a number of questions unanswered about the precise mechanism underlying these differences, so much, so that at the moment it is not possible to firmly conclude that time does not actually speed up in dangerous situations. Nonetheless, the large differences observed clearly highlight that an important effect exists and suggest clear future research strategies to explore the cause of and potential implications of these biases.

ACKNOWLEDGEMENTS

This research was partly supported by a pump-priming grant from the School of Psychology, Nottingham University. The authors would like to thank Dr Nicola Phelps for her assistance in testing and providing access to the group of older more experienced drivers.

REFERENCES

Angrilli, A., Cherubini, P., Pavese, A., & Manfredini, S. (1997). The influence of affective factors on time perception. *Perception and Psychophysics, 59*, 972–982.

Block, R.A. (1978). Remembered duration: effects of event and sequence complexity. *Memory and Cognition, 6*, 320–326.

Block, R.A. (1982). Temporal judgments and contextual change. *Journal of Experimental Psychology: Learning, Memory, & Cognition, 8*, 530–544.

Block, R.A. (2003). Psychological timing without a timer. In Helfrich, H. (Ed.), *Time and Mind II: Information Processing Perspectives* (pp. 41–60). Cambridge, MA: Hogrefe & Huber.

Block, R.A., Zakay, D., & Hancock, P.A. (1998). Human aging and duration judgments: a meta-analytic review. *Psychology and Aging, 13*, 584–596.

Boltz, M.G. (1995). Effects of event structure on retrospective duration judgments. *Perception and Psychophysics, 57*, 1080–1096.

Brown, S.W. (1998). Automaticity versus timesharing in timing and tracking dual-task performance. *Psychological Research, 61*, 71–81.

Chapman, P.R., & Underwood, G. (1998a). Visual search of driving situations: danger and experience. *Perception, 27*, 951–964.

Chapman, P., & Underwood, G. (1998b). Visual search of dynamic scenes: event types and the role of experience in viewing driving situations. In Underwood, G. (Ed.), *Eye Guidance in Reading and Scene Perception* (pp. 371–396). Oxford: Elsevier.

Centre for the Study of Emotion and Attention (1995). *The International Affective Picture System* (photographic slides). Gainesville, FL: CSEA.

Draaisma, D. (2004). *Why Life Speeds Up as You Get Older: How Memories Shape the Past.* Cambridge, UK: Cambridge University.

Hancock, P.A. (1993). Body temperature influence on time perception. *Journal of General Psychology, 120*, 197–215.

Hicks, R.E., Miller, G.W., & Kinsbourne, M. (1976). Prospective and retrospective judgments of time as a function of amount of information processed. *American Journal of Psychology, 89*, 719–730.

Hoagland, H. (1933). The physiological control of judgments of duration: evidence for a chemical clock. *Journal of General Psychology, 9*, 267–287.

Hoagland, H. (1935). *Pacemakers in Relation to Aspects of Behavior.* New York: Macmillan.

James, W. (1890/1950). *The Principles of Psychology.* Vol. 1. New York: Dover Publications, Inc.

Lang, P.J., Bradely, M.M., & Cuthbert, B.N. (2001). *International Affective Picture System (IAPS): Instruction Manual and Affective Ratings, Technical Report A-5.* Florida: The Center for Research in Psychophysiology, University of Florida.

Lang, P.J., Greenwald, M.K., Bradley, M.M., & Hamm, A.O. (1993). Looking at pictures: affective, facial, visceral, and behavioural reactions. *Psychophysiology, 30*, 261–273.

Loftus, E.F., Schooler, J.W., Boone, S.M., & Kline, D. (1987). Time went by so slowly: overestimation of event duration by males and females. *Applied Cognitive Psychology, 1*, 3–13.

Macar, F., Grondin, S., & Casini, L. (1994). Controlled attention sharing influences time estimation. *Memory and Cognition, 22*, 673–686.

Matell, M.S., & Meck, W.H. (2000). Neuropsychological mechanisms of interval timing behavior. *BioEssays, 22*, 94–103.

Ornstein, R.E. (1969). *On the Experience of Time.* Harmandsworth, England: Penguin.

Pedersen, A.C.I., & Wright, D.B. (2002). Do differences in event descriptions cause differences in duration estimates? *Applied Cognitive Psychology, 16*, 769–783.

Poynter, W.D. (1983). Duration judgment and the segmentation of experience. *Memory and Cognition, 11*, 77–82.

Treisman, M. (1963). Temporal discrimination and the indifference interval: implications for a model of the "internal clock". *Psychological Monographs, 77*, 1–31.

Underwood, G. (1975). Attention and the perception of duration during encoding and retrieval. *Perception, 4*, 291–296.

Underwood, G., & Swain, R.A. (1973). Selectivity of attention and the perception of duration. *Perception, 2,* 101–105.

Wearden, J.H., & Penton-Voak, I.S. (1995). Feeling the heat: body temperature and the rate of subjective time, revisited. *The Quarterly Journal of Experimental Psychology, 51B,* 97–120.

Zakay, D. (1993a). Time estimation methods—do they influence prospective duration estimates. *Perception, 22,* 91–101.

Zakay, D. (1993b). Relative and absolute duration judgments under prospective and retrospective paradigms. *Perception and Psychophysics, 54,* 656–664.

Zakay, D. (1998). Attention allocation policy influences prospective timing. *Psychonomic Bulletin and Review, 5,* 114–118.

Zakay, D., & Block, R.A. (1997). Temporal cognition. *Current Directions in Psychological Science, 6,* 12–16.

Zakay, D., Block, R.A., & Tsal, Y. (1999). Prospective duration estimation and performance. In Gopher, D., & Koriat, A. (Eds.), *Attention and Performance XVII Cognitive regulation of Performance: Interaction of Theory and Application* (pp. 557–580). Cambridge, MA: MIT Press.

Traffic and Transport Psychology
G. Underwood (Editor)
© 2005 Elsevier Ltd. All rights reserved.

37

DRIVING WITHOUT AWARENESS

*Katja Karrer[1], Susanne Briest[1], Thomas Vöhringer-Kuhnt[1],
Thorb Baumgarten[1] and Robert Schleicher[2]*

INTRODUCTION

In situations causing tiredness and boredom, everyone has experienced states of "absence" that seem like sleeping with open eyes. Although this phenomenon may be harmless when listening to a long speech, it poses a serious hazard on the road. Particularly, on long journeys under monotonous road conditions, many drivers experience short lapses of attention from which they seem to awaken, even if their eyes were not actually closed.

While research has established that this phenomenon poses a serious safety risk on the road, little effort has been done to systematically investigate the phenomenon. Different approaches have been taken to defining it, however, and we will review these briefly in the following.

One of the earliest publications dealing with this subject was Miles' (1929) study "Sleeping with the Eyes Open", which carried the provocative subtitle "a motorist or anyone may actually be asleep, even if the eyes are seen to be open". In it, Miles reflects on the chronological order of closing one's eyes and falling asleep, and concludes that the first is not a precondition for the second. Unwillingness to fall asleep may prevent a person's eyelids from closing, but that person may still enter what is clearly the physiological state of sleep. The will to keep one's eyes open is triggered by the importance of a certain task and the personal responsibility involved, which applies especially to the case of driving.

According to Williams and Shor (1970), an even earlier article from the year 1921 was the first to mention the phenomenon of "road hypnotism", and it was the first in a series of articles dealing with what later became known as "highway hypnosis:" driving in a trance-like state while gazing at a fixation point on the horizon, unable to react adequately to hazardous

---

[1] Centre of Human–Machine Systems, Berlin University of Technology, Berlin, Germany. *E-mail:* karrer@zmms.
tu-berlin.de (K. Karrer).
[2] University of Cologne, Cologne, Germany.

situations. Williams (1963), who coined this latter expression, suggests a number of reasons leading to this hypnosis, such as monotonous roads and bright points of fixation. He sees fatigue as a condition that promotes but is not necessary for inducing this trance-like state. Other authors like Shor and Thackray (1970) see the phenomenon as closely related to deep drowsiness and falling asleep. They report 10 conditions that must be fulfilled for highway hypnosis to occur, including repetition and monotony, minor physical fatigue, and the ease of learning the task, which leads to it becoming "automatic".

The correlation between highway hypnosis and fatigue has been described frequently but never explained. Schachter (1976) describes the hypnagogic state in general (without specific reference to highway hypnosis) as typified by the drowsy interval between waking and sleeping. Hypnosis is therefore a dreamlike state of sleep onset, with certain characteristics like visual and auditory imagery, suggestibility, slow eye movements, and low voltage waves in the electroencephalogram (EEG). Beyond providing such descriptions as the aforementioned, theories about highway hypnosis have done little to explain its origin and nature. They have, however, put forward a very accurate overall descriptive analysis of highway hypnosis as a trance-like state, with the expressionless or glassy stare as one of its typical physical characteristics (e.g. Williams, 1963).

Wertheim (1978) made important progress in the research in attempting to validate a theory about eye movements and their impact on highway hypnosis. As one of the few to conduct systematic studies of the phenomenon under experimental conditions, Wertheim can be considered a pioneer in this field of research. He proposed that highway hypnosis is in fact a shift from "attentive" oculomotor control guided by external stimuli to "intentive" activity carried out by internal motor programs. Specific eye movements in a visual surrounding of high predictability initiate this shift. More than 10 years after his experimental studies, Wertheim (1991) delivered a theoretical analysis of highway hypnosis, in which he wrote that although the term "highway hypnosis" was now en vogue, the description of this phenomenon as a hypnotic trance had not helped explain the factors generating and inducing this state. Again, he explains the attention shift from outside stimuli to internal processes, comparing it to the controlled and automatic mode proposed by Schneider and Shiffrin (1977). He emphasizes that the shift is not caused by monotony, but by predictability. Thus, if we drive into a fog bank, visual stimuli are reduced and less varied but we also become more alert.

At the same conference (Vision in Vehicles III) where Wertheim presented his theoretical analysis surveying the research landscape, other researchers presented papers on this topic as well. One of them, Kerr (1991) proposed a new term for the phenomenon: "the driving without attention mode". He sees the main characteristic of this state as the loss of awareness due to automatizing processes of perception induced by a highly predictable visual scene, which is consistent with Wertheim's suggestion. One of the main points that distinguishes his view of highway hypnosis from the earlier definitions of the phenomenon is that he does not assume it to be fatigue related. Kerr describes a state of attention failure and assumes that it might be independent of fatigue or drowsiness. At the same time, Brown (1991) claims that a new definition of the phenomenon is necessary. A differentiation between how sleep, trance and attention each influence the phenomenon would enable experimental validation. Brown (1994) himself again uses a descriptive definition of what he calls "driving without awareness" which assumes that drivers are oblivious to impending collisions.

Some newer characterizations of the phenomenon, such as the above-mentioned one by Kerr (1991), suggest that driving without awareness is not necessarily a symptom of fatigue but may be an attention or even memory lapse. The fact of failing to remember what happened on the road during a longer time interval is essential for what is also called the "time gap experience", as has been proposed by Chapman, Ismail and Underwood (2005), who refer to Reed (1972). On the other hand, some authors retain the assumption that driving without awareness (DWA), as it will be called in this article, is clearly linked to fatigue and impending micro-sleep attacks. Horne and Reyner (1999) describe DWA in the context of fatigue, while Sagberg (1999) sees it as an precursor to falling asleep. Nevertheless, he argues that even well rested drivers may experience sleep-related states like DWA under certain conditions, possibly without a preceding phase of subjectively experienced fatigue.

In our view, DWA is clearly linked to fatigue and drowsiness. Hence, we make recourse to the earlier definitions, such as those of Williams and Shor (1970), who define the state as "a tendency to become drowsy and fall asleep when driving an automobile". We claim that this state is characteristic of the drowsy interval between waking and sleeping, resulting from the will to keep the eyes open, when the importance of a task hinders a person from falling asleep. As has been stated by Galley and Churan (2002), people can learn to keep their eyes open under certain circumstances and carry out necessary activities to some degree while actually sleeping. A condition that facilitates or evokes the phenomenon is ostensibly a highly predictable road setting (e.g. Thiffault & Bergeron, 2003). We believe that an attention shift from outside stimuli to inner processes may occur before people fall asleep with their eyes open.

The aim of a series of experiments we carried out in a driving simulator was to analyse the fatigue progression of drivers in order to develop algorithms for driver state monitoring. In pilot studies in a driving simulator in 2002, some drivers left their lane with their eyes wide open. Because we wanted to learn more about this phenomenon, we developed a classification system including definitions for DWA and micro-sleep events. In a large follow-up study in 2003, which provided the data basis for the findings presented in this chapter, we systematically documented events we recognized as DWA in a video analysis of the test drives.

As mentioned above, for us DWA is a dangerous state during which drivers are unaware of oncoming road hazards and their eyes seem to glaze over. In our opinion, this is a serious warning sign of fatigue. We clearly distinguish this state from broader concepts like a lack of "situation awareness", as DWA does not refer to a momentary distraction with various possible causes. In our study, trained observers analysed video files of the series of experiments and inserted a marker in the software INTERACT when one of the following criteria for DWA was fulfilled:

- if the driver stared into space and then his/her head jolted up abruptly or nodded forward,
- if the driver's eyes rolled back,
- if the driver started to squint with his/her eyes half-open or
- if the driver stared into space and made a driving error.

The criteria for recording a micro-sleep were the following:

- The driver's eyes were fully closed (covered pupils) for at least 2 s and he/she made a driving error.
- The driver's eyes were fully closed for less than 2 s, but afterwards his/her head jolted up abruptly or nodded forward.

The difference between DWA and micro-sleep is the open or closed state of the driver's eyes. In consequence, DWA can be regarded as sleeping with open eyes.

The opening and closure of the eye and hence the blink behaviour is crucial for the prediction of driver fatigue, as it is a well-known fact that increased drowsiness correlates positively to prolonged eyelid closure (e.g. Galley & Andrés, 1996; Hargutt, Tietze & Krüger, 2003). In the development of driver support systems to prevent car accidents due to micro-sleep, the fact of sleeping with open eyes has largely been disregarded. The documentation of DWA events in this study can help us to learn more about the nature of the phenomenon. Furthermore, the relation to the occurrence of micro-sleep will help to find out how fatigue plays a role. Moreover, we want to analyse which characteristics set the subgroup of people who displayed DWA apart from the rest. The correlation of DWA to parameters from EEG recordings, electrooculogram (EOG) recordings, blink behaviour and self-rating will give evidence about the predictability of the phenomenon and its differentiation from micro-sleep events.

METHOD

The setting

Our study was conducted from July to August 2003 with 83 participants at the Berlin University of Technology. In it, we drew a stratified random sample regarding age, gender, distribution of driver licences in Germany (see Table 1), etc. and balanced it according to the time of day (morning, midday, evening). We used a between-group experimental design with different times of day, and each subject had to participate once at one time of day.

Table 1. Holders of driver licences in Germany (Federal Statistical Office, 1998).

	Male	Per cent	Female	Per cent
18–30	6280	12.66	5339	10.76
31–40	6775	13.65	5838	11.77
41–60	9756	19.66	7805	15.73
60+	4864	9.80	2964	5.97
Total	27,675	55.77	21,945	44.23

The subjects had to perform a monotonous driving task in a driving simulator. They were seated in a real car (VW Bora) with a screen in front of them (see Figure 1).

The task was to drive on a monotonous motorway without any other traffic. This highly predictable condition was used to evoke fatigue even in a relatively short driving time.

Figure 1. The setting in the driving simulator.

The average driving time was about 2 h. For the realistic feeling of driving, subjects heard motor and driving noises.

The data sources

We used different data sources in our experiment. One indicator for drowsiness consisted of a calculation of frequency and duration of alpha spindles the EEG (Tietze, 2000). Further indicators of fatigue were saccadic parameters from the EOG (Galley and Schleicher, University of Cologne), blink parameters (video-based, bright-pupil and dark-pupil measurement) from a sensory system called WakeUp by SMI, and self-rated fatigue level of the drivers (Galley & Churan, 2002) on a 10-point Likert scale (1 = extremely drowsy, 10 = fully alert). Furthermore, we used the data from the video analysis including a four-stage drowsiness rating by trained observers (Wierwille & Ellsworth, 1994) and the documented micro-sleep and DWA events, according to our definitions mentioned above.

Data preparation

All data were transferred to an SPSS file based on 1-min time sequences. The subjective assessment of fatigue was interpolated because of the small number of data points (subjects were asked every 30 min).

This file included the EEG data (alpha spindle), EOG data (saccadic amplitude, saccadic duration, saccadic velocities, etc.), interpolated subjective assessments (self-ratings), blink parameters (blink duration, opening amplitude, closure amplitude, etc.). In addition, the file contained the frequency of DWA and micro-sleep events.

RESULTS

Descriptive analysis

In total, we found that 15 of 83 (18.1%) of the subjects showed evidence of the phenomenon DWA. Thirteen of these 15 subjects showed both micro-sleep and DWA and only two subjects showed DWA only (see Figure 2).

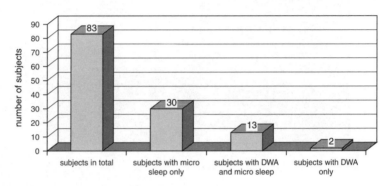

Figure 2. Number of subjects with micro-sleep and DWA.

As mentioned earlier, we drew a representative sample regarding age, gender and distribution of driver licences in Germany. Figure 3 shows the proportion of drivers within the four age groups 18–30 years, 31–40 years, 41–60 years and over 61 years for the complete sample and for the DWA sample for comparison. Whereas the proportion of 18–30- and 31–40-year-old drivers in the complete sample is the same, we find a higher percentage of young drivers (46.7%) in the DWA sample and a smaller percentage of drivers between 31–40 years (13.4%).

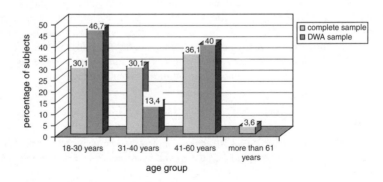

Figure 3. Distribution of age for the complete and DWA sample.

In the next step, we looked at gender differences between the overall sample and the group of subjects with DWA. We noticed that there are far more male subjects than female subjects in the sample with DWA (Figure 4). The difference in the frequencies of male and female subjects is significant (chi-square test, $p < 0.05$).

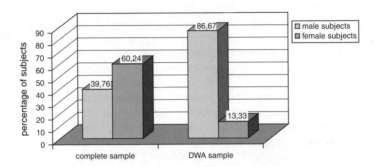

Figure 4. Gender differences between overall sample and DWA sample.

The video analysis revealed that the occurrence of DWA is related to driving errors (lane crossing). We found a total number of 260 lane-crossing events in the DWA sample, and 87 DWA events that included a driving error as such. This is a percentage of 33.5%, which means that one in three DWA events is accompanied by a driving error. For 14 of the 15 subjects with DWA, we found at least one DWA event with a driving error per subject. Figure 5 demonstrates the overall number of DWA events and the number of DWA events with a driving error.

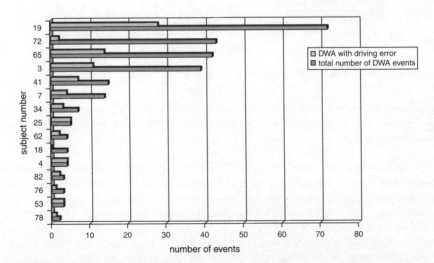

Figure 5. Total number of DWA events and DWA events with a driving error.

Interestingly, we found that two of the five drivers with two or less driving errors (subjects 72, 76 and 82) were professional drivers. This special group should be further analysed with respect to their ability to sleep with open eyes without making driving errors, as has been discussed in the theoretical literature (Galley & Churan, 2002).

Another question we wanted to answer was which phenomenon, DWA or micro-sleep, appears first over the period of driving. As stated in the introduction, the difference between DWA and micro-sleep were the open eyes of the subject. Observational criteria like the jerky body movements or driving errors were the same for DWA and micro-sleep.

Figure 6 shows the first occurrence of DWA vs. micro-sleep for each of the 13 subjects showing both phenomena. There is no clear pattern in the order of whether DWA occurs before or after micro-sleep. It is apparent that several subjects have only a minor time interval between the first occurrence of DWA and micro-sleep, with a mean value of 18 min. Seventy-seven per cent of the subjects have a maximal time difference of 15 min.

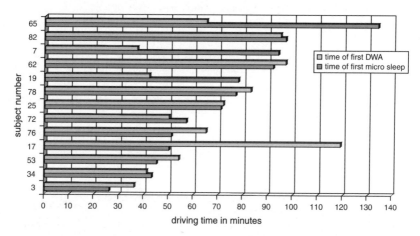

Figure 6. Time of first DWA event and micro-sleep event for each subject.

All subjects except number three had the first micro-sleep or DWA after a driving time of more than 30 min. This is probably the time span required to show the fatiguing effect of the monotonous conditions.

To summarize these descriptive results, we found that 18% of our subjects experienced the phenomenon DWA. The complete sample of 83 subjects and the DWA subgroup differed in the distribution of age and gender. We found more young subjects and a significantly higher proportion of male drivers in the DWA sample than in the complete sample. One-third of the DWA events overall include a driving error. Among the subjects with two or less DWA occurrences including a driving error, there are three professional drivers. Regarding the chronological order of the occurrence of DWA vs. micro-sleep, we find no predominant sequence worthy of note.

Correlations with EEG, EOG, blink parameters and subjective assessment

The next step in the data analysis was to calculate correlations (Spearman's rho) between the frequency of DWA events per minute and the parameters from EEG, EOG, blink parameters and subjective assessments.

Although all correlations are significant, the first two (mean alpha spindle and subjective alertness) are not substantially high. Therefore, we decided to exclude these correlations from further analysis.

The correlation between the frequency of DWA per minute is negatively correlated with the maximum of blink duration ($r = -0.363$; $p < 0.01$). The maximum blink duration decreases with a higher frequency of DWA per minute (Figure 7).

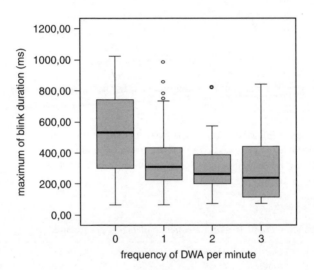

Figure 7. Box plot of maximum blink duration and frequency of DWA per minute.

This result differs from the assumptions on correlations between blink duration and increased fatigue discussed in various publications (Galley & Andrés, 1996; Hargutt et al., 2003), which also provide empirical evidence. To determine the relation between blink duration and increased fatigue in our data, we calculated the correlation between the frequency of micro-sleep (per minute) and the maximum blink duration ($r = 0.305$; $p < 0.01$). This is illustrated in Figure 8. As expected, the maximum blink duration increases with a higher frequency of micro-sleep events (per minute).

In interpreting the findings presented here, we conclude that DWA may function as a substitute for micro-sleep. The video analysis we carried out to record the micro-sleep and DWA events produced some interesting observations. The most common characteristic of all subjects who experienced DWA was that they stared and showed a general lack of eye movements.

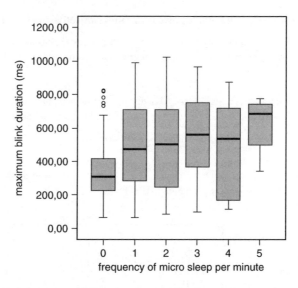

Figure 8. Box plot of maximum blink duration and frequency of micro-sleep per minute.

Consequently, we correlated the parameters from the EOG (eye movements) with the frequency of DWA (per minute). As shown in Table 2, we found two parameters with (moderately) high correlations to the frequency of DWA: the mean saccadic amplitude ($r = -0.544$) and the mean saccadic duration ($r = -0.445$).

Table 2. Correlation coefficients for frequency of DWA per minute.

	Subjective alertness	Mean alpha spindle	Maximum blink duration	Mean saccadic duration	Mean saccadic amplitude
Correlation coefficient (Spearman's rho) frequency of DWA (per minute)	$r = 0.239**$	$r = -0.308**$	$r = -0.363**$	$r = -0.445**$	$r = -0.544**$
N	290	283	410	315	315

Figure 9 shows decreasing saccadic amplitude with the higher occurrence of DWA. The subjects show no major eye movements; instead, they stare. To compare this with the stages of micro-sleep, we calculate the correlation of the mean saccadic amplitude with the frequency of micro-sleep (per minute).

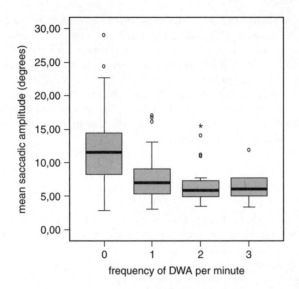

Figure 9. Box plot of mean saccadic amplitude and frequency of DWA per minute.

We found a positive relation between mean saccadic amplitude and frequency of micro-sleep as shown in Figure 10. If subjects show a higher frequency of micro-sleep, the mean saccadic amplitude increases. This is due to the fact that the subjects tend to reorient themselves after falling asleep. This can be accomplished via fast saccadic eye movements.

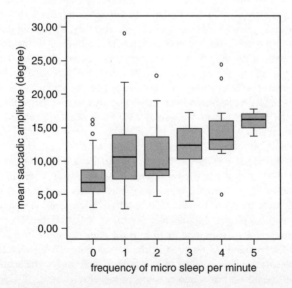

Figure 10. Box plot of mean saccadic amplitude and frequency of micro-sleep per minute.

In summary, we found (moderately) high correlations with the frequency of DWA per minute and the saccadic parameters. This finding is crucially important in the context of developing fatigue detection systems for driver monitoring. Furthermore, subjects show different tendencies concerning eye movements and blink behaviour during the occurrence of DWA and micro-sleep. With an increasing frequency of DWA events (per minute), the mean saccadic amplitude and the mean saccadic duration decrease. A possible explanation lies in the glassy stare of the subjects experiencing DWA. With the increasing frequency of micro-sleep, however, we find increasing saccadic amplitude. This can be interpreted as a reorientation tendency after the occurrence of micro-sleep.

DISCUSSION

The purpose of this study has been to learn more about a phenomenon we refer to as driving without awareness. As our experimental series in the driving simulator has shown, almost every fifth driver shows states of deep unawareness during a monotonous drive on a simulated highway. Most of the DWA that occurs while driving on real highways may go unnoticed by other drivers or even by the driver. Still, the finding that one-third of DWA events lead to driving errors like lane-crossing should be regarded as a warning sign to not underestimate the potential danger of this phenomenon.

The phases of DWA occur predominantly together with events of the so-called micro-sleep. Given that the time interval between DWA and micro-sleep is often very short, the two events would appear to be interrelated or at least caused by the same process of fatigue. We assume that DWA is not only fatigue-related, but in fact a state of sleeping with open eyes. In this assumption, we concur with a number of other authors, for example, Miles, who put forward this interpretation as early as 1929. Our findings are also in accordance with definitions from the time when the term "highway hypnosis" gained wide currency, such as those by Williams and Shor (1970), but also with newer hypotheses, for instance those of Horne and Reyner (1999) and Sagberg (1999), who see DWA as clearly sleep-related or at least as an important antecedent of falling asleep. Of course, our results could be confounded by the testing setting, which was designed to evoke fatigue in the drivers. The predictability of the setting could possibly induce both DWA and micro-sleep independently of each other without a fundamental correlation between them. However, we assume it to be somewhat unlikely that DWA and sleep are independent in reality.

The attention or memory lapses independent of fatigue that are described by Chapman et al. (2005) and Kerr (1991) might actually be a different phenomenon. With our method of video analysis, we detected short attention lapses that were clearly visible to an observer. These "acute" states of DWA are possibly precursors to falling asleep, while longer time intervals of lapsed attention without fatigue features might also occur but not be observable by another person. The phenomenon we were interested in is the allegedly more dangerous one that can lead to reaction failures and, therefore, to driving accidents. To identify these events, the method of video analysis was evaluated to be the most appropriate. The acute states of DWA documented here should be taken into account in the development of support systems for driver monitoring.

Correlations of DWA occurrence with parameters from EEG, EOG, blink behaviour and self-assessed fatigue ratings showed that the phenomenon is related in particular to saccadic parameters like mean saccadic amplitude and mean saccadic duration. The relation of DWA to eye movements was already assumed by Miles (1929), who found indications of fatigue such as a reduced saccadic velocity and a breaking of long saccadic movements into shorter movements. Our finding that both saccadic amplitude and saccadic duration decrease with a higher frequency of DWA occurrences fits well with this observation. Galley and Churan (2002) find correlations between saccadic velocity or prolonged fixation durations and increased fatigue. Comparing our results with those of other investigators, there is overall consistency in findings on saccadic movement. These parameters of eye movement could possibly be used as indicators of DWA to develop driver-monitoring systems that are able to register sleeping with open eyes. This is of particular importance because even if the same fatigue process generates both micro-sleep and DWA, they do not have the same effect on predictive parameters of blink behaviour.

Yet there are still underlying physiological and cognitive processes of the phenomenon that remain unanswered. If we assume that people can learn to keep their eyes open while actually sleeping, it would be interesting to examine a group of professional drivers more closely in future research, as has also been proposed by Galley and Churan (2002). It might not only be possible to train DWA, but also to learn how to avoid it. To counteract both impending sleep and attention lapses behind the wheel, Suinn and Richardson (1970) treated a test subject with behaviour therapy and found evidence of success after 16 meetings.

For preventative management, understanding the risk factors of DWA with regard to personality characteristics is of high interest. In our sample, which was collected according to the distribution of driver licence owners in Germany stratified by age and gender, we found that young male drivers are at a higher risk of showing DWA during monotonous drives. The reasons for this finding should be investigated. A frequently suggested method of actively preventing fatigue or DWA-related accidents is in the design of the road environment. Avoiding high predictability in road design may diminish the occurrence not only of micro-sleep attacks but also of DWA (e.g. Dewar, 2002; Tejero & Choliz, 2002).

In sum, preventive measures have been proposed in road design, detection of risk factors, elaboration of driver-monitoring devices and driver training. These suggestions can only successfully be applied if the nature and origin of DWA are examined in greater detail. A careful analysis of physiological parameters during DWA can help provide evidence about the correlation between this state and sleep. DWA might be one supplementary symptom of driver fatigue that occurs if the will to keep one's eyes open overrides the physiological need of a sleepy person to close his or her eyes and stop the visual information input. The importance of the driving task, which demands a high level of personal responsibility and response to visual stimuli, paradoxically leads to DWA with the motive of self-protection, while the actual result is ultimately harmful.

ACKNOWLEDGEMENTS

We would like to thank the Volkswagen AG (Wolfsburg, Germany) for providing the means and financing this project.

REFERENCES

Brown, I.D. (1991). Highway hypnosis: implications for road safety researchers and practitioners. In Gale, A.G., Brown, I.D., Haslegrave, C.H., Moorhead, I., & Taylor, S.P. (Eds.), *Vision in Vehicles III* (pp. 459–466). Amsterdam: Elsevier.

Brown, I.D. (1994). Driver fatigue. *Human Factors, 36* (2), 298–314.

Chapman, P.R., Ismail, R., & Underwood, G. (2005). Waking up at the wheel: accidents, attention and the time-gap experience. In Gale, A.G., Brown, I.D., Haslegrave, C.H., & Taylor, S.P. (Eds.), *Vision in Vehicles VII*. Amsterdam: Elsevier, (in press).

Dewar, R.E. (2002). Roadway design. In Dewar, R.E., & Olson, P.L. (Eds.), *Human Factors and Traffic Safety*. Tucson, AZ: Lawyers and Judges Publishing, Chapter 12.

Galley, N., & Andrés, G. (1996). Saccadic eye movements and blinks during long term driving on the autobahn with minimal alcohol ingestion. In Gale, A.G., Brown, I.D., Haslegrave, C.M., & Taylor, S.P. (Eds.), *Vision in Vehicles V* (pp. 381–388). Amsterdam: Elsevier.

Galley, N., & Churan, J. (2002). Die Ermüdung des Kraftfahrers aus der Sicht des zukünftigen Fahrzeugs. In Kubitzki, J. (Ed.), *Der sichere Fahrer—Ein Mythos? Erreichtes und Strittiges auf dem Gebiet der Verkehrssicherheit* (pp. 99–113). Köln: TÜV-Verlag.

Hargutt, V., Tietze, H., & Krüger, H.-P. (2003). A video-based method for drowsiness detection—an alternative to PERCLOS. *Journal of Psychophysiology, 17* (3), 152.

Horne, J., & Reyner, L. (1999). Vehicle accidents related to sleep: a review. *Occupational and Environmental Medicine, 56* (6), 289–294.

Kerr, J.S. (1991). Driving without attention mode (DWAM): a formalisation of inattentive states while driving. In Gale, A.G., Brown, I.D., Haslegrave, C.H., Moorhead, I., & Taylor, S.P. (Eds.), *Vision in Vehicles III* (pp. 473–479). Amsterdam: Elsevier.

Miles, W. (1929). Sleeping with the Eyes Open. *Scientific American*, 489–492, June.

Reed, G. (1972). *The Psychology of Anomalous Experience*. London: Hutchinson University Library.

Sagberg, F. (1999). Road accidents caused by drivers falling asleep. *Accident Analysis and Prevention, 31* (6), 639–649.

Schachter, D. (1976). The hypnagogic state: a critical review of the literature. *Psychological Bulletin, 83* (3), 452–481.

Schneider, W., & Shiffrin, R.M. (1977). Controlled and automatic human information processing. I: Detection, search and attention. *Psychological Review, 84*, 1–66.

Shor, R.E., & Thackray, R.I. (1970). A program of research in "highway hypnosis": a preliminary report. *Accident Analysis and Prevention, 2* (2), 103–109.

Suinn, R.M., & Richardson, F. (1970). Behavior therapy of an unusual case of highway hypnosis. *Journal of Behavior Therapy and Experimental Psychiatry, 1* (2), 175–176.

Tejero, P., & Choliz, M. (2002). Driving on the motorway: the effect of alternating speed on driver's activation level and mental effort. *Ergonomics, 45* (9), 605–618.

Thiffault, P., & Bergeron, J. (2003). Monotony of road environment and driver fatigue: a simulator study. *Accident Analysis and Prevention, 35*, 381–391.

Tietze, H. (2000). Stages of fatigue during long duration driving reflected in alpha related events in the EEG. *Paper presented at the International Conference on Traffic and Transport Psychology*, Bern.

Wertheim, A.H. (1978). Explaining highway hypnosis: experimental evidence for the role of eye movements. *Accident Analysis and Prevention, 10* (2), 111–129.

Wertheim, A.H. (1991). Highway hypnosis: a theoretical analysis. In Gale, A.G., Brown, I.D., Haslegrave, C.H., Moorhead, I., & Taylor, S.P. (Eds.), *Vision in Vehicles III* (pp. 467–472). Amsterdam: Elsevier.

Wierwille, W.W., & Ellsworth, L.A. (1994). Evaluation of driver drowsiness by trained raters. *Accident Analysis and Prevention, 26*, 571–581.

Williams, G. (1963). Highway hypnosis: a hypothesis. *International Journal of Clinical and Experimental Hypnosis, 11* (3), 143–151.

Williams, G., & Shor, R.E. (1970). An historical note on highway hypnosis. *Accident Analysis and Prevention, 2* (3), 223–225.

Traffic and Transport Psychology
G. Underwood (Editor)
© 2005 Elsevier Ltd. All rights reserved.

471

38

PROPHYLACTIC NAPS CAN REDUCE CAR ACCIDENTS RISK IN SHIFT-WORKERS

Barbara Mascialino[1], Sergio Garbarino[2,3], Maria A. Penco[4], Sandro Squarcia[4], Fabrizio De Carli[5], Lino Nobili[2], Manolo Beelke[2] and Franco Ferrillo[2]

INTRODUCTION

In physiological conditions sleep propensity is regulated by the interaction between a homeostatic process S with a circadian one C. Process C describes sleep *organisation* within the day: it has a period of about 24 h and, according to the process, sleep propensity reaches maxima at 23 and 14 (Lavie, 1986) and minima at 19. Process S determines sleep *regulation*: it describes sleep pressure accumulation and depends on the previous sleep–wake behaviour adopted (Achermann, Dijk, Brunner & Borbély, 1993).

The night-scheduled work is at higher risk of accidents (Horne & Reyner, 1995) because it coincides with the circadian nadir of vigilance oscillation, deeply linked with the circadian process C. At the same time, night-time work is accompanied by a decrease in alertness ascribable to the progressive increase of sleepiness due to prolonged wakefulness, i.e. homeostatic process S accumulation (Achermann et al., 1993).

Many investigations have demonstrated the importance of developing and implementing countermeasures to fatigue and excessive sleepiness, especially in professional drivers (Åkertedt & Landstrom, 1989; Rosekind, Gander & Dinges, 1991). It is well known that prophylactic napping is practised usually during the afternoon or early evening preceding

[1] INFN—Sezione di Genova, Via Dodecaneso 33, 16146 Genova, Italy. *E-mail:* barbara.mascialino@ge.infn.it (B. Mascialino).
[2] Center of Sleep Medicine, University of Genoa, Genoa, Italy.
[3] Center of Neurology and Medical Psychology, Health Service of the State Police, Department of the Interior, Genoa, Italy.
[4] Department of Physics, Health Physics and Medical Statistics Laboratory, Genoa, Italy.
[5] Institute of Bioimaging and Molecular Physiology, National Council of Research, Milan, Italy.

extended night work in order to develop and implement a countermeasure to sleepiness, particularly in professional drivers. Beneficial effects of prophylactic naps have been demonstrated in experimental sets and in limited samples, depending on duration of prior wakefulness, time of day of the nap and its duration (Naitoh, 1981; Lumley, Roehrs, Zorick, Lamphere & Roth, 1986; Åkerstedt, Torsvall & Gillberg, 1989; Macchi, Boulos, Ranney, Simmons & Campbell, 2002). It must be underlined that studies aimed at demonstrating naps' effectiveness have been performed involving healthy young volunteers, rather than experienced shift-workers (Gillberg, 1984; Webb, 1987; Dinges, Whitehouse, Orne & Orne, 1988; Rogers, Spencer, Stone & Nicholson, 1989; Sugerman & Walsh, 1989; Bonnet, 1991; Bonnet & Arand, 1995). The only two exceptions are represented by two studies (Gillberg, Kecklund & Åkerstedt, 1996; Sallinen, Härma, Åkerstedt, Rosa & Lillqvist, 1998), concerning, respectively, professional drivers and oil refinery process operators. In both cases subjects enrolled in the study were real shift-workers, but the effects of short naps on performance were only evaluated in conditions of simulated night work.

The present study shows that in a large population of shift-workers in everyday life conditions, napping behaviour is self-initiated as a sleepiness counteractive strategy. Moreover, its efficacy in preventing sleepiness-related accidents is mathematically estimable: accidents are on average reduced by 38%.

MATERIAL AND METHODS

Subjects and schedule description

The study included all the highway vehicle accidents occurred to Italian police drivers during the years 1993–1997. Subjects were working on fast-rotating shifts organised according to the schedule shown in Table 1. A working shift lasts 6 h, 12 free hours separate consecutive shifts, 60 h rest follow each cycle. The rotation of the schedule is counterclockwise with a continuous progression.

Table 1. The fast counterclockwise rotating schedule adopted by Italian State Police officers.

Day	Hours			
	01–07	*07–13*	*13–19*	*19–01*
Day 1				Evening
Day 2			Afternoon	
Day 3		Morning		
Day 4	Night			
Day 5				

The number of accidents recorded was 1195: 216 during the evening shift, 364 in the afternoon, 417 in the morning and 198 in the night. Figure 1 shows accidents time distribution within the day. Drivers, 96% male, were on average 28 years old (standard deviation, SD = 6 years) with a seniority of 5 years (SD = 5 years). For every accident, the official Italian police database allowed the estimation of the time of the accident, the weather conditions and the culpability of

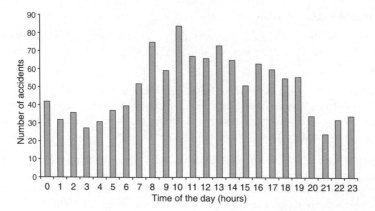

Figure 1. 24-h time distributions of highway accidents occurred to shift-working drivers of Italian Police in the years 1993–1997.

the driver (yes/no). These data were complemented with other data, provided by the Italian Highway Society:

- a dangerousness index of the specific highway section in which the accident occurred,
- the traffic intensity conditions that usually can be found in that road section, in the same day of the week and in the same hour of the day in which the accident occurred. Figure 2 shows the hourly average traffic intensity.

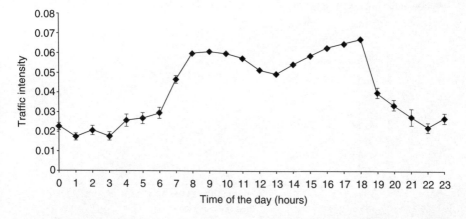

Figure 2. Italian highway average traffic intensity as a function of the hour of the day. Vertical bars represent the standard error. These data were provided by the Italian Highway Company. It must be underlined that traffic intensity is quite constant during night-time and is reduced to very low values.

Sleep processes quantification

Homeostatic sleep pressure (process S) was mathematically computed with the two-process model of sleep regulation (Daan, Domien, Beersma & Borbély, 1984), quantitatively described in Appendix A.

Data concerning the usual sleep–wake behaviour within a schedule were gathered together with post-accident telephone interviews during the year 1999. Each driver was asked to report the usual time of sleep onset and duration of the night before the same shift in which the accident occurred and the time position and duration of the intervening naps.

According to the mathematical model, the intensity of homeostatic drive towards sleep was calculated as an exponential saturating function, depending on the length of preceding sleep and wakefulness. It took into account both the time of sleep onset and of wake up; it also considered either the presence or the absence of daytime naps, their timing and duration.

The effect of naps on sleep pressure S was quantitatively evaluated by partitioning subjects into two groups: those who took a nap before the evening or night shift and those who did not. Process S levels, age and seniority of these two groups were compared by means of Kolmogorov–Smirnov (K–S) test.

Concerning the circadian sleep propensity (process C), as Daan's mathematical model does not take into account the existence of the circasemidian peak of sleep propensity, we decided to evaluate subjects' circadian process by means of an empirical model. For each subject, the circadian oscillation of sleep propensity (process C) was therefore estimated from a previous experimental study performed under bed-rest conditions (Nobili et al., 1995). Subjects were kept 32 h long in spatial and temporal isolation, in very dim light conditions. Sleep propensity (process C) was estimated as the ratio between the hourly sleep quantity and the daily average of minutes of sleep in 1 h. Figure 3 represents circadian and semicircadian sleep propensity as a function of the hour of the day: the mid-afternoon peak of sleep propensity cannot be neglected.

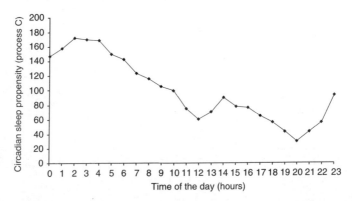

Figure 3. Circadian sleep propensity as a function of the hour of the day. These data were derived from a clinical study performed under bed-rest conditions (Nobili et al., 1995). Note that sleep propensity is at maximum levels during night-time, with a significant secondary peak in the early afternoon; the minimum level, i.e. the wakefulness peak, is reached at about 19–20.

Accident risk analysis

The influence of the driver's characteristics (age, sex and shift-work seniority), the context condition (weather, traffic intensity, road dangerousness, culpability and process C levels), and the time from the start of the shift and the process S levels on accident risk was evaluated by means of Cox's proportional hazard regression. All the variables that turned out to be significant to the analysis, contribute in increasing or reducing accident risk. The way every variable influences accident risk is quantified by means of a Hazard Ratio (HR). If the value of HR is higher than 1, that variable will increase accident risk; otherwise (HR < 1) that variable will reduce accident risk. The variables were inserted in the analysis in their standardised scale. This means that if a selected variable will increase/decrease of one standard deviation, the accident risk will be HR times higher/lower.

In order to study the effect of sleep scheduling (the napping behaviour in particular) when sleep propensity increases (Garbarino, Nobili, Beelke, De Carli & Ferrillo, 2001) and traffic influence lowers, Cox's proportional hazard regression was repeated only on night-time hours (9 p.m.–7 a.m.).

The experimental and the theoretical model

On the basis of the results obtained in the time restricted Cox hazard regression analysis, an experimental regression model estimated the influence of the hourly mean process S ($S_{observed}$) on the hourly number of accidents ($N_{observed}$):

$$N_{observed} = f(S_{observed}).$$

The model f was then used to estimate the expected accident trend as a function of the theoretical homeostatic sleep pressure ($S_{theoretical}$) that subjects would have reached in absence of naps ($N_{expected}$):

$$N_{expected} = f(S_{theoretical}).$$

The theoretical curve of expected accidents was compared with the curve of observed accidents by means of the chi-squared test.

RESULTS

The fast counterclockwise roster adopted influenced deeply the sleep–wake schedule of shift-workers. In fact, the morphology of the shift plan itself allowed workers to adopt a napping prophylactic strategy only before some working shifts spontaneously. In our sample only 15% of drivers took a nap before the evening shift, with a mean duration equal to 28 ± 1 min. Napping was not at all initiated before the afternoon shift (0%), as after the evening shift workers used to fall asleep late in the night and were free to sleep as long as they wished. Of course morning shift too was not associated with a napping prophylactic behaviour, as workers had just woken up from night sleep. Most subjects (85%) took an afternoon or early evening nap before the night shift, with a mean duration of 91 ± 3 min.

K–S test demonstrated that police officers who took a nap differed from the ones that did not as to shift-work seniority and age distribution ($p < 0.001$), the nappers being the oldest: (31 ± 7) years versus (26 ± 4) years. K–S test highlighted a difference in the process S levels distribution in the two samples, ascribing lower levels to nappers rather than to non-nappers ($p < 0.001$).

As a matter of fact, process S levels differed not only on the basis of the napping behaviour, but also in the statistical difference of their distribution even among different shifts (K–S test, $p < 0.001$). For this reason, independently of external causes, accident exposition had an hour of day component (both traffic intensity and process C levels were not uniform over the 24 h) and a working shift one (process S levels).

The influence of these three factors (traffic, process C levels and process S levels), together with driver characteristics (age, sex and shift-work seniority) and external conditions (weather, traffic, road dangerousness and culpability), on accidents distribution was evaluated with a Cox hazard proportional risk analysis.

Cox proportional regression (see Table 2) showed that the risk of accident was increased by process S levels (HR = 1.31), process C levels (HR = 2.27) and traffic intensity (HR = 2.35). The other variables (sex, age, shift-work seniority, weather conditions, road dangerousness and culpability) did not turn out to be significant and, therefore, did not influence accident risk.

Table 2. Cox proportional regression results. All the 1195 accidents were considered. Accident risk is mainly weighted by traffic intensity, circadian process C and homeostatic process S, while the other variables were not significant.

Variables	$p_{24\,h}$	$HR_{24\,h}$
Sex	0.48	–
Age	0.61	–
Shift-work seniority	0.29	–
Process C	10^{-5}	2.28
Process S	10^{-5}	1.32
Traffic	10^{-5}	2.35
Weather conditions	0.85	–
Road dangerousness	0.73	–
Culpability	0.91	–

In order to study the effect of sleep scheduling when sleep propensity increases (Horne & Reyner, 1995; Folkard, 1997; Garbarino et al., 2001;) and traffic influence lowers (K–S test, $p < 0.001$), we repeated the same regression analysis only for night-time hours, from 9 p.m. to 7 a.m. Being in this time-span traffic intensity both constant and very low, the influence of process S levels became predominant (HR = 3.71), process C levels went out of phase (HR = 0.61) and a light influence of shift-work seniority came out (HR = 1.18). Traffic intensity and the other variables inserted in the regression were not significant (see Table 3).

Table 3. Cox proportional regression results. 24 h accident risk
is influenced mainly by homeostatic process S and lightly by
shift-work seniority.

Variables	$p_{night\text{-}time}$	$HR_{night\text{-}time}$
Sex	0.45	–
Age	0.23	–
Shift-work seniority	10^{-3}	1.18
Process C	10^{-5}	0.61
Process S	10^{-5}	3.71
Traffic	0.07	–
Weather conditions	0.21	–
Road dangerousness	0.56	–
Culpability	0.62	–

In these hours, a significant exponential relationship between the mean process S levels
($S_{observed}$) and the hourly number of accidents ($N_{observed}$) was found ($R^2 = 0.40$, $p < 0.05$),
which is shown in Figure 4:

$$N_{observed} = f(S_{observed}) = 3.64\,e^{3.47 S_{observed}}$$

In order to evaluate the prophylactic role played by naps on accidents trend, a new unobservable
variable ($S_{theoretical}$) was built. In practice, in $S_{theoretical}$ nap contributions to $S_{observed}$ were omitted
from mathematical computations.

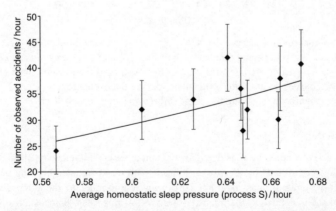

Figure 4. Experimental data (diamonds + standard error) and significant empirical
relationship (continuous line) between the hourly average homeostatic sleep pressure ($S_{observed}$)
and the number of observed accidents per hour ($N_{observed}$). The hourly number of accidents
increases as an exponential function of sleep pressure.

$S_{\text{theoretical}}$ values were necessarily either equal or greater than corresponding S_{observed} ones; this difference was small during the evening shift and became important during the night shift; as a whole, K–S test showed a significant difference ($p < 0.001$).

On the basis of the experimental model found, the number of expected accidents in absence of naps (N_{expected}) was estimated by simply replacing process S observed levels (S_{observed}) with a $S_{\text{theoretical}}$ value, computed omitting naps:

$$N_{\text{expected}} = f(S_{\text{theoretical}}) = 3.64\, e^{3.47 S_{\text{theoretical}}}$$

The expected N_{expected} values (Figure 5) were slightly greater than N_{observed} during evening hours: chi-square test did not show differences ($\chi^2 = 2.1$, $p = $ n.s.). On the contrary N_{observed} turned out to be significantly lower than N_{expected} during the night ($\chi^2 = 49.8$, $p = 10^{-11}$). More precisely, in these hours the percentage difference between the two curves ranged between a minimum decrease of 30% and a maximum of 49%, with a mean decrease of $(38 \pm 8)\%$.

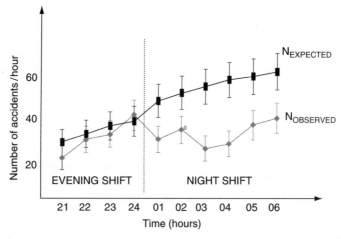

Figure 5. Number of observed accidents (N_{observed}, grey line) and number of expected accidents (N_{expected}, black line). Expected number of accidents (counts and standard error) in each working hour were calculated as a function of homeostatic drive towards sleep omitting naps. The two curves do not differ statistically during the evening shift ($\chi^2 = 2.1$, $p = $ n.s.). They differed significantly during the night shift ($\chi^2 = 49.8$, $p < 0.001$).

DISCUSSION

As process S levels could be considered as the unique variable influencing sleepiness that can be externally "controlled" by the worker himself with a self-initiated napping behaviour, we decided to investigate if naps could have had some role in reducing the number of accidents. Since process S is defined as the intensity of drive towards sleep, homeostatically increasing with the quantity of wakefulness preceding sleep, the fact that the distributions of nappers and non-nappers in process S levels differed was not trivial. In fact, it showed that the timing and duration of these naps were sufficient to generate a statistically significant difference between nappers and non-nappers, as to intensity of drive towards sleep.

Many experimental studies reported data concerning the ability and efficacy of prophylactic naps to avoid both extended night-work ascribable alertness and performance deterioration (Naitoh, 1981; Åkerstedt & Torsvall, 1985; Lumley et al., 1986; Åkerstedt et al., 1989; Rogers et al., 1989; Rosekind et al., 1991; Rosa, 1993; Åkerstedt & Landstrom, 1998; Macchi et al., 2002). However, in most cases the investigated subjects were either young volunteers or small groups of shift-workers; in any case, the investigation itself has been performed only on experimental paradigms of simulated shift-working conditions (Gillberg, 1984; Webb, 1987; Dinges et al., 1988; Rogers et al., 1989; Sugerman & Walsh, 1989; Bonnet, 1991; Bonnet & Arand, 1995).

Our data confirm that napping behaviour before night work in daily life and in a big sample in real conditions, and in real accidents, is an effective countermeasure to alertness and performance deterioration associated with night work. In fact, before extended night work, napping behaviour is a spontaneous, self-managed prophylactic strategy adopted by most drivers in our sample (85%). Its efficacy lies in its capability of reducing the levels of homeostatic pressure towards sleep proportionally to nap duration and according to its timing.

The age and shift-work seniority difference between nappers and non-nappers suggests that this self-initiated behaviour is somehow linked to subjective experience of workers in developing their own strategies of coping with the demands of night work.

However, this strategy is spontaneously adopted only before the night shift, while its practice is neglected before the so-called "evening-shift", where it could be useful as well. This may indicate that the risk of sleep-related accidents while driving during the evening and early night were underestimated. During night-time Cox hazard regression showed that process S levels were associated with high levels of HR. Moreover, the statistical significance found in the experimental relationship detected between the hourly average observed sleep pressure $S_{observed}$ and the hourly number of accidents $N_{observed}$, stresses the existence of a real link between homeostatic pressure and accidents occurrence also in the evening and in early night hours. Consequently, we would like to underline the possible effectiveness of education schemes to increase the workers' awareness of accident risk related to sleepiness and to extend the prophylactic behaviour of napping before night work.

Due to its generality, the mathematical model built is absolutely independent of the roster adopted by police officers, and could be applied to other categories of shift-workers, as truck drivers. The model itself underestimates $N_{expected}$, neglecting the influence of process C levels could have on this variable. Actually, there could be a non-linear interaction between process S levels and process C levels (Achermann, 1999; Dijk, Jewett, Czeisler & Kronauer, 1999), but its mathematical form is still unknown because it is impossible to determine which component modulates the other one. Anyhow, we believe that, independently of their exact mathematical description, process S levels and process C levels interact constructively during night-time. This means that, inserting process C levels in the model built as an independent variable, its contribution could only increase further $N_{expected}$. As the maximum propensity to sleep ascribable to process C levels is in the middle of the night (3–4 a.m.) and in the same hours we found the maximum prophylactic effects of napping behaviour, we believe that napping could be a coping strategy also with the (unknown) interaction of both process S and process C.

The weakest point of this study is the retrospective nature of the data collection and the time elapsed between the events of interest and the telephone interviews. In fact, the time difference between the accident occurrence (1993–1997) and the telephone interview (1999) may have increased recall error of the subjects involved. The importance of telephone data collection is pivotal as these data allowed the estimation of sleep pressure S accumulation at accident time. In fact, this was the crucial variable used in building the predictive mathematical model. With the aim of validating the model, we felt the need for new field-based data, collected prospectively. For these reasons, the present study was followed by a validation analysis of a smaller cohort of accidents prospectively collected during 2003 ($N = 84$ accidents) (Garbarino et al., 2004). The official data were completed by means of phone interviews within a few days from the accident. This action supplied a more precise estimation of sleep timing and homeostatic process at the time of accident and the verification of the efficacy of sleep napping behaviour. In order to validate the retrospective sleep data we compared retrospective and prospective sleep patterns: no statistical difference was found. Again, in the new sample the hourly number of accidents increased with homeostatic sleep pressure; the theoretical efficacy of napping was quantified in 48% accidents decrease. These new data confirmed the old results reported in this paper, i.e. napping before night shift is an effective countermeasure to alertness and performance deterioration associated with night work. Moreover, this self-initiated behaviour could have a prophylactic efficacy in reducing the number of car accidents.

REFERENCES

Achermann, P. (1999). Technical note: a problem with identifying nonlinear interactions of circadian and homeostatic processes. *Journal of Biological Rhythms, 14*, 602–603.

Achermann, P., & Borbély, A.A. (1999). Sleep homeostasis and models of sleep regulation. *Journal of Biological Rhythms, 14* (6), 557–568.

Achermann, P., Dijk, D.J., Brunner, D.P., & Borbély, A.A. (1993). A model of human sleep homeostasis based on EEG slow-wave activity: quantitative comparison of data and simulations. *Brain Research, 31*, 97–113.

Åkerstedt, T., & Landstrom, U. (1998). Work place countermeasures of night shift fatigue. *International Journal of Industrial Ergonomics, 11*, 17–34.

Åkerstedt, T., & Torsvall, L. (1985). Napping in shift work. *Sleep, 8* (2), 105–109.

Åkerstedt, T., Torsvall, L., & Gillberg, M. (1989). Shift work and napping. In Dinges, D.F., & Broughton, R.J. (Eds.), *Sleep and Alertness: Chronobiological, Behavioural, and Medical Aspects of Napping* (pp. 205–220). New York: Raven Press.

Bonnet, M.H. (1991). The effect of varying prophylactic naps on performance, alertness and mood throughout a 52-h continuous operation. *Sleep, 14*, 307–315.

Bonnet, M.H., & Arand, D.L. (1995). Consolidated and distributed nap schedules and performance. *Journal of Sleep Research, 4*, 71–77.

Borbély, A.A. (1982). A two process of human sleep regulation. *Human Neurobiology, 1*, 195–204.

Borbély, A.A., & Achermann, P. (1992). Combining different models of sleep regulation. *Journal of Sleep Research, 1* (2), 144–147.

Borbély, A.A., & Achermann, P. (2003). Mathematical models of sleep regulation. *Frontiers of Bioscience, 8*, s683–s693.

Daan, S., Domien, G.M., Beersma, M., & Borbély, A.A. (1984). Timing of human sleep: recovery process gated by a circadian pacemaker. *American Journal of Physiology, 246*, R161–R178.

Dijk, D.J., Jewett, M.E., Czeisler, C.A., & Kronauer, R.E. (1999). Reply to technical note: nonlinear interactions between circadian and homeostatic processes: models or metrics? *Journal of Biological Rhythms, 1* (4), 604–605.

Dinges, D.F., Whitehouse, W.G., Orne, E.C., & Orne, M.T. (1988). The benefits of a nap during prolonged work and wakefulness. *Work and Stress, 2*, 139–153.

Folkard, S. (1997). Black times: temporal determinants of transport safety. *Accidents Analysis and Prevention, 19* (4), 417–430.

Garbarino, S., Nobili, L., Beelke, M., De Carli, F., & Ferrillo, F. (2001). The contributing role of sleepiness in highway vehicle accidents. *Sleep, 24* (2), 203–206.

Garbarino, S., Mascialino, B., Penco, M.A., Squarcia, S., De Carli, F., Nobili, L., Beelke, M., & Ferrillo, F. (2004). Professional shift-work drivers spontaneously adopting prophylactic naps can reduce the risk of car accidents during night work. *Sleep, 27* (7), 1295–1302.

Gillberg, M. (1984). The effects of two alternative timings of a one-hour nap on early morning performance. *Biological Psychology, 19*, 45–54.

Gillberg, M., Kecklund, G., & Åkerstedt, T. (1996). Sleepiness and performance in professional drivers in a truck simulator—comparisons between day and night driving. *Journal of Sleep Research, 5*, 12–15.

Horne, J.A., & Reyner, L.A. (1995). Sleep related vehicle accidents. *British Medical Journal, 310*, 565–567.

Lavie, P. (1986). Ultrashort sleep-waking schedule. III. 'Gates' and 'Forbidden zones' for sleep. *Electroencephalography and Clinical Neurophysiology, 63*, 414–425.

Lumley, M., Roehrs, T., Zorick, F., Lamphere, J., & Roth, T. (1986). The alerting effects of naps in sleep-deprived subjects. *Psychophysiology, 23*, 403–408.

Macchi, M.M., Boulos, Z., Ranney, T., Simmons, L., & Campbell, S.S. (2002). Effects of an afternoon nap on nighttime alertness and performance in long-haul drivers. *Accidents Analysis and Prevention, 34*, 825–834.

Naitoh, P. (1981). Circadian cycles and restorative effects of naps. In Johnson, L.C., Tepas, D.T., Colquhoun, W.P., & Colligan, M.J. (Eds.), *Biological Rhythms, Sleep and Shift-Work.* (553–580) New York: Spectrum.

Nobili, L., Besset, A., Ferrillo, F., Rosadini, G., Schiavi, G., & Billiard, M. (1995). Dynamics of slow wave activity in narcoleptic patients under bed rest conditions. *Electroencephaography Clinical Neurophysiology, 95*, 414–425.

Rogers, A.S., Spencer, M.B., Stone, M.B., & Nicholson, A.N. (1989). The influence of a 1-h nap on performance overnight. *Ergonomics, 32*, 1193–1205.

Rosa, R. (1993). Napping at home and alertness on the job in rotating shift workers. *Sleep, 16*, 727–735.

Rosekind, M.R., Gander, P.H., & Dinges, D.F. (1991). Alertness management in flight operations: strategic napping. SAE Technical Paper Series no. 912138.

Sallinen, M., Härma, M., Åkerstedt, T., Rosa, R., & Lillqvist, O. (1998). Promoting alertness with a short nap during a night shift. *Journal of Sleep Research, 7*, 240–247.

Sugerman, J.L., & Walsh, J.K. (1989). Physiological sleep tendency and ability to maintain alertness at night. *Sleep, 12*, 106–112.

Webb, W. (1987). The proximal effects of two- and four-hour naps within extended performance without sleep. *Psychophysiology, 24*, 426–429.

APPENDIX A. THE TWO-PROCESS QUANTITATIVE MODEL OF SLEEP REGULATION

During the last 20 years many efforts were made, with the aim of describing sleep processes (circadian process C and homeostatic process S) as well as sleep regulation by means of a simple abstract mathematical formulation. One of the easiest to treat is surely the two-process model of sleep regulation (Borbély, 1982; Daan et al., 1984; Borbély & Achermann, 1992, 2003; Achermann, 1999; Achermann & Borbély, 1999). This mathematical model is based on the assumption that sleep propensity is determined by the interaction of a circadian process C with an homeostatic process S.

CIRCADIAN SLEEP PROPENSITY: PROCESS C

Circadian process C description was developed on the basis of the clinical observation of sleep organisation within the 24-h cycle. In the model sleep time organisation is converted in a theoretical process C, representing the alternation of higher and lower sleep propensity periods. In mathematical terms it is easily expressed by means of a skewed sinusoidal wave obtained with a sine wave series. Given a time t, the value of the circadian process C at the time t (C_t) is easily calculable by means of the following equation:

$$C_t = A \sum_k \alpha_k \sin[(2i\pi/\tau)(t - t_0)]$$

where A is the wave amplitude, α_k are numerical coefficients, t represents the time and t_0 is the circadian phase at the beginning of the simulation. According to this mathematical description, C_t values depend only on the specific time t.

It must be noticed that this equation represents a skewed sine wave and that its main aim is to describe the alternation between higher sleep propensity (during night-time) and lower sleep propensity (day-time) zones. For these features, it is not suitable in fitting the circasemidian peak of sleep propensity that can be experimentally measured at about 14–15 (see Figure 3).

HOMEOSTATIC SLEEP PRESSURE: PROCESS S

The homeostatic sleep propensity time course was derived from EEG slow-wave activity observations. These observations are translated in mathematics adopting a theoretical process S, decreasing exponentially during sleep episodes as a function of sleep length and simulating in this way slow-wave activity trend. On the other hand, wake time process S description is based on the assumption that it is accumulated exponentially saturating with wake length. As process S mathematical formulation must be continuous, it was based on a recursive iterative formulation, its value depending only on the preceding sleep–wake behaviour adopted:

$$S_t = S_{t-1} \exp[-\Delta t/\tau_d] \qquad \text{Sleep}$$

$$S_t = 1 - (1 - S_{t-1}) \exp[-\Delta t/\tau_r] \qquad \text{Wake}$$

τ_d and τ_r are time constants, t and $t - 1$ represent time instants, while Δt is the time step.

SLEEP EXECUTION: INTERACTION BETWEEN PROCESS C AND PROCESS S

The interaction between the two processes determines sleep timing and duration. The two-process model of sleep regulation is based on the hypothesis of a linear interaction between S and C. According to this assumption, sleep pressure S_t values vary between two thresholds (Daan et al., 1984), each one being modulated by a circadian process. If H_m and L_m represent their mean values, the two thresholds oscillate as follows:

$$H_t = H_m + C_t \quad \text{upper threshold}$$

$$L_t = L_m + C_t \quad \text{lower threshold}$$

On the basis of a linear interaction between C_t and S_t, sleep is theoretically executed when:

$$S_t = H_t \Rightarrow S_t = H_m + C_t$$

while wake up is executed when:

$$S_t = L_t \Rightarrow S_t = L_m + C_t$$

Figure A1 represents the simulation of an ideal subject with only daily habits (sleep onset 11 p.m. and awakening 7 a.m.); x-axis represents the time from the beginning of the simulation (in hours) and vertical lines indicate the midnight, while y-axis represent the oscillation of S_t between the two thresholds L_t and H_t.

In real life, of course, man can choose to remain awake ignoring the upper threshold H_t, or he can wake up earlier or later than L_t values. If we consider man as a social being, these two rules

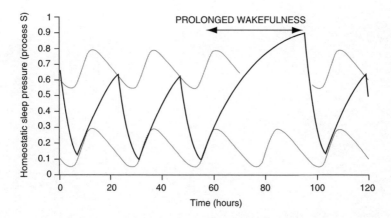

Figure A1. 5-days long simulation of process S levels (black line) for a subject respecting the assumptions of the two-process model of sleep regulation. The grey lines represent the thresholds for physiological retiring and awakening according to the two-process model. On x-axis is reported the time from the beginning of the simulation (in hours), on the y-axis the homeostatic process S. Note process S accumulation and the consequently "temporary threshold suspension effect" during the 40 h of prolonged wakefulness.

are generally ignored and

$$S_t \neq H_t \qquad \text{sleep onset}$$
$$S_t \neq L_t \qquad \text{awakening}$$

During prolonged wakefulness a subject goes on accumulating exponentially homeostatic sleep pressure. Under this condition S_t saturates exceeding the upper threshold H_t. This condition $(S_t > H_t)$ is taken into account by the model: it assumes a "temporary threshold suspension effect" (Daan et al., 1984). In Figure A1 this effect is evident during the 40 h of sleep deprivation.

POWER OF THE MODEL

This model is the most general to deal with as it can be used without the need for any clinical measurements, as EEG recordings. Self-reported sleep patterns (as the ones we obtain using questionnaire investigations) can be easily analysed in terms of sleep processes. More in particular, the model seems to be the most suitable concerning shift-work research. In fact, the mathematical formulation allows the theoretical computation of both subjective process C and process S trend within a roster.

VIOLATION AND REHABILITATION

Traffic and Transport Psychology
G. Underwood (Editor)
© 2005 Elsevier Ltd. All rights reserved.

39

DRIVERS AND TRAFFIC LAWS: A REVIEW OF PSYCHOLOGICAL THEORIES AND EMPIRICAL RESEARCH

Dana Yagil[1]

INTRODUCTION

Two fundamental assumptions ought to underlie any attempt to understand driver behavior in relation to traffic laws: first, citizens have the obligation to comply with the laws of the state; and second, traffic laws are beneficial and contribute to drivers' safety. Neither assumption, however, is universally accepted. The question of whether a citizen has a prima facie obligation to obey the law has been debated for centuries by philosophers, sociologists and legal experts. The contribution of traffic laws to drivers' safety has also been questioned, e.g. by Rothengatter (1997), who criticized traffic laws for being non-specified, disregarding the capabilities and limits of the driver, and being unrealistic. He claims that traffic laws primarily serve to allocate blame when an accident occurs and only secondarily save to prevent accidents.

Nevertheless, if the two fundamental assumptions are accepted, it is suggested that the violation of traffic laws contradicts at least two basic human motivations. First, as with other risky behaviors, violating traffic contradicts the motivation of self-preservation, which is considered a basic human motivation (Maslow, 1954) because it is a dangerous behavior that has been found to be correlated with accident liability (Parker, Reason, Manstead & Stradling, 1995). Based on these findings, Parker and Manstead (1996) claim that a successful approach to road safety might include a focus on reducing the commission of violations by influencing drivers not to deviate deliberately from safe practices.

The second contradiction reflected in the violation of traffic laws is related to people's motivation to maintain a positive self-image (Tesser, 2001), which presumably includes

[1] University of Haifa, Israel. *E-mail:* dyagil@research.haifa.ac.il (D. Yagil).

the notion of being a law-abiding citizen. Significantly, Baxter, Macrae, Stradling, Reason and Parker (1990) found that drivers attribute their own violations to situational factors, yet attribute the same behaviors in other drivers to dispositional factors.

In other words, drivers' behavior relating to traffic laws does not seem to follow the rules of logic. Drivers do not take traffic laws seriously, and behave as if these laws were fundamentally different from other laws. A possible reason for this inconsistency relates to the nature of traffic laws themselves. Certain inherent unique characteristics of traffic laws might make compliance especially difficult, namely:

(1) Traffic laws have a more ubiquitous presence in people's everyday lives than most other laws. Every day, and usually more than once, people are faced with the need to keep to a speed limit, use a seat belt, comply with traffic signs, etc. Furthermore, drivers have to comply with these laws simultaneously. Thus, the probability of violating traffic laws is higher than the probability of violating other laws, simply because there are more opportunities to violate them. Moreover, due to a process of habituation, traffic laws may become less impressive than other laws.

(2) Compliance with some traffic laws requires constant effort and alertness, e.g. maintaining a speed limit. Much less effort is required in maintaining laws in most other areas.

(3) Some traffic laws are not dichotomous, and it possible to violate them only a little, e.g. exceeding the speed limit a little, or coming to a nearly full stop at a *stop* sign. Thus, it is possible not to comply with traffic laws without feeling that one has violated them, which enables drivers to commit violations, without changing their self-perception as law-abiding citizens. This might partially explain why maintaining the speed limit, which is continuous, is the most frequently violated law, whereas using a seat belt, which is dichotomous, is an infrequently violated law. Such behavior is characteristic of many traffic laws. By comparison, laws in other areas of life are often dichotomous.

Most explanations of drivers' law-abiding behavior refer to driver motivations. Following is a review of some of these explanations, in relation to general theories about the violation of law among non-delinquent citizens.

A COMPARISON OF INSTRUMENTAL AND NORMATIVE PERSPECTIVES ON COMPLIANCE WITH THE LAW

In a comprehensive book entitled *Why do people obey the law?* Tyler (1990) observed that there are two perspectives of obedience to laws: instrumental and normative. According to the instrumental perspective, which underlies the literature on deterrence, people are motivated by gains, losses, rewards and punishments related to obeying or disobeying the law. Thus, increasing the severity and certainty of punishment is viewed as an effective way of increasing obedience. By contrast, the normative perspective, explains compliance with the law as a function of values that reflect what people feel they ought to do, and which possess a strong motivational component independent of any specific environment. In this perspective, people bring their values to their environment with the values constituting a force that shapes motivation in the environment. Values lend consistency to behavior, across situations and over time, that would not exist if people behaved according to their evaluations of the potential costs and benefits of various behaviors, within any given situation. Thus, e.g. most people will not rob a bank even if they notice that the guard is asleep and the likelihood of success appears to be high. Robbing a bank is contrary to the sense of obligation to obey the law, which they bring into the bank with them (Tyler, 2001). However, since the sense of compliance with traffic laws is weaker, many drivers will exceed the speed limit when they evaluate that there is a low risk of being apprehended by the police.

Kelman (1961) in differentiating between various levels of attitude change, also refers to instrumental and normative motives. In Kelman's view, instrumental motives are reflected in compliance, which is the most superficial level of attitude change. He described this level of attitude change as a reaction initiated solely by the desire to avoid punishment, or to receive positive rewards, and is maintained only in the presence of the change agent. Normative motives, by contrast, are the result of the internalization of an attitude, which is the deepest level of attitude change. It is reflected in the acceptance of an attitude because it is coherent with the individual's general system of values and beliefs. Arguably, the distinction between the instrumental and normative perspectives is a distinction between the perception of obedience to laws in terms of a means (leading to costs and/or rewards) or as a goal in itself.

The difference between compliance and internalization is clearly demonstrated in the area of perceived probability of detection, a major consideration in drivers' attitudes toward speed choice. Aberg (1997) discusses the effect of visible surveillance, which represents a main reason for compliance with the law. Increased enforcement leads to an increased probability of detection, and therefore also decreases the driver's tendency to commit violations. Nevertheless, studies have found that this behavioral change does not necessarily lead to a change in the driver's attitudes. Aberg concluded that the effects of enforcement activities are of short duration. Thus, there is a behavior of compliance in the presence of the enforcement authorities, but since there is no internalization of the importance of maintaining the speed limit, there is no real attitude change.

Tyler (2001) maintains that there is a general shift away from the strategies of social regulation, that are based upon the use of command and control approaches, toward a greater focus on approaches that exert social regulation through the consent and cooperation of those who are being regulated. Such self-regulation is achieved when people's internal values dictate that they ought to follow social rules. Once a control approach is replaced with a focus on self-regulation, the focus of attention is on the internal motives that shape people's behavior.

Both instrumental and normative motives interact with demographic factors to affect drivers' behavior. Yagil (1998a) found that both types of motivations are weaker among younger drivers. Nevertheless, normative motivations such as a sense of obligation to comply with the law were a better predictor of the intention to violate the law among young drivers, whereas instrumental motives were a better predictor among older drivers. In a comparison of age and gender groups (Yagil, 1998b), the lowest level of perceived importance of traffic laws relative to other laws was found among young male drivers. Instrumental motivation (i.e. perceived danger involved in the commission of a traffic violation) was found to be stronger among women than among men. Pedestrian road-crossing behavior, namely crossing against a "don't walk" sign, was predicted by the perceived consequences of the behavior, as well as by normative considerations (Yagil, 2000).

The instrumental perspective: models of rational behavior

Rational-choice theories of illegal behavior explain offenses in terms of the costs and benefits of committing violations, and suggest that the intention to commit illegal behavior is inversely related to the perceived cost of the act (Clarke & Cornish, 1994). Possible reasons for the violation of traffic laws are described by Rothengatter (1997) in terms of costs and benefits, such as being in a hurry, seeking excitement, trying to prove one's skill, or being in a bad mood. The main rational theory applied to the area of traffic law violations is Ajzen's (1985) theory of planned behavior, which is derived from Fishbein and Ajzen's (1975) theory of reasoned action. The theory of planned behavior, suggests that the decision to engage in a particular behavior is the result of a rational process, that is goal-oriented and that follows a logical sequence. Behavioral options are considered, consequences of each option are evaluated, and a decision is reached. The decision is reflected in behavioral intentions that are a strong predictor of actual behavior. These behavioral intentions themselves can be predicted by attitudes toward the specific behavior—subjective norms; and perceived behavioral control. Many studies on the planned behavior theory were conducted by the Manchester Driver Behavior Group Research project which predicted the intention to violate traffic laws based on the original model as well as added components such as personal norms (Parker, Manstead & Stradling, 1995) and situational factors, e.g. such as time of day and the presence of a passenger in the car (Parker, Manstead, Stradling & Reason, 1992a,b).

The health beliefs model which is also based on the assumption that people behave in a rational manner, was applied to road safety to predict the helmet use among cyclists (Arnold & Quine, 1994) and safe-riding behavior among motorcyclists (Rutter, Quine & Chesham, 1995).

Nevertheless, rational-instrumental explanations seem to be insufficient in explaining driver behavior relating to traffic laws: ample evidence supports the effect of emotions on the violation of traffic laws. For example Lawton, Parker, Manstead and Stradling (1997a) found various positive emotions relating to speeding such as feeling exhilarated and powerful, and concluded that the assessment of attitudes must include measures of affect and not purely cognitive measures. More broadly, various personality traits unrelated to cognitive processes but related to emotional motivations were found to affect the violation of laws generally. A well-known example is the effect of sensation-seeking defined by Zuckerman (1979) as "the need for varied, novel, and complex sensations and experiences, and the willingness to take physical and social risks for the sake of such experiences" (p. 10). Numerous studies have found a relationship between sensation seeking and risky driving (reviewed by Jonah, 1997). Yagil (2001) indicated that the intention of drivers to commit traffic violations is predicted by attitudes toward this behavior, and by sensation seeking, external locus of control, aggression and anxiety.

The normative perspective: legitimacy, procedural justice, legal culture and moral reasoning

In addition to instrumental considerations and emotions, social values also affect the violation of traffic laws. Although the normative perspective on the antecedents of such values has not been studied as widely as the instrumental perspective in regard to compliance with traffic laws, it is precisely this perspective that might explain why the sense of obligation to comply applies less to traffic laws than to other laws. The normative perspective focuses on voluntary compliance with laws rather than compliance as a response to external rewards and punishments. Voluntary compliance results from a belief that the authorities have a legitimate right to dictate behavior.

Legitimacy

Legitimacy has been defined as an issue that arises in an interaction either between two people, or between a person and a system, in which one party makes a certain claim, which the other accepts or rejects (Kelman, 2001). Acceptance or rejection depends on whether that claim is seen as rightful. Legitimacy can be evaluated on two levels: One level concerns the legitimacy of the claim itself, and the other concerns the legitimacy of the claimant—the person or system that makes the claim. Kelman explicitly associates the concept of legitimacy with the normative perspective of behavior, by suggesting that whereas the main theoretical models in the social sciences, such as rational choice, focus on the interests of the actors, the concept of legitimacy implies that there are significant aspects of social behavior and social structure that are determined not by interests but by rights and obligations. Parker and Manstead (1996) expressed a similar view in regard to compliance with traffic laws, maintaining that "internalized notions of right and wrong driver behavior, play a significant role in determining behavioral intentions over and above considerations of consequences, social norms and the perceived controllability of the behavior" (pp. 207–208).

According to Tyler (2001), feelings of obligation are central to legitimacy. Legitimacy exists to the degree that people feel a personal obligation to follow social rules and to obey social authorities. The ability to develop and maintain legitimacy is a key feature of effective authority because it is based on social values that shape people's voluntary behavior. Social values involve self-regulation because people take the responsibility to obey laws without considerations of potential benefits or costs. Thus, compliance with traffic laws is presumably affected by the driver's perception that law-enforcing authorities have the right to demand compliance with traffic laws and that traffic laws themselves are legitimate.

Procedural justice

Tyler (2001) suggests that the roots of legitimacy lie in people's assessments of procedural justice, i.e. the fairness of the decision-making procedures used by the authorities, whereas the favorability or fairness of the outcomes have little impact on legitimacy granted to the authorities. Furthermore, research suggests that the effect of procedural justice remains stronger over time than the effect of the outcomes. For example, Paternoster et al. (1997) found that the citizen's evaluation of the fairness of an encounter with the police predicted continued deterrence better than did the degree or type of sanctioning that occurred during the initial experience.

The experience of fair procedures practiced by the authorities results in an obligation to accept the authority's decisions and support its rules. Gibson and Caldeira (1996) suggest that a specific aspect of perceived fairness, the perceived neutrality of the law, strongly affects citizens' support of the law. People who view law as a neutral force are likely to value it either because it reinforces a desirable social order or because it serves the interests of all citizens. Those who view law as neutral are more likely to support it than those who doubt its neutrality.

Indeed, obedience to laws was found to be related to perceived procedural justice attributed to authorities (Lind & Tyler, 1988; Tyler & Mitchell, 1994). Smith and Tyler (1996) found that American citizens' feeling of obligation to comply with the decisions of the Congress is explained by their assessment of the quality of treatment that people receive from Congress when it makes policy decisions.

Three surveys conducted over 3 years, using representative samples of Israeli citizens, aimed to predict the willingness to take the law into one's own hands as a function of social, personal and attitudinal variables (Rattner & Yagil, forthcoming; Rattner, Yagil & Pedhazur, 2001; Yagil & Rattner, 2002). Perceived procedural justice was measured by questions about police and court conduct (e.g. "The Israeli police/courts fulfill their functions equally towards one and all"); commitment to the law was measured by questions examining the sense of obligation to comply with the law under all circumstances (e.g. "It is unnecessary to obey laws that seem unreasonable to me"). Procedural justice was repeatedly found to be positively related to commitment to the law, which in turn was negatively related to the willingness to take the law into one's own hands.

A study of the effect of procedural justice regarding traffic violations specifically (Xie & Parker, 2002) examined the relationship between violation of laws, and attitudes toward law-enforcement authorities and traffic laws among Chinese drivers. Drivers were asked about their reaction to being stopped on the road for committing a driving violation or for getting a traffic ticket, and about their concern about violating laws. The findings showed that violations were positively correlated with the perception that social hierarchy plays a role in the authorities' decisions regarding the enforcement of traffic laws, i.e. drivers who believed that authorities decisions are influenced by social status reported committing more violations.

The attribution of procedural fairness includes an important linkage to the way people are treated by the authorities. People are strongly affected by the dignity of their treatment by the authorities and by the degree of respect shown for their rights. They are influenced by evidence of neutrality, trustworthiness and benevolence on the part of the authorities whom they encounter (Tyler, 2001). This aspect of procedural justice is highly relevant to the area of compliance with traffic laws.

According to Radelet and Cartet (1994, p. 207) "by far the biggest conflict between the police and the public occurs in the enforcement of traffic laws." Encounters between police officers and citizens in traffic situations constitute a major source of citizen hostility toward the police (Wilson, 1964). According to one study (Kirkham & Wollan, 1980) for most citizens traffic incidents represent their only encounter with the police. This encounter often stimulates negative emotions on the part of drivers because the police officer is seen as a salient symbol of government authority, and being caught thus represents interference with the driver's freedom of action. Furthermore, although drivers admit to having violated a traffic law, there is often a feeling of having been unjustly singled out for punishment because drivers witness many cases in which violations are undetected. Radelet and Carter (1994) suggest that when a driver is asked to stop and pull over not only does he/she feel singled out, but also suspicious that the only reason for the police officer's behavior is the desire to fill a quota. Any feelings of guilt that might be engendered by the violation are transferred to the police officer as a defense mechanism. Indeed, Yagil (1998c) found that police officers enforcing traffic laws were perceived by drivers as disagreeable, their conduct was evaluated negatively and drivers experienced anger more than shame when they were stopped by a police officer after committing a violation. These effects were stronger for young drivers.

In a similar vein, Kirkham and Wollan (1980) found that the explanations drivers offer for being stopped by a police officer refer mainly to officers' personal motives and improper conduct. The most frequent assumption is that the officer is behind his/her daily quota, although some drivers also assume that the officer has something against sport cars, is prejudiced against blacks or whites, young or old drivers, etc. Most drivers do not consider accident prevention to be a major motive behind police officers actions.

Using Kelman's differentiation between the legitimacy of the claimant and the legitimacy of the claim as a starting point, several possible types of legitimacy can affect driver compliance with traffic laws as follows:

(1) The violation of traffic laws may reflect a lack of legitimacy attributed to the authorities who enforce these laws, as described above (Xie & Parker, 2002).

(2) More broadly, compliance with traffic laws may relate to the level of legitimacy attributed to authorities in general. This possibility is indirectly supported by evidence that the propensity to commit traffic violation is related to a more general antisocial motivation. Lawton, Parker, Stradling and Manstead (1997b) found a relationship between mild social deviance and accident rates which was mediated by the tendency to commit violations. Sivak (1983), in a study conducted across the United States found that homicide rates predicted the traffic fatality rates in 50 states. West, Elander and French (1993) explain the relationship between social deviance and the violation of traffic laws by maintaining that the tendency toward social deviance affects driving style, which is the way a person chooses to drive, as opposed to driving skill, which is the way a person is capable of driving. Suchman (1970) also claimed that the association results from the tendency of deviants to expose themselves to risky environments. Nevertheless, the relationship between social deviance and the violation of traffic laws might be mediated by drivers' attitudes toward the authorities. Underwood, Chapman Wright and Crundall (1997) suggested that people who violate traffic laws and are opposed to a stricter enforcement of traffic laws, probably demonstrate their tendency toward social deviance in other ways as well. This explanation is supported in their study examining the relationship between accident liability and drivers' attitudes toward violations and violators, which showed that both social deviance and the violation of traffic laws are related to attitudes toward violations and the enforcement of traffic laws.

(3) The legitimacy granted to the enforcement of a specific law may also play a role in driver willingness to comply with the law. Conceivably some laws are violated because drivers see them as illogical, redundant or impractical. Lawton, Parker, Stradling and Manstead (1997c) found that most drivers make judgments about the type of road on which they are driving and the degree of speeding that is acceptable, and their intention to speed varies accordingly. Although such a flexible-individualistic approach to compliance with the law

is viewed as a high level of moral reasoning in Kholberg's model (1969), Reason, Parker, and Lawton (1998) suggested that compliance involves following formal rules and procedures irrespective of whether or not the rule is a good one or wholly applicable to the situation.

Legal culture

The legitimacy granted to authorities and to laws may be conceptualized as legal culture. Gibson and Caldeira (1996) suggested that a country's culture affects the legal attitudes of its citizens when the issue of compliance with the law is not clear-cut.

Bierdbrauer (1994) observed, in this vein, that "Law and legal systems are cultural products like language, music and marriage arrangements…. This structure is passed on through socially transmitted norms of conduct, and rules of decision, that influence the construction of intentional systems, including cognitive processes and individual dispositions" (Bierdbrauer, 1994, p. 243). By way of example, Bierdbrauer found cultural differences in the respect for state laws relating to religious differences.

Gibson and Caldeira (1996) also found significant cross-national differences in citizens' attitudes toward the law. In response to the sentence, "If you don't particularly agree with a law, it is alright to break it if you are careful not to get caught," 93% of the British respondents disagreed but the rates of disagreement in France, Luxembourg and Belgium were considerably lower: one quarter of the respondents agreed. Significant differences were also found in the perceived neutrality of the law, which in West Germany, the Netherlands, Britain and Denmark was high but in Greece low. This research found that legal disobedience in European countries generally.

Legal culture is therefore viewed as a socially derived code of behavior encompassing concepts such as legitimacy, the acceptance of authority, support for the rule of law and the notion that citizens should obey the law (Bierdbrauer, 1994; Gibson & Caldeira, 1996). This definition may explain findings relating to cross-cultural differences in compliance with traffic laws. For example, Demick, Inoue, Wapner and Isinii (1992) found differences between the use of safety belts in the US and in Japan: the rates were higher in Japan. The lower American rate was related to the concern of the American sample that mandatory safety belt legislation was an invasion of privacy and a violation of human rights. This difference reflects the effect of the individualism–collectivism tendency of cultures on the support of the rule of law as discussed by Gibson and Caldeira (1996) in their description of the components of legal culture.

Moral reasoning

The normative perspective of compliance with law includes moral values and a sense of duty. Kohlberg (1969) in presenting a model of stages of moral reasoning describes the developmental changes in the individual's view of authority and the duty to comply with its laws. According to the model, "preconventional" morality is characterized by attributing legitimacy solely to powerful authorities, to the avoidance of punishment and to reward seeking. The second stage, "conventional" morality, is reflected in granting legitimacy to the authorities based on their intentions, or legitimacy that results from unquestioned respect for authority. The last stage, "postconventional" morality, grants legitimacy to a system that is seen as functioning in accordance with universal principles of justice, equality and human rights (Jasinka-Kania, 1989). According to Kohlberg's model, the issue of compliance with the law is closely associated with moral values. Research by Rattner, Yagil and Sherman-Segal (2003) indeed shows a negative relationship between the willingness to disobey the law on ideological grounds and moral reasoning.

Bianchi and Summuala (2002) examining the relationship between moral judgment and involvement in accidents did not find a conclusive relationship, although this was explained by the small variance in moral judgment in the sample. Nevertheless, morality was found to affect traffic violations in a study by Parker et al. (1995), who showed that adding a component of personal norm to the variables included in the theory of planned behavior predicted the intention to violate traffic laws. The personal norm variable consisted of moral norms, that reflects the internalization of moral rules, and anticipated regret, that reflects the expected affective consequences of breaking the rules. The researchers found that adding this component to the model heightened its predictive ability.

THE EFFECT OF THE SELF-CONCEPT ON COMPLIANCE WITH TRAFFIC LAWS

The self-discrepancy theory

According to the self-discrepancy theory developed by Tory Higgins (1989), the relationships between different types of self-beliefs cause emotional reactions. The theory refers to self-beliefs relating to three aspects of self: the actual-self which consists of the attributes the person believes he/she possesses; the ideal-self which consists of the attributes that the person would like to possess; and the ought-self which consists of the attributes that the person believes he/she ought to possess. The theory assumes that people are motivated to reach a condition in which their actual-self matches the ideal-self and the ought-self. In the case of a discrepancy between the actual-self and the ideal-self, the discrepancy represents the absence of positive outcomes and this will lead to dejection-related symptoms (sadness, dissatisfaction and lowered behavioral and physiological responses). When the actual-self is discrepant from the ought-self, the individual sees his/her current attributes as not matching the state he/she believes it is his/her duty to attain. The breach of duty could be accompanied by sanctions, and this discrepancy therefore represents the presence of negative outcomes and arouses agitation-related emotions (fear, threat and heightened behavioral and physiological responses).

Applying this theory to the area of traffic law violations, it may be assumed that the violation of such laws is part of the ought-self because it has to do with duties and obligations. Accordingly, the self-discrepancy theory would predict that whenever a driver violates a traffic law, this behavior should engender agitation relating to the fear of sanctions and criticism. Presumably, however, most drivers do not experience fear every time they violate a traffic law, otherwise such behavior would not be so common. In fact, the emotion that has been found most frequently in the research relating to driving is not fear but anger, and this probably reflects the prevailing emotion in driving.

One possible explanation for the lack of a sense of agitation whenever a driver commits a traffic violation is that the probability of having an accident, or of being stopped by a police officer is perceived as low. Thus, drivers do not expect negative outcomes as a result of a discrepancy between what they ought to do and what they are actually doing. Another explanation is that drivers are often unaware of a discrepancy between their actual-self and their ought-self. A driver who routinely exceeds the speed limit might not have a sense of doing something forbidden each and every time, especially if he/she exceeds the limit only a little. In this analysis, it is the presence of the police that stimulates agitation because it forces drivers to become aware of the discrepancy between what they are doing and what they ought to do, and increase awareness of the sanctions that follow the discrepancy. A third explanation is that there is an intrinsic contradiction between the ideal-self and the ought-self in the context of driving. Being a skillful driver is an aspect of the ideal-self, as demonstrated by studies on drivers' self-perceptions of this skill which is viewed as designed for self-enhancement (McKenna, 1993). However, the demonstration of this skill often involves risk taking and violating the law. For example, a driver can better demonstrate control of the car at a high speed than at a low speed. Indeed, Yagil (1999) found that safety orientation was weaker among professional drivers with a strong occupational commitment than among professional drivers with a weak commitment. This unexpected result might be interpreted as resulting from the perceived contradiction between skill and safety. Drivers who violate laws might at the same time engage in a demonstration of their skill. The demonstration of skill might reduce the discrepancy between the ideal-self and the actual-self, generate positive emotions and thus prevent the sense of agitation that would otherwise accompany breaking the law. This explanation is supported by a finding by Lawton et al. (1997a) that the violating traffic laws are related to positive affect.

Thus, in the driving situation the ideal-self might sometimes "compete" with the ought-self. Furthermore, being a skillful driver is associated with a positive image, namely that such a driver can cope with the unexpected, survive emergencies, is brave, self-reliant and "cool". A law-abiding driver is likely to be perceived at best as cautious which is not a very glamorous image. The other, more compelling images are likely to be strong among young drivers and to affect their driving. Essentially, campaigns that are designed to convince young drivers that complying with the law is actually a cool behavior represent an attempt to reduce the contradiction between these drivers' ideal and ought selves.

A later theory developed by Higgins, the theory of regulatory focus (1998), which stemmed from the self-discrepancy theory, distinguishes between a promotion focus, in which the individual strives toward positive outcomes and is focused on accomplishments and aspirations, and a prevention focus, in which the individual avoids negative outcomes and is focused on safety, duty and responsibility.

This difference in regulatory focus seems to be highly relevant to traffic-law violation. Conceivably, a promotion focus will be related to the motivation to achieve desired goals that might lead to the violation of laws such as getting to one's destination quickly, or enjoying fast driving. Indeed, research on the promotion focus showed it to be related to more risky behaviors (Levine, Higgins & Choi, 2000). The prevention focus by contrast, is likely to be related to compliance with laws in order to avoid negative sanctions, and therefore drivers with a prevention focus are likely to be more law abiding. Nevertheless, the regulatory focus is also affected by the situation. Situational cues that generate a prevention focus are expected to increase compliance with traffic laws.

MOTIVATIONAL BIASES RELATING TO COMPLIANCE WITH TRAFFIC LAWS

According to cognitive dissonance theory (Festinger, 1957), the awareness of an inconsistency between two or more attitudes generates an unpleasant state that induces a motivation to reduce the dissonance. Accordingly, an awareness that one is violating traffic laws would be dissonant for most people with the belief that this is dangerous behavior as well as with the person's self-perception as a law-abiding citizen. To reduce the dissonance, at least one of these attitudes must be changed. Conceivably, drivers' biases in self-perception as well as in the perception of other drivers serve to reduce dissonance by enhancing their sense of personal safety as well as allowing them to maintain a self-concept of law-abiding citizens. Thus, these biases actually enhance the violation of traffic laws.

The dissonance that results from the coexistence of the cognitions "The violation of traffic laws is dangerous" and "I violate traffic laws" are reduced by adopting the belief that traffic violations are dangerous but only for other drivers, because:

(1) I am a better driver than other drivers (the bias of an illusion of control); and

(2) The world is Just, and bad things do not happen to good people like myself (the bias of a belief in a Just World).

Illusion of control

The illusion of control is defined as the tendency to overrate one's control over one's own behavior and one's environment. In the context of driving, one example of the illusion of control is an exaggerated estimation of one's ability. Drivers hold various beliefs that have been described as illusionary, such as that they are more skillful than other drivers (Groerger & Brown, 1989; McKenna, Stainer & Lewis, 1991; Sevenson, 1981) or are less likely to be involved in an accident (McKenna, 1993). DeJoy (1992) found that overestimating one's driving ability is stronger among male drivers, who also underestimate the risks involved in various driving activities. The tendency to overrate one's driving ability is universal: Sivak, Soler and Traenkle (1989) found that there were no cross-cultural differences in driver self-assessment, as the majority of drivers in each country rated themselves positively on all driving-related scales. Horswill, Waylen and Tofield (2004) found that drivers evaluated themselves as superior to other drivers on hazard perception skills, which are related to perceived safety. While the illusion of a high level of skill and control serves the purpose of self-enhancement (McKenna, 1993), it is also likely to enhance a false sense of safety and justify risky driving. Indeed, Horswill et al. (2004) suggest that if drivers believe that they are more skilled and less likely to be involved in accidents than others, they have less reason to be cautious. Safety campaigns cannot be effective because while people might agree with the content of the campaigns, they assume that it is relevant to other drivers who are not as skilled.

Belief in a Just World

Another bias that serves to enhance a sense of safety is the belief in a Just World, described by Lerner and Miller (1978) as resulting from people's "need to believe that they live in a world where people generally get what they deserve" (p. 1030). This belief provides psychological buffers against the harsh realities of life along with a sense of personal control over one's own destiny. People feel less vulnerable and have a lower perception of risk because they believe they have done nothing to deserve negative outcomes (Furnham, 2003). The need to believe in a Just World presumably leads to the belief that accidents cannot happen to the driver him/herself but only to other drivers because they did something wrong. Montada (1998) reviewing studies on process of victim blaming to restore Just World beliefs found relationships between the belief in a Just World and blaming of many different categories of victims such as AIDS patients, rape victims, the Third World poor, and accident cases.

In order to maintain the self-concept of a law-abiding citizen, drivers need to resolve the contradiction between two cognitions: "traffic laws are laws" and "I violate traffic laws." One possible way to minimize this contradiction and the resulting dissonance is to attribute the same behavior regarding violating the law to other drivers (the bias of false consensus). By doing so, drivers create a sense of belonging to a majority group and therefore negate the possibility that they are behaving in a socially deviant manner.

False consensus

The bias of false consensus, i.e. the tendency to attribute one's own attitudes and behavior to others, was studied in a sample of drivers by Manstead, Parker, Stradling, Reason and Baxter (1992). They found that frequency of violations was related to the evaluated percentage of other drivers who commit the same violations. Furthermore, Groeger and Chapman (1997) found that information about the percentage of other drivers who were not speeding or tailgating reduced the occurrence of these traffic violations, but only if the information showed that the majority of the drivers complied with the law. Rothengatter (1988, 1991) argued that beliefs about driving norms influence drivers' behavior in that committing violations depends not only on anticipated consequences but also on the wish to behave like other drivers. It can also serve to achieve consensual validation and the feeling that one is doing the right thing. However, apart from social comparison and conformity, information about other drivers' behavior might neutralize the false consensus effect and force drivers to actually comply with the laws in order to maintain their self-concept of law-abiding citizens.

Conclusions

Several possible future research directions derive from this review:

(1) Issues relating to the normative perspective of traffic law violations have been the subject of much less study than the instrumental-rational perspective. Further research is called for to examine the extant of legitimacy attributed to the legislation of traffic laws, to the authorities' responsible for the enforcement of traffic laws and to the laws themselves. Exploring the effect of procedural justice attributed to the courts and the police regarding compliance with traffic laws would also be beneficial. Another issue relating

to the normative perspective is legal culture. Cross-cultural differences shown in various studies on the violation of traffic laws signify that legal culture ought to be explored as one of the causes of this variance.

(2) Perceptions and attributions that reduce cognitive dissonance associated with violating traffic laws also merit research. The discrepancy between attitudes and behavior has been found to be minimized when people trivialize the impact of such behavior (Simon, Greenberg & Brehm, 1995), as when drivers claim that they have exceeded the speed limit by just a little. Furthermore, it might be desirable to examine whether cognitive dissonance can be manipulated to affect drivers' behavior in the desired direction. Aronson, Fried and Stone (1991) found that when people are made aware of the contradiction between their behavior and their attitudes, they become more conscious of hypocrisy and may change their behavior accordingly.

(3) The relationship between violations and driver's self-concept constitutes another research area. Individual differences in the association of compliance with the law and the driver's self-concept are likely to affect law-abiding behavior. In this context, individual differences in the driver's regulatory focus seem to be especially relevant.

REFERENCES

Aberg, A. (1997). The role of perceived risk of detection. In Rothengatter, T., & Vaya, E.C. (Eds.), *Traffic and Transport Psychology*. Oxford: Elsevier Science Ltd.

Ajzen, I. (1985). From intentions to actions: a theory of planned behavior. In Kuhl, J., & Beckmann, J. (Eds.), *Action Control: From Cognition to Behavior* (pp. 11–39). Berlin: Springer.

Arnold, L., & Quine, L. (1994). Predicting helmet use among schoolboy cyclists: an application of the Health Belief Mode. In Rutter, D.R., & Quine, L. (Eds.), *Social Psychology and Health: European Perspectives* (pp. 101–130), Brookfield, VT: Avebury Ashgate Publishing.

Aronson, E., Fried, C., & Stone, J. (1991). Overcoming denial: increasing the intention to use condoms through the induction of hypocrisy. *American Journal of Public Health, 18,* 1636–1640.

Baxter, J.S., Macrae, C.N., Manstead, A.S., Stradling, S.G. & Parker, D. (1990). Attributional biases and driver behavior. *Social Behavior, 5,* 185–192.

Bianchi, A., & Summala, H. (2002). Moral judgment and drivers' behavior among Brazilians students. *Psychological Reports, 91,* 759–766.

Bierdbrauer, G. (1994). Toward an understanding of legal culture: variations in individualism and collectivism between Kurds, Lebanese and Germans. *Law & Society Review, 28,* 243–264.

Clarke, R.V., & Cornish, D.B. (1994). Modeling offenders' decisions: a framework for research and policy. In Farrington, D.P. (Ed.), *Psychologicl Explanations of Crime, The International Library of Criminology, Criminal Justice & Penology* (pp. 399–437). Brookfield, VT: Dartmouth Publishing Company.

DeJoy, D.M. (1992). An examination of gender differences in traffic accident risk perception. *Accident Analysis and Prevention, 24,* 237–246.

Demick, J., Inoue, W., Wapner, S., & Ishii, S. (1992). Cultural differences in impact of governmental legislation: automobile safety belt use. *Journal of Cross Cultural Psychology, 23*, 468–487.

Festinger, L. (1957). *A Theory of Cognitive Dissonance*. Evanston, IL: Row Peterson.

Fishbein, M., & Ajzen, I. (1975). *Beliefa, Attitudes, Intention and Behavior: An Introduction to Theory and Research*. Reading, MA: Addison-Wesley.

Furnham, A. (2003). Belief in a just world: research progress over the last decade. *Personality and Individual Differences, 34*, 795–817.

Gibson, J.L., & Caldeira, G.A. (1996). The legal cultures of Europe. *Law and Society Review, 30*, 55–85.

Groeger, J.A., & Brown, I.D. (1989). Assessing one's own and others' driving ability: influences of sex, age and experience. *Accident Analysis and Prevention, 21*, 155–168.

Groeger, J.A., & Chapman, P.R. (1997). Normative influences on decisions to offend. *Applied Psychology: An International Review, 46*, 265–285.

Higgins, E.T. (1989). In Berkowitz, L. (Ed.), *Self-discrepancy theory: What Patterns of Self-Beliefs Cause People to Suffer?* (pp. 93–136). San Diego, CA: Academic Press.

Higgins, E.T. (1998). Promotion and prevention: the pains and pleasures of distinct regulatory systems. In Kavanaugh, D., Zimmerberg, B., & Fein, S. (Eds.), *Emotions: Interdisciplinary Perspectives* (pp. 203–241). Mahwah, NJ: Erlbaum.

Horswill, M., Waylen, A.E., & Tofield, M.I. (2004). Drivers' ratings of different components of their own driving skill: a greater illusion of superiority for skills that relate to accident involvement. *Journal of Applied Social Psychology, 34*, 177–195.

Jasinka-Kania, A. (1989). Moral values and political attitudes. In Eisenberg, E., Reykowski, J., & Staub, E. (Eds.), *Social and Moral Values, Individual and Societal Perspectives*. Hillsdale, NJ: Lawrence Erlbaum Associates.

Jonah, B.A. (1997). Sensation seeking and risky driving. In Rothengatter, T., & Vaya, E.C. (Eds.), *Traffic and Transport Psychology*. Oxford: Elsevier Science Ltd.

Kelman, H.C. (1961). Processes of opinion change. *Public Opinion Quarterly, 25*, 57–78.

Kelman, H.C. (2001). Reflections on social and psychological processes of legitimization and delegitimization. In Jost, J.T., & Major, B. (Eds.), *The Psychology of Legitimacy*. Cambridge: Cambridge University Press.

Kirkham, J.L., & Wollan, L.A. (1980). *Introduction to Law Enforcement*. New York: Harper & Row Publishers.

Kohlberg, L. (1969). Stage and sequence: the cognitive-developmental approach to socialization. In Goslin, D.A. (Ed.), *Handbook of Socialization Theory and Research*. Chicago: Rand NoNally.

Lawton, R., Parker, D., Manstead, S.G., & Stradling, A.S.R. (1997a). The role of affect in predicting social behaviors: the case of road traffic violations. *Journal of Applied Social Psychology, 27*, 1258–1276.

Lawton, R., Parker, D., Stradling, S.G., & Manstead, A.S.R. (1997b). Predicting road traffic accidents: the role of social deviance and violations. *British Journal of Psychology, 88*, 249–263.

Lawton, R., Parker, D., Stradling, S.G., & Manstead, A.S.R. (1997c). Self-reported attitude towards speeding and its possible consequences in five different road contexts. *Journal of Community and Applied Social Psychology, 7*, 153–165.

Lerner, M.J., & Miller, D.T. (1978). Just world research and the attribution process: looking back and ahead. *Psychological Bulletin, 85*, 1030–1051.

Levine, J.M., Higgins, E.T., & Choi, H.S. (2000). Development of strategic norms in groups. *Organizational Behavior and Human Decision Processes*, *82*, 88–101.

Lind, E.A., & Tyler, T.R. (1988). *The Social Psychology of Procedural Justice*. New York: Plenum.

Manstead, A., Parker, D., Stradling, S.G., Reason, J.T., & Baxter, J.S. (1992). Perceived consensus in estimates of the prevalence of driving errors and violations. *Journal of Applied Social Psychology*, *22*, 509–530.

Maslow, H.A. (1954). *Motivation and Personality*. New York: Harper & Row.

McKenna, F.P. (1993). It won't happen to me: unrealistic optimism or illusion of control. *British Journal of Psychology*, *84*, 39–50.

McKenna, F.P., Stainer, R.A., & Lewis, C. (1991). Factors underlying illusory self-assessment of driving skills in males and females. *Accident Analysis and Prevention*, *23*, 45–52.

Montada, L. (1998). Belief in a Just World: a hybrid of justice motive and self interest? In Montada, L., & Lerner, M.J. (Eds.), *Response to Victimization and Belief in a Just World, Critical issues in social justice*, pp. 217–246). New York: Plenum Press.

Parker, D., & Manstead, A. (1996). The social psychology of driver behavior. In Semin, G.R., & Klaus, F. (Eds.), *Applied Social Psychology* (pp. 198–224). London: Sage.

Parker, D., Manstead, A.S.R., Stradling, S.G., & Reason, J.T. (1992a). Intention to commit driving violations: an application of the theory of planned behavior. *Journal of Applied Psychology*, *77*, 94–101.

Parker, D., Manstead, A.S.R., Stradling, S.G., & Reason, J.T. (1992b). Determinants of intention to commit driving violations. *Accidents Analysis and Prevention*, *24*, 117–134.

Parker, D., Reason, J.T., Manstead, A., & Stradling, S.G. (1995). Driving errors, driving violations and accident involvement. *Ergonomics*, *38*, 1036–1048.

Parker, D., Manstead, A.S.R., & Stradling, S.G. (1995). Expanding the theory of planned behavior: the role of personal norms. *British Journal of Social Psychology*, *34*, 127–137.

Paternoster, R., Bachman, R., Brame, R., & Sherman, L.W. (1997). Do fair procedures matter? The effect of procedural justice on spouse assault. *Law and Society Review*, *31*, 163–204.

Radelet, L.A., & Carter, D.L. (1994). *The Police and the Community*. New York: Macmillan College Publishing Company.

Rattner, A., & Yagil, D. Taking the law into one's own hands on ideological grounds. *International Journal of Sociology of the Law*, *32*, 85–101.

Rattner, A., Yagil, D., & Pedhazur, A. (2001). Not bound by the law: legal disobedience in Israeli society. *Behavioral Sciences and the Law*, *19*, 265–283.

Rattner, A., Yagil, D., & Sherman-Segal, C. (2003). The sense of entitlement to violate the law: legal disobedience as a public versus a private reaction. *Social Behavior and Personality*, *31*, 545–556.

Reason, J., Parker, D., & Lawton, R. (1998). Organizational controls and safety: the varieties of rule-related behavior. *Journal of Occupational and Organizational Psychology*, *71*, 289–304.

Rothengatter, T. (1988). Risk and the absence of pleasure: a motivational approach to modeling road user behavior. *Ergonomics*, *31*, 599–607.

Rothengatter, T. (1991). Automatic policing and information systems for increasing traffic law compliance. *Journal of Applied Behavior Analysis*, *24*, 85–87.

Rothengatter, T. (1997). Errors and violations as factors in accident causation. In Rothengatter, T., & Vaya, E.C. (Eds.), *Traffic and Transport Psychology*. Oxford: Elsevier Science Ltd.

Rutter, D.R., Quine, L., & Chesham, D.J. (1995). Predicting safe riding behavior and accidents: demography, beliefs, and behavior in motorcycling safety. *Psychology and Health, 10*, 369–386.

Sevenson, O. (1981). Are we all less risky and more skillful than our fellow drivers? *Psychologica, 47*, 143–148.

Simon, L., Greenberg, J., & Brehm, J. (1995). Trivialization: the forgotten mode of dissonance reduction. *Journal of Personality and Social Psychology, 68*, 247–260.

Sivak, M. (1983). Society's aggression level as a predictor of traffic fatality rate. *Journal of Safety Research, 14*, 93–99.

Sivak, M., Soler, J., & Traenkle, U. (1989). Cross cultural differences in driver self-assessment. *Accident Analysis and Prevention, 21*, 371–375.

Smith, H.J., & Tyler, R.T. (1996T). Justice and power: when will justice concerns encourage the advantaged to support policies which redistribute economic resources and the disadvantaged to willingly obey the law? *European Journal of Social Psychology, 26*, 171–200.

Suchman, E.A. (1970). Accidents and social deviance. *Journal of Health and Social Behavior, 11*, 4–15.

Tesser, A. (2001). On the plasticity of self-defense. *Current Directions in Psychological Science, 10*, 66–69.

Tyler, T. (1990). *Why People Obey the Law*. New Haven: Yale University Press.

Tyler, T. (2001). A psychological perspective on the legitimacy of institutions and authorities. In Jost, J.T., & Major, B. (Eds.), *The Psychology of Legitimacy*. Cambridge: Cambridge University Press.

Tyler, T., & Mitchell, G. (1994). Legitimacy and the empowerment of discretionary legal authority: the United States supreme court and abortion rights. *Duke Law Journal, 43*, 703–814.

Underwood, G., Chapman, P., Wright, S., & Crundall, D. (1997). Estimating accident liability. In Rothengatter, T., & Vaya, E.C. (Eds.), *Traffic and Transport Psychology*. Oxford: Elsevier Science Ltd.

West, R., Elander, J., & French, D. (1993). Mild social deviance, type-A behavior pattern and decision making style as predictors of self-reported driving style and traffic accident risk. *British Journal of Psychology, 84*, 207–219.

Wilson, O.W. (1964). Police authority in a free society. *Journal of Criminal law, Criminology and Police Science, 54*.

Xie, C.Q., & Parker, D. (2002). A social psychological approach to driving violations in two Chinese cities. *Transportation Research Part F: Traffic Psychology and Behavior, 5*, 293–308.

Yagil, D. (1998a). Instrumental and normative motives for compliance with traffic laws among young and older drivers. *Accident Analysis and Prevention, 30*, 417–424.

Yagil, D. (1998b). Gender and age differences in attitudes toward traffic laws and traffic violations. *Transportation Research Part F: Traffic Psychology and Behavior, 1*, 123–135.

Yagil, D. (1998c). I'm O.K.—you're not O.K.: drivers attitudes toward police officers' enforcing traffic laws. *Policing: An International Journal of Police Strategies and Management, 21*, 339–353.

Yagil, D. (1999). Job-related attitudes and safety orientation of professional drivers. *Journal of Traffic Medicine, 27*, 115–124.

Yagil, D. (2000). Beliefs, motives and situational factors related to pedestrians' self-reported behavior at signal-controlled crossings. *Transportation Research Part F: Traffic Psychology and Behavior, 3*, 1–13.

Yagil, D. (2001). Reasoned action and irrational motives: a prediction of drivers' intention to violate traffic laws. *Journal of Applied Social Psychology, 31*, 720–740.

Yagil, D., & Rattner, A. (2002). Between commandments and laws: religiosity, political ideology, and legal obedience in Israel. *Crime, Law and Social Change, 38*, 185–209.

Zuckerman, M. (1979). *Sensation Seeking: Beyond the Optimal Level of Arousal*. Hillsdale, NJ: Lawrence Erlbaum.

Traffic and Transport Psychology
G. Underwood (Editor)
© 2005 Elsevier Ltd. All rights reserved.

40

WHY DO DRIVERS SPEED?

Henriette M. Wallén Warner[1] and Lars Åberg

INTRODUCTION

Every year approximately 45,000 people in Europe are killed in road accidents, and it is well known that excessive speeds are indirectly the most common cause of these accidents. In urban areas, where vehicles have to interact with vulnerable road-users, the consequences of excessive speeds are even more severe. If hit by a car travelling at 50 km/h, 70 pedestrians in 100 would die, while only 10 pedestrians in 100 would die if the car was travelling at 30 km/h (Swedish National Road Administration, 1999).

Even though the risks with excessive speeds are well known many drivers are still speeding (Nilsson, 1999), and road authorities all over Europe are therefore trying different alternatives to change driver behaviour. One alternative that has recently received a lot of attention is intelligent speed adaptation (ISA). The concept of ISA (see Carsten, 2002, for an overview) is to help the drivers to adapt their speed to a static or dynamic speed limit. To enable this, different techniques have been used ranging from advisory to intervening. In designing these new devices, it is of great importance that the focus is on the drivers and why they make the decision to speed during their everyday driving. Previous studies on speeding behaviour (Åberg, 1997; Åberg, Larsen, Glad & Beilinsson, 1997; Forward, 1997; Parker, Manstead, Stradling, Reason & Baxter, 1992; Stradling & Parker, 1997; Vogel & Rotthengatter, 1984) have shown that the theory of planned behaviour (Ajzen, 1991) can be successfully used, as a conceptual framework, to predict drivers' behaviour. The difference between this study and previous ones is that previous studies have, as far as we are aware, always been based on the drivers' self-reported behaviour or measurements of speed under restricted conditions (e.g. measurements of speed at one single point or over a short distance). In this study, however, it has been possible to measure the drivers' everyday speeding behaviour on all roads with a 50 km/h speed limit, within a large urban area, under an extended period of time.

---

[1] Dalarna University, Sweden. *E-mail:* hpe@du.se (H.M.W. Warner).

The theory of planned behaviour is an extension of the theory of reasoned action (Ajzen & Fishbein, 1980; Fishbein & Ajzen, 1975). This extension was necessary due to the original model's limitation in dealing with behaviours over which people have incomplete volitional control. According to the theory of planned behaviour, people's *attitude towards the behaviour*, their *subjective norm*, and their *perceived behavioural control* determine their *behaviour* indirectly via their *intentions*. People's attitude towards a behaviour is determined by their beliefs about the likely consequences of the behaviour, their subjective norm is determined by their beliefs about the normative expectations of important others and their perceived behavioural control is determined by their beliefs about the presence of factors that may facilitate or obstruct the performance of the behaviour. The intention is defined as their willingness to try to perform the behaviour and the behaviour refers to a defined action. The more positive a person's attitude and subjective norm is, and the greater their perceived control, the stronger is their intention to perform the behaviour. Finally, given enough actual control over the behaviour, people are expected to carry out their intention as soon as an opportunity is given. For behaviours over which people have incomplete volitional control it is also useful to consider perceived behavioural control in addition to intention. When people are realistic in their judgments of behaviour's difficulty, a measure of perceived behavioural control can contribute to the prediction of the behaviour by serving as a proxy for actual control (Ajzen, 1991). Besides predicting drivers' speeding behaviour the theory of planned behaviour has also been successful in predicting behaviours such as drinking and driving (Åberg, 1993; Beck, 1981; Parker et al., 1992), dangerous overtaking (Forward, 1997; Parker et al., 1992), close following (Parker et al., 1992), and lane discipline (Parker, Manstead, & Stradling, 1995), as well as such diverse behaviours as choosing a career, deciding to donate blood, or deciding to use condoms, among many others (Ajzen, 2001; Armitage & Connor, 2001; Sutton, 1998; for reviews).

The aim of this study is to examine if, and to what extent, independent variables stipulated in the theory of planned behaviour can be used to predict drivers' everyday speeding behaviour on roads with a 50 km/h speed limit, within urban areas.

METHOD

Between 1999 and 2002 the Swedish Road Administration funded large-scale ISA field trials with approximately 4500 vehicles in four different cities. The cities differed with respect to the number of test vehicles as well as the devices used (Swedish National Road Administration, 1999, 2002). In the city of Borlänge, an ISA speed-warning device was installed in approximately 400 vehicles (250 private, 150 commercial). The device was based on a digital map covering approximately 700 km of roads within the city of Borlänge and four main roads leaving the city. Whenever the test drivers drove within this area the device continuously informed them of the current speed limit and warned them, with a flashing red light and sound signals, if they exceeded this limit. In addition, the device continuously logged the test drivers' behaviour with regards to speed and position, amongst other variables. For this study, data from all roads with a 50 km/h speed limit was used.

Test drivers

In 1999, private test drivers were recruited among 1000 randomly selected car owners (with vehicles no older than from 1984) in the town of Borlänge. Approximately 1 year later, a new recruitment was made among an additional 2000 randomly selected car owners in the area. A total of approximately 250 car owners and their co-drivers (other family members that regularly used the vehicle) chose to participate in the project. A total of 134 test drivers drove their vehicle more than 45% of the time, completed a questionnaire, and had logged data successfully retrieved from at least 10 journeys, before the warning system was activated. List-wise deletion of missing data reduced the number of test drivers to 115. In addition, data from three test drivers was deleted due to technical problems while retrieving their logged data. For this study, data from the remaining 112 test drivers was used.

The test drivers' age ranged from 25 to 88 years, with a mean of 54 years. Sixty-five per cent of the test drivers were men while 35% were women. The skewed distribution can to some extent be explained by the fact that 68% of the total number of car owners in the Borlänge municipal area are men (H. Granlund, Swedish Road Administration, personal communication, December 11, 2003).

Procedure

After recruitment an ISA-speed warning device was installed in the test drivers' vehicles. During the first 2–4 weeks the device logged the test drivers' behaviour but the warning system was not yet activated. This meant that the test drivers did not get any information about the current speed limit or any warning signals if this limit was exceeded. The warning system was then activated. For this study, the questionnaire data was collected before the device was installed in the test drivers' vehicles and the logged data was collected during the period after installation but before activation.

Target behaviour. The test drivers' behaviour (speed, position, etc.) was logged at least once every 10 s as soon as the vehicles were driven within the area covered by the digital map used by the ISA device. For this study all data retrieved from roads with a 50 km/h speed limit, during 2–4 weeks, before the warning system was activated, was used. The measure of speeding behaviour was taken as the total time exceeding the speed limit 50 km/h by at least 2 km/h, divided by the total time driven. When the ISA device showed that the speed limit had been exceeded with 2 km/h, the speedometers in most of the test drivers' vehicles showed approximately 57 km/h.

Questionnaire. A questionnaire was posted to the test drivers before they had the device installed in their vehicles. The questionnaire included questions with Ajzen's theory of planned behaviour as a frame of reference. Several sections dealing with other speed limits than 50 km/h and also other aspects of speed limits and road safety were included, but these issues will not be addressed here. Attitude, subjective norm, and perceived behavioural control were measured on 5-point scales while self-reported present behaviour was measured on a 6-point scale.

Attitude towards the behaviour was measured by asking: "How acceptable is it for you personally to exceed different speed limits? 50 km/h in urban areas?" 1 = *Not acceptable*; 3 = *Neither*; 5 = *Totally acceptable*.

Subjective norm was measured by asking: "What do you believe people important to you (family, close friends, etc.) think if you exceed speed limits? 50 km/h in urban areas?" 1 = *Not acceptable*; 3 = *Neither*; 5 = *Totally acceptable*.

Perceived behavioural control was measured by asking: "How hard is it to comply with different speed limits? 50 km/h in urban areas?" 1 = *Very hard*; 3 = *Neither*; 5 = *Very easy*.

Intention was replaced by self-reported present behaviour that was measured by asking: "If you consider your own behaviour as a driver. How often do you exceed the speed limit 50 km/h in urban areas by 10 km/h or more?" 1 = *Never*; 2 = *Very rarely*; 3 = *Rarely*; 4 = *Sometimes*; 5 = *Often*; 6 = *Very often*.

The reason for replacing the direct question about intention with self-reported present behaviour was that the test drivers received the questionnaire just before the ISA device was due to be installed in their vehicles, and it was assumed that this might affect their answers about future intention. Self-reported present behaviour was chosen instead of drivers' intention as it was thought to be an approximation of the intention. This is also supported by Haglund and Åberg (2000) who showed that the correlation between intention and self-reported behaviour is strong ($r = 0.69$).

Analyses

The data was analysed by structural equation modelling, using the LISREL 8.54 computer program (Jöreskog & Sörbom, 1993). Theory Weighted Least Squares Chi-Square was used to evaluate the fit between the final model and the data. A non-significant chi-square value and Root Mean Square Error of Approximation (RMSEA) of lesser than 0.05 indicate a close fit between the data and the model (Browne & Cudeck, 1993).

RESULTS

The median for the attitude towards the behaviour and the subjective norm was two, while the median for the perceived behavioural control was four. On average, the test drivers exceeded the speed limit 28% of the time. The inter-correlation between the independent variables was moderately high. Attitude towards the behaviour and subjective norm correlated with 0.49 ($N = 112$; $p < 0.01$) and attitude towards the behaviour and perceived behavioural control correlated with -0.31 ($N = 112$; $p < 0.01$). Subjective norm and perceived behavioural control correlated with -0.33 ($N = 112$; $p < 0.01$).

Figure 1 shows the final structural model with standardized path coefficients and explained variance for self-reported present behaviour and logged behaviour. Using structural equation modelling subjective norm was not found to add significantly, neither directly nor indirectly, to the prediction of behaviour and was therefore excluded from the model. Also, drivers' perceived behavioural control was not found to add directly to the prediction of drivers' behaviour. The direct path from perceived behavioural control to behaviour was therefore excluded. After excluding the subjective norm and the direct path from perceived behavioural control to behaviour, all remaining variables added significantly, directly or indirectly, to the prediction of behaviour. Twenty-three per cent of the variance in self-reported present behaviour, and 14% of the variance in behaviour, was explained by the model. The statistics shows that the data fitted the model quite well (χ^2 [df = 2, N = 112] = 2.48; p = 0.29; RMSEA = 0.047).

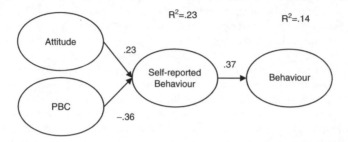

Figure 1. Structural model with standardized path coefficients and explained variance for self-reported behaviour and logged behaviour. PBC = Perceived Behavioural Control.

DISCUSSION

The aim of this study was to examine if, and to what extent, independent variables stipulated in the theory of planned behaviour can be used to predict drivers' everyday speeding behaviour on roads with a 50 km/h speed limit, within urban areas. The results show the theory to afford a level of prediction of drivers' self-reported present behaviour as well as their everyday speeding behaviour. Attitudes towards speeding, and perceived behavioural control were significant determinants of self-reported present behaviour. But contrary to the theory of planned behaviour subjective norm did not turn out to be a significant determinant. Furthermore, self-reported present behaviour, but not perceived behavioural control, contributed to the prediction of drivers' everyday speeding behaviour.

But why did subjective norm not add significantly, neither directly nor indirectly, to the prediction of drivers' everyday speeding behaviour? The results showed that there is a strong correlation (r = 0.49) between attitude towards speeding and the subjective norm. This means that a large part of the test drivers' subjective norm is already included in their answers on attitudes, which could explain why subjective norm did not contribute significantly to the prediction of behaviour.

When it comes to the direct path from perceived behavioural control to behaviour, Ajzen (1991) argues that it can be useful to consider perceived behavioural control in addition to intention for behaviours over which people have incomplete volitional control. When people are realistic in their judgments of a behaviour's difficulty, a measure of perceived behavioural control can contribute to the prediction of the behaviour by serving as a proxy for actual control. In the current study, perceived behavioural control did not account for additional variance in drivers' behaviour. This could be due to the fact that intention was replaced by self-reported present behaviour. Drivers with several years of experience might already have taken into account the actual control they have over the target behaviour when answering the question about the present behaviour.

The model was able to explain 14% of the variance in behaviour, which under the circumstances has to be considered quite good. The logged speeding behaviour was collected during 2–4 weeks whenever the test drivers drove on any of the roads, with a 50 km/h speed limit, covered by the digital map used by the ISA device. This created uncontrollable variation as the data was collected during different times of year, at different times of day and on different roads, depending on when the test drivers were recruited and when and where they then chose to drive. Also, all the test drivers participated voluntarily in the study and it is therefore reasonable to believe that the variation within the group was reduced. In addition, there were some technical constraints that should be highlighted. First, even though the digital map was thoroughly tested in the field, before it was distributed to the test drivers, it still contained several errors regarding speed limits. Second, the ISA device logged data as soon as the vehicle was driven within the mapped area and it was not possible to match the data collected with individual drivers. To combat this second constraint the data analyses only included those test drivers who used their vehicle more than 45% of the time. Further analysis showed that a majority of the test drivers included in the study did in fact drive their vehicles more than 90% of the time. Despite this, some of the target behaviour was still collected from drivers not included in the analyses. These limitations in the methodology weaken the relationships between the target behaviour and the rest of the variables in the model. This aside, the model is still able to explain a significant proportion of the variance in behaviour.

As it was shown that the drivers' attitude towards speeding and their perceived behavioural control can be used to predict drivers' everyday speeding behaviour within urban areas, a way to reduce the speed on our roads would be to affect these variables. The more positive the driver's attitude towards keeping the speed limit and the greater their perceived behavioural control, the larger should their chances to keep the speed limits be. To increase the perceived behavioural control different ISA systems might be a useful tool. As both variables affected the behaviour more or less equally at the same time, as their inter-correlation was relatively high it is reasonable to believe that a change in perceived behavioural control would also affect the drivers' attitude towards speeding. Before any of the ISA systems are implemented on a large scale, more research is needed into drivers' behaviour and the short- and long-term effects of the equipment.

The current study demonstrates that the theory of planned behaviour, with some modifications, can be used to predict drivers' everyday speeding behaviour within urban areas, even when the behaviour is measured during several weeks.

ACKNOWLEDGEMENTS

This study was financially supported by the Swedish Road Administration.

REFERENCES

Åberg, L. (1993). Drinking and driving: intentions, attitudes, and social norms of Swedish male drivers. *Accident Analysis and Prevention, 25*, 289–296.

Åberg, L. (1997). The role of perceived risk of detection. In Rothengatter, I., & Carbonell, E. (Eds.), *Proceedings of the International Conference on Traffic and Transport Psychology, Valencia (1996)*. Amsterdam: Elsevier.

Åberg, L., Larsen, L., Glad, A., & Beilinsson, L. (1997). Observed vehicle speed and drivers' perceived speed of others. *Applied Psychology: An International Review, 46,* 287–302.

Ajzen, I. (1991). The theory of planned behaviour. *Organizational Behaviour and Human Decision Processes, 50,* 179–211.

Ajzen, I. (2001). Nature and operation of attitudes. *Annual Review of Psychology, 52,* 27–58.

Ajzen, I., & Fishbein, M. (1980). *Understanding Attitudes and Predicting Social Behaviour.* Englewood Cliffs, NJ: Prentice-Hall.

Armitage, C.J., & Connor, M. (2001). Efficacy of theory of planned behaviour: a meta-analytical review. *British Journal of Social Psychology, 40,* 471–499.

Beck, K.H. (1981). Driving while under the influence of alcohol: relationship to attitudes and beliefs in a college population. *American Journal of Drug and Alcohol Abuse, 8,* 377–388.

Browne, M.W., & Cudeck, R. (1993). Alternative ways of assessing model fit. In Bollen, K.A., & Long, J.S. (Eds.), *Testing Structural Equation Models.* New York: Sage Publications.

Carsten, O. (2002, May). European research on ISA: where are we now and what remains to be done. *Proceedings of the ICTCT-extra Workshop in Nagoya, Japan.*

Fishbein, M., & Ajzen, I. (1975). *Belief, attitude, intention and behaviour: an introduction to the theory and research.* Reading, MA: Addison-Wesley.

Forward, S. (1997). Measuring driver attitudes using the theory of planned behaviour? In Rothengatter, I., & Carbonell, E. (Eds.), *Proceedings of the International Conference on Traffic and Transport Psychology, Valencia (1996).* Amsterdam: Elsevier.

Haglund, M., & Åberg, L. (2000). Speed choice in relation to speed limit and influences from other drivers. *Transportation Research Part F, 3,* 39–51.

Jöreskog, K.C., & Sörbom, D. (1993). *LISREL 8: Structural equation modelling with the SIMPLIS command language, Scientific Software International.* Hillsdale, NJ: Earlbaum.

Nilsson, A. (1999). *Hastigheter och tidluckor 1998.* Borlänge, Sweden: Vägverket.

Parker, D., Manstead, A.S.R., Stradling, S.G., Reason, J.T., & Baxter, J.S. (1992). Intentions to commit driving violations: an application of the theory of planned behaviour. *Journal of Applied Psychology, 77,* 94–101.

Parker, D., Manstead, A.S.R., & Stradling, S.G. (1995). Extending the theory of planned behaviour: the role of personal norm. *British Journal of Social Psychology, 34,* 127–137.

Stradling, S., & Parker, D. (1997). Extending the theory of planned behaviour: the role of personal norm, instrumental beliefs and affective beliefs in predicting driving violations. In Rothengatter, I., & Carbonell, E. (Eds.), *Proceedings of the International Conference on Traffic and Transport Psychology, Valencia (1996).* Amsterdam: Elsevier.

Sutton, S. (1998). Predicting and explaining intentions and behaviour: how well are we doing? *Journal of Applied Social Psychology, 28,* 1317–1338.

Swedish National Road Administration (1999). *ISA Intelligent Speed Adaptation. [Brochure].* Borlänge, Sweden: Vägverket.

Swedish National Road Administration (2002). *Results of the world's largest ISA trial. [Brochure].* Borlänge: Vägverket.

Vogel, R., & Rothengatter, J.A. (1984). *Motieven van snelheidsgedrag op autosnelwegen: een attitude onderzoek (Motivation of speeding behaviour on motorways), Report VK 84-09.* Traffic Research Centre, University of Groningen, Haren, The Netherlands.

Traffic and Transport Psychology
G. Underwood (Editor)
© 2005 Elsevier Ltd. All rights reserved.

41

EFFECTS OF SPEED CAMERAS ON DRIVER ATTITUDE AND BEHAVIOUR

Stephen G. Stradling, Lee Martin and Mhairi Campbell[1]

INTRODUCTION

Speed cameras are intended to reduce casualties by reducing accidents by reducing speeds at specific high-risk locations. In the UK, use of speed cameras to supply an evidential basis for prosecution was made possible by Section 23 of the Road Traffic Act 1991, which provided that photographs from an approved automated speed camera may be used as evidence in prosecuting drivers for exceeding speed limits without the corroboration of a police officer.

Bourne and Cooke (1993) reported that in the State of Victoria, Australia, a mobile Speed Camera Program, running since 1989 in conjunction with tougher drink-driving enforcement and advertising campaigns, had lowered traffic crashes by 25% and decreased injuries by 45%. However, three treatment variables are here confounded and it is not clear how much of the crash and injury reduction may be attributed to the camera campaign.

Hooke, Knox and Portas (1996) looked at the effectiveness of almost 500 speed camera sites in 10 UK police forces and found the installation of fixed-site speed cameras reduced accidents by 28% and lowered speeds by an average of 4.2 mph. Corbett and Simon (1999) collected self-report information from drivers in four police force areas (Thames Valley, Northumbria, West Midlands and Surrey) where speed cameras had been installed. They found that installing speed cameras produced a reduction in self-reported speeds for up to 8 months, with the drivers' speed choice and concern at being detected strongest at the initial installation of the camera. Before camera installation 63% of drivers reported that they drove at above 31 mph. Two months after camera installation 35% of drivers said they did. After 6 months this figure reduced further to 30%. At 8 months after camera installation they found 34% of drivers reporting driving above 31 mph, suggesting that the effect had peaked.

[1] Transport Research Institute, Napier University, Edinburgh, UK. *E-mail:* s.stradling@napier.ac.uk (S.G. Stradling).

In 1999, it was estimated that about 75 countries around the world rely on cameras to enforce speed limits (Insurance Institute for Highway Safety, 1999) but the UK Department for the Environment, Transport and the Regions (DETR, 2000) cautioned that speed cameras cannot be viewed as the single answer to speeding problems. DETR (2000) reported that many people do not perceive breaking the speed limit as a criminal act. These opinions on speeding were in contrast with those of drunk driving and of dangerous driving, both of which the respondents viewed as serious crimes. The punishments for these crimes were a strong deterrent to the respondents, who also saw these crimes as morally wrong.

Scottish Executive (2000) statistics showed that 35% of motor vehicle offences recorded by the police in Scotland were speeding offences, that speeding offences made up the largest single category of motor vehicle offences in Scotland, and that they were increasing. This may be partly due to the advances in the technology now available to the police to detect these offences, though the police are only able to detect a large number of speeding offences if there are many motorists driving above the posted speed limits.

The first speed cameras in the Strathclyde Police area were introduced in 1993. Location decisions regarding where these cameras should be placed were made by examining accident and speed data held by the police and the local authority to find concentrations of fatal and serious accidents. Revised guidance is now available to inform the positioning of all fixed, mobile and red light cameras. However, flexibility is given so that 15% of detections can come from cameras that do not comply with all these guidelines, but are positioned due to operational factors such as community concern. For the majority of fixed camera sites that comply with the guidelines, the location must provide up to 1 km of suitable road conditions where no other engineering measures would be appropriate for slowing traffic. On this stretch of road, there must have been at least four fatal or serious accidents in the last 3 years and the 85th percentile speed for the site must equal or exceed the Lord Advocate's current enforcement threshold for site speed limit (the 85th percentile speed is that at or below which 85% of the traffic is travelling). In addition, the camera must be clearly visible (painted in bright reflective stripes), clearly signed, and its location made available to the public prior to operation.

A Notice of Intention to Prosecute is sent to each driver detected exceeding the enforcement threshold, requiring the registered keeper to identify the person driving at the time of the offence. A Conditional Offer letter is then sent requiring the driver to either pay the fixed penalty or contest the accusation in court. Drivers detected by a speed camera exceeding the speed limit are liable for a fine of £60 plus a licence endorsement of three penalty points in force for 3 years from the time of issue. Drivers accumulating 12 penalty points are banned from driving for 6 months. Drivers exceeding the limit by a large margin (typically 20 mph) are summoned to appear at court. UK national newspaper reports suggest that over 1 million speeding citations were issued in 2003 and that around 16% of the UK driving population are currently carrying penalty points on their driving licence.

In the hypothecation pilot project that began on 1st April 2000, whereby the costs of setting up and running additional safety cameras may be recovered from fine revenue, Strathclyde was one of the eight UK regions taking part and each region was required to set up Safety Camera Partnerships involving the police, courts, local authority and other interested agencies and to introduce additional speed cameras, over and above their previous level of automated speed enforcement. The other seven regions were Cleveland, Essex, Lincolnshire, Nottingham, Northampton, South Wales and Thames Valley. An evaluation of these pilots reported a 35% reduction in casualties at camera sites. At the time of writing 40 of the 43 UK police force areas have Safety Camera Partnerships in operation.

PA Consulting and University College London (2004) were commissioned to evaluate the effectiveness of Safety Camera Partnerships. In February 2003, they published an evaluation of the eight pilot schemes that was expanded upon in 2004 to include 24 partnerships that had been operational for at least 1 year. This 3-year report covering 2000–2003 illustrated a significant reduction in speed with partnerships, on average, seeing a 7% reduction in speed and 32% fewer vehicles breaking speed limits at camera sites. The number of people killed or seriously injured at the new sites fell by 40% and there was a 33% reduction in the number of personal injury collisions. National surveys showed that on average 74% of people were in support of the use of safety cameras for targeted enforcement with 68% of people surveyed agreeing that their primary use was to save lives. The report also found that the funding mechanism and partnership arrangements had worked well. It was concluded that the Safety Camera Partnership programme had met its main objectives.

Data is reported here from three studies showing the general deterrent effects of fixed-site speed cameras on vehicle speed (Study 1), the specific deterrent effects of issuing fixed fine penalties and points on subsequent speeding behaviour (Study 2), and the relation between being detected speeding and recent collision involvement (Study 3).

STUDY 1

Methodology

Nu-metric equipment was used to measure, inter alia, the percentage of passing vehicles exceeding the speed limit at five new 30 mph fixed camera sites installed in the Glasgow area. Baseline measurement was taken in April 2000 with the cameras, warning signs and road markings installed before further measurement in July 2000. Follow-up measures were taken in October 2000 and October 2001. There were no appreciable changes in traffic flow at the sites across times of measurement (Campbell & Stradling, 2002a).

Results

Table 1 shows the percentage of drivers exceeding the speed limit at these sites.

The percentage of passing motorists exceeding the 30 mph speed limit was reduced from two-thirds (64%) to one third (37%) simply by installation of the site furniture. With the equipment operational, at time 3, it was further reduced to one quarter (23%). One year later it had crept back to one third (31%).

These fixed speed cameras at 30 mph sites served a general deterrent function, affecting drivers' speeding behaviour at the camera site.

Table 1. Effects of camera installation averaged across five new 30 mph fixed sites in the Glasgow area.

Date of measurement	Condition	Percent of passing vehicles exceeding speed limit
April 2000	Baseline	64
July 2000	Camera housing only	37
October 2000	Camera housing + grid lines (+cameras)	23
October 2001	Fully functioning for 1 year	31

STUDY 2

Methodology

Questionnaires were sent to drivers detected by speed cameras in Glasgow over a 2-month period, February and March 2001. To ensure compliance with the UK Data Protection Act (1984) the questionnaires were sent by the Camera Enforcement Unit of Strathclyde Police and returned directly to the Transport Research Institute, Napier University, thus ensuring both anonymity and confidentiality. The questionnaires were sent with a time delay of 2 months from the mailing of the conditional offer letter.

Results

Just over 500, 18% of the questionnaires were returned. The age distribution of those returning questionnaires was compared to that of those receiving questionnaires: those at the lower end of the age range were slightly under-represented amongst the returns.

Respondents, inter alia, rated their agreement with a number of items concerning their driving since receiving the speeding ticket. These responses were factor analysed (Campbell & Stradling, 2002b) and Table 2 displays the variables loading on the two factors extracted and

Table 2. Changes to driver behaviour 2 months after receiving a speeding ticket.

"Since receiving the speeding ticket..."	% Agree
Speed sensitive	
I keep more of a look out for speed limit signs	80
I pay more attention to my speed while driving	74
I look at my speedometer more often	73
I drive more carefully	58
*I drive more slowly	56
I allow more time for journeys	36
Camera sensitive	
I keep more of a look out for speed cameras	79
*I slow down when passing any speed cameras	74
I take extra care when driving past the camera at which I was caught	66

shows level of agreement (strongly agree plus agree) with each item. The factors were labelled speed sensitive and camera sensitive.

These appear initially to be encouraging levels of agreement. However, cross-tabulation of two core attitude items (shown as * in Table 2) and then of scale scores derived from the two factors, showed three separable groups (Campbell & Stradling, 2002b) whose size could be estimated:

- those who now drive more slowly necessarily including driving slowly past cameras: 54–56%

- those who only slow down at cameras and are not driving more slowly otherwise: 30–32%

- those doing neither: 14–15%

Thus, around one half of the respondents were more speed sensitive for 2 months after receipt of punishment, one third more camera sensitive, and one sixth were neither. Punishment, in the form of a £60 fine and three penalty points, had some specific deterrence function, but left other drivers unremediated.

STUDY 3

Methodology

This study combines data sets from two recent surveys of Scottish drivers, one conducted for the Scottish Executive and one for the Strathclyde Safety Camera Partnership. Both surveys involved in-home interviews with quota samples of drivers. Full details of sampling strategy and sample demographics are given in Stradling et al. (2003) for the first and Campbell and Stradling (2003) for the second survey. Data from 1088 drivers from the first survey and 1101 from the second, who held a current driving license, had driven within the previous year and who cited "car" as their main vehicle when driving are combined here.

Results

Respondents were asked on both surveys, "How many times have you been flashed by a speed camera in the past 3 years?" and "How many road traffic accidents have you been involved in as a driver in the past 3 years?"

Fifteen per cent of the sample (18% of the male drivers and 13% of the female drivers) reported having been involved in one or more road traffic accidents (RTA) as a driver within the last 3 years. While 13% of male and 11% of female non-speeders reported recent RTA involvement, the proportions reporting recent RTA involvement were significantly elevated ($p < 0.001$) to 22% for both male and female speeders.

In a separate survey for the Lothian & Borders Safety Camera Partnership, 1134 drivers were asked "As a driver, how many times have you been involved in an accident in the past 5 years in which someone was injured?" 8% of those who had been detected speeding (flashed by a speed camera in the past 3 years) compared to 4% of those who had not reported having been involved in an injury accident as a driver in the previous 5 years.

Thus, around twice as many detected speeders had been RTA involved as those who had not triggered a speed camera.

Crash involvement increases with exposure—mileage driven—(e.g. Stradling et al., 2003). Figure 1 plots the relation between crash involvement and annual mileage separately for those car drivers in the combined sample who had and who had not been flashed by a speed camera in the previous 3 years ($N = 2022$).

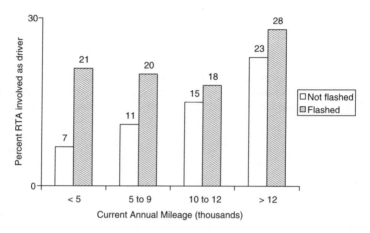

Figure 1. Percent of car drivers RTA involved in the last 3 years by mileage band for those detected speeding by safety camera and not.

For those not detected speeding, the proportion that reported RTA involvement rose inexorably with increasing mileage, from 7% of the lowest mileage group (less than 5000 miles per annum) (c8000 km pa) to 23% for the highest mileage group (above 12,000 miles per annum) (c19,000 km pa). For the "speeders", however, the proportions who had been RTA involved was elevated at each mileage band and further elevation with increased mileage appeared only to affect the highest mileage group.

CONCLUSIONS

Most safety cameras in the UK installed under the current guidelines signal the presence of hazardous locations at which people have died. Study 1 showed that fixed-site speed cameras in 30 mph areas provided a general deterrence function, slowing many, but not all, passing drivers at that location. Study 2 showed that speeding tickets have a specific deterrence effect on some drivers, with around half of the sample of recipients of speeding tickets reporting themselves more speed sensitive for 2 months after receiving their ticket. A study using the conviction and crash records of a large sample of drivers in Ontario, Canada (Redelmeier, Tibshirani & Evans, 2003) concluded that "The risk of a fatal crash in the month after a [driving] conviction was about 35% lower than in a comparable month with no conviction for the same driver... [but] The benefit lessened substantially by 2 months and was not significant by 3–4 months"

(p. 2177), suggesting that conviction—detection and punishment—for a driving offence has only a brief and temporary effect on changing driver behaviour.

Study 3 showed that speed cameras detect drivers in need of help. We have long known that speed kills. The laws of physics inexorably dictate that the higher the speed at impact the more energy must be rapidly absorbed by hard metal, soft flesh and brittle bone. From the data reported here, we have also seen that those drivers who had been flashed by a speed camera had almost double the incidence of recent crash involvement, with 22% of the detected speeders versus 12% of those who had not been detected speeding having been involved in an RTA as a driver in the previous 3 years.

The kinds of drivers who have been detected speeding are more likely to have been recently collision involved. These people pose more risk to themselves and to other, usually more vulnerable, road users. They need help with changing their driving styles (Stradling, 2005). There is support amongst the UK motoring public for such an approach. The 2002 RAC Report on Motoring (RAC Foundation, 2002) reported 57% of a large UK sample of drivers agreeing with the statement that "All drivers should receive periodic refresher training". Such driver refresher training could be duration based (and should probably be more frequent for young and old drivers) or incident based following involvement in RTAs or speeding infractions.

Driver retraining courses, where drivers pay for their own remediation, and pay more than the fixed penalty fine, combining classroom sessions ("Why to change") and on-road guided practice ("How to change") offer the possibility of undoing old habits and facilitating integrated, sustainable changes in driving style. Speed cameras spot "crash magnets" in need of change. Changing KSA, addressing the knowledge, skills and attitudes of drivers, offers a potentially powerful route to changing KSI, and reducing the numbers killed and seriously injured on the roads.

REFERENCES

Bourne, M., & Cooke, R. (1993). Victoria's speed camera program. In Clarke, R.V. (Ed.), *Crime Prevention Studies* (Vol. 1). New York: Criminal Justice Press.

Campbell, M., & Stradling, S.G. (2002a). The general deterrent effect of speed camera housings. In Grayson, G.B. (Ed.), *Behavioural Research in Road Safety XI*. Crowthorne: Transport Research Laboratory.

Campbell, M., & Stradling, S.G. (2002b). The impact of speeding tickets on speeding behaviour. In Grayson, G.B. (Ed.), *Behavioural Research in Road Safety XII*. Crowthorne: Transport Research Laboratory.

Campbell, M., & Stradling, S.G. (2003). Factors influencing driver speed choices. *Behavioural Research in Road Safety XIII*. London: Department for Transport.

Corbett, C. & Simon, F. (1999). The effects of speed cameras: how drivers respond. DETR. Road Safety Research Report No. 11.

DETR (2000). *New Directions in Speed Management: A Review of Policy*. London: DETR.

Hooke, A., Knox, J., & Portas, D. (1996). *Cost benefit analysis of traffic light and speed cameras*. Police Research Series Paper 20. London: Home Office Police Research Group.

Insurance Institute for Highway Safety (1999). *Who cares about a camera if you are not speeding?* Status Report 34(6). Arlington, VA: Insurance Institute for Highway Safety.

PA Consulting and University College London (2004). *The National Safety Camera Programme: Three-year Evaluation Report*. London: Department for Transport.

RAC Foundation (2002). *RAC Report on Motoring 2002*. London: RAC Foundation.

Redelmeier, D.A., Tibshirani, R.J., & Evans, L. (2003). Traffic-law enforcement and risk of death from motor-vehicle crashes: case-crossover study. *The Lancet, 361*, 2177–2182.

Scottish Executive (2000). *Motor Vehicle Offences in Scotland 1999*. Edinburgh: Scottish Executive Statistical Bulletin.

Stradling, S.G. (2005). Speeding behavior and collision involvement in Scottish car drivers. In Hennessy, D.A., & Wiesenthal, D.L. (Eds.), *Current Trends in Driver Behavior and Traffic Safety Research*. New York: Nova Science Publishers.

Stradling, S.G., Campbell, M., Allan, I.A., Gorrell, R.S.J., Hill, J.P., Winter, M.G., & Hope, S. (2003). *The Speeding Driver: Who, How and Why?* Edinburgh: Scottish Executive Social Research.

Traffic and Transport Psychology
G. Underwood (Editor)
© 2005 Elsevier Ltd. All rights reserved.

42

WHAT SHALL WE DO ABOUT
SPEEDING — EDUCATION?

Frank P. McKenna[1]

INTRODUCTION

There is little doubt that there is a relationship between speed and accident involvement. We can examine this relationship in a number of ways. For example, we can examine changes in the legal speed limits and show that as the speed limit goes up then so also does the casualties (Rock, 1995). Alternatively, we might observe drivers speed and show that those who are observed to drive faster have more accidents (Wasielewski, 1984). We might also simply take a self-report measure of speeding and show that those people who state that they drive faster have more accidents (French, West, Elander & Wilding, 1993). We might also try, as we have done, to devise a video simulation of speed and allow drivers to choose different speeds and show that those who choose faster speeds have more speed-related accidents (Horswill & McKenna, 1999). Whichever way we look at it we find that there is a relationship between speed and accidents. If we make the reasonable assumption that this relationship is causal then the community and individuals have a mechanism for reducing accident risk. The community could reduce speed limits and individuals could reduce their personal speeds. Where there is much activity by vulnerable users then relatively low speeds ought to be chosen by the community and by individuals since the consequences are considerable. In the UK the 30 mph limit is widespread in areas where vulnerable road users are present. The simple defence of this limit is that it is difficult for pedestrians to survive an impact that is much higher than this speed. If individuals take on board this argument which has been presented on the mass media for some time then there should be general observance of the speed limit.

It is very clear that drivers do not observe the 30 mph limit (nor for that matter any other limit). The speed limit in urban areas is of particular interest because of the potential savings in casualties. The majority of drivers break this limit. In one survey it was found that 69% of

---

[1] University of Reading, Reading, UK. *E-mail:* f.p.mckenna@reading.ac.uk (F.P. McKenna).

drivers broke the 30 mph limit (DETR, 2000). This finding presents some serious safety, democratic and legal challenges. The safety issue is transparent. If people cannot be persuaded or required to drive within the urban speed limits then casualties will continue. The democratic and legal challenges are less obvious but nonetheless challenging. How does one change the behaviour of the majority of the population? If a change is to be required or enforced then what mandate does one have when the majority of the population disobey? Given that the stakes are so high in terms of casualties it is likely that the challenge will be met with a number of measures ranging from persuasion, through requirement to enforcement. Where accident sites can be identified traffic calming and safety cameras offer the potential of reducing speed and casualties if local communities will accept them. Surveys do not reveal any great opposition to safety cameras. Measures such as safety cameras are likely to have an important role to play but like most measures they have their limitations. A question occurs as to whether safety cameras produce conformity or compliance. We can distinguish between conformity and compliance in the sense that conformity refers to an enduring change in attitude and behaviour in response to pressure while compliance refers to a transitory shift without any real change (Hogg & Vaughn, 1995). The fact that drivers reduce their speed for only several hundred metres in the area of the camera (Keenan, 2002) would suggest that compliance rather than conformity is operating. In addition, if we accept the Haight (2004) argument that a substantial proportion of accidents are difficult to locate in time and space then it would appear that measures that go beyond a specific time and place will be required.

A general change in attitude to speeding would be welcome because it would not only underpin traffic calming and safety cameras but also might prompt a consideration of general driving issues. It would appear that there is a long way to go. Campbell and Stradling (2002) note that anger was the major first reaction that drivers report when they have been caught speeding. In the context of making a move towards increasing conformity this presents a challenge. Tyler (2003) has argued that perceived fairness not only is a key determinant of whether people accept legal decisions but also whether they conform in their future behaviour. A number of measures have been introduced that are designed to increase the perceived fairness of the enforcement. The prominent colour of the safety camera and the warning signs ensure that the attentive driver can readily avoid a speeding offence. In addition, the introduction of speed awareness courses presents speeding offenders with an option of avoiding points on their licence. The idea is that while prosecution for a speeding offence offers little opportunity to change drivers' attitudes to speeding and the perceived legitimacy of enforcement spending several hours on a course does offer such opportunities.

In considering speed awareness courses an issue arises as to who should be offered these courses. Should it be those who have broken the speed limit by a small margin or those who have broken it by a large margin? This in turn raises an issue as to whether these groups are different. If the difference between those caught at low speeds versus those caught at high speeds is due to random transient factors, e.g. "on this particular occasion I was in a hurry" then we should find that there are no stable differences between the two groups in terms of their general speed choices, attitudes and personality. In fact McKenna (2004) has shown that there are differences between the two groups in their general attitudes to violations and speed choice. Those caught at higher speeds do report higher tendencies to violate and higher general speed choices. In addition, those caught at higher speeds were found to have had a higher number of accidents and twice the speed-related accidents as those caught at lower speeds.

There were two aims of the present study. The first was to determine if there were psychological differences between the high and low speed groups. The second was to determine if attending the course produced any change in the perceived legitimacy of enforcement. If Tyler (2003) is correct in arguing that perceived legitimacy is a key feature of law abiding behaviour then changing this factor should be an important element of a speed awareness course.

STUDY I

Method

Participants. A total of 9475 drivers attended the low-speed program while 567 attended the high-speed course. Of those attending the low-speed course 5403 were men and 4072 were women. Of those attending the high-speed course 429 were men and 138 were women. Age was determined in large part by participants responding in 5-year ranges, e.g. 26–30. At the young end an exception was made such that up to age 20, drivers specified their actual age. The modal age of those attending the courses was 36–40 years of age. To facilitate interaction with the trainer the maximum size of any group was 24 participants.

Procedure. The first section consisted of the computer-based assessment. The system was designed to be used by people who had little or no experience of computers. All participants were informed that their responses were anonymous and that no questions would or could be used to identify an individual. They were informed that they would receive feedback and that the accuracy of the feedback was dependent on the accuracy of their answers.

The first section took between 40–50 min and covered a broad range of topics including demographics, self-report speed, driving violations, fatigue, driving experiences and personality. For the present purposes the focus of attention was on driving experiences and personality. The Driving Experiences Questionnaire was used which produces four factors: pleasure, attention/distraction, emotional outlet and independence. The personality assessment was a measure of aggression. Digitised video tests were also included that assessed speed choice, close following and hazard perception.

On finishing the assessment each driver received a four-page printout providing (a) a personalised risk profile outlining strengths and weaknesses across a range of factors including speed choice, close following, violations and fatigue and (b) safety messages tailored to their personal responses.

The next session was with a trainer who involved all participants in the discussion, which was designed to cover both perceived barriers to enforcement (e.g. should the police enforce the speed limit, and is this just a money making exercise?) and how speed is connected with accident involvement. The latter is illustrated through examining the personal speed choices of the participants.

At the end of the course the participants rated the usefulness of the digital video tests, the computer-based assessment with feedback, and the driver trainer discussion. Each was rated on a five-point scale with 1 anchored with the label "not at all" 3 with the label "quite" and 5 with the label "very". They also indicated their future speed intentions.

Results and discussion. In order to ensure comparability, the speed limit of 30 mph was chosen for all participants. While this makes relatively little difference to the number attending the low-speed course it does make more of a difference to the number attending the high-speed course. (A significant proportion of the high-speed group had broken the 70 mph limit.)

Table 1 presents the means for the high-speed offenders and low-speed offenders. There was a significant difference between the two groups $t(9576) = 2.89$, $p < 0.01$ Cohen's $d = 0.18$, indicating that the high-speed offenders experienced more pleasure from driving than the low-speed offenders. There was no significant difference between the two groups in the level of attention devoted to the driving task $t(9576) = 1.84$, $p > 0.05$, Cohen's $d = 0.11$. There was a significant difference between the two groups in using the vehicle as an emotional outlet $t(9576) = 4.81$, $p < 0.001$, Cohen's $d = 0.30$ indicating that those attending the high-speed course more often reported using the vehicle as an emotional outlet. There was no significant difference between the two groups in the level of independence that is experienced from driving $t(9576) = 1.49$, $p > 0.05$, Cohen's $d = 0.09$. On a separate measure of aggression there was a significant difference between the groups $t(9576) = 3.28$, $p < 0.01$, Cohen's $d = 0.20$ indicating that those attending the high-speed course were more aggressive. It should be noted that the effect size for these differences is small apart from the emotional outlet difference.

Table 1. Driving experiences for high- and low-speed offenders.

	N	Pleasure	Attention	Emotion	Independence
Low speed	9316	3.25 (1.27)	3.81 (1.36)	2.42 (1.11)	6.41 (1.15)
High speed	262	3.02 (1.38)	3.60 (1.49)	2.75 (1.32)	6.51 (1.12)

One potential reason for the relatively small differences between the two groups may be that attending a high or a low speed course may be an imperfect measure of general speed choices. For example, it is entirely possible that some drivers attending the low speed course do in general choose high speeds but on this particular occasion were caught at a lower speed. One method of exploring this possibility is to define two groups, not in terms of their attendance at the high versus low speed courses, but rather in terms of their self-reported speeds. Two groups were formed by taking the top and bottom quartiles in terms of those most or least likely to report breaking speed limits. There was a significant difference between the two groups in driving pleasure $t(4622) = 6.06$, $p < 0.001$, Cohen's $d = 0.18$, indicating that those who choose faster speeds experienced more pleasure from driving than the low speed offenders. There was a significant difference between the two groups in the level of attention devoted to the driving task $t(4622) = 21.07$, $p < 0.001$, Cohen's $d = 0.59$, indicating that those who choose faster speeds reported more lapses of attention. There was a significant difference between the two groups in using the vehicle as an emotional outlet $t(4622) = 24.69$, $p < 0.001$, Cohen's $d = 0.68$ indicating that those who choose faster speeds reported more often using the vehicle as an emotional outlet. There was a significant difference between the two groups in the level independence that is experienced from driving $t(4622) = 14.84$, $p < 0.001$, Cohen's $d = 0.43$ indicating that those who choose faster speeds reported experiencing higher degrees of independence from driving. On the measure of aggression there was a significant difference between the groups $t(4622) = 13.87$, $p < 0.001$, Cohen's $d = 0.40$, indicating that those who choose faster speeds were more aggressive. From this set of analyses it is clear that not only are there significant differences between the groups but also that these differences are not small (apart from driving pleasure). Those who are more inclined to break the speed limits report more lapses of attention while driving, are more inclined to use the vehicle as an emotional outlet, derive more feelings of independence from driving and at the level of personality are more aggressive.

Figure 1 plots the future speed intentions of drivers attending the high- and low-speed courses. These intentions were expressed anonymously after they had examined their personal risk profile and had spent several hours with the trainer. It can be seen that the majority of drivers expressed the intention to drive slower in the future.

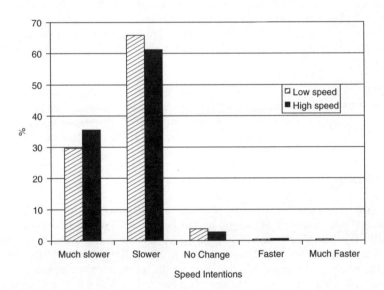

Figure 1. Speed intentions for those attending the high- and low-speed courses.

There was a significant difference between the two groups in their future speed intentions $t(9347) = 3.64$, $p < 0.001$, Cohen's $d = 0.23$ such that those attending the high-speed course intended to drive slower. It should be noted that the effect size is not large and that those attending the high-speed course tend to choose significantly faster speeds to start with so intentions to drive slower may not mean that in absolute terms the high-speed group intended to driver slower than the low-speed group.

STUDY 2

From Study 1 it was clear that following the examination of the risk profile and the discussion with the trainer there was a clear intention to drive slower. As noted in the introduction another aspect of speed awareness courses is that they offer the possibility of changing the perceived legitimacy of enforcement. By changing the perceived legitimacy of enforcement the idea is that the culture within which speed choice is judged is changed. If people acknowledge that it is legitimate to enforce they are acknowledging that the behaviour in question is not appropriate and that action to change this behaviour is acceptable. Study 2 was designed to determine if the goal of changing the perceived legitimacy of enforcement was achieved. It was decided to examine a very specific form perceived legitimacy. In particular, drivers were asked whether they thought that the police were justified in following up their particular offence. Since people are generally effective in producing excuses for their own behaviour it was thought that this would be a particularly testing form of the hypothesis.

Method

Participants. A total of 1993 drivers attended the speed awareness program. Of this total 1112 were men and 881 were women. Age was determined in large part by participants responding in 5-year ranges, e.g. 26–30. At the young end an exception was made such that up to age 20, drivers specified their actual age. The modal age of those attending the courses was 36–40 years of age.

Procedure. The same procedure was used as that in Study 1 with the following exception. In this version of the software the question on police justification was presented either early in the computer assessment or it was presented after drivers had been presented with their risk profile, tailored feedback and had been involved in the trainer discussion. The item was rated on a five-point justification scale with 0 being anchored with the label "not at all", 3 being rated with the label "quite" and 5 being rated with the label "very". On alternate days the software presented the justification question either before or after the course.

Results and discussion. The effect of the course on perceived legitimacy of police enforcement was examined by comparing the ratings of those who responded prior to receiving the course with those who responded after receiving the course. It was found that there was a significant difference between the two groups $t(1991) = 17.46, p < 0.001$, Cohen's $d = 0.73$, indicating that those who had received the course rated the legitimacy of police enforcement as higher. Another way of presenting this result is to note that 39% challenged the legitimacy of police action in their personal case before the course and this percentage went down to 10.5% after drivers had received the course. As a means of improving perceptions of procedural justice the course has had some success.

GENERAL DISCUSSION

The issue of speeding in most societies produces some important dilemmas. The evidence of a clear connection between speed choice and accident involvement is well accepted in professional circles. The observance of speed limits, however, is not great. The majority of drivers break the speed limits. A dilemma then occurs in the democratic mandate for enforcing a law that is broken by the majority of the people. One part of this issue is to consider the perceived legitimacy of action. It has been argued that perceived fairness is not only an important factor in determining whether people accept legal decisions but also in whether people conform in their future behaviour (Tyler, 2003). One approach is to introduce measures designed to improve the perceived legitimacy of action on speeding. One such measure is the introduction of speed awareness courses. By offering an educational alternative to punishment one aim is to achieve more public support. In other words, the mere presence of an educational alternative in the public domain could lead the public to see that those responsible for road safety are attempting to be flexible on the matter of speed enforcement. A second aim of the speed awareness course was to address the issue of perceived legitimacy for those who attend the course. A third aim was to change the speed intentions of those who attend the course. The latter issue was addressed in Study 1 in which it was clear that the majority of drivers did intend to drive slower. Reliance is then made on the generally reasonable connection between intentions and behaviour (Armitage & Conner, 2001). It would appear that providing drivers with feedback on their driving skills and attitudes and tailored safety messages combines with the driver training session to change drivers' intentions. McKenna (2004) found that the rating of the risk profile was the best predictor of future speed intentions.

In Study 1 two groups of drivers were examined, those who had broken the speed limit by a large margin versus those who had broken the speed limit by a small margin. Previous research had shown that these were different in their attitudes to violations and their accident involvement. The present work also shows that there are differences in their driving experiences and in their personality. Those who tend to choose higher speeds are more inclined to use the vehicle as an emotional outlet, to be less attentive to their driving and are more aggressive. The differences between the two groups are not trivial which raises an issue as to who should be offered the course. An argument in favour of offering the course to the low speed offenders might follow from a proportionality argument (von Hirsh & Ashworth, 1998) that those who break the speed limit by a small margin are those who least merit punishment. The idea of proportionality is that societal action in the form of penalties sends a signal specifying the degree of censure attached to a behaviour. More severe offences should then receive greater punishment and thus a signal is sent regarding just how reprehensible the conduct is judged. On this basis the low speed offenders would most merit education as an alternative to punishment. It might be added that the low speed offenders are large in number so as a persuasive device to change public opinion this would offer some potential. On the issue of persuasion it is worth noting that speed awareness courses have some advantage over general propaganda on at least two points. First, the speed awareness course is able to target the specific audience in a way that general propaganda cannot. In other words, on the speed awareness course the message is being delivered to those most in need of receiving it. By providing tailored feedback the aim is to provide targeting not only at the group level but also at the level of the individual. Second, on the speed awareness course it is much more possible to involve the audience with the message. Again by providing tailored individual feedback the aim is to involve the driver with the message.

The arguments for offering the speed awareness course to high-speed offenders involve a clash of principles. As noted earlier, from a proportionality point of view this group would consist of those who least merit the offer. However, from a rehabilitation or restorative justice point of view the high-speed offenders are those who are in most need of a catalyst to change their behaviour. From this perspective the group who are most vulnerable to be involved in accidents and the group who are most likely to involve other members of society in accidents are the high-speed offenders. Changing the high-speed group could then reap considerable rewards. The clash of principles is represented in the type of offer that was made to the high-speed offenders.

They still received points on their licence though the overall severity was less than they were likely to receive otherwise.

As noted in the introduction, another aim of the speed awareness course is to change perceived legitimacy of police action. The argument here is that in domains with high violation rates a core issue that needs to be addressed is the legitimacy of action. In professional circles the need for action on speeding is taken for granted. The behaviour of drivers, in general, indicates that observance of speed limits is poor. Perceived legitimacy is likely to underpin a whole range of actions on speeding from enforcement to engineering. As a result one aim of the course was to improve the perceived legitimacy of police action. Study 2 demonstrated that the course achieved this goal. The results to date indicate that speed awareness courses do offer a viable alternative to the standard punitive action.

REFERENCES

Armitage, C.J., & Conner, M. (2001). Efficacy of the theory of planned behaviour: a meta-analytic review. *British Journal of Social Psychology, 40,* 471–499.

Campbell, M., & Stradling, S.G. (2002). The impact of speeding tickets on speeding behaviour. In *Behavioural Research in Road Safety XII.* London: Department for Transport, pp. 86–93.

DETR (2000). *New Directions in Speed Management: a Review of Policy.* London: Department of the Environment, Transport and the Regions.

French, D.J., West, R.J., Elander, J., & Wilding, J.M. (1993). Decision-making style, and self-reported involvement in road traffic accidents. *Ergonomics, 36,* 627–644.

Haight, F. (2004). Accident proneness: the history of an idea. In Rothengatter, T., & Huguenin, R.D. (Eds.), *Traffic and Transport Psychology.* Oxford: Elsevier.

Hogg, M., & Vaughn, G. (1995). *Social Psychology.* London: Prentice Hall.

Horswill, M.S., & McKenna, F.P. (1999). The development, validation, and application of a video-based technique for measuring an everyday risk-taking behaviour: drivers' speed choice. *Journal of Applied Psychology, 84,* 977–985.

Keenan, D. (2002). Speed cameras—the true effect on behaviour. *Traffic Engineering and Control, 43,* 154–161.

McKenna, F.P. (2004). The Thames Valley speed awareness scheme: a comparison of high and low speed courses. In *Behavioural Research in Road Safety 2004: Fourteenth Seminar.* London: Department for Transport.

Rock, S.M. (1995). Impact of the 65 mph speed limit on accidents, deaths and injuries in Illinois. *Accident Analysis and Prevention, 27,* 207–214.

Tyler, T.R. (2003). Procedural justice, legitimacy, and the effective rule of law. In Tonry, M. (Ed.), *Crime and Justice: A Review* (Vol. 25). Chicago: University of Chicago Press.

Von Hirsh, A., & Ashworth, A. (1998). *Principled Sentencing.* Oxford: Hart Publishing.

Wasielewski, P. (1984). Speed as a measure of driver risk: observed speeds versus driver and vehicle characteristics. *Accident Analysis and Prevention, 16,* 89–103.

Traffic and Transport Psychology
G. Underwood (Editor)
© 2005 Elsevier Ltd. All rights reserved.

43

WAYS TO REHABILITATE DRUNKEN DRIVERS IN GERMANY—RECRUITING OF CLIENTS, REHABILITATION PROGRAMS, EVALUATION

Karin Müller[1]

INTRODUCTION

In Germany, the rehabilitation of traffic offenders has been a part of specific preventive provisions in order to raise safety in traffic for more than 30 years. For the treatment of the various target groups, a large range of specific courses and psycho-therapeutic programs exists. Some of them have already proven their efficiency in an impressive manner, while others are still in the phase of evaluation or planning of evaluation. All measures serve in their own way to improve drivers' qualification to drive, namely, when deficiencies have become obvious.

Here our current system of rehabilitating approaches for DUI-drivers in Germany, their actual involvement in legal authority and their developmental possibilities.

(1) The traffic situation in Germany

(2) Legal foundation and regulatory framework for the application of rehabilitation programs

(3) The assessment of qualification to drive as the basis for rehabilitation

(4) The system of rehabilitating programs

(5) Evaluation of the rehabilitation system.

THE TRAFFIC SITUATION IN GERMANY

In Germany, the number of road accidents and the number of injured and killed people have been decreasing continuously during the last years (Figure 1).

---

[1] Medico-Psychological Institute of the TÜV Rheinland Group, Berlin, Germany. *E-mail:* Karin.Mueller@de.tuv. com (K. Müller).

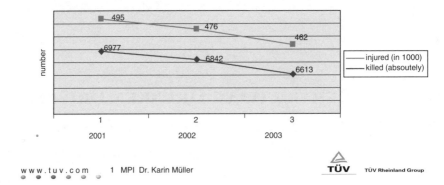

Figure 1. People injured or killed on German roads.

However, it can be observed that the group of young road users in the age between 18 and 25 still represent an alarmingly large proportion of the accident victims. In terms of fatal crashes, the quotient of victims, referring to 100,000 inhabitants of that age group, is more than three times higher than in the group of drivers aged 25–65 (Figure 2).

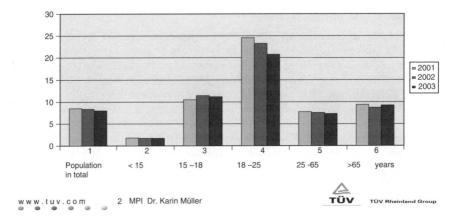

Figure 2. People killed in traffic per 100,000 population.

This relation to age can also be observed in the group of injured people.

Moreover, the age group of 15–18 is affected above average, mainly caused by smaller motor-bikes. This phenomenon, that has hardly changed during the last years, led to the development of quite a number of specific rehabilitation programs especially created for younger drivers.

When we look at accident statistics in terms of "reasons for accidents" then detected driving under the influence of alcohol (DUI) lay at position 6 of road accident statistics for about 2 years. However, one has to be aware of the fact that the estimated number of unknown offences under alcohol is very high. A research by Müller (1992), who observed all fatal crashes that happened in the German Saarland within a year, showed that 50% of all people killed drove under the influence of alcohol. Owing to the extremely grave effects of accidents that proceed from intoxicated drivers, and therefore the extreme danger of driving under the influence of alcohol, drunken drivers are the centre of interest regarding the development of new rehabilitation models.

The figures of driving suspension because of DUI have been declining for about 2 years (Figure 3). To a large extent, this can be traced back to the efficacy of a reconciled system of rehabilitating and sanctioning programs, which are based on German traffic law.

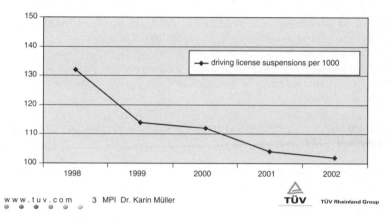

Figure 3. License suspensions caused by DUI.

LEGAL PROVISIONS AND REGULATORY FRAMEWORK FOR THE APPLICATION OF REHABILITATION PROGRAMS

The legislator in Germany provides that motorists who applied for a driving license for the first time initially receive a "probationary license" having passed all checks. This period usually lasts for 2 years. It is prolonged for another 2 years if the motorists commit one or more offences within the first 2 years.

In the extremely endangered group of young drivers in particular, early educating and psychological programs take effect, which can be adjoined to the system of special rehabilitation programs.

For example, a young driver who has committed either one grave road violation (e.g. leaving an accident without permission, extreme speeding) or two less grave violations (e.g. slight speeding) is requested to participate at a special continuation seminar of four sessions of 135 min (i.e. 9 h in total).

This continuation seminar takes places at a driving school and is given by a driving instructor. It includes group conversations where the infraction and its reasons are discussed. Additionally, in order to observe the behavior pattern of driving, an on-the-road-test is conducted.

If the young driver's "grave violation" is drunken driving, the driver is assigned to a "specific continuation program," that may only be given by graduate psychologists with an additional training in traffic psychology. Individual habits of alcohol consumption and the clear separation of drinking and drug ingestion from driving are the main topics of this course, which needs to be officially recognized by government.

Unlike almost all other rehabilitation models, in such an obligatory course that is created especially for young drivers, there is no diagnosis made at the beginning of the program. In this course model, the actual extent of the alcohol problem is not taken into consideration, because it has only been developed for the status of driving beginners.

If the young driver commits another violation in traffic after having passed the seminar, he is requested to take part in an individual traffic psychological advice.

In 3–4 individual sessions, led by an especially for this concerns qualified and also officially recognized traffic psychologist, the individual motives for the infraction and their future prevention are discussed.

This option is inapplicable if the young person apprehended was caught with a blood alcohol concentration of 0.11% or more.

If a road user of no matter which age is apprehended with such a BAC, he is no longer allowed to drive and the driving license is suspended by law (Table 1).

Table 1. Legal consequences at certain levels of BAC in Germany

0.00–0.05	No consequences
>0.03 + driving with faults or causing an accident	Fine, eventually license suspension (at least 6 months)
>0.03 + probationary license	Fine, rehabilitation program for driving beginners
From 0.05	Fine, entry in the central register of penalty points, driving prohibition (1–3 months)
From 0.11	License suspension (at least 6 months), *voluntary* rehabilitation program
From 0.16 or repeated DWI	Medical-Psychological Assessment (MPA), combined with a rehabilitation program

In the context of license suspension, the German law lays down a ban period, during which the responsible public authority may not hand out a new driving license.

Depending on the gravity of the infraction, the ban period amounts to 6–12 months, or in most cases 9–18 months, and sometimes even for the rest of life.

This period can be used by the alcohol-impaired driver for voluntary rehabilitating programs. In fact, he will only do so if he is afraid that the license authority will not give him back his license after the ban period and if it is probable that an examination of his qualification to drive is ordered. The order for such an assessment is always made in cases of drunken driving with a BAC of 0.16% or more, and in case of repeated drunken driving, with a BAC of 0.05% or more.

The examination, which is a medico-psychological assessment, takes place at the end of the ban period. It will be presented briefly in "Assessment of the Qualification to Drive as a Precondition for Rehabilitation" section of the presentation.

The drunken driver can make practical use of the ban period for working up the personal reasons for the infraction in a psychological rehabilitation process, and for starting and establishing the modification of his drinking habits. If he did so, he had incidentally a perfect preparation for the assessment that is necessary at the end of the ban period, for which he would start well prepared. In fact, that thoughtful and time-saving approach is only used by the minority. There are no concrete figures, but it is remarkable that the majority of the applicants come to the assessment without any preparation. Specific advice in the assessment offices themselves, but also independent traffic psychologists, should support the client to work out as soon as possible the ways to regain the qualification to drive and to work out the individual rehabilitation possibilities.

ASSESSMENT OF THE QUALIFICATION TO DRIVE AS A PRECONDITION FOR REHABILITATION

A well founded medico-psychological diagnostic is an essential and indispensable precondition for a successful rehabilitation of alcohol-affected motorists. The use of rehabilitation programs by alcohol-affected drivers in Germany takes place in most cases on the basis of advice, which is given in a legally ordered medico-psychological examination.

Those assessments may generally only be conducted by officially recognized assessment authorities. The executive body of those assessment authorities needs to be accredited for the target by the Federal Highway Research Institute according to the international norm EN 45013, and it also has to be officially recognized in each state by the responsible highest Federal State Authority. Therefore, the submission of a quality-management handbook and the demonstration of continuous approval of the work are required.

The executive body is a private organization that works without governmental subsidy. The client has to pay for the assessment himself. The prices are prescribed by law and the amount is currently between 320 and 700 Euro, depending on the reason for the assessment.

The report about drunken drivers is conducted on the basis of German-wide binding regulations for the assessment of alcohol-affected drivers, as well as different assessment criteria and behavior indicators.

These assessment and behavioral indicators are applied to check the following risk-relevant areas:

  I.   Alcoholism

  II. Lack of control of drinking behavior

III. Habituation to alcohol

IV. Drinking and driving (conditions for changes in drinking and driving behavior)

V. Additional traffic or general offences not obviously connected with the consumption of alcohol

VI. Organic impairment

VII. Psychic-functional condition

VIII. Potential for improvement

THE SYSTEM OF REHABILITATION PROGRAMS

Generally speaking, an assessment for fitness for drive can lead to the following results:

(1) The qualification to drive is confirmed unlimited. In this case, no further rehabilitation programs are necessary.

(2) During the time of assessment, the fitness for driving cannot be confirmed.

In case 2, an individual report with regard to rehabilitation advice is given by the assessors, depending on the reasons for the disqualification (Figure 4):

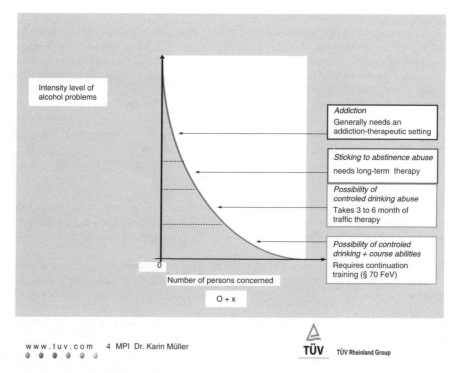

Figure 4. The four diagnosis groups for alcohol-taking motorists.

If the person concerned is addicted to alcohol, according to the international diagnosis system ICD 10, he will only be able to re-establish the qualification to drive by stationary or an ambulant addiction therapy. This kind of rehabilitation is only carried out by institutions that specialized in addiction therapies.

If an abuse of alcohol that has not been overcome sufficiently is diagnosed within the assessment process, specific rehabilitation programs are advised by the assessors that may lead to the reestablishment of the qualification to drive.

They depend on the current extent of the alcohol abuse, the personal motivation to change, and on the efforts already begun to modify the drinking behavior.

If the alcohol abuse is still apparent, e.g. if the motorist, despite drunken driving, still has no understanding of his own problems with alcohol at the time of the assessment, only target-group-specified long-term measures, i.e. traffic-orientated behavior therapies, can be applied in order to re-establish the qualification to drive.

If a stable abstinence is necessary or if a modified, well controlled consumption of alcohol is sufficient has to be defined by the assessors. They have to deliver a specific diagnosis in order to assure a successful rehabilitation.

At the moment, no legal definition of those models for traffic therapeutic long-term rehabilitation exists regarding their scientific foundation, evaluation, and the qualification of the course leader.

Because of this situation, there is no generally binding and German-wide unique standard. The term "traffic therapy" is not recognized by law.

This has the consequence that the spectrum of rehabilitation programs offered ranges from serious, competent suppliers of traffic therapies to sellers of "crash-courses" without any behavior-modifying effects.

It should be emphasized that the participation at those long-term rehabilitation programs is always voluntary. After completing it, another medico-psychological assessment is prescribed.

If it becomes known that the case history of alcohol abuse had not been very great, that the person concerned is generally able to control the consumption of alcohol, and furthermore shows first understanding for the necessity of a modification of his drinking habits, a shorter rehabilitation model can be conducted. In this case, the candidate has the legally based possibility (§70 of Driving License Regulation) to re-establish his qualification to drive immediately by the use of a model developed especially for this situation and well established. Here, the qualification to drive does not have to be checked by another medico-psychological assessment after the course.

The executive body of such a course must be accredited by the corresponding European norm DIN EN 45013 (§72 Driving License Regulation) and must be officially recognized by the responsible highest Federal State Authority. The task of accreditation is also accomplished by the Federal Highway Research Institute. The course leaders, must have attained a university degree as psychologists. Additionally, the leaders need to have attended traffic psychological training at a University or College, or any office that is qualified to deal with the subject of assessment or reestablishment of the qualification to drive. They need to have the necessary knowledge for assessing the qualification of motorists, as well as special training for leading a course.

Figure 5 sums up the system of rehabilitation programs in Germany.

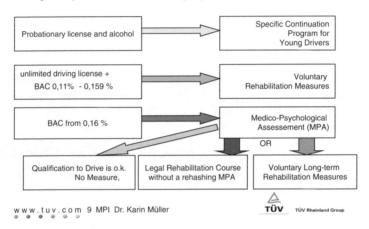

Figure 5. The system of rehabilitation programs in Germany.

EVALUATION OF THE REHABILITATION SYSTEM

The efficiency of legally based courses for DUI with the consequence of regranting the driving license immediately has been proved by a state-of-the-art evaluation process. The advised period of evaluation amounts to 3 years. A course for DUI can be considered as successful if the recidivism rate of the participants is not higher than the one of the parallel control group of positive-assessed persons. The reference rate of 18.8% for positive-assessed persons that is used at the moment proceeds from one of the most important German researches on the subject of evaluation, named ALKOEVA (Winkler, Jacobshagen & Nickel, 1988). The figures for the ALKOEVA research originate from more than 3000 alcohol offenders (experimental, course participants $n = 1740$, control group $n = 1489$). It was shown that alcohol-taking motorists who had taken part at one of the programs for reestablishing the qualification to drive only had a recidivism rate of 13.3% compared with the abovementioned 18.8% in the case of positive-assessed persons. Newer research led by Jacobshagen and Utzelmann from 1987 to 1989 on more than 3000 drunken drivers (EVAGUT) proved again that by participating at the specific program for re-establishing the qualification to drive, the recidivism rate could be reduced over a period of 3 years to 13.8% (Jacobshagen & Utzelmann, 1997). In comparison, positively assessed persons in the MPA showed a recidivism rate of 11.2%, a proof for the continuous improvement of diagnosis methods throughout the years. Finally, an evaluation research with more than 1600 motorists from 1994 to 1996 (BUSS) showed the reduction of the recidivism rate for participants at a specific model for re-establishing the qualification to drive of 8.3% compared with 6.5% in case of those positively assessed (Jacobshagen, 2001) (Figure 6).

sample	year of assesm.	positive in MPA	course recommended
ALKOEVA (1988)	79–83	18,8	13,3
EVAGUT (1997)	87–89	11,2	13,8
BUSS-control-group (2001)	94–96	6,5	8,3

www.t u v . c o m   10 MPI Dr. Karin Müller   △ TÜV   TÜV Rheinland Group

Figure 6. Results of evaluation: relapse rates (%) at 36 months follow-up after reinstatement of license.

These figures can be interpreted entirely in the sense of a continuously improving efficiency of the combination of "qualification to drive diagnoses" in the assessment and advancement of qualification to drive carried out by specific, quality-assured rehabilitation programs.

Furthermore, apart from the main criterion, "legal confirmation", the evaluation criteria "variable knowledge improvement", "modification of attitudes", "reported behaviour", and "acceptance of the programs by the participants" should be mentioned. These criteria can also be controlled in a "pre–post design" that also has to take a control group into consideration. The already mentioned research ALKOEVA proved in a pre–post examination that the participation at a program can lead to an improvement of the knowledge about alcohol consumption and traffic, and can also lead to a modification of the traffic-relevant attitudes, especially in terms of finding a solution for the drink-driving conflict.

The wide range of long-term rehabilitation programs are not bound to legal consequences up to the present. Therefore, in this group of traffic therapeutic intervention models, no legally prescribed requirements in terms of quality management are requested. Nevertheless, multivarious and some very high qualitative measures have been developed in this group as well. Some suppliers of those rehabilitation programs have bound themselves to norms within the quality management systems by voluntary obligation.

REFERENCES

Jacobshagen, W. (2001). Die Wirksamkeit des Modells BUSS-Beratung, Untersuchung und Schulung in der Sperrfrist. *Blutalkohol*, *38*, Heft 4.

Jacobshagen, W., & Utzelmann, H.-D. (1997). Prognosesicherheit der MPU. *Zeitschrift für Verkehrssicherheit*, *43*, 28–36.

Müller, A. (1992). Alkoholeinfluss als Ursache bei tödlichen Verkehrsunfällen: Stimmen die amtlichen Zahlen? *Blutalkohol, 29,* 242–251.

Winkler, W., Jacobshagen, W., & Nickel, W.-R. (1988). Wirksamkeit von Kursen für wiederholt auffällige Kraftfahrer. Bundesanstalt für Straβenwesen (Hrsg.). *Unfall- und Sicherheitsforschung,* Heft 64, Bremerhaven.

Traffic and Transport Psychology
G. Underwood (Editor)
© 2005 Elsevier Ltd. All rights reserved.

44

SETTING UP AND ASSESSING A COMMITMENT PROCEDURE IN REHABILITATION TRAINING COURSES FOR TRAFFIC REGULATION OFFENDERS IN FRANCE

Patricia Delhomme[1]

INTRODUCTION

In many countries, demerit points system or credit of points system for drivers exist. When our research was conducted in France in 2002, the credit of points system had been in place for more than 10 years. After license, drivers start with a credit of 12 points and rehabilitation training courses for traffic regulation offenders are carried out. These courses last for two consecutive days with between 6 and 20 participants. They are conducted by two instructors, a psychologist and a specialized driving trainer. In these courses, all drivers have, at some point, driven over the speed limit. This is not surprising because speeding is the most frequent violation (Moget, 1980; Reason, Manstead, Stradling, Baxter & Campbell, 1990; Manstead, Parker, Stradling, Reason & Baxter, 1992) and is one of the main accident risks (Brown, 1962; Deen & Godwin, 1985; West, French, Kemp & Elander, 1993; Parker, Reason, Manstead & Stradling, 1995; Lajunen, Karola & Summala, 1997; Delhomme & Cauzard, 2000; Delhomme, 2002). This speeding is produced with a large stability across driving situations (Ahlin, 1979; Rothengatter, 1988) and allows drivers to fit in with traffic in car following situations (Saad, 1996). Our objective in this research was to make the course participants observe speed limits.

From theoretical and empirical work, we know that there are two strategies to lead people to modify their behaviour with the idea that the initiative of change must come from them:

(1)   one to directly influence attitudes towards the target behaviour (for instance preventive campaigns);

---

[1] INRETS, Laboratory of Driving Psychology, Arcueil, France. *E-mail:* delhomme@inrets.fr (P. Delhomme).

(2)   and to act directly on the targeted behaviour in leading people to undertake involving acts which prepare them to produce the target behaviour in the future. These involving acts can also modify attitudes or reinforce them in favour of targeted behaviour according to whether or not their initial attitudes were against the targeted behaviour.

In our research, we chose the second strategy. We set up an intervention in rehabilitation training courses to lead the participants to publicly commit themselves to observing speed limits and we tested the effect of this intervention on self-reported behaviour.

THEORETICAL FRAMEWORK

Numerous studies are conducted in the field of Psychology of Commitment. The origin of this line of research on commitment is attributed to Lewin's (1947) work. In 1943 in the United States, the difficulties of victualling and health problems made it necessary for people to change their food practices. But we know that it is difficult to modify habits, that is to say frequent and regular behaviour like food practices. That is why the Institute of Technology of Cambridge asked Kurt Lewin which would be the best strategy to lead the housewives to modify their eating habits, traditional information campaigns having failed. Lewin (1947) conducted several experimental researches to answer this question. From his consistent seminal work, we know that change of behaviour is all the more likely when participants can express their point of view themselves in favour of change in a context where they can speak openly without explicit pressure from the instructor and where they freely take the decision to change their behaviour in public. In the same vein, a few years later, Freedman and Fraser (1966) developed an intervention framework of compliance without pressure in order to increase the likelihood that people comply. They called this intervention: "The foot-in-the-door". Two different cost requests are made: a small request which is the initial request and a larger request which is the targeted request. The intervention consists of asking little the first time (initial request) to obtain more the second time (targeted request). "Carrying out a small request increased the likelihood that the participant would agree to a similar larger request made by the same person" (p. 201), so the initial request produces an increase in compliance. In 1971, Kiesler gave a new impulse to this line of research that he called Psychology of Commitment. Other intervention frameworks were developed to lead people to accept requests that they could not accept spontaneously in putting them in a context where they freely committed themselves, that is to say without feeling forced to do so (for instance, the door-in-the-face technique, Cialdini et al., 1975; the law-ball procedure, Cialdini, Cacioppo, Bassett & Miller, 1978).

A synthesis of experimental work (Joulé & Beauvois, 1998) shows that some factors increase the likelihood of people accepting an involving act:

(1)   The visibility of the act: the involving act should be carried out in public, be explicit, be irreversible, the effect of commitment is all the greater when it is both verbal and written (Katzev & Wang, 1994) and being performed on several occasions.

(2)   The importance of the act: it should have serious consequences and be time consuming or costly.

(3)   The motives of the act: it should be felt as the result of a deliberate choice from the individual, a feeling of self-determination. Preferably, the act should not be undertaken for

external reasons (for instance for money) as these prove to be less effective. Internal reasons on the other hand (for instance doing something to be seen as a responsible person) reinforce the perceived link between the individual and their act.

Many studies tested the effect of commitment in the short term, few of them in the long term (Joulé & Beauvois, 1998). The effectiveness of commitment has been largely proved in the short term and has been shown in the long term, for instance a reduction of gas and electricity consumption a year after the intervention (Pallak & Cummings, 1976). However, the explanations remain unclear. Some hypotheses are in terms of a process of cognitive rationalization, that is to say a reduction of cognitive dissonance (Festinger, 1957) or the need for consistency insofar as the individual who has made the commitment would rationalize their motives in favour of the targeted behaviour. Other explanations have been put forward like self-perception (Bem, 1972) or reactance (reaction to a perceived threat of one's personal freedom, Brehm, 1966).

The commitment procedure has been set up to increase the production of very different behaviours in various fields (health, road safety for wearing seat belts, environment protection, marketing, etc.). But to our knowledge, it has never been introduced in an imposed legal framework such as rehabilitation training courses. At first glance, this legal framework could be at odds with a sense of self-determination, a precondition for commitment.

EMPIRICAL RESEARCH

Participants

Our research was carried out among 624 participants in 2002 in 43 training courses of 2 days. The average age of participants was 34 years (18–80 years). The sample was made up of 90% of men and 10% of women, which is near the national breakdown of participants in training courses in France. Participants attended the rehabilitation training course for three reasons:

– to get back lost points for 55.3% of them;

– as an alternative to legal sanctions (21.6%);

– as "novices" if they had their driving license for less than 2 years and had been fined for an offence which cost at least four points (23.1%).

Procedure

Our commitment procedure is mixed. In order to increase the likelihood that participants freely commit to observing speed limits, we used a foot-in-the-door intervention framework and created a context to encourage people to express points of view in favour of observing speed limits before introducing a public act of commitment.

Initial small request. At the end of the first day, the instructors made a small request which virtually everyone agreed with. The instructors asked participants to fill in a short questionnaire in favour of safe driving specifying that they were free to accept or refuse to do so. This questionnaire was a first step towards a future commitment to observing speed limits.

Targeted request introduced in an ad hoc context. At the end of the second day, the instructors began a discussion by asking participants what they could do to decrease the accident risk. The aim of this was to influence people to speak about the importance of observing speed limits. At the end of the discussion, participants were asked, in public, to commit to observing speed limits each time they drive and to signing a commitment form.

The experimental design

We used three groups to test the effect of the intervention:

- *an experimental group* where the intervention was introduced by five different instructors in two courses out of three;

- *a comparison group* where these same five instructors did not introduce the intervention in one course out of three in order to increase the chance of obtaining two comparable groups except in commitment;

- *a control group* where two other instructors did not introduce the intervention at all during the courses.

We chose to have more participants in the experimental group compared to the other groups (see Figure 1) in order to know how many of them commit or refuse to commit to observe the speed limit and to test the effect of this commitment on self-reported behaviour.

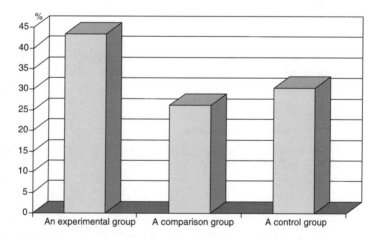

Figure 1. Percentage of participants in the three groups used to test the effect of the intervention.

The test of the impact of commitment

The participants ended their rehabilitation training without being allowed to contact each other afterwards. But to test the impact of commitment, it was necessary to contact them after the rehabilitation training courses. So, we asked them to take part in a 5-min phone survey on their driving trips. The instructors asked the three groups of participants if they accepted to give their phone number to take part in this phone survey during the third half-day of the courses. That is to say, before asking the participants of the experimental group to commit to observing speed limits in order to distinguish these two requests. The advantage of this procedure is obvious. This procedure made the survey appear as being separate from the research on commitment. However, this procedure was limited insofar as only volunteers taking part in the phone survey on driving trips were contacted.

The interviews were carried out by interviewers who did not know which group the participants were in. The interviews were repeated four times about (see Table 1):

– 12 days,

– 45 days,

– 3.5 months,

– 5 months after the courses.

Participants were interviewed by phone on their driving trips for these time periods:

– the last 8 days for the first interview;

– the last 3 weeks for the second interview;

– the last 4 weeks for the third and fourth interview.

Table 1. Time schedule for the four interviews and period concerned.

	First interview	*Second interview*	*Third interview*	*Fourth interview*
Time schedule	12 days after course	45 days after course	3, 5 months after course	5 months after course
Period concerned	Last 8 days	Last 3 weeks	Last 4 weeks	Last 4 weeks

Dependant variables

During the phone interviews, we recorded among these volunteers who drove during the time period considered:

– on which type of road they drove;

– the duration of their trips;

– if they observed or broke speed limits in general and according to the type of road on which they drove;

– if they modified their speed in comparison to 1 year ago (the same, increase or decrease in speed).

Other variables were registered by instructors before the courses like number of accidents, the last offences for which they came to the courses.

Results

In our sample of participants, 100% accepted to fill in the small questionnaire (initial request of foot-in-the-door intervention framework) at the end of the first day of the training course.

Among the participants of the experimental group, 53.1% ($N = 144$) committed to observe speed limits each time they drove and 46.9% ($N = 127$) refused such a commitment. The percentage of commitment is comparable according to whether they attended the rehabilitation training course to get back lost points or as an alternative to legal sanctions whereas there was slightly less commitment among the "novices" (see Figure 2). These results are similar in proportion among men and women.

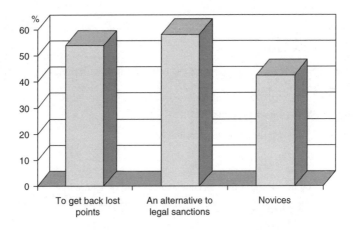

Figure 2. Percentage of commitment according to reasons for following course.

Interview participation rates

The percentage of participants for whom the commitment was tested:

– during the first interview, there were less than half of the participants,

– during the second interview, more than a third,

– during the third interview, more than a quarter,

– and for the last interview, a quarter.

The participation rate in the phone driving trips survey was similar between the four groups (see Figure 3).

The effect of commitment

The commitment had a positive effect on self-reported speed limits in all four interviews (see Figure 4): significantly more drivers who committed declared that they observed speed limits during the time period before each interview whereas there were significantly less than in

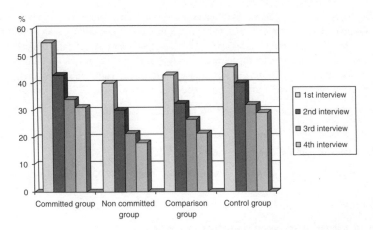

Figure 3. The participation rate in the four interviews according to the four groups.

the other three groups. About 12 days after courses, 53.4% of those who committed claimed to have observed speed limits whereas there were less than 36% in the other three groups. About 5 months after courses, this was still the case although the successive interviews carried out among the participants had an effect in each group: 48.1% of those who committed claimed to have observed speed limits whereas the percentages were lower among the non-committed group (less than 10%) and among comparison and control groups (28.6 and 20%).

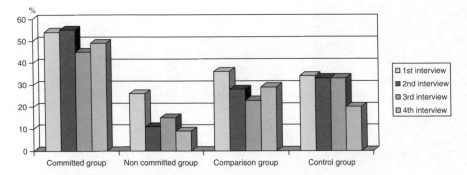

Figure 4. Percentage of participants who claimed to have observed speed limits in the four interviews according to the four groups.

The effect in favour of commitment, however, seems more effective in two categories of drivers: those who attended the course as "an alternative to legal sanctions" and the "novices" and not for those who wanted to get back lost points.

This effect observed at a general level, was also found on specific roads where they were driving, compared to those who refused to commit or those in the comparison or in the control group only for the first three interviews. The effect was not significant during the fourth interview because the number of participants was lower. However, the results tend to follow the same direction as our hypothesis. Proportionally, more participants who committed, compared to other three groups, claimed to have observed speed limits:

- downtown and on dual carriageways during the first three interviews,
- on county roads during the first two interviews,
- on highways during the third interview.

No commitment effect was observed during the four interviews on ring roads and on country roads.

Changes in self-reported speed compared to 1 year ago

Globally, the participants in the committed group claimed to have reduced their speed (scale from 1 "low reduction" to 5 "high reduction") more than those in other groups, particularly during the first interview (cf. Figure 5). But this effect in favour of commitment was significantly found only among those who attended the course to get back lost points during the first three interviews. This effect was not significant among those who attended the course as "an alternative to legal sanctions" or among "novices".

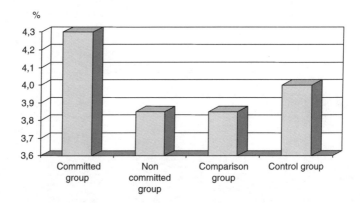

Figure 5. Reducing one's speed compared to 1 year ago according to the four groups.

CONCLUSION

With a legal context that does not seem favourable to lead a commitment, about half of participants to rehabilitation training courses committed to observe speed limits each time they drove. The percentage of commitment is comparable according to whether they attended the rehabilitation training course to get back lost points or as an alternative to legal sanctions whereas there was slightly less commitment among the "novices". We found a positive effect of commitment: about 12 days after courses, 53.4% of those who committed claimed to have observed speed limits whereas there were less than 36% in the other groups. About 5 months after courses, this was still the case: 48.1% of those who committed claimed to have observed speed limits whereas there were less than 29% in the other groups. Although we did not expect very large effect among this population of offenders and for the behaviour we were seeking to modify, that is to say the speed. The size of the effect produced by the commitment is between 20 and 40% concerning the percentages of participants who claimed to have observed the speed limits.

Commitment seems less effective among those who attend the courses to regain lost points, who have often committed more offences, especially with regard to speeding. In fact there are more people in this group who claim to have been fined for speeding at their last offence compared to those who attend the courses as "an alternative to legal sanctions" or as "novices". Those in "alternative to legal sanctions" freely chose to attend the course. "Novices" were forced to follow the course but they have less driving habits. As a result, commitment could have two different meanings:

–   for those who attend the courses as "an alternative to legal sanctions" or as "novices", it could mean observing speed limits;

–   for those who attended to get points back, it could mean reducing their speed without necessarily observing the speed limits.

As suggested by the theoretical framework, we found a positive effect of commitment. This effect occurred with participants who took part in rehabilitation training courses, i.e. in a legal context that could be described as a forced choice situation. Thus, our results expand the robustness of the positive effect of commitment. This leaves us with a question: can this positive effect of commitment on self-reported data be observed on the road?

ACKNOWLEDGEMENTS

This research was supported by Minister of Transport. The author thanks V. Kreel, F. Bragagnolo, D. Ducamp, G. Korn, C. Lardon, M.-P. Laurent, J.-F. Lequellenec, I. Ragot, C. Rodon, A. Schamelhout and P. de Vit who took part in this research.

REFERENCES

Ahlin, F.J. (1979). *An Investigation into the Consistency of Drivers' Speed Choice.* Toronto, Ontario: Department of Civil Engineering, University of Toronto.

Bem, D.J. (1972). Self-perception theory. In Berkowitz, L. (Ed.), *Advances in Experimental Social Psychology* (Vol. 6, pp. 1–62). New York: Academic.

Brehm, J.W. (1966). *A Theory of Psychological Reactance.* New York: Academic.

Brown, I.D. (1962). Studies of component movements, consistency and spare capacity of car drivers. *Annuals of Occupational Hygiene, 5,* 131–143.

Cialdini, R.B., Vincent, J.E., Lewis, S.K., Catalan, J., Wheeler, D., & Darby, B.L. (1975). Reciprocal concessions procedure for inducing compliance: the door-in-the-face technique. *Journal of Personality and Social Psychology, 31,* 206–215.

Cialdini, R.B., Cacioppo, J.T., Bassett, R., & Miller, J.A. (1978). The law-ball procedure for producing compliance: commitment then cost. *Journal of Personality and Social Psychology, 36*, 463–476.

Deen, T.B., & Godwin, S.R. (1985). Safety benefits of the 55 mph speed limit. *Transportation Quarterly, 39*, 321–343.

Delhomme, P. (2002). Croyances des jeunes automobilistes en matière de vitesse. Rapport final. Convention DSCR-INRETS N° 00/010/T-étude N° 7, décembre 2002.

Delhomme, P., & Cauzard, J.-P. (2000). Comparer sa vitesse à celle d'autrui: comparaison sociale et représentation de la conduite chez les automobilistes européens. *Recherche Transports Sécurité, 67*, 39–64.

Festinger, L. (1957). *A Theory of Cognitive Dissonance*. Standford, CA: Standford University Press.

Freedman, J.L., & Fraser, S.C. (1966). Compliance without pressure: the foot-in-the-door technique. *Journal of Personality and Social Psychology, 4*, 195–202.

Joulé, R.V., & Beauvois,, J.L. (1998). *La soumission librement consentie*. Paris: Presses Universitaires de France.

Katzev, R., & Wang, T. (1994). Can commitment change behavior? A case study of environmental actions. *Journal of Social Behavior and Personality, 9*, 13–26.

Lajunen, T., Karola, J., & Summala, H. (1997). Speed and acceleration as measures of driving style in young male drivers. *Perceptual and Motor Skills, 85*, 3–16.

Lewin, K. (1947). Group Decision and Social Change. In Maccoby, E.E., Newcomb, T.M., & Hartley, E.L. (Eds.), Reading in Social Psychology (pp. 197–211). New York: Holt, Rinehart & Winston, réédité en 1958.

Manstead, A.S.R., Parker, D., Stradling, S.G., Reason, J.T., & Baxter, J.S. (1992). Perceived consensus in estimates of the prevalence of driving errors and violations. *Journal of Applied Social Psychology, 22* (7), 237–254.

Moget, M. (1980). *Une contribution au problème du risque dans l'activité de conduite: Les mécanismes de régulation du "comportement de base" de l'usager de la route*, Inrets, Rapport interne.

Pallak, M., & Cummings, N. (1976). Commitment and voluntary energy conservation. *Personality and Social Psychology Bulletin, 2*, 27–31.

Parker, D., Manstead, A.S.R., & Stradling, S.G. (1995). Extending the theory of planned behaviour: the role of personal norm. *British Journal of Social Psychology, 34*, 127–137.

Reason, J.T., Manstead, A.S.R., Stradling, S.G., Baxter, J.S., & Campbell, K.A. (1990). Errors and violations on the road: a real distinction? *Ergonomics, 33*, 1315–1332.

Rothengatter, T. (1988). Risk and the absence of pleasure: a motivational approach to modelling road user behaviour. *Ergonomics, 31* (4), 599–607.

Saad, F. (1996). Driver strategies in car-following situations. In Gale, A.G., Brown, I.D., Haslegrave, C.M., & Taylor, S.P. (Eds.), *Vision in Vehicles V* (pp. 61–70). Amsterdam: Elsevier Science.

West, R., French, D., Kemp, R., & Elander, J. (1993). Direct observation of driving, self reports of driver behaviour, and accident involvement. *Ergonomics, 36*, 557–567.

TRAVEL DEMAND MANAGEMENT AND TRAVEL MODE CHOICE

Traffic and Transport Psychology
G. Underwood (Editor)
© 2005 Elsevier Ltd. All rights reserved.

45

CHANGES OF PRIVATE CAR USE IN RESPONSE TO TRAVEL DEMAND MANAGEMENT

Tommy Gärling[1]

INTRODUCTION

Increasing availability and speed of motorized vehicles have had beneficial impacts on human living conditions. This applies in particular to the increase in accessibility due to the daily use of private cars for travel to work places, shopping facilities, and recreational places. At the same time social costs of the use of private cars are becoming intolerably high (Goodwin, 1996; Greene & Wegener, 1997). These costs include congestion, accidents, health hazards caused by noise and air pollution, and excessive use of energy and land. Counter-measures are on the political agenda in many countries; few seem, however, to be implemented at a scale that promises to make them effective.

In this chapter different measures for managing the demand for car use is first discussed. A theoretical framework is then presented with the aim of providing a means of analyzing of how these measures affect car use. In the proposed theoretical framework car users' responses are conceptualized as adaptations of their daily activities and travel. An overview follows of some research examining this adaptation process that my collaborators and I have conducted recently. The chapter finishes with conclusions followed by a discussion of needs and directions for future research.

TRAVEL DEMAND MANAGEMENT MEASURES

There are several conceivable measures to abate the adverse effects of private car use. A subset of these measures (e.g. increased capacity of road infrastructure, improved car technology, and limiting speed) does not necessitate a reduction in car use, at least not in the immediate future.

[1] Department of Psychology, Göteborg University, P.O. Box 500, SE-40530 Göteborg, Sweden. *E-mail:* Tommy.Garling@psy.gu.se (T. Gärling).

A general assessment of the current state is, however, that measures that reduce demand for car use must be implemented (e.g. Hensher, 1998). In addition, it is desirable in order to reduce congestion to change car use with respect to when and where people drive, particularly at peak hours in urban areas or on major arteries. Since the proposed measures focus on changing or reducing demand for car use, they are referred to as travel demand management (TDM) (Kitamura, Fujii, & Pas, 1997; Pas, 1995). Other terms with similar meanings include, for instance, transport system management (Pendyala, Kitamura, Chen, & Pas, 1997) or mobility management (Kristensen & Marshall, 1999).

Several attempts have been made to classify TDM measures. At a more specific level, Litman (2003) distinguishes five classes: improvements in transport options; provisions of incentives to switch mode; land-use management; policy and planning reforms; and support programs. A partly overlapping set is proposed by May, Jopson, and Matthews (2003) as land-use policies, infrastructure provision (for modes other than the private car), management and regulation, information provision, attitudinal and behavioral change measures, and pricing. Vlek and Michon (1992) suggest the following classes: physical changes such as, for instance, closing out car traffic or providing alternative transportation; law regulation; economic incentives and disincentives; information, education, and prompts; socialization and social modeling targeted at changing social norms; and institutional and organizational changes such as, for instance, flexible work hours, telecommuting, or "flexplaces." Louw, Maat, and Mathers (1998) note that there are policies encouraging mode switching, destination switching, changing time of travel, linking trips, substitution of trips with technology (e.g. teleworking), and substitution of trips through trip modification (e.g. a single goods delivery in lieu of a series of shoppers' trips). At a more general level, Gatersleben (2003) distinguishes measures aimed at changing behavioral opportunities from measures aimed at changing perceptions, motivations, and norms. In a similar vein, Jones (2003), Steg and Vlek (1997), Stradling, Meadows, and Beatty (2000), and Thorpe, Hills, and Jaensirisak (2000) distinguish between push and pull measures. Push measures discourage car use by making it less attractive; pull measures encourage the use of alternative modes to the car by making such modes more attractive.

Partly based on these different systems of classification, Loukopoulos, Gärling, Jakobsson, and Fujii (2004a) proposed that TDM measures may be characterized as varying with respect to *targeting latent* vs. *manifest travel demand, time scale, spatial scale, coerciveness, top−down* vs. *bottom−up process*, and *market-based* vs. *regulatory mechanism*. Brief definitions of each are given in Table 1 together with assessments on these dimensions of *Individualized Marketing* (IM), *Road Pricing* (RP), and *Prohibition* (Pn) (see Appendix A). Any TDM measure may thus be characterized as to whether it targets observed or unobserved travel (e.g. measures reducing congestion targeting manifest travel demand vs. measures increasing public transport capacity targeting latent demand),[2] with respect to time and area of operation (e.g. weekday morning peak on major arteries to downtown), and the degree to which the measure affects voluntary control or freedom of choice. Coercive measures (such as prohibition) target change in manifest travel demand by declining car users' voluntary control. Other measures are designed to empower car users to increase voluntary control (e.g. information campaigns trying to affect

---

[2] A measure such as individualized marketing targeting latent travel demand does not change the travel alternatives open to car users. Some would therefore hesitate to call it a TDM measure.

attitudes toward coercive measures) or make voluntary control costly (e.g. pricing travel). It may be seen that IM is non-coercive, whereas Pn is coercive. RP tends to fall in between since it is coercive for those who cannot afford the fees, non-coercive for those who can. Apparently, they also differ on other dimensions. Loukopoulos, Jakobsson, Gärling, Schneider, and Fujii (2004e), furthermore, observed differences between these measures in car-users' and non-car-users' attitudes, beliefs, and evaluations related to them.

The proposed dimensions may be related to acceptance and effectiveness of TDM measures. If so, drawing on them may, for instance, facilitate the choice of combinations of TDM measures for different purposes. They may, furthermore, suggest reasons why TDM measures are effective. However, this also requires an understanding of how car users respond.

Table 1. Proposed system of classifying TDM measures.

Dimension with definition	IM	RP	Pn
Targeting latent (vs. manifest) demand: changing unobserved (vs. observed) car use	Yes	Partly	No
(Restriction of) time scale: hours of operation	No	Yes	Yes
(Restriction of) spatial scale: area of operation	No	Yes	Yes
Coerciveness: declining car users voluntary control	No	Partly	Yes
Bottom–up (vs. top–down) process: empowering car users to increase voluntary control	Yes	Partly	No
Market-based (vs. regulatory) mechanism: increasing voluntary control at a cost	No	Yes	No

IM = Individualized marketing, RP = Road pricing, Pn = Prohibition.

RESPONSES TO TDM MEASURES

Fulfilling biological needs, social obligations, and personal desires requires that people move from one place to another place to perform goal-directed behaviors such as work, maintenance activities (e.g. shopping), and various leisure activities (Gärling & Garvill, 1993). The basic tenet of the activity-based approach to travel behavior (e.g. Axhausen & Gärling, 1992; Bhat & Koppelman, 1999; Ettema & Timmermans, 1997; Jones, Dix, Clarke, & Heggie, 1983; Kitamura, 1988; Recker, McNally, & Roth, 1986; Vilhelmson, 1999) is that demand for travel is derived from this requirement.

The way a society is spatially organized is an essential determinant of the degree and type of travel demand. For instance, the boost in motorized travel is partly a consequence of that urban areas have grown in size to accommodate a rising population, thereby increasing demand for fast, motorized travel. Another factor is that changes in life style have increased the complexity of travel demand far beyond the home-to-work journeys on weekdays. Existing alternative travel modes such as public transport lacks the versatility of the private car necessary to satisfy such a complex travel demand. This versatility is in turn a consequence of the advancement in automobile technology and huge investments in road infrastructure.

These propositions are summarized in Figure 1. Degree and type of travel demand depend on activity choice and the spatial organization of the environment. Mediating between travel demand and travel (sometimes referred to as manifest travel demand or only travel demand) is *travel choice* that is influenced by attributes of the transportation system such as speed, frequency, reliability, safety, and cost. It is thus implied that some degree of freedom exists (see Timmermans et al., 2003) in choosing to travel or not, where to travel, how to travel, and when to travel.

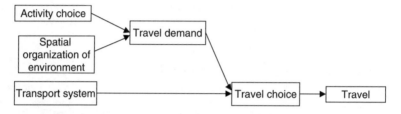

Figure 1. Determinants of travel.

Extensive research has provided knowledge of how travel choices are made (Gärling, Gillholm, Gärling, 1998a). Traditionally, this research has focused choices for single trips of travel mode (e.g. for home-to-work journeys) (e.g. Golob, 1989), shopping locations (e.g. Timmermans & Golledge, 1990), or departure times (e.g. Mahmassani & Jou, 2000). Travel time and monetary costs are found to be important determinants. The significant role of aversion towards wait time, uncertain delays, and changes are other recurrent research findings. An important distinction has, furthermore, been made between habitual, impulsive, compulsive, and planned travel (Doherty & Miller, 2000; Jakobsson, 2004). Commuting to work is an example of habitual travel. Shopping trips are more frequently impulsive (less planned or planned with a short time horizon). Travel in cases of emergencies is compulsive. Long-distance travel is more meticulously planned than any other travel. Research shows that pre-choice information search and deliberation are reduced when travel becomes habitual (Verplanken, Aarts, & Knippenberg, 1997). It has also been demonstrated how easily a car-use habit is developed and generalized across situational contexts (Gärling, Fujii, & Boe, 2001).

Car travel frequently has multiple purposes at multiple destinations. A more recent aim of research is therefore to understand the *interrelated choices* preceding such trip chains or tours (Axhausen & Gärling, 1992; Gärling, 2004), for instance, choices related to all trips from home and back to home during a day. It is proposed that choices related to trip chains are made of all or a subset of activity (type and duration), destination, mode, departure time, and route. Many other related choices are made but have not been extensively investigated. The need to understand interrelated travel choices became an impetus to improve the traditional mathematical–statistical tools for analyses of single-trip choices (Ben-Akiva & Lerman, 1985). Several generations of computer simulations[3] or computational process models (CPM)

---

[3] This work is closely related to computer simulation of thinking processes such as problem solving pioneered in psychology by Newell and Simon (1972), or decision making (Payne et al., 1993) (see Gärling et al., 1989).

have therefore been developed (e.g. Arentze & Timmermans, 2000; Gärling, Kwan, & Golledge, 1994). The most recent generation of CPMs aims at modeling how people learn about and represent the environment as well as how they learn to choose alternatives with positive outcomes (Arentze & Timmermans, 2003). In CPMs realism of the travel plan frequently replaces the traditional criterion of utility maximization under generalized cost constraints. Given a complex household agenda of activities, speed of travel then becomes the single most important property of the transportation system. Although speed of car travel has slowed down in many urban areas, driving is typically still the fastest travel mode and therefore likely to be chosen. The reason is that the car is superior to other motorized travel in being always available and moving people from door to door.

More recent research has highlighted the role of feelings of personal freedom, joy, security, and status as determinants of the choice of the private car (Steg, Geurs, & Ras, 2002) Cost factors may also play a more important role than assumed. Some of the costs of driving are non-transparent, and thus may be largely discounted (Everett & Watson, 1987). Conversely, the capital cost of a car is probably not perceived as a sunk cost that should be discounted. Even though the cost of an alternative is lower compared to the variable cost of driving, it is therefore perceived to be unnecessary when the investment in the car once has been made.

The potential effectiveness of TDM measures for reducing private car use depends on how car users respond to them. Given that private car use primarily results from needs, desires, and social obligations to participate in out-of-home activities, car-use reduction needs to be viewed broadly as an adaptation by car users to changes in travel alternatives that potentially have consequences for their engagement in different activities and the satisfaction they experience from this. A central issue is whether theories of travel choice that apply in equilibrium are transferable to conditions of change. As has been noted (Goodwin, 1998), it may take a long time before equilibrium is reached. Furthermore, theories of choice in equilibrium may not include factors that are important for understanding change processes. For this reason several recent attempts have been made to conceptualize the change process (Arentze, Hofman, & Timmermans, 2004; Cao & Mokhtarian, 2004a,b; Gärling, Gärling, & Johansson, 2000; Gärling, Gärling, & Loukopoulos, 2002b; Kitamura & Fujii, 1998; Pendyala et al., 1997, Pendyala, Kitamura, & Reddy, 1998). In the following the theoretical framework proposed by Gärling et al. (2002a) will be described. This theoretical framework aims at analyzing the multi-facetted nature of car users' responses to TDM measures.

As illustrated in Figure 2, travel alternatives are defined as bundles of attributes describing trip chains (including purposes, departure and arrival times, travel times, routes, and monetary costs). Choices of travel alternatives are influenced by these bundles of attributes. Another determinant is the reduction or change goals that households set. In self-regulation theory in social psychology (Carver & Scheier, 1998),[4] such goals form a hierarchy from concrete

---

[4] The theory of reasoned action (Fishbein & Ajzen, 1975), its successor the theory of planned behavior (Ajzen, 1991), or the norm-activation theory proposed by Schwartz (1977) and later revised by Stern, Dietz, and Black (1986) have frequently been proposed as a theoretical foundation. However, although these theories have many points of communality with the goal setting and self-regulation theories, they do not as easily capture change processes.

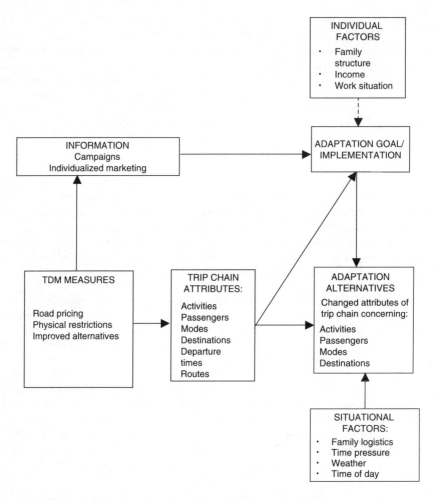

Figure 2. Theoretical framework. (adapted from Gärling et al., 2002a.)

programs to abstract principles functioning as reference values in negative feedback loops regulating ongoing behavior or changes in behavior. If a discrepancy between the present state and the goal is detected, some action is carried out with the aim of minimizing it. For instance, after implementing a road pricing scheme, a car-use reduction goal may be set if households experience increased monetary travel costs. On the other hand, if other changes are simultaneously encountered such as shorter travel times (due to less congestion) or concomitant reduced living costs (e.g. children moving out, a salary raise), no such goal may be set. In effect, a simple relationship does not exist between increasing the cost of driving and the setting of car-use reduction goals.

Needs, desires, attitudes, and values influence the goals that people set and strive to attain (Austin & Vancouver, 1996). Sociodemographics are frequently proxies for these determining factors. The set goals vary in content and intensity (Locke & Latham, 1984, 1990). Content is related to (i) difficulty or lack of skill required to attain the goal, (ii) specificity of the goal, (iii) complexity of the goal (the number of outcome dimensions), and (iv) the degree of conflict with other goals at the same or higher levels. Intensity refers to perceived importance and degree of commitment. Research in other areas on goal setting and attainment (e.g. Lee, Locke, & Latham, 1989) has shown that specific, more difficult goals increase the likelihood that they are attained. Skills, commitment to the goal, and immediate clear feedback about goal attainment are moderating factors.

After having set a car-use reduction goal, households are assumed to form a plan for how to achieve this goal and to make commitments to execute the formed plan. In social psychological research, this process is referred to as the *formation of implementation intentions* (Gärling & Fujii, 2002; Gollwitzer, 1993). The plan that is formed consists of predetermined choices contingent on specified conditions (Hayes-Roth & Hayes-Roth, 1979). In making plans for how to reduce car use, households may consider a wide range of alternatives such as staying at home suppressing trips and activities, using electronic communications means instead of driving, car pooling, or changing the effective choice set of travel options with respect to purposes, destinations, modes, or departure times. Households may also consider longer-term strategic changes such as moving to another residence or changing work place or hours.

It is hypothesized that individuals and households seek and select adaptation alternatives that lead to the achievement of the goal they have set. We do not assume, however, that this process necessarily entails a simultaneous optimal choice among all alternatives. Experimental laboratory-based research (Payne, Bettman, & Johnson, 1993) has shown that people make tradeoffs between accuracy and (mental and tangible) costs, and that these tradeoffs are frequently optimal. A vital difference to microeconomic utility-maximization theories (e.g. McFadden, 2001) is that it is not assumed that people invariably invest the required degree of effort. Whether they do or not is in the theoretical framework assumed to depend on properties of the set goal (e.g. the degree of commitment). Furthermore, if the cost of an effective adaptation is too high, even a small and specific reduction goal to which a household is highly committed may be abandoned or reduced.

Consistent with the notion of bounded rationality (Gigerenzer, Todd, & The ABC Research Group, 1999; Simon, 1990), a second important difference to microeconomic utility-maximization theories is that choices are made sequentially over time. This implies that the change process is prolonged and fails to instantaneously result in outcomes beneficial to society. Furthermore, although both benefits (effectiveness or goal achievement) and costs of chosen alternatives are evaluated, costs are assumed to be attended to first since in general they are immediately felt. Effectiveness is evaluated *over time* on the basis of negative feedback. If such evaluations indicate a discrepancy with the goal, more costly changes are chosen. Thus, we propose that a *sequential cost-minimizing principle* dictates the choices of change or adaptation alternatives. Even though it has been shown that people make optimal accuracy–cost tradeoffs in laboratory experiments, they may not in real life when making complex travel choices. Several facts speak to this. As has been noted (Gärling & Axhausen, 2003), habitual car use and related habitual and routine activities cause inertia. Research has also demonstrated that a bias exists such that the current state is overvalued (e.g. Samuelson & Zeckhausen, 1988), thus making changes less attractive. In particular if the car-use reduction goal is vague, evaluating whether or not a change is effective may possibly be biased toward confirming the expectation that it is (e.g. Einhorn & Hogarth, 1978; Klayman & Ha, 1987). Furthermore, previous research has demonstrated that immediate clear feedback is essential (e.g. Brehmer, 1995).

A nested hierarchy of change alternatives that vary from less to more costly is hypothesized to exist. In Table 2 this hypothesis is operationalized by specifying three different classes of potential change alternatives together with their associated costs. An ordering of them from less to more costly is based on the assumption that car users' belief that switching from using the car to another mode is more costly than suppressing activities. An additional assumption is that adding change alternatives to each other increases costs and effectiveness. Furthermore, each change alternatives may be performed to varying degrees (frequency over time), thereby also increasing both its costs and effectiveness. Summarizing, it is assumed that the less costly change alternatives are chosen before the more costly. Assuming a direct relationship between cost and effectiveness for these changes, more costly alternatives are expected to be chosen for larger reduction goals. By choosing more alternatives and increasing the frequency of each, effectiveness and costs are also increased. As a consequence, more changes are expected to be chosen at a higher frequency when the size of the reduction goal increases.

Table 2. Adaptations to TDM measures.

Adaptations	Costs
More efficient car use Trip chaining Car pooling Choosing closer destinations	Additional planning
More efficient car use Trip suppression	Additional planning Activity suppression
More efficient car use Trip suppression Mode switching	Additional planning Activity suppression Increased time pressure Inconveniences

As indicated in Table 2, the first stage involves making car use more efficient by chaining trips, car pooling, or choosing closer destinations. The cost is an increased need to plan ahead. The resulting change in car use may, however, not be sufficient to achieve a set car-use reduction goal.

In a second stage trips may also be suppressed in order to achieve larger car-use reduction. In addition to increased planning, trip suppression implies changes in activities. Although in extreme cases this may necessitate lifestyle changes, the required changes are generally likely to be minor, perhaps only involving the suppression of isolated shopping trips. Leisure activities are next most likely to be removed from the activity agenda or substituted by in-home activities. Least likely are more consequential changes in work hours.

The car-use reduction goal may still not be attained unless other modes are chosen. For instance, since work cannot easily be suppressed, public transport may be chosen for such trips. Additional planning, increased time pressure, and inconveniences are possible costs associated with switching to public transport.

In order to understand how TDM measures affect car use, the theoretical framework implies that four processes need to be examined. First, how does a particular TDM measure change the travel alternatives that households face, and since households are a heterogeneous group, how do these changes differ among households with different characteristics. Some empirical studies addressing these questions have been reported. For instance, Loukopoulos, Gärling, and Vilhelmson (2004b) showed that in Gothenburg, Sweden, prohibition of car use in the city center during the morning peak or in the middle of the day yielded the expected effects on different types of trips, larger effects the larger the area of prohibition. Yet, the effects were not substantial and they differed for different groups of residents varying in employment, income, age, and sex. If road pricing had been implemented, it may favor some and disfavor some (cf. Santos & Rojey, 2004).

Second, how does a TDM measure affect the size and type of car-use reduction goals set by households with different characteristics? Which of the properties listed in the previous section for describing TDM measures, if any, are related to the goal-setting process? One may speculate that coercive measures more directly would lead to that car-use reduction or change goals are set. However, the outcome is clearly dependent on the imposed time and area restrictions. At the same time, voluntary-change measures may lead to a higher commitment to car-use reduction goals. Road pricing is the measure most likely to induce goals unrelated to car use.

If a TDM measure does not lead to the setting of car-use reduction or change goals, we assume it cannot have the intended effect. If it does, it may however still not have the intended effect. This follows from the fallibility of the third process that needs to be examined: the formation and implementation of a plan to achieve the car-use reduction or change goal. It is documented that attitudes and intentions may have a weak correspondence with actual behavior (Fujii & Gärling, 2003; Gärling et al., 1998a). Several reasons for this have been identified. In this chapter some of them have been alluded to. Self-regulation theory (Carver & Scheier, 1998) highlights yet others.[5] In particular, it is assumed here that the principle of sequential cost-minimization is important for understanding how households attempt to attain set car-use reduction goals. If the cost is too high, the goal may be abandoned or changed. Evaluation of feedback about effectiveness (goal attainment) is another element. If it is delayed and vague, suboptimal adaptation alternatives may continue to be chosen.

Fourth, although outside the scope of this chapter, it should be noted that it is important to examine the system effects of the car-use reduction any TDM measure leads to. Short-term system effects include reduced congestion, less air pollution, and less noise that all may have effects on the travel alternatives such that the initial effects of the TDM measure are weakened or strengthened. For instance, reduced congestion may increase car use by some households due to improvement of

---

[5] It should be noted that the theories referred to in footnote 3 have little to say about the process of implementation attitudes or intentions.

travel alternatives. At some point in time equilibrium is attained. Assessing the effectiveness of TDM measures thus needs to both consider the process of change and the future equilibrium.

EMPIRICAL EVIDENCE

A first survey (Loukopoulos, Jakobsson, Gärling, Schneider, & Fujii, 2004d) was conducted to test implications of the proposed sequential cost-minimizing principle of choosing change alternatives. From the assumptions described above and given that participants believe or experience that a direct relationship exist between effectiveness and costs of the change alternatives, more changes and more costly changes are expected to be chosen more frequently when the size of the reduction or change goal increases. A caveat is that cost and effectiveness may vary for given adaptation alternatives depending on factors such as trip purpose and household characteristics (Gärling et al., 2000). Thus, the nested hierarchy of change alternatives shown in Table 2 may not be observed, although the number of chosen alternatives and their frequency are still expected to increase. IM, RP, and prohibition of car traffic in the city center (Pn) were compared in an internet-based survey of 291 (52.6% response rate) faculty and staff employed at Göteborg University. Only data for those with a driving license and access to a car were included, thus reducing sample size to 199. The respondents were presented with the descriptions of the TDM measures given in Appendix A. They indicated both how much they would reduce car use (size of car-use reduction goal), and what changes (adaptations) they would choose if any of the TDM measures were implemented in their place of living (Gothenburg, Sweden, pop. 475,000). Nine alternatives were provided which were grouped in *efficient car use* (conducting more errands per trip, car-pooling with others, choosing closer destinations, changing the departure time), *trip suppression* (conducting fewer shopping trips, work more from home, perform fewer out-of-home leisure activities), and *switching mode* (from car to public transport, choosing other destinations not requiring car use).

The first survey was followed up with another in which explicit car-use reduction goals were induced (Loukopoulos, Jakobsson, Gärling, Meland, & Fujii, 2004c). Thus, it was assumed that only the size of the car-use reduction goal would determine choice of adaptation alternative, not the particular TDM measure that was implemented. In other respects the second survey was essentially identical to the first survey. Another sample of employees at Göteborg university participated. After discarding outlying respondents and respondents with missing values, 171 (32.0% response rate) remained.

Analyses were also made of unpublished data obtained from a travel survey conducted in 1992 after the implementation of a toll ring in Trondheim, Norway (pop. 138,000) (Loukopoulos et al., 2004c; Meland, 1994). A population-based sample of car owners (68.6% response rate) answered questions about how much they had changed car use (size of change goal) and what changes they had made. Although only retrospective reports were obtained, in contrast to the preceding surveys the reported changes were actual rather that intended.

The results of all three surveys partially supported the sequential cost-minimizing principle. In the first survey, on average respondents indicated for all three TDM measures that they would change their car use very little. Still, the more coercive TDM measures (RP and Pn) made respondents set larger car-use reduction goals than did the less coercive measure (IM). Furthermore, a stronger relation with the size of the car-use reduction goal was as expected obtained for the more costly adaptation alternatives *mode switching* than the less costly adaptation alternatives *activity/trip suppression* which in turn was more closely related to the size of the goal than the least costly adaptation alternatives *more efficient car use*. However, when data were analyzed for specific adaptation alternatives, differences were observed both between TDM measures and trip purposes (work, shopping, leisure). As noted, a possible explanation is that the same adaptation alternative varies in costliness (and effectiveness) depending on these factors. An obvious example is that choice of closer destinations are not always feasible (e.g. for work trips). Choice of public transport may also differ in costs depending on trip purpose (being, for instance, less costly for work trips than for shopping or leisure trips). As another example, some changes in response to road pricing (for instance, change of departure time) that steer clear of paying the fee may be less costly.

The small changes in car use observed in the first survey made it difficult to examine the choice of adaptation alternatives. In the second survey respondents were therefore asked to imagine that they would be forced to reduce car use to different extents (5, 25, and 50% in counterbalanced order). In each case they stated how frequently they would choose different specified adaptation alternatives for work, shopping, and leisure trips. Given that the first study showed that the adaptation alternatives that were grouped together tended to differ in frequency across trip purpose, no a priori grouping of them was made. Instead, as shown in Table 3,

Table 3. Changes in stated frequency of adaptation alternatives related to size of car-use reduction goal for different trip purposes.

Work trips	Shopping trips	Leisure trips
Low frequency/low slope		
Closer destinations	Car poolingActivity/trip	Activity/trip suppression
Car pooling	suppression (shop from home,	(leisure at home, use IT)
Activity/trip suppression	use IT)	
(reducing frequency)		
Mode switching (walking)		
Low frequency/high slope		
		Closer destinations
		Activity/trip suppression
		(reducing frequency)
High frequency/low slope		
Mode switching (cycling)	Mode switching (cycling)	Mode switching (walking)
High frequency/high slope		
Trip chaining	Closer destinations	Car pooling
Activity/trip suppression	Trip chaining	Trip chaining
(work at home, use IT)	Activity/trip suppression	Mode switching
Mode switching	(reducing frequency)	(cycling)
(public transport)	Mode switching (walking)	Mode switching
	Mode switching	(public transport)
	(public transport)	

a grouping of the different adaptation alternatives were based on the average frequency (low vs. high) and slope (low vs. high) of the linear increase with the car-use reduction goal. It should first be noted that the results supported the hypothesis in that the frequency of all change alternatives showed linear increases.[6] Thus, as a consequence, the expected increase in average frequency was confirmed.

An implication of the assumed differences in costs for different adaptation alternatives (see Table 2) is that one should expect to find the less costly in the category high frequency and low slope, the most costly in the category low frequency and high slope. Such a pattern is, however, not evident in Table 3. Furthermore, it is also clear that there were differences due to trip purpose. In future research it would be advisable to measure the costs and effectiveness of specific change alternatives to establish how they differ in these respects.

A summary of the results of the Trondheim travel survey is given in Table 4. One striking feature is that a large majority of respondents did not change their travel as a result of the implementation of the toll ring. The percentage of respondents indicating that they had made no change and that they had adopted a particular adaptation alternative was accordingly very small for all trip purposes. As expected, this number increased from no to small change for all adaptation alternatives and trip purposes. Furthermore, for shopping trips there were also increases from small to large change. On the other hand, for work trips some changes decreased in frequency from small to large change. All adaptation alternatives were significantly related to both small and large change with the single exception of "more trips with others" for shopping trips. However, there were only a few significant differences between small and large change: for work trips "fewer trips" was significantly less frequently chosen for large than for small change; for shopping trips "change in timing" was significantly more frequently chosen for a large than for a small change. For shopping trips, the increase in the number of chosen change alternatives was significant.

In line with the assumed differences in costs and effectiveness, for shopping trips the most frequently chosen adaptation alternatives were associated with more efficient car use (change in timing, change of destination), the next most frequently with trip suppression (fewer trips), and less frequently with mode switching. However, conducting more trips with others (car pooling) was less frequently chosen. Change of route was more frequently chosen. The existence of a toll ring might have motivated some to drive around it.

Work trips differed, however, in that the frequency of some adaptation alternatives decreased, most clearly "fewer trips" and "more trips with others." This resulted in no increase of the number of chosen change alternatives with the size of the change. Conducting "more trips with others" for work trips may be costly in terms of planning and coordination, and conducting "fewer trips" may also be costly if it implies a change in work hours or scheduling. Additionally, a change in mode may be relatively less costly for work trips (presumably because most public transport is geared to supporting the work commute). Such changes naturally reduce the need for or even prevent some other adaptations. Thus, substitutions of change alternatives are also a possibility that should be taken into account.

---

[6] However, it appears illogical that choices of closer destinations or trip chaining are increased for work trips.

Table 4. Frequency of choices of adaptation alternatives in response to the implementation of a toll ring in Trondheim related to self-reported size of change for work and shopping trips.

Work trips (n = 2155)		Shopping trips (n = 2299)	
Small change (11.5%)	Large change (5.5%)	Small change (29.2%)	Large change (10.3%)
Change of mode (35.2%)[a]	Change of mode (43.6%)[a]	Change in timing (50.1%)[a]	Change in timing (66.9%)[a,b]
Change of route (20.6%)[a]	Change of route (18.8%)[a]	Change of destination (30.3%)[a]	Change of destination (36.4%)[a]
More trips with others (16.6%)[a]	Change in timing (13.9%)[a]	Fewer trips (26.9%)[a]	Fewer trips (30.1%)[a]
Change in timing (13.8%)[a]	More trips with others (6.9%)[a]	Change of route (11.9%)[a]	Change of route (19.9%)[a]
Fewer trips (11.7%)[a]	Fewer trips (2.0%)[a,b]	Change of mode (4.5%)[a]	Change of mode (8.5%)[a]
Change of destination (1.6%)[a]	Change of destination (2.0%)[a]	More trips with others (2.4%)	More trips with others (1.7%)
M = 1.0; Range: 0–3	M = 0.9; Range: 0–3	M = 1.3[a]; Range: 0–4	M = 1.6[a,b]; Range: 0–4

[a]Statistically significant increase from no change; [b]Statistically significant increase from small to large change.

It is concluded that for both intended changes and actual changes the results showed that the number of chosen adaptation alternatives as well as their frequency increased with the size of the car-use reduction or change goal. However, these changes varied with adaptation alternative, trip purpose, and TDM measure. Although not reported here, household characteristics such as income, age of household members, current car use, and residential location may also affect the choice of adaptation alternatives. Thus, consistent with the proposed theoretical framework, changes in response to TDM measure are multi-faceted and cannot simply be collapsed into a single unidimensional effect measure. Assuming that the choices are guided by cost and effectiveness may still provide a more parsimonious description.

SUMMARY AND CONCLUSIONS

This chapter focused on measures for TDM targeting private car use in urban areas. After discussion and classification of TDM measures, a theoretical framework was presented that may be used to analyze the effects of these measures. In this theoretical framework, it is hypothesized that car users respond by setting car-use reduction or change goals. Setting larger goals is more likely in response to coercive command-and-control measures such as prohibition of car use (Pn). The same may to some extent apply to market-based TDM measures such as RP that fall in between coercive and non-coercive voluntary-change measures depending on households' wealth. Non-coercive TDM measures such as IM may, however, strengthen commitment to the goal, thus may to some degree compensate for that smaller goals are set.

It was further proposed that goal attainment entails choices of available change alternatives following a sequential cost-minimizing principle. In addition it was speculated what the costs are. The principle implies a sequential satisficing choice process that may not necessarily achieve an optimal cost–benefit tradeoff. Whether it does or not may depend on effective change options being made less costly and on immediate clear feedback about goal attainment. Coercive TDM measures (and for some households road pricing) do not empower car users to attain their car-use reduction or change goals. Other TDM measures targeting changed latent demand are presumably needed for this.

Any implementation of TDM measures would benefit from forecasts of their likely effects. With the proposed theoretical framework as a basis, mathematical–statistical models of the goal-setting and adaptation process need to be developed. Such developments may draw on previous research developing the Activity–Mobility Simulator or AMOS (Kitamura & Fujii, 1998; Pendyala et al., 1997, 1998). AMOS reproduces how travelers modify their activity/travel choices in response to specified TDM measures. It uses as input an observed daily activity/travel pattern to sequentially generate adaptation options, then computes and evaluates each new activity/travel pattern.

ACKNOWLEDGEMENTS

Financial support has been obtained through grant #2002-00434 from the Swedish Agency for Innovation Systems, and grant #25.9/2001-1763 from the Swedish Research Council for Environment, Agricultural Sciences, and Spatial Planning.

Among many colleagues and students who have made valuable contributions, I would in particular like to mention Satoshi Fujii, Cecilia Jakobsson, and Peter Loukopoulos.

REFERENCES

Ajzen, I. (1991). The theory of planned behavior. *Organizational Behavior and Human Decision Processes, 50*, 179–211.

Arentze, T., & Timmermans, H.P.J. (2000). *ALBATROSS: a learning based transportation oriented simulation system.* Eindhoven, The Netherlands: Technical University of Eindhoven, European Institute of Retailing and Services Studies.

Arentze, T., & Timmermans, H.P.J. (2003). Modeling learning and adaptation processes in activity–travel choice. *Transportation, 30*, 37–62.

Arentze, T., Hofman, F., & Timmermans, H.P.J. (2004). Predicting multi-faceted activity–travel adjustment strategies in response to possible pricing scenarios using an Internet-based stated adaptation experiment. *Transport Policy, 11*, 31–41.

Austin, J.T., & Vancouver, J.B. (1996). Goal constructs in psychology: structure, process, and content. *Psychological Bulletin, 80*, 286–303.

Axhausen, K., & Gärling, T. (1992). Activity-based approaches to travel analysis: conceptual frameworks, models, and research problems. *Transport Reviews, 12*, 323–341.

Ben-Akiva, M., & Lerman, S.R. (1985). *Discrete choice analysis.* Cambridge, MA: MIT Press.

Bhat, C.R., & Koppelman, F.S. (1999). A retrospective and prospective survey of time-use research. *Transportation, 26*, 119–139.

Brehmer, B. (1995). Feedback delays in complex dynamic decision making. In Frensch, P.A., & Funke, J. (Eds.), *Complex Decision Making: The European Perspective* (pp. 103–130). Hillsdale, NJ: Erlbaum.

Cao, X., & Mokhtarian, P.L. (2004a). How do individuals adapt their personal travel? A conceptualk exploration of the consideration of travel-related strategies. *Transport Policy*, in press.

Cao, X., & Mokhtarian, P.L. (2004b). How do individuals adapt their personal travel? Objective and subjective influences on the consideration of travel-related strategies. *Transport Policy*, in press.

Cambridgeshire County Council. (2003a). *Roads and Transport—Cars in Cambridge*, http://www.cambridgeshire.gov.uk/sub/eandt/highways/cambridge/cb_car.htm, Retrieved 10 March, 2003.

Cambridgeshire County Council. (2003b). *Roads and Transport—Cambridge City Centre Deliveries*, http://www.cambridgeshire.gov.uk/sub/eandt/highways/cambridge/cb_del.htm, Retrieved 10 March, 2003.

Carver, C.S., & Scheier, M.F. (1998). *On the Self-Regulation of Behavior.* Cambridge: Cambridge University Press.

Doherty, S.T., & Miller, E. (2000). A computerized household activity scheduling survey. *Transportation, 27*, 75–97.

Ettema, D., & Timmermans, H.P.J. (1997). Theories and models of activity patterns. In Ettema, D., & Timmermans, H.J.P. (Eds.), *Activity-Based Approaches to Travel Analysis* (pp. 1–36). Oxford: Pergamon.

Everett, P.B., & Watson, B.G. (1987). Psychological contributions to transportation. In Stokols, D., & Altman, I. (Eds.), *Handbook of Environmental Psychology* (Vol. 2, pp. 987–1008). New York: Wiley.

Einhorn, H.J., & Hogarth, R.M. (1978). Confidence in judgment: persistence of the illusion of validity. *Psychological Review, 85*, 396–416.

Fishbein, M., & Ajzen, I. (1975). *Belief, Attitude, Intention, and Behavior: an introduction to Theory and Research*. Reading, MA: Addison-Wesley.

Foo, T.S. (1997). An effective demand management instrument in urban transport: the Area Licensing Scheme in Singapore. *Cities, 14*, 155–164.

Foo, T.S. (1998). A unique demand management instrument in urban transport: the Vehicle Quota System in Singapore. *Cities, 15*, 27–39.

Foo, T.S. (2000). An advanced demand management instrument in urban transport. *Cities, 17*, 33–45.

Fujii, S., & Gärling, T. (2003). Application of attitude theory for improved predictive accuracy of stated preference methods in travel demand analysis. *Transportation Research A, 37*, 389–402.

Gärling, T. (2004). The feasible infeasibility of activity scheduling. In Schreckenberg, M., & Selten, R. (Eds.), *Human Behaviour in Traffic Networks* (pp. 231–250). Berlin: Springer.

Gärling, T., & Axhausen, K. (2003). Habitual travel choice (introduction to special issue). *Transportation, 30*, 1–11.

Gärling, T., & Fujii, S. (2002). Structural equation modeling of determinants of implementation intentions. *Scandinavian Journal of Psychology, 43*, 1–8.

Gärling, T., Laitila, T., & Westin, K. (Eds.) (1998b). *Theoretical Foundations of Travel Choice Modeling*. Amsterdam: Elsevier.

Gärling, T., Brännäs, K., Garvill, J., Golledge, R.G., Gopal, S., Holm, E., & Lindberg, E. (1989). Household activity scheduling. In *Transport Policy, Management and Technology Towards 2001* (Vol. IV, pp. 235–248). Ventura, CA: Western Periodicals.

Gärling, T., Gillholm, R., & Gärling, A. (1998a). Reintroducing attitude theory in travel behavior research: the validity of an interactive interview procedure to predict car use. *Transportation, 25*, 147–167.

Gärling, T., & Garvill, J. (1993). Psychological explanations of participation in everyday activities. In Gärling, T., & Golledge, R.G. (Eds.), *Behavior and Environment: Psychological and Geographical Approaches* (pp. 270–297). Amsterdam: Elsevier/ North-Holland.

Gärling, T., Kwan, M.-P., & Golledge, R.G. (1994). Computational-process modeling of household activity scheduling. *Transportation Research B, 25*, 355–364.

Gärling, T., Eek, D., Loukopoulos, P., Fujii, S., Johansson-Stenman, O., Kitamura, R., Pendyala, R., & Vilhelmson, B. (2002a). A conceptual analysis of the impact of travel demand management on private car use. *Transport Policy, 9*, 59–70.

Gärling, T., Gärling, A., & Johansson, A. (2000). Household choices of car-use reduction measures. *Transportation Research A, 34*, 309–320.

Gärling, T., Gärling, A., & Loukopoulos, P. (2002b). Forecasting psychological consequences of car-use reduction: a challenge to an environmental psychology of transportation. *Applied Psychology: An International Review, 51*, 90–106.

Gärling, T., Fujii, S., & Boe, O. (2001). Empirical tests of a model of determinants of script-based driving choice. *Transportation Research F, 4*, 89–102.

Gatersleben, B. (2003). On yer bike for a healthy commute. In Hendrickx, L., Jager, W., & Steg, L. (Eds.), *Human Decision Making and Environmental Perception: Understanding and Assisting Human Decision Making in Real-Life Settings* (pp. 161–182). Groningen, The Netherlands: University of Groningen.

Gigerenzer, G., Todd, P.M., & The ABC Research Group (Eds.) (1999). *Simple Heuristics That Make Us Smart*. Oxford: Oxford University Press.

Goh, M. (2002). Congestion management and electronic road pricing in Singapore. *Journal of Transport Geography, 10,* 29–38.

Gollwitzer, P.M. (1993). Goal achievement: the role of intentions. *European Review of Social Psychology, 4,* 141–185.

Golob, T.F. (1989). The causal influences of income and car ownership on trip generation by mode. *Journal of Transport Economics and Policy, 23,* 141–162.

Goodwin, P.B. (1996). Simple arithmetic. *Transport Policy, 3,* 79–80.

Goodwin, P. (1998). The end of equilibrium. In Gärling, T., Laitila, T., & Westin, K. (Eds.), *Theoretical Foundations of Travel Choice Modeling* (pp. 103–132). Amsterdam: Elsevier.

Greene, D.L., & Wegener, M. (1997). Sustainable transport. *Journal of Transport Geography, 5,* 177–190.

Hayes-Roth, B., & Hayes-Roth, F. (1979). A cognitive model of planning. *Cognitive Science, 3,* 275–310.

Hensher, D.A. (1998). The imbalance between car and public transport use in urban Australia: why does it exist? *Transport Policy, 5,* 193–204.

Jakobsson, C. (2004). Accuracy of household planning of car use: comparing prospective to actual car logs. *Transportation Research F, 7,* 31–42.

Jones, P. (2003). Acceptability of transport pricing strategies: meeting the challenge. In Schade, J., & Schlag, B. (Eds.), *Acceptability of Transport Pricing Strategies* (pp. 27–62). Oxford: Elsevier.

Jones, P., Dix, M.C., Clarke, M.I., & Heggie, I.G. (1983). *Understanding Travel Behavior.* Aldershot, UK: Gower.

Kitamura, R. (1988). An evaluation of activity-based travel analysis. *Transportation, 15,* 9–34.

Kitamura, R., & Fujii, S. (1998). Two computational process models of activity–travel choice. In Gärling, T., Laitila, T., & Westin, K. (Eds.), *Theoretical Foundations of Travel Choice Modeling* (pp. 251–279). Amsterdam: Elsevier.

Kitamura, R., Fujii, S., & Pas, E.I. (1997). Time-use data, analysis and modeling: toward the next generation of transportation planning methodologies. *Transport Policy, 4,* 225–235.

Klayman, J., & Ha, Y.-W. (1987). Confirmation, disconfirmation, and information in hypothesis testing. *Psychological Review, 94,* 211–228.

Kristensen, J.P., & Marshall, S. (1999). Mobility management to reduce travel: the case of Aalborg. *Built Environment, 25,* 138–150.

Lee, T.W., Locke, E.A., & Latham, G.P. (1989). Goal setting theory and performance. In Pervin, L.A. (Ed.), *Goal Concepts in Personality and Social Psychology* (pp. 291–326). Hillsdale, NJ: Lawrence.

Litman, T. (2003). The online TDM encyclopedia: mobility management information gateway. *Transport Policy, 10,* 245–249.

Locke, E.A., & Latham, G.P. (1984). *Goal Setting: A Motivational Technique That Works.* Englewood Cliffs, NJ: Prentice-Hall.

Locke, E.A., & Latham, G.P. (1990). *A Theory of Goal-Setting and Task Performance.* Englewood Cliffs, NJ: Prentice-Hall.

Loukopoulos, P., Gärling, T., Jakobsson, C., & Fujii, S. (2004a). A cost-minimization principle of adaptation of private car use in response to road pricing schemes. In Jensen-Butler, C., Larsen, M., Madsen, B., Nielsen, O.A., & Sloth, B. (Eds.), *Road Pricing, the Economy, and the Environment.* Oxford: Elsevier, in press.

Loukopoulos, P., Gärling, T., & Vilhelmson, B. (2004b). Mapping the potential consequences of car-use reduction in urban areas. *Journal of Transport Geography*, in press.

Loukopoulos, P., Jakobsson, C., Gärling, T., Meland, S., & Fujii, S. (2004c). Cost and effectiveness of adaptation to car-use reduction goals. Manuscript submitted for publication.

Loukopoulos, P., Jakobsson, C., Gärling, T., Schneider, C.M., & Fujii, S. (2004d). Car user responses to travel demand management measures: goal setting and choice of adaptation alternatives. *Transportation Research D*, *9*, 263–280.

Loukopoulos, P., Jakobsson, C., Gärling, T., Schneider, C.M., & Fujii, S. (2004e). Public attitudes towards policy measures for reducing private car use. *Environmental Science and Policy*, *8*, 57–66.

Louw, E., Maat, K., Mathers, S. (1998). *Strategies and Measures to Reduce Travel by Car in European Cities*. Paper Presented at the Eighth World Conference on Transport Research, Antwerp, Belgium, July.

Mahmassani, H.S., & Jou, R.-C. (2000). Transferring insights into commuter behavior dynamics from laboratory experiments to field surveys. *Transportation Research A*, *34*, 243–260.

May, A.D., Jopson, A.F., & Matthews, B. (2003). Research challenges in urban transport policy. *Transport Policy*, *10*, 157–164.

McFadden, D. (2001). Disaggregate behavioral travel demand's RUM side—a 30 years retrospective. In Hensher, D.A. (Ed.), *Travel Behavior Research* (pp. 17–63). Amsterdam: Elsevier.

Meland, S. (1994). *Road pricing in urban areas: the Trondheim toll ring—results from panel travel surveys*. [Report STF63 S94006], Trondheim, Norway: SINTEF.

Newell, A., & Simon, H.A. (1972). *Human Problem Solving*. Englewood Cliffs, NJ: Prentice-Hall.

Pas, E.I. (1995). The urban transportation planning process. In Hanson, S. (Ed.), *The Geography of Urban Transportation* (pp. 53–77). Amsterdam: Elsevier.

Payne, J.W., Bettman, J.R., & Johnson, E.J. (1993). *The Adaptive Decision Maker*. New York: Cambridge University Press.

Pendyala, R.M., Kitamura, R., Chen, C., & Pas, E.I. (1997). An activity-based micro-simulation analysis of transportation control measures. *Transport Policy*, *4*, 183–192.

Pendyala, R.M., Kitamura, R., & Reddy, D.V.G.P. (1998). Application of an activity-based travel demand model incorporating a rule-based algorithm. *Environment and Planning B*, *25*, 753–772.

Recker, W.W., McNally, M.G., & Roth, G.S. (1986). A model of complex travel behavior: theoretical development. *Transportation Research A*, *20*, 307–318.

Santos, G., & Rojey, L. (2004). Distributional impacts of road pricing: the truth behind the myth. *Transportation*, *31*, 21–42.

Samuelson, W., & Zeckhausen, R. (1988). Status quo bias in decision making. *Journal of Risk and Uncertainty*, *1*, 7–59.

Schwartz, S.H. (1977). Normative influences on altruism. In Berkowitz, L. (Ed.), *Advances in Experimental Social Psychology* (Vol. 10, pp. 221–279). New York: Academic Press.

Simon, H.A. (1990). Invariants of human behavior. *Annual Review of Psychology*, *41*, 1–19.

Steg, L., & Vlek, C. (1997). The role of problem awareness in willingness-to-change car use and in evaluating relevant policy measures. In Rothengatter, T., & Carbonell Vaya, W. (Eds.), *Traffic and Transport Psychology. Theory and Application* (pp. 465–475). Amsterdam: Pergamon.

Steg, L., Geurs, K., & Ras, M. (2002). The effects of motivational factors on car use: a multidisciplinary modeling approach. *Transportation Research A, 35,* 789–806.

Stern, P.C., Dietz, T., & Black, J.S. (1986). Support for environmental protection: the role of social norms. *Population and Environment, 8,* 204–222.

Stradling, S.G., Meadows, M.L., & Beatty, S. (2000). Helping drivers out of their cars. Integrating transport policy and social psychology for sustainable change. *Transport Policy, 7,* 207–215.

Thorpe, N., Hills, P., & Jaensirisak, S. (2000). Public attitudes to TDM measures: a comparative study. *Transport Policy, 7,* 243–257.

Timmermans, H.J.P., & Golledge, R.G. (1990). Applications of behavioral research on spatial problems II: preference and choice. *Progress in Human Geography, 14,* 311–354.

Timmermans, H.J.P., van der Waerden, P., Alves, M., Polak, J., Ellis, S., Harvey, A.S., Kurose, S., & Zandee, R. (2003). Spatial context and the complexity of daily travel patterns: an international comparison. *Journal of Transport Geography, 11,* 37–46.

Verplanker, B., Aarts, H., & van Knippenberg, A. (1997). Habit, information acquisition and the process of making travel mode choices. *European Journal of Social Psychology, 27,* 539–560.

Vilhelmson, B. (1999). Daily mobility and the use of time for different activities: the case of Sweden. *GeoJournal, 48,* 177–185.

Vlek, C., & Michon, J. (1992). Why we should and how we could decrease the use of motor vehicles in the future. *IATSS Research, 15,* 82–93.

APPENDIX A

TDM measure	Description
Prohibiting car traffic in city center (Cambridge, UK) (Cambridgeshire County Council, 2003a,b).	The city of Cambridge is a lively trafficked historic city in England. Its streets date from the Middle Ages and are not designed for today's traffic flows. Instead of expanding the road network, Cambridgeshire County has chosen another solution. The Council has decided to impose considerable restrictions on private car traffic in the central parts of the city. The policy package is comprised of two parts. Firstly, the area inside the ring road, which is called the Inner Ring Area, has been divided into eight sub-areas. These eight sub-areas have only one entry and exit point to and from the inner ring road. Secondly, pedestrian zones have been created in the liveliest business areas and in residential areas. Parking is not permitted in the pedestrian zones 24 h a day, 7 days a week. Car traffic is not permitted between the hours of 10 a.m. and 4 p.m., Monday to Saturday, except for those vehicles that have a special permit. Time-activated traffic barriers have been designed so as to sink into the ground for cars or busses with a special permit in the form of an electronic id-card. This applies, for example, to taxis.
Road Pricing (Singapore) (Foo, 1997, 1998, 2000; Goh, 2002).	In Singapore, a city-state with about 3.5 million inhabitants, various forms of road pricing in the city center have been implemented by the government over the past 30 years. The latest system in Singapore is called Electronic Road Pricing (ERP). This means that one has to pay to be able to drive his or her car within a zone referred to as the "Restricted Zone", which is about 7 km^2 in size and has about 30 entry points. All entry points are clearly marked with portals over the road and when the ERP system is in operation, the words "In Operation" flash on screens situated on the portals. ERP works with the assistance of these portals, an in-vehicle unit which is in every type of vehicle and a smart card system. There are antennae, cameras, and optical detectors situated on the portals. When a vehicle approaches the portal, the ERP system communicates with the in-vehicle unit, identifies what type of vehicle it is (i.e. car, taxi, truck, motorcycle etc.), deducts the appropriate fee from the card which is loaded with money and, if a transgression is detected

(continued)

Continued.

TDM measure	Description
	(e.g. no in-vehicle unit or insufficient funds on the card etc.) the vehicle and license plate is photographed. The prices vary depending on vehicle type and time of entry into the "Restricted Zone". For example, the average price for a private car is SGD 1.00. The price levels are reviewed every 3 months. If the congestions levels are too high then the prices are raised, if the roads are not being sufficiently utilized then the prices are lowered.
Individualized marketing (Perth, Australia) (Department of Transport Western Australia, 1999, 2001).	The city of Perth, Western Australia has a population of approximately 1 million. In an attempt to reduce traffic by 10%, a program known as "TravelSmart" has been introduced. In the suburb South Perth (population 37,000), a part of the TravelSmart program known as Individualized marketing has been introduced. Individual households are contacted. Information is gathered about the type of car users living in the household and if they are interested in using alternatives to the car. The decision to participate in the program is left to the household. Those households that are interested in beginning to use alternative modes of transport to the car are provided with information about the various modes in the Perth area (cycle, busses, walking, etc.). They are offered personal advice about their trips. This information consists of personalized timetables, which can be sent by post, received over the phone or by a home visit from a consultant who analyzes the household's trips and provides suggestions for alternatives to the car. It has been found that an important reason as to why people do not refrain from using the car more often is that they believe that the same trip with another transport mode (walking, cycling, public transport) would take twice as long and cost one third more than is actually the case. About half of the households with easily implemented alternatives are unaware of the individualized marketing service. The TravelSmart Program contributes with correct information. It is then up to the household to decide whether or not they wish to continue using the car.

Traffic and Transport Psychology
G. Underwood (Editor)
© 2005 Elsevier Ltd. All rights reserved.

46

CHILDHOOD INFLUENCES ON ADULT TRAVEL MODE CHOICE

Maria Johansson[1]

INTRODUCTION

Children's freedom to travel alone has significantly decreased and a large amount of European children are today chauffeured by car to school and leisure activities (Hillman, 1993; Sissons Joshi & MacLean, 1995; Björklid, 2001; Gatersleben, Leach & Uzzell, 2001; Balzani & Borgogni, 2003). The increased car usage for children's trips affects the local and global environment negatively. Many benefits would be achieved for the children's physical health and psychological well being if children independently could walk and cycle (Johansson, 2004a). It seems very likely that the levels of car use for children's trips will continue to increase in the future. Children who from early age are chauffeured by car will get little experience of other travel modes and may, therefore, not achieve the skills necessary to walk and cycle in adulthood. This might have adverse impacts on future policies aimed at reducing car use (Mackett, 2002).

Parents have a crucial role in the decision of travel mode choice. In a study of 357 Swedish children aged 8–11 years, the parents had decided upon travel mode for 73% of the children's trips (Johansson, 2004b). Research in the related fields of driving behaviour show that the parents' attitudes and behaviour may transfer to young drivers, partly through modelling of parental life style and driving style (for overviews see Bianchi & Summula, 2004; Rämet & Summula, 2004). So far the parental influence on adult travel mode choice has however largely been ignored. This chapter discusses the impact of parental attitudes and mode choice in childhood on adult choice of travel mode.

Previous research

Swedish children and adolescents seem to have a rather positive view of the private car (Bernow, 1991; Johansson, 2000). In Johansson's study, most children and adolescents were

[1] Department of Environmental Psychology, Lund Institute of Technology, Sweden. *E-mail:* Maria.Johansson@ mpe.lth.se (M. Johansson).

highly concerned about the environment and perceived urban traffic as hazardous for environment and human health. Still, they expressed a high level of affection for the car and approximately 85% wanted their own car when they grew up. Moreover, the children and adolescents who expressed a high level of affection for the private car were more likely to have parents who thought the car was a pleasant and convenient travel mode. Sandqvist and Kriström, (2001) identified, however, widely divergent views of the car among adolescents in Stockholm depending on whether their families had access to a car or not. The adolescents in general expressed lower affection for the car than did their parents. Still, the adolescents' level of affection was partly predicted by their parents' attitude. The relationship was, however, not significant for more instrumental views of the car such as the environmental impact of private cars (Sandqvist, 2004). Contradictory to these results Andréasson and Sjöberg, (1996) in interviews with 32, 17–18 year-olds, found that they held a very critical view of their parents' unreflected car usage, although most of the young adults themselves frequently had been chauffeured by car to leisure activities during their childhood. Studies of adults point to a relation between childhood travel and present travel patterns. In an analysis of parents' reasons for accompanying their children to school in the UK Sissons Joshi, MacLean and Carter (1997) found that parents who had themselves first travelled independently to school at a later age were more likely to accompany their own children to school.

Problem and theoretical considerations

This chapter is based on two separate investigations with the common purpose to analyse the impact of childhood travel experiences on the attitudes and travel mode choice in adulthood. The parental influence may be based on genetic as well as environmental factors. The two studies consider environmental aspects only and therefore the genetic relation between parent and child has not been asked for. It is recognised that the parents' attitudes towards and choice of travel mode may be transferred to the children via paths defined in social-learning theory (Bandura, 1977, 1986). The theory has been successfully applied for the explanation of young people's social behaviour and more recently drug abuse and health behaviour (Smith, Cowie & Blades, 1998). Social-learning theory states that people develop certain behaviour patterns in response to environmental contingencies. Some behaviour may be rewarded while others may produce unfavourable results. Through the process of differential reinforcement people select the more successful behaviour patterns. A child who expresses a strong desire to walk and cycle independently, but is constantly told by the parent that it is safer to travel by car and consequently chauffeured may in response change opinion. Further, the role of models in transmitting both specific behaviours and emotional responses is emphasised. By observing others, e.g. parents, one forms an idea of how new behaviours are performed, and at later occasions this information serves as a guide for action. Social-learning theory also stresses the importance of vicarious learning, e.g. learning by watching the behaviours of others and observing the consequences it produces for them. The main questions put forward in the present research were:

(a) Do parents differ in their approach to various travel modes because of different travel experiences in their own childhood? It was hypothesised that parents who were chauffeured in their childhood today would express a more positive attitude towards motorised transports and that they would to a larger extent let their own children travel by car. Parents who were never chauffeured were expected to hold a more positive attitude towards their children walking and cycling independently. Their children were further expected to travel independently to a higher degree.

(b) Are young adults' present attitudes and travel mode choice influenced by their childhood travel experiences? The hypotheses were that young adults who were frequently chauffeured in childhood and whose parents used to have a positive attitude towards motorised transports would be more favourable towards the car and to a higher degree travel by car. Young adults who travelled independently and whose parents held a positive attitude towards independent travel would presently express a more positive attitude towards walking and cycling as well as more frequently travel by these travel modes.

The debate on children's travel has largely focused on children's journey to school, but also other trips are increasingly made by car (Mackett, 2002). In a survey, in the city of Lund, Sweden, 84% of children were chauffeured to their leisure activities (Trivector Information, 1999). This study therefore particularly focus on leisure travel, e.g. mode choice to and from friends and organised leisure activities.

STUDY I: METHOD

The first study was carried out as a questionnaire survey including 357 Swedish parents (corresponding to a response rate of 67%) of children aged 8–11 years (50% girls, 50% boys, mean age $= 9{:}6$ years). The questionnaire was directed to the parent with the main responsibility for the child's travel. It was predominantly answered by the mother (78%). A majority (71%) of the households used one car, 15% regularly used two or more cars, whereas 14% did not own a car. Car-less families are somewhat over-represented as compared to the national level (3% among families with children aged 7–18 years) (Statistics Sweden, 1999). The deviation from the national figure is likely to depend on the urban sample.

Based on focus group discussions with parents a questionnaire was developed to collect data on parents' travel mode choice for children's leisure trips (Johansson, 2004b). The items analysed for the present purpose were: one question about how frequently the parents themselves were given a lift to leisure activities in their childhood, answered by a 4-point Likert scale (almost never—almost always). Nine scales where different travel modes were to be rated at 7-graded scales according how desirable or undesirable they were perceived for children's trips within the urban environments where the families lived. In addition, data collected by a 1-week travel diary of the children's trips have been analysed. This data covered the aim of the trip, the company, and choice of travel mode. Furthermore items concerning the child's and the parents' demographics were included.

Data was collected in four public schools in the cities of Lund (100,000 inhabitants) and Malmö (250,000) inhabitants, south of Sweden. The questionnaire, the travel diary and a free-post envelope were sent to the parents via their children. The parents were sent two reminders and 70% of them were randomly called to make sure they had received the questionnaire. In order to further increase the response rate, returned questionnaire were part of a prize draw of approximately £20 per school.

Data has been treated by frequency analysis, analysis of reliability, factor analysis and analysis of variance (ANCOVA) in SPSS version 11. Due to the large sample the general level of significance was set to $p = 0.01$.

RESULTS OF STUDY I

The parents' attitudes towards travel modes for children's trips

A factor analysis of the nine scales measuring attitudes towards various travel modes resulted in three dimensions explaining 66% of the total variance. The first factor expressed the parent's attitude towards motorised transports including the child being chauffeured in the family car, as part of a carpool, and travelling by bus together with an adult. The second factor described the attitude towards independent travel (e.g. the child independently take a bus, walk and cycle alone, walk with a friend/sibling). The third factor included the attitude towards walking and cycling with adult company. One index was created for each factor, which could vary between 1 (undesirable) and 7 (desirable). Motorised transport ($M = 5.44$, Mdn $= 6$, SD $= 1.65$, Cronbach's alpha $= 0.77$), independent travel ($M = 3.54$, Mdn $= 3.25$, SD $= 1.49$, Cronbach's alpha $= 0.70$), and adult company ($M = 5.89$, Mdn $= 6$, SD $= 1.20$, Cronbach's alpha $= 0.57$).

The children's leisure time trips

In the travel diaries (which were completed by a somewhat smaller sample $N = 325$), 83% of the parents reported their children had made trips to leisure activities during that particular week. Based on the factor analysis above again three variables were created, but this time relating to actual travel mode choice. *Independent trips*: trips made alone or with friends by walking, cycling or public transport, *accompanied trips*: walking and cycling with adult company and *motorised trips*: trips made by car or public transport together with adults. For each one of the variables the subject's score were calculated by dividing the number of trips made in each category of travel by the number of trips reported to leisure activities. Because of the low amount of trips made by walking and cycling in adult company, this category was excluded in further analyses. In order to get an approximate normal distribution of independent, respectively, motorised trips the obtained amount of trips within each category were recoded into a three-step scales (hardly any trips $= 1$, some trips $= 2$, almost all trips $= 3$, independent trips: $M = 1.63$, Mdn $= 1$, SD $= 0.70$, motorised trips: $M = 2.06$, Mdn $= 2$, SD $= 0.76$).

Parents' travel to leisure activities in their childhood

Sixty-five per cent of the parents were almost never chauffeured to leisure activities in their childhood, 18% sometimes, 10% often and 7% almost always. For the further analyses, the subjects who were chauffeured sometimes, often and almost always were treated as one group.

The impact of parents' childhood travel

The impact of the parents' childhood travel on their present attitude towards various travel modes for their child's trips were analysed in analysis of variance with the child's age and gender as covariates. Parents who sometimes were chauffeured to their leisure activities expressed a more favourable attitude towards motorised transports for their own children's trips (sometimes chauffeured: $M = 5.81$, never chauffeured: $M = 5.26$ $F(1, 342) = 9.77, p < 0.01$). Parents who were sometimes chauffeured also tended to express a more negative attitude towards their child travelling independently ($p = 0.03$). In corresponding analyses with travel mode choice for children's leisure trips as the dependent variable results in the same direction were obtained. Children of parents who had been chauffeured, more frequently travelled by car to their leisure activities than those children whose parents were never chauffeured (sometimes chauffeured: $M = 2.22$, never chauffeured: $M = 1.97$, $F(1, 259) = 7.41, p < 0.01$). Additionally, a tendency of children, whose parents had been chauffeured, travelling less independently was identified ($p = 0.05$).

STUDY II: METHOD

Study II was a questionnaire survey among young adults aged 19–25 years and the parent who was responsible for the young adult's travel at the age of 10. The sample included 76 pairs of young adult-parent, corresponding to a response rate of 32%. The young adults included 75% females and 25% males (mean age 22 years) and 78% of the parents were mothers and 22% fathers.

At the age of 10 years, 93% of the young adults lived in households with at least one car. Today 72% of the young adults had a driving license. Only 14% owned a car, but many could borrow a car from their parents or friends. According to national statistics, 42% of 16–24 year olds have obtained a driving license and that 44% have access to a car (Statistics Sweden, 1999). The higher degree of driving license in the present sample is likely to depend on the somewhat older sample.

The instrument applied in Study I was adapted to the present purpose. One version of the questionnaire was developed for the young adults and another version for the parents. From the young adult-questionnaire the following items have been analysed: eight scales where different travel modes were to be rated at 7-graded scales according how desirable or undesirable they at present were perceived for leisure trips within their hometown. Four items about the most frequent travel mode for trips to friends and leisure activities during daylight and darkness. One item about how frequently the young adult was chauffeured to leisure activities at the age of 10 (almost never—almost always). In addition, items about socio-demographics were included. The parent-questionnaire related to the time when the young adult was about 10-years old. To a large extent it covered the same questions as employed in the children's study. Travel mode choice was however measured by the most frequent travel mode for friends, respectively, leisure activities at daylight and darkness.

The personnel manager/course administrator of different workplaces and educational settings were contacted in the cities of Lund and Malmö. At 19 places with a significant number of employees/students aged 19–25 years the project was introduced as a study of young people's travel mode choice in urban areas. The set of questionnaires and a free-post envelope were then distributed to the young adults either by the personnel manager or a member of the research team. The young adult was asked to hand over the parent version to his/her parent. All returned complete sets of questionnaires participated in a prize draw of cinema vouchers.

Data has been treated by frequency analysis, analysis of reliability, chi-squared analysis and analysis of variance (ANOVA) in SPSS version 11. Due to the smaller sample, the conventional level of significance ($p = 0.05$) was employed in Study II.

RESULTS OF STUDY II

The young adults' childhood travel experiences

The parent's attitudes towards various travel modes when the young adult was 10-years old were treated according to the factors motorised transport and independent travel obtained in Study I. The reliability of the index motorised transport in this sample substantially increased if the scale "public transport in adult company" was dropped. Similarly, the reliability of the index of independent travel increased if the scale "public transport on his/her" own was excluded. Consequently the index motorised transport consists of two items ($M = 5.82$, Mdn $= 6.50$, SD $= 1.67$, Cronbach's alpha $= 0.92$) and the index independent travel is based on three items ($M = 4.48$, Mdn $= 4.67$, SD $= 1.59$, Cronbach's alpha $= 0.81$). The results are therefore not directly comparable with those obtained in Study I.

The level of motorised trips at the age 10 was assessed by adding the number of times the parent had mentioned car or carpooling as the most frequent travel modes to friends and leisure activities. The level of independent trips at the age of 10 was assessed by adding the number of times the parent had replied with cycle on his/her own, walk with friends/siblings and walk on his/her own as the most frequent travel mode. The two indices of travel mode choice could vary between 0 and 4, with 4 indicating that the type of travel mode was mentioned as the most frequent in all of the four situations (travel to friends in daylight/darkness, respectively, travel to leisure activities in daylight/after darkness) (Motorised trips: $M = 1.59$, Mdn $= 2$, SD $= 1.35$; Independent trips: $M = 1.91$, Mdn $= 2$, SD $= 1.31$).

Seventeen per cent of the young adults responded that they were almost never chauffeured to their leisure activities, 21% answered sometimes, 31% often and 31% said that they were almost always chauffeured. In comparison with the parents' answers at the same question in Study I, the young adults to a significantly higher degree had been chauffeured (*Chi-squared* $= 54.24$, df $= 3$, $p < 0.01$).

The reliability of the variables measuring childhood travel experience is supported by the consistency in the parents' attitudes, assessment of travel modes and the young adults' assessment. The correlation coefficients and level of significance are shown in Table 1.

The young adults' present attitudes and choice of travel mode

At present the young adults expressed the most favourable attitude towards walking and cycling in company with friends for leisure time trips within their home town, whereas taxi was the least preferred travel mode (Table 2).

Table 1. Correlations between attitudinal and behavioural measures (*N* varies between 74 and 76).

	Parent's attitudes		Parent's assessment of travel mode choice		Young adult's assessment
	Motorised transport	*Independent travel*	*Motorised trips*	*Independent trips*	*Chauffeuring to leisure activities*
Parent's attitudes					
Motorised transport					
Independent travel	− 0.27*	–			
Parent's assessment of travel mode choice					
Motorised trips	0.42**	− 0.39**	–		
Independent trips	− 0.17 n.s.	0.44**	− 0.74**	–	
Young adult's assessment					
Chauffeuring to leisure activities	0.36**	− 0.19 n.s.	0.64**	− 0.45**	–

*correlation is significant at $p < 0.05$, **correlation is significant at $p < 0.01$.

Table 2. Young adults' present attitude towards various travel modes.

Attitude towards	*M*	*Mdn*	*SD*
Go by car	4.58	5	2.05
Share lifts or carpool	5.16	5	1.72
Take a taxi	4.03	4	1.83
Go by bus	4.83	5	1.52
Cycle in company with someone you know	5.72	6	1.59
Cycle alone	5.67	6	1.74
Walk together with someone you know	5.89	6	1.43
Walk alone	4.70	5	1.80

The travel mode reported as the most frequent during daylight as well as after dark was to cycle alone. In daylight it was also common to walk alone, whereas public transport was reported more frequently for trips after dark (Figure 1). Based on these frequencies, two indices were computed, car trips including the items car, carpool, taxi, respectively, trips by walking and cycling (walk/cycle alone or with someone you know) by counting the number of times the young adult mentioned these travel modes as the most frequent for the four categories of trips. These indices could vary between 0 times and 4 times (car trips: $M = 0.93$, Mdn = 1, SD = 1.05; walk/cycle: $M = 3.05$, Mdn = 3.5, SD = 1.20).

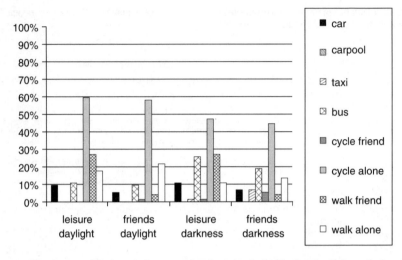

Figure 1. The young adults' most frequent travel mode choice during daylight and after dark.

The impact of childhood experiences on the young adults' present travel

The influence of the parent's attitude towards motorised transport, respectively, independent travel at the young adults' present attitudes and travel was analysed by means of one-way ANOVAS. No significant effects of either the parent's attitudes could be found at the young adults present attitudes, respectively, travel mode choice. The parent's assessment of motorised, respectively, independent trips did however have some influence. Young adults who to a high degree had made independent trips in childhood expressed a more favourable attitude towards cycling alone ($M = 6.02$) than those who rarely had travelled independently ($M = 5.15$) ($F(1, 75) = 5.38$, $p < 0.05$). Tendencies in the same direction were found for young adults who had made independent trips to be more positive towards cycling with friends ($p = 0.06$) and walking alone ($p = 0.08$). No significant effects could be found of motorised trips in childhood, but tendencies for those who to a large extent had made motorised trips to be less positive towards cycling alone ($p = 0.06$) and travelling by public transport ($p = 0.08$) were identified.

Young adults who responded that they almost always had been chauffeured expressed a less positive attitude towards cycling in company with someone they knew (almost never chauffeured: $M = 6.54$, sometimes: $M = 5.88$, often: $M = 6.04$, almost always: $M = 4.91$, $F(3, 71) = 3.91, p = 0.01$) and cycling alone (almost never chauffeured: $M = 6.23$, sometimes: $M = 5.94$, often: $M = 6.26$, almost always: $M = 4.65$, $F(3, 71) = 4.69$, $p < 0.01$) than those who more rarely had been chauffeured.

No significant effects were found, neither of the parent's attitudes or the parent's assessment of most frequent travel mode at the young adult's present travel mode choice. The young adult's own assessment did however have an influence at their present level of walking and cycling. Young adults who had rarely been chauffeured reported more often walk and cycle as the most frequent travel mode to friends and leisure activities than those who thought they were almost always chauffeured in childhood (almost never chauffeured: $M = 3.61$, sometimes: $M = 3.19$, often: $M = 3.22$, almost always: $M = 2.56$, $F(3, 71) = 2.65$, $p = 0.05$).

DISCUSSION

During the last 20 years the amount of passenger car transports in Europe have increased by 15%, resulting in expanding environmental, safety and congestion problems (European Environment Agency, 2003). One source of the growth is the amount of children's trips made by car (European Commission, 2002). Today, these trips are deficient for children's health and well being as well as the environment. The present study indicates that these car trips may also cause a future escalation of the negative environmental and health consequences of car usage.

The results confirm that the amount of children who are chauffeured have increased. Among the parents in Study I 7% almost always had been chauffeured, whereas the corresponding figure among the young adults in Study II was 31%. The children of the parents in Study I was chauffeured to an even higher degree (approximately 50%). In line with the hypotheses, the results points to a direct impact of childhood travel experiences on adulthood attitudes and travel mode choice. The influence of actual experiences seems to be strongest, particularly as oneself remember the situation. Parental attitudes towards various travel modes were contrary to the expectations of no importance. It might be that the parents never verbally expressed their attitudes towards various travel modes to their children, and the attitudes thereby were never reinforced.

Among the young adults, the influence was directed towards attitudes related to walking and cycling as well as the actual frequency of walking and cycling, whereas among parents in Study I, the influence was strongest on attitudes towards motorised transport as well the choice of such travel modes. It might be that the influence of childhood travel experiences varies over the lifetime and between different situations. As shown in previous research teenagers may become critical to their parents' choice of travel mode (Andréasson & Sjöberg, 1996). Young adults also have limited possibilities to travel by car due to lack of driver's license and/or access to a car (Statistics Sweden, 1999). These factors together may reduce the influence of childhood travel experiences in adolescence and early adulthood. This might be the case in Study II, where driver's license and access to car was lower than among the parents in Study I. As described by Klöckner (2004) the travel mode choice is likely to change as a consequence of significant life events. Buying the first car, moving to a new town or changing workplaces are events that will have an effect on travel mode choice. Also new travel demands for the children, e.g. to get to and from one certain leisure activity might elicit new travel patterns among parents. Still, these changes may mirror childhood travel patterns. This conclusion is confirmed by previous focus groups discussions with parents. One reason frequently mentioned for chauffeuring children was that the parent him or herself had been chauffeured to leisure activities and now he/she wanted to return this to the own child (Johansson, 2002).

In order to break a negative spiral of more parents chauffeuring their children, thereby model car usage, planners and policy makers must provide realistic alternatives that parents feel are safe and secure. This includes the design of the traffic environment as well as social issues (Björklid, 2001; Johansson, 2002, 2004b). Also the limited use of public transport for children's trips should be noted.

Retrospective measures are sensitive to forgetting and distortion of memories. The congruence between the information obtained from the young adults, respectively, their parents suggests, however, that this has not been a major problem in this study. Additional studies with a longitudinal approach would however be desirable. The study of young adults and parents was mainly based on mothers–daughters. It is suggested that further studies, in line with social-learning theory should account for gender differences. There is also a need of a deeper understanding of the processes behind the parental influence on travel mode choice. Social-learning theory may provide one theoretical framework. In addition inheritance might need to be considered, e.g. in terms of physical and psychological preconditions.

Travel mode choice is based on a large number of factors, including more psychological variables such as values and norms, attitudes, and habits, but also the physical environment, more practical matters such as time and weather conditions, and health aspects play a role in individual travel patterns. Future studies should make an attempt to identify how important the childhood travel experiences are in relation to these other factors and how the childhood theoretically could be integrated in the models of theory of planned behaviour (Ajzen, 1991) and the norm activation theory (Schwartz, 1977a,b) commonly employed to analyse travel mode choice.

ACKNOWLEDGEMENTS

This research was financed by the Swedish Agency for Innovation Systems (VINNOVA). Special thanks are due to the colleagues at the Environmental Psychology Unit, Lund Institute of Technology, for their advice during the course of the study. The author would also like to thank Anna-Maria Grage for her assistance in the collection of data for Study II and all the participants for their support.

REFERENCES

Ajzen, I. (1991). The theory of planned behavior. *Organizational Behavior and Human Decision Processes*, *50*, 179–211.

Andréasson, H., & Sjöberg, A. (1996). *Ungdomars syn på kollektivtrafik och bil* [Young people's view of public transport and the car] (Report 9:1996). Göteborg: Trafikkontoret Göteborgs Stad.

Balzani, M., & Borgogni, A. (2003). The body goes to the city project: research on safe routes to school and playgrounds in Ferrara. In Garciá-Mira, R., Cameselle, J.M.S., & Martinez, J.R. (Eds.), *Culture, Environmental Action and Sustainability* (pp. 299–312). Cambridge, MA: Hogrefe &Huber.

Bandura, A. (1977). *Social Learning Theory*. New Jersey: Prentice Hall.

Bandura, A. (1986). *Social Foundations of Thought and Action. A Social Cognitive Theory*. New Jersey: Prentice Hall.

Bernow, R. (1991). *Ungdomars värderingar om rörlighet, resvanor och miljö* [Young people's appraisal of mobility, travel habits and environment]. Borlänge: Vägverket.

Bianchi, A., & Summula, H. (2004). The "genetics" of driving behavior: parents' driving style predicts their children's driving style. *Accident Analysis and Prevention, 36*, 655–659.

Björklid, P. (2001). Rätten till staden—barnens eller bilens? [The right to the city—the children's or the cars'?]. In Nyström, L., & Lundström, M. (Eds.), *Barn i stan? Om barns tillgång till stadsbygden.* [Children in the city? On children's access to the urban environment] (pp. 105–126). Karlskrona: Stadsmiljörådet.

European Commission (2002). *Kids on the Move.* Luxembourg: Office for Official Publications of the European Commission.

European Environment Agency (2003). *Europe's Environment: The Third Assessment.* Copenhagen: European Environment Agency.

Gatersleben, B., Leach, R., & Uzzell, D. (2001). *Travel to school. Studying and reporting walking and cycling to school in four junior and one secondary school in Ash, Surrey.* Guildford: Department of Psychology, University of Surrey.

Hillman, M. (1993). *Children, Transport and the Quality of Life.* London: The Policy Studies Institute.

Johansson, M. (2000). *Identification and promotion of attitudes related to pro-environmental travel behaviour.* Doctoral Dissertation. Lund: Environmental Psychology Unit, Lund University.

Johansson, M. (2002). I am a parent and a driver—a study of parents' environmental trust and children's travelling. In Uth Thomsen, T. (Ed.), *Workbook for the Workshop on Children and Traffic,* www.flux.teksam.ruc.dk/FLUX_UK/ChildrenMob/2002%20workshop/ workbook.pdf

Johansson, M. (2004a). *Independent Travel among 8–11 year-olds—A Comparison between Sweden and the UK,* manuscript.

Johansson, M. (2004b). *Environmental and Parental Aspects of Travel Mode Choice for Children's Leisure Activities,* in manuscript.

Klöckner, C.A. (2004). *How Single Events Change Travel Mode Choice—A Life Span Perspective.* Paper presented at the third International Conference on Traffic and Transport Psychology, Nottingham, UK. www.psychology.nottingham.ac.uk/ IAAPdiv13/

Mackett, R. (2002). Increasing car dependency of children: should we be worried? *Proceedings of the Institution of Civil Engineers-Municipal Engineer, 151* (1), 29–38.

Rämet, T., & Summula, H. (2004). *Young Drivers' and Their Parents' Driving Habits and Attitudes.* Paper presented at the third International Conference on Traffic and Transport Psychology, Nottingham, UK.

Sandqvist, K. (2004). *Car-Related Attitudes of Adolescents and Their Parents. A Comparison Between Car-Owning and Car-Less Households in Suburban and Inner-City Stockholm.* Paper presented at the third International Conference on Traffic and Transport Psychology, Nottingham, UK. www.psychology.nottingham.ac.uk/IAAPdiv13/

Sandqvist, K., & Kriström, S. (2001). *Getting along without a family car. The role of an automobile in adolescents' experiences and attitudes. Part I. Inner city Stockholm.* Stockholm: Institutionen för individ, omvärld och lärande, Lärarhögskolan i Stockholm.

Schwartz, S.H. (1977a). Normative influences on altruism. *Advances in Experimental Social Psychology, 10,* 221–279.

Schwartz, S.H. (1977b). Normative influences on altruism. *Advances in Experimental Social Psychology, 25,* 1–65.

Sissons Joshi, M., & MacLean, M. (1995). Parental attitudes to children's journeys to school. *World Transport Policy & Practice, 1* (4), 29–36.

Sissons Joshi, M., MacLean, M., & Carter, W. (1997). Children's journeys to school—new data and further comments. *World Transport Policy & Practice, 3* (4), 17–22.

Smith, P.K., Cowie, H., & Blades, M. (1998). *Understanding Children's Development* (3rd ed.). Oxford: Blackwell.

Statistics Sweden (1999). *Undersökningen om levnadsförhållande.* [The survey of living conditions] http://www.scb.se/templates/Standard_22862.asp

Trivector Information (1999). *Gå och cykla till skolan. En redovisning av resultaten från enkäten genomförd vid samtliga lågstadieskolor i Lunds kommun våren 1999.* [Walk and cycle to school]. Lund: Lunds Kommun.

Traffic and Transport Psychology
G. Underwood (Editor)
© 2005 Elsevier Ltd. All rights reserved.

47

Temporary Structural Change: a Strategy to Break Car-Use Habit and Promote Public Transport

Satoshi Fujii[1] and Tommy Gärling[2]

Introduction

Congestion, excessive energy and resource consumption, adverse environmental effects such as noise, vibration and the emission of various pollutants, global warming are known negative consequence of automotive transportation. As part of a solution to these problems, use of public transport should increase. Inducing automobile drivers' to change to public transport use requires breaking *habits* that impede behavioural change (Ronis, Yates & Kirscht, 1989; Verplanken, Aarts, Van Knippenberg & Van Knippenberg, 1994; Dahlstrand & Biel, 1997; Verplanken, Aarts & Van Knippenberg, 1997; Verplanken & Faes, 1999; Gärling, Fujii & Boe, 2001). A habit refers to "goal-directed automaticity" in behaviour (Verplanken & Aarts, 1999). For this reason, a habitual driver is unlikely to consider public transport to be a possible alternative and to acquire information that is necessary for using public transport (Verplanken et al., 1997; Gärling et al., 2001).

With the purpose of changing drivers' behaviour into public transport use, one must ask how car-use habits may be changed (Dahlstrand & Biel, 1997). A basic tenet is that if driving habits could be broken, drivers will consciously evaluate available travel modes and select public transport that their car-use habit has prevented them from doing in the past. In addition, if habitual drivers develop a new habit of using public transport, the behavioural change may be lasting.

[1] Department of Civil Engineering, Tokyo Institute of Technology, 2-12-1, Ookayama, Meguro-ku, Tokyo 152-8552, Japan. *E-mail:* fujii@plan.cv.titech.ac.jp (S. Fujii).
[2] Department of Psychology, Göteborg University, P.O. Box 500, SE-405 30 Göteborg, Sweden.
E-mail: Tommy.Garling@psy.gu.se (T. Gärling).

Ronis et al. (1989) and Dahlstrand and Biel (1997) proposed that a habit would be broken by engagements in alternative behaviours. However, it is unlikely that habitual drivers voluntarily would stop driving. Thus, in some way they need to be forced to do so. Practically, temporary forced choices may be possible to achieve. However, if the forced choice is only temporary, will it result in changes that last?

This chapter highlights the possible effectiveness of *temporary structural change* for breaking habits of using the automobile. For instance, people who develop a strong habit of using the automobile may be forced to use public transport when the automobile is temporally unavailable (e.g. because it is on maintenance or repair). If the automobile has been unavailable for some time, the driver furthermore must use public transport repeatedly. Thus, the frequency of using public transport increases whereas the frequency of using the automobile decreases. These changes in relative frequencies may weaken or break the old habit of using the automobile as well as strengthen or develop the new habit of using public transport. Examples of feasible temporary structural changes include freeway closures due to maintenance work, offering free public transport on selected days, distributing free public transport tickets to frequent drivers, and implementing road pricing on a temporary basis. These strategies may induce the use of alternative modes which may break the habit of using the automobile.

EFFECTS OF FORCED BEHAVIOURAL CHANGE ON CAR-USE HABIT

The authors conducted a panel survey entailing observations of both actual choices of automobile and public transport before and after changes of residences and work places (Fujii & Gärling, 2003). The samples were students who graduated from four universities in Japan. The first wave was carried out approximately 2 months before the graduation. Sixty-seven students recruited to the panel responded to a questionnaire administered in classes. After graduation they were employed by companies in different locations. Due to changes in residences and work places, in many cases commuting behaviour changed. In the second wave carried out approximately 3 months after graduation, 53 (79.1%) of the students responded to a mail questionnaire. On the basis of questions asked in the questionnaire in each wave, measures were constructed of frequencies of past choice of automobile and public transport and of habits in using automobile and public transport. The measure of habit was similar to that developed by Verplanken et al. (1994, 1997) and used by Gärling et al. (2001).

For the analysis of the data from the panel survey, the sample was split into three groups (i.e. low-change group, median-change group, and high-change group) on the basis of the change of relative frequency of using automobile to that of using public transport from the first wave to the second wave. The results shown in Figure 1(a) indicate that the strength of habit of using automobile significantly increased from the low-change group over the median-change group to the high-change group. An opposite significant trend was shown in Figure 1(b) for the habitual strength of using public transport. The results thus showed that the car-use habit was broken and that a public transport use habit developed some time after the forced change.

(a) Script-based choice of automobile

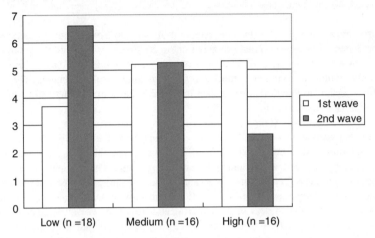

(b) Script-based choice of public transport

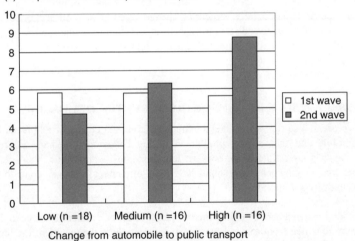

Change from automobile to public transport

Figure 1. Degree of script-based choice of (a) automobile and (b) public transport in first and second wave related to degree of change from automobile to public transport. (Adapted from Fujii & Gärling, 2003.)

SHORT-TERM EFFECTS OF TEMPORARY STRUCTURAL CHANGE ON CAR-USE HABIT

Although the results reported above suggest that a forced behavioural change influences car-use habit strength, it is necessary to directly show that a temporary structural change induces a behavioural change. This was the aim of the field experiment reported in Fujii and Kitamura (2003). Furthermore, another question concerns whether a temporary structural change affects attitudes toward automobile and public transport use. Such changes in attitudes may be necessary for lasting behavioural changes.

Forty-three drivers in Kyoto, Japan, were recruited. A 1-month free bus ticket was given to 23 drivers assigned to the experimental group but not to 20 drivers assigned to the control group. Attitudes toward, habits of, and frequency of using automobile and bus were measured immediately before, immediately after, and 1 month after the intervention. The measure of habit was again similar to that developed by Verplanken et al. (1994, 1997) and used by Gärling et al. (2001).

The result showed that monthly frequency of using bus doubled for the drivers who received a 1-month free bus ticket (from 4.13 to 9.34). This signifies that the temporary structural change induced a temporary behavioural change. The comparison of the data collected immediately before the intervention and 1 month after the intervention furthermore yielded increases in positive attitudes toward bus and decreases in habits of using automobile for the drivers in the experimental group. It was also indicated that the drivers in the experimental group used bus more frequently 1 month after the intervention. The increase was 20% higher than the frequency of using bus before the intervention (4.13 per month before, and 4.95 per month after). These results imply that a temporary behavioural change induced by a structural change leads to a modification of attitudes toward using bus in a positive direction as well as a decrease in the strength of habits of using automobile. The changes in attitudes and habits may be expected to cause lasting changes in public transport use.

LONG-TERM EFFECTS OF TEMPORARY STRUCTURAL CHANGE

The results presented so far support that a temporary structural change would break habits of using automobile and that it may promote a lasting behavioural change. However, the behaviour changes investigated in both reviewed studies were rather short term. Yet, the strategies for changing behaviour should have long-term effect if they are going to solve the problems caused by automobile use.

The third study reviewed here examines the long-term effect of a temporary structural change. The data were obtained from a two-waves panel survey, where the results of the first survey is reported in Fujii, Gärling and Kitamura (2001) and that of the second survey in Fujii and Gärling (2003).

The first survey was conducted during an 8-day closure of the Hanshin Expressway Sakai Route, a toll road between Osaka City and Sakai City in Japan. This closure caused commuting time by automobile to increase, and for many drivers public transport was faster. We took advantage of this temporary freeway closure to study how it affected the frequency of commuting by public transport. The first survey targeted 335 drivers who commuted regularly on the Sakai Route. Questionnaires distributed to these drivers requested them to indicate the frequencies of commuting by auto and by public transport (bus or train) before the closure. The questionnaires also requested respondents to indicate on each day during the freeway closure which mode they used, what time they departed from home and arrived at work, and what they, at the time of departure, expected to be arrival times of their commute trips. Based on the reported numerical estimates, the *expected commute time* was calculated as the difference between the departure time and the expected arrival time and the *actual commute time* as the difference between the departure and arrival times.

The results showed that the 8-day freeway closure increased public transport use by commuting drivers from 9 to 20%. The results also showed that the frequency of switching to public transport during the closure was inversely related to the frequency of auto commuting before the closure. Since it is plausible that this frequency is positively related to the strength of a habit of automobile commuting (Ronis et al., 1989; Verplanken & Aarts, 1999; Gärling et al., 2001), the results imply that habitual driving impedes behavioural change.

The results also showed that the commute time by public transport was overestimated by the respondents, more so the more frequently they commuted by automobile. Data obtained from drivers who commuted every day by automobile before the freeway closure and used public transport during the freeway closure indicated that expected commute time by public transport was about 5 min longer than actual commute time by public transport. However, this overestimate of commute time by public transport for less frequent automobile commuters was from 1 to 2 min. Thus, habitual drivers held negative beliefs about the alternative travel mode, and the size of these negative beliefs increased with driving habit. After the drivers' first public transport use during the closure, overestimates of commute time by public transport were, however, more accurate. Furthermore, those whose overestimates were affected continued to use public transport (during the freeway closure) to a larger extent than those whose overestimates were not affected. This suggests that if high-frequency drivers use public transport at least once, their overestimates of public transport commute time are corrected leading to an increase in the frequency of public transport use.

The second survey was conducted about 1 year after the first survey. Questionnaires were distributed to the respondents in the first survey. In the new questionnaires, they were again asked to indicate the frequency of commuting to their work place by automobile and public transport. As a result, panel data were obtained from 111 respondents in both the first and second waves who before the closure commuted by car every day and whose work place and home address had not changed. The results indicated that those drivers who used public transport during the closure increased public transport use significantly more from before to after (average individual share of using public transport before the closure was 6%, after the closure 16%, see Figure 2), but there were no significant difference between frequency of using public transport between before and after the closure for those who did not use public transport during the closure (3% before, 5% after). In addition, the results showed that expected commute time for those who used public transport during the closure, which had been become more accurate after experiencing use of public transport during the closure, was not changed after the closure. Thus, the estimates of commute times made by high-frequently drivers remained accurate. In summary, a temporary structural change of freeway closure had long-term effects on beliefs about the service level of alternative travel modes (i.e. public transport), and on commuting behaviour.

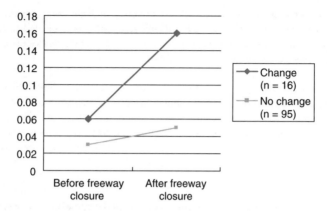

Figure 2. Monthly frequency of public transport use before and 1 year after a freeway closure related to change vs. no change to public transport use during the freeway closure. (Adapted from Fujii & Gärling, 2003.)

CONCLUSIONS

Taken together the results from three studies demonstrate that a temporary structural change breaks car-use habits and promotes public transport use. As shown in Figure 3, Studies 1 and 3 indicated that the temporary structural change induced a temporary behavioural change from car use to public transport use. As Studies 1 and 2 showed, the temporary behavioural change

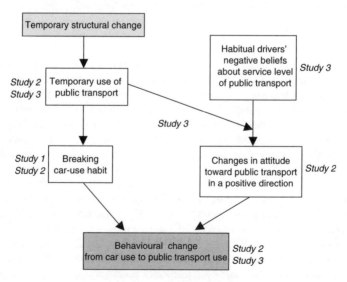

Figure 3. Effects of temporary structural change on belief, habit, attitude and behavioural change.

broke car-use habits. In addition, as found in Study 3, the temporary behavioural change corrected habitual drivers' negative beliefs about the service level of public transport. The results of Study 2 showed that temporary behavioural change had a positive effect on attitudes toward public transport. This attitude modification was perhaps caused by corrections of negative beliefs about public transport.

Thus, temporary changes from car use to public transport use that was induced by a temporary structural change may have two consequences: one is to break car-use habits, the other is to modify attitudes toward public transport use in a positive direction. As was actually shown in Studies 2 and 3 to be the case, both these consequences may be expected to contribute to lasting behavioural changes.

It is, however, not claimed here that a temporary structural change would invariably be effective in promoting a behavioural change. For example, Cone and Hayes (1980) reported several field experiments showing that the effects of a temporary structural change were only temporary. However, the experiments they reported did not target habit change. The point here is that *habit* would be broken because of the temporary structural change, and therefore behavioural modification would be more than temporary. The effectiveness of a temporary structural change should thus increase if it is targeted at habitual drivers.

Furthermore, the effectiveness of the temporary structural change may increase with strength of habit. This is implied by the results of Study 3 showing that weak and medium strong habitual drivers did not always overestimate commute time by public transport, although strong-habitual drivers did. This might be because some experiences of commuting by public transport are sufficient to correct the negative beliefs. Therefore, correction of negative beliefs about public transport due to temporary structural change occurs only for strong-habitual drivers who never uses public transport.

Based on the results presented here, it is suggested that temporary structural change such as providing free public transport ticket may be an effective ingredient of a practical communication program targeting travel behaviour modification, for instance travel feedback programs (TFP; cf. Taniguchi, Hara, Takano, Kagaya & Fujii, 2003) including Individualized Marketing (Brög, 1998), Travel Blending (Rose & Ampt, 2001), and other similar programs. However, it should be noted that the effectiveness of such programs may not be successful unless the participants have strong car-use habits. Such participants are likely to have unjustified negative beliefs that are corrected. This could be the motive they need to change to public transport. Once they have started to use public transport, a new habit is presumably developed and maintained.

REFERENCES

Brög, W. (1998). Individualized marketing: Implications for TDM. CD-ROM of Proceedings of *77th Annual Meeting of Transportation Research Board*.

Cone, J.D., & Hayes, S. (1980). *Environmental Problems/Behavioral Solutions*. Monterey, CA: Brooks/Cole.

Dahlstrand, U., & Biel, A. (1997). Pro-environmental habit: propensity levels in behavioral change. *Journal of Applied Social Psychology, 27*, 588–601.

Fujii, S., & Gärling, T. (2003). Development of script-based travel mode choice after forced change. *Transportation Research F: Traffic Psychology and Behavior, 6* (2), 117–124.

Fujii, S., & Kitamura, R. (2003). What does a one-month free bus ticket do to habitual drivers? An experimental analysis of habit and attitude change. *Transportation, 30*, 81–95.

Fujii, S., Gärling, T., & Kitamura, R. (2001). Changes in drivers' perceptions and use of public transport during a freeway closure: effects of temporary structural change on cooperation in a real-life social dilemma. *Environment and Behavior, 33* (6), 796–808.

Gärling, T., Fujii, S., & Boe, O. (2001). Empirical tests of a model of determinants of script-based driving choice. *Transportation Research F: Traffic Psychology and Behavior, 4*, 89–102.

Ronis, D.L., Yates, J.F., & Kirscht, J.P. (1989). Attitudes, decisions, and habits as determinants of repeated behavior. In Pratkanis, A.R., Breckler, S.J., & Greenwald, A.G. (Eds.), *Attitude Structure and Function* (pp. 213–239). Hillsdale, NJ: Erlbaum.

Rose, G., & Ampt, E. (2001). Travel blending: an Australian travel awareness initiative. *Transportation Research, 6D*, 95–110.

Taniguchi, A., Hara, F., Takano, S., Kagaya, S., & Fujii, S. (2003). Psychological and behavioral effects of Travel Feedback Program for travel behavior modification. *Transportation Research Record, 1839*, 182–190.

Verplanken, B., & Aarts, H. (1999). Habit, attitude and planned behaviour: is habit an empty construct or an interesting case of goal-directed automatic? *European Review of Social Psychology, 10*, 101–134.

Verplanken, B., & Faes, S. (1999). Good intentions, bad habits, and effects of forming implementation on health eating. *European Journal of Social Psychology, 29*, 591–604.

Verplanken, B., Aarts, H., Van Knippenberg, A., & Van Knippenberg, C. (1994). Attitude versus general habit: Antecedents of travel mode choice. *Journal of Applied Social Psychology, 24*, 285–300.

Verplanken, B., Aarts, H., & Van Knippenberg, A. (1997). Habit, information acquisition, and the process of making travel mode choices. *European Journal of Social Psychology, 27*, 539–560.

EPILOGUE

Traffic and Transport Psychology
G. Underwood (Editor)
© 2005 Elsevier Ltd. All rights reserved.

48

Traffic Psychology and Road Safety: Separate Realities

Talib Rothengatter[1]

Introduction

There are large differences in accident-involvement between different groups of drivers. Young drivers have more—and more serious—crashes per kilometre driven; women have fewer crashes per kilometre driven. These differences can be explained in roughly two ways. The first explanation is functional. Young drivers are less experienced and therefore make more errors. These errors are in perception, decision-making and action. Groeger and Chapman (1996) and McKenna and Crick (1991) argue that the perception of road hazards is age-dependent and that this may in part explain the differences in accident involvement. It has also been argued that over time drivers shift from rule-based to skill-based action, thus allowing them to respond adequately to changing circumstances. The differences in accident-involved between males and females are less easily explained on this basis, unless it is assumed that skill-based action in driving is innate in females and can only be acquired by males. The second explanation is in terms of social or differential psychology; some drivers are more inclined than others to deviate from the normative—that is normative in task analysis terms, normative need not be "normal"—behaviour, and young or male drivers have a larger propensity to do so than adult or female drivers. Reason, Manstead, Stradling, Baxter and Campbell (1990) distinguished "errors and violations on the road" maintaining that violations, not errors are associated with accident involvement. The instrument they used—the Driver Behaviour Questionnaire (DBQ)—is still widely in use. It also has evolved over time. As a result, many different versions are in use, which makes the results difficult to compare. The three distinct factors reported by Reason et al. have been replicated but the use of confirmatory factor analysis is not frequently reported. Nonetheless, the assertion that intentional deviations from normative behaviour are a major explanation for increased accident-involved in specific groups of drivers, has had a tremendous impact on research.

---

[1] Department of Psychology, University of Groningen, Groningen, The Netherlands. *E-mail:* j.a.rothengatter@ppsw.rug.nl (J.A. Rothengatter).

The question is whether traffic psychology as applied field of research is now better positioned in the area of road safety research. Can traffic psychology contribute to traffic safety and are these contributions incorporated in road safety policy? My contention is that this is not the case. In a recent report by the European Council for Traffic Safety (prepared by scientific experts) the most important, cost-effective transport safety measures were identified as: (a) daytime running lights, (b) random breath testing, (c) audible seat belt reminders, (d) use of EuroNCAP as an incentive for developing safer cars, and (e) road safety engineering (ECTS, 2003). This report sets the agenda for EU transport safety policy. Yet, no mention is made of driver education and training, or attitudes and attitude changes or driver rehabilitation. In the list of possible engineering countermeasures, no mention is made of perception, visual search, decision-making or drivers' information-processing capabilities, let alone hazard perception.

This is in striking contrast with the famous statements made in the 1980s that a sizeable amount (estimates went as high as 84%) of road accidents are due to road user behaviour. Psychologists, but apparently only psychologists, interpreted these statements as indicating that understanding and changing road user behaviour would be the only way to achieve tangible improvements in road safety. Since Reason et al. claimed that violations, not errors, are related to accident-involvement, it seems appropriate to examine what studies in this area have produced in terms of results that can be applied in road safety measures.

SOCIAL PSYCHOLOGY OF DRIVING

Social-psychological literature applied to driving has been dominated by the attitude construct; more specifically, by the theory of planned behaviour. The model, albeit in different forms, has been applied to driving behaviour such as speeding on and off motorways, close following, drinking and driving, seat belt use, lane changing, driving in residential areas, overtaking, flashing headlights, running red at traffic lights (see for an overview Rothengatter & Manstead, 1997; Stradling & Parker, 1997), cyclist behaviour (e.g. Maring & Van Schagen, 1990) and less frequently, to pedestrian behaviour (e.g. Diaz, 2002). Typically, these studies find moderate to low correlations between the attitude, social norm, perceived behavioural control components and intention and between intention and behaviour. However, Rothengatter and Manstead noted a bias towards attitude or social norm as dominant factor in the relation between the model components dependent on the type of measurement used (direct versus indirect). Over the years, the model has been extended by several other components (see Stradling & Parker, 1997), thus enhancing its complexity. A methodological problem is the measurement of the behaviour component. As behaviour is predicted on the basis of the attitude model components, the measurement of that behaviour should follow the measurement of the attitude model components. In practice, the model components and the behaviour are measured concurrently, not sequentially. Also, most studies refrain from actually observing or recording the target behaviour and use self-reported behaviour as proxy. These methodological issues may inflate the correlations found between the model components and behaviour. Some experimental work has been carried in relation to speed behaviour. West, French, Kemp and Elander (1993) found self-reported speed to be a reliable predictor of speed choice on motorways. This study was criticized by Lajunen and Summala (2003) on the ground that self-reports and observations were collected in highly public settings in which the participants were well aware of the presence of the observer and the non-anonymity of their self reports. However, in their own study Lajunen and Summala did not find evidence for a social-desirability bias. This finding is in line with the reasoning that driving behaviour such as violation of speed limits does not constitute socially undesirable behaviour in the view of the driving populations—nor in the view of the police for that matter (Rothengatter, 1993). Haglund and Åberg (2002) studied the stability of speed choice of drivers at two different locations and found that repeated speed measure correlation coefficients ranged from 0.49 and 0.81 for free-flowing vehicles. However, this finding cannot be construed as evidence that speed choice is stable over longer time periods. It also cannot be assumed that the correlation between observed and reported driving behaviour is as high as was found for speed choice. Other behaviour—for example, drinking driving—may be considered much more social undesirable and, therefore, more prone to a social-desirability bias.

The relation between attitudes and accident involvement also requires further examination. Assum (1997) found that attitudes and accident involvement are related in a sample representative of the driving population, but also found that when age is taken into account, this relation disappears. Yagil (1998) reports large differences between older and younger drivers in terms of correlations between evaluative statements and propensity to violate traffic law. While the evaluation of traffic law was significantly correlated with behaviour in younger drivers, it was not in older drivers. Conversely, perceived gains involved in the commission of violations were significantly correlated with behaviour in older drivers, but not in younger drivers. The latter finding complies with the results of an analysis of motives for speeding indicating that attitudes towards speeding are determined by the assessment of the positive outcomes rather than the perceived risk of negative outcomes of speeding. These finding suggest that possibly attitudes amongst younger drivers are thrill-seeking/risk-avoidance based, while they are based on rational decision-making in older drivers. That would explain why attitude–accident involvement correlations are limited to the younger segment of the driving population and why older drivers are much less accident-involved than younger drivers, even though they maintain their propensity to commit traffic violations.

In contrast to the attitude construct, the construct of attribution has received little attention in road user research. Baxter, Macrae, Manstead, Stradling, and Parker (1990) carried out a study in which they demonstrated the fundamental attribution error (i.e. deviant behaviour was attributed to situational factors when committed by the subjects themselves but attributed to dispositional factors when committed by others). This lack of research is regrettable because, as Parker (2004) suggests, attribution may well provide the basis for understanding the causes of aggressive behaviour and provide a basis for studying aggressive behaviour. At present, a lack of a usable definition of what aggressive behaviour entails hampers progress. Definitions of aggressive driving range from the extreme cases when driving intentionally (attempt to) inflict harm to other drivers to behaviour that can possibly harm others (such as running red at traffic lights) or even behaviour that in general shows disrespect to others (see Porter & Berry, 2004). Also, the relation between anger and aggressive behaviour is less than clear-cut (Mesken, Hagenzieker & Rothengatter, this volume). Of particular interest are the factors that evoke the impression of others' aggression. Some studies have attempted to attribute the incidence of aggression to road conditions and congestion, but that may well be beside the point. It is more likely that behaviour of others is interpreted as aggressive when road conditions or congestion pose a high demand or potential threat on drivers, while that same behaviour is interpreted as merely instrumental in less demanding circumstances. It is also likely that behaviour that is judged instrumental by the driver is considered aggressive by others.

Stereotyping may well enhance these mechanisms. Rothengatter and De Bruin (1988) found that perceived driving speed is dependent of vehicle characteristics and make, with Italian sports cars producing the largest overestimation of speed and Swedish-made cars producing the largest underestimation of speed.

Other social-psychological constructs that have been studied in relation to road user behaviour involve the perception of self. Svensson (1981) reported that drivers consider themselves more skilful then others. Although these results have been subject to debate on methodological grounds (who is the other?), the tendency to believe oneself to be better than others prevails. This bias in perception has been related to self-enhancement, optimism bias, illusion of control and self-justification (see Parker, 2004; Rothengatter, 2002 for a more detailed discussion). Evidence supporting the notion that these constructs offer an explanation why young or female drivers are less at risk is not apparent.

ROAD SAFETY MEASURES

In the early implementation of engineering measures to increase road safety, the road safety improvements were found to be less than calculated. Improvements in road safety were "used" by road users to adapt to the changed environment to optimize their benefit. This phenomenon that led to a plethora of risk-related theories and models indicates that road users are, in a way as yet not understood, able to perceive their momentary risk either on an aggregate or disaggregate level, and are able to weight that risk against other possible outcomes of their behaviour—such as task demand, pleasure in driving, esteem from others, or any other factor that may move the road user. The implication is that drivers not only adapt to environmental factors but also adapt to individual factors. They may be prone to trait anger, they may have a negative attitude towards speed limits or considered themselves better than others, or may be impatient, in a hurry or pleasantly aggressive, but most drivers seem to have sufficient skills to adapt to prevailing circumstances which in this case means ignore their trait or state and act responsively. That adaptive skill may be more developed in female and/or in older drivers. Road rage or other pathological behaviour occurs where this adaptive skill fails.

Traffic psychology can then contribute in two ways to improve road safety. It can develop training programs, or more generally, interventions that increase the willingness to adaptation. Hazard perception training can be a component, although improved hazard perception, as a skill may only be a by-product of this training. Reduced illusion-of-control or rather the increased preparedness to adapt to hazardous circumstance may be a more important educational objective. Calibration training as proposed by Kuiken and Twisk (2001) can be another competent as it specifically has adaptive behaviour as objective, albeit adaptive to task demands rather than individual intentions. Traffic psychology can also support engineering measures. Behavioural engineering is nothing new. Social behavioural engineering could be.

Whether traffic psychology needs to produce measures to improve road safety still is an open question, at least for psychologists. Complex traffic behaviour is Groeger's view a very important and worthwhile test-bed for psychology and psychological theory (Groeger, 2002). My contention that the reason of being for traffic psychology is that it focuses on a specific societal problem, as does health or work psychology, and has to contribute to improving road safety, as health or work psychology contributes to solving problems in those areas. At present, traffic psychology needs no comma, but a question mark.

REFERENCES

Assum, T. (1997). Attitudes and road accident risk. *Accident Analysis and Prevention, 29*, 153–159.

Baxter, J.S., Macrae, C.N., Manstead, A.S.R., Stradling, S.G., & Parker, D. (1990). Attributional biases and driving behaviour. *Social Behaviour, 5*, 185–192.

Diaz, E.M. (2002). Theory of planned behaviour and pedestrians' intentions to violate traffic regulations. *Transportation Research F, 5*, 169–176.

ECTS (2003). *Cost-Effective Transport Safety Measures*. Brussels: European Council of Transport safety.

Groeger, J.A. (2002). Trafficking in cognition: applying cognitive psychology to driving. *Transportation Research F, 5*, 235–248.

Groeger, J.A., & Chapman, P.R. (1996). Judgement of traffic scenes: the role of danger and difficulty. *Applied Cognitive Psychology, 10*, 349–364.

Haglund, M., & Åberg, L. (2002). Stability in drivers' speed choice. *Transportation Research F, 5*, 177–188.

Kuiken, M.J., & Twisk, D. (2001). *Safe Driving and the Training of Calibration*. Leidschendam: SWOV.

Lajunen, T., & Summala, H. (2003). Can we trust self-reports of driving? Effects of impression management on driver behaviour questionnaire responses. *Transportation Research F, 6*, 97–107.

Maring, W., & Van Schagen, I. (1990). Age dependence of attitudes and knowledge in cyclists. *Accident Analysis and Prevention, 22*, 127–136.

McKenna, F.P., & Crick, J.L. (1991). Experience and expertise in hazard perception. In Grayson, G.B., & Lester, J.F. (Eds.), *Behavioural Research in Road Safety*. Crowthorne, UK: Transport and Road Research Laboratory.

Mesken, J., Hagenzieker, M.P., Rothengatter, J.A. (this volume). Effects of emotions on optimism bias and illusion of control in traffic.

Parker, D. (2004). Road safety: what has social psychology to offer. In Rothengatter, J.A., & Huguenin, R.D. (Eds.), *Traffic and Transport Psychology*. Oxford: Elsevier.

Porter, B.E., & Berry, T.D. (2004). Abusing the roadway commons: understand aggressive driving through an environmental preservation theory. In Rothengatter, J.A., & Huguenin, R.D. (Eds.), *Traffic and Transport Psychology*. Oxford: Elsevier.

Reason, J.T., Manstead, A.S.R., Stradling, S.G., Baxter, J.S., & Campbell, K. (1990). Errors and violations on the roads: a real distinction? *Ergonomics, 33*, 1315–1332.

Rothengatter, J.A. (1993). *Attitudes towards law violations and enforcement, Proceedings 37th Annual Conference of the Association for the Advancement of Automotive Medicine*. Portland, Oregon: Association for the Advancement of Automotive Medicine.

Rothengatter, J.A. (2002). Drivers' illusions—no more risk. *Transportation Research F, 5*, 249–258.

Rothengatter, J.A., & De Bruin, R.A. (1988). The influence of drivers' attitudes and vehicle characteristics on speed choice on highways and its safety consequences. *International Journal of Vehicle Design, 9*, 579–585.

Rothengatter, J.A., & Manstead, A.S.R. (1997). The role of subjective norm in predicting the intention to commit traffic violations. In Rothengatter, J.A., & Carbonell Vaya, E. (Eds.), *Traffic and Transport Psychology: Theory and Application*. Oxford: Pergamon.

Stradling, S.G., & Parker, D. (1997). Extending the theory of planned behaviour: the role of personal norm, instrumental beliefs and affective beliefs in predicting diving violations. In Rothengatter, J.A., & Carbonell Vaya, E. (Eds.), *Traffic and Transport Psychology: Theory and Application*. Pergamon: Oxford.

Svensson, O. (1981). Are we all less risky and more skillful than our fellow drivers? *Acta Psychologica, 47*, 143–148.

West, R., French, D., Kemp, R., & Elander, J. (1993). Direct observation of driving, self reports of driver behaviour, and accident involvement. *Ergonomics, 36*, 557–567.

Yagil, D. (1998). Gender and age-related differences in attitudes toward traffic law and traffic violations. *Transportation Research F, 1*, 123–135.

NAME INDEX

SUBJECT INDEX

accident analyses, 155, 156
accident involvement, 18, 21, 23, 157, 215–217,
   219, 223–225, 431, 432, 521, 523, 526, 527,
   595, 597
accident prevention, 3, 9, 327, 493
accident rate, 18, 22, 38, 46, 169, 215, 245, 493
accidents, 17–23, 27, 28, 38, 64, 91, 101, 103,
   116, 129–131, 137–139, 141, 142, 157–160,
   176–178, 181, 216, 217, 219–221, 223–225,
   273, 274, 293, 296, 297, 304, 327–329, 333, 336,
   352, 355, 420, 431, 458, 466, 467, 471–473,
   475–480, 487, 495, 497, 498, 505, 513, 514,
   517, 521, 522, 527, 529–531, 543, 551, 596
accompaniment, 6, 50, 157, 172, 173, 177, 178,
   343, 352, 461, 471, 495, 576
adaptive cruise control (ACC), 231, 244, 247,
   274, 297–300
advanced driver assistance systems (ADAS), 231,
   233, 273–276, 304–306, 312
age differences, 102, 103, 111, 197
ageing populations, 79, 80
aggression, 182, 203, 217, 223, 433, 438, 490, 523,
   524, 597
alertness, 144, 232, 273, 299, 463, 464, 471, 479,
   480, 488
anger, 75, 181–188, 191–194, 196–200,
   203–205, 207, 209, 210, 391, 439, 493, 496,
   522, 597, 598
atomic beliefs, 428
attention, 7, 18, 22, 64, 84, 87, 102, 110, 115, 118,
   120, 121, 123, 144, 224, 235, 240, 258, 276,
   290, 296, 303, 323, 327, 340, 348, 353, 357,
   369, 389, 408, 414, 417, 419, 420, 433, 434,
   444, 445, 455–457, 466, 467, 489, 505, 516,
   523–525, 597
attention failure, 22, 456
attention lapses, 389, 466, 467
attention shift, 456, 457
attitudes, 6–8, 11, 72, 158–160, 216, 232, 294,
   489, 490, 492–494, 497–499, 509, 519, 522,
   527, 537, 539, 540, 553, 557, 559, 573–576,
   578–582, 588, 591, 596, 597
attractiveness, 64, 68, 69, 73
attributions, 181–183, 185, 187, 188, 499
audio warnings, 258, 264, 268, 271
automated driving, 231, 232, 243–247, 249, 250,
   252, 253, 293, 294, 296, 297, 299, 300

automation, 130, 233, 241, 243, 246, 247,
   273–276, 293, 296, 300
awareness, 51, 53, 61, 109, 153, 154, 232–234,
   239, 241, 258, 261, 270, 296, 307, 339, 432,
   437, 439, 455–457, 466, 479, 496, 497, 522,
   523, 526–528

behavioural adaptation, 138, 244, 245, 276, 304,
   384, 387, 389, 391
bicycle, 7, 50, 65, 66, 317
bidimensional regression, 55, 59
Big Five personality characteristics, 215–225
blink behaviour, 458, 466, 467
blink duration, 358, 365, 366, 459, 463, 464
blinks, 357, 366, 367

car following, 231, 243, 247–249, 282, 305, 327,
   330, 332, 333, 335, 336, 358, 365, 371, 386,
   402, 539
car use, 49–51, 60, 61, 551–562, 564, 571, 573,
   585–587, 590, 591
car-use reduction, 555–562, 564
categorization, 38, 39, 42, 46, 413
chauffeuring, 579, 581
child pedestrian, 27, 28, 35, 38
childhood, 573–576, 578, 580–582
children, 27–35, 37–47, 49–61, 573–582
coding, 30, 41, 42, 216
cognitive bias, 205, 211, 212
cognitive limitations, 18
cognitive maps, 49, 51, 61
cognitive schemata, 37
cohort studies, 158, 160
collision warning, 240, 271
comfort zone, 386, 389–391
comfort, 65, 71, 73, 252, 273–274, 297, 384, 386,
   388–391
commitment, 492, 496, 539–547, 557, 559, 564
comprehension, 121, 122, 124, 233, 352, 369
compulsory, 153, 420, 421, 424
concept mapping, 308, 309
concept of danger, 38
conceptual knowledge, 38
connecting database and measurement tool (DBT),
   143